19.93

D0014515

The Minister's Library™
Volume 1

The Minister's Library™
Volume 1

The Minister's Library™

Volume 1

by
Cyril J. Barber

MOODY PRESS
CHICAGO

Library of Congress Cataloging in Publication Data

Barber, Cyril J.
  The minister's library.

  Includes indexes.
  1. Theological libraries.   2. Theology—Bibliography.
3. Christianity—Bibliography.   4. Religion—
Bibliography.   5. Libraries, Private.   I. Title.
Z675.T4B3   1985   027.6′7   84-25500
ISBN 0-8024-5296-5 (v. 1.)

1 2 3 4 5 6 7 Printing/RR/Year 89 88 87 86 85

Printed in the United States of America

This book is for
Aldyth,
Allan, and Stephen

This book is for
Aldyth,
Allan, and Stephen

Contents

Foreword to the 1985 Edition

Dr. Cyril Barber and I have been close friends and colleagues in ministry for over twenty years. I realized early in our relationship that the man was destined to make a significant contribution to the cause of Christ, but little did I realize how extensively he would be used!

An author with as prolific a pen as this man must be well read, which he is. This means he must also possess a sizable library, which he does. And that means he ought to have much to say about books, which he has! It is contained in this fine volume you are holding in your hands—*The Minister's Library*.

Many bibliographical works are studies in futility for ministers and ministers-to-be. Some are so heavy and detailed that they become a source of frustration to pastors and seminary students alike. *Or* they are so general and superficial that they lack the resourcefulness a book of this nature should provide. This volume is different. It is thorough without being tedious, and that makes it practically useful to those of us who are busily engaged in tasks that have deadlines.

For the past ten years I have returned to *The Minister's Library* again and again. I cannot recall a time when I have sought the counsel of this reference work without being steered in the right direction. I'm confident you will derive the same benefits as you keep it on a shelf near your fingertips. Of one thing I am sure—it will gather no dust.

I am delighted to know that Moody Press has published this new edition. Dr. Barber has added a few new entries that have come to his attention during the past decade. What we now have is essentially the same excellent content as before—a work that informs the reader of those books that will prove personally helpful and enhance public ministry.

The Minister's Library is a masterful work. Without reservation, I commend it to you.

CHARLES R. SWINDOLL

Foreword to the 1974 Edition

The Minister's Library, by Cyril Barber, is an outstanding volume for several reasons. It has a lofty goal, which is to acquaint the pastor and Christian worker with the finest and best expository literature and aids available. It accomplishes its goal with perceptive insight and exhaustive thoroughness.

This book is outstanding in that it not only points out what books the Bible expositor ought to have, but it also shows him how to set up his personal libarary so that these expository helps do not become mere shelf-fillers and academic ornaments, but are ready tools easily accessible for immediate use.

It is obvious at the outset how extremely practical this work is. Those who desire to know what the Word of God says and have the call of God upon their lives to expound it will find *The Minister's Library* indispensable. They will discover themselves consulting it time and again. It will prove a constant guide in evaluating books already in one's library, and it will serve as an invaluable aid when new purchases are to be made. It will soon repay its purchaser many times over in time saved and through avoidance of bad selections.

Often the minister, who is a sincere man of faith and prayer and who depends upon the teaching ministry of the Holy Spirit, is hamstrung on the human plane in the matter of his personal library. This volume will be a special boon to him in enriching his ministry. He will be able to rejoice in what the Lord reveals to him personally, as well as what the Lord will make known to him through what He has disclosed to other faithful students of the Scriptures.

Rarely does a work come from the press that is of more practical value to the Christian minister and Bible expositor than this monumental work. We recommend it most warmly and wish for it the widest sphere of usefulness.

MERRILL F. UNGER

Introduction

Speaking at a chapel service at seminary one day, a district superintendent of long standing mentioned a startling fact. He said: "The length of a man's stay in any one pastorate is frequently determined by the size of his library." He went on to explain that as he traveled up and down the country visiting men in the ministry, he had come to the conclusion that a man's personal library had a direct bearing upon (1) the quality of his ministry and (2) the length of his pastorates. He illustrated his point by showing that great men of the past invariably had large personal libraries. H. A. Ironside, W. Graham Scroggie, George W. Truett, Alexander Whyte, Jonathan Edwards, A. T. Pierson, Charles H. Spurgeon, Andrew Bonar, Clarence Edward Macartney, Alexander Maclaren, T. T. Shields, Henry Ward Beecher, F. B. Meyer and others were reviewed in turn. They were well read and could pass on to their congregations the fruit of their study.

It should be pointed out at the very beginning of this work that books are not a substitute for the inner working and empowering ministry of the Holy Spirit. Rather, the man of God, under the Spirit's control, can have his ministry enriched as a result of a well-balanced reading program. Lest some should imagine that they do not need to avail themselves of the works of others, let us remind ourselves of Spurgeon's counsel on the subject:

> In order to be able to expound the Scriptures, . . . you will need to be familiar with the commentators: . . . Of course, you are not such wiseacres as to think or say that you can expound the Scripture without assistance from the works of divine and learned men who have labored before you in the field of exposition. . . . It seems odd that certain men who talk so much of what the Holy Spirit reveals to themselves, should think so little of what He has revealed to others.[1]

1. C. H. Spurgeon, *Commenting and Commentaries* (reprint ed., London: Banner of Truth Trust, 1969), p. 1. Used by permission.

Assuming that we realize the value and benefit of good books, two major problems face us today. One is the rising cost of books, and the other is the overwhelming volume of new books that are being published each year. As to the cost, we should buy judiciously and add to our shelves only those books that are of lasting value. Other books can be obtained from a local library or through interlibrary loan facilities.

The second problem facing us is quite staggering. So many new books are coming from the presses that people need counsel regarding the value and content of each. Last year alone, 45,000 new books were printed in the United States, bringing the total number of books presently available to more than 479,000 separate titles. If British, Canadian, and European publications are added to this figure, the total output is truly staggering. It is true that not all of these books are "religious" ones; but even the 3,270 religious books (excluding pamphlets and privately circulated materials) published last year are beyond the ability of any one person to read and comprehend.

As a result of this vast avalanche of printed materials, students in the different institutions in which I have served have frequently approached me with the request that I make available to them a comprehensive, annotated list of books that they could use as a "buying guide" in the development of their own libraries. These students have invariably been preparing for pastoral ministry and were particularly interested that the suggestions focus upon expository preaching and the tools that would enable them to effectively teach the Word. In its initial phase, this list of books was to contain about 1,000 entries.

When the first edition of *The Minister's Library* was in preparation, it was suggested that I include titles by men who do not necessarily hold to a conservative, evangelical position but whose works are nonetheless widely known throughout the country. It was at his suggestion that I use an asterisk (*) to mark those works that are worthy of a pastor's investment and a dagger (†) symbol to identify those written from a theologically "liberal" point of view.

In following these suggestions, I have retained the original purpose of the list, namely, to be a tool in the hands of pastors who wish faithfully to expound the Scriptures. This work is geared, therefore, toward the needs of the expository preacher and Bible teacher. Having served as a pastor, Bible college and seminary professor, and seminary librarian, I have some general familiarity with the needs of the pastorate and the resources ministers require in preparation of their messages.

This book is not intended for the scholar or academician. Its aim is to be practical and helpful, and it is geared to the needs of men in the ministry or who are preparing for the ministry.

Originally, the plan was to follow the same general format as the Union (Va.) Theological Seminary's *Essential Books for a Pastor's Library* and to utilize the wide margin for the classification (i.e., call) number of each book. This would have the effect of placing the entries in the same sequence as the books on one's shelf. Later, however, a decision was made to place the classification at the end of each entry. The sequence of entries still preserved the "shelf lift" order, but to the casual user it was not as easy to use. In this resetting of the type, an alphabetic sequence has been preserved. Because this work is *not designed for the scholar*, I have continued to try to identify the theological perspective of the major authors whose books I cite.

In drawing up this list I have been conscious of the contributions of others, but I have not used their works as a basis for my own. For example, several seminaries have issued book lists. These have invariably been geared to the needs of a scholarly community. Several of them have also manifested a marked weakness in the area of Bible commentaries. It is my hope that this weakness has been corrected in the present volume. Likewise, no attempt has been made to duplicate the work of Raymond P. Morris who, in his *Aids to a Theological Library* (1969), provided a valuable desiderata list for theological seminaries. Those who possess a copy of Spurgeon's *Commenting and Commentaries* will find that very little duplication occurs. Whereas Spurgeon's strength lay in his extensive knowledge of post-Reformation works, the present treatment concentrates on more recent publications, most of which are available at the present time.

With all works of this kind there are, of course, limitations. The reader needs to know what has been expressly included and what has been purposefully omitted from the list of books. First, as has been previously mentioned, the emphasis of this treatment is on exposition. Therefore, books on pastoral theology, homiletics, counseling, philosophy of religion, and historical theology, while not ignored, are subordinated to the primary purpose of the work. Only those reference tools that are of particular value to the pastor have been included.

Second, foreign language publications have been omitted with the exception of works such as Mandelkern's *Veteris Testamenti Concordantiae* and other Greek and Hebrew grammars and lexicons.

Furthermore, I have tried as far as possible to be nonsectarian. I have listed the significant works of individuals irrespective of their denominational affiliation.

Basically, this book falls into two major sections. Part 1 is designed to provide a simple explanation of *how* the busy pastor may easily and painlessly classify and catalog his entire library. Information is provided on how to arrive at call numbers for books and how to organize the information on 3″ × 5″ cards. Examples of each step of the process are given, and an explanation of the reason for each is provided in nontechnical terms.

Part 2 contains a list of books with the Dewey Decimal Classification and the author "Cutter number" at the end of each entry.

It is inevitable that in a work of this size some errors of judgment (both with regard to the inclusion and exclusion of certain books, and in the annotations) should occur. These will be corrected in a later edition. Because new books are constantly coming from the presses throughout the world, it is imperative that a work of this nature be kept up-to-date. In the providence of God, I hope to be able to continue to keep abreast of developments in the disciplines associated with the pastoral ministry and to revise this work as time goes by. In this way, redundant titles can be dropped and new, significant works added.

While serving on the faculty of the Trinity Evangelical Divinity School, I was able to benefit from the special training and expertise of my colleagues. The content of this book has been freely discussed with them, and I am particularly grateful to them for their help. In addition, Professor Patrick Williams of the Graduate School of Library Science, Rosary College, Illinois, read through chapters 1 and 2 and offered his wise counsel regarding their improvement. I would also like to express my appreciation to Dr. Kenneth S. Kantzer for encouraging me to undertake this task. Since then I have enjoyed the counsel of my colleagues on the faculties of the Rosemead Graduate School of Psychology and the Talbot Theological Seminary.

The first edition of this manuscript was read through by Dr. and Mrs. Robert J. Williams of Clarks Summit, Pennsylvania. The revision has been checked carefully by my research assistant, Mrs. Steve (Janet) McCracken. Any fluidity of style and ease of comprehension is due to their indefatigable efforts. Special thanks are also due my secretary, Mrs. Richard (Jeane) Huett, and to Mrs. Eldred (Jane) Gillis for their help in typing the manuscript.

This introduction would be incomplete if I failed to mention my wife, Aldyth, and my two sons, Allan and Stephen. They graciously put up with me during many long months while I spent a major portion of each evening working on the manuscript.

I also wish to express my profound thanks to Dr. Charles R. Swindoll for so kindly writing the foreword to this 1985 reprinting of the original work.

My indebtedness to my family and these colleagues and friends of mine is impossible to calculate. In the final analysis, however, I bear the responsibility for any imperfections in this work.

Abbreviations

ANEP	*Ancient Near East in Pictures*
ANET	*Ancient Near Eastern Texts*
ASV	*American Standard Version,* 1901
BDB	Gesenius's *Hebrew-English Lexicon of the Old Testament,* ed. by Brown, Driver, and Briggs
BIP	*Books in Print*
BPR	*Book Publishers' Record*
CBI	*Cumulative Book Index*
DAC	Hastings, *Dictionary of the Apostolic Church*
DCG	Hastings, *Dictionary of Christ and the Gospels*
DDC	Dewey Decimal Classification
EA	*Encyclopedia Americana*
EB	*Encyclopedia Britannica*
HDB	Hastings, *Dictionary of the Bible*
HERE	Hastings, *Encyclopedia of Religion and Ethics*
IB	*Interpreter's Bible*
IDB	*Interpreter's Dictionary of the Bible*
ICC	International Critical Commentary
IRPL	*Index to Religious Periodical Literature*
ISBE	*International Standard Bible Encyclopedia*
KD	Keil and Delitzsch, *Commentary on the Old Testament*
LC	Library of Congress
LXX	Septuagint
MM	Moulton and Milligan, *The Vocabulary of the Greek Testament*
MT	Masoretic Text
NBD	*New Bible Dictionary*
NEB	*New English Bible*
NICNT	New International Commentary on the New Testament

NICOT	New International Commentary on the Old Testament
NT	New Testament
OED	*Oxford English Dictionary*
OT	Old Testament
PAIS	*Public Affairs Information Service*
RSV	*Revised Standard Version*
RV	*Revised Version*
TDNT	*Theological Dictionary of the New Testament*
TNTC	Tyndale New Testament Commentaries
TOTC	Tyndale Old Testament Commentaries

PART ONE

How to Set Up Your Library

1

Classifying Your Library

INTRODUCTION

Classification and cataloging are the two prerequisites for an orderly library. Most pastors of my acquaintance, and particularly those who have been in the ministry for any length of time, have extensive collections of books. Few, however, really use their books to the best advantage. It seems that the more books person possesses, the harder it is for him to remember where to go to find the information he needs. Most pastors are familiar with a few well-used reference volumes, but the books in their collection are not put to the best advantage because they lack a proper, systematic arrangement.

Proper classification and cataloging is designed to make the pastor's resources more readily available—to bring order out of chaos and cohesion out of confusion. Classification will make your library a more useful tool in the work of the ministry than it is at present.

Some pastors will arrange a book according to its topic or content. This kind of arrangement is generally adequate for smaller libraries. It frequently parallels other classification systems, but it omits the numbers or symbols that are placed upon the spine.

For those who wish to arrange their books in this way, the following list of subject headings may prove helpful.

CHRISTIANITY (RELIGION)
Bible
  Inspiration, canonicity
  Concordances
  Dictionaries
  Text and versions
  Interpretation, criticism
  Commentaries on entire Bible
  Geography, history, archaeology

Old Testament
  Commentaries on specific books or portions of the OT.
    Follow sequence of the books of the OT.
New Testament
  Same as OT above.
Apocrypha
Theology, doctrine
  Godhead, Trinity, attributes
  God the Father
  God the Son, Christology
    Life of Christ
    Public ministry
    Teachings
    Transfiguration
    Passion week, Lent
    Crucifixion and death
    Resurrection, appearances, ascension
  God the Holy Spirit
  Man, Doctrine of
  Salvation
  Spirits, angels, Satan
  Eschatology, prophecy
  Eternal state
  Apologetics
Devotional works
  Ethics, Christian
  Daily Bible readings
Christian Home
Christian church
  Local church
  Preaching, homiletics
    Preparation
    Illustrations
    Sermons
  Ordinances, sacraments
    Baptism
    Lord's Supper
  Special occasions
    (The arrangement in this section can follow the church calendar or can include
    books on specific topics such as Christmas, New Year, ordination, confirmation,
    commencement addresses, and so on.)
  Counseling
    (The arrangement of this section can be alphabetical according to topic: e.g.,
    alcoholism, bereavement, divorce, premarital, marital, servicemen, sick and
    dying, youth, problems of, and so on.)
  Evangelism

Church leaders
   Elders
   Deacons
   Other orders
Church administration
   Public worship
   Hymns, hymnology
Missions
   Home missions
   Foreign missions
   Missionary biographies
Christian education
   (Arrange books by age group)
Church history
   Apostolic era to A.D. 100
   Struggle for survival 100-313
   Supremacy of the old Catholic imperial church 313-590
   Medieval church 590-1517
   Modern church 1517-
      Reformation and Counter Reformation
   Rationalism, revivalism, denominationalism
   Missions, modernism
   Twentieth-century church
      Ecumenism
      Fundamentalism
   Church creeds, history of doctrine
Denominations and sects
   (Include history and biography)
   Primitive, Oriental
   Roman Catholic
   Anglican, Episcopal
   Lutheran
   Calvinistic, Reformed
   Anabaptist, Mennonite, Free churches, and so on
   Baptist
   Disciples of Christ, Seventh Day Adventist
   Methodist
   Unitarian
   Sects
      (Arrange alphabetically)
Comparative religions
   (Arrange alphabetically)

Whereas this method of arrangement is orderly and is satisfactory for use in small libraries, it is essentially a one-man system. It does not lend itself to use by others. The church secretary, for example, will not be able to reshelve the books used by the busy pastor when once his sermon preparation has been completed.

As libraries grow larger and the need for help increases, a system similar to the one outlined above, but including numerical or alphabetical symbols, becomes a necessity.

Proper classification, then, may be looked upon as the process of (1) grouping books into logical order according to their subject matter, (2) assigning to each book a class number that will indicate the particular group to which that book belongs, and then (3) giving it a specific place on the bookshelf. Although many different methods of arrangement have been tried in the past, only those methods that arrange books according to their subject content are now prevalent.

Several systems are in use. Some of these are for large libraries; others have been developed for technical libraries. The most common system is the Dewey Decimal Classification System. It is easy to use and is found in public schools and libraries across the country.

Before enlarging upon the Dewey Decimal Classification, let us take a brief look at the other available systems. You will need to have some familiarity with them when you use university and college libraries.

CLASSIFICATION SCHEMES

There are many different kinds of subject classifications, and it is necessary for you to choose one of them.

The *Library of Congress Classification* system is designed for large, technical collections. It is kept up-to-date with frequent revisions and is far too elaborate for private use.

A second system has been designed by the Union Theological Seminary in New York City. It is called the *Classification of the Library of Union Theology Seminary* and is specifically designed for theological libraries. Its general usefulness is limited, and it has now been abandoned by the library of Union Seminary.

Other schemes like the one by Henry Evelyn Bliss, *A Bibliographic Classification,* 4 vols. (2d ed.; New York: H. W. Wilson, 1952), have been developed, but these have never enjoyed widespread acceptance.

DEWEY DECIMAL CLASSIFICATION SCHEME

The Dewey Decimal Classification (DDC) system is probably the most popular one for general use. It is a simple system to follow; is widely used in public, private, college, and technical libraries; enjoys an international reputation, and forms the basis of the *Universal Decimal Classification* system (3d ed.; London: British Standards Institution, 1961). This system was devised by Melvin Dewey in 1873 and since then has been kept up-to-date with a number of revisions. The unabridged 18th edition, published in 1972, covers every facet of human knowledge and is not too costly (particularly when compared to the Library of Congress Classification system).

The entire system may be outlined in the following manner.

NUMBER	ANSWERING THE QUESTION . . .	SUBJECT MATTER
000		General Works
100	Who am I?	Philosophy and Psychology
200	Who made me?	Religion
300	What about other people?	Social Sciences and Education
400	How may I communicate with others?	Philosophy and Language
500	How may I understand the world around me?	Science
600	How may I use what I have learned about nature and science?	Applied Arts and Sciences
700	How may I enjoy my leisure times?	Fine Arts and Recreation
800	How may I pass on to posterity what I have learned?	Literature
900	How may I leave a record for the future?	History, Biography, and Geography

Each one of these major groups may be broken down decimally in the following way. Because pastors will use the 200 division dealing with RELIGION more frequently than any other, we will use this as an illustration.

200 RELIGION
210 Natural theology
220 Bible
230 Doctrine, theology
240 Devotional literature
250 Homiletical and pastoral
260 The church: institutions and work
270 History of the Christian church
280 Christian churches and sects
290 Non-Christian religions

The other sections of the DDC are similarly divided into ten subdivisions each. Each of these groups includes the chief related subject areas within the group, and each of these groups consists of one hundred general areas of study.

The DDC is flexible, may be expanded indefinitely, and contains many thousands of minor subdivisions. Few pastors will ever need to use these subdivisions even in the 200 category. To further illustrate the way in which the RELIGION section may be broken down, we shall take as an illustration the 220 subdivision.

220 Bible: General works
221 Old Testament: Texts, introduction, etc.
222 Old Testament, Historical books
223 Old Testament, Poetical books
224 Old Testament, Prophetic books
225 New Testament: Texts, introductions, etc.
226 New Testament, Gospels and Acts
227 New Testament, Epistles
228 New Testament, Revelation
229 Apocrypha

The way in which the 220 section is broken down illustrates what may be done for each one of the RELIGION 200-299 categories.

To further demonstrate the flexibility and scope of this system, we shall examine the 226 ("New Testament, Gospels and Acts") subdivision.

226   Gospels and Acts
226.1 Harmonies
226.2 Matthew
226.3 Mark
226.4 Luke
226.5 John
226.6 Acts
226.7 Miracles
226.8 Parables
226.9 Lord's Prayer

Whatever method you choose to use, it should be instituted with thoroughness and pursued with vigor. Of course, it should be a method that can be set up with the least possible labor and difficulty and yet at the same time achieve the greatest possible efficiency. Only in this way will your library serve a useful purpose and be changed from a mass of material into a well-organized collection arranged according to its subject content.

In order to facilitate the speedy classification of your library, the writer has assigned the DDC number to each of the books listed in the bibliography. Of course, the best time to begin classifying your library is when it is small. Then it is a relatively simple matter to assign each volume a class number as you buy it. However, even those who are fortunate enough to possess large libraries will find that their books can be classified easily and speedily by referring to the author and title indexes at the end of this book or to the subject guide (relative index) to the DDC contained in chapter 3.

When the task of proper classification and cataloging has been done, it will richly repay your time and effort, make study more profitable, and have a beneficial effect upon those to whom you minister. Furthermore, you will have the sense of satisfaction that comes from having transformed your collection of books into a well-ordered, efficient, and functional library.

Once you have caught up with the backlog of books you already possess, the task of keeping pace with future purchases will be pleasant and unhurried.

Before we outline the successive steps involved in classification, we must focus our attention on the need for and benefits of accessioning.

ACCESSIONING

Accessioning may seem like a lot of busywork, but pastors should keep an accession record. This need not be as detailed as the accession record kept by public, college, or university libraries, but it can serve a variety of purposes. One of the purposes served by an accession record is to support *income tax deductions.* All ordained ministers are entitled to deduct from their gross earnings the amount they have spent on books for their own self-improvement and the work of the ministry. All who claim this deduction are already keeping some form of record. It is a very simple matter to blend this record with the accession record of their library holdings.

In addition, some ministers claim as a legitimate deduction the *depreciation* of books in their library. I can think of no better way of keeping a record of this than in the book that, at the same time, records your acquisitions.

A third reason for keeping an accession record is *insurance.* In the event of the loss of or damage to your library—either by fire, storm, broken water pipes, or whatever—insurance companies will require some form of evidence to substantiate a claim. Here again, a brief but accurate accession record is of the utmost value.

A sample of a page in an accession record is given in Figure 1.

Each book that is taken into the library is given an accession number. This number is lettered in the book on the page following the title page (i.e., the verso page). It should be about one inch from the top of the page and fairly close to the spine of the book. In most libraries the accession number is also placed on the shelf list card. However, as a shelf list card is not necessary in small private libraries, the accession number may be placed on the author or main entry card, which will be discussed in the next chapter. The only details that need to be entered in the accession book are the name of the author, title of the book, and cost. However, some pastors may also wish to include the name of the publisher, year of publication, and source from which the book was obtained.

Once these brief details have been noted, you are all set for the task of classifying the book.

Number	Author	Title	Publisher	Date	Source	Cost	Remarks
26							
27							
28							
29							
30							
31							
32							
33							
34							
35							
36							
37							
38							
39							
40							
41							
42							
43							

Fig. 1. Accession Record

CLASSIFICATION

Classification may be defined as the process whereby books are assigned an appropriate place on a library shelf in accordance with their content. In order to ascertain the classification number of a particular book, reference should be made to the title page, the table of contents, and the preface. Of course, you may be familiar with the contents of the book. In this case, classification will be relatively easy. One rule to bear in mind is this: classify *broadly*. If you are familiar with the contents of the book, reference can easily be made to the relative index (a subject classification) in chapter 3, or to volume 3 of the unabridged edition of the Dewey Decimal Classification (DDC) system. For convenience, Broadman Press of Nashville, Tennessee, has issued in an inexpensive format the RELIGION 200 section of the DDC.

ASSIGNING CLASSIFICATION NUMBERS

When the classification number has been found, reference should still be made to the schedules in volume 2 of the DDC, because only in this way can you determine which of the suggestions or alternatives is correct. For example, books on evangelism may be placed in the following categories: 248.5, 253.7, or 269.2. Each of these classifications is perfectly valid in itself. It is important, however, to determine the exact nature and scope of the book and then to assign to it the proper number. For example, if the book in question deals with personal evangelism, it should go in the 248.5 category. If it is designed for pastors, then the class number 253.7 is more appropriate. If, however, it is concerned with mass evangelism, then obviously 269.2 is a better place for it.

By using the information in the relative index and the schedules of the DDC, you will be able to classify all the books in your library.

Encyclopedias of religion will receive a 200.3 classification; Bible dictionaries and encyclopedias will receive a 220.3 classification; commentaries on the whole Bible will be assigned the 220.7 class number; works in the field of doctrine and theology will be placed in the 230 category; those dealing with the different aspects of the life of Christ will be subdivided under 232; books on pastoral theology under 250, and so on.

EDITIONS

Frequently a book is revised and a second or third edition is printed. Because the call number would look odd with "3d ed." at the bottom, an accepted procedure for indicating a revision or a new edition of a book is to include the date in the call number. For example, the fifth edition of *Building a Successful Marriage*, by Judson T. and Mary G. Landis, would carry the call number 301.42.L23 1968, and the date would immediately distinguish it from the fourth edition, which was published in 1963.

STANDARD SUBDIVISION

Before leaving the subject of general classification, there are a few matters that need to be discussed. The DDC system makes provision for certain works on a similar topic to be distinguished from one another by the addition of standard subdivisions. For example, books dealing with the philosophy or theory of a particular subject may, at your discretion, be distinguished from books dealing with the study and teaching of that subject. And periodicals on a given subject may be separated on the shelf from collected writings by assigning the periodical an additional number to distinguish it from collected works on the same subject. These additions are called standard subdivisions and generally consist of the addition of a .01 to the class number for books on the philosophy or theory of a subject; .03 for dictionaries, encyclopedias, and concordances; .05 for serial publications; .07 for works on the study and teaching of the subject in question; .08 for collected writings; and .09 for the historical or geographical treatment.

The standard subdivisions are listed on pages 1-13 of volume 1 of the DDC. There are times when the schedules (vol. 2 of the DDC) will indicate that these numbers are to change with a specific division (e.g., to .01-.09 or .001-.009, etc.). However, for your own convenience, and particularly while you are learning some of the finer points of the DDC classification scheme, these additions have been made for you and are included in the classification assigned to each book in the bibliography. They are separated from the essential part of the classification number by an apostrophe (e.g., 230'.09 for the history of Christian doctrine). Depending on the size of your library and your own personal wishes, you may prefer to omit these standard subdivisions from your call number.

BIBLE COMMENTARIES

Individual Bible commentaries will follow the breakdown contained in the 222-228 schedules. The DDC makes provision for critical works to be distinguished from expository studies. Additional numbers may be added to the basic number in accordance with the information contained in a note on page 105 of volume 2. In this case, the general subdivisions mentioned above are 001-009.

To the basic number you are instructed to add 0, and then to this 0 the number found in the general principles summary on pages 98-99 of volume 2. Expository studies are, therefore, distinguished from works on interpretation and criticism by the addition of .07, whereas books devoted solely to critical and introductory matters have .06 following the class number. For example, Leon Morris has written two works on John's gospel. The first, *Studies in the Fourth Gospel,* deals with such matters as the problems of authorship, form-criticism, and the relationship of John's writings to the Essene community at Qumran; while the second, *The Gospel According to John,* is an exposition. The class number assigned to John's gospel in the schedules is 226.5. In large libraries, librarians frequently wish to distinguish between introductory studies and expository treatments. They do so by assigning an extra number to the books in question. *Studies in the Fourth Gospel* would, therefore, receive a number 226.506, and *The Gospel According to John* the number 226.507. In small libraries, however, the addition of these extra numbers is not necessary. In part 2 of this work, the extra numbers have been added and are indicated by an apostrophe (e.g., 226.5'06 and 226.5'07). The numbers following the apostrophe may be omitted at your discretion.

EXPOSITION OF PART OF A BOOK

If a book expounds only a portion of a book of the Bible, it should still be given a class number for that book. For example, Marcus Rainsford's *Our Lord Prays for His Own* covers John 17. The classification for this book should, therefore, be 226.5. To set it apart from other books that cover the entire gospel, the portion covered in this treatment is placed after the classification number of the book (in this instance 17). The complete classification would look like this:

226.5

17   ⟩

R13

Further, to distinguish Martyn Lloyd-Jones's *Studies in the Sermon on the Mount* from his *Expositions of Matthew's Gospel,* "5—7" should be added as the call number. The call number would be:

226.2

5—7

L77

This is very simple. You can understand how the number for Rainsford's book was arrived at (John's gospel) and why Martyn Lloyd-Jones's book received a 226.2 classification number; but where did the R13 and the L77 come from? These are author "Cutter numbers," which are explained in the next section.

ASSIGNING AUTHOR NUMBERS

Once the classification number has been assigned to a particular work, your next task will be to provide each book with an author number. This will distinguish it from other books on the same subject. Librarians have used different methods, depending upon their own needs. For example, a popular method of assigning a specific number to a book is to provide the first two letters of the author's name followed by a space, and then the first two letters of the title of the book (omitting definite and indefinite articles). For example, Francis A. Schaeffer's book *The Church at the End of the Twentieth Century* will be assigned the number:

261.8

SC CH

The "SC" represents the name "Schaeffer," and the "CH" stands for the first word of the title "church."

A more satisfactory way of assigning numbers is to consult the *C. A. Cutter's Two-Figure Author Table* (distributed by Libraries Unlimited, Inc., P.O. Box 263, Littleton, CO 80160). The edition of the *C. A. Cutter's Author Tables* I have used in assigning cutter numbers is the Swanson-Swift Revision of 1969.

From Figure 2, which gives a portion of the *Author Tables* for the letters "O" through "S," it is clear why the cutter number for Rainsford is R13 and the number for Lloyd-Jones is L77.

To illustrate further, if you were placing the book *Major Bible Themes,* by Lewis Sperry Chafer, in your library, you would assign it the number 230 because it deals with Bible doctrine. This is the classification (or class) number.

C. A. CUTTER'S Two-Figure Author Table (SWANSON-SWIFT REVISION)   3

O			P	Q	R	S			
Oa 1	Oj 1	Ot 1	Pa 11	Qa 1	Ra 11	Sa 1	Scu 1	Sk 1	Sta 1
Oad 2	Oje 2	Oto 2	Pack 12	Qu 2	Rae 12	Sai 2	Scud 2	Ske 2	Stam 2
Oag 3	Oji 3	Otg 3	Pad 13	Que 3	Rai 13	Sal 3	Scug 3	Ski 3	Ste 3
Oai 4	Ojl 4	Oti 4	Paf 14	Qui 4	Ram 14	Sam 4	Scuk 4	Skl 4	Stem 4
Oal 5	Ojo 5	Otl 5	Pah 15	Quo 5	Ran 15	San 5	Scum 5	Sko 5	Sti 5
Oan 6	Ojr 6	Oto 6	Pain 16	Quq 6	Rane 16	Sao 6	Scun 6	Skr 6	Sto 6
Oar 7	Ojt 7	Otr 7	Pak 17	Quv 7	Rann 17	Sar 7	Scur 7	Sku 7	Ston 7
Oat 8	Ojv 8	Ott 8	Palm 18	Quz 8	Rao 18	Sat 8	Scut 8	Skw 8	Str 8
Oaw 9	Ojx 9	Otu 9	Pam 19	Qv 9	Rau 19	Sav 9	Scuv 9	Sky 9	Stu 9
Ob 1	Ok 1	Ou 1	Par 21		Rax 21	Sb 1	Scy 1	Sl 1	Su 1
Obc 2	Oke 2	Ouc 2	Parke 22		Re 22	Sbc 2	Scyd 2	Sle 2	Sud 2
Obi 3	Oki 3	Oue 3	Parkm 23		Ream 23	Sbi 3	Scyg 3	Sli 3	Sug 3
Obl 4	Okl 4	Oug 4	Parm 24		Reb 24	Sbl 4	Scyk 4	Sij 4	Suj 4
Obo 5	Oko 5	Oul 5	Pars 25		Ree 25	Sbo 5	Scym 5	Slo 5	Sul 5
Obr 6	Okr 6	Oun 6	Pas 26		Reg 26	Sbr 6	Scyn 6	Sir 6	Sum 6
Obs 7	Okt 7	Our 7	Pau 27		Rei 27	Sbu 7	Scyr 7	Slu 7	Sun 7
Obu 8	Okv 8	Ous 8	Pau 28		Rem 28	Sbv 8	Scyt 8	Slun 8	Sus 8
Obw 9	Okx 9	Ouv 9	Pay 29		Ren 29	Sby 9	Scyv 9	Sly 9	Suw 9
Oc 1	Ol 1	Ov 1	Pe 31		Rer 31	Sca 1	Sd 1	Sm 1	Sv 1
Oce 2	Ole 2	Ovc 2	Peas 32		Rev 32	Scad 2	Sde 2	Smam 2	Svc 2
Och 3	Oli 3	Ovg 3	Peh 33		Rey 33	Scag 3	Sdi 3	Sme 3	Svi 3
Ocj 4	Olir 4	Ovi 4	Ped 34		Rh 34	Scak 4	Sdl 4	Smi 4	Svl 4
Oco 5	Olm 5	Ovl 5	Pei 35		Ri 35	Scam 5	Sdo 5	Smith 5	Svo 5
Ocp 6	Oln 6	Ovo 6	Pok 36		Rice 36	Scan 6	Sdr 6	Smith J 6	Svr 6
Ocs 7	Olo 7	Ovr 7	Pen 37		Rich 37	Scar 7	Sdu 7	Smo 7	Svu 7
Ocu 8	Ols 8	Ovu 8	Penm 38		Richa 38	Scat 8	Sdw 8	Smu 8	Svun 8
Ocw 9	Olu 9	Ovw 9	Poo 39		Richards 39	Scav 9	Sdy 9	Smy 9	Svy 9
Od 1	Om 1	Ow 1	Per 41		Richm 41	Se 1	Sced 1	Sn 1	Sw 1
Ode 2	Ome 2	Owe 2	Perl 42		Rick 42	Seb 2	Sede 2	Snc 2	Swam 2
Odi 3	Omg 3	Owi 3	Pers 43		Rid 43	Sec 3	Seg 3	Sni 3	Swe 3
Odl 4	Omh 4	Owl 4	Pet 44		Rie 44	Seh 4	Sek 4	Snj 4	Swem 4
Odo 5	Omi 5	Owo 5	Pett 45		Ril 45	Seem 5	Sem 5	Sno 5	Swi 5
Odr 6	Omo 6	Owr 6	Peu 46		Rim 46	Scen 6	Seo 6	Snow 6	Swim 6
Ods 7	Omr 7	Owt 7	Pf 47		Rin 47	Secr 7	Ses 7	Snu 7	Swo 7

Fig. 2. C.A. Cutter's Two-Figure Author Table: Portions of "O" through "S"

C. A. CUTTER'S Two-Figure Author Table (SWANSON-SWIFT REVISION, 1969)   1

© RICHARD A. CUTTER, 1969

A			B	C	D	E			F
Aa 1	Aj 1	As 1	Ba 11	Ca 11	Da 11	Ea 1	Ej 1	Es 1	Fa 11
Aad 2	Aje 2	Asc 2	Bac 12	Cai 12	Dad 12	Ead 2	Eje 2	Esd 2	Fad 12
Aag 3	Aje 3	Ash 3	Baco 13	Call 13	Dae 13	Eag 3	Eje 3	Esg 3	Faf 13
Aak 4	Ajg 4	Asi 4	Bad 14	Cam 14	Dai 14	Eai 4	Ejg 4	Esk 4	Fah 14
Aan 5	Aji 5	Ass 5	Bail 15	Camp 15	Dal 15	Eak 5	Eji 5	Esm 5	Fai 15
Aap 6	Aji 6	Asp 6	Bain 16	Can 16	Dall 16	Eam 6	Eji 6	Esp 6	Fairc 16
Aar 7	Ajo 7	Ass 7	Bak 17	Cap 17	Dalt 17	Ear 7	Ejo 7	Esr 7	Fais 17
Aau 8	Aju 8	Ast 8	Bal 18	Carc 18	Dam 18	Eat 8	Eju 8	Est 8	Fal 18
Aax 9	Ajy 9	Asu 9	Bald 19	Carf 19	Dan 19	Eaw 9	Ejy 9	Esv 9	Fall 19
Ab 1	Ak 1	At 1	Ball 21	Carm 21	Danf 21	Eb 1	Ek 1	Et 1	Fam 21
Abbo 2	Akb 2	Atc 2	Ban 22	Caro 22	Dani 22	Ebc 2	Eke 2	Ete 2	Far 22
Abd 3	Akc 3	Ath 3	Bar 23	Carr 23	Dank 23	Ebe 3	Ekh 3	Eth 3	Farn 23
Abg 4	Akg 4	Athe 4	Bark 24	Cart 24	Dar 24	Ebh 4	Ekk 4	Eti 4	Farr 24
Abi 5	Aki 5	Atic 5	Barm 25	Caru 25	Darm 25	Ebk 5	Ekl 5	Etn 5	Fars 25
Abk 6	Ako 6	Atl 6	Barne 26	Cas 26	Das 26	Ebl 6	Ekm 6	Eto 6	Fas 26
Abn 7	Akr 7	Ato 7	Barr 27	Casm 27	Dav 27	Ebo 7	Eko 7	Etr 7	Fau 27
Abr 8	Aku 8	Att 8	Bars 28	Cat 28	Davi 28	Ebt 8	Eku 8	Etu 8	Faw 28
Abu 9	Aky 9	Atw 9	Bas 29	Catm 29	Davis 29	Ebu 9	Eky 9	Ety 9	Fay 29
Ac 1	Al 1	Au 1	Bat 31	Cau 31	Davj 31	Ec 1	El 1	Eu 1	Fe 31
Acc 2	Ald 2	Auc 2	Batf 32	Cc 32	Daw 32	Ecc 2	Eld 2	Euc 2	Fee 32
Ace 3	Alg 3	Aue 3	Bax 33	Cel 33	Day 33	Ecc 3	Elg 3	Eue 3	Fel 33
Ach 4	Ali 4	Aug 4	Bay 34	Ce 34	Db 34	Ech 4	Eli 4	Eug 4	Felt 34
Acj 5	Ali 5	Aul 5	Be 35	Chal 35	Deb 35	Eck 5	Elk 5	Eul 5	Fen 35
Acl 6	Alm 6	Aur 6	Beal 36	Chan 36	Ded 36	Ecl 6	Elm 6	Eun 6	Fenn 36
Aco 7	Alo 7	Aus 7	Beam 37	Char 37	Del 37	Eco 7	Elr 7	Eur 7	Fer 37
Act 8	Alu 8	Aut 8	Bear 38	Charles 38	Dell 38	Ect 8	Elt 8	Eut 8	Ferg 38
Acu 9	Alw 9	Aux 9	Bed 39	Chat 39	Dem 39	Ecu 9	Ely 9	Eux 9	Fern 39
Ad 1	Am 1	Av 1	Bel 41	Che 41	Den 41	Ed 1	Em 1	Ev 1	Fer 41
Add 2	Ame 2	Avc 2	Bem 42	Chem 42	Denn 42	Edd 2	Emc 2	Eve 2	Fes 42
Ade 3	Ame 3	Ave 3	Ben 43	Chi 43	Deno 43	Edg 3	Eme 3	Evi 3	Fet 43
Adh 4	Amg 4	Avg 4	Beno 44	Chim 44	Deo 44	Edi 4	Emh 4	Evk 4	Fi 44
Adk 5	Ami 5	Avi 5	Beo 45	Chl 45	Des 45	Edl 5	Emk 5	Evl 5	Fie 45
Adm 6	Amm 6	Avi 6	Bers 46	Chr 46	Desi 46	Edo 6	Emm 6	Evo 6	Fieldi 46
Ado 7	Amp 7	Avo 7	Bi 47	Ci 47	Desr 47	Edr 7	Emp 7	Evr 7	Fih 47
Adr 8	Ams 8	Avr 8	Big 48	Ci 48	Det 48	Edt 8	Ems 8	Evt 8	Fill 48
Adu 9	Amu 9	Avt 9	Bil 49	Cim 49	Dev 49	Edw 9	Emy 9	Evy 9	Fin 49

Fig. 3. C.A. Cutter's Two-Figure Author Table: Portions of "A" through "F"

Now, however, it should be distinguished from other works on the same subject written by different authors. By consulting the Cutter Table for the letter "C" (Fig. 3), you will find that 34 is the numerical equivalent of the author's name. "C" preceeds the number, for it is the first letter of the writer's name (Chafer).

The Cutter number would then be "C34." The entire *call number* would look like this:

230

C34

To distinguish this book from Chafer's eight-volume *Systematic Theology* (which would also carry the classification 230), you may wish to add to the Cutter number the first letter of the title. The Cutter number for *Major Bible themes* would then read C34M. Chafer's *Systematic Theology* would then bear the call number:

230

C34S

The Cutter-Sanborn system is exceedingly easy to use. It is accompanied by a brief but descriptive manual. Depending on the size of your library, you may wish to use one letter of the alphabet to distinguish an author, except for names beginning with vowels (Ironside, which should be IR; Oman, which should be OM; and names beginning with Sc or Sch).

CLASSIFYING BIOGRAPHIES

Biographies are treated differently from other books. Some librarians dispense with a classification number altogether and use a "B" instead of the DDC number. Then, instead of assigning an author number underneath the classification number, they print the first three or four letters of the name of the subject. For example, if they were classifying a book on the life of D. L. Moody, the call number according to this system would be:

B

MOOD

A better way of classifying biographies, particularly if one is to view the contribution of great leaders of the Christian church in the light of their times, is to assign the biography a number in the 280 (denominations and sects) category. It is divided up as follows:

281 Primitive and Oriental Churches
282 Roman Catholic Church
283 Anglican Churches
284.1 Lutheran Churches
284.2 Calvinistic Reformed Churches in Europe

285   Presbyterian, American Reformed, and Congregational Churches
285.7 Reformed Churches in America
285.8 Congregationalism
286   Baptist, Disciples of Christ, Adventist Churches
287   Methodist Churches
288   Unitarianism
289   Other Denominations and Sects

For example, a biography on the life of the renowned Methodist revivalist John Wesley would receive a classification number 287.1. The same number would be assigned to a biography dealing with his American contemporary Francis Asbury. If you wish to keep biographies distinct so that they are arranged by country or continent, then Wesley's classification number can have the area notation 42 added to it. It would then be 287.142. In like manner, Asbury's classification number could have the area notation[1] for the United States added to it. It would then be 287.173.

Biographies about Martin Luther will be assigned the number 284.1 (Lutheran Churches), and, if it is your desire to distinguish German Lutherans from Lutherans in other countries, then the area notation for Germany should be added to it. The classification for Martin Luther would therefore be 284.143.

William Cunningham was a Scottish Presbyterian. The classification for Calvinistic churches of European origin is 284.2. To this number may be added the area notation for Scotland, 41. The classification would then be 284.241.

A biography of the British Baptist preacher Charles Haddon Spurgeon would carry the initial classification number of 286.1. To distinguish Spurgeon from American Baptists, the area notation for the country in which he labored could be added to the basic number. The classification would therefore be 286.142. On the other hand, an American Baptist like George W. Truett, former pastor of the First Baptist Church, Dallas, would have the area notation 73 added to the classification 286.1. Truett's class number would therefore be 286.173.

CUTTER NUMBERS FOR BIOGRAPHIES

Cutter numbers given to biographies are also different. To have all the works on or about men like Hodge, Luther, or Spurgeon in their respective places on the shelves, the Cutter number for biographies is the number for the

---

1. Area notations are to be found in volume 1 of the DDC (pp. 14-386). They are never used alone. They are added to a basic classification number to indicate locality. They may be omitted without jeopardizing the system. For your convenience, they have been included in the classification of the books in the bibliography that follows.

subject, not the biographer. In other words, the Cutter number for Charles Hodge would be H66 regardless of who wrote the book. Luther would be assigned the Cutter number L97, and a biography on the life of Spurgeon would be given the number SP9. A problem arises when you try to distinguish between biographies on Luther written by different men. Quite obviously you would like Roland Bainton's *Here I Stand,* Thomas Lindsey's *Luther and the German Reformation,* and A. Skevington Wood's *Captive to the Word* in the same place on your shelves. To arrange them in proper order, it is an easy matter to add to the Cutter number the first letter of the writer's name. For example, the Cutter number for Bainton's *Here I Stand* would be L97B. The call number would look like this:

284.143

L97B

Likewise Lindsey's *Luther and the German Reformation* would have the Cutter number L97L, and Wood's *Captive to the Word* would have the Cutter number L97W.

The same problem arises when assigning Cutter numbers to Bible biographies. Once again, the problem is solved by providing the Cutter number for the subject. However, what happens when you have five biographical treatments of Paul's life and the name of the writer of each begins with the letter M? For example, Clarence E. Macartney wrote *Paul the Man,* John R. McDuff wrote *Footsteps of St. Paul,* F. B. Meyer published a series of addresses under the title: *Paul: Servant of Jesus Christ,* Donald G. Miller wrote a discerning study he called *Conqueror in Chains,* and Olaf Moe has a volume on *The Apostle Paul.* The Cutter number for each one would be P28. To end each Cutter number with the first letter of the biographer's name (M) would not distinguish one work from the other. In these instances, many librarians add a third line. These lines carry the Cutter number, the first for Paul and the second for Macartney. The Cutter number would look like this:

227.092

P28

M11

In this way it differs from McDuff's work, because his Cutter number would be M14. Likewise, Meyer's Cutter number would be M57; Miller's M61; and Moe's M72. By following this elementary procedure, each book is given its rightful place on the bookshelf and distinguished from other books on the same subject.

General biographical sketches dealing with characters in both Old and New Testaments are assigned the number 220.92 and are followed by the Cutter number for the name of the writer or compiler. This is done for obvious reasons. The contents of the book cover more than one Bible character and, therefore, cannot be assigned a Cutter number for any one person. For example, Clovis G. Chappell's book on *Familiar Failures* contains character sketches of people in both Old and New Testaments. It would be assigned the Cutter number C36. To distinguish it from his other book *Feminine Faces*, "F" can be added to the Cutter number. The Cutter number would then be C36F. General works by a particular writer may, therefore, be distinguished from one another by addition of the first letter of the title to the end of the Cutter number.

CUTTER NUMBERS FOR SPECIAL BOOKS

Before leaving this discussion of Cutter numbers, mention needs to be made of works of a general nature that are sometimes given a general classification .8 or .08, plus the number that would normally be assigned to them if they did not treat a biblical or theological theme. For example, works on astrology carry a DDC number 133.52. When a book is written about astrology from a biblical point of view, the number 220 (for Bible) and .8 (general) is added to the regular classification, making for a long number—in this case 220.813352 (as in the instance of Kenneth C. Moore's *God's Voice in the Stars*). Rather than have such a long call number to somehow or another place on the spine of the book, it may be preferable to assign a Cutter number to astrology—for example, AS8 (AS because the word begins with a vowel)—in place of 133.52 and place this immediately below the general classification. The Cutter number for Moore would then follow on the third line. The classification of his book would then look like this:

220.8
AS8
M78

In addition, in areas of one's library that tend to grow rapidly, but for which there is no established form of subdivision (e.g., pastoral counseling, 253.5), the same policy of assigning special Cutter numbers may be followed so that works dealing with the counseling of alcoholics, the aged, the bereaved, drug addicts, and so on, may be grouped together.

With these few elementary principles, you will be able to classify your entire library.

Before focusing our attention on cataloging, we need to discuss two small but important aspects of preparing your books for their assigned place on your shelves. One is lettering, and the other deals with the marks of identification.

LETTERING

After you have gone to all the trouble of classifying your books, you will need to have the call numbers lettered on the spine. Different methods have been used. Some use India ink and letter the numbers on the spine (or, if the book is a very thin one, on the side cover) with a pen. Others use an electric pencil. (See Fig 4.) Still others obtain pressure-sensitive labels that are mounted on backing sheets so that they can be typed on easily and then removed for sticking on the spine. (See Fig. 5.) These pressure-sensitive labels stick without

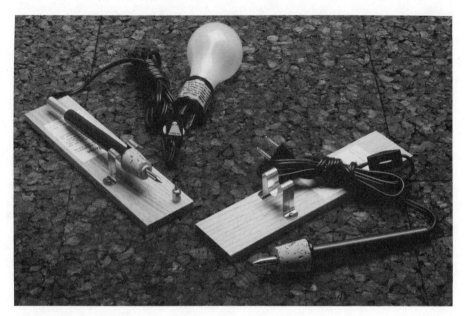

Fig. 4. Electric Stylus

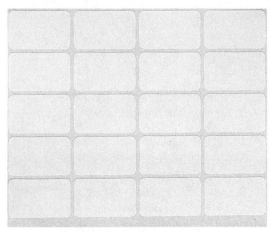

Fig. 5. Pressure-Sensitive Labels

moisture and have extra gripping qualities so that they can stay permanently in place. The size generally preferred by librarians is $\frac{3}{4}'' \times 1''$. They are inexpensive and, should the cover of the book cause a label to lift off, can easily be secured in position with a one inch strip of clear tape.

2

Cataloging Your Library

Henry Ward Beecher is one of the great names in the annals of the American pulpit. He said: "It is a man's duty to have books. A library is not a luxury, but one of the necessities of life." Great preachers of the past have invariably been lovers of good books. To have well-selected works as an aid in the ministry is an indispensible asset, but it is just as important for you to have these books recorded in a way that will enable you to make the greatest use of them. This is the task of cataloging. Without proper cataloging, you will hardly know what is in your library or how to find the information you need when you need it.

To aid you in your search for material, libraries arrange books in a convenient order. This is the task of classification. Cataloging describes the book in a standard manner and assigns subject headings to each work. In other words, cataloging is involved with the description of each work[1] and the preparation of cards for filing in a card catalog.

In the previous chapter, we dealt with *classification* and showed how this enables you to arrange your books according to their subject content. *Cataloging* makes a record of each item in the collection and provides subject headings to further aid you in research. Standard terminology is used to describe the contents of the book, and this enables you to know exactly what is in the library.

It is essential that every library, regardless of its size, have a card catalog. The card catalog may be arranged in one of two ways. A *dictionary card catalog* contains all the entries in one sequential file. These entries pertain to the author, title, subject, series, and so on, and are arranged in one general alphabet. A *divided catalog* has author and title entries filed together and the subject cards filed in a separate section. Divided catalogs are only used in larger libraries. Some ministers of my acquaintance have more than twelve

---

1. Librarians use the term *bibliographic description*.

thousand volumes in their private collections and file their cards in one catalog without any loss of efficiency.

CATALOG CARDS

INTRODUCTION

The cards filed in the catalog are generally three in number. Essentially the same information appears on each of these cards; however, one is called the *author,* or *main entry, card.* (See Fig. 8.) It is filed under the name of the author or the corporate body responsible for preparing the material.

A second card contains the same information on it except for the fact that the title of the book is typed above the author's name, and it is filed according to the title. This is called the *title card.* (See Fig. 10.)

Lastly, there will be a card or cards containing the same type of information except for the fact that the subject heading or headings will be typed in capitals above the author entry. This *subject card* is filed alphabetically by subject entry. (See Fig. 11.)

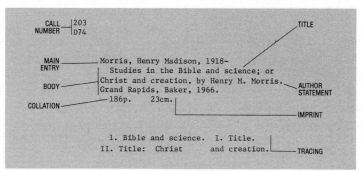

Fig. 6. A Shelf List Card

Public, academic, and institutional libraries always have a separate card, identical to the author card, that is filed separately by call number. It is called the *shelf list card.* (See Fig. 6.) Each of the library cards will be discussed in detail in this chapter.

The easiest way to develop a card catalog is to order the cards from the Library of Congress, Building 159, Navy Yard Annex, Washington, D.C. 20541. The Library of Congress order number is usually found on the verso of the title page and should be supplied with your order. The Library of Congress supplies order forms free of charge, and these forms must be used, because the information put on them is read by an optical reader at the Library of Congress offices. The cost of each set of cards varies, but it is relatively inexpensive when compared with the cost of employing someone to type multiple copies of the same card. When one considers the amount of material on the cards and the ease with which they can be acquired, the cost is very reasonable. (See Fig. 7 for a sample of a Library of Congress Card.)

> **The New international dictionary of New Testament theology /**
> Colin Brown, general editor. — Grand Rapids, Mich. : Zondervan Pub. House, c1975-1978.
>> 3 v. ; 25 cm.
>> Dictionary of New Testament theology.
>> "Translated, with additions and revisions, from the German Theologisches Begriffslexikon zum Neuen Testament, edited by Lothar Coenen, Erich Beyreuther and Hans Bietenhard."
>> "Companion volume: The new international dictionary of the Christian Church."
>> Includes bibliographical references and indexes.
>> ISBN 0-85364-177-3 (v. 1)
>> 1. Bible. N.T.—Theology—Dictionaries. 2. Bible. N.T.—Dictionaries.
>> I. Brown, Colin, 1932-   . II. Title: Dictionary of New Testament theology.
>> BS2397.N48   1975   225'.3—dc19   75-38895
>>   MARC
>
>> Library of Congress   75[8301r83]rev3

Fig. 7. Library of Congress Card

Some pastors, however, have their secretaries or volunteers from the church type up cards for them.

AUTHOR, OR MAIN ENTRY, CARD

The primary purpose of the author, or main entry, card is to indicate the full name of the author (if known—even if his full names do not appear on the title page), the year of his birth, and, if deceased, the year of his death. (See Fig. 7.) These dates may be omitted if the information is not readily available. However, if the author's name is a common one (e.g., Brown, John), you should try to obtain his date of birth to help distinguish him from someone else of the same name.

The author's name(s) appears four lines from the top of the card and begins nine spaces in from the left-hand edge of the card. This is called the *first indention*. The author's last name is typed first, and this is followed by his other names, year of birth, and so on. The bulk of this material can probably be obtained from the title page, foreword, or dust cover of the book.

Whenever the name of the author is incomplete, space is left in the main entry for the name to be filled in. This is done on the assumption that at some future time information regarding his full names may be forthcoming.

The author statement in the body of the card, however, must always reflect

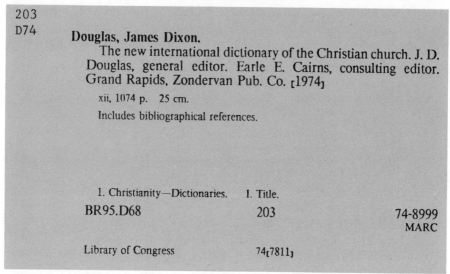

203
D74

Douglas, James Dixon.
    The new international dictionary of the Christian church. J. D.
Douglas, general editor. Earle E. Cairns, consulting editor.
Grand Rapids, Zondervan Pub. Co. ₁1974₁

    xii, 1074 p.   25 cm.

    Includes bibliographical references.

    1. Christianity—Dictionaries.   I. Title.

    BR95.D68   203   74-8999
                                                                   MARC

    Library of Congress   74₁7811₁

Fig. 8. An Author, or Main Entry Card

what is on the title page. In this way the author or main entry differs from the author statement. The only exception to this rule is if the author statement is an integral part of the title.

Titles like Sir, Dr., Ph.D., and Professor are generally omitted from the card.

In the event that a book has been written by more than one person and the words "by" and "and" do not appear on the title page, those words are added and are placed in brackets [   ].

If the book was written by more than one person, only the name of the first-mentioned author is put in the author entry. The names of the other contributors, editors, or compilers are reserved for the body of the card. (See Fig. 9.)

If the book was written by a committee, the main entry will bear the name of the committee or the association sponsoring the work.

The body of the card follows the main entry and begins on the second line. This material is typed eleven spaces in from the left edge of the card (the *second indention*), and the succeeding lines of the body of the card begin at the first indention. The body of the card consists of (1) title, (2) subtitle, (3) author statement, (4) edition statement and (5) imprint (i.e., the place of publication, the name of the publisher, and the date). Illustrations and material pertaining to a foreword are included only if they appear on the title page. If this is the case, they go between the author statement and the edition statement.

Only the first letter of the title is capitalized unless other words in the title are proper nouns. A subtitle, if included, follows immediately after the title and is separated from it by a comma, semicolon, or colon, depending upon the rules of grammar. The title or subtitle is generally followed by a comma (when the title and/or subtitle is short), and this in turn is followed by the author statement. When the word "by" does not appear on the title page, it is enclosed in brackets. The author statement is always followed by a period and appears exactly the same way it is found on the title page. If there is more than one author, then the other names are listed in the author statement exactly as they appear on the title page.

If there is no author statement (i.e., if the author's name is given in full on the title page and there are no additional authors), the *edition statement* follows the title or subtitle. The edition statement is always placed in brackets if the information has to be taken from the verso of the title page. If the information is found on the title page, the brackets are omitted. Periods or commas never follow the use of brackets.

In the same paragraph, but leaving four spaces to separate it from the author or edition statement, we have the *imprint*. This deals with the place of publication, followed by a period. If, however, the year of publication does not appear on the title page and the date can be obtained from the verso of the title page, the date should be placed within brackets. In this case it is not preceded by a comma, nor is it followed by a period. The name of the publisher is generally shortened so that Harper and Row becomes "Harper"; and Baker Book House becomes "Baker." University presses, however, are never abbreviated.

When turning to the title page, you may find that more than one city is listed. If, for example, you find that the book is published simultaneously in

Theological wordbook of the Old Testament / R. Laird Harris, editor, Gleason L. Archer, Jr., associate editor, Bruce K. Waltke, associate editor. — Chicago : Moody Press, c1980.

2 v. ; 26 cm.

Includes bibliographies and index.
ISBN 0-8024-8631-2 (set) : $34.95

1. Bible. O.T.—Dictionaries—Hebrew. 2. Bible. O.T.—Theology—Dictionaries. I. Harris, Robert Laird. II. Archer, Gleason Leonard, 1916-
III. Waltke, Bruce K.

BS440.T49   221.4'4'0321—dc19   80-28047
                                                  MARC

Library of Congress   ₁8304r83₁rev

Fig. 9. A Card Listing Other Contributors

"London, New York, and Paris," it is quite acceptable to type the first city and, if it is not an American city, the first American city as well. The imprint would then read: "London, New York." If, however, no place of publication is recorded, put [n.p.] for "no place." Such a notation is always placed in brackets.

A new paragraph at the second indention introduces the *collation*. The collation deals with the extent of the text (i.e., the number of pages, illustrations and maps, if any) and the height of the book in centimeters. When recording the number of pages, include the last numbered page of each section. For example, if the introduction or preface is numbered in Roman numerals, include the Roman figures as well as the Arabic figure when indicating the number of pages in the book (i.e., xii, 237).

If the book is in a series, the series statement follows on the same line as the collation, but it is separated from it by four spaces. The title of the series is always placed in parentheses, and only the first letter of the first word is capitalized (e.g., "International critical commentary").

Any *notes* that follow the collation are separated from the body of the card by a line. Although some libraries make a practice of putting notes on almost every card, this procedure is not necessary and consumes a great deal of time. Notes are designed to alert the reader of a translation of a book, or to show the fact that a book published in England under one title is now available in the United States under another title. For example, F. F. Bruce's book *This Is That* was published in America under the title *New Testament Development of Old Testament Themes.* A note recording this change is quite in order. Pastors will find contents notes particularly helpful. They are frequently used for *Festschriften* and other similar publications, but they may also be used to good effect for books of sermons. A contents note would list each sermon in the order in which it appears. In this way, by browsing through the card catalog, you can readily refresh your mind on exactly what material is contained in your collection.

The *tracing* makes up the last entry on the card. It begins near the bottom of the card and at the second indention. It contains a record of all headings (other than the main entry) where a card pertaining to this book may be found. Subject headings are preceded by Arabic numerals, whereas added entries are preceded by Roman numerals. The subject headings describe the content of the book. The added entries refer to joint authors, or translators, and the title. The value of these lie in the fact that they bring together all works on a particular subject. For example, books dealing with administration may be found under 254 (church administration) or 658 (management). The principles of secular management may apply equally as well to the administration of a church. By consulting the subject cards, you will be able to find all the material that you have on a particular subject. Or, if you have an inquiry from one of your teachers regarding the teaching of adolescents, material may be found under 155.5 (psychology of adolescence), 268.433 (Christian education of youth), or 373.2 (secular education). Only by using a card can you obtain access to material in these different areas.

This point may be further illustrated by considering the topic of evil. The Christan doctrine of theodicy is found under 231.8. Those interested in the ontological aspect of this study will find material under 111.84, and information from comparative religions and folklore will be found under 291.216 and 398.4 respectively. Occultism also has its doctrine of evil, and books dealing with this specific facet of study will be classified under 133.423. Finally, books dealing with the vindication of God's justice and goodness in permitting the existence of evil and suffering will be classified under 214. With such a divergency of subject material on topics such as "evil" and "suffering," it is imperative that you consult the different facets of the subject to obtain full information. Only by means of a well-arranged card catalog can you find all the material you may have on any one subject.

An indispensable aid in arriving at consistent, logical subject headings is the *Sears List of Subject Headings,* edited by Barbara M. Westby (10th ed.; New York: H. W. Wilson Company, 1972). It is less expensive than the *Library of Congress Subject Headings* (2 vols.), which is used in most academic libraries.

Special rules govern the subject headings given the Bible or parts of it. To the general heading "Bible" may be added the designation of a part of the Bible; the language of the text; the name of a version, translator, or reviser; and the year of the edition. For example, the tracing for a commentary on Genesis would read:

Bible. O.T. Genesis—Commentary.

Groups of the books such as the "prison epistles" or the Catholic epistles are entered in the following way:

Bible. N.T. Prison epistles; or, Bible. N.T. Catholic epistles.

Versions are entered in accordance with the language, version, selections (if any), and date. A copy of the Greek text would be entered as follows:

Bible. N.T. Greek.

Further information on these special rules may be obtained by consulting the *Anglo-American Cataloging Rules* in your nearest public library.

While this is the *approved* method, there is nothing to prevent pastors from dispensing with this formality and assigning expository works the tracing of Genesis, or Matthew, as the occasion requires.

TITLE CARD

The title card is designed to record the entry of the book in the card catalog by the title. (See Fig. 10.) It will be typed exactly the same as the author card except for one entry. Above the author entry and thirteen spaces in from the left-hand edge of the card (the *third indention*), the title is recorded. Only the first letter and proper nouns are capitalized.

The title is typed in full exactly as it appears on the title page. Even if it is long, it should not be abbreviated.

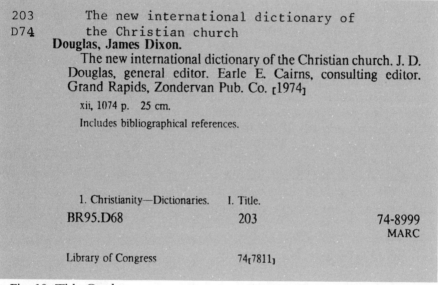

```
203          The new international dictionary of
D74            the Christian church
          Douglas, James Dixon.
             The new international dictionary of the Christian church. J. D.
          Douglas, general editor. Earle E. Cairns, consulting editor.
          Grand Rapids, Zondervan Pub. Co. ₍1974₎

          xii, 1074 p.  25 cm.

          Includes bibliographical references.




             1. Christianity—Dictionaries.   I. Title.
          BR95.D68                    203                    74-8999
                                                             MARC

             Library of Congress         74₍7811₎
```

Fig. 10. Title Card

SUBJECT CARD

The function of the subject card is to provide a brief standard description of the subject of the book. This has been discussed at length under *tracing*. The subject card will be identical to the author card except for the fact that the subject heading(s) will appear in capital letters above the main entry and will begin at the third indention. A separate card will be typed for each major subject treated in the book. (See Fig. 11.)

SHELF LIST CARD

As mentioned earlier, public, academic, and institutional libraries have shelf list cards. (See Fig. 6.) This card is identical to the main entry, or author, card, but it is filed separately by call number. It is checked whenever new books are

203   CHRISTIANITY--DICTIONARIES
D74   **Douglas, James Dixon.**
         The new international dictionary of the Christian church. J. D.
       Douglas, general editor. Earle E. Cairns, consulting editor.
       Grand Rapids, Zondervan Pub. Co. [1974]

         xii, 1074 p.   25 cm.

         Includes bibliographical references.

         1. Christianity—Dictionaries.   I. Title.
         BR95.D68   203   74-8999
                                                                     MARC

         Library of Congress   74[7811]

Fig. 11. A Subject Card

added to the library to insure that the call numbers have not been duplicated. In a small library this is unlikely, and, if a duplication should occur, it can easily and speedily be corrected.

FILING

When the cards have been typed, they are ready for filing in a 3″ × 5″ card catalog. They may be filed either word by word or letter by letter. However, the tendency today is to file word by word. Foreign accent marks and punctuation should be ignored. Initials are treated as one letter words. Abbreviations like St. for Saint, and Dr. for Doctor are regarded as if spelled in full. Exceptions are single letter abbreviations for geographic place names, for example, D. C., VT, GA.

The cards are filed in alphabetic order giving preference to (1) author cards, with (2) title and (3) subject cards coming next. In the early stages of your library, the filing of cards will be easy. However, as more and more cards are added to your catalog, you will want to read the little booklet *ALA Rules for Filing Catalog Cards,* by Pauline A. Seely (2d ed.; Chicago: American Library Association, 1968).

All of this is designed to make the books in your library more usable to you in your ministry. As you progress, classification will become easy, and cataloging will not seem like a chore. And the important thing to remember is that it serves as a reminder to you of what you have in your library! However, the processing of books always takes second place to their selection, and the next few chapters are designed to help you select the best books for your own personal library. Such reference tools as multi-volume sets—*New York Times Index, Public Affairs Information Service (PAIS), Facts on File,* and *Cambridge Ancient History,* for example—need not be bought or subscribed to. They can always be used in your nearest public library or a nearby college or university library. Read wisely, but choose with care the books you want to have in your own library. Buy them for the lasting value they will have and the benefit they will be to you in your ministry.

3

Subject Guide
to Dewey Decimal
Classification

The following Subject Guide or Relative Index is one of the most important aids in proper classification. When once you have determined the subject matter of the book, the tentative classification may be arrived at by consulting the Subject Guide. This does not do away with the need for checking the tentative classification against the schedules. It can be of great help to you, however, in outlining the different areas in which books may be classified.

In the following classification, the entries in italics differ from the Dewey system, but not so as to impair the value of Melvin Dewey's work.

32 **The Minister's Library**

PART TWO

A Guide to Books for Your Library

4

General Reference Works and Bible Commentaries

As a pastor, your primary responsibility is to preach the Word. While the other tasks involved in the ministry are important, pastors should be, above everything else, expositors! In a perceptive and greatly needed article entitled "Pastor of All Trades,"[1] Dr. Earl D. Radmacher, president of Western Conservative Baptist Theological Seminary, deplores the "jack-of-all-trades" syndrome into which many pastors fall. In applying the truths of Acts 6:1-7 to this situation, Radmacher points the way out of the cul-de-sac and stresses the need for priorities in the ministry. He emphasizes the importance of a teaching ministry that will edify and feed the flock of God over which we have been made overseers.

The following list of books is designed to guide pastors in their choice of good books, to facilitate study, and to help them fulfill their God-appointed role of being pastor-teachers (Eph. 4:11). The books regarded as most important and worthy of acquisition here have been marked with an asterisk (*). Books of general interest are included for the sake of those who desire to read broadly in a particular area. Books espousing a theological viewpoint not in keeping with a conservative, evangelical position have been identified with a dagger (†). This does not necessarily mean they are not worthy of consultation or acquisition. It does avoid repetition of annotations in regard to this point.

GENERAL REFERENCE WORKS

Bumpus, John Skelton. *A Dictionary of Ecclesiastical Terms.* New York: Gordon Press, 1969.

Originally published in 1910. Contains definitions of hundreds of ecclesiastical terms associated with doctrines, theories,

---

1. Earl D. Radmacher, "Pastor of All Trades," *The Christian Reader* 9, no. 6 (December 1971—January 1972): 44-48.

ceremonies, and rituals that have been held to or practiced by religious bodies since the first century. Provides a full etymology and concise history of the development, changes, and uses of the particular word, name, or phrase. Remains a valuable reference work, and frequently explains the origin of present-day practices and beliefs. Of particular importance to Roman Catholics. 203.B88

Catholic University of America. *New Catholic Encyclopedia.* 15 vols. and index. Washington, D.C.: Catholic University of America, 1967.

An entirely new work, and, in spite of its title, it bears no relation to the earlier *Catholic Encyclopedia* (17 vols., 1907-22). Researchers who consult both works will find that this new one reflects the more tolerant views and policies of the post-Vatican II era. Arranged alphabetically, the articles reflect maturity as well as reliability. And although manifesting a tendency to devote more space to the Catholic church in the United States and Latin America, they cover virtually every aspect of Catholic history, theology, and ministry. Each of the 17,000 articles is signed, and helpful bibliographies are appended to many of them. 282.03.C28

Encyclopedia Americana. 30 vols. New York: Americana Corp., 1966.

The leading competitor of the *Encyclopedia Britannica.* First published in 1829-33. Since 1936 kept current under a policy of continuous revision. Major emphasis given to scientific and technological subjects, including a careful consideration of material in the fields of nuclear science and space exploration. Noted for its accuracy and fullness of information on American towns and cities. Contemporary biographies and historical data relating to important events, persons, and inventions included among its special features. Includes a comprehensive index of 325,000 entries, 34,000 cross references, and maps covering every state of the United States and Canada, all the continents and major countries, and many other regions of the world. 031.AM3

Encyclopedia Britannica: A New Survey of Universal Knowledge. 24 vols. Chicago: Encyclopedia Britannica, 1968.

The oldest and most famous English encyclopedia available today. Since 1932 published under a policy of continuous revision. The eleventh edition published in 1910-11 is the most famous and certainly the most extensive. With the fourteenth edition published in 1929, the *EB* became more practical in character, and articles were shorter and grouped under specific headings. The trend in modern times has been toward a more visually attractive and more readable encyclopedia. Illustrations and maps are excellent, the writing style simple, and the bibliographies suggestive. Two accurate and comprehensive indexes are found in volume 24, together with a handy atlas. 032.B77

Encyclopedia of Religion and Ethics. Edited by James Hastings. 13 vols. Edinburgh: T. and T. Clark, 1925.

The fullest work of its kind. Contains comprehensive articles on all religions, ethical systems and movements, religious beliefs and customs, philosophical ideas and moral practices, anthropology, mythology, folklore, biology, psychology, economics, sociology, and names of persons and places connected with these subjects. An extensive index volume completed the set and enhances its general usefulness. Found in all major public, university, and college libraries. 203.H27

Index to Religious Periodical Literature: An Author and Subject Index to Periodical Literature . . . Including an Author Index to Book Reviews. Prepared by Libraries of the American Theological Library Association. Compiled and edited by J. S. Judah and L. J. Ziegler. Chicago: American Theological Library Association, 1953.

IRPL is a semiannual index with biennial cumulations. It has long been regarded as one of the most important resource tools for theological research. The *IRPL* originally indexed only 31 journals, but the coverage increased to 58 in 1955-56, 113 in 1965-66, and 203 in 1975-76. Essays dealing with aspects of church history, the history of religions, sociology, psychology of religion, the humanities, and current events are given a prominent place in *IRPL*. Church music and counseling, however, are also fairly represented. *IRPL* places its emphasis primarily on English-language periodicals, although about 25 percent of those indexed bear foreign titles. Many of these foreign titles, however, have essays in English in every issue. Protestant, Catholic, and Jewish journals are included without religious bias. Later volumes were divided into three sections: A subject index that adheres closely to the approved subject headings of the Library of Congress, an author index that includes a brief abstract of the article, and a book review index listing alphabetically by author those works that received scholarly review during the preceding two years. Journal articles on different books of the Bible (or parts of books of the Bible) are arranged under "Bible. (O.T.)" or "Bible. (N.T.)." To find an article dealing with Paul's thought in Romans 5:12-21, the investigator will need to check the entries in *IRPL* under "Bible. (N.T.) Romans" and then look down the entries for those articles discussing chapter 5. 016.205.IN2

*McClintock, John and *James Strong.* *Cyclopedia of Biblical, Theological and Ecclesiastical Literature.* 12 vols. Grand Rapids:

Baker Book House, 1968-70.

One of the most exhaustive encyclopedias ever to be published in the English language. Covers virtually every field of religious knowledge in its 31,000 articles. First published in 1895, but still of great value today. Few researchers will be disappointed by what they find in this work. 203.M13

*New Schaff-Herzog Encyclopedia of Religious Knowledge. Edited by Samuel Macauley Jackson. 13 vols. Grand Rapids: Baker Book House, 1949.

First published in 1908. Covers biblical and extrabiblical material. Biographical articles and ancient and modern religions receive considerable attention. Two supplementary volumes update the material. The bibliographies are representative and helpful. 203.SCHI

*Smith, William and **S. Cheetham.** *Dictionary of Christian Antiquities.* 2 vols. Hartford, Conn.: J. B. Burr, 1880.

Provides a full account of the leading persons, institutions, art, social life, and so on, of the Christian church from the earliest times to Charlemagne. 271ʹ.009.SM6A

Universal Jewish Encyclopedia. Edited by Isaac Landman. 11 vols. New York: Universal Jewish Encyclopedia Co., 1930-44.

Replete with information about the "Jews and Judaism since the earliest times." It consists of a compilation of 10,000 lengthy, signed articles on Jewish history, religion, culture, and customs, and is ideal for Bible character studies (e.g., Aaron, Barak, David, Elijah, Gehazi, Moses, Jonah). Also gives an explanation of Jewish feasts (Trumpets, Purim) and fasts *(Yom Kippur)*. 296.03.UN3

The World Book Encyclopedia. 20 vols. Chicago: Field Enterprises Educational Corp., 1962.

An outstanding juvenile encyclopedia issued annually under a policy of continuous revision. A reading and study guide (issued separately) combines with a classified index to make this an ideal set. The *World Book* Year Book updates the encyclopedia. While designed specifically for young people, the usefulness of this encyclopedia need not be limited to the young. 031.W89

INTRODUCTORY STUDIES ON RELIGION

*Babbage, Stuart Barton. *The Vacuum of Unbelief.* Grand Rapids: Zondervan Publishing House, 1969.

A brilliantly written series of essays containing refreshing and illuminating studies on the profound truths of Christian faith and their relevancy to the closing decades of this century. 208.B11

Bellinzoni, Arthur J., Jr. and **Thomas V. Litzenburg, Jr.** *Intellectual Honesty and Religious Commitment.* Philadelphia: Fortress Press, 1969.

The answers given by the writers to the problem of intellectual honesty are widely divergent because the contributors have varying conceptions of religious commitment. These differences will cause more confusion than certainty. 201.B41

Bush, Douglas. *The Renaissance and English Humanism.* Toronto: Toronto University Press, 1939.

The Alexander Lectures for 1939. True to the title of the book. 211.6.B96

Carnell, Edward John. *A Philosophy of the Christian Religion.* Grand Rapids: Wm. B. Eerdmans Publishing Co., 1954.

A scholarly attempt to make Christianity intellectually acceptable. Evaluates the varied religious and pseudoreligious views of a wide variety of people, but fails to include an evaluation of existentialism. Now dated. 201.C21

*Clark, Gordon Haddon. *Religion, Reason, and Revelation.* Philadelphia: Presbyterian and Reformed Publishing Co., 1961.

A carefully reasoned attempt to refute the traditional philosophies of knowledge, religion, and mortality, and to replace these inadequate views with a philosophy in harmony with the Scriptures. 201.C54

Erasmus, Desiderius. *Christian Humanism and the Reformation: Selected Writings.* Translated and edited by John C. Olin. New York: Harper and Row, n.d.

Contains primary source material but is not as helpful to the pastor as Bainton's *Erasmus of Christendom.* Heavy reading. 211.6.ER1

Ferm, Robert O. *The Psychology of Christian Conversion.* Westwood, N.J.: Fleming H. Revell Co., 1959.

A clear, simple analysis of the basic problems of the psychology of religion, with authoritative answers that demand respect and, in the majority of cases, acceptance. 201.6. F38

Ford, Leighton. *One Way to Change the World.* New York: Harper and Row, 1970.

Challenging studies stressing the need for the spreading of the gospel among the nations. 209.04.F75

Freeman, David Hugh. *A Philosophical Study of Religion.* Philadelphia: Presbyterian and Reformed Publishing Co., 1964.

An examination of the nature of religion, religious claims to revelation, a biblical view of science, and so on. 201.F87

Hackett, Stuart Cornelius. *The Resurrection of Theism: Prolegomena to Christian Apology.* Chicago: Moody Press, 1957.

A well-written, logical defense of the traditional arguments for the existence of God. 211.H11

Henry, Carl Ferdinand Howard. *Faith*

at the Frontiers. Chicago: Moody Press, 1969.

Makes Christianity meaningful and relevant. Attacks the problems of today's milieu, and offers some concrete solutions. 208.H39

Holmes, Arthur F. *Christian Philosophy in the Twentieth Century.* Nutley, N.J.: Craig Press, 1969.

An essay in philosophical methodology. 201.H73

James, William. *The Varieties of Religious Experience: A Study in Human Nature.* London: Wm. Collins, Sons, 1960.

†Originally published in 1902 in a scientific attempt to analyze religious experience in terms of psychological phenomenon. Describes two distinct types of religious orientation—the healthy and the sick. Of value for its histories and case-studies. However, James was a pragmatist and was antisupernaturalistic in his approach to spiritual conversion. 201.6.J23 1960

Lewis, Clive Staples. *Christian Reflections.* Edited by Walter Hooper. Grand Rapids: Wm. B. Eerdmans Publishing Co., 1967.

A series of essays dealing with the immortality of all men and the reality of heaven and hell. 208.L58

Lloyd-Jones, David Martyn. *Conversions: Psychological and Spiritual.* London: Inter-Varsity Press, 1959.

An inadequate reply to William Sergant's antisupernatural work *The Battle of the Mind.* 201.6.L77

Maritain, Jacques. *The Degrees of Knowledge.* Translated by Gerald E. Phelan. New York: Charles Scribner's Sons, 1959.

Regarded as the magnum opus of this contemporary philosopher. Records his attempt to develop a complete metaphysical synthesis along Thomist lines. 201.M33

Moltmann, Jurgen. *Religion, Revela-* *tion, and the Future.* New York: Charles Scribner's Sons, 1969.

†Studies presented during Moltmann's visit to the United States, providing an introduction to his thought. Primarily philosophical in their approach. 201.M73

Montgomery, John Warwick. *The Suicide of Christian Theology.* Minneapolis: Bethany Fellowship, 1970.

A collection of essays and reviews by one of America's leading sacramental theologians. 201.1'08.M76

*Morris, Leon. *The Abolition of Religion.* Chicago: Inter-Varsity Press, 1964.

A series of essays on "religionless Christianity." 201.M83

Niebuhr, Helmut Richard. *The Purpose of the Church and Its Ministry.* New York: Harper and Row, 1956.

†A sociological study. Valuable for its insights, but marred by the writer's theological presuppositions. 207.N55

Niebuhr, Reinhold. *Beyond Tragedy: Essays on the Christian Interpretations of History.* New York: Charles Scribner's Sons, 1937.

†Working from a strong sociological premise, the writer believes that a biblical view of life offers the only true approach to the meaning of history. He insists that the center, source, and fulfillment of history lie beyond its boundaries. 201.N51

Paine, Thomas. *The Age of Reason.* Indianapolis: Bobbs-Merrill Co., 1968.

Written initially in 1794-95 to rescue the essentials of deism from oblivion. Has long been regarded as a rationalistic attempt to discredit Christianity. 211.4.P16 1968

Ramsey, Arthur Michael. *Sacred and Secular.* New York: Harper and Row, 1965.

†In an endeavor to extricate man from compartmentalizing his secular and religious life, the archbishop of Canterbury

provides a study of the otherworldly and this-worldy aspects of Christianity. 208.R14

Rian, Edwin Harold, ed. *Christianity and World Revolution.* New York: Harper and Row, 1963.

A series of scholarly addresses designed to stimulate the church to social action. 208.2.R35

Sayers, Dorothy L. *Christian Letters to a Post-Christian World.* Edited by Roderick Jellema. Grand Rapids: Wm. B. Eerdmans Publishing Co., 1969.

A collection of clear, sometimes witty, always relevant papers on apologetic themes. 208.SA9

Schilling, Sylvester Paul. *God in an Age of Atheism.* Nashville: Abingdon Press, 1969.

Limited to data from the nineteenth century and onward, this volume summarizes the grounds on which philosophers and theologians have tended to reject a belief in God. 211.8.SCH3

Temple, William. *Mens Creatrix.* New York: St. Martin's Press, 1917.

†The former archbishop of Canterbury pleads for a Christian theism that is akin to an evolutionary idealism. 211.3.T24

Tennant, Frederick Ross. *Philosophical Theology.* 2 vols. Cambridge: At the University Press, 1928.

†A classic treatment of the teleological argument for the existence of God. 210.T25

Young, Warren Cameron. *A Christian Approach to Philosophy.* Grand Rapids: Baker Book House, 1964.

A conservative introduction. 201.Y8

CREATION, SCIENCE, AND THE BIBLE

Bube, Richard H., ed. *Encounter Between Christianity and Science.* Grand Rapids: Wm. B. Eerdmans Publishing Co., 1967.

†This book has been described as "essays full of creative bending and stretching by generally conservative Christians" to make the Bible fit the findings of modern science. The chapters on astronomy, geology, the physical and biological sciences, psychology, and sociology relate the theory of evolution to theology. 215.B85

***Carron, T. W.** *Evolution: The Unproven Hypothesis.* Worthing, Eng.: Lindisfarne Press, 1957.

A brief discussion of discrepancies in the evolutionary theory. 575.C23

Clark, Gordon Haddon. *The Philosophy of Science and Belief in God.* Nutley, N.J.: Craig Press, 1964.

A small volume that summarizes the reasons for the widespread rejection of religion by scientists. Points out that science does not and cannot imply the nonexistence of God or of spiritual realities. 501.C54

Clark, Robert Edward David. *The Christian Stake in Science.* Chicago: Moody Press, 1967.

A British scientist defends his belief that Christians should not abandon their trust in an inerrant Bible in favor of "inexorable scientific laws," but that scientific inquiry, rightly undertaken and properly interpreted, confirms the Bible. 215.C54

*_____. *Darwin: Before and After.* London: Paternoster Press, 1958.

Subsequently published by Moody Press, this examination and assessment of Darwin's life and evolutionary theory deserves widespread reading. 575.016.C54

*_____. *The Universe: Plan or Accident?* Philadelphia: Muhlenberg Press, 1961.

A confirmed creationist here provides a constructive study of the religious implications of modern science. 215.C54U

Clark, Robert T., and **James D. Bales.** *Why Scientists Accept Evolution.* Grand Rapids: Baker Book House, 1966.

Does not evaluate the pros and cons of evolution, but examines the reasons for its widespread acceptance. 575.C54

Criswell, Wallie Amos. *Did Man Just Happen?* Grand Rapids: Zondervan Publishing House, 1957.

Deals with the factual material relating to the creation of man, the evidence of biology for special creation, and the mystery of man. A popular treatment. 215.C86

Davidheiser, Bolton. *Evolution and Christian Faith.* Nutley, N.J.: Presbyterian and Reformed Publishing Co., 1969.

An antievolutionary work containing a careful definition of evolution as it relates to the Christian faith. Commendable for its attempt to state accurately the essential views of all writers quoted. At the same time, the writer presents a biologist's view of special creation. 213.D28E

_____. *Science and the Bible.* Grand Rapids: Baker Book House, 1971.

A biologist's critical evaluation of the methods used and conclusions reached by scientists in their attempt to prove the evolutionary hypothesis. 215.D28

Everest, F. Alton. *The Prior Claim.* Chicago: Moody Press, 1953.

This book forms the basis of the Moody Institute of Science film and deals with the amazing way in which plants and animals have anticipated man's greatest inventions. 215.EV2

Frair, Wayne and **P. William Davis.** *Case for Creation.* Chicago: Moody Press, 1967.

Two biologists show the limitations and weaknesses of the evolutionary hypothesis. 213.F84

Hardy, Alister Clavering. *The Living Stream.* London: Wm. Collins, Sons, 1965.

Comprising the Gifford Lectures on Science, Natural History and Religion, University of Aberdeen, Scotland, 1963-65, these studies assess the theory of evolution and its relationship to the spirit of man. This is a scholarly volume that, while supporting a modified evolutionary hypothesis, exposes many of its weaknesses as well. 575.H22

Heim, Karl. *The World: Its Creation and Consummation, the End of the Present Age and the Future of the World in the Light of the Resurrection.* Translated by Robert Smith. Edinburgh: Oliver and Boyd, 1962.

Part of a six-volume work that tries to reconcile science with a Christian understanding of the world. Roman Catholic. 213.H36

Huxley, Julian Sorell. *Evolution in Action.* New York: Harper and Row, 1953.

†Containing the Patton Foundation Lectures delivered at Indiana University in 1950-51, these studies by a renowned evolutionary writer, philosopher, and scientist unwittingly demonstrate the fixity of species. 575.H98

James, Edwin Oliver. *Creation and Cosmology.* Studies in the History of Religions. Leiden: E. J. Brill, 1969.

A historical and comparative study. Antisupernaturalistic. 213.J23

Kelly, Howard Atwood. *A Scientist's Belief in the Bible.* Philadelphia: Sunday School Times Co., 1925.

A professor of gynecology discusses his spiritual pilgrimage and how he came to faith in Christ and a belief in the inerrancy of the Scriptures. 215.K29

Kerkut, G.A. *Implications of Evolution.* New York: Pergamon Press, 1960.

The professor of physiology and biochemistry, University of Southhampton, England, writes concerning his misgivings about evolution. In his chapter on basic assumptions, he shows that even evolutionists have assumptions that are not scientifically verifiable. A very extensive bibliography concludes this important work. 575.K45

*Klotz, John William. *Genes, Genesis and Evolution.* 2d revised ed. St. Louis: Concordia Publishing House, 1970.

Following the discovery of the molecular structure of DNA, RNA, and protein synthesis in heredity, Klotz felt it necessary to revise his earlier work, which was published in 1955. This revision provides the reader with a great deal of knowledge and understanding concerning the present-day theories of evolution and creation. 213.K69 1970

_____. *Modern Science in the Christian Life.* St. Louis: Concordia Publishing House, 1961.

A masterly treatment. Ideal for young people. 215.K69

*Lammerts, Walter Edward, ed. *Scientific Studies in Special Creation.* Grand Rapids: Baker Book House, 1971.

_____, **comp.** *Why Not Creation?* Grand Rapids: Baker Book House, 1970.

These scholarly studies support the special creation view and must be answered by those advocating a theistic concept of evolution. 213'.08.L18

Leakey, Louis Seymour Bazett. *Adam's Ancestors: The Evolution of Man and His Culture.* 4th ed. New York: Harper and Row, 1960.

Leakey's work at Olduvai Gorge in central Africa has been popularized by the National Geographic Society. He spent his entire life trying to substantiate the evolutionary theory. This book is the result of his extensive study and research. 575'.016.L47 1960

Maatman, Russell W. *The Bible, Natural Science, and Evolution.* Grand Rapids: Baker Book House, 1970.

Taking the Bible as the norm for arriving at the truth, the author makes a sincere attempt to evaluate the information provided by science. 215.M11

MacBeth, Norman. *Darwin Retried.* Boston: Gambit Publishing Co., 1971.

Building upon the laws of evidence, the writer evaluates Darwinism and concludes that the basis upon which it rests cannot be closely scrutinized without leading to the collapse of the system. 575.M12

Moorehead, Alan. *Darwin and the Beagle.* New York: Harper and Row, 1969.

A penetrating, modern assessment of Darwin's famous voyage. Well written, but lacking a scientist's perception. 508.309.M78

Morris, Henry Madison. *The Bible and Modern Science.* Chicago: Moody Press, 1951.

One of the writer's earliest works. Shows that the findings of science, when properly interpreted, confirm the teachings of Scripture. 215.M83B

*_____. *Evolution and the Modern Christian.* Grand Rapids: Baker Book House, 1967.

A brief, scholarly refutation of evolution. 575.M83

*_____. *Studies in the Bible and Science.* Grand Rapids: Baker Book House, 1966.

An important series of essays that does not minimize the problems confronting Christians in the realm of science. Morris, however, justifies faith in an infallible Bible and furnishes his readers with an important apologetic. 215.M83S

*_____. *The Twilight of Evolution.* Grand Rapids: Baker Book House, 1964.

Contains a valuable discussion of the laws of thermodynamics and the inconsistency of the evolutionary hypothesis when compared with these laws. 215.M83T

Morrison, Abraham Cressy. *Man Does Not Stand Alone.* Westwood, N.J.: Fleming H. Revell Co., 1944.

A scientist unfolds an almost unbelievable range of data showing God's direct involvement in the order of creation and the preservation of the universe. 215.M83

Nelson, Bryon Christopher. *After Its Kind.* Minneapolis: Augsburg Publishing House, 1965.

By building upon the findings of paleontologists, the writer provides a strong refutation of the evolutionary hypothesis. 215.6.N33

Ramm, Bernard Lawrence. *Christian View of Science and Scripture.* Grand Rapids: Wm. B. Eerdmans Publishing Co., 1954.

†A scholarly discussion of the problems associated with this area of study. The writer denounces "hyperorthodoxy" but leaves his readers with serious doubts regarding his own view of biblical infallibility. While his *Protestant Biblical Interpretation* contains excellent hermeneutical principles, the reader will find that these are waived in order to make concessions to scientists by making the Bible fit their theories. In spite of its scholarship, this remains a disappointing treatise. 215.R14

Rushdoony, Rousas John. *Mythology of Science.* Nutley, N.J.: Craig Press, 1967.

A study of creationism that succeeds in exposing many of the naive theories long held by scientists. 215.R89

*Short, Arthur Rendle. *Modern Discovery and the Bible.* 3d ed. London: Tyndale Press, 1952.

A comprehensive, consistent analysis of the nature of the universe, together with evidence justifying a belief in special creation. 215.SH8 1952

Shute, Evan. *Flaws in the Theory of Evolution.* Nutley, N.J.: Craig Press, 1966.

First published in England in 1961, these essays by a medical doctor, endocrinologist, and geriatrics specialist center in the study of the human body and show how the facts of anatomical science are in violent contradiction to the theories of evolution. 575.SH9

A Symposium on Creation. Grand Rapids: Baker Book House, 1968.

These studies by leading geologists, biologists, scientists, chemists, and engineers have been appearing annually. The essays are scholarly, and all support the creationist belief in special creation. They can be read with profit and are particularly suited to the needs of those who work with collegiates. 213.SY6 1968

*Whitcomb, John C., Jr. *Creation According to God's Word.* Grand Rapids: Reformed Fellowship, 1966.

A carefully researched essay by a leading creationist. 213.W58

*_____. *Origin of the Solar System.* Philadelphia: Presbyterian and Reformed Publishing Co., 1964.

In his usual thorough way, the writer explains the origin of the solar system from a creationist's point of view. 523.2.W58

*Wilder-Smith, A. E. *Creation of Life.* Wheaton: Harold Shaw Publishers, 1970.

This holder of three earned doctorates in the fields of organic chemistry, pharmacology, and science probes the very means by which scientific materialists have attempted to support the theory of evolution. 213.5.W64

_____. *Man's Origin, Man's Destiny.* Wheaton: Harold Shaw Publishers, 1968.

A critical survey of the principles of evolution and Christianity, with emphasis upon the often neglected aspect of man's destiny, or life after physical death. 573.2.W64M

Zimmerman, Paul Albert, ed. *Darwin, Evolution, and Creation.* St. Louis: Concordia Publishing House, 1959.

Studies by creationists on the inconsistencies of the evolutionary hypothesis. 213.5.Z6

_____, ed. *Rock Strata and the Bible Record.* St. Louis: Concordia Publishing House, 1970.

A research team of seven scientists and theologians provides enlightening essays on the controversy between science and religion. This book is a repository of information on the earth, rock strata, and fossils. 215.Z6

BIBLE ENCYCLOPEDIAS AND DICTIONARIES

Allmen, Jean-Jacques von. *A Companion to the Bible.* New York: Oxford University Press, 1958.

A dictionary of the major theological ideas and terms found in the Bible. Based on the RSV. Published in England under the title *Vocabulary of the Bible.* Articles by theological liberals and conservatives appear side-by-side. Still helpful. 220.3.AL5

Cruden, Alexander. *Dictionary of Bible Terms.* London: Pickering and Inglis, 1958.

Contains the helpful notes on scriptural terms found interspersed throughout Cruden's unabridged concordance. These have been culled and made available in book form for easy reference. 220.3.C88

*Douglas, James Dixon, ed. *New Bible Dictionary.* Grand Rapids: Wm. B. Eerdmans Publishing Co., 1962.

Represents the finest British conservative scholarship (only a few American authors were included). Less complete and less consistent than Unger's, but provides fuller information on some critical subjects. 220.3.D74

Fairbairn, Patrick, *Imperial Bible Dictionary.* 6 vols. Grand Rapids: Zondervan Publishing House, 1957.

First published in 1889. Particularly good on biblical biography, with thorough articles on leading biblical places and events. Has been superseded by more recent sets. 220.3.F15 1957

Harper's Bible Dictionary. Edited by Madeleine Sweeny Miller and J. Lane Miller. New York: Harper and Brothers, 1952.

†Advocates the documentary hypothesis of the Pentateuch, explains away miracles, denies the prophetic fulfillment of the book of Revelation, contradicts the biblical teaching on the personality of Satan, and in general fails to provide Bible students with the type of information they need. 220.3.H23

*Hastings, James, ed. *Dictionary of the Bible.* 5 vols. Edinburgh: T. and T. Clark, 1951.

†First published in 1898. Retains its value although now somewhat dated. Particularly rich in historical data. 220.3.H27

Hastings Dictionary of the Bible. Edited by F. C. Grant and H. H. Rowley. Rev. ed. New York: Charles Scribner's Sons, 1963.

†A revision of an earlier one-volume abridgement of *HDB,* this edition contains helpful historical information and some excellent articles. 220.3.H27 1963

The Interpreter's Dictionary of the Bible. Edited by G. A. Buttrick, et al. 4 vols. Nashville: Abingdon Press, 1962.

†A scholarly dictionary that defines and explains every proper name, major incident, and place mentioned in the Bible, pays close attention to details contained in the Apocrypha, comments on all the ceremonies and rites of both OT and NT, and provides definitive articles on every major doctrine and theological concept. Well illustrated with full-color maps. Pronunciation is given for difficult words, and the cross references and bibliographies are particularly helpful. 220.3.IN8

Miller, Madeleine Sweeny and **J. Lane Miller.** *Encyclopedia of Bible Life.* New

York: Harper and Brothers, 1955.

†A monumental work on the agriculture, animals, arts and crafts, business, homes, nutrition, transportation, and social and professional life of those living in the ancient Near East. Dated. 220.3.M61

***Orr, James, ed.** International Standard Bible Encyclopedia.* 5 vols. Grand Rapids: Wm. B. Eerdmans Publishing Co., 1939.

An old work presently undergoing revision. Not as scholarly as *Hastings' Dictionary of the Bible,* and not as up-to-date as the *Interpreter's Dictionary of the Bible,* but still valuable. Contains indices to Hebrew and Greek words. 220.3.OR7

Pictorial Biblical Encyclopedia. Edited by Gaalyahu Cornfield. New York: Macmillan Co., 1964.

A thoroughly conservative Jewish work reflecting the theological stance of the writers. Contains excellent articles on Aaron, the Aegean civilization, the Tel el Armarna letters, Canaanite gods and idols, and so on. 220.3.P58C

Seventh-Day Adventist Bible Dictionary. Edited by S. H. Horn. Washington, D.C.: Review and Herald Publishing Co., 1961.

Contains biblical and extrabiblical information about people and places, countries and customs, objects and beliefs mentioned in the Bible. Illustrated with photographs, drawings and maps.

Indexed. 220.3.H78

***Unger, Merrill Frederick, ed.** Unger's Bible Dictionary,* 3d ed. Chicago: Moody Press, 1961.

One of the best single-volume Bible dictionaries. More complete and reliable than the *New Bible Dictionary.* 220.3.UN3 1961

Westminster Dictionary of the Bible. Edited by John D. Davis and Henry S. Gehman. Philadelphia: Westminster Press, 1944.

A once highly respected volume marred in revision by its handling of chronological data and biblical incidents. Articles on such topics as the virgin birth, canonicity, salvation, hermeneutics, biblical theology, the atonement, and sin are inadequate. 220.3.W52

Zondervan Pictorial Bible Dictionary. Edited by Merrill C. Tenney. Grand Rapids: Zondervan Publishing House, 1969.

Beautifully illustrated and containing Trans-Vision maps. Over five thousand entries, more than seven hundred photographs, charts, and drawings, and many full-color maps make this volume a kaleidoscope of sacred sites and customs. While better illustrated than the dictionaries by Unger and Douglas, it lacks cohesion, and the material is generally inferior to those works. 220.3.Z7

BIBLE CONCORDANCES

Cruden, Alexander. *Cruden's Unabridged Concordance.* Grand Rapids: Baker Book House, 1953.

Contains the author's original notes and comments on Bible places, names, and types; an alphabetic listing of every word in the Bible; a complete concordance to proper names; a valuable listing of names and titles given to Jesus Christ; and a dictionary to the original meaning of proper names used in Scripture. Includes a concordance to the apocryphal books and a biographical sketch of the author. Originally published in 1737, this complete concordance to the AV has never been surpassed. Do not buy an abridged edition. 220.2.C88 1953

Clarke, Adam, ed. *Clarke's Bible Concordance.* Grand Rapids: Kregel Publications, reprint, 1968.

Complete and inexpensive. Gives definitions, parts of speech, quotations, and references for all the key words of the Bible, including proper names. A handy reference tool. Originally published in 1846. 220.2.C54 1968

The Complete Concordance to the American Standard Version of the Holy Bible in the Revised Edition. Compiled by Marshall Curtis Hazard. New York: Thomas Nelson and Sons, 1922.

This concordance omits material relating to Hebrew and Greek words but makes up for this omission by including references to most group words, arranging them under phrases in which one word predominates. 220.2.H33

Complete Concordance of the Bible. Douay Version. Edited by N. W. Thompson and Raymond Stock. St. Louis: Herder Book Co., 1945.

This present edition of the concordance to the Douay Version of the Bible is considerably enlarged and contains many additional words and references not found in the first edition. Originally published in 1942. 220.2.T37

Inglis, James. *A Topical Dictionary of the Bible Texts.* Grand Rapids: Baker Book House, 1968.

Valuable in sermon preparation. Originally published in 1861 under the title *Bible Text Cyclopedia.* 220.2.IN4 1968

Nelson's Complete Concordance to the Revised Standard Version. Compiled by J. W. Ellison. New York: Thomas Nelson and Sons, 1957.

Fills a very real need among those who have become accustomed to working with the RSV. Was compiled by a Univac 1 computer, and, as a result, the context and location of each word found in the RSV is listed. 220.2.EL5

*Strong, James. *Exhaustive Concordance of the Bible.* New York: Abingdon Press, 1890.

The most complete concordance to the AV and RV, with a brief dictionary of Hebrew and Greek words. More exhaustive than *Young's Analytical Concordance,* this work is of the utmost value, particularly when working from the English text. 220.2.ST8

*Young, Robert. *Analytical Concordance to the Bible.* Grand Rapids: Wm. B. Eerdmans Publishing Co., 1955.

A lexicon designed specifically for those who want to see at a glance the way Hebrew, Greek, and Aramaic words were used. Originally published in its present edition in 1881. Ideal for word studies. Augmented by a chapter on "Recent Discoveries in Bible Lands" by William F. Albright. 220.2.Y8

BIBLE STUDY

*Danker, Frederick W. *Multipurpose Tools for Bible Study.* 2d rev. ed. St. Louis: Concordia Publishing House, 1966.

Designed specifically for pastors and students of theology, and geared toward assisting them to use the basic reference works in each area of OT and NT study. Grapples with the problems of textual criticism, and shows the importance of resource tools like dictionaries, lexicons, and commentaries. 220.07.D23 1966

*Gettys, Joseph Miller. *How to Enjoy Studying the Bible.* Rev. ed. Richmond: John Knox Press, 1962.

A brief, information booklet, helpful in independent study and ideal for use in discussion groups. 220.07.G33 1962

Gray, James Martin. *Synthetic Bible Studies.* New ed. rev. Westwood, N.J.: Fleming H. Revell Co., 1959.

Informative synthetic studies containing an outline of each book of the Bible, accompanied by suggestive sermonic materials. First published in 1906. No longer as valuable as it once was. 220.07.G79 1959

Hudson, Roland Vernon. *Bible Survey Outlines.* Grand Rapids: Wm. B.

Eerdmans Publishing Co., 1954.

Provides his readers with numerous suggestive preaching outlines. 220.07.H86

*Jensen, Irving Lester. *Independent Bible Study.* Chicago: Moody Press, 1963.

Highlights the use of the analytical chart and the inductive method of Bible study. Shows how Bible study can become an exciting experience and a meaningful learning process. 220.07.J45

Manley, George Thomas, ed. *The New Bible Handbook.* London: Inter-Varsity Press, 1950.

A compact, topical handbook to the Scriptures. 220.07.M31

Manson, Thomas Walter, ed. *A Companion to the Bible.* Edinburgh: T. and T. Clark, 1963.

†This work is of mixed value because of the varying theological commitments of the authors. 220.07.M31

Morgan, Frank Crossley. *Importance of the Study of the English Bible.* London: Westminster Chapel, 1949.

The Campbell Morgan lectureship. Stimulating. 220.07.M82

Perry, Lloyd Merle and **Robert Duncan Culver.** *How to Search the Scriptures.* Grand Rapids: Baker Book House, 1967.

A practical book for those who wish to study the Bible for themselves. 220.07.P42

Pierce, Rice Alexander. *Leading Dynamic Bible Studies.* Nashville: Broadman Press, 1969.

A well-written book that applies contemporary group methods to Bible study. 220.07.P61

Pink, Arthur Walkington. *Profiting from the Word.* London: Banner of Truth Trust, 1970.

A basic guide to effective Bible study. 220.07.P65

Smith, Wilbur Moorehead. *A Treasury of Books for Bible Study.* Grand Rapids: Baker Book House, 1960.

Significant for the books it recommends. A companion volume to *Profitable Bible Study.* 016.22.SM6

Scroggie, William Graham. *Know Your Bible.* 2 vols. London: Pickering and Inglis, 1965.

Now available in one volume, this work contains useful outlines and other illustrative material. 220.07.SCRS

*_____. *Unfolding Drama of Redemption.* 3 vols. London: Pickering and Inglis, 1953-71.

A valuable set for the expositor. Treats each canonical book thematically. 220.07.SCR5U

Spurgeon, Charles Haddon. *Commenting and Commentaries.* London: Banner of Truth Trust, 1969.

Contains an extensive catalog of Bible commentaries and other expository works. Of particular value for its listing of works from the time of the Reformation of the middle of the nineteenth century. First published in 1876. 016.22'07.SP9 1969

Stibbs, Alan Marshall, ed. *Search the Scriptures.* London: Inter-Varsity Press, 1968.

A systematic course of daily Bible study designed to cover the whole of Scripture in three years. 220.07.ST5

*Traina, Robert A. *Methodical Bible Study: A New Approach to Hermeneutics.* Wilmore, Ky.: The Author, 1966.

Designed as a hermeneutical manual; also ideally suited for advanced Bible study. Abounds in helpful information, stresses the different kinds of charts and diagrams that can be used in personal study. Suggests a step-by-step approach whereby any passage of Scripture may be studied effectively and in the light of the context. 220.07.T68

*Wald, Oletta, *Joy of Discovery.* Minneapolis: Bible Banner Press, n.d.

One of the finest study guides of its kind. Brief, but full of important insights. 220.07.W14

BIBLE VERSIONS

INTRODUCTORY STUDIES

Grant, Frederick Clifton. *Translating the Bible.* London: Thomas Nelson and Sons, 1961.

An easy-to-read account of the history of Bible translations. 220.52'01.G76

Nida, Eugene Albert. *Bible Translating.* New York: American Bible Society, 1947.

A series of studies on the principles of translation. 220.52'01.N54

————. *Toward a Science of Translating: With Special Reference to Principles and Procedures Involved in Bible Translating.* Leiden: E. J. Brill, 1964.

A study solidly based upon contemporary developments in linguistics, anthropology, and psychology. 220.52'01.N54T

OLD TESTAMENT: INTRODUCTORY STUDIES

Ap-Thomas, Dafydd Rhys. *A Primer of Old Testament Text Criticism.* Philadelphia: Fortress Press, 1966.

Easier to read than Wurthwein, but not as up-to-date. 221.66.AP8

Engnell, I. *A Rigid Scrutiny.* Nashville: Vanderbilt University Press, 1969.

†Despite the unquestioned value of these essays, they do not reflect a conservative position on biblical criticism and therefore are of little lasting value. 221.66.EN3

Ginsberg, Christian David. *Introduction to the Massoretico-Critical Edition of the Hebrew Bible.* Philadelphia: Ktav Publishing House, 1966.

A scholarly Jewish study. 221.44.G43

*Kittel, Rudolph. *Biblica Hebraica.* New York: American Bible Society, 1937.

A standard critical edition of the MT. 221.44.K65

*Robert, Bleddyn Jones. *Old Testament Text and Versions.* Cardiff: University of Wales Press, 1951.

Presents judicious judgments and sound conclusions. Coverage superior to Wurthwein. An excellent treatment. 221.44.R54

Sandmel, Samuel. *The Hebrew Scriptures: An Introduction to Their Literature and Religious Ideas.* New York: Alfred A. Knoff, 1963.

One of the best Jewish critical introductions. 221.66.SA5

Snaith, Norman Henry, ed. *Hebrew Old Testament.* London: British and Foreign Bible Society, 1958.

A usable text for general nontechnical study. 221.44.SN1

Wurthwein, Ernst. *The Text of the Old Testament: An Introduction to Kittel-Kahle's "Biblica Hebraica."* Translated by Peter R. Ackroyd. Oxford: Basil Blackwell, 1957.

A translation made from the author's revision of his *Der Text des alten Testaments,* 1952. Incorporates references to recent literature on textual criticism. 221.44.W96

DEAD SEA SCROLLS

Bruce, Frederick Fyvie. *Biblical Exegesis in the Qumran Texts.* London: Tyndale Press, 1960.

Incorporates information about the Zadokites, the Messianic expectation of the Essenes, an interpretation of Daniel, and an interesting section on the "Servant of the Lord and the Son of Man." 221.4.B83

Dupont-Sommer, Andre. *The Essene Writings from Qumran.* Translated by G. Vermes, New York: World Publishing Co., 1962.

A corpus of Qumran writings presenting all the nonbiblical scrolls and scroll fragments in translation, with comments. Evaluates the problems raised by these new texts. Of particular value is the historical data on the Essene community. 221.4.D92

Gaster, Theodor Herzl. *Dead Sea Scriptures.* Rev. and enl. ed. Garden City: Doubleday and Co., 1964.

An English translation of the Scrolls. Easy-to-read. Enlightening. 221.4.G21 1964

Mansoor, Menahem. *Thanksgiving Hymns.* Studies in the Texts of the Desert of Judah. Grand Rapids: Wm. B. Eerdmans Publishing Co., 1961.

A translation accompanied by a comprehensive introduction. 296.817.M31T

Waard, Jan de, ed. *A Comparative Study of the Old Testament Text in the Dead Sea Scrolls and in the Desert of Judah.* Grand Rapids: Wm. B. Eerdmans Publishing Co., 1966.

A detailed examination of the OT and NT texts of the Dead Sea Scrolls. A work for the scholar. 221.4.W11

Wernberg-Møller, Preben. *Manual of Discipline.* Studies in the Texts of the Desert of Judah. Edited by J. Vander Ploeg. Leiden: E. J. Brill, 1957.

A translation of and commentary on one of the most important discoveries found in the Qumran caves. Designed to help serious students of the Scrolls understand the theology and practice of Essenes. 296.817.W49

SEPTUAGINT

Jellicoe, Sidney. *The Septuagint and Modern Study.* Oxford: At the Clarendon Press, 1968.

An excellent work that brings Swete up-to-date. More comprehensive than Ottley's *Handbook to the Septuagint.* 221.48.J39

*Rahlfs, Alfred, ed. *Septuaginta.* 2 vols. Stuttgart: Privilegierte Württembergische Bibelanstalt, 1935.

The finest modern critical work available. 221.48.R13

The Septuagint Version of the Old Testament and Apocrypha with an English Translation. London: Samuel Bagster and Sons, n.d.

A handy volume, with the Greek and English in parallel columns. 221.48.SE6B

*Swete, Henry Barclay. *An Introduction to the Old Testament in Greek.* Revised by R. R. Ottley. New York: Ktav Publishing House, 1968.

First printed in 1902, and revised in 1914. An indispensable, scholarly work long regarded as the standard critical introduction to the Septuagint. 221.48.SW41 1968

_____, **ed.** *The Old Testament in Greek According to the Septuagint.* 4th ed. 3 vols. Cambridge: At the University Press, 1912.

A valuable but extremely-hard-to-find set giving the different texts of the LXX. 221.48.SW4S 1912

Tischendorf, Lobegott Friedrich Constantin von. *Vetus Testamentum Graece Iuxta LXX Interpretes.* 2 vols. Lipsig: F. A. Brochhaus, 1869.

Contains an extensive introduction, together with the text of Codex Sinaiticus and notes. 221.48.T52

NEW TESTAMENT

Colwell, Ernest Cadman. *What Is the Best New Testament?* Chicago: University of Chicago Press, 1952.

†A modern approach to the problems of NT textual criticism. 225.4.C72

The Greek New Testament. Edited by Kurt Aland, et al. New York: American Bible Society, 1966.

A new critical edition of the Greek text prepared by Kurt Aland, Matthew Black, Bruce Metzger, and Allen Wikgren. Designed with the specialized needs of Bible translators in mind. 225.48.AM3

The Greek New Testament. Edited by R. V. G. Tasker. London: Oxford University Press, 1964.

The 1961 Greek text of the New Testament of the NEB. Lacks critical apparatus. 225.48.G81

*Greenlee, Jacob Harold. *Introduction to New Testament Textual Criticism.* Grand Rapids: Wm. B. Eerdmans Publishing Co., 1964.

A reliable introduction to the subject of textual criticism. Partially helpful to beginners for its excellent section on the use of the textual apparatus. Conservative. 225.4.G84

Kenyon, Frederick George. *Handbook to the Textual Criticism of the New Testament.* Grand Rapids: Wm. B. Eerdmans Publishing Co., reprint.

While older than Colwell and Greenlee's, this work is reliable and complete. Published in 1901. 225.4.K42

————. *The Text of the Greek Bible.* London: Gerald Duckworth, 1949.

A knowledgeable, balanced treatment. Reprinted from the 1937 edition. Now superseded by Metzger's *The Text of the New Testament* and Greenlee's *Introduction to New Testament Textual Criticism.* 225.4.K42T

Kilpatrick, George Dunbar, ed. *The Greek New Testament.* London: British and Foreign Bible Society, 1958.

One of the most useful critical editions available today. Includes material omitted in the Nestle text. 225.48.K55

Lake, Kirsopp. *The Text of the New Testament.* London: Rivingtons, 1959.

An older work that needs to be read with B. B. Warfield. Now superseded by Metzger's *Text of the New Testament.* 225.4.L14

Metzger, Bruce Manning. *Chapters in the History of New Testament Textual Criticism.* New Testament Tools and

Studies. Grand Rapids: Wm. B. Eerdmans Publishing Co., 1963.

A stimulating volume emphasizing the tasks associated with investigating the transmission of the Greek NT. 225.4.M56N

*————. *The Text of the New Testament.* 2d ed. New York: Oxford University Press, 1970.

An extensive treatment of the transmission, corruption, and restoration of the text of the NT. 225.4.M56T 1970

Milligan, George. *The New Testament Documents.* London: Macmillan Co., 1913.

Contains some very fine material on the transmission of the NT mss. 225.4.M62

*Nestle, Eberhard, ed. *Novum Testamentum Graece.* 24th ed. Revised by K. Aland. Stuttgart: Wurttembergische Bibelanstalt, 1960.

The most recent edition of Nestle's famous critical text. Soon to be revised. 225.48.N37

Novum Testamentum Graece et Latine. Edited by Augustus Merk. 7th ed. Rome: Pontifical Biblical Institute, 1951.

The critical footnotes of this edition are far more detailed than those found in the latest Nestle-Aland text. The Latin and Greek texts are given on alternate pages. 225.48.M 1951

Robertson, Archibald Thomas. *An Introduction to the Textual Criticism of the New Testament.* Nashville: Broadman Press, 1925.

A brief, elementary introduction containing much valuable information. Now superseded by Metzger's *The Text of the New Testament* and Greenlee's *Introduction to New Testament Textual Criticism.* 225.4.R54

Souter, Alexander. *Novum Testamentum Graece.* Oxford: At the Clarendon Press, 1947.

Represent British scholarship behind the RV of 1881. The text of the 1910 edition remains unchanged in this edition. Essentially, Souter's work reproduces Edwin Palmer's edition, which was based upon the third edition of Stephanus (1550). Orthography and spelling of proper names remain unchanged. 225.48.508 1947

Taylor, Vincent. *The Text of the New Testament.* 2d ed. London: Macmillan Co., 1963.

A brief, inadequate treatment. 225.4.T21 1963

Tischendorf, Almothens Fredericus Constantinus. *Novum Testamentum Graece.* 2 vols. Lipsig: Adolph Winter, 1859.

Contains the text of Codex Sinaiticus with extensive footnotes. 225.48.T52

Warfield, Benjamin Breckenridge. *An Introduction to the Textual Criticism of the New Testament.* 5th ed. London: Hodder and Stoughton, 1886.

Informative, but out of date. 225.4.W23 1886

ENGLISH TRANSLATIONS

The Amplified Bible. Translated by Frances E. Siewert. Grand Rapids: Zondervan Publishing House, 1965.

The "amplifications" to the text consist mainly in enumerating all the varieties of meanings that the original word or phrase bears. While this may help in personal meditation, it does not add precision or accuracy to Bible study. 220.52'06.SI1A

The Companion Bible. Edited by E. W. Bullinger. London: Lamp Press, 1964.

Whenever the outline of the text follows the grammatical structure of the original, this work is of real value to the pastor. When Bullinger's comments are more elaborate, the value of the work is

diminished. An appendix of 198 pages contains notes on word studies, maps, charts, and other topical material. 220.52'04.B87

The Holy Bible. American Standard Version. New York: Thomas Nelson and Sons. 1901.

A generally accurate translation of the Bible designed to correct many of the errors of the British RV of 1881. 220.52'04.AM3 1901

The Holy Bible. The Berkeley Version. Grand Rapids: Zondervan Publishing House, 1959.

The NT was translated by Gerrit Verkuyl and first published in 1945. The translation of the OT is the product of a score of American scholars and is very commendable. Now available under the title *The Modern Language Bible.* 220.52'06.B45

The Holy Bible. Confraternity Version of the Holy Bible. Patterson: St. Anthony Guild Press, 1941.

A thorough revision of the Douay-Rheims version. 220.52'05.C76

The Holy Bible. New English Bible with the Apocrypha. New York: Oxford and Cambridge University Presses, 1971.

Includes the second edition of the NT together with the translation of the OT and Apocrypha. The translators failed to avail themselves of the Ugaritic materials that could have been used to good advantage in translating numerous OT passages. In spite of its excellent literary qualities, this translation is disappointing in that it too often reflects the theological biases of the translators. 220.52'06.N42

The Holy Bible. Revised Standard Version. New York: Thomas Nelson and Sons, 1946-52.

†An easy-to-read translation of the Bible. Widely regarded as being weak in OT translation and in its rendition of the messianic psalms, but nevertheless the

best translation in modern English. 220.52'04.R32 1951

The Jerusalem Bible. Garden City: Doubleday and Co., 1966.

†An annotated edition translated from the French and containing scholarly introductions and notes. Unfortunately, the French translators ignored Ugaritic parallels when working from the Hebrew text. Their adherence to the documentary hypothesis and other higher critical tenets impairs the usefulness of this translation and its notes. 220.52'05.J48

Knox, R. A. *The Holy Bible*. London: Burns and Oates, 1954.

A translation from the Latin Vulgate with due regard for the Hebrew and Greek originals. Combines lucidity with relative accuracy, resulting in a work of distinction. Roman Catholic. 220.52'05.K75

The Living Bible. Paraphrased by Kenneth N. Taylor. Wheaton: Tyndale House Publishers, 1971.

Being a paraphrase, this is not and should not be regarded as an accurate version of the Holy Scriptures. When seen as such, it is a deservedly famous work. It appeals to young Christians and young people. 220.52'06.T21

Moffatt, James. *A New Translation of the Bible*. London: Hodder and Stoughton, 1926.

†Moffatt's helpful translation of difficult portions into a free, colloquial idiom is marred by the liberties he takes in rearranging the text. 220.52'04.M72

The New American Bible. Translated by Members of the Catholic Biblical Association of America. New York: P. J. Kennedy and Sons, 1970.

First complete American version of the Scriptures translated directly from the original Hebrew, Arabic, and Greek. 220.52'05.N42

*The New American Standard Bible. Carol Stream, Ill.: Creation House, 1971.

This work by an outstanding team of biblical scholars is perhaps the most accurate and reliable translation presently available. 220.52'06.AM3 1971

New Analytical Bible. Authorized Version. Chicago: John A. Dickson Publishing Co., 1950.

The special feature of this Bible is that it begins each book with a chart of the contents and closes with an outline and notes on special subjects contained in the book. The references are printed in the text in smaller type immediately after the verse. Indexes at the back of the Bible contain a number of tables on the lives of famous personalities, miracles, prayers, prophecies, and so on. 220.52'03.D56

The New Chain-Reference Bible. Authorized Version. Edited by Frank Charles Thompson. Indianapolis: B. B. Kirkbride Bible Co., 1934.

Contains marginal paragraph headings accompanied by a large number of subject headings, as well as a cyclopedia of topics and texts running into 293 pages and containing diagrams and maps of the travels of Christ during His earthly ministry, plus the journeys of Paul. 220.52'03.T37

Rotherham, Joseph Bryant, ed. *The Emphasized Bible*. Grand Rapids: Kregel Publications, 1959.

A literal translation of the Greek and Hebrew texts, with particular stress upon the grammatical emphasis of each verse by use of diacritical marks. The style is stilted, and it will be of help only to pastors whose knowledge of Greek and Hebrew is limited. 220.52'03.R74

The Scofield Reference Bible. Authorized Version. Rev. ed. New York: Oxford University Press, 1967.

One of the most popular widely used reference Bibles in existence. The revised edition retains the footnotes and introductory paragraphs of the early edition, eliminates some of the misleading notes about dispensationalism, and updates many of the archaic expressions. Regardless of their prophetic position, readers will find this reference Bible very helpful. 220.52'03.SCO2 1967

HISTORY OF THE BIBLE

*Bruce, Frederick Fyvie. *The English Bible: A History of Translations from the Earliest English Versions to the New English Bible.* New rev. ed. New York: Oxford University Press, 1970.

The new edition includes a chapter on the New English Bible and Apocrypha. It traces the history of the English Bible from its first beginnings in the seventh century to the present times. Bruce is disappointing in that he does not interact with many of the criticisms leveled against the NEB. However, the earlier part of this work remains a most valuable survey. 220.52'09.B83 1970

The Cambridge History of the Bible. 3 vols. Cambridge: At the University Press, 1963-1970.

†A brilliant and extensive treatment of the transmission of the Bible, beginning with the ancient world and tracing the transmission of the Bible through the biblical period to Jerome, then west from Jerome to the Reformation, and lastly from the Reformation to the present day. 220.52'09.C14

Deanesly, Margaret. *The Lollard Bible and Other Medieval Biblical Versions.* Cambridge: At the University Press, 1920.

An important, readable account of the labors of John Wycliffe and the Lollards. 220.52'09.D34

Gulston, Charles. *The English Bible: Our Greatest Heritage.* Grand Rapids: Wm. B. Eerdmans Publishing Co., 1961.

Presents the drama of the birth of the English Bible. Covers more than 1300 years of history, and reveals the thrilling story and vital contributions made by those who translated and defended the English Bible. 220.52'09.G95

Hamilton-Hoare, Henry William. *Our English Bible: The Story of Its Origin and Growth.* London: John Murray, 1911.

At one time, Hoare's work was one of the most widely read works of its kind. It is now dated, but it still makes good reading. 220.5'09.H65

Kenyon, Frederick George. *The Story of the Bible.* Grand Rapids: Wm. B. Eerdmans Publishing Co., 1967.

A clear and compelling account of the human history surrounding the origin, transmission, and translation of the Bible. A final chapter by F. F. Bruce updates the material. Originally issued in 1936. 220.52'09.K42S 1967

_____. *Our Bible and the Ancient Manuscripts.* Revised by A. W. Adams. New York: Harper and Brothers, 1958.

A popular treatment of the development of the Bible. Contains a helpful analysis of each translation and revision of the Scriptures. 220.4.K42 1958

MacGregor, John Geddes. *The Bible in the Making.* London: John Murray, 1961.

Designed for laypeople, this work presents in thorough, though popular fashion, the history of the English Bible through the various manuscript traditions to modern versions. While seldom favoring evangelical scholars, this work contains many valued insights. 220.5'09.M17

_____. *A Literary History of the Bible.* Nashville: Abingdon Press, 1968.

A fascinating history of the translations of the Bible from the Middle Ages to the present day. 220.52'09.M17

Mozley, James Frederic. *Coverdale and His Bibles.* London: Lutterworth Press, 1953.

An important study that bridges the gap between Tyndale and Coverdale, records the labors, trials, and tribulations of Coverdale as a translator, exposes some of the weaknesses inherent in his translations, and gives him an honored place in the history of the church. 220.52'09.M87

Robinson, Henry Wheeler, ed. *The Bible in Its Ancient and English Versions.* Westport, Conn.: Greenwood Press, 1970.

Originally published in 1940. Surveys the history of the Hebrew, Greek, Syriac, Latin, and English versions of the Bible. Provides a considerable amount of background material on the committees, translations, unique features, and peculiarities of each translation. A work of real scholarship. Not as up-to-date or as easy to read as Bruce's *The English Bible,* but frequently more discerning. 220.52'09.R56 1970

MODERN VERSIONS

Allis, Oswald Thompson. *The New English Bible: The New Testament of 1961.* Philadelphia: Presbyterian and Reformed Publishing Co., 1963.

A study designed to expose the weaknesses of the NEB NT as compared with the AV. 225.5.AL3

————. *Revision or New Translation?* Philadelphia: Presbyterian and Reformed Publishing Co., 1940.

A careful evaluation of the RSV that exposes the theological presuppositions of the translators. 225.5.AL5R

Beck, William F. *The New Testament in the Language of Today.* St. Louis: Concordia Publishing House, 1963.

A scholarly translation that stresses idiomatic expressions. 225.52.B38

Bratcher, Robert G. *Good News for Modern Man: The New Testament in Today's English Version.* New York: American Bible Society, 1966.

†Highly popular due to its simple, unconventional English style rather than its accuracy. 225.52.B73

*Dennett, Herbert. *A Guide to Modern Versions of the New Testament.* Chicago: Moody Press, 1965.

Written to guide pastors and their parishioners in their choice of NT versions. 225.5'09.D41

*Phillips, John Bertram. *The New Testament in Modern English.* New York: Macmillan Co., 1958.

A suggestive and free modern paraphrase that brings to light many important shades of meaning found in the original. Makes good reading. Pastors especially will appreciate its originality. 225.52.P54

————. *The Ring of Truth.* New York: Macmillan Co., 1967.

Contains the translator's own testimony to his belief in the validity and veracity of the Scriptures. 225.5'08.P54R

Rieu, Emile Victor. *The Four Gospels: A New Translation.* Baltimore: Penguin Press, 1952.

A translation that manifests real insight into the purpose of the gospel writers. 226.52.R44

Rieu, C. H. *The Acts of the Apostles: A New Translation.* Baltimore: Penguin Press, 1957.

A translation by a classical scholar that combines accuracy in dealing with the intricacies of the original text with the best literary style. 226.52.R44A

*The Twentieth Century New Testament.

Chicago: Moody Press, 1961.

A praiseworthy translation based upon the Greek text of Westcott and Hort. 225.52.T91

Vaughan, Curtis, ed. *New Testament from 26 Translations.* Grand Rapids: Zondervan Publishing House, 1967.

A one-volume work that provides, at a glance, variations from twenty-six different translations of the NT. 225.52.V46

Way, Arthur Sanders. *The Letters of St. Paul.* London: Marshall, Morgan and Scott, 1950.

In addition to the Pauline epistles, includes the letters to the seven churches and the letter to the Hebrews. This translation clarifies the meaning and is stimulating and challenging. 227.052.W36 (Alt. DDC 225.52)

*Weymouth, Richard Francis. *The New Testament in Modern Speech.* New York: Harper and Brothers, 1909.

A most readable translation that combines a lucid style with grammatical accuracy. Old, familiar phrases take on new significance. 225.52.W54

Williams, Charles Bray. *The New Testament.* Chicago: Moody Press, 1954.

A translation known for its accuracy and general reliability. 225.52.W67

ORIGIN AND AUTHENTICITY OF THE BIBLE

Arndt, William Frederick. *Does the Bible Contradict Itself?* 5th ed. St. Louis: Concordia Publishing House, 1955.

An unusually illuminating discussion of alleged contradictions in the Bible. Not complete, but helpful. 220.1.AR6 1955

Bowman, Allen. *Is the Bible True?* New York: Free Press, 1965.

A brief, well-written apologetic for the reasonableness and realiability of the biblical record. 220.1.B68

*Can I Trust My Bible? Chicago: Moody Press, 1963.

A symposium dealing with topics such as "Can We Believe in the Miraculous?" "Does Science Contradict the Bible?" "What Books Belong in the Canon of Scripture?" and "Is the History of the Old Testament Really Accurate?" Now available in paperback. Can be used effectively in study groups. 220.1.C16

*Criswell, Wallie Amos. *Bible for Today's World.* Grand Rapids: Zondervan Publishing House, 1965.

Sermons underlining the immutable nature of God's Word and defending the inerrancy of the Scriptures against the various tenets of higher criticism that have questioned the supernatural inspiration of the Bible. A timely work. 220.081.C86

*———. *Why I Preach that the Bible Is Literally True.* Nashville: Broadman Press, 1969.

A well-written, eloquent defense of the verbal inspiration and inerrancy of the Bible. 220.1.C86

Lloyd-Jones, David Martyn. *Authority.* London: Inter-Varsity Press, 1966.

A persuasive plea for believers and the church to return to the authority of Christ, the Word, and the Holy Spirit. 220.1.L77

Ramm, Bernard Lawrence. *The Pattern of Religious Authority.* Grand Rapids: Wm. B. Eerdmans Publishing Co., 1957.

Ramm's thesis is that there is no single doctrine of authority for believers today, but rather a threefold authority: the authority of the Scriptures, the authority of the Holy Spirit, and the authority of Jesus Christ. 220.1.R14

Scroggie, William Graham. *What if There Had Never Been a Bible?* London: Westminster Chapel, 1950.

The second G. Campbell Morgan lecture. An inspiring address. 220.1.SCR5

CANONICITY

Barclay, William. *The Making of the Bible.* Bible Guides. Nashville: Abingdon Press, 1961.

An introductory guide. 220.12.B23

Filson, Floyd Vivian. *Which Books Belong in the Bible?* Philadelphia: Westminster Press, 1957.

†A modern treatment of the canon. 220.12.F48

*Green, William Henry. *General Introduction to the Old Testament: The Canon.* London: John Murray, 1899.

An excellent treatment of the problem of canonicity from the conservative point of view. 220.12.G82

*Harris, Robert Laird. *Inspiration and Canonicity of the Bible.* Grand Rapids: Zondervan Publishing House, 1957.

A masterly approach to the subject of bibliography. 220.12.H24

*Lightner, Robert Paul. *The Savior and the Scriptures.* Philadelphia: Presbyterian and Reformed Publishing Co., 1966.

Presents Christ's view of the Scriptures and stresses His absolute reliance upon the irrevocable authority of the Word. 220.12.L62

Ryle, Herbert Edward. *The Canon of the Old Testament.* London: Macmillan Co., 1892.

†A study on the gradual growth and formation of the Hebrew canon of Scripture. 221.12.R98

REVELATION AND INSPIRATION

Beegle, Dewey M. *The Inspiration of Scripture.* Philadelphia: Westminster Press, 1963.

A scholarly attempt to prove that the Bible is an authoritative but errant book. Questions the value of some of the canonical books. 220.13.B39

*Custer, Stewart. *Does Inspiration Demand Inerrancy?* Nutley, N.J.: Craig Press, 1968.

A study of the biblical doctrine of inspiration in the light of inerrancy. A clear, informative statement. 220.13.C96

*Engelder, Theodore Edward William. *Scripture Cannot Be Broken.* St. Louis: Concordia Publishing House, 1945.

A vigorous defense of the doctrine of verbal plenary inspiration. 220.13.EN3

Gaussen, Francois Samuel Robert Louis. *Divine Inspiration of the Bible.* Grand Rapids: Kregel Publications, n.d.

A classic defense of the conservative view and authority of the Scriptures. Contains a valuable subject index. 220.13.G32

Gerstner, John H. *Bible Inerrancy Primer.* Grand Rapids: Baker Book House, 1965.

A brief, nontechnical presentation of biblical inerrancy. 220.13.G32

Henry, Carl Ferdinand Howard, ed. *Revelation and the Bible.* Contemporary Evangelical Thought. Grand Rapids: Baker Book House, 1958.

Contains chapters by twenty-four Christian writers of repute. Deals with crucial subjects in today's theological debate. 220.13.H39

Kirkpatrick, Alexander Francis. *The Divine Library of the Old Testament.* London: Macmillan Co., 1909.

Five lectures on the origin, preservation, inspiration, and permanent value of the OT Scriptures. 221.7'06.K63

Orr, James. *Revelation and Inspiration.* Grand Rapids: Wm. B. Eerdmans Publishing Co., 1952.

Provides a healthy discussion of the issues involved. Advocates a view that accepts verbal but not plenary inspiration. 220.13.OR7

*Pache, René. *Inspiration and Authority*

of Scripture. Translated by Helen I. Needham. Chicago: Moody Press, 1969.

Re-examines the doctrine of inerrancy, and upholds the complete authenticity and supernatural origin of the Bible. 220.13.P11

Packer, James Innell. *God Speaks to Man: Revelation and the Bible.* Philadelphia: Westminster Press, 1966.

Points out that critical views of the Bible have always impoverished students of the Word. Urges believers to return to a careful study of what the Scriptures say, unadorned by contemporary trappings. 220.13.P119

Pinnock, Clark H. *A Defense of Biblical Infallibility.* Philadelphia: Presbyterian and Reformed Publishing Co., 1967.

Composed of the Tyndale Lecture in Biblical Theology delivered at Cambridge in 1966. Admirably answers the liberal and neoorthodox theologians who have insisted that orthodoxy's affirmation of infallibility is irrelevant. 220.13.P65

Rahner, Karl. *Inspiration in the Bible.* Translated by Charles H. Henkey. London: Thomas Nelson and Sons, 1961.

†Proceeds from the premise that both God and man are responsible for the "authorship" of Holy Writ, and advances the author's reasons for believing in the authority of the Bible and the formation of the canon. Roman Catholic. 220.13.R12

Reid, John Kelman Sutherland. *The Authority of Scripture: A Study of the Reformation and Post-Reformation Understanding of the Bible.* New York: Harper and Brothers, 1957.

Following in the footsteps of Karl Barth, the writer studies the historical development of the doctrine of authority from the time of the Reformation to the emergence and development of neoorthodoxy. 220.13'09.R27

Robinson, Henry Wheeler. *Inspiration*

and Revelation in the Old Testament. Oxford: At the University Press, 1967.

†Lectures delivered at the University of Oxford dealing with the revelation of God in nature, in man, and in history. From this premise considers the media through which this revelation was expressed, namely, the prophet, the priest, the wisdom writer, and the psalmist. 221.13.R54

Runia, Klaas. *Karl Barth's Doctrine of Holy Scripture.* Grand Rapids: Wm. B. Eerdmans Publishing Co., 1962.

An objective treatment showing the error of Barth's views, together with the valuable truths that may be salvaged from Barth's theology. 220.13.R87

Stonehouse, Ned Bernard and **Paul Woolley.** *The Infallible Word: A Symposium.* Philadelphia: Presbyterian and Reformed Publishing Co., 1946.

A carefully reasoned series of essays dealing with the general character of biblical authority, containing a chapter on the canonicity of the Scriptures, and concluding with an emphasis upon their relevancy, place in preaching, and distinctive characteristics of the Word of God. By members of the faculty of Westminster Theological Seminary. 220.13.ST7

Tenney, Merrill Chapin, ed. *The Bible: The Living Word of Revelation.* Grand Rapids: Zondervan Publishing House, 1968.

Ten essays presented by members of the Evangelical Theological Society, focusing on the meaning of Logos, the necessity of revelation, the means of communication in revelation, the problem of communication, the fact of inerrancy, and so on. 220.13.T25

Thomson, James G. S. S. *The Old Testament View of Revelation.* Grand Rapids: Wm. B. Eerdmans Publishing Co., 1960.

A biblical work dealing with special (not general) revelation and containing two supplementary chapters on the attributes and names of God. 221.13.T38

Walvoord, John Flipse, ed. *Inspiration and Interpretation.* Grand Rapids: Wm. B. Eerdmans Publishing Co., 1957.

A symposium by members of the Evangelical Theological Society. 220.13.W17

Warfield, Benjamin Breckenridge. *Revelation and Inspiration.* New York: Oxford University Press, 1927.

Originally published in a limited edition only. Because of its unique value, reprinted with additions in *The Inspiration and Authority of the Bible.* 220.13.W23R

*———. *The Inspiration and Authority of the Bible.* Philadelphia: Presbyterian and Reformed Publishing Co., 1958.

A work deserving a place on every pastor's desk. 220.13.W23

Woychuk, N. A. *Infallible Word.* Chicago: Moody Press, 1963.

A consistently evangelical defense of the doctrine of infallibility 220.13.W91

*Young, Edward Joseph.** *Thy Word Is Truth.* Grand Rapids: Wm. B. Eerdmans Publishing Co., 1957.

A forthright defense of the Bible as the infallible and inerrant Word of God. 220.13.Y8

PROPHETIC MESSAGE

Coder, Samuel Maxwell and **George F. Howe.** *Bible, Science and Creation.* Chicago: Moody Press, 1965.

A theologian and a biologist team up to demonstrate the harmony that exists between God's words and His works. Premillennial. 220.15.C65

Girdlestone, Robert Baker. *The Grammar of Prophecy: A Systematic Guide to Biblical Prophecy.* Grand Rapids: Kregel Publishing Co., 1955.

Using the principles of biblical hermeneutics, this volume emphasizes truths that might otherwise be overlooked and seeks to show the remarkable harmony of the whole of prophetic revelation. 220.15.G44

Orelli, Conrad von. *The Old Testament Prophecy of the Consummation of God's Kingdom.* Edinburgh: T. and T. Clark, 1892.

By one of the best German commentators and a contributor to *ISBE.* Fairly reliable, but makes some concessions to those who espouse liberal views. 221.15.OR3

Oxtoby, Gurdon C. *Prediction and Fulfillment in the Bible.* Philadelphia: Westminster Press, 1966.

Because the concerns of modern man find their locus in the present rather than the past, the writer labors under the illusion that the Bible has become an irrelevant book. This book attempts to solve the problem. 220.15.OX8

*Pentecost, John Dwight.** *Prophecy for Today.* Grand Rapids: Zondervan Publishing House, 1965.

A series of expository messages on major prophetic themes that, beginning with the "Next Event in the Prophetic Program," trace the entire history of prophetic Scripture from the rapture to the eternal state. Premillennial. 220.15.P38

Rowley, Harold Henry, ed. *Studies in Old Testament Prophecy.* Naperville, Ill.: Alec R. Allenson, 1957.

A collection of articles on a variety of OT themes. 221.15.R79

*Sauer, Erich Ernst.** *From Eternity to Eternity.* Grand Rapids: Wm. B. Eerdmans Publishing Co., 1954.

A study on God's plan of salvation, His dealings with mankind, and the coming Kingdom from the premillennial viewpoint. An appendix discusses the differences between Israel and the church. 220.15.SA8

Scroggie, William Graham. *Prophecy and History.* London: Marshall, Morgan and Scott, n.d.

A study of the place of Jews, Gentiles,

and the church of God in God's plan of the ages. 220.15.SCR5P

*_____. *Ruling Lines of Progressive Revelation.* London: Marshall, Morgan, and Scott, n.d.

A series of studies on the unity and harmony of the Scriptures. Premillennial. 220.15.SCR5R

Talbot, Louis Thompson. *God's Plan of the Ages.* Grand Rapids: Wm. B. Eerdmans Publishing Co., 1936.

A comprehensive view of God's plan from eternity to eternity. Serves well for use in adult Bible classes. 220.15.T14

Tatford, Frederick Albert. *God's Program of the Ages.* Grand Rapids: Kregel Publications, 1967.

Stressing the imminency of the second advent, these studies survey the scope of prophecy from a premillennial point of view. The writer avoids setting dates and demonstrates remarkable charity when dealing with those with whom he disagrees. 220.15.T18

Wood, Arthur Skevington. *Prophecy in the Space Age.* Grand Rapids: Zondervan Publishing House, 1963.

A British Methodist theologian draws attention to the signs heralding the imminent return of Christ and explains future events in the light of the Scriptures. Premillennial. 220.15.W85

INTERPRETATION AND CRITICISM OF THE BIBLE

Barr, James. *Old and New in Interpretation.* New York: Harper and Row, 1966.

The Currie Lectures at Austin Presbyterian Theological Seminary, Texas, 1964. Generally difficult to understand, and philosophical rather than exegetical in handling of OT quotations in the NT. 220.6.B27

_____. *The Semantics of Biblical Language.* London: Oxford University Press, 1961.

†An important discussion of linguistic hermeneutics aimed at clarifying for theologues the importance of the culture that gave rise to different literary forms. 220.8.H.B27

Briggs, Charles Augustus. *A General Introduction to the Study of the Holy Scripture.* Grand Rapids: Baker Book House, 1970.

†A classic treatment by a leading nineteenth-century theologian. 220.6.B76

Butler, Basil Christopher. *The Church and the Bible.* London: Barton, Longman and Todd, 1960.

A significant study by a British Roman Catholic scholar. 220.6.B97

*Geisler, Norman L., and **William E.**

Nix. *General Introduction to the Bible.* Chicago: Moody Press, 1968.

Covers the inspiration, canonicity, text, and translation of the entire Bible from an evangelical point of view. 220.6.G27

*Horne, Thomas Hartwell. *An Introduction to the Critical Study and Knowledge of the Holy Scriptures.* 5 vols. 8th ed. Grand Rapids: Baker Book House, 1970.

Of great value to the Bible expositor. Provides a comprehensive compendium of biblical knowledge covering hermeneutics, history and geography, and apologetics. 220.6.H78

Hyatt, James Phillip, ed. *The Bible in Modern Scholarship.* Nashville: Abingdon Press, 1965.

Papers read at the centennial meeting of the Society of Biblical Literature, New York City. Interfaith and international in scope. Designed for the scholar. 220.6'09.H99

Pierson, Arthur Tappan. *The Bible and Spiritual Criticism.* Grand Rapids: Baker Book House, 1970.

The reprinting of a series of lectures delivered at Exeter Hall, England, in

1904, on the occasion of the centenary year of the British and Foreign Bible Society. Encourages a true criticism of the Scriptures with the purpose of demonstrating the real nature of the Bible. 220.007.P61 1970

Rowley, Harold Henry. *The Unity of the Bible.* Philadelphia: Westminster Press, 1955.

Discusses the unity of the Bible in the midst of diversity, interpretation, and the *Sitz im Leben* of each Testament. Based on a mediating position. 220.6.R79

OLD TESTAMENT

*Archer, Gleason Leonard, Jr. *A Survey of Old Testament Introduction.* Chicago: Moody Press, 1964.

A definitive study that takes its place among the front rank of works in the field, ably defends the conservative position against the attacks of critics, and is essential for evangelicals who wish to have an intelligent grasp of the OT. 221.61.AR2

Cook, Stanley Arthur. *The Old Testament: A Reinterpretation.* Cambridge: W. Heffer and Sons, 1936.

†Seeks to establish a basis for understanding the OT based upon critical theories in vogue at the time. Dated, and of little value. 221.6.C77

Eissfeldt, Otto. *The Old Testament: An Introduction.* Translated by Peter R. Ackroyd. London: Basil Blackwell, 1965.

†An analysis of literary forms, with heavy stress upon the importance of form-criticism in current OT study. Includes sections on the Apocrypha and Pseudepigrapha. 221.61.E18

Ellison, Henry L. *The Message of the Old Testament.* Grand Rapids: Wm. B. Eerdmans Publishing Co., 1970.

A fascinating study of the Judeo-Christian tradition. 221.61.EL5

Gottwald, Norman Karol. *A Light to the Nations: An Introduction to the Old Testa-*

ment. New York: Harper and Row, 1959.

†A popular presentation of the position presently held by the post-Wellhausen school of biblical criticism. 221.61.G71

Kyle, Melvin Grove. *The Problem of the Pentateuch.* Oberlin, Ohio: Bibliotheca Sacra Co., 1920.

Provides a detailed and technical introduction to Pentateuchal criticism based on a consideration of the literary forms, technical terms, and natural divisions. Includes a consideration of the technical law-words found in other OT books, evidence from archaeology, and a harmony of the style and diction contained in the different divisions. 221.1'06.K98

Mowinckel, Sigmund Olaf Plytt. *The Old Testament as Word of God.* Translated by Radar B. Bjornard. Oxford: Basil Blackwell, 1960.

†A series of popular lectures designed to make the OT intelligible to laymen. Stresses the cultic background of the *Sitz im Leben* as the only viable basis for interpreting the OT. 221.6.M87

Noordtzy, A. *The Old Testament Problem.* Translated by Miner B. Stearns. Dallas: Bibliotheca Sacra, 1941.

An appraisal of the Wellhausen school of thought that readily reveals the weaknesses of the documentary hypothesis. 221.6.N73

Noth, Martin. *The Laws in the Pentateuch and Other Studies.* Translated by D. R. Ap-Thomas. Philadelphia: Fortress Press, 1967.

†A fresh interpretation of OT archaeological and historical material and its bearing upon OT study today. 221.6.N84

*Orr, James. *The Problem of the Old Testament.* New York: Charles Scribner's Sons, 1931.

A standard work refuting the documentary hypothesis. 221.6.OR7

Preus, James Samuel. *From Shadow to Promise: Old Testament Interpretation from*

Augustine to the Young Luther. Cambridge, Mass.: Belknap Publishers, 1969.

Stresses the need for a return to the great classical tradition of exegesis maintained by Luther and Calvin, and to the systems of theology they founded. 221.63.P92

Raven, John Howard. *Old Testament Introduction.* New York: Fleming H. Revell Co., 1910.

An old, conservative introduction. Valuable, but not as comprehensive as Archer's *Survey of Old Testament Introduction.* 221.61.R19

Robinson, Theodore Henry. *An Introduction to the Books of the Old Testament.* London: E. Arnold Publishers, 1948.

A popular work attempting to provide readers with a contemporary introduction to literary criticism. 221.61.R54

Rowley, Harold Henry. *Growth of the Old Testament.* London: Hutchinson's University Library, 1950.

†A brief introduction to each book of the OT based upon the latest critical scholarship. 221.R77

_____, ed. *The Old Testament and Modern Study.* London: Oxford University Press, 1961.

†A series of scholarly essays written by members of the Society for Old Testament Study and covering notable discoveries and significant research during the past generation. 221.41.R79

*Schultz, Samuel Jacob. *Old Testament Speaks.* New York: Harper and Brothers, 1960.

Covers the entire OT and provides the reader with a clear popular presentation of the archaeological, geographical, historical, and linguistic background to each book of the OT. A helpful introduction described as "careful, critical, and conservative." 221.61.SCH8

*Unger, Merrill Frederick. *Introductory Guide to the Old Testament.* Grand Rapids: Zondervan Publishing House, 1951.

An extensive treatment ably setting forth the Mosaic authorship and unity of the Pentateuch, the date of the Exodus, Israel's conquest of Canaan, and the chronological problems of Joshua-Judges. Refutes the duetero-Isaiah theory and rejects a late date for the book of Daniel. 221.61.UN3

Weiser, Artur. *Introduction to the Old Testament.* Translated by Dorthea M. Barton. London: Darton, Longman and Todd, 1961.

†A scholarly form-critical approach. 221.61.W43

_____. *The Old Testament: Its Formation and Development.* Translated by Dorthea M. Barton. New York: Association Press, 1961.

†A careful blending of literary criticism and biblical theology. Contributes little to an understanding of the purpose of OT revelation, but does acquaint readers with the view of other OT scholars. 221.61.W430

Westermann, Claus. *The Old Testament and Jesus Christ.* Minneapolis: Augsburg Publishing House, 1970.

The translation of a brief but important work that pleads for a fresh understanding of the place of Christ in the OT. 221.6.W52

*Young, Edward Joseph. *An Introduction to the Old Testament.* Rev. ed. Grand Rapids: Wm. B. Eerdmans Publishing Co., 1960.

While older than Archer's *Survey of Old Testament Introduction,* this work ably treats the major critical problems facing students in their study of the OT. 221.61.Y8 1960

NEW TESTAMENT

Anderson, Hugh. *Jesus and Christian Origins.* New York: Oxford University Press, 1964.

†A modern critical inquiry into the sources behind NT books. Adheres to

the form-critical approach, and endeavors to discover the historical facts behind the proclamation of the early church. 225.6.AN2

Bultmann, Rudolph Karl. *Jesus Christ and Mythology.* London: SCM Press, 1958.

†An exposition of the German theologians' radical theories. 225.6.B87

Feine, Paul and **Johannes Behm.** *Introduction to the New Testament.* Edited by Werner George Kuemmel. Translated by A. J. Mattill, Jr. 4th rev. ed. Nashville: Abingdon Press, 1966.

†One of the most up-to-date introductions available to the English reader. Representative of the latest continental scholarship. 225.61.F32 1966

Fuller, Reginald Horace. *A Critical Introduction to the New Testament.* London: Gerald Duckworth, 1966.

†A concise account of the critical opinions of NT scholars, with an inadequate evaluation of their theories. 225.61.F95

Godet, Frederic Louis. *Introduction to the New Testament.* Translated by William Affleck. Edinburgh: T. and T. Clark, 1899.

A handy introduction to the gospels, but now dated. 225.61.G54

―――. *Studies on the New Testament.* London: Hodder and Stoughton, 1873.

Now superseded by more recent works. 225.61.G54S

Grant, Robert McQueen. *A Historical Introduction to the New Testament.* New York: Harper and Row, 1963.

A work by a leading form-critical scholar supporting many of the conclusions conservative NT scholars have held for years. 225.67.G76

Hadjiantoniou, George A. *New Testament Introduction.* Chicago: Moody Press, 1957.

Chief value lies in the author's familiarity with the writings of the church Fathers. 225.61.H11

*Harrison, Everett Falconer. *Introduc-*

tion to the New Testament. Grand Rapids: Wm. B. Eerdmans Publishing Co., 1964.

Vies with Guthrie for the number one position among modern conservative introductions. An excellent work. 225.61.H24

*Hiebert, David Edmond. *New Testament Introduction.* In process. Chicago: Moody Press, 1954.

One of the finest conservative introductions available today. Each book is meticulously outlined, critical issues are dealt with fairly, and the concluding bibliography acquaints readers with important literature. 225.61.H53

Hunter, Archibald Macbride. *Bible and Gospel.* London: SCM Press, 1969.

Hunter grapples with the Bultmannian proposals that inevitably lead to "a faceless eschatological event" and a "dehydrated gospel," as he tries to extricate from what is left the kerygma of the historical Jesus. 225.6.H91

―――. *Interpreting the New Testament, 1900-1950.* Philadelphia: Westminster Press, 1951.

An important study subsequently updated by the author's article "New Testament Survey, 1939-1964," *Expository Times* 76 (October 1964). 225.63.H91

―――. *Introducing the New Testament.* 2d ed. Philadelphia: Westminster Press, 1957.

A simple, nontechnical presentation based upon the latest source criticism. Concentrates upon the essentials and presents the material so as to appeal to laymen. 225.61.H91 1957

―――. *The Message of the New Testament.* Philadelphia: Westminster Press, 1954.

Expounds the themes of "One Lord," "One Church," and "One Salvation." Published in England under the title *The Unity of the New Testament.* 225.6.H91M

Jeremias, Joachim. *The Central Message of the New Testament.* New York: Charles

Scribner's Sons, 1965.

A scholarly form-critical study of "Abba," "Christ's Sacrificial Death," "Justification by Faith," and "The Revealing Word." 225.6'081.J47

Käsemann, Ernst. *New Testament Questions of Today.* London: SCM Press, 1965.

†Fifteen essays that originally were contributions to Festschriften or lectures to learned societies. They survey a wide variety of subjects. Will have little appeal to the pastor. 225.6.K15

Ladd, George Eldon. *The Pattern of New Testament Truth.* Grand Rapids: Wm. B. Eerdmans Publishing Co., 1968.

Studies growing out of the Nils W. Lund Memorial Lectures, North Park Seminary, Chicago, 1966. Shows the continuity of NT thought, particularly as relates to the teachings of Jesus and Paul. 225.6.L12

Lamsa, George Mamishisho. *More Light on the Gospels.* Garden City: Doubleday and Co., 1968.

Accepting as fact that Jesus spoke Aramaic, the writer attempts to highlight many incidents in the gospels from the common idiomatic expressions, customs and mannerisms, teaching and traditions of this Semitic group. 225.6'08.L21

McNeile, Alan Hugh. *An Introduction to the Study of the New Testament.* 2d ed. Revised by C. S. C. Williams. Oxford: At the Clarendon Press, 1953.

†A work of the finest scholarship. 225.61.M23 1953

Moffatt, James. *An Introduction to the Literature of the New Testament.* International Theological Library. 3d rev. ed. Edinburgh: T. and T. Clark, 1961.

†A time-worn volume containing a mine of important information on the history of interpretation. Designed for the serious student of of the NT. Reprinted from the 1918 edition. 225.61.M72 1961

Moule, Charles Francis Digby. *The*

Phenomenon of the New Testament: An Inquiry into the Implications of Certain Features of the New Testament. London: SCM Press, 1967.

†A short work purporting to give the general reader an insight into the circumstances that prompted the early Christians to give expression to their faith in the documents now composing the NT. 225.6.M86

***Neill, Stephen Charles.** *The Interpretation of the New Testament, 1861-1961.* New York: Oxford University Press, 1966.

An instructive survey of the historical development of NT criticism during the past century. 225.6'09.N31

Robertson, Archibald Thomas. *Studies in the New Testament.* Nashville: Broadman Press, 1949.

Deals briefly with the historical background to the NT, the life of Christ, and the history of the apostolic age. Much of this material is now superseded by later works. First published in 1915. 225.66.R54

***Robertson, James Alexander.** *The Hidden Romance of the New Testament.* London: James Clarke and Co., 1923.

A delightful, imaginative, and scholarly study. Contains preaching values that expositors will welcome. 225.6.R54

Salmon, George. *An Historical Introduction to the Study of the Books of the New Testament.* 10th ed. London: John Murray, 1913.

In many respects dated, but later editions are still helpful. Provides some exceptionally valuable material on the Pauline epistles, Hebrews, and the Apocrypha and Pseudepigrapha. 225.61.SA3 1913.

Tenney, Merrill Chapin. *New Testament Survey.* Grand Rapids: Wm. B. Eerdmans Publishing Co., 1961.

A revision of the author's historical and analytical survey published in 1953.

Combines historical accuracy with a loyalty to the text. Helpful for use on a college level, but also of value to the pastor. 225.61.T25

*Theron, Daniel Johannes. *Evidence of Tradition.* Grand Rapids: Baker Book House, 1958.

A handy volume containing selective source material for the study of the history of NT times, the NT books, and the development of the canon. Source material is cited in the original Greek or Latin, with a translation for English readers. 225.67.T34

Thiessen, Henry Clarence. *Introduction to the New Testament.* Grand Rapids: Wm. B. Eerdmans Publishing Co., 1943.

Still valuable. Some prefer Thiessen's handling of such matters as the synoptic problem to the newer treatments by Guthrie and Harrison. 225.61.T34

*Zahn, Theodore. *Introduction to the New Testament.* 3 vols. Grand Rapids: Kregel Publications, 1953.

A fine conservative introduction, though in some respects dated. First published in English in 1909. 225.61.Z2

HERMENEUTICS, INTERPRETATION

HERMENEUTICS

Berkhof, Louis. *Principles of Biblical Interpretation.* Grand Rapids: Baker Book House, 1950.

A textbook covering the history and principles of interpretation and advocating a special hermeneutic for the study of prophecy. 220.63.B45

*Farrar, Frederic William. *History of Interpretation.* Grand Rapids: Baker Book House, 1961.

Valuable for its treatment of the history of interpretation from the earliest times to the rise of the higher critical school of interpretation. 220.63'09.F24 1961

Fisher, Fred L. *How to Interpret the New Testament.* Philadelphia: Westminster Press, 1966.

Provides help in NT hermeneutics in spite of the writer's neoorthodox terminology. Includes valuable chapters on "Tools of Interpretation" and "Seek a General Understanding of the Book." 225.63.F53

Kistemaker, Simon. *Interpreting God's Word Today.* Grand Rapids: Baker Book House, 1970.

A survey of past and present attitudes toward the OT and NT, the doctrine of the Scriptures, the ecclesiastical confessions, and apologetics. 220.63.K64

Mickelsen, A. Berkley. *Interpreting the Bible.* Grand Rapids: Wm. B. Eerdmans Publishing Co., 1963.

Deals with the principles and historic precedents of interpretation, but fails to clarify many of the problems facing exegetes and expositors today. 220.63.M58

*Ramm, Bernard Lawrence. *Protestant Biblical Interpretation.* 3d rev. ed. Grand Rapids: Baker Book House, 1970.

An introductory textbook to the science of hermeneutics from a conservative theological viewpoint. The last three chapters are disappointing. 220.63.R14 1970.

Smart, James D. *The Interpretation of Scripture.* Philadelphia: Westminster Press, 1961.

Attempts to study the interpretation and authority of the Scriptures as part of biblical theology. 220.63.SM2

*Terry, Milton Spense. *Biblical Hermeneutics.* Grand Rapids: Zondervan Publishing House, 1968.

First published in 1883. An exhaustive

work that, despite its age, contains valuable material for those who will take the time to read it. 220.63.T27

Unger, Merrill Frederick. *Principles of Expository Preaching.* Grand Rapids: Zondervan Publishing House, 1955.

A fine treatment of biblical interpretation—but with a misleading title. 220.63.UN3

Ward, Wayne E. *The Word Comes Alive.* Nashville: Broadman Press, 1969.

Discusses the relevancy of the Word of God and the reasons why people dismiss it today. 220.63.W21

Westermann, Claus, ed. *Essays on Old Testament Hermeneutics.* Translated by James Luther Mays. Richmond: John Knox Press, 1963.

†Essays manifesting an acceptance of the authority of the OT but showing no agreement concerning how this authority is to be understood. 221.63.W52

Wood, Arthur Skevington. *Principles of Biblical Interpretation.* Grand Rapids: Zondervan Publishing House, 1967.

A study of the interpretative principles set forth by Irenaeus, Origen, Augustine, Luther, and Calvin. Valuable for its historic materials. 220.63'09.W85

TYPOLOGY

*Fairbairn, Patrick. *The Typology of Scripture.* 5th ed. Grand Rapids: Zonder-

van Publishing House, 1963.

A systematic treatment of typology. Possibly the best ever written on this subject. 220.64.F15 1963

Foulkes, Francis. *The Acts of God.* London: Tyndale Press, 1958.

A study of the basis of typology in the OT. 220.64.F82

Habershon, Ada Ruth. *Study of the Types.* Grand Rapids: Kregel Publications, 1961.

A detailed devotional study of OT types and their fulfillment in the NT. 220.64.H11

Koch, Klaus. *The Growth of the Biblical Tradition.* Translated by S. M. Cupitt. New York: Charles Scribner's Sons, 1969.

†A detailed explanation of the five aspects that make up form-criticism. Portrays many of the "beneficial advantages" of form-criticism, but ignores the fact that God used human experience to record His revelation to man in the original inspired writings. A capable work spoiled because the writer ignores divine revelation. 220.6'6.K81

Lampe, Geoffrey William Hugo and **Kenneth John Woolcombe.** *Essays on Typology.* Studies in Biblical Theology. London: SCM Press, 1957.

†An analysis of the reasonableness of typology, with an assessment of the biblical origins and patristic development of this system of interpretation. 220.64.L19

BIBLE COMMENTARIES

Abingdon Bible Commentary. Edited By F. C. Eiselen, Edwin Lewis, and D. G. Downey. New York: Abingdon Press, 1929.

†The introductory articles on the Bible as a whole, the OT, and the NT are, in many respects, of greater value than the commentary on the text. 220.7.AB5

Anchor Bible. Edited by W. F. Albright and D. N. Freedman. Garden City, NY:

Doubleday and Company, 1964.

†This set, when completed, will include the canonical books of the OT and NT, together with the Apocrypha. The contributors have been drawn from Protestant, Catholic, and Jewish backgrounds. Their philological scholarship is unquestioned. Significant volumes include Speiser (Genesis), Dahood (Psalms), Bright (Jeremiah), Anderson

and Freedman (Hosea), R. Brown (John's gospel and epistles), M. Barth (Ephesians). 220.7.AN2

Baxter, James Sidlow. *Explore the Book.* Grand Rapids: Zondervan Publishing House, 1962.

Helpful for personal study, particularly when approaching a book of the Bible not previously studied in depth. Designed for laypeople. 220.7.B33E

_____. *The Strategic Grasp of the Bible.* Grand Rapids: Zondervan Publishing House, 1970.

A series of stimulating and informative studies dealing with the structure and characteristics of the Bible. Well outlined, ably illustrated, and of particular value for use with adult study groups. 220.7.B33S

Beacon Bible Commentary. Edited by H. F. Harper, et al. 10 vols. Kansas City: Beacon Hill Press, 1964-69.

An evangelical Wesleyan commentary claiming to work from the original languages, but consisting mainly of an exposition based on the English text. 220.7.35

Black, Matthew and **Harold Henry Rowley, eds.** *Peake's Commentary on the Bible.* New York: Thomas Nelson and Sons, 1963.

†First published in 1924, but since updated. Includes the "generally accepted results of Biblical Criticism, Interpretation, History, and Theology." 220.7.B56

Broadman Commentary. Edited by Clifton J. Allen. 12 vols. Nashville: Broadman Press, 1969.

†A controversial work. Writers on the OT quote with approval the works of those who deny the Mosaic authorship of the Pentateuch, hold to the documentary hypothesis, attack the doctrine of inspiration, adhere to a belief in a primitive cosmology, accept with apparent agreement contradictions in the text, and reject certain events as unhistorical. Volume 1 has been withdrawn from circulation. The NT commentaries reflect a more generally accepted position and so far have escaped censure. 220.7.B78

***Calvin, John.** *Calvin's Commentaries.* 22 vols. Edinburgh: Calvin Translation Society, 1849.

"Of all commentators I believe John Calvin to be the most candid," wrote Spurgeon. "In his expositions he is not always what moderns would call Calvinistic; ... inasmuch as some Scriptures bear the impress of human free action and responsibility, he does not shun to expound their meaning in all fairness and integrity." 220.7.C13 1849

Cambridge Bible for Schools and Colleges. Edited by J. J. Stewart Perowne. Cambridge: At the University Press, 1916.

Based upon the RV, these works have now been superseded, though some retain their value. 220.7.C14

A Catholic Commentary on Holy Scripture. Edited by Bernard Orchard, et al. New York: Thomas Nelson and Sons, 1953.

A critical commentary based upon the Douay version. Places particular emphasis upon the doctrinal and spiritual teachings of the canonical books and Apocrypha. Exceptionally well indexed. 220.7.C28

The Century Bible. Edited by W. F. Adeney. 34 vols. London: Caxton Publishing Co., n.d.

†Originally published 1901-3. Based upon the RV. Commentators' remarks too brief and too old to be of particular value. 220.7.C33

Clarke, Adam. *Adam Clarke's Commentary.* Edited by Ralph Earle. Grand Rapids: Baker Book House, 1967.

A one-volume edition of this famous writer's six-volume work. For laypeople.

Arminian. 220.7.C54

The Clarendon Bible. Edited by Walter F. Adeney. 34 vols. Oxford: At the Clarendon Press, n.d.

†Limited in usefulness by the critical position adopted by some of the writers, and by the brevity of their comments. 220.7.C54A

Cook, F. C., ed. *The Bible Commentary.* 10 vols. New York: Charles Scribner's Sons, 1871-81.

Known also as the *Speaker's Bible Commentary* and published in England under the title *The Holy Bible According to the Authorized Version (A.D. 1611), with an Explanatory and Critical Commentary . . .* , this work contains mixed material. Among the outstanding contributors are B. F. Westcott and E. H. Gifford. Westcott's study of John's gospel and Gifford's remarkable work on Romans were deemed to be so outstanding that they were published separately. 220.7.C77

Ellicott, Charles John. *A Bible Commentary for English Readers.* 8 vols. London: Cassell and Co., n.d.

Originally published 1877-84. Though useful, does not serve the broad purpose of a work like Lange's commentary. 220.7.EL5

*The Expositor's Bible. Edited by William Robertson Nicoll. 6 vols. Grand Rapids: Wm. B. Eerdmans Publishing Co., 1956.

This set, originally completed in 1903, contains expositions by both conservation and liberal theologians. The most important works are by Kellogg (Leviticus), Blaikie (Joshua, I and II Samuel), Adeney (Ezra, Nehemiah—though Esther is weak), Maclaren (Psalms), Moule (Romans), Findlay (Galatians and Ephesians), Plummer (pastoral epistles and the epistles of James and Jude), Lumby (epistles of Peter), and Milligan (Revelation). 220.7.EX7 1956

Gaebelein, Arno Clemmens. *The An-* *notated Bible,* 9 vols. Chicago: Moody Press, 1913.

Of particular help to laymen. 220.7.G11

*Geikie, John Cunningham. *Hours with the Bible.* 10 vols. London: Hodder and Stoughton, 1884.

Does not fulfill the role of a commentary, but abounds in practical sermonic material. Of value to the expository preacher. 220.7.G27

Gill, John. *Exposition of the Bible.* 6 vols. Feltham, Middlesex, Eng.: W. H. Collingridge, 1952.

A deeply devotional but highly allegorical exposition. Originally published in 1852. 220.7.G41 1952

Gore, C., H. L. Goudge and **A. Guillaume, eds.** *A New Commentary on Holy Scripture.* London: S.P.C.K., 1928.

†Among the noteworthy commentaries in this volume are the works on Matthew by Levertoff and C. H. Turner's expositon of Mark. 220.7.G66

Henry, Matthew. *Commentary on the Whole Bible.* 6 vols. Westwood, N.J.: Fleming H. Revell, reprint.

Matthew Henry lived at a time when little emphasis was placed on the history and geography of the Holy Land. However, he was skilled in applying the truths of Scripture to the needs of those to whom he preached. His commentary, first published in 1708-10, may still be consulted with profit today. An abridged edition has been published by Zondervan Publishing House. 220.7.H39

The Interpreter's Bible. Edited by G. A. Buttrick, et al. 12 vols. Nashville: Abingdon Press, 1953-1956.

†Containing the latest in liberal scholarship, these volumes are complete with lengthy introductions, the AV and RSV text, exegetical and expository notes, and bibliography. Volume 12 contains additional articles on the "Transmission

of the New Testament," "Illustrated History of the Biblical Text," "The Dead Sea Scrolls," and a "Literary Chronology" combining the OT Apocrypha and Pseudepigrapha, and the NT. 220.7.IN8B

International Critical Commentary. Edited by Samuel Rolles Driver. Alfred Plummer, and Charles A. Briggs. 39 vols. New York: Charles Scribner's Sons, 1896-1937.

†While not complete, this set covers the greater portion of the Bible. Each commentary has been written by a different author, and they vary in quality and theological presuppositions. Each volume contains its own index. 220.7.IN8

Jamieson, Robert, A. R. Fausset and **David Brown.** *A Commentary, Critical, Experimental, and Practical on the Old and New Testaments.* 6 vols. Grand Rapids: Wm. B. Eerdmans Publishing Co., 1945.

Originally published in 1871, this work grows on the user. It is based on the original languages, and is not overly technical. It contains helpful comments on each passage. 220.7.J24 1945

The Jerome Biblical Commentary. Edited by Raymond E. Brown, Joseph A. Fitzmyer, and Roland E. Murphy. Englewood Cliffs, N.J.: Prentice Hall, 1968.

†Originally published in two volumes, this helpful work has now been made available in one volume. It is designed to meet the needs of educated readers who wish to study the Scriptures for themselves. Based upon the most recent scholarly research, it contains eighty articles written by competent Roman Catholic theologians, reflects an ecumenical thrust, and supplies a remarkable contemporary interpretation that at times is at variance with accepted Catholic dogma. The general articles on such topics as biblical theology, history, geography, and archaeology, plus the assessment of the significance of modern discoveries such as the apocryphal gospels

and the Dead Sea Scrolls, are of particular importance. 220.7.J47

***Lange, John Peter, ed.** Commentary on the Holy Scriptures.* Translated and edited by Philip Schaff. 24 vols. Grand Rapids: Zondervan Publishing House, 1960.

One of the best multivolume commentaries available. It is helpful on the OT, though it is dated archaeologically, historically, and philologically. 220.7.L25 1960

Maclaren, Alexander. *Expositions of Holy Scripture.* 25 vols. New York: George H. Doran Co., n.d.

Originally published in 1908, these expository studies do not cover every chapter and verse of the Bible. In these volumes, preachers, will find a fine example of expository preaching. 220.7.M22

Morgan, George Campbell. *Living Messages of the Books of the Bible.* Westwood: Fleming H. Revell Co., n.d.

Previously printed in four volumes, this work contains perceptive essays on each book of the Bible. First published in 1912. 220.7.M82

The New Bible Commentary. Edited by Francis Davison, et al. 2d ed. Grand Rapids: Wm. B. Eerdmans Publishing Co., 1954.

This work is prefaced with a series of general articles on the authority of Scripture, revelation and inspiration, the literature of the OT, an evaluation of apocryphal material, and so on. The expository material is generally helpful. Interspersed throughout the text are appendices on such topics as the Ark of the Covenant and the documentary hypothesis. The writers all adhere to the Reformed tradition. 220.7.N42D 1954

The New Bible Commentary: Revised. Edited by Donald Guthrie, et al. Grand Rapids: Wm. B. Eerdmans Publishing Co., 1970.

Follows essentially the same format as

the earlier edition by Francis Davidson. The general articles are particularly noteworthy and include an appraisal of the authority of Scripture, revelation and inspiration, the history of Israel, apocalyptic literature, the intertestamental period, and so on. In this edition there has been a tendency to include more American, Canadian, and Australian authors. 220.7.N42G 1970

The New Century Bible. Edited by R. E. Clement and M. Black. London: Marshall, Morgan and Scott, in process.

These commentaries are intended to update the earlier series issued at the turn of the century. They are based upon the latest critical source material, reflect a tendency toward the acceptance of higher critical theories, and are supposedly based upon the RSV, although for the most part the writers work from the original texts. Among the significant volumes are those by Rowley on Job, Ellis on Luke, Bruce on the Corinthian epistles, and Guthrie on Galatians. 220.7.N42

Poole, Matthew. *A Commentary on the Holy Bible.* 3 vols. London: Banner of Truth Trust, 1962.

J. C. Ryle said of this work: "Matthew Poole is sound, clear, sensible, and taking him for all in all, I place him at the head of English commentators." While his comments elucidate the text and reveal the writer's insights into the depths of the Word, they do not provide a sequential exposition of the text. Originally published in 1685. 220.7.P78 1962

The Preacher's Complete Homiletical Commentary. 32 vols. New York: Funk and Wagnalls Co., 1892-96.

Of limited usefulness. Whatever may have been the homiletic value of this set at one time, it now suffers from all the disadvantages of age, with none of the advantages. 220.7.P91

The Pulpit Commentary. Edited by H. D. M. Spence and Joseph S. Exell. 23 vols. Grand Rapids: Wm. B. Eerdmans Publishing Co., 1963.

This work, originally published between 1880 and 1919, remains valuable. The brief homilies contain many well-indexed sermonic ideas. In all there are 26,512 pages containing information on 9,500 subjects. 220.7.P96 1963

***Unger, Merrill Frederick.** *Unger's Bible Handbook.* Chicago: Moody Press, 1966.

The best handbook of its kind from the conservative viewpoint. Ideal for laypeople. 220.7.UN3

The Wesleyan Bible Commentary. Edited by Charles W. Carter, Ralph Earle, and W. Ralph Thompson. Grand Rapids: Wm. B. Eerdmans Publishing Co., 1964-69.

A popular Bible commentary, "evangelical, expositional, practical, homiletical, and devotional." Authors show familiarity with secondary material and occasionally discuss the meaning of specific Hebrew and Greek words. In general, the writers tend to hold to a mediating position and frequently fail to discuss problems that arise from a study of the text. Arminian. 220.7.W51

Westminster Commentaries. Edited by Walter Lock. Incomplete. London: Methuen and Co., 1901-.

These volumes tend to reflect the Anglo-Catholic point of view. However, a few volumes do stand out as being of real expository value. 220.7.W52

Wycliffe Bible Commentary. Edited by C. F. Pfeiffer and E. F. Harrison. Chicago: Moody Press, 1962.

Brief comments by evangelicals on each book of the Bible. 220.7.W97

OLD TESTAMENT

Alleman, Herbert Christian and **E. E. Flack, eds.** *Old Testament Commentary.* Philadelphia: Fortress Press, 1948.

Reflects the historic Lutheran approach to the Scriptures; emphasizes the message of the OT canonical books, the setting out of which they came, and the life they tend to cultivate. 221.7.AL5

*Keil, Johann Karl Friedrich and **Franz Julius Delitzsch.** *Biblical Commentary on the Old Testament.* 25 vols. Grand Rapids: Wm. B. Eerdmans Publishing Co., reprint.

Originally published in 1875. An invaluable work combining sound exegesis with solid exposition. 221.7.K26

Margolis, Max Leopold. *The Holy Scripture with Commentary.* Philadelphia: Jewish Publication Society of America, 1908.

An old, Jewish commentary. 221.7.M33

Soncino Books of the Bible. Edited by A. Cohen. 13 vols. London: Soncino Press, 1947-52.

A set of commentaries by Jewish scholars containing the Hebrew text with an English translation and an exposition based upon classical Jewish expositon. 221.7.S95

*New International Commentary on the Old Testament. Edited by E. J. Young and R. K. Harrison. Grand Rapids: Wm. B. Eerdmans Publishing Co., 1976-present.

This series, like its New Testament counterpart, is representative of the best of modern, evangelical scholarship. Each book is judiciously introduced and carefully expounded. Documentation is reserved for the footnotes. Extensive use is made of data from archaeological "digs," and philological comparisons are made between the Masoretic Text and information gleaned from the Dead Sea Scrolls or other Near Eastern sources. Although varying in quality, the volumes produced thus far have added a new dimension to the study of the Old Testament. 221.7.N42

*Tyndale Old Testament Commentaries. Edited by Donald J. Wiseman. Grand Rapids: Wm. B. Eerdmans Publishing Co., 1968.

A popular series of commentaries that aims at achieving evangelical scholarship without becoming overly technical. Concerned with deriving the true meaning of the text and applying the teaching of each book to the needs of the present day. Volumes manifest a slight adherence to the higher critical documentary theories. This minimizes their value and usefulness for laymen or adult Bible discussion groups. 221.7.T98

NEW TESTAMENT

Alford, Henry. *The Greek Testament.* Revised by E. F. Harrison. 4 vols. Chicago: Moody Press, 1958.

Not spectacular, but provides considerable help in areas where there are few capable commentaries. Premillennial. Anglican. Based on the 1894 edition. 225.7.AL2 1958

An American Commentary on the New Testament. Edited by Alvah Hovey. 7 vols. Philadelphia: American Baptist Publication Society, 1886.

An old work that, apart from Broadus on Matthew and Hackett on Acts, offers little to expositors today. 225.7.AM3

Barclay, William. *Daily Study Bible.* 2d ed. Philadelphia: Westminster Press, 1955-60.

Comments on each book of the NT. Rich in historic and linguistic data; weak in theology. 225.7.B23

Barnes, Albert. *Barnes' Notes on the New Testament.* Grand Rapids: Kregel Publications, 1966.

Of uneven value. Appeals to the layman, but too brief for the expositor. 225.7.B26

Bengel, Johann Albrecht. *Gnomon of*

the New Testament. 5 vols. Revised and edited by Andrew R. Fausset. Edinburgh: T. and T. Clark, 1857-95.

An old work that contains valuable insights into the Greek of the NT and is still sought after. 225.7.B43

*Calvin, John. *Calvin's Commentaries.* 12 vols. Edited by David W. Torrance and Thomas F. Torrance. Grand Rapids: Wm. B. Eerdmans Publishing Co., 1959-73.

The translation is outstanding, and the style is lucid and forceful. The long sentences of the original have been skillfully shortened, resulting in an adequate conveyance of Calvin's thought to the mind of the English reader. A well-executed revision. 225.7.C13

The Cambridge Greek Testament for Schools and Colleges. Edited by J. Stewart Perowne. Cambridge: At the University Press, 1916.

Dated, but still valuable for brief exegetical comments. 225.7.P42

*Erdman, Charles Rosenbury. *Commentaries on the New Testament Books.* 17 vols. Philadelphia: Westminster Press, 1916-36.

Brief commentaries that adequately explain the theme of each book of the NT and ably expound its central message. Provides preachers with numerous vignettes that can be developed into sermons. Premillennial. 225.7.ER2

The Expositor's Greek Testament. Edited by William Robertson Nicoll. 5 vols. Grand Rapids: Wm. B. Eerdmans Publishing Co., 1951.

Weak in theology and somewhat dated, but contains some good exegetical insights on the epistles of the NT. 225.EX7

Howley, George Cecil Douglas, F. F. Bruce and **H. L. Ellison.** *A New Testament Commentary.* Grand Rapids: Zondervan Publishing House, 1970.

This work is of marginal value. It is based upon the RSV and contains essays and comments from twenty-five contributors. 220.7.H84

*Lenski, Richard Charles Henry. *Interpretation of the New Testament.* 14 vols. Minneapolis: Augsburg Publishing House, 1946.

A conservative, very extensive, and generally helpful exposition. Arminian in doctrine, rigid in its approach to Greek grammar, and follows an amillennial interpretation of eschatology. Contains exceedingly helpful background material, and abounds in good preaching values. 225.7.L54

Meyer, Heinrich August Wilhelm, ed. *A Critical and Exegetical Commentary on the New Testament.* 20 vols. Edinburgh: T. and T. Clark, 1877.

While the German commentaries in this series have been updated, the English have not and are in need of revision. They are marked by fine scholarship, however, and close attention is paid to critical details. Theology is blended with exegesis in expounding the text. 225.7.M57

The Moffatt New Testament Commentary. 17 vols. New York: Harper and Row, 1927-72.

†Aims to bring out the meaning of the NT books, but most of the volumes fail to make any lasting contribution. 225.7.M72

*New International Commentary on the New Testament. Edited by N. B. Stonehouse and F. F. Bruce. Grand Rapids: Wm. B. Eerdmans Publishing Co., 1951-present.

Generally representative of the best of modern Reformed scholarship from many countries and, when complete, will probably take its place among the most serviceable works for the minister and the more advanced Bible student. Each expository study, although ostensibly based on the English text of 1881 Revised Version and the American Standard Version (1901), has in reality been established upon an exacting study of the original. Critical comments have been largely confined to footnotes. Elaboration on important issues, grammatical and textual factors highlighting some facet of the text, and historical details will be found in special notes in the appendices. Of particular significance to the researcher will be Lane's work on Mark, Morris's treatment of John's gospel, Bruce's expositions of Acts and Hebrews, Hughes's magisterial handling of II Corinthians, and Marshall's treatment of John's epistles. 225.7.N42

*Robertson, Archibald Thomas. *Word Pictures in the New Testament.* 6 vols. Nashville: Broadman Press, 1930-33.

A work of thorough scholarship stressing the meaningful and pictorial suggestions that are often implicit in the original text but lost in translation. Of particular help whenever one undertakes the study of a NT book for the first time. 225.7.R54

Tyndale New Testament Commentaries. Edited by R. V. G. Tasker. 20 vols. Grand Rapids: Wm. B. Eerdmans Publishing Co., 1957-71.

An up-to-date, moderately priced, evangelical series of commentaries written by British and Australian theolo-

gians. While these works vary in value, each writer bases his exposition upon an exegesis of the Greek text. Reformed. 225.7.T97

Vincent, Marvin Richardson. *Word Studies in the New Testament.* 4 vols. Grand Rapids: Wm. B. Eerdmans Publishing Co., 1957.

Surpassed by other exegetical and expository works and now of little value to the pastor. 225.V74

Williams, George. *The New Student's Commentary.* Revised by Charles R. Wood. Grand Rapids: Kregel Publications, 1970.

A comprehensive one-volume Bible commentary. Thoroughly conservative, with ultradispensational leanings. 225.7.W67 1970

Wordsworth, Christopher. *The New Testament of Our Lord and Savior Jesus Christ.* 2 vols. London: Rivingtons, 1862.

Painstaking notes covering the entire NT, ably supplemented with quotations from the church Fathers and revealing the writer's devout spirit. Bibliographic references are interspersed throughout the text. 225.7'07.W89

Wuest, Kenneth Samuel. *The New Testament.* 4 vols. Grand Rapids: Wm. B. Eerdmans Publishing Co., 1961.

Of particular value for those students of the Scriptures who lack a personal knowledge of Greek. 225.7.W95

SPECIAL SUBJECTS

Arndt, William Frederick. *Bible Difficulties.* St. Louis: Concordia Publishing House, 1962.

A frank discussion of some perplexing problems and apparent contradictions in the Bible. 220.8'239.AR6

Babbage, Stuart Barton. *Christianity and Sex.* Chicago: Inter-Varsity Press, 1963.

A careful investigation of the nature and problems of sex from a theological and historical perspective. 220.8.ET3.B11

Barrett, Charles Kingsley. *Biblical Problems and Biblical Preaching.* Philadelphia: Fortress Press, 1964.

A brief, scholarly study. 220.8'251.B27

Bodenheimer, Friedrich Simon. *Ani-*

mal and Man in Bible Lands. Leiden: E. J. Brill, 1960.

A very readable manual by the late professor of zoology, Hebrew University, Jerusalem. 220.8591.B63

Bright, John. *The Authority of the Old Testament.* Nashville: Abingdon Press, 1967.

†Stresses the need for a Western kind of biblical theology as the answer to the confusion facing many preachers and teachers. Emphasizes principles that may be used in solving critical problems. 221.8.AU8.B76

*Bullinger, Ethelbert William. *Figures of Speech Used in the Bible.* Grand Rapids: Baker Book House, 1968.

Contains a comprehensive and detailed study of figures of speech used in the Bible. Although first published in 1898, the material has never been replaced or superseded. 220.88'08.B87

Cansdale, George. *Animals of the Bible Lands.* London: Paternoster Press, 1970.

A fascinating, well-illustrated volume. 220.859.C16

Childs, Brevard S. *Biblical Theology in Crisis.* Philadelphia: Westminster Press, 1970.

An appeal for a reassessment of the role of biblical theology in the light of the present demise it faces as an academic discipline. Calls for a return to the Christian canon as the only authoritative basis upon which to develop a biblical theology, voices concern about the attempts to build a biblical theology upon *Heilsgeschichte,* language phenomenology, or some mode of consciousness illustrated by the text, and stresses the need for viewing Scripture as a whole rather than in fragmented sections. 220.823.C43

Cole, William Graham. *Sex and Love in the Bible.* New York: Association Press, 1959.

†A candid examination of the cultural and historical factors that influenced the people of God in Bible times. Manifests an inadequate view of inspiration, misunderstands completely the nature of betrothal, and flirts with the idea that the Bible permits premarital sexual relations. In spite of these glaring weaknesses, contains valuable information. 220.8.ET3.C67

Cook, Stanley Arthur. *The "Truth" of the Bible.* Cambridge: W. Heffer and Sons, 1938.

Seeks to make clear the relevance and abiding value of the Bible. Unfortunately, by adopting higher critical theories concerning God's Word, Cook fails to present a convincing case. As scholarly as these essays are, they will invariably disappoint the reader. 220.8.C77

Daube, David. *Studies in Biblical Law.* New York: Ktav Publishing House, 1970.

First published in 1947. Emphasizes comparative law in Israel, and points out many interesting distinctions between biblical law, Roman law, and ancient Near Eastern codes. 220.8.L41.D26

Davis, John James. *Biblical Numerology.* Grand Rapids: Baker Book House, 1968.

A careful and helpful study of the use of numbers in the Bible. 220.6'8.D29

DeHoff, George Washington. *Alleged Bible Contradictions Explained.* Murphreesboro, Tenn.: DeHoff Publications, 1950.

A modern treatment of the alleged contradictions and discrepancies in the Bible. Not as comprehensive as Haley's *Alleged Discrepancies in the Bible.* 220.8'239.D67

Guillebaud, H. E. *Some Moral Difficulties of the Bible.* London: Tyndale Press, 1941.

Discusses the origin of sin, God's choice of Israel, the problem of preterition, God's wrath and jealousy, the imprecatory psalms, and so on. 220.8.ET3.G94

Hooke, Samuel Henry. *Alpha and*

Omega: A Study in the Pattern of Revelation. London: James Nisbet and Company, 1961.

The text of the Speaker's Lecture, University of Oxford, 1956-61, these essays focus on the life of Christ and draw from the pages of the OT and NT relevant information showing how He was the revelation of God to man. 220.13.H76

Kraemer, Hendrik. *The Bible and Social Ethics.* Philadelphia: Fortress Press, 1965.

†Sets forth the theory that the revival of interest in a new social ethic and the ecumenical movement are interrelated. 220.8.ET3.K86

Little, Robert J. *Insight.* Chicago: Moody Press, 1971.

Provides answers to some of the questions featured on "Moody Presents" and "The Question Box." Covers topics such as "Was Jesus a Revolutionary?" "The If's and Ought's of Prayer," and "Christian Ethics." 220.8.L72

Madden, Frederic William. *History of Jewish Coinage and of Money in the Old and New Testament.* Prolegomenon by M. Avi-Yonah. New York: Ktav Publishing House, 1967.

Reveals the importance of numismatics to the study of the OT and NT. A valuable work. 220.8.N91.M26 1967 (Alt. DDC 737.4933)

Maston, Thomas Bufford. *Biblical Ethics.* Cleveland: World Publishing Co., 1967.

A thoughtful and comprehensive survey of biblical ethics, with the major emphasis on the ethical unity of the Bible. The author is convinced that the dynamic and ethical unity of the Bible are derived from the nature of God, whose grace and truth are discoverable in the message and ministry of Christ. 220.8.ET3.M39

Møller-Christensen, V. and **K. E. Jordt Jørgensen.** *Encyclopedia of Bible Creatures.* Edited by M. Theodore

Heinecken. Translated by Arne Unhjem. Philadelphia: Fortress Press, 1965.

Ably correlates biological information with biblical facts and historical references. Illustrated with numerous black-and-white photographs. 220.859.M73

*****Morris, Henry Madison.** *Biblical Cosmology and Modern Science.* Grand Rapids: Baker Book House, 1970.

Supports biblical creationism, catastrophism, naturalism, and eschatology, and exposes the failings of pagan cosmologies, uniformitarianism, and anti-supernaturalism. Timely and authentic. 220.857.M83

Mouldenke, Harold N. *The Plants of the Bible.* Waltham, Mass.: Chronica Botanica Co., 1952.

An important work by the former curator and administrator of the Herbarium, New York Botanical Gardens. The bibliographies are full and very helpful. 220.858.M86

*****Moulton, Richard Green.** *The Literary Study of the Bible.* London: Isbister and Co., 1899.

An old, standard work that is always worthy of consideration. 220.8.L71.M86

Parmelee, Alice. *All the Birds of the Bible.* London: Lutterworth Press, 1960.

A handy, helpful volume containing stories with the identification and meaning of each of the birds named in the Bible. 220.859.P24

Patal, Raphael. *Family, Love and the Bible.* (n.p.) MacGibbon and Kee, 1960.

A historical treatment from a Jewish perspective. 220.8.F21.P27

Pinney, Roy. *The Animals in the Bible.* Philadelphia: Chilton Books, 1964.

Of help in classifying accurately the many references to animals in the Bible. Valuable as an aid in preaching as well. 220.859.P65

Scorer, Charles Gordon. *The Bible and Sex Ethics Today.* Downers Grove, Ill.: Inter-Varsity Press, 1966.

A biblical and historical treatment of the contemporary views of sex. 220.8.ET3.SC7

Smith, Willard S. *Animals, Birds and Plants of the Bible.* Needham Heights, Mass.: Church Art, 1971.

A recent, colorful, reliable work. 220.859.SM6

Vester, Bertha Hodges (Spafford). *Flowers of the Holy Land.* Garden City: Doubleday and Co., 1962.

A popular, practical work with seventeen color reproductions of original watercolors. Meets a real need, for there are few reliable works treating this area of biblical study. 220.858.V63

*__Vos, Gerhardus.__ *Biblical Theology: Old and New Testaments.* Grand Rapids: Wm. B. Eerdmans Publishing Co., 1948.

A representative work from an evangelical point of view. Although it does not consider certain areas of Israel's thought (e.g., the wisdom literature) and was issued prior to the more recent theological research, it has much to contribute historically. Based on covenant theology. 220.823.V92

Walker, Winifred. *All the Plants of the Bible.* London: Lutterworth Press, 1958.

Contains exquisite photographs captioned with the English, Latin, and Hebrew names of the plants, with text on the opposite page, complete with the characteristics and lore of each plant. 220.858.W15

Wright, George Ernest. *The God Who Acts: Biblical Theology as Recital.* Naperville, Ill.: Alec R. Allenson, 1952.

†A survey of the great acts of God as developed in the *Heilsgeschichte* of the OT and NT. 220.823.W93

Wright, Ruth V. and **Robert L. Chadbourne.** *Gems and Minerals of the Bible.* New York: Harper and Row, 1970.

A fascinating book dealing with the sixty-two gems and minerals known in Bible times, used by well-known Bible

personalities, and which have frequently become surrounded by legends, superstitions, and myths. A highly informative work. 220.8'549.W93

OLD TESTAMENT

Anderson, Bernard Word, ed. *The Old Testament and Christian Faith: A Theological Discussion.* New York: Harper and Row, 1963.

†A contemporary discussion of the relation of the OT to the NT, with a complete division of thought on the part of the contributors over Bultmann's "Significance of the Old Testament for the Christian Faith." 221.823.AN3

Autrey, C. E. *Revivals of the Old Testament.* Grand Rapids: Zondervan Publishing House, 1960.

Sermons by the director of evangelism, Southern Baptist Convention. May be regarded as seed-thoughts for a series of messages. 221.8.R32.AU8

*__Baron, David.__ *Rays of Messiah's Glory.* Grand Rapids: Zondervan Publishing House, reprint.

An inspirational study on OT Christology, with appendices on "The Seed of the Woman," "Until Shiloh Comes," "Psalm 22," and so on. 221.8'07.B26

*_____. *Types, Psalms, and Prophecies.* 2d ed. London: Hodder and Stoughton, 1907.

A series of studies covering such topics as the Sabbath, the feasts of Israel, expositions of selected psalms, and a study of "the Suffering Servant of Jehovah and the Glorious Fruits of His Missions." 221.8.B26 1907

Bruce, W. S. *The Ethics of the Old Testament.* 2d ed. Enlarged. Edinburgh: T. and T. Clark, 1960.

This concise discussion of the teaching of the OT on moral behavior grounds the distinctive lifestyle of the Hebrews in God's revelation to them, ably distinguishes between Israel's laws and those of the surrounding nations, and provides a perceptive evaluation of the intent of the ethical principles of the OT. 221.8.ET3.B83 1960

Childs, Brevard Springs. *Myth and Reality in the Old Testament.* Studies in Biblical Theology. London: SCM Press, 1960.

Analyzes the mythical concept of reality as it relates to biblical research and, while cognizant of Bultmann's approach to the NT, offers a different approach to the problem, particularly as it relates to the study of the OT. 221.1.C43

Davidson, Andrew Bruce. *Old Testament Prophecy.* Edited by J. A. Paterson. Edinburgh: T. and T. Clark, 1903.

An intriguing résumé of the history of prophecy from the time of Moses to the postexilic period. Includes a discussion of symbolism, the nature of revelation, typology, the teaching of false prophets, messianism, and so on. 221.8.P94.D28

————. *Theology of the Old Testament.* International Theological Library. Edited by S. D. F. Salmond. Edinburgh: T. and T. Clark, 1961.

A moderately liberal work that can be consulted with profit. 221.823.D28

Delitzsch, Franz Julius. *Old Testament History of Redemption.* Translated by S. I. Curtiss. Edinburgh: T. and T. Clark, 1881.

A rare work devoted to exploring the concept of salvation in OT times. Provides a solid foundation for NT study as well. 221.8.R24.D37

Dentan, Robert Claude. *The Knowledge of God in Ancient Israel.* New York: Seabury Press, 1968.

†By focusing upon the doctrine of God in the OT, the writer seeks to explain the relationship of God to Israel and how Israel came to understand more about God and His ways. 221.8.D43

————. *Preface to Old Testament Theology.* New York: Seabury Press, 1963.

†Important for its concise treatment of the subject. 221.823.D43

Eichrodt, Walther. *Man in the Old Testament.* Translated by K. and R. G. Smith. Studies in Biblical Theology. London: SCM Press, 1951.

A definite contribution to our understanding of the OT teaching of the purpose of God in creation, as well as man's obligation to his Creator. 221.8.M32.EI2

————. *Theology of the Old Testament.* Translated by J. A. Baker. 2 vols. Philadelphia: Westminster Press, 1961.

†Based upon the covenant concept as the unifying principle of the OT, Eichrodt's work is rooted in the historical response of the people of God to His self-revelation. 221.823.E12

Ellison, Henry Leopold. *The Centrality of the Messianic Idea for the Old Testament.* London: Tyndale Press, 1957.

A helpful consideration of the central theme of the OT Scriptures. Presented in such a way that the NT becomes more meaningful. An enlightening work. Amillennial. 221.823.EL5

Evangelical Theological Society. *New Perspectives on the Old Testament.* Edited by John Barton Payne. Waco: Word Books, 1970.

A compilation of seventeen essays prepared and presented at the twentieth anniversary meeting of the Evangelical Theological Society. 221.8.EV1

Gaebelein, Arno Clemens. *The Harmony of the Prophetic Word: A Key to Old Testament Prophecy Concerning Things to Come.* New York: Fleming H. Revell Company, 1907.

Contains nine chapters covering a variety of themes from the "Day of Jehovah" to the setting up of Christ's "Theocratic Kingdom." Dated, but still stimulating. 221.8.P94.G11

Jacob, Edmond. *Theology of the Old Testament.* Translated by Arthur W. Heathcote and Phillip J. Allcock. New York: Harper and Brothers, 1958.

Stresses God's mastery of history, and is useful for collateral reading in a course on OT theology. 221.823.J15

Johnson, Aubrey Rodway. *The One and the Many in the Israelite Conception of God.* Cardiff: University of Wales Press, 1961.

A popularized but obtuse presentation of H. Wheeler Robinson's studies on corporate personality. 221.8.J63

Knight, George Angus Fulton. *A Christian Theology of the Old Testament.* Philadelphia: Westminster Press, 1959.

†A specifically Christian approach to an understanding of the OT message. Not as reliable as Barton Payne's *Theology of the Old Testament.* 221.823.K74

Köhler, Ludwig Hugo. *Old Testament Theology.* Translated by A. S. Todd. Philadelphia: Westminster Press, 1957.

†While disappointing in theology, the value of this work lies in its useful word studies. 221.823.K81

*Kurtz, Johann Heinrich. *Sacrificial Worship of the Old Testament.* Translated by J. Martin. Edinburgh: T. and T. Clark, 1858.

Thoroughly conservative and evangelical, Kurtz's treatment even today makes rewarding reading and serves as an effective counter-balance to other more liberal works whose viewpoints continue to recur in modern discussions. 221.8.SA1.K96

Leathes, Stanley. *Old Testament Prophecy: Its Witness as a Record of Divine Knowledge.* London: Hodder and Stoughton, 1880.

The text of the Warburton Lectures, 1876-80, these chapters deal with the indestructibility of supernaturalism and provide a scholarly apologetic for the authority of the OT Scriptures. 221.8.P94.L48

Norden, Rudolph F. *Parables of the Old Testament.* Grand Rapids: Baker Book House, 1964.

Sermons by a Lutheran pastor. Seminal. 221.8.P21.N75

Noth, Martin and D. Winton Thomas, eds. *Wisdom in Israel and the Ancient Near East.* Leiden: E. J. Brill, 1960.

†A fine collection of essays that presumes readers are thoroughly conversant with Jewish wisdom literature and can readily interact with the material. Of value to the scholar, but holds little for the novice. 221.8.N84

*Oehler, Gustave Friedrich. *Theology of the Old Testament.* Translated by George E. Day. Grand Rapids: Zondervan Publishing House, n.d.

A classic study. Originally published in 1873-74. Reformed. 221.823.OE5

*Payne, John Barton. *The Theology of the Older Testament.* Grand Rapids: Zondervan Publishing House, 1962.

An impressive work in the field of biblical theology. Written from a thoroughly Reformed point of view. 221.823.P28

Peake, Arthur Samuel. *Brotherhood in the Old Testament.* New York: George H. Doran Company, 1923.

Traces the idea of corporate personality through the history of divine relation as it bears upon Israel's political and social structure, attitude towards other ethnic groups, and treatment of the poor and afflicted. 221.8.B79.P31

_____, ed. *The People and the Book.* Oxford: At the Clarendon Press, 1925.

A selection of essays by members of the Society for OT Studies. Deals with Israel's neighbors, religious environment, and history; the methods of higher criticism; status of OT studies; the worship of Israel; Jewish interpretation of Scripture; and so on. 221.8.P31

*_____. *The Problem of Suffering in the Old Testament.* London: Robert Bryant, 1904.

Studies surveying Habakkuk's problem regarding why Yahweh is indifferent to suffering, the problems faced by Ezekiel during his ministry, the "Servant of Yahweh" passages in Isaiah, the problem of suffering as found in the book of Job, and so on. Not all readers will agree with the writer's approach, but he makes a valuable contribution. 221.824.P31

Rad, Gerhard von. *Old Testament Theology.* Translated by D. M. G. Stalker. 2 vols. New York: Harper and Row, 1962.

†As with Eichrodt, von Rad rejects the traditional categories of dogmatic theology and bases his work squarely upon *Heilsgeschichte.* In addition, von Rad's typological exegesis makes many of his conclusions questionable. 221.823.R11

*Raven, John Howard. *The History of the Religion of Israel: An Old Testament Theology.* New Brunswick Theological Seminary, 1933.

Says J. Barton Payne, "A genuine theology of the OT—not just what men thought, but what God taught, authoritatively preserved in inspired Scripture." 221.8'09.R27.R19

Robinson, Henry Wheeler. *The Religious Ideas of the Old Testament.* Studies in Theology. 2d rev. ed. London: Gerald Duckworth, 1956.

A mediating work by a higher critical scholar who, while modifying some of the destructive theories of Wellhausen's system, tries to establish a constructive biblical theology with an evaluation of Israel's religious practices. 221.823.R54

Rowley, Harold Henry. *The Faith of Israel: Aspects of Old Testament Thought.* London: SCM Press, 1956.

A brief sketch of OT theology. Too brief and too biased to be of value. 221.823.R79

————, ed. *The Old Testament and Modern Study: A Generation of Discovery and Research.* Oxford: At the Clarendon Press, 1951.

A collection of essays by members of the British Society for OT Study. 221.8.R79

————. *The Servant of the Lord.* 2d ed. Oxford: Basil Blackwell, 1965.

†A collection of studies that includes a discussion of "The Marriage of Ruth," "The Interpretation of the Song of Songs," and "The Unity of the Book of Daniel." 221.8.R79S 1965

Schultz, Hermann. *Old Testament Theology: The Religion of Revelation in Its Pre-Christian Stage of Development.* 2 vols. Translated by J. A. Peterson. Edinburgh: T. and T. Clark, 1895.

Representative of a school of thought current in Germany toward the end of the last century. Adopts a mediating position being neither identified with conservatives such as Oehler nor radicals of the caliber of Stade. Succeeds in elucidating God's revelation in the OT. 221.823.SCH8

Smith, William Robertson. *The Old Testament in the Jewish Church: A Course of Lectures on Biblical Criticism.* 2d. ed. rev. and enl. London: Adam and Charles Black, 1907.

†Provocative essays that are often insightful, but are also misleading. An example of the negative results of biblical criticism. 221.8.SM5 1907

Snaith, Norman Henry. *The Distinctive Ideas of the Old Testament.* New York: Schocken Books, 1964.

†Building upon the conviction that a unique concept of God is the root of the distinctiveness of the OT, Snaith enlarges upon God's holiness, righteousness, covenant-love, election-love, and Spirit as a life-giving power. 221.823.SN1

Toombs, Lawrence E. *The Old Testament in Christian Preaching.* Philadelphia: Westminster Press, 1961.

Explores the riches of the OT and the relevancy of its message in the life of the church. 221.8.P91.T61

Trumbull, Henry Clay. *The Blood Covenant: A Primitive Rite and Its Bearing Upon Scripture.* Philadelphia: John Wattles, Publisher, 1893.

A detailed work explaining the background of the "blood covenant," the occasions when it would be used, and its significance. Informative and enlightening. 221.8.C83B.T77

―――. *The Covenant of Salt as Based on the Significance and Symbolism of Salt in Primitive Thought.* New York: Charles Scribner's Sons, 1899.

A volume welcomed by scholars on both sides of the Atlantic. Highlights a Near Eastern custom and shows its relevance to OT study. 221.8.C83S.T77

―――. *The Threshold Covenant; or the Beginning of Religious Rites.* Edinburgh: T. and T. Clark, 1896.

A work of considerable erudition. Traces the origin of this covenant and shows how it permeated the society of the ancient Near East. 221.8.C83T.T77

Vriezen, Theodorus Christiaan. *An Outline of Old Testament Theology.* Translated by S. Nevijen. Philadelphia: Westminster Press, 1958.

May be distinguished from other treatments on the same subject by the novel way in which it looks at time-worn themes. 221.823.V96

*Wilson, Robert Dick. *A Scientific Investigation of the Old Testament.* Revised by Edward J. Young. Chicago: Moody Press, 1959.

An examination of the text, grammar, vocabulary, history, and religion of the OT based squarely upon the "laws of evidence." Repudiates such theories as the documentary hypothesis of the Pentateuch, and defends the evangelical position on such matters as transmission of the text. 221.821.W69 1959

*Wright, George Ernest. *The Old Testament and Theology.* New York: Harper and Row, 1969.

†Concerned with demonstrating the relationship of the OT to the life of the contemporary Christian, and argues persuasively against theologians who "dissolve theology into Christology." 221.823.W93

Young, Edward Joseph. *A Study of Old Testament Theology Today.* Westwood, N.J.:

Fleming H. Revell Co., 1959.

A brief work. Young grounds his theology upon God's involvement in Israel's history. 221.823.Y8

Zimmerli, Walther. *Man and His Hope in the Old Testament.* Studies in Biblical Theology. Naperville, Ill.: Alec R. Allenson, 1968.

†Traces the theme of hope through the OT, beginning with the book of Job, then in the different eras of history, and concludes with an assessment of hope in Israel's apocalyptic literature. 221.8.H77.Z6

NEW TESTAMENT

*Abrahams, Israel. *Studies in Pharisaism and the Gospels.* New York: Ktav Publishing House, 1967.

First published in two volumes in 1917 and 1924. Now available in one volume. Long regarded as a pioneer work that revolutionized an understanding of the character and development of Pharisaism. 225.8.P49.AB8 1967 (Alt. DDC 296.81)

Akerman, John Younge. *Numismatic Illustrations of the Narrative Portions of the New Testament.* Chicago: Argonaut Publishers, 1966.

Written by the first editor of the *Numismatic Journal.* Adds meaning, value, and historic insights to the study of the NT. 225.8.N91.AK3 (Alt. DDC 737.4933)

*Bernard, Thomas Dehany. *The Progress of Doctrine in the New Testament.* Grand Rapids: Zondervan Publishing House, n.d.

These Bampton Lectures, delivered at the University of Oxford in 1864, survey the entire scope of NT theology and are, to quote Dr. Wilbur M. Smith, "the product of sound scholarship, and a profound belief in the Divine origin of the Holy Scriptures." 225.823.B45

Blaiklock, Edward Musgrave. *Word*

Pictures from the Bible. Grand Rapids: Zondervan Publishing House, 1971.

This work, by a very gifted writer and classical scholar, lacks depth but is an ideal reference work in the pastor's library. 225.84.B57

Bornkamm, Gunther. *Early Christian Experience.* Translated by P. L. Hammer. London: SCM Press, 1969.

†Eleven essays representative of the writer's careful, balanced scholarship. This ably illustrates his blending of historical, theological, and critical data with his exegesis. Of little value to pastors because of the author's theological position. 225.824.B65

Brandon, Samuel George Frederick. *Jesus and the Zealots.* New York: Charles Scribner's Sons, 1967.

†A futile attempt to identify Jesus Christ with the revolutionary party of His times. 296.8'1.B73

Bruce, Frederick Fyvie. *The New Testament Development of Old Testament Themes.* Grand Rapids: Wm. B. Eerdmans Publishing Co., 1968.

Published in England under the title *This Is That,* these essays, based on the Payton Lectures delivered at the Fuller Theological Seminary, California, in 1968, deal with the NT events forecast and foreshadowed in OT times. 225.84.B83

_____. *Tradition: Old and New.* Grand Rapids: Zondervan Publishing House, 1970.

Traces the history and development of Christian tradition, and probes the establishment of standards that have long been used to measure Christian thought and practice. Bruce warns of the dangers of form-criticism, but builds some of his own theories upon form-critical presuppositions. This is tantamount to a denial of inspiration. Otherwise very helpful. 225.8.B83

Bultmann, Rudolf Karl. *Theology of the New Testament.* 2 vols. London: SCM Press, 1956.

†A radical approach to NT theology. 225.823.B87

Burton, Ernest De Witt. *Spirit, Soul, and Flesh.* Chicago: University of Chicago Press, 1918.

Traces the usage of *pneuma, psuche,* and *sarx* through the writings of the Greeks to A.D. 225. One of the most thorough treatments ever attempted. 225.8.M29.B95

Conzelmann, Hans. *An Outline of the Theology of the New Testament.* London: SCM Press, 1969.

†A delineation of the standard dogmas that have come to be identified with this German theologian. 225.823.C76

***Daube, David.** *The New Testament and Rabbinic Judaism.* London: Athlone Press, 1956.

Composed of the Jordan Lectures for 1952, this work contains a mine of information. The author's training in law serves him admirably in interpreting and evaluating contemporary source material. Regrettably omits a consideration of the Qumran materials and their impact upon biblical scholarship. 225.8.R11.D26

Davies, William David. *Christian Origins and Judaism.* London: Darton, Longman and Todd, 1962.

Stresses the Jewish background of NT thought. 225.8.D28

Deissmann, Gustav Adolf. *Biblical Studies.* Translated by Alexander Grieve. Edinburgh: T. and T. Clark, 1923.

A valuable contribution to our understanding of koine Greek, but not as important as the writer's famous volume *Light from the Ancient East.* 225.848.D36B

*_____. *Light from the Ancient East.* Translated by Lionel R. M. Strachan. Grand Rapids: Baker Book House, 1965.

The product of fifteen years of study of the Greek text and other documents of the Hellenistic East. Elucidates the text, language, literature, and history of the NT. 225.848.D36L 1965

Dodd, Charles Harold. *According to the Scriptures.* London: James Nisbet and Co., 1961.

†Part of the Stone Lectures delivered at Princeton Theological Seminary in 1950. Focus on the substructure of NT theology. Too critical to be of value to the pastor. 225.823.D66

_____. *The Apostolic Preaching and Its Developments.* London: Hodder and Stoughton, 1970.

Contains three lectures delivered at King's College, University of London, in 1935, together with an appendix on eschatology and history. Includes an exhaustive and enlightening treatment of the kerygma. First published in 1936. 225.825.D66 1970

_____. *More New Testament Studies.* Grand Rapids: Wm. B. Eerdmans Publishing Co., 1968.

†Basing his studies solidly upon form-criticism, Dodd shows that he has again shifted his position toward greater acceptance of the historicity of the gospels. Questions the acceptance of the priority of Mark, and holds out hope for a possible return to some of the original *logia* of Jesus. 225.84.D66

_____. *The Old Testament in the New* Philadelphia. Fortress Press, 1952.

A brief introduction to the methodology of textual comparison, with selected illustrations. 225.84.D66

Edersheim, Alfred. *The Temple, Its Ministry and Services.* Grand Rapids: Wm. B. Eerdmans Publishing Co., 1954.

A singularly helpful work by a Christian Jewish scholar. Provides essential information pertaining to the Temple in the time of Christ. 225.829.ED2

Ellis, Edward Earle. *Paul's Use of the Old Testament.* Grand Rapids: Wm. B. Eerdmans Publishing Co., 1957.

Combines evangelical scholarship with

a detailed analysis of the literature of the NT. Analyzes Paul's attitude toward Scripture, his relationship to Judaism and the teachings of Christ, and his exegesis. 225.84.EL5

Filson, Floyd Vivian. *Jesus Christ, the Risen Lord.* Nashville: Abingdon Press, 1956.

†A serious attempt to find some form of unity within the framework of a biblical theology. 225.823.F48

France, R. T. *Jesus and the Old Testament.* London: Tyndale Press, 1971.

A valuable study that provides generally conservative, thorough, and scholarly examination of the OT passages in the gospels that apply to Christ and His mission. It stops short, however, of adherence to a belief in inspiration. 225.848.F84

Henderson, Ian. *Myth in the New Testament.* London: SCM Press, 1952.

A discerning critique of Bultmann's theory of demythologization. 225.823.H38

Hill, David. *Greek Words and Hebrew Meanings: Studies in the Semantics of Soteriological Terms.* Society for New Testament Studies. Cambridge: University Press, 1967.

A scholarly study of the Greek words for "propitiation," "ransom," "righteousness," "eternal life," and "spirit." 225.84.H55

Jones, Arnold Hugh Martin. *Studies in Roman Government and Law.* Oxford: Basil Blackwell, 1960.

A brief, fact-packed study explaining the complexity of Roman law and making the material understandable to laymen. 225.8.G74.J41

Ladd, George Eldon. *Jesus and the Kingdom.* Waco: Word Books, 1969.

A comprehensive, scholarly study of the preaching of Jesus concerning the kingdom of God. 225.823.L12

Lightfoot, Joseph Barber. *Dissertations*

on the Apostolic Age. London: Macmillan Co., 1892.

Contains essays originally appearing in Lightfoot's exegetical studies of the Pauline epistles, including "The Brethren of Our Lord," "The Christian Ministry," "St. Paul and Seneca," and "The Essenes." 225.8.L62D

————. *Biblical Essays.* London: Macmillan Co., 1893.

Helpful studies on the authenticity of John's gospel, Paul's preparation for the ministry, the chronology of Paul's life and letters, the mission of Titus to Corinth, and so on. 225.8.L62

*McDonald, Hermit Dermot. *Living Doctrines of the New Testament.* London: Pickering and Inglis, 1970.

Lacks penetrating insight and fails to do justice to many critical questions of interpretation that frequently blur theological distinctions. In spite of this, an important work. 225.823.M14

Manson, William. *Jesus and the Christian.* Grand Rapids: Wm. B. Eerdmans Publishing Co., 1967.

Contains a series of essays published in various journals between 1925 and 1957. The "depth exegesis" moves from a clarification of Jesus' ministry to the significance of His life for the Christian and for world evangelism today. Accepts many of the higher-critical theories, but renounces the methods and conclusions of form-criticism. 225.8.M31

Milligan, George. *Here and There Among the Papyri.* London: Hodder and Stoughton, 1923.

A readable work surveying the earlier discoveries and relating their importance to the study of the NT. 225.84.M62

Moffat, James. *Grace in the New Testament.* London: Hodder and Stoughton, 1931.

A companion volume to Moffat's exemplary study of love in the NT. This work likewise is deserving of repeated consultation. 225.8.G75.M72

————. *Love in the New Testament.* London: Hodder and Stoughton, 1929.

A work that must be consulted when doing a study of the NT teaching on love. 225.8.L94.M72

*Morris, Leon. *The Apostolic Preaching of the Cross.* Grand Rapids: Wm. B. Eerdmans Publishing Co., 1965.

Brilliant word studies on redemption, covenant, blood, propitiation, reconciliation, and justification. Deserves a place in every preacher's library. 225.823.M83A

Mounce, Robert H. *The Essential Nature of New Testament Preaching.* Grand Rapids: Wm. B. Eerdmans Publishing Co., 1960.

By tracing the kerygma through the NT and LXX, the author seeks to show the theological and ethical content that should characterize biblical preaching. The kerygma is defined as the proclamation of the death, resurrection, and exaltation of Jesus, His reception as both Lord and Christ, and the summons to repent and receive forgiveness of sins. 225.8.P91.M86

Richardson, Alan. *An Introduction to the Theology of the New Testament.* New York: Harper and Row, 1958.

†Follows the topical method of approach. Arbitrary in selection of material, but scholarly in content. Its limited scope and the writer's bias toward the theological left militate against its general acceptability as biblical theology. 225.823.R39

Riesenfeld, Harold. *The Gospel Tradition.* Translated by Margaret Rowley and Robert Kraft. Philadelphia: Fortress Press, 1970.

Articles previously published in British and European journals and *Festschriften.* Includes the author's famous essay "The Gospel Tradition and Its Beginnings." 225.8.R44

Robertson, Archibald Thomas. *The Pharisees and Jesus.* London: Gerald Duckworth, 1920.

Composed of the Stone Lectures at Princeton Theological Seminary for 1915-16. Surveys the Pharisaic outlook on doctrine and life and the resentment by the Pharisees of the words and works of Jesus. Provides a clear delineation of the events that led up to His condemnation by the Pharisees. 225.8.P49.R54

*****Ryrie, Charles Caldwell.** *Biblical Theology of the New Testament.* Chicago: Moody Press, 1959.

A valuable treatment of biblical theology based upon historical, exegetical, critical, and theological data. 225.823.R99B

*****Sherwin-White, Adrian Nicholas.** *Roman Society and Roman Law in the New Testament.* Oxford: At the Clarendon Press, 1963.

An exemplary treatment that confirms NT history and ably demonstrates from legal documents that the events of the canonical books could only have taken place under the judicial system of the first century of the Christian era. 225.8.L41.SH5

Soli Deo Gloria: New Testament Studies in Honor of William Charles Robinson. Edited by J. McDowell Richards. Richmond: John Knox Press, 1968.

A *Festschrift* containing essays running the gamut from NT theology to Calvin's polemic against idolatry. 225.8.R56S

Stevens, George Barker. *The Theology of the New Testament.* International Theological Library. 2d rev. ed. Edinburgh: T. and T. Clark, 1918.

An old but valuable contribution. 225.823.ST3 1918

Stonehouse, Ned Bernard. *Paul Before the Areopagus.* Grand Rapids: Wm. B. Eerdmans Publishing Co., 1957.

Essays dealing in a scholarly way with a wide variety of NT themes, including a refutation of the theories advanced by Bultmann and Dibelius. 225.839.ST7

Tasker, Randolph Vincent Greenwood. *The Old Testament in the New Testament.* 2d ed. Grand Rapids: Wm. B. Eerdmans Publishing Co., 1963.

†Provides an introductory study to the problems of OT quotations found in the NT. 225.84.T18 1963

Wenham, John William. *Our Lord's View of the Old Testament.* London: Tyndale Press, 1961.

An evaluation of the credibility of OT history, the authority of OT teaching, and the inspiration of the OT writing. 225.84.W48

BIBLE GEOGRAPHY ATLASES

*****Aharoni, Yohanan** and **Michael Avi-Yonah.** *Macmillan Bible Atlas.* New York: Macmillan Co., 1968.

†A Jewish work so arranged that each page has its own description of the maps and illustrations on it, and each map deals with specific biblical events. Has a map for most of the events in Scripture, with locations pinpointed with great accuracy. Considerable detail provided in each map and annotation. 220.9.AH1

Baly, Denis and **A. D. Tushingham.** *Atlas of the Biblical World.* Cleveland: World Publishers, 1970.

Contains fourteen good color relief maps, together with a series of less-helpful black-and-white ones. The photographs are particularly fine. Nearly 200 pages of text deal with the typography, climate, and archaeology of the biblical world. The bibliography is particularly good and contains a large number of post-1957 publications. 220.9.B21

Blaiklock, Edward Musgrave, ed. *Zondervan Pictorial Bible Atlas.* Grand Rapids: Zondervan Publishing House, 1969.

A well-illustrated atlas bearing adequte evidence to the editor's interest in the classics and knowledge of Near Eastern places and events. 220.9.B57

Grollenburg, Lucas Hendricus Antonius. *Atlas of the Bible.* Translated and edited by J. M. H. Reed and H. H. Rowley. New York: Thomas Nelson and Sons, 1956.

A Roman Catholic work with thirty-five beautiful color maps, two large maps on the end papers, and 408 illustrations, some of which are remarkable photographs of ancient art. Includes the ground plans of palaces, temples, cities, harbors, and so on. Factual and helpful in historical details, but deficient because of the low view of inspiration held by the writer. 220.9.G89

———. *Shorter Atlas of the Bible.* Translated by Mary F. Hedlund. London: Thomas Nelson and Sons, 1959.

A student's edition. 220.9.G89S

Kraeling, Emil Gottlieb Heinrich, ed. *Rand McNally Bible Atlas.* New York: Rand McNally and Co., 1956.

Contains 22 color maps and 136 numbered photographs, diagrams, and plans of buildings. Provides a valuable survey of the geography of Bible lands, but reflects little respect for the accuracy and authentiticity of biblical text. 220.9.K85

May, Herbert Gordon, ed. *Oxford Bible Atlas.* London: Oxford University Press, 1962.

†Lavishly illustrated, with 26 color maps and 77 illustrations, and relief maps showing vegetation and rainfall in biblical lands. Has much to commend it, but value of text limited by the liberal leanings of the contributors. 220.9.M45

——— and Chester C. McCown. *A Remapping of the Bible World: Nelson's Bible Maps.* New York: Thomas Nelson and Sons, 1949.

Contains 44 simple black-and-white maps similar to those found in Nelson Bibles. Handy. 220.9.M45R

Negenman, Jan H. *New Atlas of the Bible.* Garden City: Doubleday and Co., 1969.

†Noteworthy for the relief maps and exceptionally fine color photographs. 220.9.N31

*Pfeiffer, Charles Franklin, ed. *Baker's Bible Atlas.* Grand Rapids: Baker Book House, 1961.

An important work incorporating a geographical gazetteer to assist the reader in identifying biblical places with present-day names. 220.9.P48

Rowley, Harold Henry. *Student's Bible Atlas.* Cleveland: World Publications, 1965.

†A brief, helpful work. 220.9.R79

*Wright, George Ernest and **Floyd Vivian Filson.** *Westminster Historical Atlas to the Bible.* Rev. ed. Philadelphia: Westminster Press, 1956.

A large work containing 18 colorful maps and 77 illustrations, with a comprehensive index that will be of great value to the expositor. Helpful in geographical and historical information. 220.9.W93. 1956

GEOGRAPHY, SACRED SITES, MANNERS, AND CUSTOMS

Adams, James McKee. *Biblical Backgrounds.* Revised by Jos. A. Calaway. Nashville: Broadman Press, 1965.

A well-illustrated, up-to-date work on the geography of the ancient Near East. 220.91.AD1 1965

*Aharoni, Yohanan. *The Land of the Bible.* Translated by A. F. Rainey. Philadelphia: Westminster Press, 1967.

A brilliant work by a Jewish scholar. 220.91.AH1

Baly, Denis. *Geographical Companion to the Bible.* New York: McGraw Hill Book Co., 1963.

A series of lectures supplementing the author's masterly *Geography of the Bible.* 220.91.B21C

*_____. *The Geography of the Bible.* New York: Harper and Brothers, 1957.

"Combines the magical narrative style of George Adam Smith's classical volume with some of the technical information of the two great volumes by Father F. M. Abel." 220.91.B21

Budden, Charles William and E. Hastings. *The Local Color of the Bible.* Edinburgh: T. and T. Clark, 1923.

An old work now largely superseded. 220.91.B85

Croswant, W. *Dictionary of Life in Bible Times.* Translated by Arthur Heathecote. London: Hodder and Stoughton, 1960.

An exceptionally well-adjusted work that covers in detail the whole range of life in Bible times. 220.91.C88

Echholz, Georg. *Landscapes of the Bible.* New York: Harper and Row, n.d.

One hundred and three magnificent color plates in a work of 152 pages. 220.91.EC4

Glueck, Nelson. *River Jordan.* New York: McGraw-Hill Book Co., 1968.

A well-written book dealing with the civilizations that have flanked the Jordan River. Includes information on Bible places, events, and personalities. 220.91.G52

Hoade, Eugene. *Guide to the Holy Land.* 4th ed. Jerusalem: Franciscan Press, 1971.

An impressive and valuable travel guide. 913.3.H65 1971

Hopkins, W. J. *Jerusalem: A Study in Urban Geography.* Grand Rapids: Baker Book House, 1970.

A brief study guide on the city in ancient and modern times. 915.94.H77

*Kitchen, J. Howard. *Holy Fields: An Introduction to the Historical Geography of the Holy Land.* London: Paternoster Press, 1955.

A very helpful handbook to the typography of the Holy Land. 220.91.K64 (Alt. DDC 915.694)

Mackie, G. M. *Bible Manners and Customs.* Westwood, N.J.: Fleming H. Revell Co., n.d.

An old work by a man who spent many years living in Palestine and Syria. Originally printed in 1898. 220.913.M21 (Alt. DDC 913.33)

Mazar, Benjamin. *Views of the Biblical World.* 5 vols. Jerusalem: Intercultural Publishing Co., 1959-61.

A lavishly illustrated work republished under the title *World of the Bible* (New York: Educational Heritage, 1965). Thorough in coverage, beautiful in color. Provides ready access to archaeological, biological, and topographical material organized according to the sequence of the biblical books. 220.91.M45

*National Geographic Society. *Everyday Life in Bible Times.* Washington, D.C.: National Geographic Society, 1967.

†A brilliantly illustrated, fascinating portrayal of the Holy Land in its historic setting. With its 412 full-color photographs and drawings, it is the next best thing to a tour of the Holy Land. 220.91.N21

Pearlman, Moshe and Yaacov Yannai. *Historical Sites in Israel.* New York: Vangard Press, 1964.

Contains many color and black-and-white plates, but is of shorter compass than the National Geographic Society production. 220.91.P31

Peters, John Punnett. *Bible and Spade.* Edinburgh: T. and T. Clark, 1922.

Highlights the culture and customs, history and worship of people in Bible lands. 220.91.P44

*Pfeiffer, Charles Franklin and **Howard F. Vos.** *Wycliff Historical Geography of Bible Lands.* Chicago: Moody Press, 1967.

A modern, evangelical treatment of the ten areas of the Near Eastern and Mediterranean world. Blends the historical, geographical, biblical, and archaeological material to form a factual, informative reference tool. Enhanced with 459 excellent illustrations, 45 black-and-white maps, 16 pages of color maps, and helpful diagrams of local areas and many ancient cities. 220.91.P47

*Robinson, Edward. *Biblical Researches in Palestine and the Adjacent Regions.* 3 vols. 2d. ed. London: John Murray, 1856.

Contains a "journal of travels" in the Holy Land during which copious notes were kept, and these are now made available to those engaged in biblical research. The material covers topography as well as the customs observed. Many of these facts and features are correlated with the biblical record. The value of these volumes lies in their antiquity. They were written before modern civilization had impacted the major cities. 220.91.R56 1856

Robinson, Godfrey Clive and **Stephen Frederick Winward.** *In the Holy Land: A Journey Along the King's Highway.* London: Scripture Union, 1963.

A helpful work containing 16 color plates, maps, and diagrams. Ideal for visitors to the Holy Land who wish to take along a handy, light "travel guide." 220.91.R56

Rowley, Harold Henry. *Dictionary of Bible Place Names.* Old Tappan, N.J.: Fleming H. Revell Co., 1970.

A layman's guide. Too brief to be of lasting value to serious Bible students. 220.91'03.R79

Smith, George Adam. *Historical Geography of the Holy Land.* 16th ed. London: Hodder and Stoughton, 1910.

A classic study by a renowned scholar of the past century. 220.91.SM5 1910

Stanley, Arthur Penrhyn. *Sinai and Palestine.* London: John Murray, 1889.

A clear presentation of the typography and geography of the Sinai peninsula and other areas of interest to Bible students. 915.69.ST2

Terrien, Samuel. *Lands of the Bible.* New York: Simon and Schuster, 1957.

Not as brief as Rowley nor as extensive as Negenman. Has over 100 photographs and colored relief maps. 220.91.T27

*Thompson, William McClure. *The Land and the Book.* 3 vols. New York: Harper and Brothers, 1886.

An indispensable work based upon the author's thirty years of missionary work in the Near East. Adds color to the numerous social customs mentioned in Scripture. A one-volume abridgment is available. 220.81.T37

Trumbull, Henry Clay. *Kadesh-Barnea; Its Importance and Probable Site, Including Studies of the Route of the Exodus. . . .* London: Hodder and Stoughton, 1884.

An exceedingly rare work, but one regarded by many as supplying an accurate identification of the location of Kadesh-Barnea, together with informative details about the route of the Exodus to the southern border of the Holy Land. 220.91.K11.T77

*Turner, George Allen. *Historical Geography of the Holy Land.* Grand Rapids: Baker Book House, 1973.

A well-outlined, beautifully illustrated, and admirably executed volume. Deserves a place on every Bible student's book shelf. 220.91.T84

OLD TESTAMENT

Alt, Albrecht. *Essays on Old Testament History and Religion.* Translated by R. A. Wilson. Garden City: Doubleday and Co., 1968.

†First published in 1929. A landmark book. Significant for Alt's epic-making essay on "The God of the Father's," which contended that Abraham, Isaac, and Jacob worshiped separate ancestral deities—the theory that forms the basis of modern higher critical scholarship. 221.9'08.A17

Noth, Martin. *The Old Testament World.* Translated by Victor I. Gruhn. Philadelphia: Fortress Press, 1966.

†An exacting survey of the lands of the Bible, with considerable attention paid to the geography, identification of sites, and appreciation of the relationship between history and the setting in which the events took place. 221.91.N84

Simons, Jan Jozef. *The Geographical and Topographical Texts of the Old Testament.* Leiden: E. J. Brill, 1959.

Exhibits unusual breadth of scholarship. Covers over 1700 passages of Scripture in the Bible and the Apocrypha that contain data on geographical identifications. A work for the scholar. 221.91.S15G

*Vaux, Roland de. *Ancient Israel: Its Life and Institutions.* Translated by John McHugh. New York: McGraw-Hill Book Co., 1961.

†By a French Roman Catholic priest. Vast in scope and covers virtually every aspect of Israelite life and culture. 221.91.V46 (Alt. DDC 913.33)

―――. *The Bible and the Ancient Near East.* Translated by Damain McHugh. Garden City: Doubleday and Co., 1971.

A selection of fifteen articles translated from the author's *Bible et Orient.* 221.91.V46B

*Wright, George Ernest. *The Old Testa-ment Against Its Environment.* Naperville, Ill.: Alec R. Allenson, 1950.

†Devoted to a survey of the uniqueness of the world of the Bible. Helpful as an introduction to biblical theology. 221.91.W93

NEW TESTAMENT

Blaiklock, Edward Musgrave. *Cities of the New Testament.* London: Pickering and Inglis, 1965.

Relies heavily upon the writings of Sir William Ramsay, and is not abreast of the latest archaeological findings. 225.91.B57

Bouquet, Alan Coates. *Everyday Life in New Testament Times.* New York: Charles Scribner's Sons, 1953.

A full and fascinating account of the culture and customs of the people living during the first century of the Christian era. 225.91.B66

Bruin, Paul and **Phillipp Giegel.** *Jesus Lived Here.* New York: William Morrow and Co., 1958.

A pictorial study of the places referred to in the gospels. The illustrations have been chosen with taste and distinction and comprise color as well as black-and-white prints. 225.91.B83 (Alt. DDC 915.694)

*Dalman, Gustav Hermann. *Sacred Sites and Ways.* Translated by Paul P. Levertoff. New York: Macmillan and Co., 1935.

One of the best modern works on the geography of Palestine. 225.91.D16 (Alt. DDC 915.69)

Daniel-Rops, Henri (pseud.) *Daily Life in the Time of Jesus.* Translated by Patrick O'Brien. New York: Hawthorne Books, 1962.

A vivid re-creation of life in first-century Palestine by a Roman Catholic scholar whose real name is Jules Charles Henri Petiot. 225.91.D22

Downey, Glanville. *Ancient Antioch.* Princeton: Princeton University Press, 1963.

A scholarly study of the history of Antioch in Syria from the time of the Seleucids to the Arab conquest. 939.4.D75

Edersheim, Alfred. *Sketches of Jewish Social Life in the Days of Christ.* London: James Clark and Co., 1961.

First published in 1883, this work is still one of the most important treatments of daily life in Palestine in the first century A.D. 225.91.ED2 1961

Filson, Floyd Vivian. *The New Testament Against Its Environment.* London: SCM Press, 1950.

†A careful survey of the many facets making up the background of early Christianity. 225.91.F48

*Jeremias, Joachim. *Jerusalem in the Time of Jesus.* Translated by F. H. and C. H. Cave. Philadelphia: Fortress Press, 1967.

A valuable investigation into the economic and social conditions that prevailed during NT times. Fully abreast of the latest archaeological data. 225.91.J48J

Morton, Henry Canova Vollam. *In the Steps of St. Paul.* London: Methuen and Co., 1963.

A clear description of the writer's journey through Syria, Palestine, Cyprus, Turkey, Macedonia, Greece, Rhodes, Malta, and Italy as he followed the footsteps of the apostle Paul from his birthplace in Tarsus to the scene of his martyrdom in Rome. 225.91.M84 (Alt. DDC 915.6)

————. *In the Steps of the Master.* New York: Dodd, Mead and Co., 1966.

A vivid account of the writer's journey throughout Palestine, Trans-Jordan, and Syria, with an evaluation of the culture and the places associated with the life and ministry of Christ. 225.91.M84

*Ramsay, William Mitchell. *The Cities of St. Paul.* Grand Rapids: Baker Book House, 1960.

An indispensable work first published in 1907. Focuses attention upon the cities of eastern Asia Minor, draws heavily upon the historical background, and traces their influence upon Paul's life and thought. Dated. 225.91.R14 1960 (Alt. DDC 915.6)

*————. *The Historical Geography of Asia Minor.* London: John Murray, 1890.

An old, standard work. 225.91.R14

*————. *St. Paul the Traveller and Roman Citizen.* Grand Rapids: Baker Book House, 1960.

Reprinted from the 1897 edition. Deals with the cities made famous by Paul. Includes a chronology of early church history from A.D. 30-40 and a chapter on the composition of the book of Acts. 225.91.P28.R14 1960

Sanday, William. *Sacred Sites of the Gospels, with Illustrations, Maps and Plans.* Oxford: At the University Press, 1903.

An old, moderately helpful survey of sights made famous by Christ during His earthly life and ministry. 225.91.SA5

*Tenney, Merrill Chapin. *New Testament Times.* Grand Rapids: Wm. B. Eerdmans Publishing Co., 1965.

A valuable reconstruction of the cultural milieu into which Christ was born and in which the apostolic church developed. Includes an evaluation of three cultural tensions that existed simultaneously, namely, Judaism, Roman imperialism, and Hellenism. Well illustrated. 225.91.T25

Unnik, Willem Cornelis van. *Tarsus or Jerusalem: The City of Paul's Youth.* Translated by G. Ogg. London: Epworth Press, 1962.

A scholarly study of the place where Paul is supposed to have spent his youth. 225.91.T17.UN5

BIBLE CHARACTERS

Baxter, James Sidlow. *Mark These Men.* London: Marshall, Morgan and Scott, 1955.

Vivid portrayals of lesser-known Bible characters. A good illustration of this type of preaching. 220.92.B33

*Blaikie, William Garden. *Heroes of Israel.* London: Thomas Nelson and Son, 1894.

Limited to a discussion of Abraham, Isaac, Jacob, Joseph, and Moses. A helpful aid when preaching on Bible characters. 221.92.B57

Kunz, Marilyn. *Patterns for Living with God.* Downers Grove, Ill.: Inter-Varsity Press, 1961.

A study of the lives of selected Bible characters. 220.92.K96

*LaSor, William Sanford. *Great Personalities of the Bible.* Westwood, N.J.: Fleming H. Revell Co., 1965.

Formerly published in two volumes. Eighteen studies from each testament survey the background of the personalities, assess their strengths and weaknesses, and draw lessons for life today from their experiences. 220.92.L33

*Macartney, Clarence Edward Noble. *Trials of Great Men of the Bible.* New York: Abingdon Press, 1946.

Covers material from Job to Paul. Shows the place and purpose of trials in the development of Christian character. 220.92.M11 (Alt. DDC. 252.051)

Ockenga, Harold John. *Women Who Made Bible History.* Grand Rapids: Zondervan Publishing House, 1962.

A collection of sermons recording the saga of biblical events as seen through the eyes of saintly (and not-so-saintly) women of the Bible. 220.92.OC2

Redding, David A. *What Is Man?* Waco: Word Books, 1970.

A collection of studies about notable men of the Bible and outstanding leaders of church history. 220.92.R24

Sanders, John Oswald. *Robust in Faith.* Chicago: Moody Press, 1965.

Focuses on the methods God uses to prepare and train His instruments for the work to which He has appointed them. 220.92.SA5

Stevenson, Herbert F. *Galaxy of Saints.* London: Marshall, Morgan, and Scott, 1957.

Illuminating studies of some "lesser lights" of the OT and NT. 220.92.ST4

Vander Velde, Frances. *She Shall Be Called Woman.* Grand Rapids: Kregel Publications, 1968.

Thirty-one stimulating, imaginative, and devotional studies of women of the Old and New Testaments. Ideal material for discussion groups. 220.92.V28

Whyte, Alexander. *Bible Characters.* 2 vols. London: Oliphants Press, 1952.

An epochal work that increases in value the more it is used. 220.92.W62

OLD TESTAMENT

*Blaikie, William Garden. *David, King of Israel.* London: James Nisbet and Company, 1861.

Extremely rare, these brief chapters can be read with profit by laypeople. Recommended. 221.91.D28.B57

Bruce, John. *The Life of Gideon.* Edinburgh: Edmonston and Douglas, 1879.

A very full, devotional exposition. 221.92.G36B

Carlson, R. A. *David: The Chosen King: A Traditio-historical Approach to the Second Book of Samuel.* Stockholm: Almqvist and Wiksell, 1964.

†Form-critical. Nevertheless, one of the best treatments on II Samuel. 221.92.D28C

Corvin, R. O. *David and His Mighty*

Men. Freeport, N.Y.: Book for Libraries Press, 1970.

Clear, concise and suggestive. Reprinted from the 1950 edition. 221.92.C81 1970.

Cox, Samuel. *Balaam: An Exposition and a Study.* London: Kegan Paul, Trench and Co., 1884.

A careful exposition and study of the life and times of Balaam. Devotional. 221.92.B18C

Deane, Henry. *Daniel: His Life and Times.* London: James Nisbet and Co., 1888.

Valuable for its historic material. 221.92.D22D

Deane, William John. *David: His Life and Times.* London: James Nisbet and Co., n.d.

A rewarding devotional work. 221.92.D28D

_____. *Joshua: His Life and Times.* London: James Nisbet and Co., 1889.

A historic study of the book of Joshua. Dated, but still of value. 221.92.J78D

_____. *Samuel and Saul: Their Lives and Times.* London: James Nisbet and Co., n.d.

A pleasing exposition of the biblical text. Dated, but with numerous suggestions for the application of the truth of God's Word to life. 221.92.SA4D

Dykes, J. Oswald. *Abraham, the Friend of God.* London: James Nisbet, 1877.

Seventeen devotional messages based upon Genesis 12-25. Still valuable. 221.92.AB8D

Farrar, Frederic William. *Solomon: His Life and Times.* London: James Nisbet and Co., n.d.

Leans too heavily upon the LXX to be of outstanding worth, but presents some helpful historic observations. 221.92.SO4F

***Hamilton, James.** *Moses, the Man of God.* London: James Nisbet and Company, 1871.

Highly recommended by C. H. Spurgeon in *Commenting and Commentaries,* this work deserves a place on the bookshelf of every pastor. 221.92.M85.H18

***Kirk, Thomas.** *Samson: His Life and Work.* Edinburgh: Andrew Elliot, 1891.

Six moving messages based upon Judges 13-16. Well reasoned, deeply devotional, and true to the Scriptures. 221.92.SA4.K63

*_____. *Saul: The First King of Israel.* Edinburgh: Andrew Elliot, 1896.

Postmortem of a king. Devotional and perceptive. 221.92.SA9.K63

*_____. *Solomon: His Life and Works.* Edinburgh: Andrew Elliot, 1915.

Stimulating, as are all Kirk's writings. Exhibits an understanding of human nature and the needs of the spirit, as well as the provisions of God. Contains a happy combination of helpful historical material and edifying application. 221.92.SO4.K63

*_____. *The Life of Joseph.* Edinburgh: Andrew Elliot, 1900.

Of utmost value for the pastor who preaches on Bible characters. 221.92.J77.K63

Kittel, Rudolf. *Great Men and Movements in Israel.* New York: Ktav Publishing House, 1966.

†Studies of OT life and literature recounting the thoughts and deeds of leading Bible personalities. First published in 1928. 221.92.K65 1966

Kraeling, Emil Gottlieb Henrich. *The Prophets.* Chicago: Rand McNally and Co., 1969.

†Divided into three distinct historical eras in Jewish history. Stresses the fact that time and again the prophets emerged to rebuke the people of Israel for their sins and call them to repentance. Shows that the implication of these pronouncements has a wider sphere of application than to Judaism alone, and

that the prophets' message has stimulated men and movements throughout history. Impaired by adherence to the tenets of higher criticism. 221.92.K85

*Krummacher, Frederick William. *David: The King of Israel.* Translated by M. G. Easton. Edinburgh: T. and T. Clark, n.d.

Presents the life of David from his obscure roots in a village in Judah to his leadership as Israel's king. While the book makes no pretense at originality, preachers will find it permeated with rich homiletic ideas. 221.9.D28.K94

———. *Elijah the Tishbite.* Grand Rapids: Zondervan Publishing House, n.d.

A German evangelical theologian's meaty exposition. First published in German in 1826. 221.92.EL4K

———. *Elisha.* Translated by R. F. Walter. Grand Rapids: Zondervan Publishing House, n.d.

First published in 1837. A careful devotional exposition emphasizing the uniqueness of Elisha's ministry. 221.92.EL4K

*MacDuff, John Ross. *Elijah, the Prophet of Fire.* Grand Rapids; Baker Book House, 1956.

The reading of this book is a moving experience. The writer's power of description can hardly be equaled. Dramatic and dynamic. 221.92.EL4M

Meyer, Frederick Brotherton. *Abraham: The Obedience of Faith.* London: Marshall, Morgan and Scott, 1953.

Simple, perceptive devotional messages. Meyer is always good. 221.92.AB8.M57 1953.

———. *David: Shepherd, Psalmist, King.* London: Marshall, Morgan and Scott, 1953.

Stresses the way in which David's character was formed and his sweetest Psalms composed. First published in 1895. 221.92.D28.M57 1953

———. *Elijah: And the Secret of His Power.* London: Marshall, Morgan and Scott, 1954.

Describes Elijah as a "colossus among ordinary men," yet shows him to be a "man of like passions" as well as a man of God. An edifying work. First published in 1887. 221.92.EL4.M57 1954

———. *Israel: A Prince with God.* London: Morgan and Scott 1909.

Devotional thoughts on the life of Jacob. First published in 1887. 221.92.J15.M57 1909

———. *Jeremiah: Priest and Prophet.* London: Morgan and Scott, n.d.

A fascinating, topical study of the life and prophecies of Jeremiah. Originally published in 1894. 221.92.J47.M57

———. *Joseph: Beloved, Hated, Exalted.* London: Marshall, Morgan and Scott, 1955.

A careful unfolding of the fascinating story of Joseph and God's dealing with him. Devotional. Ideal for laymen. Originally published in 1890. 221.92.J77.M57 1955

———. *Moses, the Servant of God.* London: Marshall, Morgan and Scott, 1953.

A series of devotional studies by a leading British Baptist preacher of a generation or two ago. First published in 1892. 221.92.M85.M57 1953

———. *Samuel the Prophet.* London: Marshall, Morgan and Scott, 1902.

Similar to his other works on David, Elijah, Joseph, et al. Well worth reading. 221.92.SA4.M57

*Pink, Arthur Walkington. *The Life of David.* 2 vols. Grand Rapids: Zondervan Publishing House, 1958.

A masterful exposition that unfolds the lessons David learned as a result of God's dealings with him. 221.92.D28.P65

———. *The Life of Elijah.* Swengel, Penn.: Bible Truth Depot, 1956.

An in-depth study. Revealing and challenging. 221.92.EL4.P65

Rawlinson, George. *Ezra and Nehemiah: Their Lives and Times.* London: James Nisbet and Co., 1890.

A historically valuable work that students may consult with profit. 221.92.EZ7.R19

_____. *Isaac and Jacob: Their Lives and Times.* London: James Nisbet and Co., 1890.

Beautifully written, these studies still contain valuable insights for preachers today. 221.92.S1.R19

_____. *Moses: His Life and Times.* London: James Nisbet and Co., 1887.

Although dated historically and archaeologically, the abiding value of these studies lies in the writer's ability to combine Scripture with Scripture, and to draw upon his knowledge of history to illuminate the biblical text. 221.92.M85.R19

*Redpath, Alan. *The Making of a Man of God.* Westwood, N.J.: Fleming H. Revell Co., 1962.

Devotional studies in the life of David delivered from the pulpit of the Moody Memorial Church, Chicago. 221.92.D28.R24

Ridout, Samuel. *King Saul: The Man After the Flesh.* New York: Loizeaux Brothers, n.d.

An exacting study by a Plymouth Brethren writer. 221.92.SA8R

Taylor, William Mackergo. *Daniel the Beloved.* New York: Harper and Brothers, 1878.

A relevant, timely study that readily reveals this great preacher's knowledge of human nature and ability to apply the text to the needs of his congregation. 221.92.D22.T21

*_____. *David: King of Israel.* Grand Rapids: Baker Book House, 1961.

Devotional expositions manifesting a depth seldom attained by preachers today. First published in 1886. 221.92.D28.T28 1961.

*_____. *Joseph the Prime Minister.* Grand Rapids: Baker Book House, 1961.

Dynamic and inspiring messages by a former Lyman Beecher lecturer at Yale and L. P. Stone lecturer at Princeton. Originally published in 1886. 221.92.J77.T21 1961

*_____. *Moses: The Law Giver.* Grand Rapids: Baker Book House, 1961.

These rich and edifying expositions reflect the author's familiarity with the original text of Scripture, but they manifest a tendency to accept the LXX over the MT. Originally published in 1879. 221.92.M85.T21 1961

_____. *Ruth the Gleaner, and Esther the Queen.* Grand Rapids: Baker Book House, 1961.

Expository messages by the famous preacher of the Broadway Tabernacle, New York City. First published in 1891. 221.92.R93.T21 1961

NEW TESTAMENT

Babbage, Stuart Barton. *The Light Beneath the Cross.* Grand Rapids: Zondervan Publishing House, 1966.

A study of personalities connected with Christ's passion. Refreshing sketches probe deeply into the fabric of life and reveal the texture in which many unforgettable deeds—both good and evil—originated. 225.92.B11L

Barclay, William. *The Master's Men.* New York: Abingdon Press, 1959.

Discourses on each of the apostles. Frequently places greater stress upon tradition than upon what is revealed in the Scriptures. 225.922.B23.B23

_____. *The Mind of St. Paul.* New York: Harper and Brothers, 1959.

A critical study stressing the crucial role of the apostle as "a man of two worlds," bridging the Judaeo-Christian and Graeco-Roman cultures of his time. At times goes well beyond the evidence contained in the epistles. 225.92.P23

Birks, H. A. *Studies in the Life and Character of St. Peter.* London: Hodder and Stoughton, 1887.

This series of messages on selected incidents in the life of Peter contains an analysis of the relationship of Peter and Judas as contenders for the position of leader of the apostles. 225.92.P44.B53

Carpenter, William Boyd. *The Son of Man Among the Sons of Men.* New York: Thomas Whittaker, 1898.

Messages ranging from Herod to Pilate—including John the Baptist, some of the disciples, blind Bartimaeus, and the restored demoniac. Abounds in seed thoughts for sermons. 225.92.C22

*Coneybeare, William John and **John Saul Howson.** *The Life and Epistles of Paul.* Grand Rapids: Wm. B. Eerdmans Publishing Co., 1953.

Excellent background material on the life of the apostle Paul, coupled with a valiant attempt to fit the events of the book of Acts and the epistles into a chronological framework. First published more than a century ago (1852), but still worth consulting. 225.92.P28.C76 1953

Davidson, Donald. *God Chose Them.* Grand Rapids: Zondervan Publishing House, 1965.

Thirty informative character studies of NT personalities following the tradition of the late Alexander Whyte. 225.922.D28

Deane, Anthony. *New Testament Studies.* London: Skeffington and Son, 1909.

A series of biographical sketches on NT personalities. 225.92.D34

———. *St. Paul and His Letters.* London: Hodder and Stoughton, 1942.

An elementary survey designed to encourage readers to study the Pauline epistles for themselves. 225.92.P28.D34

*Deissman, Gustav Adolf. *Paul: A Study in Social and Religious History.* Trans-

lated by William E. Wilson. 2d ed. New York: Harper and Row, 1957.

A chatty, popular evaluation of Paul resulting from the writer's travels through ancient Turkey. Places Paul in the lower level of Jewish society. 225.92.P28.D36

Dibelius, Martin. *Paul.* Edited and completed by Warner Georg Kummel. Translated by Frank Clarke. London: Longmans, Green and Co., 1953.

†A form-critical study. Rarely consulted today. 225.92.P28.D54

Dodd, Charles Harold. *The Mind of Paul: Change and Development.* Manchester: John Rylands Library, 1934.

†This companion volume to *The Mind of Paul: A Psychological Approach* argues for a dichotomous eschatology. Dodd believes that Paul, in his early writings, stressed an embodiment at the time of the parousia, but that he later changed his views and, in his later epistles, departed from a resurrection doctrine. 225.92.P28.D66

Eadie, John. *Paul the Preacher.* London: Richard Griffin and Co., 1859.

A series of popular, practical expositions of Paul's discourses and speeches contained in the book of Acts. 225.92.P28.EA2

English, Eugene Schuyler. *The Life and Letters of St. Peter.* New York: "Our Hope," 1941.

Consists of a series of messages on the high points in the life of Peter, together with an exposition of his epistles. 225.92.P44.EN3

Farrar, Fredric William. *The Herods.* London: James Nisbet and Co., 1899.

Part of the Popular Biblical Library. Begins with the Jews after the Babylonian captivity, highlights their history under the Ptolemies and Seleucids, and traces in graphic style the rise of the Hasmonaean family. 225.92.H43.F24

Foakes-Jackson, Frederick John. *The*

Life of St. Paul. London: Jonathan Cape, 1927.

An important, popular treatment explicating the development of Paul's theology. 225.92.P28.F69

Gardner, Percy. *The Religious Experiences of St. Paul.* London: Williams and Norgate, 1913.

†A psychological analysis of Paul's conversion and spiritual experience. 225.92.P28.G17

Gloag, Paton J. *The Life of St. John.* Bible Class Primers. Edinburgh: T. and T. Clark, 1950.

A brief résumé of material enlarged upon in the writer's *Introduction to the Johannine Writings.* 225.92.J61G

Goodspeed, Edgar Johnson. *Paul.* Philadelphia: John C. Winston, Co., 1947.

Makes use of all the critical data current at the time, and provides an intensely interesting, highly readable, and captivating account of Paul's voyages and journeys, letters, and followers. 225.92.P28.G62

Grant, Michael. *Herod the Great.* New York: American Heritage Press, 1971.

A fascinating account of the crafty politician who ruled Judea at the time of Christ's birth. Disappointing in that the writer considers the biblical account of Herod's massacre of the children in Bethlehem a myth. Enhanced by beautiful photographs. 225.92.H43G

Harris, James Rendel. *The Twelve Apostles.* Cambridge: W. Heffer and Sons, 1927.

A scholarly study of the identity of the apostles of Christ. 225.922.H24

Hoehner, Harold Walter. *Herod Antipas.* Cambridge: University Press, 1972.

A brilliantly written, scholarly study of the life, political career, and historical background of this son of Herod the Great who was also tetrarch of Galilee. 225.92.H43H

Holden, John Stuart. *The Master and*

His Men. London: Marshall, Morgan and Scott, 1953.

Penetrating studies on the disciples of Christ by one of the memorable preachers of the early twentieth century. 225.922.H71

Howson, John Saul. *The Companions of St. Paul.* New York: American Tract Society, n.d.

Twelve messages on lesser known NT characters. Originally published in 1871. 225.922.H83

Iverach, James. *St. Paul: His Life and Times.* London: Wilkes and Co., 1890.

A brief historical treatment. 225.92.P28.IV3

Jones, John Daniel. *The Glorious Company of the Apostles: Being Studies in the Characters of the Twelve.* London: James Clarke and Company, 1904.

Combines a thorough knowledge of human nature with an understanding of the manner in which Christ developed the leadership abilities of His disciples. Helpful. 225.92.AP4.J71

Knox, John. *Chapters in the Life of Paul.* Nashville: Abingdon-Cokesbury Press, 1950.

The discussion of the chronology of Paul's life is helpful, but the treatment of his theology leaves much to be desired. 225.92.P28.K75

Kraeling, Emil Gottlieb Heinrich. *I Have Kept the Faith: The Life of the Apostle Paul.* New York: Rand McNally, 1965.

An imaginative popularization of the biblical evidence. 225.92.P28.K85

Lees, Harrington C. *St. Paul's Friends.* London: Religious Tract Society, 1917.

Twelve expositions explaining Paul's missionary methods and introducing readers to the leaders of the Christian church. Excellent. 225.922.L51

Loane, Marcus Lawrence. *John the Baptist: As Witness and Martyr.* Grand Rapids: Zondervan Publishing House, 1968.

A series of studies dealing in depth

with the life, labors, personality, and influence of the greatest of all prophets. A devotional gem. 225.92.J61L

_____. *Mary of Bethany.* London: Marshall, Morgan and Scott, 1949.

A valuable discussion of a woman who occupies a central place in the gospel records. 225.92.M36

*Longenecker, Richard Norman. *Ministry and Message of Paul.* Grand Rapids: Zondervan Publishing House, 1971.

A clear and concise introduction to the ministry and message of Paul. 225.92.P28.L85

*Macartney, Clarence Edward Noble. *"Of Them He Chose Twelve."* Philadelphia: Corrance and Co., 1927.

Indispensable studies of the apostles. 225.922.M11

_____. *Paul: The Man.* Westwood, N.J.: Fleming H. Revell Co., 1961.

An appraisal of Paul's life and ministry unobstructed by theological debate or erudite scholarship. 225.92.P28.M11

*MacDuff, John Ross. *The Footsteps of St. Paul.* London: James Nisbet and Co., 1856.

A verbose but very picturesque account of the life of the celebrated apostle to the Gentiles. Makes captivating reading. 225.92.P28.M14

Mackay, William Macintosh. *The Men Whom Jesus Made.* London: Hodder and Stoughton, 1924.

A series of character studies of the twelve apostles. 225.922.M19

McNeile, Alan Hugh. *St. Paul: His Life, Letters, and Christian Doctrine.* Cambridge: At the University Press, 1932.

†A work characterized by the writer's usual thorough scholarship. 225.92.P28.M23

*Maier, Paul L. *Pontius Pilate.* Garden City, N.Y.: Doubleday and Co., 1968.

A historical novel that deserves a place in every minister's library. Based upon a thorough acquaintance with the political pressures, economic trends, and cultural milieu of the first century of the Christian era. Excellent. 225.92.P64

Martin, Hugh. *Simon Peter.* London: Banner of Truth Trust, 1967.

This volume concentrates on the aspects of Peter's character that he shares with Christians in all walks of life. 225.92.P44.M36

Meyer, Frederick Brotherton. *John the Baptist.* London: Marshall, Morgan and Scott, 1954.

A valuable, informative, devotional study. 225.92.J61M 1954

_____. *Paul: A Servant of Jesus Christ.* London: Marshall, Morgan and Scott, 1953.

A brief devotional study of Paul's life and labors. First appeared in print in 1897. 225.92.P28.M57 1953

_____. *Peter: Fisherman, Disciple, Apostle.* London: Marshall, Morgan and Scott, 1953.

An exposition of the humanness of the fisherman who became a pillar in the church. First published in 1919. 225.92.P44.M57 1953

Miller, Donald G. *Conqueror in Chains: A Story of the Apostle Paul.* Philadelphia: Westminster Press, 1951.

A dramatic and deeply moving account of Paul's life. Surveys his journeys, discourses, trials, shipwreck, and imprisonments. 225.92.P28.M61

*Moe, Olaf Edvard. *The Apostle Paul: His Life and Word.* Translated by L. A. Vigness. Grand Rapids: Baker Book House, 1968.

First appeared in German in 1923; translated into English and published in the U.S. in 1950. Comprehensive in scope, and fully abreast of the major criticisms leveled against the apostle. 225.92.P28.M72 1968

*Perowne, Stewart. *The Life and Times of Herod the Great.* London: Hodder and Stoughton, 1958.

A remarkable work by a secular historian. Indispensable in studying the history leading up to the birth of Christ. 225.92.H43.P41

*_____. *The Later Herods.* London: Hodder and Stoughton, 1958.

A sequel to *The Life and Times of Herod the Great.* Surveys the political background of the NT, and reveals the shortcomings and follies, failures and compromises of those who were quick to "render unto Caesar the things that are Caesar's" but never learned to "render unto God the things that are God's." 225.92.H43L.P41

Pollock, John Charles. *The Apostle: A Life of Paul.* Garden City: Doubleday and Co., 1969.

A lucid biography of Paul as revealed in the NT and as seen by his contemporaries. 225.92.P28.P76

Redrich, E. Basil. *St. Paul and His Companions.* London: Macmillan Co., 1913.

A study of Paul and his friends and helpers in the light of the history of Acts and the epistles. Contains some good "seed thoughts" for sermons. 225.92.P28.R24

Robertson, Archibald Thomas. *Epochs in the Life of Paul.* New York: Charles Scribner's Sons, 1937.

A clear, well-outlined study of the development of Paul's thought and ministry. 225.92.P28.R54

_____. *Epochs in the Life of Simon Peter.* New York: Charles Scribner's Sons, 1933.

A clear, chronological presentation of the life, ministry, and writings of the apostle. 225.92.P44.R54

_____. *John the Loyal.* New York: Charles Scribner's Sons, 1923.

A series of studies in the life and ministry of John the Baptist. As with all of Robertson's character studies, this one gives evidence of having been written hastily. 225.92.J61R

Sandmel, Samuel. *Herod: Profile of a Tyrant.* Philadelphia: J. B. Lippincott Co., 1967.

A provocative study of a brilliant and ruthless politician who never rose above the position of a "client king" of Rome. 225.92.H43S (Alt. DDC 933).

Scott, Charles Archibald Anderson. *Saint Paul, the Man and the Teacher.* Cambridge: At the University Press, 1936.

A well-written, popular biographical interpretation of Pauline thought. Based upon a modified form-criticism. 225.92.P28.SC08

*Seekings, Herbert S.** *The Men of the Pauline Circle.* London: Charles H. Kelly, 1914.

Deals first with the distinguished members of Paul's company, then those who were obscure, thirdly with the officials whom he contacted during his ministry, and lastly with the unrecorded. A suggestive work. 225.922.SE3

*Shepard, John Watson.** *The Life and Letters of St. Paul.* Grand Rapids: Wm. B. Eerdmans Publishing Co., 1950.

An exegetical study that makes use of both grammatical and historical data and provides a lucid, adequate explanation of each of the Pauline epistles. 225.91.P28.SH4

*Smith, David.** *The Life and Letters of St. Paul.* New York: Harper and Brothers, n.d.

†A monumental work combining readability and scholarship with accuracy and a vivid portrayal of the historical events surrounding the ministry of the apostle. Thorough, and still of value today. First published in 1919. 225.92.P28.SM5

Stalker, James. *The Life of St. Paul.* Westwood, N.J.: Fleming H. Revell Co., 1950.

An ideal work for laymen. 225.92.P28.ST1

_____. *The Two St. Johns in the New*

Testament. London: Isbister and Co., 1895.

A historic study of John the apostle and John the elder. 225.92.J61S

*Taylor, William Mackergo. *Paul the Missionary.* Grand Rapids: Baker Book House, 1962.

Popular messages that deserve serious study. Reprinted from the 1909 edition. 225.92.P28.T21 1962

*_____. *Peter the Apostle.* New York: Harper and Brothers, 1876.

An excellent biographical study. 225.92.P44.T21

*Thomas, William Henry Griffith. *The Apostle Peter: Outline Studies in His Life, Character and Writings.* Grand Rapids: Wm. B. Eerdmans Publishing Co., 1950.

Drawing heavily upon Peter's natural characteristics, the writer shows how these were transformed by the Holy Spirit. A timely, devotional study. 225.92.P44.T36

White, Ernest. *St. Paul: The Man and His Mind.* Fort Washington, Penn.: Christian Literature Crusade, 1958.

A practicing psychologist grounds his theories about Paul's life and personality upon the scriptural narrative and ably defends Paul's conversion and calling as an apostle. 225.92.P28W.W58

*White, Reginald Ernest Oscar. *Apostle Extraordinary: A Modern Portrait of St. Paul.* Grand Rapids: Wm. B. Eerdmans Publishing Co., 1962.

A clear, concise interpretation of Paul's life and ministry. Ably combines historical and exegetical, theological and devotional emphases. 225.92.P28.W58

Whyte, Alexander. *Saul Called Paul.* London: Oliphants Ltd., 1955.

Eloquent, discerning studies by a great Scottish preacher of a generation past. First published in 1903. 225.92.P28.W62 1955

Wiles, Maurice F. *The Divine Apostle.* Cambridge: At the University Press, 1967.

†An able and persuasive defense of the value of the early patristic teaching on the life of Paul. 225.92.P28.W64

BIBLICAL ARCHAEOLOGY

Avi-Yonah, Michael. *Jerusalem.* New York: Orion Press, 1960.

A strongly Jewish account of the history of the city of Jerusalem. Profusely illustrated. 220.93.J47.AV5

*_____. and **Emil Kraeling.** *Our Living Bible.* New York: McGraw-Hill Book Co., 1962.

A condensed version of Benjamin Mazar's *Views of the Biblical World,* which provides readers with a lavishly illustrated guide to the history, geography, and antiquities of the ancient Near East. 220.93.AV5L

Bailey, Albert Edward. *Daily Life in Bible Times.* New York: Charles Scribner's Sons, 1943.

No longer abreast of the latest archae-

ological findings, but does provide a helpful study of daily life in Bible lands. 220.93.B15D

Barton, George Aaron. *Archaeology in the Bible.* Philadelphia: American Sunday School Union, 1916.

An old standby, but now very much out-of-date. 220.93.B28

Burroughs, Miller. *What Mean These Stones?* New Haven, Conn.: American Schools of Oriental Research, 1941.

A technical treatment of biblical archaeology, but one in need of revision. 220.93.B94

*Chiera, Edward. *They Wrote on Clay.* Chicago: University Press, 1938.

A richly illustrated account of the clay tablets from Babylon. 913.358.C43

*Finegan, Jack. *Light from the Ancient Past.* 2d ed. Princeton: Princeton University Press, 1959.

†Packed with interesting detail, but not as consistent or as reliable as Unger's *Archaeology of the Old Testament.* 220.93.F49 1950

*Free, Joseph P. *Archaeology and Bible History.* Wheaton: Scripture Press, 1964.

Shows how archaeology confirms Bible history, and illuminates the events of the OT and NT. An introductory work. 220.93.F87

Freedman, David Noel and **Jonas C. Greenfield, eds.** *New Directions in Biblical Archaeology.* Garden City: Doubleday and Co., 1969.

Ably bridges the gap between painstaking interpretation of archaeological data and theological truth. 220.93.F87

Gilbertson, Merle T. *Uncovering Bible Times.* Minneapolis: Augsburg Publishing House, 1968.

A brief account of biblical archaeology. Too limited to be of lasting value. 220.93.G37

Glueck, Nelson. *Rivers in the Desert.* New York: Grove Press, 1959.

†An archaeological survey of the Negev from the earliest times to the Nebataean era. Upon the basis of surface excavations and the examinations of pottery, the author concludes that these areas were not inhabited when the Bible says they were. 220.93.G52

Heaton, Eric William. *Everyday Life in Old Testament Times.* New York: Charles Scribner's Sons, 1956.

A widely read sourcebook that serves as an able supplement to de Vaux's *Ancient Israel.* 221.93.H35

Kenyon, Frederick George. *The Bible and Archaeology.* New York: Harper and Brothers, 1940.

An old, reliable work that retains its significance because of who the author was, but now is very much out-of-date. 220.93.K42B

Kenyon, Kathleen Mary. *Archaeology in the Holy Land.* New York: Frederick A. Praeger, 1960.

More than half of this volume is devoted to the pre-Israelite period. Based upon primary source material, which is skillfully blended into an easy-to-read narrative. Reliance upon carbon-14 dating makes the reconstruction of the chronology before 1400 B.C. liable to error. A scholarly work that ably supplements those archaeological studies concentrating solely on the biblical period. 220.93.D42A (Alt. DDC 913.3945)

————. *Digging Up Jericho.* London: Ernest Benn, 1957.

Attempts to place Garstang's work in limbo, but fails to include information from the nearby cemetery. 220.93.J47.K42

————. *Jerusalem: Excavating 3000 Years of History.* New York: McGraw-Hill Book Co., 1967.

Major emphasis falls upon Miss Kenyon's own archaeological "digs." Covers the history of the city from ancient times to the present. Of particular value and importance is the discussion of the walls of the Jebusite city. 220.93.J48.K42

Kyle, Melvin Grove. *The Deciding Voice of the Monuments in Biblical Criticism.* Oberlin, Ohio: Bibliotheca Sacra Co., 1924.

A perceptive account of the role archaeology is playing in biblical criticism. Dated. 220.93.K98

Lloyd, Seton. *Mounds of the Near East.* Edinburgh: Edinburgh University Press, 1963.

Provides a commendable discussion of ancient sites, with a reconstruction of technical evidence pertaining to the identification and excavation of each. Very little of the material deals with biblical sites. 913.39.L77

Owen, George Frederick. *Archaeology and the Bible.* Westwood, N.J.: Fleming H. Revell Co., 1961.

A good work for beginners. Focuses attention on the OT and, in a lucid, fascinating way, uses archaeological information to illumine the biblical narrative. Handles archaeological evidence with restraint, and avoids drawing conclusions from scanty evidence. 220.93.OW2

Parrot, André. *Discovering Buried Worlds.* Studies in Biblical Archaeology. Translated by Edwin Hudson. London: SCM Press, 1955.

An introductory monograph designed to acquaint the busy minister with some of the latest archaeological discoveries and the importance of these "finds" to biblical study. 220.93.P24D

————. *Samaria: The Capital of the Kingdom of Israel.* Translated by S. H. and B. E. Hooke. Studies in Biblical Archaeology. New York: Philosophical Library, 1958.

A historical survey dealing with the story of Samaria from the time of Omri to the Roman period. 220.93.P24S

***Pfeiffer, Charles Franklin.** *The Biblical World.* Grand Rapids: Baker Book House, 1966.

Arranged in dictionary format, this valuable reference work contains articles from "Abgar" to "Ziusudra" and provides adequate coverage of the relevance of archaeology and the way in which such knowledge illumines the biblical text. 220.93.P47

————. *Jerusalem Through the Ages.* Studies in Biblical Archaeology. Grand Rapids: Baker Book House, 1967.

A brief treatment of the history of Jerusalem through the centuries. Incorporates a survey of both sacred and secular history, and includes the significant archaeological findings and their bearing upon the text of Scripture. 913.3.J48.P47 (Alt. DDC 956.94)

Thompson, John Arthur. *Bible and Archaeology.* Grand Rapids: Wm. B. Eerdmans Publishing Co., 1962.

Chief value lies in the author's correlation of the history of the nations surrounding Palestine with the history of the Israelites. 220.93.T37

Vos, Howard Frederick. *Introduction to Bible Archaeology.* Chicago: Moody Press, 1956.

A book for the beginner. 220.93.V92

Williams, Walter George. *Archaeology in Biblical Research.* New York: Abingdon Press, 1965.

An introductory manual designed to acquaint readers with archaeological information that will enable them to read other works intelligently. 220.93.W67

Wiseman, Donald John. *Illustrations from Biblical Archaeology.* Grand Rapids: Wm. B. Eerdmans Publishing Co., 1959.

An informative pictorial survey of biblical archaeology by the professor of Assyriology, University of London, England. Contains over 100 photographs, charts, and drawings, with explanations alongside each plate. 220.93.W75

Wright, Fred H. *Highlights of Archaeology in Bible Lands.* Chicago: Moody Press, 1955.

A popular survey of important biblical sites. 220.93.W93

Wright, George Ernest. *Biblical Archaeology.* Rev. ed. Philadelphia: Westminster Press, 1962.

An excellent, lavishly illustrated volume. 220.93.W93 1962

OLD TESTAMENT

Albright, William Foxwell. *The Archaeology of Palestine.* London: Penguin Books, 1954.

A short, technical introduction. 221.93.AL1P

————. *Archaeology and the Religion of Israel.* 4th ed. Baltimore: Johns Hopkins

Press, 1956.

Lectures given at Colgate-Rochester Divinity School, 1941, dealing with the mental outlook of the peoples of the Near East, their religion and deities, and their influence upon Israel. Dated, but much of the material can still be read with profit. 221.93.AL1R 1956

*Bible and the Ancient Near East. Edited by George Ernest Wright. Garden City: Doubleday and Co., 1965.

Contains essays on important Near Eastern themes by leading OT scholars. An important reference book, and a useful guide to the study of present-day biblical archaeology. 221.93.W93

Garstang, John and J. B. E. Garstang. The Story of Jericho. New ed., rev. London: Marshall, Morgan and Scott, 1948.

An old work that supports the biblical evidence for an early destruction of the city. This revision answers Kenyon's criticisms. 221.93.J47.G17 1948

Gray, John. Archaeology and the Old Testament World. London: Thomas Nelson and Sons, 1962.

†Makes available the archaeological discoveries of the last forty years, and highlights the importance of the findings at Ras Shamra. 221.93.G79

———. The Legacy of Canaan: The Ras Shamra Texts and Their Relevance to the Old Testament. 2d rev. ed. Leiden: E. J. Brill, 1965.

Of value in spite of the negative aspects to which the writer's presuppositions lead him. 221.93.G79L 1965

Kapelrud, Arvid Schou. Ras Shamra Discoveries and the Old Testament. Translated by G. W. Anderson. Norman, Okla.: University of Oklahoma Press, 1963.

A well-written introduction to the findings of the Ugaritic texts and their influence upon biblical research. 221.93.UG1.K14

Kelso, James L. Archaeology and the Ancient Testament. Grand Rapids: Zondervan Publishing House, 1968.

Written for laymen. Adheres to a late date for the Exodus. The chief value of this book lies in the contrast drawn between the religion of the Canaanites and the beliefs of God's people. 221.93.K29

Kenyon, Kathleen Mary. Royal Cities of the Old Testament. London: Barrie and Jenkins, 1971.

This competent archaeological report is comprehensive, well illustrated, and surveys the ancient Jebusite city, as well as Jerusalem during the united and divided kingdom periods, Megiddo, Hazor, Gezer, and Samaria. Should be read with discrimination. 221.93.K42

Kyle, Melvin Grove. Moses and the Monuments: Light from Archaeology on Pentateuchal Times. Oberlin, Ohio: Bibliotheca Sacra Co., 1920.

Originally presented as the 1919 Stone Lectures at Princeton Theological Seminary. Covers a wide variety of philological, historical, cultural, and eschatological themes, all of which have been enriched by archaeological discoveries. Dated. 221.93.K98

Marston, Charles M. The Bible Comes Alive. 6th ed. Joplin, Mo.: College Press, 1969.

An old but interesting work on OT archaeology. First published in 1937. 221.93.M35 1969

Parrot, André. The Temple of Jerusalem. Translated by B. E. Hooke. Studies in Biblical Archaeology. London: SCM Press, 1957.

A handy, helpful archaeological treatment. Not up-to-date since it was printed before the results of Kathleen Kenyon's excavations were published. 221.93.P24T

*Pfeiffer, Charles Franklin. Ras Shamra and the Bible. Grand Rapids:

Baker Book House, 1962.

A concise presentation of the significance of these discoveries. 221.93.UG1.P47

*_____. *Tell El Amarna and the Bible*. Studies in Biblical Archaeology. Grand Rapids: Baker Book House, 1963.

A recounting of the story of the Tell El Amarna tablets and their bearing upon a knowledge of the Bible and Bible times. 913.32.P47T

Pritchard, James Bennett. *Archaeology and the Old Testament*. Princeton: Princeton University Press, 1958.

†A brief outline of the major archaeological finds and their influence upon biblical study. 221.93.P93

*_____, ed. *The Ancient Near East in Pictures Relating to the Old Testament*. Princeton: Princeton University Press, 1955.

A companion volume to *ANET*. Contains 769 illustrations classified according to the peoples and their dress, daily life, scenes from history, royalty and dignitaries, gods and their emblems, the practice of religion, and myths, legends, and rituals. A paperback edition entitled *The Ancient Near East* contains the most significant photographs from this volume and the most important texts from *ANET*. 221.93.P93P

*_____, ed. *Ancient Near Eastern Texts Relating to the Old Testament*. Princeton: Princeton University Press, 1955.

Popularly referred to as *ANET*, this is an indispensable aid in understanding the background and culture of the peoples in the ancient Near East. 221.93.P93T

*_____. *Ancient Near East: Supplementary Texts and Pictures Relating to the Old Testament*. Princeton: Princeton University Press, 1969.

This supplement to *ANET* contains an abundance of material from recent archaeological excavations. 221.93.P93S

_____. *Gibeon: Where the Sun Stood Still*. Princeton: Princeton University Press, 1962.

An enlightening account of four seasons of extensive excavation at the biblical city of Gibeon. 221.93.G35.P93

Rowley, Harold Henry. *From Joseph to Joshua: Biblical Traditions in the Light of Archaeology*. London: British Academy, 1950.

†An old work written from a mediating point of view. 221.93.R79

Simons, Jan Jozef. *Jerusalem in the Old Testament: Researchers and Theories*. Leiden: E. J. Brill, 1952.

Somewhat dated but, nevertheless, quite comprehensive. 221.93.S15J

Thomas, David Winton, ed. *Archaeology and Old Testament Studies*. Oxford: At the Clarendon Press, 1967.

A companion volume to *Documents from Old Testament Times*. Contains essays by leading OT scholars on Palestinian sites and geographical areas, plus selected sites in Egypt, Mesopotamia, Anatolia, and Syria. 221.93.T36

_____, **ed.** *Documents from Old Testament Times*. New York: Thomas Nelson and Sons, 1958.

Not as comprehensive as *ANET*, but adequate for most purposes and available in an inexpensive paper format. Helpful introductory comments concerning each of the documents. 221.93.T36D

***Unger, Merrill Frederick.** *Archaeology and the Old Testament*. Grand Rapids: Zondervan Publishing House, 1966.

Informative, fascinating, and perhaps the best book written on the subject. Enables the reader to obtain an overall picture of the world and peoples of the OT. 221.93.UN3

Wright, George Ernest. *Shechem: The Biography of a Biblical City*. New York:

McGraw-Hill Book Co., 1965.

Based upon the Norton Lectures delivered at Southern Baptist Seminary in 1963. Reconstructs the life and culture of this ancient city. 221.93.SCH2.W93

Yadin, Yigael. *Masada: Herod's Fortress and the Zealots' Last Stand.* New York: Random House, 1966.

An authoritative, well-illustrated, expensive monograph. 221.93.M37.Y1

NEW TESTAMENT

*Barrett, Charles Kingsley, ed. *The New Testament Background: Selected Documents.* New York: Harper and Brothers, 1956.

Of great value to those who do not possess or do not have access to large libraries. Includes and suitably introduces the reader to the Greek, Roman, and Jewish literature of the period. Provides a survey of the writings of the philosophers, together with valuable data on the mystery religions, rabbinic Judaism, the Septuagint, literary forms of apocalyptic literature, and the Jewish sectarian documents. 225.93.B27

Blaiklock, Edward Musgrave. *The Archaeology of the New Testament.* Grand Rapids: Zondervan Publishing House, 1970.

A helpful work. More recent than Unger's treatment, but less comprehensive. 225.93.B57

*Finegan, Jack. *Archaeology of the New Testament: The Life of Jesus and the Beginning of the Early Church.* Princeton: Princeton University Press, 1969.

A scholarly and intriguing volume. Fully abreast of the latest archaeological developments. Less complete than Unger's treatment, and manifests a tendency to accept secondary source material in place of biblical data. 225.93.F49

Gasque, Woodrow Ward. *Sir William*

M. Ramsay: Archaeologist, and New Testament Scholar. Grand Rapids: Baker Book House, 1966.

An evaluation of the unique contribution made by this renowned historian and archaeologist. 225.93'092.R14G

Harrison, Roland Kenneth. *Archaeology of the New Testament.* New York: Association Press, 1964.

A generally conservative introduction. 225.93.H24

Kelso, James Leon. *An Archaeologist Follows the Apostle Paul.* Waco: Word Books, 1970.

A picturesque account of Paul's life and ministry, ably supplemented by archaeological information. 227.093.K29

Parrot, André. *Golgotha and the Church of the Holy Sepulcher.* Translated by Edward Hudson. Studies in Biblical Archaeology. London: SCM Press, 1957.

Where was Christ crucified, and where was He buried? The writer presents his evidence for the traditional Roman Catholic view. 225.93.P24

*Ramsay, William Mitchell. *The Bearing of Recent Discovery on the Trustworthiness of the New Testament.* 2d ed. London: Hodder and Stoughton, 1915.

A book by a brilliant historian and archaeologist in which he time and again proves the reliability of the text of the NT and provides an abundance of helpful background material. 225.93.R14 1915

*Unger, Merrill Frederick. *Archaeology and the New Testament.* Grand Rapids: Zondervan Publishing House, 1962.

A lucid, fascinating work ably covering the whole range of NT archaeology. Profusely illustrated. Indispensable. 225.93.UN3

DEAD SEA SCROLLS

Black, Matthew. *The Scrolls and Chris-*

tian Origins. New York: Charles Scribner's Sons, 1969.

Examines the question of the origin and identity of the Qumran sect, and discusses the religious institutions and theological beliefs contained in the scrolls. 296.817.B56

Bruce, Frederick Fyvie. *Teacher of Righteousness in the Qumran Texts.* London: Tyndale Press, 1956.

An introductory study to the teaching of the Qumran community on the "Teacher of Righteousness" and the belief of Christianity in Jesus Christ. 296.817.B83

*Cross, Frank Moore, Jr. *Ancient Library of Qumran and Modern Biblical Studies.* London: Gerald Duckworth and Co., 1958.

Text of the Haskell Lectures for 1956-57. Has long been looked upon as a standard work in the field. 296.817.C88

Driver, Godfrey Rolles. *The Judaean Scrolls: The Problem and a Solution.* Oxford: Basil Blackwell, 1965.

A proposed solution to some of the enigmas surrounding the "Teacher of Righteousness," the War Scroll, "Thanksgiving Hymns," Zadokites, and so on, referred to in the scrolls or associated with the Qumran community. Dated. 296.817.D83

Dupont-Sommer, Andre. *The Dead Sea Scrolls.* Translated by E. M. Rowley. Oxford: Blackwell's, 1952.

A preliminary survey of the significance of the scrolls in OT study. 296.817.D92

———. *The Jewish Sect of Qumran and the Essenes.* Translated by R. D. Barnett. London: Vallentine, Mitchell and Co., 1954.

Provides a basic work on the identification of the community, their enemies, and the relationship of their literature to Christianity. 296.817.D92J

Harrison, Roland Kenneth. *The Dead Sea Scrolls: An Introduction.* New York: Harper and Brothers, 1961.

A brief, popular presentation of the finding and significance of the scrolls in biblical study. 296.827.H24

Leaney, Alfred Robert Clare. *The Rule of Qumran and Its Meaning.* Philadelphia: Westminster Press, 1966.

A comprehensive study of the "Manual of Discipline." 296.81.L47

Mansoor, Menahem. *Dead Sea Scrolls.* Grand Rapids: Wm. B. Eerdmans Publishing Co., 1964.

Provides interesting information on the Jewish sects, the Bar Kochba revolt, and Jewish eschatology during the Qumran period. 296.817.M31

*Milik, Jozef Takeusz. *Ten Years of Discovery in the Wilderness of Judaea.* Translated by J. Strugnell. London: SCM Press, 1959.

A scholarly discussion of the theological, historical, archaeological, textual, and paleographic issues involved in translating and interpreting the scrolls. 296.817.M59

*Pfeiffer, Charles Franklin. *The Dead Sea Scrolls and the Bible.* Rev. ed. Grand Rapids: Baker Book House, 1969.

A popular treatment of the story of the Dead Sea Scrolls and the origin and teachings of the Qumran community. 221.44.P47 1969

Ploeg, J. P. M. van der. *The Excavations at Qumran.* Translated by K. Smythe. London: Longmans, Green, and Co., 1958.

A scholarly survey of the discovery of the Dead Sea Scrolls and the significance of the ideals of the Essenes to biblical scholarship. 296.817.P729

Rowley, Harold Henry. *Dead Sea Scrolls and the New Testament.* London: SPCK, 1957.

A brief survey of the significance of the

scrolls in the study of the NT.
296.817.R79

Stendahl, Krister, ed. *The Scrolls and the New Testament.* New York: Harper and Brothers, 1957.

†A valuable, critical study summarizing the links between Qumran and Christianity. 296.817.ST4

Unger, Merrill Frederick. *Dead Sea Scrolls.* Grand Rapids: Zondervan Publishing House, 1957.

Part 1 deals with the Dead Sea Scrolls. Part 2 deals with other archaeological discoveries, including the Rosetta Stone, the Moabite Stone, Hezekiah's tunnel inscription, and so on. 221.93.UN3D

BIBLE HISTORY

Avi-Yonah, Michael. *Holy Land from the Persian to the Arab Conquest.* Grand Rapids: Baker Book House, 1966.

A historical geography by a leading Jewish archaeologist. An excellent introductory study. 933.AV5

Bright, John. *Early Israel in Recent History Writing: A Study in Method.* Studies in Biblical Theology. London: SCM Press, 1956.

An important study in methodology for students of the OT. 220.95.B76

Dentan, Robert Claude, ed. *The Idea of History in the Ancient Near East.* New Haven: Yale University Press, 1955.

Chapters by recognized authorities on each of the major countries in the ancient Near East. Provides a summary of the history of each area. 930.D43

*Finegan, Jack. *Handbook of Biblical Chronology.* Princeton: Princeton University Press, 1964.

†Does not attempt to deal with all the data or solve all the problems of biblical chronology, but contains principles for the reckoning of time in the ancient world. 220.94.F49

Grant, Michael. *The Ancient Historians.* New York: Charles Scribner's Sons, 1971.

Deals with the techniques, literary goals, and biases of the great classical historians. Important to Bible students since it deals with pagan historians who lived in Bible times. 907.2.G76

*Josephus, Flavius. *Complete Works of Josephus.* Translated by William Whiston.

Grand Rapids: Kregel Publications, 1963.

A classic! Valuable as a guide to the study of the OT, and helpful in understanding the history of the Jewish people. 933.J77 1963

*Kitto, John. *Kitto's Daily Bible Illustrations: Being Original Readings for a Year....* Edited and revised by J. L. Porter. 8 vols. Edinburgh: Oliphant and Company, 1901.

While not intended to be a commentary, the material in these volumes is excellent. The originality of Kitto's thought and his extensive research and commitment to the truth make these indispensible to the expository preacher. 220.95.K65

Prideaux, Humphrey. *The Old and New Testament Connected in the History of the Jews and Neighbouring Nations; From the Declension of the Kingdoms of Israel and Judah to the Time of Christ.* 2 vols. New York: Harper and Brothers, n.d.

A scholarly attempt to illumine the "400 silent years." Gives evidence of painstaking research. Now dated, but still of antiquarian interest. First published in 1715. 220.95.P93

Skrobucha, Heinz. *Sinai.* New York: Oxford University Press, 1967.

The emphasis is on the peninsula, and particularly the famous St. Catherine's monastery. Many of the illustrations are in full color. 915.3'1'03.SK6

Smith, George Adam. *Jerusalem.* 2 vols.

London: Hodder and Stoughton, 1907.

Provides considerable detail on the topography, economics, and history of Jerusalem from the earliest times to A.D. 70. 220.95.J47.SM5

Thackeray, Henry St. John. *Josephus, the Man and the Historian.* New York: Ktav Publishing House, 1967.

Based upon the writer's lectures delivered at the Jewish Institute of Religion, Hebrew Union College, in 1929. Provides present-day Bible students with an analysis of the character of Josephus and his reliability as a historian. 933.072.T363 1967

Vilnay, Zev. *The Guide to Israel.* Cleveland: World Publishing Co., 1970.

Similar in scope to Hoade. Contains modern maps and descriptions, is revised annually, has a strong archaeological emphasis, and is exceptionally helpful. 913.3.V71

OLD TESTAMENT

Ackroyd, Peter R. *Exile and Restoration.* Old Testament Library. Philadelphia: Westminster Press, 1969.

†An important work by a British OT scholar. 221.95.AC5

Albright, William Foxwell. *The Biblical Period from Abraham to Ezra.* New York: Harper and Row, 1963.

A well-known synopsis of the period. The footnotes are of particular value. 221.95.AL1B

Anati, Emmanuel. *Palestine Before the Hebrews: A History, from the Earliest Arrival of Man to the Conquest of Canaan.* London: Jonathan Cape, 1963.

†A full and richly rewarding study that draws information from the geography, geology, and paleography of the area and marshals the data so as to form a mosaic of ancient life and culture. 933.AN1

Anderson, Bernhard W. *Understand-ing the Old Testament.* Englewood Cliffs, N.J.: Prentice-Hall, 1957.

†After reconstructing the biblical text in accordance with the theories of modern scholarship, the writer traces the literary and theological development of Israel from the time of Abraham to the beginning of the Christian era. 221.95.AN3

*Bright, John. *A History of Israel.* Philadelphia: Westminster Press, 1960.

†Although Bright's views on critical questions relating to the date of Deuteronomy, the time of the Exodus, the unity of Isaiah, and the integrity of Daniel will not be acceptable to most evangelicals, his work is still the most eagerly sought-after OT history available today. 221.95.B76

Bruce, Frederick Fyvie. *Israel and the Nations.* Grand Rapids: Wm. B. Eerdmans Publishing Co., 1963.

†Presents, with apparent approval, support for the documentary hypothesis of the Pentateuch, a late date for the Exodus, a Persian date of composition of Isaiah 40-66, and a Maccabaean date for the prophecy of Daniel. 221.95.B83

Cooke, George Albert. *A Textbook of North Semitic Inscriptions.* Oxford: At the Clarendon Press, 1903.

Makes available to researchers translations of Moabite, Hebrew, Phoenician, Aramaic, Nabataen, and Palmyrene materials. 221.46.C77

Daniel-Rops, Henry (pseud.) *The Book of Books: The Story of the Old Testament.* Translated by Donald O'Kelly. London: Burns and Oates, 1958.

This work by Jules Charles Henri Petiot is characterized by the writer's usual scholarship. Clear and informative. Roman Catholic. 221.95.P44

Edersheim, Alfred. *Bible History.* 2 vols. Grand Rapids: Wm. B. Eerdmans Publishing Co., 1954.

A clear, simple review of the history of

Israel from before the Flood to the time of the Babylonian captivity. 221.95.ED2 1954

Ewald, Georg Heinrich August von. *The History of Israel.* Translated by J. Eslin Carpenter. 5 vols. London: Longmans, Green and Co., 1874.

†An extensive, scholarly, and critical study of Israel's history from its beginnings to the institution of the hagiocracy in Israel. Includes the events that immediately preceded the birth of Christ. 221.94.EW1

Gordon, Cyrus Herzl. *The Ancient Near East.* New York: W. W. Norton and Co., 1965.

Formerly published under the titles of *The World of the Old Testament* and *Introduction to Old Testament Times.* Focuses upon biblical history, includes important information from Canaanitish literature, and is based upon the latest archaeological data. 221.95.G65

Harrison, Roland Kenneth. *History of Old Testament Times.* Grand Rapids: Wm. B. Eerdmans Publishing Co., 1962.

A blending of the history and religion, languages and literature, economy and culture of the peoples of the Near East, with due emphasis upon and regard for the geographic and political interdependence of the different nations. 221.95.H24

Heaton, Eric William. *The Hebrew Kingdoms.* New Clarendon Bible. Oxford: At the Clarendon Press, 1968.

†A serious introduction to Israel's history during the period of the divided monarchy. 221.95.H35

Join-Lambert, Michael. *Jerusalem.* New York: G. P. Putnam's Sons, 1958.

A thorough history of the city of Jerusalem, generously illustrated with 135 photographs and maps. 220.95.J66 (Alt. DDC 913.33)

*Kitchen, Kenneth Anderson. *Ancient Orient and Old Testament.* London: InterVarsity Press, 1966.

Together with John Bright's *History of Israel,* this work is one of the best. Because Bright and Kitchen follow certain higher critical views, the pastor needs to keep Archer's *Introductory Survey to the Old Testament* close at hand. 221.95.K64

Kurtz, Johann Heinrich. *History of the Old Covenant.* 3 vols. Translated by A. Edersheim. Edinburgh: T. and T. Clark, 1859.

While failing to emphasize the place and importance of the theocracy in the OT, Kurtz nevertheless deals adequately with the historic developments and provides perceptive insights into the different events—insights preachers will find useful in fleshing out their messages. 221.95.K96

*Merrill, Eugene H. *Historical Survey of the Old Testament.* Nutley, N.J.: Craig Press, 1966.

A conservative presentation of Israel's history, with special concentration on the early chapters of Genesis. 221.95

Montet, Pierre. *Egypt and the Bible.* Translated by Leslie R. Keylock. Philadelphia: Fortress Press, 1968.

Discusses in chronological order those instances of contact between Israel and Egypt that are reported in the OT. Marred by Montet's naivete where Palestinian history and archaeology are concerned. 221.95.M84

Noth, Martin. *The History of Israel.* Translated by Stanley Godman. New York: Harper and Brothers, 1958.

†This brief introductory volume builds upon the evidence from Ras Shamra, Mari, and Tell el Amarna in describing the prevailing urban and rural culture of the biblical period. The writer's treatment of the patriarchal period, the conquest of Canaan, and the time of the judges is flimsy and structured around Noth's own theories regarding tribal constitution and rule. From the kingdom period onward, he is helpful. However, he is inferior to

Bright's *History of Israel* and most unreliable when dealing with the early chapters of Genesis. 933.N84

*Owen, George Frederick. *Abraham to the Middle East Crisis*. London: Pickering and Inglis, 1957.

A brilliant, captivating treatment of the history of Palestine from the time of Abraham to David Ben-Gurion. One of the few books of which it might be said, "It is hard to put down." 933.OW2

*Payne, John Barton. *An Outline of Hebrew History*. Grand Rapids: Baker Book House, 1954.

An excellent, well-documented text of particular value for its loyalty to the Scriptures and the way in which the writer synchronizes the history and chronology of Israel with the events of the surrounding nations. 221.95.P29

Pedersen, Johannes. *Israel: Its Life and Culture*. 4 vols. Oxford: At the University Press, 1959.

Without a peer as a sociological and psychological analysis of life and culture of the Israelites. Very expensive, and the philological data is unreliable. 221.95.P34 (Alt. DDC 933)

Rowley, Harold Henry. *From Moses to Qumran*. New York: Association Press, 1963.

†A series of studies concerned with such subjects as the teaching of the Pentateuch on monotheism, sacrifice in the OT, the meaning of the book of Job, proselyte baptism, and a study of the Qumran sect. 221.081.R79

Russell, David Syme. *The Jews from Alexander to Herod*. New York: Oxford University Press, 1967.

Provides a detailed historical sketch of Hellenism down to the death of Herod the Great. Contains an appraisal of significant religious institutions during the centuries since the Exile, and praises the different religious parties that have appeared within Judaism. 221.95.R91

Russell, Michael. *A Connection of Sacred and Profane History, From the Death of Joshua to the Decline of the Kingdoms of Israel and Judah*. 3 vols. London: C. and J. Rivington, 1827-37.

Continues the work of Shuckford and precedes the contribution of Prideaux on the intertestamental period. Well researched and painstakingly compiled; and while obviously dated, nevertheless provides a fitting introduction to the history and politics of the period. 221.95.R91

Shuckford, Samuel. *The Sacred and Profane History of the World Connected from the Creation of the World to the Dissolution of the Assyrian Empire . . . With a Treatise on the Creation and Fall of Man*. Oxford: At the University Press, 1847.

First published in 1727, this work was motivated by the appearance of Prideaux's "Historical Connection." Shuckford shows himself to be a man of unusual learning and masterfully blends biblical history with what was then known of the history of other nations. 221.95.SH9 1847

Smith, Henry Preserved. *Old Testament History*. International Theological Library. Edinburgh: T. and T. Clark, 1903.

†Many of the critical theories adopted by the writer have been drastically modified, and his work is obviously devoid of the archaeological material that began to come to light in the 1930's. 221.95.SM5

*Wood, Leon James. *A Survey of Israel's History*. Grand Rapids: Zondervan Publishing House, 1970.

A strongly conservative book written with the undergraduate student in mind. Meets a definite need in that it is a selective rather than exhaustive treatment of Israel's history. 221.95.W85

NEW TESTAMENT

Blaiklock, Edward Musgrave. *The Century of the New Testament*. Chicago:

Inter-Varsity Press, 1962.

A well-balanced study of the history of the first century A.D. Very readable. 225.95.B57

Filson, Floyd Vivian. *A New Testament History: The Story of the Emerging Church.* London: SCM Press, 1964.

†Helpful for its chronological data. 225.95.F48

Pfeiffer, Robert Henry. *History of New Testament Times with an Introduction to the Apocrypha.* New York: Harper and Row, 1949.

†A comprehensive, radical treatment. The intervening two decades have witnessed the setting aside of many of the theories proposed in this volume. 225.95.P48

Reicke, Bo Ivar. *New Testament Era: The World of the Bible from 500 BC to AD 100.* Philadelphia: Fortress Press, 1968.

†Includes a treatment of the cultural, social, and economic conditions of the Hellenistic and Roman eras, as well as a well-balanced account of the persecution of Christians during the reigns of Nero and Domitian. 225.95.R27

Smallwood, E. M. *Documents Illustrating the Principles of Nerva, Trajan, and Hadrian.* Cambridge: At the University Press, 1966.

A collection of documents that parallel apostolic church history in the crucial years between A.D. 96 and 138. Contains inscriptions, coins, and a few papyri, together with a list of the consuls who served in various areas. Well indexed. 937.07.SM1

Toynbee, Arnold, ed. *The Crucible of Christianity.* London: Thames and Hudson, 1969.

A magnificent, beautifully illustrated portrayal of Judaism, Hellenism, and the historical background to the Christian faith. 225.95.T66

Turner, Henry Ernest William. *Historicity and the Gospels.* London: A. R. Mowbray and Co., 1963.

†A critical work in which a distinguished British scholar evaluates the gospels to determine what is historically true as opposed to a mere expression of faith in Christ. Relying upon his own integrity as a historian, he subjectively proposes to exclude from the NT the very element that, he claims, underlies all historical writing. 225.95.T85

―――. *Jesus, Master and Lord.* London: A. R. Mowbray, 1953.

A study in the historical truth of the gospels. 225.95.T85J

GENERAL HISTORY OF BIBLE TIMES

Caldwell, Wallace Everett and **Mary Francis Gyles.** *The Ancient World.* New York: Holt, Rinehart and Winston, 1966.

A textbook on the early history of the Mediterranean and Near Eastern world. 913.03.C13

The Cambridge Ancient History. Edited by J. B. Bury, S. A. Cook, and F. E. Adcock. 12 vols. 2d ed. Cambridge: At the University Press, 1929-39.

Has long been regarded as a standard history of the ancient world. The treatment of ancient Egypt and Babylon, the Hittite Empire, Assyria, Persia, Greece, and Rome (including the Roman Republic, the imperial peace, etc.), makes this set a valuable reference tool. The text is augmented by five volumes of plates. A new edition is in process, and this set, when completed, will update the earlier work and bring it abreast of the latest archaeological material and historical data. 930.C14

Frankfort, Henri. *The Birth of Civilization in the Near East.* Garden City: Doubleday and Co., 1956.

After scoring Spengler and Toynbee for failing to view ancient civilizations within the context of their times, the writer explores the "form" and inner "dynamics" of Mesopotamia and Egypt respectively from earliest paleolithic times to the end of the third millennium B.C. 930.F85

Grant, Michael. *The Ancient Mediterranean.* New York: Charles Scribner's Sons, 1969.

This treatment of the history of lands surrounding the Mediterranean parallels the events from Abraham to the end of the first century of the Christian era and provides an important backdrop to the emergence of the different cultures, the spread of commerce and industry, and the influence of the different religions upon neighboring countries. 913.3'098.G76

McNeill, William H. *A World History.* New York: Oxford University Press, 1967.

A brief, secular approach to world history by the chairman of the department of history, University of Chicago. 909.M23

Moscati, Sabatino. *Ancient Semitic Civilizations.* New York: G. P. Putnam's Sons, 1957.

A sketch of the interplay between the ancient Babylonians, Assyrians, Canaanites, Hebrews, Aramaeans, Arabs, and Ethiopians. 572.892.M85

———. *The Face of the Ancient Orient.* Garden City: Doubleday and Co., 1962.

Contrasts the dominant cultures of the Fertile Crescent from 3000 to 300 B.C., and shows how these led ultimately to the flowering of the Persian Empire. Well-chosen excerpts from ancient texts

enliven the presentation. 901.M85

Rawlinson, George. *The Five Great Monarchies of the Ancient World.* 3 vols., 3d ed. London: John Murray, 1871.

A well-written and very thorough study of the history, geography, and antiquities of Chaldea, Assyria, Babylon, Media, and Persia. Remains an important sourcebook for ministers today. 935.R19

Schwantes, Siegfried J. *A Short History of the Ancient Near East.* Grand Rapids: Baker Book House, 1965.

Illumines the background of the OT, and gives perspective to the student of the Scriptures. 935.SCH9

Starr, Chester G. A. *History of the Ancient World.* New York: Oxford University Press, 1965.

A comprehensive and readable survey beginning with the earliest civilizations of man and continuing through to the fifth century A.D. Recommended for those who require a reliable guide to add perspective to their study of the Scriptures. 930.ST2

ANCIENT EGYPT

Breasted, James Henry. *Ancient Records of Egypt.* 5 vols. New York: Russell and Russell, 1962.

A collection of ancient historical documents first published in 1906. Traces the history of Egypt from the earliest times to the Persian conquest, and sheds light on biblical events from the time of Abraham to Alexander the Great. 932.01.B74

———. *A History of Egypt.* New York: Charles Scribner's Sons, 1969.

A classic treatment by a leading Egyptologist, but one that is now out of date. 932.01.B74H

Cottrell, Leonard. *The Lost Pharaohs: The Romance of Egyptian Archaeology.* New York: Greenwood Press, 1969.

An account of the amazing archaeological discoveries that have taken place
in the land of Egypt from the time of
Napoleon Bonaparte to the present.
932.01.C82

*Gardiner, Alan Henderson. *Egypt of
the Pharaohs.* New York: Oxford University Press, 1961.

More up-to-date than Breasted. Makes
a valuable contribution to the study of
Egyptian history. 932.01.G16

Petrie, William Matthew Flinders.
Egypt and Israel. London: SPCK, 1911.

An old study tracing the contacts between Abraham and his descendants in
Egypt. While Petrie's chronological reconstruction is helpful, his interpretation of biblical data shows a marked
tendency toward the acceptance of his
own findings over the biblical record
until the period of the United Kingdom.
932.01.P44

―――. *Social Life in Ancient Egypt.*
London: Constable and Co., 1932.

Provides readers with the "cream" of
Petrie's extensive exposure to ancient
Egyptian culture. 932.01.P44S

Rawlinson, George. *History of Ancient
Egypt.* 2 vols. London: Longmans, Green
and Company, 1881.

Composed of the author's extensive,
personal research (with many of his own
drawings), this work, though now dated,
bears mute testimony to the prodigious
labors of those whose investigation and
research now find their way into more
popular, less comprehensive treatises.
932.R19

Seters, John van. *The Hyksos: A New
Investigation.* New Haven: Yale University
Press, 1966.

Fully abreast of the latest archaeological information, and possibly the
best statement of current scholarship on
the Hyksos. 932.01.SE7

*Steindorff, George and **Keith C.
Steele.** *When Egypt Ruled the East.* 2d ed.
Revised by Keith C. Steele. Chicago:

University of Chicago Press, 1957.

An excellent treatment that includes
the more recent archaeological discoveries, together with a description of
the latest trends in Egyptology. Particularly helpful for its reconstruction of
the chronology of the Old and New
Kingdoms, treatment of prehistory, and
the Hyksos occupation. 932.01.ST3
1957.

*Wilson, John Albert. *Burden of Egypt.*
Chicago: University Press, 1965.

An interpretation of ancient Egyptian
culture. Published in paperback under
the title of *The Culture of Ancient Egypt.* A
significant contribution to Egyptology.
932.01.W69

ANCIENT MESOPOTAMIA

Bibby, Geoffrey. *Looking for Dilmun.*
New York: Alfred A. Knopf, 1969.

A popular account of the work of the
Danish archaeological expedition in the
area along the Persian Gulf and the
maritime highway between Mesopotamia and India, including the discovery of a civilization that antedates
Sumer. One of the most important discoveries of the expedition indicates that
South Arabia was once a very verdent
area, and this has given support to the
speculation about its being the first true
home of human civilization.
910.01'1'1824.B47

Cottrell, Leonard. *The Land of Shinar.*
London: Souvenir Press, 1965.

Fully in accord with all that we have
come to expect of this author. Ably recreates the culture of the ancient Sumerians, and provides a concise background for our understanding of the
early chapters of Genesis. 913.5.C82

―――. *The Quest for Sumer.* New York:
G. P. Putnam's Sons, 1965.

By studying the archaeological remains, Cottrell has been able to reconstruct the history of Sumerian culture

and resurrect from the ashes of the past the prebiblical versions of the stories of the fiery furnace, the massacre of the innocents, the Tower of Babel, and the Flood. 913.35031.C82

Gordon, Cyrus Herzl. *Hammurabi's Code: Quaint or Forward-Looking?* New York: Holt, Rinehart and Winston, 1965.

A brief booklet answering many questions about the relationships between Moses and the renowned Babylonian lawgiver. 221.8.G65

Heidel, Alexander. *Gilgamesh Epic and Old Testament Parallels.* 2d ed. Chicago: University of Chicago Press, 1949.

A translation and interpretation of the Gilgamesh Epic and related Babylonian and Assyrian documents. 221.93.H36 1949

Jacobsen, Thorkild. *Toward the Image of Tammuz and Other Essays on Mesopotamian History and Culture.* Edited by W. L. Moran. Cambridge, Mass.: Harvard University Press, 1970.

These studies, by a distinguished authority, treat specific areas of the life and culture of those who lived in the "Land between the Rivers" including their religious beliefs, social mores, legal and political institutions. 913.35.T15.J15

Kramer, Samuel Noah. *History Begins at Sumer.* Garden City: Doubleday and Co., 1959.

Includes a treatment of the first flood narrative, the first law code, and highlights twenty-five other "firsts" among the Sumerian people. 935.4.K86

_____. The Sumerians: Their History, Culture and Character. Chicago: University of Chicago Press, 1963.

Provides one of the best general treatments of Sumerian history and culture. 913.35.K86

Larue, Gerald A. *Babylon and the Bible.* Grand Rapids: Baker Book House, 1969.

A brief, informative introduction to the history of Babylon from its beginnings to the reign of Nebuchadnezzar.

913.5.L32

*Olmstead, Albert Ten Eyck. *History of Assyria.* Chicago: University of Chicago Press, 1951.

Traces the rise of the Assyrian Empire, deals with the most important kings of the period, correlates the history of Assyria with the fortunes of Israel, and records the eventual overthrow and replacement of Assyria by the Neo-Babylonian Empire. Reprinted from the 1923 edition. 935.2.OL5 1951

_____. History of the Persian Empire. Chicago: University of Chicago Press, 1948.

A valuable reconstruction of the Persian rise to supremacy in the Near East. The historical pageant portrayed by the writer adds color and meaning to the OT narrative. 935.05.OL5

Oppenheim, A. Leo. *Ancient Mesopotamia: Portrait of a Dead Civilization.* Chicago: University of Chicago Press, 1964.

Numerous clay tablets were discovered in the area now called Iraq. The study of these findings led the writer to describe the long-dead culture of the Babylonian and Assyrian races. Bible students have much to learn from this work, and from the writer's *Letters from Mesopotamia.* (1967). 913.35.OP5

Pallis, Svend Aage. *The Antiquity of Iraq: A Handbook on Assyriology.* Copenhagen: Ejnas Munksgaard, 1956.

An indispensable study of the culture and writing, history and religion of the ancient Assyrians and Babylonians. Contains a complete listing of the sites that have been excavated, together with extensive material on the language and grammar of these ancient peoples. 935.03.P17

Parrot, André. *Babylon and the Old Testament.* Studies in Biblical Archaeology. Translated by B. E. Hooke. London: SCM Press, 1958.

A careful review of the history of

Babylon, with an account of the exploration of the ruins of the city and the relationship between Babylon and the OT. 221.93.P24

———. *Nineveh and the Old Testament.* Translated by B. E. Hooke. Studies in Biblical Archaeology. London: SCM Press, 1955.

A slender volume into which the writer has managed to compress all the archaeological material pertaining to the biblical narrative and the relationships that existed between Assyria and the countries to the western end of the Fertile Crescent. 935.2.P24

Saggs, H. W. F. The Greatness That Was Babylon. New York: Hawthorn Books, 1962.

Depicts the splendor and degradation, religion and economy, politics and art, literature and social mores that characterized the culture of Mesopotamia from before 2000 B.C. to the Persian conquest. 935.02.SA1

Sayce, Archibald Henry. *Assyria: Its Princes, Priests, and People.* London: Religious Tract Society, 1926.

Though now seriously dated, this work succeeded in popularizing the study of the Bible by using archaeology to illumine the life and culture of those whose expansion and conquests intersected with God's ancient people, Israel. 935.SA9

Wiseman, Donald John. *Chronicles of the Chaldean Kings (626-556 B.C.)* London: British Museum, 1956.

While not specifically concerned with the history of Palestine, this work nevertheless provides basic additional information on the capture of Jerusalem. 492.19.W75

———. *The Vassal Treaties of Esarhaddon.* London: British School of Archaeology in Iraq, 1958.

Of basic importance in understanding the nature and scope of vassal treaties.

Presents the original texts, with a translation and commentary on each. 935.03.W75

Woolley, C. Leonard. *Ur of the Chaldees.* London: Ernest Benn, 1935.

A well-written, captivating record of seven years of excavation in ancient Mesopotamia. 935.02.W88

Yamauchi, Edwin M. *Greece and Babylon.* Grand Rapids: Baker Book House, 1966.

A brief and informative treatment dealing with the early contacts between the Aegean and the Near East. 913.3'03.Y1

ANCIENT HITTITES

Ceram, C. W. (pseud.). *The Secret of the Hittites.* Translated by Richard and Clara Winston. New York: Alfred A. Knopf, 1967.

Writing under a pseudonym, Kurt W. Marek unfolds the drama surrounding the discovery of this ancient empire in a popular way. 939.M33

Garstang, John. *The Land of the Hittites.* London: Constable and Co., 1910.

Deals with the then-recent explorations and discoveries in Asia Minor, and the descriptions of Hittite history and culture contained in their monuments. Dated. 956.101.G19

Gurney, Oliver Robert. The Hittites. Rev. ed. Baltimore: Penguin Books, 1964.

Makes available to laymen information about the history and religion, life and customs, law and institutions, methods of warfare, literature, and art of this race referred to in the Bible. 939.G96 1964

ANCIENT SEMITIC RACES

Alexander, Paul Julius. *The Oracle of Baalbek.* Washington: Dunbarton Oaks Center for Byzantine Studies, 1957. Distributed by J. J. Augustine, Locust Valley, N.Y.

A scholarly study that includes the Greek text of the oracular utterances with an English translation. Furnishes a graphic picture of the religious beliefs of Israel's northern neighbors.
133.3'248.AL2

Glueck, Nelson. *Deities and Dolphins.* New York: Farrar, Straus and Giroux, 1965.

An important study of the Nabataeans. 913.39403.G52

*Hindson, Edward E. *The Philistines and the Old Testament.* Grand Rapids: Baker Book House, 1971.

By reconstructing the history and drawing heavily upon recent archaeological excavations, the writer provides an informative study highlighting the significance of the Philistines in the early history of Israel. 933.H58

Kenyon, Kathleen Mary. *Amorites and Canaanites.* London: Oxford University Press, 1966.

Records the life and culture of the inhabitants of Palestine in the time of Abraham, and during the Intermediate, Early, and Middle Bronze periods. 913.33.K42

Macalister, Robert Alexander Stewart. *The Philistines: Their History and Civilization.* London: The British Academy, 1914. Reprinted by Argonaut Publishers, Chicago.

An exacting study of the "sea people" who ruled the Palestinian coastline long before the Exodus and remained there after the fall of Judah. Written by a pioneer archaeologist who personally excavated sites in the Near East before coming to some surprising conclusions about this ancient people. 913.3.M11

Olmstead, Albert Ten Eyck. *History of Palestine and Syria to the Macedonian Conquest.* Grand Rapids: Baker Book House, 1965.

A classical treatment that should be read by students of biblical history despite its occasional inaccuracies. 933.OL5

Rawlinson, George. *History of Phoenicia.* London: Longmans, Green and Co., 1889.

An old but very thorough study. 933.R19

Unger, Merrill Frederick. *Israel and the Aramaeans of Damascus.* London: James Clarke and Co., 1957.

An authoritative work. 913.3.UN3

GREECE

Burn, Andrew Robert. *A Traveller's History of Greece.* London: Hodder and Stoughton, 1965.

The author, an authority in the history of ancient Greece, furnishes his readers with a nontechnical résumé of Greek life and culture from the first neolithic settlements to the close of the philosophical schools of Athens. His work is beautifully illustrated with black-and-white photographs. 938.B93

Bury, John Bagnell. *A History of Greece to the Death of Alexander the Great.* London: Macmillan and Company, 1913.

Recounts the history of ancient Hellas with the verve and skill of a novelist, so that the battles fought, the gods worshiped, and the empire established live in the mind of the reader as if he were seeing the recreation of the events on the television screen. 938.B95

Dickinson, Goldsworthy Lowes. *The Greek View of Life.* Ann Arbor: University of Michigan Press, 1966.

Provides a fascinating view of Greek religion, their concept of the state, view of the individual, and appreciation for art. Contains informative background material for students of the NT. 938.6.D56

Glover, Terrot Reaveley. *Democracy in*

the Ancient World. New York: Cooper Square Publishers, 1966.

First published in 1927, these studies were based in part on lectures delivered at Rice Institute (later University), Houston. Provides a fine discussion of the rise of democracy from the time of Homer to Pericles, and afterward in the Roman state. Shows at the same time the decline of these same principles of government under the Greeks and Romans. 321.4'09.G51 1966.

*Greece and Rome, Builders of Our World. Washington: National Geographic Society, 1968.

A brilliantly written, fascinating volume dealing with everything from the Graecian games to Alexander's conquests. Provides an abundance of material that parallels the biblical era. 913.38.N21

Hamilton, Edith. *The Greek Way.* New York: W. W. Norton and Co., 1930.

Traces the significance of Greek life and culture, literature and philosophy, art and sculpture, and the impact of these upon the nations surrounding the Mediterranean Sea. 880.1.H18

Hooper, Finley Allison. *Greek Realities.* New York: Charles Scribner's Sons, 1956.

A full and up-to-date account of the life and thought of the ancient Greeks. Includes a discussion of the economic and social forces that molded the Greek city-states and their colonies. 913.38'03.H76

Kitto, Humphrey Davy Findley. *The Greeks.* Chicago: Aldine Publishing Co., 1964.

A scholarly study of Greek life and thought and the influence of Greek culture upon the biblical world. 913.38.K65

Melas, Evi, ed. *Temples and Sanctuaries of Ancient Greece.* London: Thames and Hudson, 1970.

This is the kind of book people who may never have the opportunity to visit Greece should acquire. It provides colorful descriptions of the Acropolis, the sanctuary of Artemis, the temple of Apollo, and so on. 913.38.M48

Murray, Gilbert. *Five Stages of Greek Religion.* Garden City: Doubleday and Co., 1955.

An authoritative monograph containing lectures delivered at Columbia University. 292.M96

Smith, William, ed. *Dictionary of Greek and Roman Biography and Mythology.* 3 vols. London: Walton and Maberly, 1864.

Possibly the best work of its kind—the product of painstaking scholarship. 913.38.SM6

ROME

Arnold, Thomas. *History of Rome.* 3 vols. London: F. and J. Rivington, 1848.

One of the most detailed works of its kind. Describes with exacting care the history of the Romans from the early legends to the end of the second Punic War. Apart from the interest that attaches to this period of history, the reader is able to assess the trends that took place during this era. Sociologically, politically, religiously, and from the point of view of Daniel's visions, readers will learn much from this excellent work. 937.AR6

————. *History of the Later Roman Commonwealth, From the End of the Punic War to the . . . Reign of Augustus: With a Life of Trajan.* 2 vols. London: F. and J. Rivington, 1849.

Contains material previously published in the *Encyclopedia Metropolitana.* Provides an indispensable backdrop to the time of Christ and the NT era. 937.AR6L

Balsdon, John Percy Vyvian Dacre. *The Emperor Gauis.* Oxford: At the Clarendon Press, 1934.

An important contribution to the history of the early empire. Provides a helpful backdrop to the study of the early history of the Christian church. 937.07.B21

Barrow, Reginald Haynes. *The Romans.* Chicago: Aldine Publishing Co., 1964.

A superb treatment of Roman history and its influence upon Christianity. 913.37.B27

Bishop, John. *Nero: The Man and the Legend.* London: Robert Hale, 1964.

A scholarly study based upon original sources and ably illustrating conditions in Rome and the empire during Nero's reign. Helps Bible students understand the political setting in which Paul lived and ministered, and the background for his Roman letter. 923.137.B54

Benko, Steven and **John J. O'Rourke.** *The Catacombs and the Colosseum.* Valley Forge: Judson Press, 1971.

Papers setting forth the primitive origin of Christianity. 913.703.B43

Carcopino, Jerome. *Daily Life in Ancient Rome: The People and the City at the Height of the Empire.* Translated by E. O. Lorimer. Edited by Henry T. Tolell. New Haven: Yale University Press, 1966.

Provides a fascinating reconstruction of daily life in the imperial city during the second century A.D., including the population and residences, society and social classes, family life and status of women, education and religion, social customs and the culture of the first century. 937.6.C17

Charlesworth, Martin Percival. *Documents Illustrating the Reigns of Claudius and Nero.* Cambridge: The University Press, 1939.

A scholarly work providing an abundance of primary source material pertaining to the first century of the Christian era. 937.07.C38

Hamilton, Edith. *The Roman Way.* New York: W. and W. Norton and Co., 1932.

While focusing specifically upon the literature of the period, this book furnishes the reader with a brilliant introduction to the life and literature of the Romans from Cicero to Juvenal. 870.1.H18

MacMullen, Ramsey. *Enemies of the Roman Order: Treason, Unrest and Alienation in the Empire.* Cambridge: Harvard University Press, 1967.

An excellent account of the intellectual unrest and disorder within the framework of the Roman imperial system. 937.06.M22

McCrum, Michael and **A. G. Weekhead.** *Select Documents of the Principates of the Flavian Emperors, A.D. 68-96.* Cambridge: At the University Press, 1961.

Valuable because these documents parallel the apostolic church and provide primary source material for the study of this period. 937.07.M13

Sherwin-White, Adrian Nicholas. *The Roman Citizenship.* 2d ed. Oxford: At the Clarendon Press, 1973.

Widely used as a textbook, this study of Roman citizenship has been greatly enlarged with the addition of several new chapters. Makes available background information for an understanding of the privileges enjoyed by the apostle Paul, as well as the freedoms enjoyed by certain cities throughout the empire. 323.6.R66 SH5

Starr, Chester G. *The Ancient Romans.* New York: Oxford University Press, 1970.

Includes an analysis of Roman laws and government, human values, and the *Pax Romana.* Enhanced by full color and halftone plates, together with eight maps and six color charts. 937.03.ST2

5

Old Testament

Few of us can begin to calculate the value of good books. They can help shape our ministry, strengthen our faith, and enrich our lives. A speaker at a businessmen's luncheon said: *"The kind of person you are in five years will be determined by two things—the company you keep, and the books you read."*

In few areas, however, have there been written so many books reflecting pragmatic bias or a lack of skill as in the area of Old Testament studies. Some of these aim at being devotional but are based upon an allegorical interpretation of Scripture. Their value is seriously impaired. Others undermine the authority of the Word and erode one's faith. The last two centuries have witnessed a brand of modern scholarship that seeks to reconstruct the Old Testament in the light of prevailing views of authorship. This critical approach has denied the veracity of the inspired record and has emphasized the negative results of higher criticism. As a result, many pastors have found that it has robbed the Old Testament of its meaning and value, and they rarely preach on Old Testament themes and passages.

These destructive critics have brought down upon their own heads the opprobrious censure of a historian such as Sir Winston Churchill who, while not an Old Testament scholar, could nevertheless recognize the absurdity of their approach. He wrote: "We reject with scorn all these learned and labored myths. . . . We believe that the most scientific view, the most up-to-date and rationalistic conception, will find its fullest satisfaction in taking the Bible literally. . . . We may be sure that all these things happened just as they are set out according to Holy Writ. The impressions these people received were faithfully recorded and have been transmitted across the centuries with far more accuracy than many of the telegraphed accounts of goings-on today. In the words of a forgotten work of Mr. Gladstone, we rest with assurance upon 'The impregnable rock of Holy Scripture.' Let the men of science and learning expand their knowledge . . . and prove with their research every detail of the records which have been preserved to us from those dim ages. All they will do is to fortify the grand simplicity and essential accuracy of the recorded truths which have lighted so far the pilgrimage of man."[1]

On the other hand, there have been those who have recognized in the Old Testament God's progressive revelation to man and have regarded historic, poetic, and prophetic literature as reliable and trustworthy. They have also come to appreciate the value of a thorough knowledge of the Old Testament in the study of the New. As with Augustine of Hippo, they have realized that "the New is in the Old concealed; the Old is in the New revealed." A thorough awareness of all that the Old Testament teaches is, therefore, essential if we are to come to a proper understanding of the New Testament.

Our knowledge of Old Testament times has been greatly enriched as a result of archaeological investigation over the last forty years. The following list of books attempts to survey some of the most significant works—both liberal and conservative—in the areas of philology, geography, history, manners and customs, archaeology, exposition, and exegesis. The annotations have been geared to the needs of preachers, and it is hoped that these will assist them to achieve a greater appreciation and awareness of the Old Testament and its message.

HEBREW LEXICONS AND GRAMMARS

Davidson, Andrew Bruce. *An Introductory Hebrew Grammar.* 26th ed. Edinburgh: T. and T. Clark, 1962.

Frequently used as an intermediate Hebrew grammar. Valuable in spite of its age, but inferior to Weingreen's *Practical Grammar of Classical Hebrew.* Tapes available from the publishers may be used in conjunction with these studies. 492.45.D28 1962

Gesenius, Friedrich Heinrich Wilhelm. *Hebrew and Chaldee Lexicon to the Old Testament Scriptures.* Translated by Samuel Prideaux Tregelles. Grand Rapids: Wm. B. Eerdmans Publishing Co., n.d.

A well-abridged lexicon long regarded as a standard work for students. Well indexed and containing more than twelve thousand entries. Less comprehensive than *BDB* or Köehler-Baumgartner, but ideal to keep on one's desk. First English translation published in 1846. 492.43.G33

————. *A Hebrew and English Lexicon of the Old Testament.* Translated by Edward Robinson. Edited by Francis Brown, S. R. Driver, and Charles A. Briggs. Oxford: At the Clarendon Press, 1952.

BDB exhibits greater understanding of the nuances of Hebrew than does Köehler-Baumgartner, and provides an indispensable tool in the biblical preachers workshop. First published in 1891-1906. 492.43.G33B 1952

*————. *Hebrew Grammar.* Edited by E. Kautsch. Revised by A. E. Cowley. 2d ed. London: Oxford University Press, 1910.

---

1. Winston S. Churchill, "Moses: The Leader of a People," *Sunday Chronicle,* 8 November 1931, p. 7. Subsequently reprinted in *Thoughts and Adventure.*

A brilliant, comprehensive classical and technical grammar. Indispensable for serious study. 492.45.G33 1910

*Girdlestone, Robert Baker. *Synonyms of the Old Testament.* 2d ed. Grand Rapids: Wm. B. Eerdmans Publishing Co., n.d.

A standard work on the synonyms of the OT and their bearing on Christian doctrine. Reprinted from the 1897 edition. 221.4.G44

*Holladay, William L. *A Concise Hebrew and Aramaic Lexicon of the Old Testament.* Grand Rapids: Wm. B. Eerdmans Publishing Co., 1970.

A recent, up-to-date work. Not as extensive as *BDB*, but easy to use and will greatly facilitate the rapid reading of Hebrew. 492.43.H71

Köehler, Ludwig Hugo and **W. Baumgartner.** *Lexicon in Veteris Testimenti Libros.* Leiden: E. J. Brill, 1953.

More recent than *BDB*, and updated with a supplement. Arranges words by alphabetic letter rather than by root (a factor that may be of help to a student who has forgotten how weak verbs really work), but does not exhibit the same "feeling" for the Hebrew idiom found in *BDB*. 492.43.K81

Lisowsky, Gerhard. *Konkordanz zum Hebräischen Alten Testament.* Graz, Austria: Wurttenbergische Bibelanstalt, 1958.

The best concordance for Hebrew word studies. Photographically reproduced from Lisowsky's handwritten MS. Indispensable to the serious Bible student. 492.43.L69

*Mandelkern, Solomon. *Veteris Testamenti Concordantiae: Hebräicae Atque Chaldaicae.* Tel Aviv: Schocken, 1969.

The best concordance for a grammatical analysis of the forms. 492.45.M31

Watts, John D. W. *Lists of Words Occurring Frequently in the Hebrew Bible.* 2d ed. Grand Rapids: Wm. B. Eerdmans Publishing Co., 1968.

A list of over 800 words that facilitates the learning of Hebrew vocabulary. 492.42.W34 1968

Weingreen, Jacob. *A Practical Grammar for Classical Hebrew.* 2d ed. Oxford: At the Clarendon Press, 1959.

A widely used grammar that, for comprehensive coverage and close attention to detail, has replaced Davidson's *Introductory Hebrew Grammar.* 492.45.W43 1959

Williams, Ronald J. *Hebrew Syntax: An Outline.* Toronto: University of Toronto Press, 1967.

An outline of the syntactical options that exist when a student is confronted with a given particle or preposition. The index is of great importance. 492.45.W67

THE HISTORICAL BOOKS

*Allis, Oswald T. *The Five Books of Moses.* 2d ed. Philadelphia: Presbyterian and Reformed Publishing Co., 1949.

A re-examination of the documentary hypothesis combined with a careful weighing of the evidence and a testing of the conclusions reached by higher critics. An indispensable work for the serious Bible student. 222.1'061.AL5 1949

Cassuto, Umberto. *The Documentary Hypothesis and the Composition of the Pentateuch.* Jerusalem: Magnus Press, 1961.

An excellent critical appraisal by a leading, though now deceased, Jewish scholar. Refutes those theories long held by adherents to negative Bible criticism. 222.1'06.C27

Criswell, Wallie Amos. *The Gospel According to Moses.* Nashville: Broadman Press, 1950.

A series of challenging, evangelical messages. 222.1'08.C86

Erdman, Charles Rosenbury. *The Pentateuch.* Old Tappan, N.J.: Fleming H. Revell Co., n.d.

A concise commentary incorporating the writer's previous works on the Pentateuch published between 1949 and 1953. Contains good preaching values. 222.1'07.ER2

Gettys, Joseph Miller. *Teaching the Historical Books.* Richmond: John Knox Press, 1963.

A careful introduction to the books of Joshua through II Kings. 222'.07.G33T

―――. *Surveying the Historical Books.* Richmond: John Knox Press, 1963.

Very helpful for personal study. Follows the chronology proposed by the *Westminster Historical Atlas.* 222'.07.G33S

*Green, William Henry. *The Higher Criticism of the Pentateuch.* New York: Charles Scribner's Sons, 1906.

A clear, concise refutation of the Graf-Wellhausen hypothesis. 222.1'06. G82

Lockyer, Herbert. *The Gospel in the Pentateuch.* Chicago: Bible Institute Colportage Association, 1939.

Contains an abundance of practical material, and aims at expounding Luke 24:27 and its relationship to the Pentateuch. Complete with numerous helpful charts. 222.1'06.L81

Martin, William James. *Stylistic Criteria and the Analysis of the Pentateuch.* London: Tyndale Press, 1955.

A brief, discerning analysis. 222.1'06.M36

Meyer, Frederick Brotherton. *The Five Books of Moses.* London: Marshall, Morgan and Scott, 1955.

A devotional commentary on each chapter, with a homiletic outline and notes on the text. Too brief to be of lasting value. 222.1'07.M57

Moorehead, William Gallogly. *Studies in the Mosaic Institutions.* New York: Fleming H. Revell Co., 1895.

An edifying study by one of the great evangelical scholars of the past century. 222.1'08.M78

*Thomas, William Henry Griffith. *Through the Pentateuch Chapter by Chapter.* Grand Rapids: Wm. B. Eerdmans Publishing Co., 1957.

Well outlined and contains helpful thoughts on the text. 222.1'07.T36

GENESIS

Barnhouse, Donald Grey. *Genesis: A Devotional Commentary.* Grand Rapids: Zondervan Publishing House, 1970.

A verse-by-verse treatment containing pithy gems of devotional thought, but covering only chapters 1-22. 222.11'07.1—22.B26G

Bonhoeffer, Dietrich. *Creation and Fall: A Theological Interpretation of Genesis 1-3.* New York: Macmillan Co., 1959.

†A philosophical interpretation of Genesis 1-3 that manifests some unusual views. 222.11'07.1—3.B64

*Candlish, Robert S. *Commentary on Genesis.* 2 vols. Grand Rapids: Zondervan Publishing House, n.d.

Originally published in 1863. Expository messages rich in their devotional emphasis, containing helpful theological discussions. Thoroughly conservative and of special value to the pastor. 222.11'07.C16

Cassuto, Umberto. *A Commentary on the Book of Genesis.* Jerusalem: Magnus Press, 1961.

Inferior to the author's work on Exodus. Covers only the first thirteen chapters. 222.11'07.—13.C27

Davis, John D. *Genesis and Semitic Traditions.* New York: Charles Scribner's Sons, 1894.

A comparison of the Genesis account

of creation and the deluge with Babylonian, Assyrian, and Egyptian traditions. 222.11'06.D29

De Haan, Martin Ralph. *Portraits of Christ in Genesis.* Grand Rapids: Zondervan Publishing House, 1966.

A series of devotional radio messages stressing the typology and prophecies of Genesis. 222.11'064.D36

*Delitzsch, Franz Julius. *A New Commentary on Genesis.* 2 vols. Edinburgh: T. and T. Clark, 1888.

†Originally published in 1852. A critical commentary on the Hebrew text that holds to the Mosaic authorship of Genesis but leaves room for final redaction in the post-exilic period. Advocates an early form of the documentary hypothesis, and holds to the "long day" theory of creation. The treatment of chapters 12-50 is greatly superior to the material in volume one and is essential whenever anyone preaches on the lives of Abraham, Isaac, Jacob, and Joseph. 222.11'07.D37 1888

Dillmann, August. *Genesis: Critically and Exegetically Expounded.* 2 vols. Edinburgh: T. and T. Clark, 1897.

†A thoroughly critical commentary on the Hebrew text. Advocates the documentary hypothesis, holds that the creation account is contradicted by science, that the Flood was local, and that the patriarchal narratives are legends. 222.11'07.D58

Driver, Samuel Rolles. *The Book of Genesis.* Westminster Commentary. London: Methuen and Co., 1943.

†First published in 1904. Follows the critical theories of the Wellhausen-Graf school of thought. Still worth consulting, for Driver was a capable, cautious scholar. 222.11'07.D83 1943

Elliott, Ralph H. *The Message of Genesis.* Nashville: Broadman Press, 1961.

†Denies the Mosaic authorship of Gen-

esis, advocates the documentary hypothesis, holds that materials in the early chapters were borrowed from Babylonian legends, makes adequate provision for evolution by adherence to the long days of creation, and so on. 222.11'06.EL5

Erdman, Charles Rosenbury. *The Book of Genesis: An Exposition.* New York: Fleming H. Revell Co., 1950.

Brief, practical, devotional expositions centered on seven main characters: Adam, Enoch, Noah, Abraham, Isaac, Jacob, and Joseph. 222.11'092.ER2

Filby, Frederick A. *The Flood Reconsidered.* London: Pickering and Inglis, 1970.

Reviews the evidences of geology, archaeology, ancient literature, and the Bible in an endeavor to give an enlightened exposition of this biblical event. Draws lessons and applications from the Scripture to the lives of people today. Holds to a limited flood. 222.11'06.6—9.F47

Finegan, Jack. *In the Beginning: A Journey Through Genesis.* New York: Harper and Brothers, 1962.

†A brief survey that claims the account of creation is a poem and not to be taken literally; that the Fall is something that happened, but not according to the Genesis account; and that the Flood is a legend. 222.11'06.1—11.F49

Gaebelein, Arno Clemens. *The Book of Genesis.* New York: Our Hope, 1912.

Brief, biblical studies. Attacks the documentary hypothesis, holds to a "gap theory" between Genesis 1:1 and 2, and looks upon the "sons of God" in chapter 6 as angelic beings. Generally helpful. 222.11'07.G11

*Green, William Henry. *The Unity of the Book of Genesis.* New York: Charles Scribner's Sons, 1895.

A thorough, scholarly refutation of

the documentary hypothesis.
222.11'06.G82

Gunkel, Hermann. *The Legends of Genesis: The Biblical Saga and History.* New York: Schocken Books, 1964.

†While the writer's scholarship and learning are unquestioned, his categorical denial of the historicity of Genesis would remove it from the canon and leave unanswered questions pertaining to the origin of man, sin, and so on. 222.11'06.G95

Heidel, Alexander. *The Babylonian Genesis.* 2d ed. Chicago: University of Chicago Press, 1951.

A study of the Babylonian creation stories and the OT parallels. 299.219.H36 1951

Law, Henry. *Christ Is All: The Gospel in Genesis.* London: Banner of Truth Trust, 1961.

One of a series of books by the author in which the subject matter of Genesis is treated from the viewpoint of typology. Contains some useful ideas for preachers, but needs to be used cautiously. 222.11'064.L41 1961

*Leupold, Herbert Carl. *Exposition of Genesis.* 2 vols. Grand Rapids: Baker Book House, 1942.

A most thorough, helpful exposition from the conservative standpoint. Defends the Mosaic authorship, refutes the documentary hypothesis, holds to six literal days for creation, believes that the "sons of God" were Sethites, and argues for universal flood. Lutheran. Amillennial. 222.11'07.L57

Lewis, Jack Pearl. *A Study of the Interpretation of Noah and the Flood in Jewish and Christian Literature.* Leiden: E. J. Brill, 1968.

An important, scholarly study that treats the issues pertaining to, and evidence for, the Deluge as found in the Bible, the Apocrypha and Pseudepigrapha, Philo of Alexandria, Josephus, the LXX, the Targums, rabbinic writings, and early Christian literature. 222.11'06.5—10.L58

Mackintosh, Charles H. *Notes on the Book of Genesis.* Neptune, N.J.: Loizeaux Brothers, 1965.

First published in the United States in 1880. Devotional, premillennial, and heavily typological. Plymouth Brethren. 222.11'07.M21 1965

Murphy, James Gracey. *A Critical and Exegetical Commentary on the Book of Genesis.* Andover: W. R. Draper, 1868.

Contains reverent scholarship based upon sound exegesis, but has now been superseded by more recent treatments. 222.11'07.M95

Nelson, Byron Christopher. *The Deluge Story in Stone.* Minneapolis: Bethany Fellowship, 1968.

A geologically based defense for the universal flood. 222.11'06.6—9.N33

Parker, Joseph. *Genesis.* Preaching Through the Bible. Grand Rapids: Baker Book House, reprint.

Eloquent expositions of major passages of the book of Genesis by a famous nineteenth-century British Congregationalist. At times builds his exposition upon faulty hermeneutics. 222.11'07.P22

Parrot, André. *The Flood and Noah's Ark.* Studies in Biblical Archaeology. London: SCM Press, 1955.

Summarizes the literary and archaeological evidence, recounts the Gilgamesh Epic and various legends of Atrahasis, comments on the Sumerian King Lists, and so on. Depreciates the size and seaworthiness of Noah's ark, and fails to deal decisively with the biblical teaching of a universal flood. Despite these limitations, this work deserves to be read. 222.11'06.6—9.P24F

_____. *The Tower of Babel.* Translated by Edwin Hudson. New York: Philosophical Library, 1955.

Mainly valuable for the writer's "archaeological evidence" and scale drawings of the Tower of Babel based on excavations in Mesopotamia. 222.11'06.11.P24T

Patten, Donald W. *The Biblical Flood and the Ice Epoch: A Study in Scientific History.* Seattle: Pacific Meridian Publishing Co., 1966.

Advances evidence to support a catastrophic, universal flood. Answers the objections of uniformitarians and those who support the idea of a local flood. 222.11'06.6—9.P27

Pfeiffer, Charles Franklin. *The Book of Genesis.* Grand Rapids: Baker Book House, 1958.

A brief study guide. 222.11'07.P48

Pieters, Albertus. *Notes on Genesis.* Grand Rapids: Wm. B. Eerdmans Publishing Co., 1943.

Strongly Reformed, these notes on different sections of Genesis make interesting reading. The author, however, while adhering to "verbal" inspiration, rejects "plenary" inspiration. He entertains the possibility of organic evolution, rejects the documentary hypothesis, refuses to commit himself on the "sons of God" in Genesis 6, appears to prefer a local flood, and feels that Stephen was in error when he made certain statements in his speech in Acts 7. 222.11'07.P61

Pink, Arthur Walkington. *Gleanings in Genesis.* Chicago: Moody Press, 1922.

Heavily typological, but contains helpful, practical observations on the text. 222.11'07.P65.

Rad, Gerhard von. *Genesis: A Commentary.* Old Testament Library. Philadelphia: Westminster Press, 1961.

†A thoroughly critical exposition based on the documentary hypothesis. The most helpful portions are the writer's treatment of Hammurabi's code, the relationship between Sarah and Hagar, and his use of archaeology to aid

in understanding the text. At times rejects the narrative as being "historically impossible" or regards it a legend. Those who speak well of this work do so because of von Rad's advocacy of *Heilsgeschichte.* 222.11'07.R11

Rehwinkel, Alfred Martin. *The Flood.* St. Louis: Concordia Publishing House, 1951.

A vigorous defense of the universal flood based upon evidence from archaeology and geology. 222.11'06.6—9.R26

Richardson, Alan. *Genesis I-XI.* London: SCM Press, 1953.

†Brief comments, based upon the documentary hypothesis. Rejects a considerable amount of the biblical text as folklore. 222.11'07.1—11.R39

Robertson, Frederick William. *Notes on Genesis.* London: Henry S. King, 1877.

Eloquent sermons by a conservative British Anglican minister. Contains excellent expository values. 222.11'07.R54

Ryle, Herbert Edward. *The Book of Genesis.* Cambridge Bible for Schools and Colleges. Cambridge: At the University Press, 1921.

†Similar to the works by Driver, Skinner, and Dillman. 222.11'07.R98

_____. *The Early Narratives of Genesis: A Brief Introduction to the Study of Genesis I-XI.* London: Macmillan Co., 1900.

†While strongly advocating the critical tenets of his day and denying the scientific accuracy of Genesis 1-11, the writer holds to a literal twenty-four hour day in chapter 1 and argues that the "sons of God" in chapter 6 are angelic beings. 222.11'07.1—11.R98

Skinner, John. *A Critical and Exegetical Commentary on Genesis.* International Critical Commentary. 2d ed. New York: Charles Scribner's Sons, 1930.

†Thoroughly critical work based upon the documentary hypothesis. Regards Genesis as a "collection of legends" borrowed from foreign mythology. Dry, ster-

ile scholarship. 222.11'07.SK3 1930

Simpson, Albert Benjamin. *Genesis.* Harrison, Penn.: Christian Publications, n.d.

Brief devotional messages stressing the typology of the book. Arminian. 222.11'07.S15

Speiser, Ephraim Avigdor. *The Anchor Bible: Genesis.* Garden City: Doubleday and Co., 1964.

†Adopts and defends the documentary hypothesis, and interprets the entire book in the light of liberal presuppositions. The translation of the text, word studies, comments on the customs and culture, and use of archaeology to illumine the events of the times are particularly helpful. 222.11'07.SP3

Spurrell, George James. *Notes on the Text of the Book of Genesis.* Oxford: At the Clarendon Press, 1896.

A critical work of help to students studying the grammar of Genesis. 222.11'06.SP9

Strahan, James. *Hebrew Ideals—A Study of Genesis from Chapters XI-L.* 4th ed. Edinburgh: T. and T. Clark, 1915.

A rich and rewarding study. Does not permit critical considerations to mar his work. 222.11'06.11—50.ST8 1915

Thielicke, Helmut. *How the World Began.* Philadelphia: Muhlenberg Press, 1961.

†Eloquent sermons on Genesis 1-11 by a leading German theologian. At times the writer appears to be thoroughly evangelical, and at other times his statements reflect the liberalism of his training. 222.11'06.1—11.T34

*Thomas, William Henry Griffith. *Genesis: A Devotional Commentary.* Grand Rapids: Wm. B. Eerdmans Publishing Co., 1946.

Possibly the most helpful devotional exposition of Genesis available. Pastors will find the material on Abraham, Isaac, Jacob, and Joseph (chaps. 12-50) to be unsurpassed. 222.11'07.T36

*Whitcomb, John Clement, Jr. and **Henry M. Morris.** *The Genesis Flood.* Philadelphia: Presbyterian and Reformed Publishing Co., 1962.

Information is gathered from linguistics, paleontology, and geology. The claims of uniformitarianism are evaluated in the light of the evidence, and the final conclusion of the writers is overwhelmingly in support of a universal flood. 222.11'06.6—9.W58

Wiseman, Donald John. *Word of God for Abraham and Today.* London: Westminster Chapel, 1959.

The Campbell Morgan lectureship for 1959. Insightful. 222.11'08.W75

Wiseman, Percy John. *New Discoveries in Babylonia About Genesis.* London: Marshall, Morgan and Scott, 1958.

The writer is known for his theory of the compilation of Genesis (which structures the book of Genesis around the recurring statements: "The book of the generations of . . .") and his claim that these were the sources used by Moses in the composition of the book. 222.11'06.W75

*Young, Edward Joseph. *Genesis Three: A Devotional and Expository Study.* London: Banner of Truth Trust, 1966.

A devotional study based upon a careful exegesis of the original text. Helpful. 222.11'07.Y83

*_____. *Studies in Genesis One.* Philadelphia: Presbyterian and Reformed Publishing Co., 1964.

A careful and critical commentary. Of value for its treatment of problems associated with creation. 222.11'07.Y81

EXODUS

*Bush, George. *Notes, Critical and Practical, on the Book of Exodus.* 2 vols. Boston: Henry A. Young, 1871.

Expository studies of considerable value to preachers. 222.12'07.B96

Cassuto, Umberto. *A Commentary on*

the Book of Exodus. Translated by Israel Abrahams. Jerusalem: Magnus Press, 1967.

A critical commentary by a recognized Jewish scholar. Can be read with profit even by those whose knowledge of Hebrew has grown dim with the passing of time. 222.12'07.C27

Driver, Samuel Rolles. *The Book of Exodus.* Cambridge Bible for Schools and Colleges. Cambridge: At the University Press, 1953.

A highly critical work of value only as it aids in a technical study of the text. 222.12'07.D83

Hyatt, James Philip. *Exodus.* The New Century Bible. London: Oliphants, 1972.

†Reconstructs the historical and theological developments of this epoch of Israel's history by combining the methodology of tradition-history and form-criticism. 222.12'07.H99

Law, Henry. *The Gospel in Exodus.* London: Banner of Truth Trust, reprint.

A devotional discussion of the typological aspects in the book of Exodus, with emphasis upon the law and its relationship to the preaching of the gospel. The writer's hermeneutic leaves much to be desired. 222.12'07.L41

MacGregor, J. *Exodus: With Introduction, Commentary and Special Notes.* Edinburgh: T. and T. Clark, 1909.

An evangelical work presenting excellent background material. 222.12'07.M17

Mackintosh, Charles Henry. *Notes on the Book of Exodus.* New York: Loizeaux Brothers, 1959.

This work by a Plymouth Brethren writer is still read by many today. Devotional. First published in 1880. 222.12'07.M21 1959

Meyer, Frederick Brotherton. *Exodus.* 2 vols. London: Marshall, Morgan and Scott, 1952.

Devotional messages by a leading Keswick speaker of a generation past.

222.12'07.M57 1952

*Murphy, James Gracey. *A Critical and Exegetical Commentary on the Book of Exodus.* Boston: Estes and Lauriat, 1874.

Is not abreast of the latest archaeological discoveries, but the treatment of the text reveals painstaking exegesis and is helpful to expositors. 222.12'07.M95

Wilson-Haffenden, D. J. *Operation Exodus.* London: Marshall, Morgan and Scott, 1957.

By a major-general in the British Army, responsible for maintaining supplies to British troops in the Middle East during World War II. A comparison of his own efforts with those of Moses at the time of the Exodus makes interesting reading. Special emphasis is placed on the qualities of character of those whom God chooses to lead His people. 222.12'08.W69

Wit, C. de. *The Date and Route of the Exodus.* London: Tyndale Press, 1960.

Advances a view for a late date of the Exodus and a route through the "Sea of Reeds." 222.12'08.W77

LEVITICUS

*Bonar, Andrew Alexander. *A Commentary on the Book of Leviticus.* Grand Rapids: Zondervan Publishing House, 1959.

One of the great works on this portion of God's Word. Devotional. First published in 1846. Not as valuable, however, as Kellogg. 222.13'07.B64 1959

Buksbazen, Victor. *The Gospel in the Feasts of Israel.* Philadelphia: The Friends of Israel, 1954.

A handy manual on the significance of Israel's feasts. 222.13'07.1—7.B86

*Bush, George. *Notes, Critical and Practical, on the Book of Leviticus.* Boston: Henry A. Young, 1870.

A book that pastors will find exceedingly useful. 222.13'07.B96

Ironside, Henry Allan. *Lectures on the*

Levitical Offerings. New York: Loizeaux Brothers, 1951.

Basing his exposition upon a literal interpretation of Scripture, Ironside ably expounds Leviticus 1 through 7. 222.13'07.1—7.1R6

Jukes, Andrew John. *The Law of the Offerings.* Grand Rapids: Kregel Publications, 1966.

Beginning with a defense of biblical typology, the writer analyzes the five offerings of the Levitical system and discusses the typical significance of each. 222.13'07.1—7.J93

*Kellogg, Samuel Henry. *The Book of Leviticus.* The Expositor's Bible. New York: George H. Doran and Co., n.d.

An exemplary study that was first published as a separate monograph in 1891. Should be in every pastor's library. 222.13'07.K29

Murphy, James Gracey. *A Critical and Exegetical Commentary on the Book of Leviticus.* Andover: Warren F. Draper, 1874.

Combines a devotional emphasis with sound exegesis. 222.13'07.M95

Pfeiffer, Charles Franklin. *The Book of Leviticus.* Grand Rapids: Baker Book House, 1957.

Very brief. Useful with study groups. 222.13'07.P48

Seiss, Joseph Augustus. *The Gospel in Leviticus.* Grand Rapids: Zondervan Publishing House, reprint.

Expository sermons by a nineteenth-century Lutheran pastor. Although valuable, not as thorough or as helpful as Kellogg's work. 222.13'07.SE4

NUMBERS

*Bush, George. *Notes, Critical and Practical on the Book of Numbers.* New York: Ivison, Phinney and Co., 1858.

Succinct, helpful comments based upon the Hebrew text. 222.14'07.B96

Gray, George Buchanan. *A Critical and Exegetical Commentary on Numbers.* International Critical Commentary. Edinburgh: T. and T. Clark, 1903.

†Like the other works in this series, this study has both good and weak features. While dated from archaeological and historical points of view, the exegetical comments are still helpful. 222.14'07.G78

*Greenstone, Julius Hillel. *The Holy Scripture with Commentary: Numbers.* Philadelphia: Jewish Publication Society of America, 1939.

By a conservative Jewish scholar. Provides insightful historical details the expositor will find valuable. 222.14'07.G85

Jensen, Irving Lester. *Numbers: Journey to God's Rest Land.* Chicago: Moody Press, 1964.

A brief explanation of the text, with numerous practical applications. 222.14'07.J45

Mackintosh, Charles Henry. *Notes on the Book of Numbers.* New York: Loizeaux Brothers, 1959.

Originally published in 1880. Opens up to the Bible student this portion of God's Word. Devotional. 222.14'07.M21 1959

DEUTERONOMY

*Manley, George Thomas. *The Book of the Law.* Grand Rapids: Wm. B. Eerdmans Publishing Co., 1957.

Critical studies centering in the date of Deuteronomy. An excellent treatment. 222.15'06.M31

Driver, Samuel Rolles. *A Critical and Exegetical Commentary on Deuteronomy.* International Critical Commentary. 3d ed. Edinburgh: T. and T. Clark, 1965.

A highly critical work that is helpful for exegesis. Driver adheres to the late origin of the book (7th cent.). Originally published in 1895. 222.15'07.D83 1965

Francisco, Clyde T. *The Book of Deu-*

teronomy. Grand Rapids: Baker Book House, 1964.

A work which makes concessions to modern criticism and is inclined to accept a late date for the composition of the book of Deuteronomy. 222.15'07.F85

*****Kline, Meredith G.** *Treaty of the Great King: The Covenant Structure of Deuteronomy.* Grand Rapids: Wm. B. Eerdmans Publishing Co., 1963.

A bold, original, and suggestive study by a Semitic scholar who uses the tools of form-criticism in his analysis of the text in an endeavor to exemplify the structural outline of the suzerainty treaties of the second millennium B.C. 222.15'07.K68

Mackintosh, Charles Henry. *Notes on the Book of Deuteronomy.* 2 vols. Neptune, N.J.: Loizeaux Brothers, 1965.

First published in 1880. Devotional in nature like the other works in this series. 222.15'07.M21

Rad, Gerhard von. *Studies in Deuteronomy.* Translated by David Stalker. Old Testament Library. London: SCM Press, 1966.

†A fresh, form-critical study. 222.15'07.R11

Reider, J. *The Holy Scripture with Commentary: Deuteronomy.* Philadelphia: Jewish Publication Society of America, 1937.

Written from a conservative Jewish point of view. Ably expounds the final messages Moses delivered to the children of Israel. 222.15'07.R27

Schultz, Samuel J. *Deuteronomy: The Gospel of Love.* Chicago: Moody Press, 1971.

A simple, thought-provoking exposition that sees the theme of this portion of God's Word as emphasizing the love of God. 222.15'07.SCH8

TEN COMMANDMENTS

Chappell, Clovis Gillham. *Ten Rules*

for Living. New York: Abingdon Press, 1938.

A practical study by a well-known Methodist preacher. 222.16'07.C36

Davidman, Joy. *Smoke on the Mountain.* Philadelphia: Westminster Press, 1971.

The wife of C. S. Lewis interprets the Ten Commandments and passes on observations she has made concerning those who have attempted to order their lives according to the Decalogue. 222.16'07.D28

Flowers, Harold Joseph. *The Permanent Value of the Ten Commandments.* London: George Allen and Unwin, 1927.

A popular presentation. 222.16'07.F65

Herklots, Hugh Gerard Gibson. *The Ten Commandments and Modern Man.* London: Ernest Benn, 1958.

A series of sermons by an evangelical Anglican. 222.16'07.H42

Hopkins, Ezekiel. *An Exposition of the Ten Commandments.* Rev. ed. New York: American Tract Society, n.d.

A brilliantly written treatise by a leading Puritan writer. Long out of print, it should be purchased if found. 222.16'07.H77

Strauss, Lehman. *The Eleven Commandments.* Neptune, N.J.: Loizeaux Brothers, 1955.

Formerly published under the title *From Sinai to Calvary.* Focuses on the law given to Moses and "the sovereign law of love." 222.16'07.ST8

*****Tatford, Frederick Albert.** *The Message of Sinai.* London: Victory Press, 1957.

A study of the meaning of the Ten Commandments and their message for today. 222.16'07.T18

Watson, Thomas. *The Ten Commandments.* London: Banner of Truth Trust, 1962.

A portion of an old Puritan work that originally appeared in *A Body of Divinity.*

Strongly Calvinistic. 222.16'07.W33

JOSHUA

*Blaikie, William Garden. *The Book of Joshua.* The Expositor's Bible. New York: A. C. Armstrong and Son, 1908.

One of the most capable treatments available today. Reverent, practical, and revealing of the writer's knowledge of the history, geography, customs, and culture of the times. 222.2'07.B57

*Davis, John James. *Conquest and Crisis.* Grand Rapids: Baker Book House, 1969.

A systematic consideration of the central themes of Joshua, Judges, and Ruth, incorporating into its material the latest archaeological findings in the Near East. Deals with the difficult problems, including Joshua's "long day" and the supernatural collapse of the walls of Jericho. A commendable volume. 222.2'06.D29

Garstang, John. *Joshua-Judges.* Foundations of Bible History. London: Constable and Co., 1931.

In spite of its age and adherence to the documentary hypothesis, this work contains some valuable information on the historic background to Joshua-Judges, Joshua's military campaigns, the settlement of the tribes, and the period of the Judges. 222.2'07.G19

Jensen, Irving Lester. *Joshua: Rest-Land Won.* Chicago: Moody Press, 1966.

A brief treatment of the historical data and spiritual truths of this book. 222.2'07.J45

Kaufmann, Yehezel. *The Biblical Account of the Conquest of Palestine.* Jerusalem: Magnus Press, 1953.

While not defending the biblical record of the conquest nor an early date for the settlement of the tribes in Canaan, this Jewish scholar does contribute one of the best answers to certain aspects of destructive higher criticism. 222.2'06.K16

Maclear, George Frederick. *The Book of Joshua.* Cambridge Bible for Schools and Colleges. Cambridge: At the University Press, 1894.

Brief expository notes. 222.2'07.M22

Pink, Arthur Walkington. *Gleanings in Joshua.* Chicago: Moody Press, 1964.

Among the last writings of the author, with chapters 20-23 completed by James Gunn of Ontario. Deeply devotional, manifests a comprehensive grasp of Scripture, contains clear outlines, and abounds in edifying material. 222.2'07.P65

*Redpath, Alan. *Victorious Christian Living.* London: Pickering and Inglis, 1955.

Devotional studies covering the major portion of Joshua. 222.2'07.R24

*Scroggie, William Graham. *The Land and Life of Rest.* Glasgow: Pickering and Inglis, 1950.

A series of devotional Bible readings on the book of Joshua. 222.2'07.SCR5

Smith, Thornley. *The History of Joshua.* Edinburgh: William Oliphant, 1870.

While making use of the topography of Canaan and the customs of the times in which Joshua lived, the chief value of this work now lies in its devotional content. 222.2'09.SM6

JUDGES AND RUTH

Burney, Charles Fox. *Notes on the Hebrew Texts of Judges and Kings.* 2 vols. New York: Ktav Publishing House, 1966.

Originally published in 1903 and 1930. Now reissued with an extensive introduction by William F. Albright. Abounds in textual, philological, historical, geographical, and archaeological material that translators and those who preach from a careful exegesis of the text will find helpful. 222.3'07.B93 1966

*Bush, George. *Notes, Critical and Practical, on the Book of Judges.* New York:

Ivison, Phinney and Co., 1862.

Expository notes based upon the original text. Of particular value to the preacher with little or no knowledge of Hebrew. 222.3'07.B96

Cooke, George Albert. *The Book of Judges.* Cambridge Bible for Schools and Colleges. Cambridge: At the University Press, 1913.

Critical notes based upon the RV. 222.3'07.C77

*Cox, Samuel. *The Book of Ruth.* London: Religious Tract Society, 1922.

The devotional nature of this commentary does not detract from its expository value. While popular in style, it exhibits a remarkable understanding of human nature. A work of real merit. 222.35'07.C83

Cundall, Arthur E. and **Leon L. Morris.** *Judges and Ruth.* Tyndale Old Testament Commentaries. London: Tyndale Press, 1968.

Judges follows many of the critical theories of our day, and Cundall makes allowance for later redaction of the text. The exposition, however, is clear and helpful. *Ruth* is written by Morris, who exhibits the same acumen in handling the OT as he does the NT. He incorporates the most recent archaeological research in his exposition and provides a satisfying verse-by-verse study. 222.3'07.C91

*Fausset, Andrew Robert. *A Critical and Expository Commentary on the Book of Judges.* London: James Nisbet and Co., 1885.

Remains one of the finest comprehensive and scholarly treatments for the expositor. 222.3'07.F27

Kennedy, A. R. S. *The Book of Ruth.* New York: Macmillan Co., 1937.

This work contains helpful comments on the Hebrew text. 222.35'07.K38

Knight, George Angus Fulton. *Ruth and Jonah: The Gospel in the Old Testament.* London: SCM Press, 1966.

†Two critical studies based upon an exegesis of the text. 222.35'07.K74

Lang, John Marshall. *Gideon and the Judges.* London: James Nisbet and Co., 1890.

An old, well-reasoned work. Helpful for its historical material. 222.3'092.L25

*Lawson, George. *Expositions of Ruth and Esther.* Evansville, Ind.: Sovereign Grace Publishers, 1960.

A book highly esteemed by C. H. Spurgeon for its wise counsel and gracious teaching. 222.35'07.L44

McGee, John Vernon. *Ruth: The Romance of Redemption.* 2d ed. Wheaton: Van Kampen Press, 1954.

A detailed dispensational treatment. 222.35'07.M17 1954

Mauro, Philip. *Ruth: The Satisfied Stranger.* Swengel, Penn.: Bible Truth Depot, 1963.

A helpful study with discussions on such topics as "kinsman," Ruth's happening to light on a part of the field belonging to Boaz, and "the name of the dead." 222.35'07.M44

Myers, Jacob Martin. *The Linguistic and Literary Form of the Book of Ruth.* Leiden: E. J. Brill, 1955.

A critical study adhering to a two-fold composition of the book, yet it contains some helpful insights. 222.35'07.M99

Moore, George Foot. *A Critical and Exegetical Commentary on Judges.* International Critical Commentary. New York: Charles Scribner's Sons, 1895.

†Remains a valuable commentary, with numerous historical insights. Modifies many of the liberal views held by his contemporaries, but the chronology is unreliable. 222.3'07.M78

Ridout, Samuel. *Lectures on the Books of Judges and Ruth.* New York: Loizeaux Brothers, 1958.

Popular in Plymouth Brethren circles since its appearance in 1900. Devotional and doctrinal. Can be read with profit. 222.3'07.R43 1958

I AND II SAMUEL

Ackroyd, Peter R. *The First Book of Samuel.* Cambridge Bible Commentary. Cambridge: At the University Press, 1971.

†Based upon the NEB, this source-critical work by a leading comparative religionist contains an up-to-date evaluation of the archaeological material relating to the period of Samuel and Saul. Adheres to a modified documentary theory. 222.43'07.AC5

Blackwood, Andrew Watterson. *Preaching from Samuel.* New York: Abingdon-Cokesbury Press, 1946.

A series of sermons showing how the pastor may introduce variety into his preaching and still expound the text. 222.4'08.B56

*Blaikie, William Garden. *The First Book of Samuel.* The Expositor's Bible. London: Hodder and Stoughton, 1898.

Exceedingly helpful expositions for preachers who want something substantial and satisfying. 222.4'07.B57

*_____. *The Second Book of Samuel.* The Expositor's Bible. New York: A. C. Armstrong and Son, 1908.

See Blaikie, *First Samuel.* As is true of all Blaikie's works, this one is excellent. 222.44'07.B57

Crockett, William Day. *A Harmony of the Books of Samuel, Kings and Chronicles.* Grand Rapids: Baker Book House, 1959.

An attempt to reconcile and correlate the history of the books of Samuel, Kings, and Chronicles into chronological sequence. Helpful. 222.4'05.C87

*Davis, John James. *The Birth of a Kingdom.* Old Testament Studies. Grand Rapids: Baker Book House, 1970.

Illuminates the historical record of the books of Samuel and Kings, draws information from the comparative literature of the ancient Near East on social and political conditions prevailing at the time, and highlights the biblical text with material from archaeological investigations. A valuable book. 222.4'06.D262

Driver, Samuel Rolles. *Notes on the Hebrew Text and the Typography of the Books of Samuel.* Oxford: At the Clarendon Press, 1913.

†Marred by Driver's theological position, but indispensable for the study of the original text. 222.4'07.D83

Hertzberg, Hans Wilhelm. *I and II Samuel: A Commentary.* Translated by J. S. Bowden. Old Testament Library. Philadelphia: Westminster Press, 1964.

†Based on the second revised edition of *Die Samuelbücher,* 1960, this form-critical work fails to incorporate into its scope the materials in the Dead Sea Scrolls, recent archaeological data, and a vast amount of data from the epigraphic literary texts. 222.4'07.H44 1964

Kirkpatrick, Alexander Francis. *The Second Book of Samuel.* Cambridge Bible for Schools and Colleges. Cambridge: At the University Press, 1930.

First published in 1880 and thoroughly revised in 1930, this book, like others in this series, contains critical notes on the text. 222.44'07.K63 1930

Smith, Henry Preserved. *A Critical and Exegetical Commentary on the Books of Samuel.* International Critical Commentary. Edinburgh: T. and T. Clark, 1904.

†A scholarly treatment of the linguistic materials that also attempts to discuss the parallels between the books of Samuel and Chronicles. Chronology is helpful, but needs to be modified in the light of recent findings. 222.4'07.SM5

I AND II KINGS

Barnes, William Emery. *The Two Books of Kings.* Cambridge Bible for Schools and Colleges. Cambridge: At the University Press, 1908.

Expository notes based upon the RV. 222.5'07.B26

*Farrar, Frederic William. *The First*

Book of Kings. The Expositor's Bible. New York: A. C. Armstrong and Son, 1908.

†Valuable expository studies by a great preacher, a profound scholar, and a man of unparalleled literary activity who exercised considerable influence as a theologian and lecturer. Manifests a marked tendency to accept the text of the LXX over the MT. 222.53'07.F24

*_____. *The Second Book of Kings.* The Expositor's Bible. New York: A. C. Armstrong and Son, 1908.

†See Farrar, *First Kings.* 222.54'07.F24

Lumby, Joseph Rawson, *The First Book of Kings.* Cambridge Bible for Schools and Colleges. Cambridge: At the University Press, 1892.

Brief expository comments. Helpful. 222.53'07.L97

_____. *The Second Book of Kings.* Cambridge Bible for Schools and Colleges. Cambridge: At the University Press, 1891.

Critical notes on the text. 222.54'07.L97

Montgomery, James Alan. *A Critical and Exegetical Commentary on the Books of Kings.* International Critical Commentary. New York: Charles Scribner's Sons, 1951.

†One of the foremost critical studies on the Hebrew text. 222.5'07.M76

*Rawlinson, George.** *Lives and Times of the Kings of Israel and Judah.* London: James Nisbet and Co., 1889.

Still valuable for its correlation of sacred and profane history. 222.5'092.R19

*Thiele, Edwin Richard.** *The Mysterious Numbers of the Hebrew Kings.* Rev. ed. Grand Rapids: Wm. B. Eerdmans Publishing Co., 1965.

While not eliminating all the problems of chronology in the period of the kings of Israel and Judah, Thiele's work has helped Bible students reconcile many aggravating problems. 222.5'067.T34 1965

*Whitcomb, John Clement, Jr.** *Solomon*

to the Exile: Studies in Kings and Chronicles. Grand Rapids: Baker Book House, 1971.

An ideal book for discussion groups. Recreates the OT setting, graphically depicts the cause of decline in Israel and Judah, and draws valid lessons from these incidents that are applied to the needs of the present. 222.5'06.W58

I AND II CHRONICLES

Myers, Jacob Martin. *The Anchor Bible: II Chronicles.* Garden City: Doubleday and Co., 1965.

Attempts to validate the text, focuses upon the theology of II Chronicles, and is particularly helpful for the way the writer blends archaeological data with the narrative. 222.64'07.M99

EZRA, NEHEMIAH, AND ESTHER

Batten, Loring Woart. *A Critical and Exegetical Commentary on the Books of Ezra and Nehemiah.* International Critical Commentary. Edinburgh: T. and T. Clark, 1913.

†Has been superseded in everything except its grammatical analysis. 222.7'07.B31

Carson, Alexander. *God's Providence Unfolded in Esther.* Evansville, Ind.: Sovereign Grace Publishers, 1960.

Contains a thoroughly biblical exposition of the doctrine of God's providential care of His people. Frequently bound together with Lawson's *Expositions of Ruth and Esther.* 222.9'07.C23

Cumming, James Elder, *The Book of Esther.* 2d ed. London: Religious Tract Society, n.d.

A devotional commentary. Brief, pointed comments. 222.9'07.C91

Ironside, Henry Allan. *Notes on the Books of Ezra, Nehemiah and Esther.* New York: Loizeaux Brothers, 1951.

Containing helpful devotional material originally published in 1905, 1913, and 1915. These expository messages are prone to be heavily typological. 222.7'07.IR6 1951

*McGee, John Vernon. *An Exposition on the Book of Esther.* Wheaton: Van Kampen Press, 1951.

A historical and cultural approach. 222.9'07.M17

Moore, Carey A. *The Anchor Bible: Esther.* Garden City: Doubleday and Co., 1971.

†A higher critical study. Archaeologically illuminating, but intended for the advanced student of Hebrew rather than the pastor. 222.9'07.M78

Myers, Jacob Martin. *The Anchor Bible: Ezra, Nehemiah.* Garden City: Doubleday and Co., 1965.

Important because there are few exegetical and historical works of its kind. The character studies, the handling of the meaning of names, and the archaeological information are helpful. 222.7'07.M99

Paton, Lewis Byles. *A Critical and Exegetical Commentary on the Book of Esther.* International Critical Commentary. Edinburgh: T. and T. Clark, 1908.

†A higher critical study of value for its linguistic comments on the text. 222.9'07.P27

*Raleigh, Alexander. *The Book of Esther.* Edinburgh: Adam and Charles Black, 1880.

A devotional study with practical lessons based upon the dramatic scenes of this book. Excellent. 222.9'07.R13

*Redpath, Alan. *Victorious Christian Service.* Westwood, N.J.: Fleming H. Revell Co., 1958.

Edifying and enriching expository studies on the book of Nehemiah. Incomplete. 222.8'07.R24

Ryle, Herbert Edward. *The Books of Ezra and Nehemiah.* Cambridge Bible for Schools and Colleges. Cambridge: At the University Press, 1917.

†A brief, critical treatment. 222.7'07.R98

Thomas, W. Ian. *If I Perish . . . I Perish.* Grand Rapids: Zondervan Publishing House, 1966.

Building his hermeneutic upon a Christological principle, Thomas looks upon the book of Esther as an allegory and expounds it as such. Of little value as an exposition. 222.9'06.T36

White, K. Owen. *Nehemiah Speaks Again.* Nashville: Broadman Press, 1964.

Twelve sermons by a Southern Baptist preacher. Geared to the times. 222.8'07.W58

Wright, John Stafford. *The Building of the Second Temple.* London: Tyndale Press, 1958.

A valuable though brief monograph on the historical setting surrounding the return of the exiles from Babylon, the ministry of Haggai and Zechariah, and the events of 520-516 B.C. 222.7'06.W93B

————. *The Date of Ezra's Coming to Jerusalem.* London: Tyndale Press, 1958.

A careful chronological study by the principal of Tyndale Hall, Bristol, England. 222.7'06.W93D

Poetical Books

Gray, George Buchanan. *The Forms of Hebrew Poetry.* London: Hodder and Stoughton, 1915.

A scholarly work that, while dated, synthesizes a vast amount of material. Reprinted by Ktav Publishing House. 223'.06.G79

Yoder, Sanford Calvin. *Poetry of the Old Testament.* Bronxville, N.Y.: Herald Books, 1948.

A popularization of OT hymnic material, but now in need of revision. 223'.06.Y7

JOB

Bennett, T. Miles. *When Human Wisdom Fails.* Grand Rapids: Baker Book House, 1971.
A perceptive analysis and exposition of the book of Job. Zeroes in on the age-old question of suffering, and enables believers to investigate their problems and reach their own conclusions. 223.1'07.B43

Blackwood, Andrew Watterson, Jr. *A Devotional Introduction to Job.* Grand Rapids: Baker Book House, 1970.
A brief work abounding in homiletic value. 223.1'07.B56

Blair, J. Allen. *Living Patiently.* Neptune, N.J.: Loizeaux Brothers, 1966.
Devotional messages on the book of Job. 223.1'07.B57

*Caryl, Joseph. *An Exposition of Job.* Grand Rapids: Kregel Publications, reprint.
An abridgment of the author's famous eight-volume work. Retains sufficient seed thoughts to prod the thinking of any preacher. 223.1'07.C19

Chambers, Oswald. *Baffled to Fight Better.* 4th ed. Oxford: Alden and Co., n.d.
Expository messages on the book of Job. Originally published in 1955. 223.1'07.C35

*Cox, Samuel. *Commentary on the Book of Job.* London: C. Kegan Paul and Co., 1880.
An exemplary treatment. Buy it if you can find a copy. Out-of-print. 223.1'07.C83

*Davidson, Andrew Bruce. *The Book of Job.* Cambridge Bible for Schools and Colleges. Cambridge: At the University Press, 1903.
A capable exposition by a renowned Scottish Hebraist. Easier to obtain than Gibson's masterly work. 223.1'07.D28

Dhorme, Edouard Paul. *A Commentary on the Book of Job.* Translated by Harold Knight. New York: Thomas Nelson and Sons, 1967.
The introductory essays are extensive and of great value. They cover a theological assessment of the theme of the book, textual matters, the shorter endings, and the credibility of Elihu's speeches. The exposition of the text is not as significant. 223.1'07.D53

Ellison, Henry Leopold. *From Tragedy to Triumph: The Message of the Book of Job.* Grand Rapids: Wm. B. Eerdmans Publishing Co., 1958.
An elementary guide to the study of this book. 223.1'07.EL5

*Gibson, Edgar Charles Summer. *The Book of Job.* Westminster Commentaries. 3d ed. London: Methuen and Co., 1919.
A valuable exposition. Deserves a place in the library of every pastor. 223.1'07.G35 1919

Gordis, Robert. *The Book of God and Man: A Study of Job.* Chicago: University of Chicago Press, 1965.
A highly critical, Jewish work that contains an excellent introduction to the study of this portion of God's Word. 223.1'06.G65

*Green, William Henry. *The Argument of the Book of Job Unfolded.* New York: Robert Carter. 1874.
Recently republished under the title of *Job's Triumph over Satan,* this excellent study ably expounds the theme of this book. A most valuable acquisition. 223.1'07.G82

Hulme, William Edward. *Dialogue in Despair.* Nashville: Abingdon Press, 1968.
A pastoral commentary. Shows the relevancy of the theme of Job to counseling and the assuaging of grief and suffering. 223.1'07.H87

*MacBeath, Andrew. *The Book of Job.*

Grand Rapids: Baker Book House, 1966.

A delightful study manual that adequately expounds the central theme of the book. Ideal for personal study or Bible class use. 223.1'07.M12

Morgan, George Campbell. *The Book of Job.* Analyzed Bible. London: Hodder and Stoughton, 1909.

Contains an enlightening analysis. One of the better volumes in this series. 223.1'07.M82

Penn-Lewis, Jessie. *The Story of Job.* Fort Washington, Penn.: Christian Literature Crusade, 1902.

Emphasizes the lessons of obedience and devotion, and that fellowship with God can be established and enlarged as a result of suffering. Guides the reader into the very heart of the meaning and message of Job. 223.1'07.P37

Ralph, E. H., ed. *The Voice Out of the Whirlwind: The Book of Job.* San Francisco: Chandler Publishing Co., 1960.

A collection of highly significant articles relating to the literary form, style and theme, source and influence, identification and analysis of character, and development of ideas contained in the book of Job. 224.1'06.R13

Snaith, Norman Henry. *The Book of Job: Its Origin and Purpose.* Studies in biblical theology. Naperville, Ill.: Alec R. Allenson, 1968.

†A critical and technical study. 223.1'06.SN1

Strahan, James. *The Book of Job.* 2d ed. Edinburgh: T. and T. Clark, 1914.

One of the best expository treatments, but difficult to obtain. Based upon a moderate form-criticism. 223.1'07.ST8 1914

PSALMS

*Alexander, Joseph Addison. *The Psalms, Translated and Explained.* Grand

Rapids: Zondervan Publishing House, reprint.

First published in Edinburgh in 1864. Contains genuine scholarship and evangelical warmth that are singularly missing from many commentaries today. 223.2'07.AL2

Alexander, William. *The Witness of the Psalms to Christ and Christianity.* New York: E. P. Dutton and Co., 1877.

An apologetic for the Christian religion based upon the testimony of the Psalms. 223.2'06.AL2

Briggs, Charles Augustus. *A Critical and Exegetical Commentary on the Book of Psalms.* International Critical Commentary. 2 vols. New York: Charles Scribner's Sons, 1906.

†More radical than Briggs's other writings. He frequently amends the text to suit his personal ideas, and he rejects the Davidic authorship of the Psalms usually ascribed to David. Lacking in exegetical and textual values. 223.2'07.B76

Buttenwieser, Moses. *The Psalms: Chronologically Treated with a New Translation.* New York: Ktav Publishing House, 1969.

†An encyclopedic work that first appeared in print in 1938. Contains textual, philological, stylistic, and exegetical material, and ably expounds the prophetic nature of Israel's hymnic literature. 223.2'06.B98 1969

Chambers, Talbot Wilson. *The Psalter.* New York: Anson D. F. Randolph and Co., 1876.

The writer uses the Psalms as a polemic for the defense of Christianity. His appreciation of the literary value of these hymns and prayers is unquestioned, and his defense of the messianic prophecies is of great value. In some respects his work is dated, but may still be studied with profit. 223.2'06.C35

Clarke, Arthur G. *Analytical Studies in*

the Psalms. Kilmarnock: John Ritchey, n.d.

Prefaced with a comprehensive introduction to the Psalms, their nature, scope, and use in Israel's worship. Complete with outlines based on the Hebrew text, notes on the text, and exegetical comments. Exceedingly helpful for preachers. 223.2'06.C55

*Cox, Samuel. *The Pilgrim Psalms: An Exposition of the Psalms of Degrees.* New York: Anson D. F. Randolph and Company, n.d.

James Moffat said, "Dr. Cox . . . was probably the greatest expositor of his day." His works are among the best that have come down to us. This book could easily form the basis for a series of expository messages. 223.2'07.120—134.C83

Cummings, John Elder. *The Psalms.* 3 vols. London: Religious Tract Society, n.d.

A devotional exposition pastors will find helpful. Captions for each of the Psalms are accurate and readily lend themselves for use as catchy sermon titles. 223.2'07.C91

*Dahood, Mitchell. *The Anchor Bible: Psalms.* 3 vols. Garden City: Doubleday and Co., 1965-70.

†A highly critical work in which the author, relying heavily upon contemporary linguistic materials and stressing the relationship of hymnic literature to the Ugaritic texts found at Ras Shamra, tries to capture and present the meaning of the original Hebrew. Helpful. 223.2'07.D13

Davis, Noah Knowles. *Juda's Jewels.* Nashville: Publishing House of the Methodist Episcopal Church, South, 1896.

A brief but intriguing study of the Davidic Psalms in their historic setting. 223.2'07.D29

Dickson, David. *A Commentary on the Psalms.* London: Banner of Truth Trust, 1959.

A richly devotional exposition by a Scottish Covenanter of the seventeenth century. 223.2'07.D56

Fausset, Andrew Robert. *Studies in the CL Psalms.* London: Church Book Society Press, 1876.

A series of lectures on the events in the life of David that are subsequently reflected in the Psalms. 223.2'07.F27

Gunkel, Hermann. *The Psalms: A Form-Critical Introduction.* Philadelphia: Fortress Press, 1962.

†A foundational work that attempts to locate the Psalms in their different sociological settings (*Sitz im Leben*) and their corresponding literary form (*Gattung*). Radical in its approach, but helpful for its analysis of literary forms. 223.2'06.G95

Harris, Arthur Emerson. *The Psalms Outlined.* Philadelphia: Judson Press, 1925.

A well-alliterated series of outlines. 223.2'06.H24

*Hengstenberg, Ernst Wilhelm. *A Commentary on the Psalms.* Translated by P. Fairbairn. Edinburgh: T. and T. Clark, 1876.

An evangelical, scholarly work still worth consulting. 223.2'07.H38

Howard, Henry. *The Threshold.* New York: George H. Doran, 1926.

Devotional messages based on Psalm 1. 223.2'07.1.H831

Inch, Morris A. *Psychology in the Psalms: A Portrait of Man in God's World.* Waco: Word Books, 1969.

A topical study of the Psalms that confronts modern man with ancient hymnic literature and new insights about himself as a person, and gives a new and refreshing perspective on life. 223.2'08.IN2

Johnson, Aubrey Rodway. *Sacral Kingship in Ancient Israel.* Cardiff: University of Wales Press, 1967.

†Stresses the corporate personality of Israel's kingship. Treats Psalm 72 as an ascension poem, and sees in Psalm 47 an earlier Canaanite worship poem or song. Explains many OT festivals in the light of Canaanitish mythology. Needs to be read with discernment. 223.2'06.J63

Jowett, John Henry. *Springs in the Desert.* New York: George H. Doran Co., 1924.

A series of masterful sermons on individual texts in the book of Psalms. Good illustrations of textual preaching. 223.2'08.J83

Ker, John. *The Psalms in History and Biography.* Edinburgh: Andrew Elliot, 1886.

Similar in scope to Ernle's *The Psalms in Human Life.* Emphasizes the inspiration and encouragement different people have received as a result of their meditation upon the Psalms. 223.2'09.K45

*Ketcham, Robert Thomas. *"I Shall Not Want."* Chicago: Moody Press, 1953.

Addresses that are fervent and practical, edifying and enriching. 233.2'07.23.K49

King, Guy Hope. *All Through the Day.* London: Church Book Room Press, 1948.

Devotional studies centering in Psalm 23. 223.2'07.23.K58

Leslie, Elmer Archibald. *The Psalms.* Nashville: Abingdon Press, 1949.

†Groups various psalms together under topics that suggest their *Sitz im Leben.* Emphasizes the aspect of worship in ancient Israel, and stresses the liturgical value of the Psalms rather than their spiritual and devotional content. 223.6'06.L56

*Leupold, Herbert Carl. *Exposition of the Psalms.* Minneapolis: Augsburg Publishing House, 1959.

A rewarding expository treatment. 223.2'07.L57

*Lloyd-Jones, David Martyn. *Faith on Trial.* Grand Rapids: Wm. B. Eerdmans Publishing Co., 1965.

Warm, devotional meditations on Psalm 73 showing how true joy may be found only in man's awareness of the presence of God. 223.2'07.73.L77

*MacDuff, John Ross. *The Hart and the Water-Brooks.* St. Paul: D. D. Merrill Co., n.d.

In these devotional studies on Psalm 42, the author rises to heights of eloquence as he expounds the text. First published in 1860. 223.2'07.42.M14

*Maclaren, Alexander. *The Psalms.* The Expositor's Bible. 3 vols. London: Hodder and Stoughton, 1893.

A masterful treatment. Defends the messianic content of the Psalms, builds upon a detailed grammatical analysis of the text, provides valuable and informative historical material that supports the composition of many of these Psalms, and abounds in practical comments. 223.2'07.M22

Meyer, Frederick Brotherton. *The Shepherd Psalm.* New York: H. M. Caldwell Co., n.d.

A warmly devotional exposition. 223.2'07.23.M57

Morgan, George Campbell. *Notes on the Psalms.* New York: Fleming H. Revell Co., 1947.

Valuable for Morgan's handling of Psalms 22-24 dealing with Christ as Savior, Shepherd, and Sovereign. 223.6'06.M82 1947

Mowinckel, Sigmund Olaf Plytt. *The Psalms in Israel's Worship.* Translated by D. R. Ap-Thomas. 2 vols. Nashville: Abingdon Press, 1962.

†A comprehensive treatment based solidly upon the principles of form-criticism and seeing in many psalms a cultic background. 223.2'06.M87

Murphy, James Gracey. *Critical and Exegetical Commentary on the Book of Psalms.* Edinburgh: T. and T. Clark, 1875.

A classic. Still helpful in spite of the passing of time. 223.2'07.M95

Murray, Andrew. *Have Mercy upon Me.* New York: Anson D. F. Randolph Co., 1895.

A brilliantly worded, deeply devotional, phrase-by-phrase study of Psalm 51. 223.2'07.51.M96

Owen, George Frederick. *The Shepherd Psalm of Palestine.* Grand Rapids: Wm. B. Eerdmans Publishing Co., 1958.

Rich and rewarding, and vividly recreates the historic setting that gave rise to this psalm. 223.2'07.23.OW2

Patton, John Hastings. *Canaanite Parallels in the Book of Psalms.* Baltimore: Johns Hopkins University Press, 1943.

†A critical work of limited value. 223.2'06.P27

*Perowne, John James Stewart. *The Book of Psalms.* 2 vols. Grand Rapids: Zondervan Publishing House, 1966.

Reprinted from the fourth revised edition of 1878. Contains valuable exegetical studies by an Anglican theologian. The introductory essays on the poetry of the Hebrew, the theology of the Psalms, the probable origin and formation of the Psalter, and the inscriptions of the Psalms make rewarding reading. 223.2'07.P42 1966

Phillips, Ordis E. *Exploring the Messianic Psalms.* Philadelphia: Hebrew Christian Fellowship, 1967.

Lists 55 psalms as being messianic, and expounds these with a devotional emphasis. Includes an interesting note on the imprecatory psalms and interprets them in the light of the tribulation period. 223.2'06.P54

*Robinson, Haddon W. *Psalm Twenty-Three.* Chicago: Moody Press, 1968.

A well-written exposition combining accuracy in interpretation and relevancy in application. 223.2'07.23.R56

*Spurgeon, Charles Haddon. *The Treasury of David.* 6 vols. Grand Rapids: Zondervan Publishing House, 1963.

A classic in its field. Richly rewarding, deeply devotional, and pleasingly relevant. Provides not only the thoughts of the great "Prince of Preachers" of the last century, but also an abundance of quotations taken from the writings of those who have preceded him in the ministry of the Word. 223.2'07.SP9

*Westermann, Claus. *The Praise of God in the Psalms.* Translated by Keith R. Crim. Richmond: John Knox Press, 1965.

†Following in the footsteps of Hermann Gunkel, the writer concentrates on psalm types and the categories through which an exegesis of the OT psalms may most profitably be studied. 223.2'06.W52

PROVERBS

Arnot, William. *Laws from Heaven for Life on Earth.* London: Thomas Nelson and Sons, 1882.

Perceptive studies of selected verses in the book of Proverbs. 223.7'07.AR6

*Bridges, Charles. *An Exposition of Proverbs.* Evansville, Ind.: Sovereign Grace Book Club, 1959.

First published in 1846, this work has become a classic of Protestantism. It is rich in thought, valued for its exposition, and provides valuable material for the preacher. 223.7'07.B76

*Greenstone, Julius Hillel. *The Holy Scripture with Commentary: Proverbs.* Philadelphia: Jewish Publication Society of America, 1950.

Another valuable work in this series. Jewish. 223.7'07.G85

Ironside, Henry Allan. *Notes on the Book of Proverbs.* New York: Loizeaux Brothers, n.d.

Still in print after sixty years of continuous circulation, this book provides perceptive comments and appropriate illustrations on each verse. Originally issued
in 1908. 223.7'07.IR6

Kidner, Derek. *The Proverbs.* Tyndale
Old Testament Commentary. London:
Inter-Varsity Press, 1964.

The introductory material is exceedingly helpful, but the textual treatment is
extremely brief. 223.7'07.K54

Toy, Crawford Howell. *A Critical and
Exegetical Commentary on the Book of Prov-
erbs.* International Critical Commentary.
Edinburgh: T. and T. Clark, 1959.

A critical work. First published in
1899. Too negative in its handling of the
text to be of real value to the preacher.
223.7'07.T66 1959

***Wardlaw, Ralph.** *Lectures on the Book
of Proverbs.* 3 vols. Edited by J. S. Wardlaw.
London: A. Fullerton and Company,
1861.

Contains some of the finest material
for preachers ever produced on this portion of God's Word. Rich, insightful,
practical. 223.7'07.W21

ECCLESIASTES

Barton, George Aaron. *A Critical and
Exegetical Commentary on the Book of Ecclesiastes.* International Critical Commentary. Edinburgh: T. and T. Clark, 1908.

A scholarly work in which 25 percent
of the space is devoted to introductory
matters. Rejects the Solomonic authorship and places the time of its composition at the beginning of the second century B.C. 223.8'07.B28

Bridges, Charles. *An Exposition of the
Book of Ecclesiastes.* London: Banner of
Truth Trust, 1960.

A series of sermons on each verse.
Deeply devotional, but manifesting a
weakness in the exposition of the succes-

sive stages of the biblical writer's thought.
223.8'07.B76

***Cox, Samuel.** *The Book of Ecclesiastes.*
The Expositor's Bible. New York: A. C.
Armstrong and Son, 1908.

A learned treatment by the former
editor of *The Expositor.* 223.8'07.C83

Erdman, William J. *Ecclesiastes: A
Study.* New York: Gospel Publishing
House, n.d.

Expounds the book of Ecclesiastes
from the viewpoint of the striving of the
natural man to find meaning and satisfaction in life. 223.8'07.ER2

Ginsburg, Christian David. *Choeleth
and Song of Songs.* New York: Ktav Publishing House, 1968.

In spite of the fact that the writer never
completed this work, and never had access to the materials from Ras Shamra,
he has left for posterity a scholarly book
that retains much of its original value
and interest. 223.8'07.G43

Ginsberg, Harold Louis. *Studies in
Koheleth.* New York: Jewish Theological
Seminary of America, 1950.

A work for the advanced student. Jewish. 223.8'06.G43

Gordis, Robert. *Koheleth: The Man and
His World: A Study of Ecclesiastes.* New
York: Bloch Publishing Co., 1955.

A scholarly though overly pessimistic
study that attempts to arrive at an outline
of the book based upon a detailed grammatical analysis. Jewish. 223.8'06.G65

***Hengstenberg, Ernst Wilhelm.** *Com-
mentary on Ecclesiastes.* Translated by
D. W. Simon. Grand Rapids: Kregel Publications, reprint.

A conservative exposition based upon
a thorough study of the original text.
223.8'07.H38

Jennings, Frederick Charles. *Old
Groans and New Songs.* New York: Loizeaux Brothers, 1946.

Rewarding devotional meditations

by a Plymouth Brethren writer.
223.8'07.J44

*Leupold, Herbert Carl.** *Exposition of Ecclesiastes.* Grand Rapids: Baker Book House, 1966.

An exceptional treatment based upon a careful exegesis of the text and revealing the emptiness of formalism and the discontent with life that follows attempts to solve its problems outside implicit faith and trust in God's providence. Originally printed in 1952. 223.8'07.L57 1966

*MacDonald, James Madison.** *The Book of Ecclesiastes Explained.* New York: M. W. Dodd, 1856.

Perhaps the finest work produced on Ecclesiastes in the nineteenth century. Clear, authoritative, reliable.
223.8'07.M14

*Wardlaw, Ralph.** *Exposition of Ecclesiastes.* Philadelphia: William S. Rentoul, 1868.

Expository sermons by one of Scotland's greatest preachers. Recommended.
223.8'07.W21

SONG OF SOLOMON

Burrowes, George. *A Commentary on the Song of Solomon.* London: Banner of Truth Trust, 1960.

A devotional exposition rather than a commentary. Does not consider the historic setting, does not deal with the two- or three-character theory, and applies the text directly to the church.
223.9'07.B94

Durham, James. *Clavis Cantici; or, An Exposition of the Song of Solomon.* Aberdeen: George and Robert King, 1840.

First published in 1668, Durham's work on Solomon's *Song* has been the standard devotional treatment for over two hundred years. Interprets each section in light of Christ's relationship with His church. 223.9'07.D93 1840

Gill, John. *An Exposition of the Book of Solomon's Song: Commonly Called Canticles.* Marshalltown, Delaware: National Foundation for Christian Education, reprint.

A full, devotional, typological exposition in which the writer stresses the relationship of Christ to the believer. Originally published in 1776. 223.9'07.G41

Gordis, Robert. *The Song of Songs: A Study, Modern Translation and Commentary.* New York: Jewish Theological Seminary of America, 1954.

Rejects the allegorical interpretation of Catholics and the theory of the Near Eastern ritual of the dying and reviving of a god, and interprets the Song as a collection of lyrics composed over a period of five centuries. 223.9'07.G65

*Ironside, Henry Allan.** *The Song of Solomon.* Neptune, N.J.: Loizeaux Brothers, 1833.

A warmly devotional work that, like other Brethren commentaries, approaches the Song from an allegorical and typological point of view. Adheres to the two-character theory. 223.9'07.IR6

LaBotz, Paul. *The Romance of the Ages.* Grand Rapids: Kregel Publications, 1965.

A strongly typological interpretation of the Song of Solomon. 223.9'07.L11

Miller, Andrew. *Meditations on the Song of Solomon.* London: G. Morrish, n.d.

A devotional treatment that interprets the Song as stressing a believer's relationship to Christ. 223.9'07.M61

Nee, Watchman [pseud.]. *Song of Songs.* Translated by Elizabeth K. Mei and Daniel Smith. Fort Washington, Penn.: Christian Literature Crusade, 1965.

Writing from prison in communist China, Nee discusses spiritual fellowship with the Lord in the hidden, secret recesses of the heart. Allegorical.
223.9'07.N28

Pouget, Guillaume and **Jean Guitton.** *The Canticle of Canticles.* Translated by Joseph F. Lilly. New York: Declan X. McMullen Co., 1946.

Building upon the three-character view, this work is helpful for its application of the text. The interpretation of this portion of Scripture is not to our liking.

223.9'07.P86

Taylor, James Hudson. *Union and Communion.* Chicago: Moody Press, n.d.

Thoughts on the relationship of Christ and His church based upon an allegorical interpretation of Solomon's Song. Devotional. First published in 1893. 223.9'07.T21

PROPHETIC BOOKS

Beecher, Willis Judson. *The Prophets and the Promise.* Grand Rapids: Baker Book House, 1963.

Stresses the unity of the Testaments, and attempts to work with Jewish motifs without a proper understanding of Jewish thought. Also attempts to understand Hebraic thought in terms of Grecian categories. First published in 1905. 224.06.B39 1963

Blackwood, Andrew Watterson. *Preaching from Prophetic Books.* New York: Abingdon Press, 1946.

Focuses on the preaching values in the prophetic writings rather than exegesis. 224.B56

Ellison, Henry Leopold. *Men Spake from God: Studies in the Hebrew Prophets.* Grand Rapids: Wm. B. Eerdmans Publishing Co., 1958.

A survey and an analysis of all the OT prophetic books, including Daniel and Lamentations. The general tenor is conservative, but the writer does make concessions to liberal higher criticism. 224'.06.EL5

_____. *The Prophets of Israel.* Grand Rapids: Wm. B. Eerdmans Publishing Co., 1969.

A concise, readable introduction to the life and writings of those prophets who ministered to the northern tribes, with emphasis on Amos and Hosea. Amillennial. 224'.06.EL5P

Ewald, Georg Heinrich August von. *Prophets of the Old Testament.* Translated by J. Frederick Smith. 5 vols. London: Williams and Norgate, 1881.

The main strength of this work lies in the use made of Arabic literature. Ewald criticizes the source-critical hypothesis, yet accepts a modified view of the development of the OT documents. Needs to be read with discernment. 224'.06.EW1

Kirkpatrick, Alexander Francis. *The Doctrine of the Prophets.* 3d ed. London: Macmillan and Co., 1932.

Comprises the Warburtonian Lectures for 1886-90. More conservative than W. Robertson Smith's *Religion of the Semites,* but manifests a rationalistic approach to the text. 224'.06.K63 1932

Leavell, Roland Quinche. *Prophetic Preaching Then and Now.* Grand Rapids: Baker Book House, 1963.

A discussion of seven different kinds of preaching that the writer feels exemplify the prophetic tradition. 224'.08.L48

Robinson, Henry Wheeler. *The Hebrew Prophets.* London: Lutterworth Press, 1948.

†Representative of early twentieth-century liberal scholarship. Pays considerable attention to the psychology of prophets. Of marginal value today. 224'.06.R54

Schultz, Samuel J. *The Prophets Speak: The Law of Love.* New York: Harper and Row, 1968.

An introduction to the mission, style, and background of the biblical prophets. 224'.06.SCH8

Yates, Kyle Monroe. *Preaching from the Prophets.* New York: Harper and Brothers, 1942.

Reminds preachers of the great preaching values of the OT. 224'.08.Y2

Yoder, Sanford Calvin. *He Gave Some Prophets: The Old Testament Prophets and Their Message.* Scottsdale, Penn.: Herald Press, 1964.

Commendable in the way it relates the teachings of the prophets and their messages to the moral issues of the present. 224'.06.Y7

*Young, Edward Joseph. *My Servants, the Prophets.* Grand Rapids: Wm. B. Eerdmans Publishing Co., 1952.

Combines fidelity to the Scriptures with the characteristic Reformed interpretation of the text. Includes the origin of the prophets, their relation to the theocracy, the difference between true and false prophets, and the prophets as the recipients of God's revelation. 224'.092.Y8

ISAIAH

*Alexander, Joseph Addinson. *Commentary on the Prophecies of Isaiah.* Grand Rapids: Zondervan Publishing House, 1962.

A verse-by-verse treatment based upon a comprehensive knowledge of Hebrew. Makes the writer's genuine scholarship and evangelical warmth available to a new generation of expositors. A classic. Amillennial. First published in 1846. 224.1'07.AL2 1962

*Allis, Oswald Thompson. *The Unity of Isaiah: A Study in Prophecy.* Philadelphia: Presbyterian and Reformed Publishing Co., 1950.

A valuable rebuttal to the deutero-Isaiah theory. 224.1'06.AL5

Archer, Gleason Leonard, Jr. *In the Shadow of the Cross.* Grand Rapids: Zondervan Publishing House, 1957.

An excellent evangelical exposition of Isaiah 53. 224.1'07.53.AR2

Boutflower, Charles. *The Book of Isaiah, Chapters 1-39.* London: SPCK, 1930.

Relies heavily upon archaeological material excavated in ancient Assyria. Provides valuable historical material highlighting chapters 1-39. 224.1'07.1—39.B66

*Brown, John. *The Sufferings and Glories of the Messiah.* Evansville, Ind.: Sovereign Grace Publishers, 1959.

This exposition of Isaiah 52:13—53:12 places in the hands of the busy pastor some of the finest expository material available today. Includes a study of Psalm 18. First published in 1852. 224.1'07.52:13—53:12.B81 1959

*Culver, Robert Duncan. *The Sufferings and Glory of the Lord's Righteous Servant.* Moline, Ill.: Christian Service Foundation, 1958.

An exposition of Isaiah 52:13—53:12. Contains a thought-provoking analysis and exposition of this key portion of holy Scripture. 224.1'07.52:13—53:12.C89

Driver, Samuel Rolles. *Isaiah: His Life and Times.* London: James Nisbet and Co., n.d.

†Helpful studies full of insights into the man and his times. First published in 1888. 224.1'092.D83

Erdman, Charles Rosenbury. *The Book of Isaiah: An Exposition.* Westwood, N.J.: Fleming H. Revell Co., 1954.

A valuable synopsis, with an adequate explanation of Isaiah's times and prophecies. 224.1'07.ER2

Engnell, Ivan. *The Call of Isaiah: An Exegetical and Comparative Study.* Uppsala: Uppsala Universitetes Arsskrift, 1949.

†A capable exegetical study of Isaiah 6. 224.1'07.6.EN3

Gray, George Buchanan and **Arthur S. Peake.** *A Critical and Exegetical Commentary on the Book of Isaiah.* International

Critical Commentary. 2 vols. New York: Charles Scribner's Sons, 1912.

†Worth consulting, but marred by liberal criticism and historical reconstruction. 224.1'07.G779

Ironside, Henry Allan. *Expository Notes on the Prophet Isaiah.* New York: Loizeaux Brothers, 1952.

Written in the language of the "man in the street." Expounds the moral and prophetic teaching of this prophecy. 224.1'07.IR6

Jennings, Frederick Charles. *Studies in Isaiah.* Neptune, N.J.: Loizeaux Brothers, 1966.

A study by a Plymouth Brethren writer. Surveys the entire scope of Isaiah's prophecies. First published in 1935. 223.1'07.J44 1966

*Kelly, William. *An Exposition of the Book of Isaiah.* 4th ed. London: C. A. Hammond, 1947.

A premillennial exposition based upon the RV. First published in 1896. An excellent treatment. 224.1'07.K28 1947

Knight, George Angus Fulton. *Deutero-Isaiah: A Theological Commentary on Isaiah 40-55.* New York: Abingdon Press, 1965.

†Purports to be a doctrinal commentary, but ends up as a translation of mixed quality with comments interspersed throughout the text. 224.1'07.40-55.K74

*Leupold, Herbert Carl. *Exposition of Isaiah.* 2 vols. Grand Rapids: Baker Book House, 1968-71.

Defends the unity of this prophecy, and furnishes a satisfying exposition. Amillennial. 224.1'07.L57

Martin, W. J. *The Dead Sea Scroll of Isaiah.* London: Westminster Chapel, 1954.

The G. Campbell Morgan Memorial Lectures for 1954. Defends the integrity of the scroll, and presents perceptive comments on the transmission and vari-

ants in the text. 224.1'04.M36

Morgan, George Campbell. *The Prophecy of Isaiah.* Analyzed Bible. 2 vols. London: Hodder and Stoughton, 1910.

One of the best works in this series. 224.1'07.M82

Neubauer, Adolf and **S. R. Driver.** *The Fifty-Third Chapter of Isaiah According to the Jewish Interpreters.* 2 vols. New York: Ktav Publishing House, 1968.

Rejects the interpretation that sees in this chapter a foreview of the sufferings of the Messiah. Covers a vast amount of material, and shows great ingenuity in sidestepping the obvious. 224.1'06.53.N39

North, Christopher Richard. *Isaiah 40-55, Introduction and Commentary.* Torch Bible Commentaries. New York: Harper and Brothers, 1952.

While denying inspiration, the writer attempts to provide a religious and theological commentary on the text. 224.1'07.40-55.N84

————. *The Second Isaiah.* Oxford: Clarendon Press, 1964.

Exhibits the writer's ability to handle critical and technical data. Fails to show any awareness of conservative views. The sections on *Heilsgeschichte,* the literary structure, and so on, hold little value for the pastor. 224.1'07.40-66.N84S

————. *The Suffering Servant in Deutero-Isaiah: A Historical and Critical Study.* Oxford: At the Clarendon Press, 1956.

†A standard, critical work. 224.1'06.N84

Orelli, Conrad von. *The Prophecies of Isaiah.* Edinburgh: T. and T. Clark, 1889.

Of value for its exegesis. See comments under the writer's *Old Testament Prophecy.* 224.1'07.OR3

Rosenbloom, Joseph R. *The Dead Sea Isaiah Scroll.* Grand Rapids: Wm. B. Eerdmans Publishing Co., 1970.

A consideration of the variance between the St. Mark's Isaiah Scroll and the MT. Provides a list of the variants with a consideration of parallel passages in the LXX, Peshitta, and the Targums. 224.1'04.R72

Sayce, Archibald Henry. *The Life and Times of Isaiah.* 3d ed. London: Religious Tract Society, 1896.

A brief study that relies heavily upon archaeological data then current and ties in the ministry of Isaiah with the records of Tiglath-Pileser, Sargon, and Sennacherib. Dated. 224.1'092.SA9 1896

Smith, George Adam. *The Book of Isaiah.* The Expositor's Bible. 2 vols. New York: A. C. Armstrong and Son, 1908.

†A brilliant and suggestive work. Needs to be read with discernment. 224.1'07.SM5

Vine, William Edwy. *Isaiah: Prophecies, Promises, Warning.* London: Oliphants Limited, 1953.

A devotional commentary. 224.1'07.V75

*Young, Edward Joseph. *The Book of Isaiah.* New International Commentary on the Old Testament. 3 vols. Grand Rapids: Wm. B. Eerdmans Publishing Co., 1965-72.

Has established itself as one of the most important Reformed expositions on the subject. Amillennial. 224.1'07.Y8

*_____. *Isaiah 53: A Devotional and Expository Study.* Grand Rapids: Wm. B. Eerdmans Publishing Co., 1952.

An informative, edifying study. 224.1.53.Y8

*_____. *Who Wrote Isaiah?* Grand Rapids: Wm. B. Eerdmans Publishing Co., 1958.

A vigorous apologetic for the unity of Isaiah's prophecy. 224.1'06.Y8

JEREMIAH AND LAMENTATIONS

*Bright, John. *The Anchor Bible:*
Jeremiah. Garden City: Doubleday and Co., 1965.

†A surprisingly conservative commentary in a predominantly liberal series. Contains an extensive introduction, a new translation, and critical notes. 224.2'07.B76

Cheyne, Thomas Kelly. *Jeremiah: His Life and Times.* London: James Nisbet and Co., 1888.

†Contains a considerable amount of valuable material. 224.2'092.C42

Erdman, Charles Rosenbury. *The Book of Jeremiah and Lamentations.* Westwood, N.J.: Fleming H. Revell Co., 1955.

A clear analysis of both books. 224.2'07.ER2

Gottwald, Norman Karol. *Studies in the Book of Lamentations.* Studies in Biblical Theology. Naperville, Ill.: Alec R. Allenson, 1962.

†Although textual questions are omitted and critical problems are confined to the introduction, the author studies the book as a link in the spiritual history of Judaism and Christianity. 224.3.G71

Ironside, Henry Allan. *Notes on the Prophecy and Lamentations of Jeremiah.* New York: Loizeaux Brothers, 1952.

Interprets the similies and metaphors, prophecies and predictions of Jeremiah. Particularly helpful for its thematic development of the content of these books. First published in 1906. 224.2'07.IR6 1952

*Jensen, Irving Lester. *Jeremiah: The Prophet of Judgment.* Chicago: Moody Press, 1966.

A valuable, elementary study. Ideal for study groups. 224.2'07.J45

*Laetsch, Theodore Ferdinand Karl. *Bible Commentary: Jeremiah.* St. Louis: Concordia Publishing House, 1952.

An adequate explanation of the indictment upon Judah for her corruption, immorality, materialism, idolatry, covetousness, and indifference. 224.2'07.L12

Leslie, Elmer Archibald. *Jeremiah: Chronologically Arranged, Translated, and Interpreted.* Nashville: Abingdon Press, 1954.

†A critical work of greater value for its general information than for its specific details. 224.2'06.L56

Morgan, George Campbell. *Studies in the Prophecy of Jeremiah.* London: Oliphants Press, 1963.

Expository messages by one of the great preachers of all time. Amillennial. 224.2'07.M82 1963

Orelli, Conrad von. *The Prophecies of Jeremiah.* Edinburgh: T. and T. Clark, 1889.

A moderately conservative, exegetical and expository work. See comments under *Old Testament Prophecy.* 224.2'07.OR3

Thomson, John G. S. S. *The Word of the Lord in Jeremiah.* London: Tyndale Press, 1959.

A thematic study. 224.2'06.T37

EZEKIEL

Blackwood, Andrew Watterson, Jr. *Ezekiel, Prophecy of Hope.* Grand Rapids: Baker Book House, 1965.

Consists of a series of expository sermons on the prophecy of Ezekiel. Amillennial. 224.4'07.B56E

————. *The Other Son of Man: Ezekiel/ Jesus.* Grand Rapids: Baker Book House, 1966.

An informative series of sermonettes on Ezekiel's prophecy. 224.4'08.B56

Cooke, George Albert. *A Critical and Exegetical Commentary on the Book of Ezekiel.* International Critical Commentary. Edinburgh: T. and T. Clark, 1936.

†Designed for advanced students of Hebrew. Contains a serious discussion of grammar and syntax. 224.4'07.C77

Eichrodt, Walther. *Ezekiel: A Commen-*

tary. Old Testament Library. Translated by Cosslett Quin. Philadelphia: Westminster Press, 1970.

†Frequently tampers with the text, passes over many verses with a paucity of exposition, and introduces lengthy critical speculation. Often relates incidents that took place in the history of Israel to heathen origin. Scholarly, but not for the casual reader. 224.4'07.EI2

Ellison, Henry Leopold. *Ezekiel: The Man and His Message.* Grand Rapids: Wm. B. Eerdmans Publishing Co., 1956.

Studies the important religious principles taught by Ezekiel, and evaluates his prophecies in the light of their local setting and the needs of the present day. Simplistic. 224.4'06.EL5

Fairbairn, Patrick. *An Exposition of Ezekiel.* Grand Rapids: Zondervan Publishing House, 1960.

Highlights the historical setting of the book. Of value to expositors. 224.4'07.F15

***Feinberg, Charles Lee.** *The Prophecy of Ezekiel.* Chicago: Moody Press, 1969.

Emphasizing the glory of the Lord, these premillennial studies explain Ezekiel's visions, elaborate upon his symbolic acts, and harmonize his predictions with other prophecies. The best work on the subject! 223.8'07.F32

Gaebelein, Arno Clemens. *The Prophet Ezekiel.* Philadelphia: Our Hope, 1918.

A concise exposition for those limited to the English text. Premillennial. 224.4'07.G11

Ironside, Henry Allan. *Expository Notes on Ezekiel the Prophet.* New York: Loizeaux Brothers, 1949.

Clear, concise, premillennial notes of expository value. 224.4'07.IR6

Rowley, Harold Henry. *The Book of Ezekiel in Modern Study.* Manchester: John Ryland's Library, 1953.

Critical essays of importance for their

survey of the commentaries written and the different positions held by people who have studied Ezekiel's prophecy. 224.4'06.R79

Taylor, John Bernard. *Ezekiel.* Tyndale Old Testament Commentary, Downers Grove, Ill.: Inter-Varsity Press, 1969.

†A handy volume, but one that must be read with discernment. 224'.4'07.T21

DANIEL

*Anderson, Robert. *The Coming Prince.* 14th ed. Grand Rapids: Kregel Publications, 1957.

Focuses upon Daniel's prophecy of the seventy weeks, and traces its chronological development through to the time when Messiah was "cut off" at the end of the sixty-ninth week. Provides reconstruction of the chronology, and deals with the times of the Gentiles, the tribulation period, and the second advent of Christ. 224.5'07.9:24-27.AN2 1957

*_____. *Daniel in the Critic's Den.* London: James Nisbet and Co., 1902.

A scholarly reply to and refutation of Driver's treatise on Daniel. 224.5'06.AN2

Auberlen, Karl August. *The Prophecies of Daniel and the Revelations of St. John, Viewed in Their Mutual Relation.* Translated by Adolph Saphir. Edinburgh: T. and T. Clark, 1856.

An informative study by a distinguished Swiss theologian. 224.5'07.AU1

Boutflower, Charles. *In and Around the Book of Daniel.* Grand Rapids: Zondervan Publishing House, 1963.

Contains excellent historical material. A valuable acquisition. 224.5'09.B66 1963

*Criswell, Wallie Amos. *Expository Sermons on the Book of Daniel.* In process. Grand Rapids: Zondervan Publishing House, 1971-.

A series of expository messages that draws upon history, philology, and archaeology as it unfolds the meaning and message of Daniel's prophecy. Premillennial. 224.5'07.C86

*Culver, Robert Duncan. *Daniel and the Latter Days.* Chicago: Moody Press, 1954.

A scholarly and well-documented premillennial approach to the book of Daniel. 224.5'08.C89

DeHaan, Martin Ralph. *Daniel—The Prophet.* Grand Rapids: Zondervan Publishing House, 1967.

A premillennial exposition by a renowned Bible class teacher. 224.5'07.D36

Dougherty, Raymond Philip. *Nabonidus and Belshazzar: A Study of the Closing Events of the Neo-Babylonian Empire.* New Haven: Yale University Press, 1929.

A valuable reconstruction of events that proves conclusively the coregency of these kings and verifies the historical reliability of Daniel. 224.5'092.D74

*Gaebelein, Arno Clemens. *The Prophet Daniel.* Grand Rapids: Kregel Publications, 1955.

A chapter-by-chapter treatment of the visions and prophecies of Daniel. Presents the essence of the predictive ministry of the prophet, and expounds the prophecy in an enlightening and helpful way from the premillennial perspective. 224.5'07.G11

Hieronymus. *Commentary on Daniel.* Translated by Gleason L. Archer, Jr. Grand Rapids: Baker Book House, 1958.

This work by Jerome, a famous church Father, has been highly esteemed by Bible students through the centuries. This translation places the work within reach of every student. 224.5'07.J48

Ironside, Henry Allan. *Lectures on Daniel the Prophet.* New York: Loizeaux Brothers, 1953.

A premillennial work in the tradition of William Kelly, Robert Anderson, and A. C. Gaebelein. A capable treatment. First published in 1911. 224.5'07.IR6 1953

King, Geoffrey R. *Daniel.* Grand Rapids: Wm. B. Eerdmans Publishing Co., 1966.

Originally published in a British journal called the *Midnight Cry,* these studies are thoroughly researched and will appeal to students of prophecy. 224.5'07.K58

Kirk, Thomas. *Daniel the Prophet.* Edinburgh: Andrew Elliot, 1906.

Expository sermons abounding in practical application and ably countering Driver's higher critical theories. 224.5'07.K63

***Lang, George Henry.** The Histories and Prophecies of Daniel.* 4th ed. London: Paternoster Press, 1950.

Based primarily upon the RV, this premillennial, posttribulation work, by a leading Plymouth Brethren writer, combines extensive research with a comprehensive view of the prophetic Scriptures. 224.5'07.L25 1950

***Leupold, Herbert Carl.** Exposition of Daniel.* Minneapolis: Augsburg Publishing Co., 1961.

A scholarly work from a conservative amillennial viewpoint. Of particular value for its exegetical treatment of the text. 224.5'07.L57

Luck, G. Coleman. *Daniel.* Chicago: Moody Press, 1958.

A clear, concise introduction to the authorship, date, language, and purpose of the book, followed by a clear, thorough explanation of the biblical text. Premillennial. 224.5'07.L96

***McClain, Alva J.** Daniel's Prophecy of the Seventy Weeks.* 7th ed. Grand Rapids: Zondervan Publishing House, 1940.

A popular presentation of the material contained in Robert Anderson's *The Coming Prince.* Helpful for its explanation of

Daniel 9:24-27. 224.5'07.M12.9:24-27 1940

Montgomery, James Alan. *A Critical and Exegetical Commentary on the Book of Daniel.* International Critical Commentary. Edinburgh: T. and T. Clark, 1927.

†Of value for its exegesis, but pastors should be aware of the marked negativism of this work. 224.5'07.M76

Porteous, Norman W. *Daniel, A Commentary.* Philadelphia: Westminster Press, 1965.

†Starts from the premise that Daniel borrows from ancient myths, prophecy, psalms, and wisdom literature. Expounds it as history, not prophecy, and thereby robs it of its unique place in apocalyptic literature. 224.5'07.P83

Pusey, Edward Borverie. *Daniel the Prophet.* Oxford: James Parker, 1869.

An extensive, scholarly treatment. Ably defends the authorship and integrity of Daniel's prophecy. Amillennial. 224.5'06.P97

Stevens, W. C. *The Book of Daniel: A Composite Revelation of the Last Days of Israel's Subjugation to Gentile Powers.* Los Angeles: Bible House of Los Angeles, 1949.

An exposition that traces the times of the Gentiles from 606 B.C. to the end of the age. Premillennial. 224.5'07.ST3

***Strauss, Lehman.** The Prophecies of Daniel.* Neptune, N.J.: Loizeaux Brothers, 1969.

Expository messages on Daniel's prophecy. Thoroughly researched, premillennial, evangelical. 224.5'07.ST8

Tregelles, Samuel Prideaux. *Remarks on the Prophetic Visions in the Book of Daniel.* 7th ed. London: Sovereign Grace Advent Testimony, 1965.

A premillennial work based upon a thorough knowledge of the original text. Contains some exceptional material. First published in 1847. 224.4'07.T71 1965

***Walvoord, John Flipse.** Daniel: The*

Key to Prophetic Revelation. Chicago: Moody Press, 1971.

Fully abreast of the latest archaeological material. Emphasizes the genuineness of the prophet and his writings, and provides a clear interpretation of the book. Thorough, well outlined, and well documented. Premillennial. 224.5'07.W17

*Whitcomb, John Clement, Jr. *Darius the Mede: A Study in Historical Identification.* Grand Rapids: Wm. B. Eerdmans Publishing Co., 1959.

A brilliant study that ably blends archaeological discoveries and historical data into a most thought-provoking work. 224.5'06.W58

Young, Edward Joseph. *Daniel's Vision of the Son of Man.* London: Tyndale Press, 1958.

An amillennial study of messianic interpretation. 224.5'06.Y8

*_____. *The Prophecy of Daniel: A Commentary.* Grand Rapids: Wm. B. Eerdmans Publishing Co., 1949.

A painstaking exegetical exposition. Amillennial. 224.5'07.Y8

MINOR PROPHETS

Farrar, Fredric William. *The Minor Prophets.* London: Francis Griffiths, 1907.

Historical studies on the lives and times of the Minor Prophets. Not as reliable as Farrar's other works. Amillennial. 224.6'07.F24

*Feinberg, Charles Lee. *Major Messages of the Minor Prophets.* 5 vols. New York: American Board of Missions to the Jews. 1947-52.

Valuable studies by a leading Hebrew Christian scholar. Premillennial. 224.6'07.F32

*Gaebelein, Frank Ely. *Four Minor Prophets.* Chicago: Moody Press, 1970.

Devotional expositions of Obadiah, Jonah, Habakkuk, and Haggai. Stress is on the relevancy of their message for today. 224.6'07.G11

*Ironside, Henry Allan. *Notes on the Minor Prophets.* New York: Loizeaux Brothers, 1909.

Studies by a leading premillennial Bible student in which the scope of each prophecy is related to the total program of God for the ages. 224.6'07.IR6

Kelly, William. *Lectures Introductory to the Study of the Minor Prophets.* London: C. A. Hammond Trust Bible Depot, reprint.

Has been used continuously by premillennial Bible teachers since its original publication in 1874. 224.6'07.K29

*Laetsch, Theodore Ferdinand Karl. *The Minor Prophets.* St. Louis: Concordia Publishing House, 1956.

Valuable devotional studies with exegetical notes, historical data, and helpful exposition. Amillennial. 224.6'07.L12

Orelli, Conrad von. *The Twelve Minor Prophets.* Edinburgh: T. and T. Clark, 1893.

A most valuable study by a moderately conservative German theologian. 224.6'07.OR3

*Pusey, Edward Bouverie. *The Minor Prophets: A Commentary, Explanatory and Practical.* 2 vols. Grand Rapids: Baker Book House, 1961.

An extensive and exhaustive study of the Minor Prophets containing homiletical material, historical information, and a scholarly, practical commentary. Amillennial. First published in 1860. 224.6'07.P97 1961

Robinson, George Livingstone. *The Twelve Minor Prophets.* Grand Rapids: Baker Book House, 1952.

A helpful introductory textbook that, despite its brevity, has stood the test of time. First published in 1926. 224.6'07.R56 1952

Smith, George Adam. *The Book of the Twelve Prophets.* Expositor's Bible. 2 vols.

New York: A. C. Armstrong and Son, 1908.

†A scholarly, critical study. See Smith, *The Book of Isaiah*. 224.6'07.SM5

HOSEA

Feinberg, Charles Lee. *Hosea: God's Love for Israel*. Major Messages on the Minor Prophets. New York: American Board of Missions to the Jews, 1947.

An evangelical commentary emphasizing Israel's sin and idolatry, and God's call to repentance and assurance of future glory. 224.6'07.F32 v. 1

Hubbard, David Allan. *With Bands of Love: Lessons from the Book of Hosea*. Grand Rapids: Wm. B. Eerdmans Publishing Co., 1968.

Adapted from material given at the Conservative Baptist Seminary, Denver, and to a Bible study class in Pasadena, these devotional messages stress the main lessons of the book of Hosea. 224.7'07.H86

Knight, George Angus Fulton. *Hosea: Introduction and Commentary*. Torch Bible Commentaries. London: SCM Press, 1960.

†A clear, concise introduction, with moderately conservative comments on the text. 224.7'07.K74

Logsdon, S. Franklin. *Hosea: People Who Forgot God*. Chicago: Moody Press, 1959.

A brief, helpful exposition. Devotional. 224.7'07.L82

Mays, James Luther. *Hosea, A Commentary*. Old Testament Library. Philadelphia: Westminster Press, 1969.

This critical study is one of the better works in this series. 224.7'07.M45

Morgan, George Campbell. *Hosea: The Heart and Holiness of God*. Westwood, N.J.: Fleming H. Revell Co., 1934.

Frequently regarded as one of Morgan's finest expository studies. Amillennial. 224.7'07.M82

Snaith, Norman Henry. *Mercy and Sacrifice: A Study of the Book of Hosea*. London: SCM Press, 1953.

†Stands in the tradition of this writer's other works. Surveys the distinctive ideas of mercy and sacrifice in the OT, and uses the book of Hosea as a springboard for these word studies. 224.7'06.SN1

JOEL

Di Gangi, Mariano. *The Book of Joel*. Grand Rapids: Baker Book House, 1970.

A brief, handy study manual. Of value to laymen. 224.8'07.D56

Driver, Samuel Rolles. *The Books of Joel and Amos*. Cambridge Bible for Schools and Colleges. Cambridge: At the University Press, 1897.

Based upon the RV, these brief studies attempt to illuminate the English text with pertinent archaeological and philological information. Dated. 224.8'07.D83

Feinberg, Charles Lee. *Amos: The Righteousness of God*. Major Messages of the Minor Prophets. New York: American Board of Missions to the Jews, 1948.

A clear study of the Day of the Lord, the outpouring of the Spirit, and the judgment of all nations. 224.6'07.F32 v. 2

Kapelrud, Arvid Schou. *Joel Studies*. Uppsala: Lundquistska, 1948.

A scholarly study. 224.8'06.K14

AMOS

Cripps, Richard Stafford. *A Critical and Exegetical Commentary on the Book of Amos*. London: SPCK, 1969.

First published in 1929, this work was thoroughly revised in 1955. Not abreast of the latest archaeological material. The exposition, however, is very full. 224.9'07.C86 1969

Harper, William Rainey. *A Critical and Exegetical Commentary on Amos and Hosea*. International Critical Commentary.

Edinburgh: T. and T. Clark, 1905.

†Valuable for its textual analysis and discussion of the traditional views of these prophecies, but of limited value to the preacher who is interested in getting to the heart of a passage. 224.9'07.H23

Honeycutt, Roy Lee. *Amos and His Message.* Nashville: Broadman Press, 1963.

Provides a well-written, interpretative analysis of this prophecy. 224.9'07.H75

***Howard, James Keir.** *Amos Among the Prophets.* Grand Rapids: Baker Book House, 1967.

After carefully analyzing the two main sections of the prophecy, the author discusses the "reformation movement" and interprets the prophecy both in relation to its historical background, and also in terms of its abiding principles of conduct. 224.9'07.H83

Kelley, Page H. *The Book of Amos.* Grand Rapids: Baker Book House, 1966.

An inductive study. 224.9'07.K29

Kapelrud, Arvid Schou. *Central Ideas in Amos.* Oslo, Norway: Aschenhoug, 1971.

A valuable introductory study to the meaning and message of this prophecy. 224.9'06.K14

***Mays, James Luther.** *Amos: A Commentary.* Old Testament Library. Philadelphia: Westminster Press, 1969.

Building upon the historical setting, expounds the contents and form of the book. A capable treatment. 224.9'07.M45

OBADIAH

Hillis, Don W. *The Book of Obadiah.* Grand Rapids: Baker Book House, 1968.

Studies based upon the English text. Will serve to introduce the layman to this particular prophecy. 224.91'07.H55

Watts, John D. W. *Obadiah: A Critical, Exegetical Commentary.* Grand Rapids: Wm. B. Eerdmans Publishing Co., 1969.

A brief, scholarly treatment. 224.91'07.W34

JONAH

Aalders, G. Ch. *The Problem of the Book of Jonah.* London: Tyndale Press, 1948.

A conservative approach. 224.92'06.AA4

***Banks, William L.** *Jonah: The Reluctant Prophet.* Chicago: Moody Press, 1966.

A helpful exposition that admirably blends historic data with Hebrew word studies and a devotional emphasis. 224.92'07.B22

***Fairbairn, Patrick.** *Jonah: His Life, Character, and Mission.* Grand Rapids: Kregel Publications, 1964.

First published over 120 years ago and since then regarded as one of the ablest expository treatments available. 224.92'07.F15 1964

***Feinberg, Charles Lee.** *Jonah: God's Love for All Nations.* The Major Messages of the Minor Prophets. New York: American Board of Missions to the Jews, 1951.

A brief but valuable exposition of the theme of this book. 224.6'07.F32 v. 3

***Martin, Hugh.** *The Prophet Jonah: His Character and Mission to Nineveh.* London: Banner of Truth Trust, 1958.

By one of the outstanding ministers in the Scottish galaxy in the middle half of the nineteenth century. Spurgeon said, "No one who has it will need any other." Reprint of the 1877 edition. 224.92'07.M36 1958

MICAH

Bennett, T. Miles. *The Book of Micah.* Grand Rapids: Baker Book House, 1968.

Included in the exposition of the text are numerous seed thoughts for sermons. 224.93'07.B43

***Feinberg, Charles Lee.** *Micah: Wrath upon Samaria and Jerusalem.* The Major Messages of the Minor Prophets. New

The Minister's Library

York: American Board of Missions to the Jews, 1951.

Shows that this prophecy contains some of the severest pronouncements of judgment upon guilty people, together with some informative portraits of Christ and His kingdom. 224.6'07.F32 v. 3

NAHUM

Bennett, T. Miles. *Books of Nahum and Zephaniah.* Grand Rapids: Baker Book House, 1968.

Contains an excellent treatment of the historical sections of these books. Amillennial. 224.94'07.B43

Driver, Samuel Rolles. *The Minor Prophets: Nahum, Habakkuk, Zephaniah, Haggai, Zechariah, Malachi.* The Century Bible. Edinburgh: T. C. and E. C. Jack, 1906.

†An explanation of these prophetic writings that is not overly critical, but builds upon the higher critical data current at the turn of the century. 224.95'07.D83

*Feinberg, Charles Lee. *Nahum: Judgment on Nineveh.* The Major Messages of the Minor Prophets. New York: American Board of Missions to the Jews, 1951.

A brief, descriptive study of the judgment of God on Nineveh. 224.6'07.F32 v. 3

*Maier, Walter A. *The Book of Nahum.* St. Louis: Concordia Publishing House, 1959.

A lengthy, critical commentary in which every word of each verse is evaluated and expounded in the light of the theme of the book. A valuable study. 224.94'07.M28

HABAKKUK

*Feinberg, Charles Lee. *Habakkuk: Problems of Faith.* The Major Messages of the Minor Prophets. New York: American Board of Missions to the Jews, 1951.

An exposition highlighting the age-old problem of why the innocent suffer, and pointing to the solution in the assurance of faith. 224.6'07.F32 v. 4

*Lloyd-Jones, David Martyn. *From Fear to Faith.* London: Inter-Varsity Fellowship, 1964.

Expository studies in the book of Habakkuk. 224.95'07.L77

ZEPHANIAH

*Feinberg, Charles Lee. *Zephaniah: The Day of the Lord.* The Major Messages of the Minor Prophets. New York: American Board of Missions to the Jews, 1951.

A portrayal of the Day of the Lord and the relationship of this prophecy to the tribulation period. 224.6'07.F32 v. 4

HAGGAI

*Feinberg, Charles Lee. *Haggai: Rebuilding the Temple.* The Major Messages of the Minor Prophets. New York: American Board of Missions to the Jews, 1951.

Emphasizes the historic events that gave rise to Haggai's ministry, and draws parallels to conditions prevailing at the present time. 224.6'07.F32 v. 4

Moore, Thomas V. *A Commentary on Haggai and Malachi.* London: Banner of Truth Trust, 1960.

Studies that are loyal to the text, endear themselves to the reader, and edify and enrich the soul. Reformed. 224.97'07.M78

Wolff, Richard. *The Book of Haggai.* Grand Rapids: Baker Book House, 1967.

A plain and practical study guide that should be used by all who have not studied this prophecy before. 224.97'07.W83

ZECHARIAH

*Baron, David. *The Visions and Prophecies of Zechariah.* Fincastle, Va.: Scripture

Truth Book Co., 1962.

First published in 1918. Provides a helpful elucidation of the messianic prophecies contained in this book. 224.98'07.B26 1962

Feinberg, Charles Lee. *God Remembers.* Wheaton, Ill.: Van Kampen Press, 1950.

A valuable study expounding in depth and detail the amazing prophecy of Zechariah. 224.98'07.F32

*Leupold, Herbert Carl. *Exposition of Zechariah.* Grand Rapids: Baker Book House, 1970.

Provides a serious, technical study of the prophetic predictions of Zechariah from an amillennial viewpoint. Very helpful. Originally published in 1956. 224.98'07.L57 1970

Luck, G. Coleman. *Zechariah.* Chicago: Moody Press, 1957.

A study of the prophetic visions of Zechariah from a premillennial viewpoint. Ideal for group use. 224.98'07.L96

Meyer, Frederick Brotherton. *The Prophet of Hope: Studies in Zechariah.* London: Marshall, Morgan and Scott, 1952.

Typological and devotional studies. Premillennial. 224.98'07.M57

Moore, Thomas Verner. *A Commentary on Zechariah.* London: Banner of Truth Trust, 1958.

A devotional commentary. Reformed. 224.98'07.M78

*Unger, Merrill Frederick. *Zechariah: Prophet of Messiah's Glory.* Grand Rapids: Zondervan Publishing House, 1963.

A valuable exposition based upon the original text. 224.98'07.UN3

MALACHI

*Feinberg, Charles Lee. *Malachi: Formal Worship.* The Major Messages of the Minor Prophets. New York: American Board of Missions to the Jews, 1951.

A forthright study denouncing formalism and heartlessness in worship. 224.6'07.F32 v. 4

Logsdon, S. Franklin. *Malachi: Will a Man Rob God?* Chicago: Moody Press, 1961.

A brief, helpful exposition. Devotional. 224.99'07.L82

*Morgan, George Campbell. *Wherein Have We Robbed God?* New York: Fleming H. Revell Co., 1898.

Messages on the prophecy of Malachi that contain pertinent truths still true of society today. 224.99'07.M82

6

New Testament

Most of our preaching centers in the New Testament. This is also the area in which the greatest number of works are available. With such an abundance from which to choose, it will *not* be hard for you to obtain the best books on any given subject. Of course, there is always the problem of finances. You cannot afford to buy all these books. However, you can buy a few of the most important ones (e.g., Erdman, Hendriksen, Lenski, Lightfoot, Westcott, Hodge, Bruce, Morris, etc.) and obtain others whenever you preach or teach on a particular book or subject.

A friend of mine who now pastors a large church in the East plans his buying of books around his preaching schedule. If, for example, he is to preach a series of sermons on Paul's epistle to the Ephesians, he buys five or six of the best books on Ephesians. He is careful to select different kinds of books and includes one or two that deal with exegesis (e.g., J. A. Robinson, B. F. Westcott), one or two good expositions (e.g., H. C. G. Moule and W. Hendriksen, or F. Foulkes and C. Hodge), and then one or two devotional works such as Ruth Paxson's *Wealth, Walk and Warfare of the Christian,* Lehman Strauss's *Devotional Studies in Galatians and Ephesians,* or Watchman Nee's *Sit, Walk, Stand.* In this way he avoids the dual dangers of superficiality and over-technicality.

This method of judicious buying builds a library without extravagance, and it gears one's purchases to the preaching and teaching needs and ministry of the individual pastor. It possesses the additional characteristic of balance and leads to a well-rounded ministry.

The suggestions of books follow essentially the same sequence begun in the two previous chapters. The library of a Bible college or seminary in your area can readily supplement what you may lack in your own library, and most librarians are happy to extend their services to men in the ministry.

RESOURCE TOOLS

New Testament Abstracts. Edited by George W. MacRae and Simon E. Smith. Weston, Mass.: Weston College, 1956-.

Published three times a year. A resource tool that is arranged alphabetically by subject, has numbered entries, and contains abstracts and critical reviews of scholarly articles and papers published in Catholic, Jewish, and Protestant periodicals. An index in each volume. 225.05.N42

ORIGIN AND AUTHENTICITY

Bruce, Frederick Fyvie. *The New Testament Documents.* 5th rev. ed. Downers Grove, Ill.: Inter-Varsity Fellowship, 1966.

Deals with the reliability of the NT documents. Evaluates the canon, the reliability of gospel miracles, the importance of Luke's writings, the role of archaeological evidence, and the importance of early Jewish and Gentile writers. 225.1.B83 1966

_____. *The Books and the Parchments; Some Chapters on the Transmission of the Bible.* 3d ed. Westwood. N.J.: Fleming H. Revell, 1963.

Of great help in understanding the history and transmission of the documents of the NT. Fully abreast of all the latest discoveries and trends in NT criticism. 225.4B 1963

Grant, Robert McQueen. *The Formation of the New Testament.* New York: Harper and Row, 1965.

Studies based upon Christian and Gnostic sources alike. Elaborates upon the development of the NT canon. 225.12.G76

Martin, James. *Origin and History of the New Testament.* 5th ed. London: Hodder and Stoughton, 1884.

A balanced study of the NT canon. Now dated. 225.12.M36 1884

Montgomery, John Warwick. *History and Christianity.* Downers Grove, Ill.: Inter-Varsity Press, 1971.

A helpful apologetic for the historical reliability of the gospels. 226.1'67.M84

Ribberbos, Herman Nicholas. *The Authority of the New Testament Scriptures.* Translated by H. De Jongste. Philadelphia: Presbyterian and Reformed Publishing Co., 1963.

A scholarly study that stops short of affirming the inspiration of the original autographs. 225.12.R43

Souter, Alexander. *The Text and Canon of the New Testament.* 2d ed. Revised by C. S. C. Williams. London: Gerald Duckworth, 1954.

†An approach to many of the recent developments in NT scholarship, with an appraisal of manuscripts discovered in recent years and an evaluation of those manuscripts that have recently been regrouped in the light of current development and research. 225.12.SO8 1954

*Westcott, Brooke Foss. *A General Survey of the History of the Canon of the New Testament.* 7th ed. London: Macmillan Co., 1896.

Many aspects of this work are still foundational in a study of the canon of the NT. Worthy of study by all seminarians. 225.12.W52 1896

GREEK LEXICONS AND GRAMMARS

Abbott-Smith, George. *Manual Greek Lexicon of the New Testament.* 3d ed. New York: Charles Scribner's Sons, n.d.

A handy lexicon that is easy to keep on the desk, fairly up-to-date, and contains helpful appendices. 487.3.AB2

*Arndt, William Frederick and **F. Wilbur Gingrich.** *Greek-English Lexicon of the New Testament.* 4th rev. ed. Chicago: University of Chicago Press, 1957.

A translation and adaptation of Walter Bauer's *Griechisch-Deutsches Wörterbuch zu den Schriften des Neuen Testaments und der ubrigen urchistlichen Literatur.* Has now replaced all previous English lexicons on the NT. 487.3.AR6 1957

*Blass, Friedrich William and **A. de Brunner.** *Greek Grammar of the New Testament and Other Early Christian Literature.* Translated and revised by Robert W. Funk. Chicago: University of Chicago Press, 1961.

The finest grammar for advanced students of NT Greek. 487.3.B61 1961

Blackwelder, Boice W. *Light from the Greek New Testament.* Anderson, Ind.: Warner Press, 1958.

An old work containing numerous insights into the Greek texts. 487.35.B56

Bullinger, Ethelbert William. *A Critical Lexicon and Concordance to the English and Greek New Testament.* London: Lamp Press, 1957.

First published in 1908. Has been eclipsed by Arndt and Gingrich. 487.3.G43 1957

Burton, Ernest DeWitt. *Syntax of the Moods and Tenses in the New Testament Greek.* 3d ed. Edinburgh: T. and T. Clark, 1965.

While Moule's *Idiom-book of New Testament Greek* has tended to replace this work, Burton's treatment of direct and indirect discourse remains one of the best. 487.5.B95 1965

Cremer, Heinrich. *Biblico-Theological Lexicon of New Testament Greek.* 3d English ed. Edinburgh: T. and T. Clark, 1880.

Brings extrabiblical usage of Greek words to bear upon biblical terms and demonstrates their biblical meaning. A valuable predecessor to Kittle's *Theological Dictionary of the New Testament.* 487.2.C86 1880

*Dana, Harvey Eugene and **Julius R. Mantey.** *A Manual Grammar of the Greek New Testament.* New York: Macmillan and Co., 1957.

An intermediate grammar for students of the NT. 487.5.D19

Dennison, J. D. *The Greek Particles.* 2d ed. Oxford: At the Clarendon Press, 1959.

A very complete work. Seeks to prove that the theology of the NT is based upon the Greek particles. A very thorough, complete study. 487.5.D42 1959

Gingrich, Felix Wilbur. *Shorter Lexicon of the Greek New Testament.* Chicago: University of Chicago Press, 1965.

An abridgment of the famous Arndt and Gingrich *Greek-English Lexicon of the New Testament,* which was published in 1957. 487.3.G43

Greek-English Lexicon of the New Testament. Translated and edited by Joseph Henry Thayer. Grand Rapids: Zondervan Publishing House, 1962.

A translation of *Clavis Novi Testamenti.* Replaced by other, more recent lexicons, but still worth consulting for its word studies. 487.3.T33 1962

Greenlee, J. Harold. *A Concise Exegetical Grammar of the New Testament Greek.* Grand Rapids: Wm. B. Eerdmans Publishing Co., 1963.

An elementary introduction to the principles of NT grammar. 487.5.G84

*Hatch, Edwin and Henry A. Redpath. *Concordance to the Septuagint.* 2 vols. Graz, Austria: Akademische Druk-U. Verlagsanstant, 1954.

Indispensable for Greek word studies. Enables the student to trace the usage of NT words in the OT and Apocrypha. 487.3.H28

Jay, Eric George. *New Testament Greek.* London: SPCK, 1965.

An excellent introductory grammar designed to lessen the trauma of the first year of Greek. 487.5.J33

*Liddell, Henry George and Robert Scott. *Greek-English Lexicon.* New ed. Revised by Henry Stuart Jones. Oxford: At the Clarendon Press, 1966.

Often referred to as "the last word in Greek lexicography." Supplies students of the NT with information about the usage of Greek words in classical and koinē literature, and includes information from the classics, papyri, and so on. Brought up-to-date with a *Supplement* prepared by E. A. Barber (1968). 483'.3.L61 1966

Metzger, Bruce Manning. *Lexical Aids for Students of New Testament Greek.* New ed. Princeton: Theological Book Agency, 1970.

Designed to facilitate the memorization of Greek vocabulary. Its arrangement according to frequency of use makes it particularly helpful. 487.32.M56 1970

Morrison, Clinton and David H. Barnes, eds. *New Testament Word Lists.* Grand Rapids: Wm. B. Eerdmans Publishing Co., 1964.

A list of words aimed at helping students read through the NT with greater rapidity. 487.32.M83

*Moule, Charles Francis Digby. *Idiom-Book of New Testament Greek.* 2d ed. Cambridge: At the University Press, 1963.

A valuable book on the syntax of the NT, with an up-to-date treatment of the idioms. An important supplement to Moulton's *Grammar of the New Testament Greek.* 487.5.M86 1963

*Moulton, James Hope, W. F. Howard and N. Turner. *Grammar of the New Testament Greek.* 3 vols. Edinburgh: T. and T. Clark. 1908-63.

An extremely worthwhile study: vol. I on *Prologomena* written by Moulton; vol. II by Howard covers *Accidence;* and vol. III on *Syntax* written by Turner. Indispensable. 487.5.M86

*Moulton, William Fidian and A. S. Geden. *Concordance to the Greek Testament.* 4th ed. Revised by H. K. Moulton: Edinburgh: T. and T. Clark, 1963.

The best concordance on the Greek text of Westcott and Hort. 487.3.M86 1963

———— and George Milligan. *The Vocabulary of the Greek Testament.* Grand Rapids: Wm. B. Eerdmans Publishing Co., n.d.

An old but invaluable volume on the contribution of the papyri to NT study. For the advanced student. 487.3.M86

*Robertson, Archibald Thomas. *Grammar of the Greek New Testament in the Light of Historical Research.* Nashville: Broadman Press, 1934.

Very full and complete. Covers the history of Greek grammar, accidence, and syntax. 487.5.R54

Summers, Ray. *Essentials of New Testament Greek.* Nashville: Broadman Press, 1950.

Well organized and ideally suited for review purposes. Not intended to serve as a beginning grammar. Widely used in seminaries. 487.5.SU6

Thackeray, Henry St. John. *A Grammar of the Old Testament in Greek.* Cambridge: At the University Press, 1909.

An extremely helpful work on the grammar of the LXX. The proposed volume on syntax was never published. Excellent material on orthography, phonology, and morphology makes this a valuable OT grammar. 221.48.T32

Theological Dictionary of the New Testament. Edited by Gerhard Kittel. Translated and edited by Geoffry W. Bromiley. In process. Grand Rapids: Wm. B. Eerdmans Publishing Co., 1964-.

†The pioneer work of Cremer is greatly enlarged in this monumental theologial dictionary. Since the death of Kittel, the work has been carried on by G. Friedrich. Scheduled for nine volumes, volumes 1-8 are presently available in English. The words selected are studied historically with respect to several areas of investigation: the OT, rabbinic Judaism, the LXX, classical and Hellenistic usage, and the word as it is used in the NT. The writers follow the *Heilsgeschichte* concept and are influenced by the existentialist school of NT interpretation. 487.2.K65

Trench, Richard Chenevix. *Synonyms of the New Testament.* Grand Rapids: Wm. B. Eerdmans Publishing Co., 1953.

A reprint of the 9th edition published in London in 1880. Will assist the student of the Word to distinguish between the different shades of meaning of similar NT Greek words. 487.2.T72 1953

Turner, Nigel. *Grammatical Insights into the New Testament.* Edinburgh: T. and T. Clark, 1965.

Focuses on the many aspects in which a knowledge of Greek grammar and syntax illuminates and enhances the significance of the biblical text. While the theology is questionable in many places, this work does contain helpful preaching values. 487.5.T85

Vine, William Edwy. *Expository Dictionary of the New Testament Words.* London: Oliphants, 1963.

A useful work for those who lack a knowledge of Greek. Arranged with the English word at the top of each section and the Greek words with their precise meaning and cognate forms underneath. Of great value to Bible students who work solely from the AV or some other English translation. Shows the rich nuances of thought inherent in the Greek words, emphasizes their doctrinal importance, and includes material from the papyri. 487.3.V75 1963

[Wigram, G. W.] *The Englishman's Greek Concordance of the New Testament.* 9th ed. London: Samuel Baxter and Sons, n.d.

A helpful work for those who lack a knowledge of Greek. 487.3.EN3

GOSPELS AND ACTS

Barclay, William. *The First Three Gospels.* London: SCM Press, 1966.

†A presentation of the critical views of the origin of the synoptic gospels. 226'.061.B23

Beasley-Murray, George Raymond. *Preaching the Gospel from the Gospels.* Valley Forge, Penn.: Judson Press, 1956.

A widely read treatise by a British Baptist theologian. 226'.08.B38

Black, Matthew. *An Aramaic Approach to the Gospels and Acts.* Oxford: At the University Press, 1954.

Serves as a valuable corrective of those who see Hellenizing or Hellenistic sources behind practically everything in the early books of the NT. 226'.06.B56

Brown, David. *The Four Gospels: A Commentary, Critical, Experimental, and Practical.* London: Banner of Truth Trust, 1969.

Reprinted from the 1864 edition. Scholarly and devotional. Contains some fresh and vital ideas for a series of sermons. 226'.07.B81 1969

Dale, Robert William. *The Living Christ and the Four Gospels.* London: Hodder and Stoughton, 1895.

Studies in the historical trustworthiness of the gospel narratives.
226'.06.D15

Denney, James. *Jesus and the Gospel: Christianity Justified in the Mind of Christ.* New York: A. C. Armstrong and Son, 1909.

A series of studies centering in the gospel records and dealing primarily with the self-revelation of Jesus Christ. 226'.08.D41

*Fairweather, William. *Background of the Gospels.* Edinburgh: T. and T. Clark, 1920.

A very important older work tracing the historical and doctrinal themes of the intertestamental period and the preparation of the Graeco-Roman world for the coming of Christ. 226'.09.F16

Gloag, Paton James. *Introduction to the Synoptic Gospels.* Edinburgh: T. and T. Clark, 1895.

A most valuable treatment that has been largely ignored by contemporary writers because it is hard to obtain. 226'.061.G51

Grant, Frederick Clifton. *An Introduction to New Testament Thought.* New York: Abingdon Press, 1950.

†A comprehensive survey of the world of the NT. 225'.61.G76

*Hastings, James, ed. *Dictionary of Christ and the Gospels.* 2 vols. New York: Charles Scribner's Sons, 1907-9.

†Follows a similar format to *HDB* and is primarily the product of British scholarship. It is designed to focus attention specifically on the person, work, and teaching of Christ. Its emphasis is "mainly with things biographical, historical, geographical, or antiquarian" as those areas of interest have a bearing on the ministry of Christ. It is replete with indices of subjects, Greek terms, and Scripture texts and will handsomely repay the researcher for his efforts. Excellent articles highlight the places of

Christ's ministry, the traditions and practices of the Jews, the preaching style of the Lord Jesus, and topics like "Only Begotten" and "the Brethren of Our Lord," which are based upon the biblical record. In all, 2,000 topics have been covered. 226'.03.H27

Johnson, Sherman Elbridge. *The Theology of the Gospels.* London: Duckworth Co., 1966.

†A survey of the doctrinal teaching of the gospels that regards the preexistence of Christ as a myth and looks upon the greater part of the Christian revelation as alternating between "myth" and history. 226'.082.J63

Jukes, Andrew John. *The Differences of the Four Gospels.* London: Pickering and Inglis, n.d.

Recently republished by Kregel Publications under the title of *Four Views of Christ.* Considers the differences found in each of the gospels, and relates these to the thematic purpose of each writer. An enriching and rewarding study. 226'.06.J93

Kelso, James Leon. *An Archaeologist Looks at the Gospels.* Waco: Word Books, 1969.

Designed for laymen. Illuminates the gospel records. Contains some misleading views on salvation and the spiritual life. 226'.093.K29

Maclaren, Alexander. *Bible Class Expositions.* 5 vols. London: Hodder and Stoughton, 1892.

Expository studies on the gospels and Acts. Not worthy of serious consideration. 226'.07.M22

Major, Henry Dewsbury Aives, T. W. Manson and **C. J. Wright.** *The Mission and Message of Jesus: An Exposition of the Gospels in the Light of Modern Research.* New York: Macmillan Co., 1940.

†A work in which Manson contributes his *Sayings of Jesus.* The authors rely heavily upon "Q" to explain their

sources. Of mixed value. 226'.066.M28

*Mattill, A. J. and M. B. Mattill. *A Classified Bibliography of Literature on the Acts of the Apostles.* New Testament Tools and Studies. Leiden: E. J. Brill, 1966.

Similar in scope to Metzger's *Index to Periodical Literature on Christ and the Gospels.* Contains 6,646 numbered entries drawn from approximately 200 journals and is divided into 9 main sections. Lists material from the period of the church Fathers to 1961. Includes index of authors. 016.226.M43

*Metzger, Bruce Manning [comp.] *Index to Periodical Literature on the Apostle Paul.* New Testament Tools and Studies. Leiden: E. J. Brill, 1960.

A valuable reference tool. Of primary importance to students of the epistles. Contains entries leading to articles in approximately 135 journals and covering material from the earliest time to 1957. There are 2,987 numbered entries in 6 separate sections. Includes an author index. 016.226.M56

*_____ [comp.] *Index to Periodical Literature on Christ and the Gospels.* New Testament Tools and Studies. Leiden: E. J. Brill, 1966.

This is an indispensable aid to the study of the gospels. It contains 10,090 numbered entries from approximately 160 journals, helpfully arranged in sections. No annotations. Includes an author index. 016.226.M56P

Olshausen, Hermann. *Biblical Commentary on the Gospels and on the Acts of the Apostles, . . .* Clark's Foreign Theological Library. 4 vols. Edinburgh: T. and T. Clark, 1850-63.

C. H. Spurgeon in *Commenting and Commentaries* says, "*Olshausen* is mentioned by *Alford* as so rich in original material, that he has often cited him. . . . He is one of the most devout German [expositors], and a great scholar." 226'.07.OL8

Pfeiffer, Robert Henry. *History of New Testament Times.* New York: Harper and Brothers, 1949.

†Valuable for its scholarship, but impaired by the author's theological bias. 226'.09.P

Rawlinson, Alfred Edward John. *Christ in the Gospels.* Oxford: At the Clarendon Press, 1940.

†An approach to the Christology of the gospels. A moderately liberal work. 226.082.R19

Ryle, John Charles. *Expository Thoughts on the Gospels.* 4 vols. Grand Rapids: Zondervan Publishing House, 1951.

A masterly commentary. Very suggestive, and offers helpful devotional thoughts on every passage. 226'.07.R98

*Scroggie, William Graham. *Guide to the Gospels.* London: Pickering and Inglis, 1962.

Worth an entire shelf of books on the same subject. 226'.07.SCR5

*Stott, John Robert Walmsey. *Christ the Controversialist.* Downers Grove, Ill.: Inter-Varsity Press, 1970.

An original, challenging, and stimulating series of messages on the essentials of the evangelical religion. Highly recommended. 226'.08.ST7

Tasker, Randolph Vincent Greenwood. *The Nature and Purpose of the Gospels.* Richmond: John Knox Press, 1962.

An explanation of the essence and function of the gospel in the Christian experience. 226'.06.T18

Taylor, Vincent. *The Formation of Gospel Tradition.* London: Macmillan and Co., 1953.

†Vincent is not at his best as a critic of the form-critic. He tries to counteract the radical tendencies of form-criticism, but with little success. 226'.066.T21

_____. *The Gospels: A Short Introduction.* 5th ed. London: Epworth Press, 1945.

†A brief, introductory survey from a source-critical viewpoint. Fourth edition published in 1878. 226'.06.T21 1945

Tenney, Merrill Chapin. *The Genius of the Gospels.* Grand Rapids: Wm. B. Eerdmans Publishing Co., 1951.

Deals with the historicity of the gospels, the biographical sketches they contain, their purpose as homiletic treatises, and their place and importance as spiritual guides. A valuable introductory work. 226'.061.T25

Trench, Richard Chenevix. *Studies in the Gospel.* 5th ed. London: Kegan Paul. Trench and Co., 1886.

A miscellaneous assortment of essays including the temptation of Christ, the calling of Philip and Nathaniel, the Samaritan woman, a consideration of the transfiguration, and the unfinished tower. 226'.08.T72 1886

Westcott, Brooke Foss. *An Introduction to the Study of the Gospels.* 8th ed. London: Macmillan Co., 1895.

Remains a most valuable treatment of the preparation of the NT world for the reception of the gospel, the Jewish expectation of a Messiah, the place of oral tradition in the transmission of the NT, the individual characteristics of the gospels, and the analysis of the difference between the gospel of John and the synoptic gospels. 226'.067.W52 1895

Wink, Walter. *John the Baptist in the Gospel Tradition.* New York: Cambridge University Press, 1968.

†Basing his study on *Redaktionsgeschichte,* the writer pursues his "quest for the historical Baptist." Fails to sufficiently analyze the literary structures within the gospels, and invariably atomizes the text. 226'.06.W72

HARMONIES

*Aland, Kurt, ed. *Synopsis Quattuor Evangeliorum.* Stuttgart: Wurttembergische Bibelanstalt, 1964.

The latest critical harmony of the four gospels in Greek. 226.1'48.AL1

Burton, Ernest DeWitt and **Edgar Johnson Goodspeed.** *Harmony of the Synoptic Gospels in Greek.* Chicago: University of Chicago Press, 1947.

A standard harmony based on the text of Westcott and Hort. 226.148.B95

Greenleaf, Simon. *The Testimony of the Evangelist.* Grand Rapids: Baker Book House, 1965.

Using the laws of evidence, an attorney examines the gospel records to determine their credibility. The introduction (pp. 1-54) is of the utmost value. The appendix, by Tischendorff, contains a history of the most ancient manuscript copies of the NT and a comparison of their text with that of the AV. Also included in this work is a review of the trial of Jesus. First published in 1846. 226.1.G84 1965

*Robertson, Archibald Thomas. *A Harmony of the Gospels for Students of the Life of Christ.* New York: Harper and Brothers, 1922.

Regarded by many as one of the most helpful harmonies available today. 226.1.R54

Throckmorton, Burton Hamilton, Jr. ed. *Gospel Parallels: A Synopsis of the First Three Gospels.* London: Thomas Morrison and Sons, 1967.

A critical harmony based upon the RSV. 226'.1.T41

Titianus. *The Earliest Life of Christ, Being the Diatessaron of Tatian.* Translated by J. Hamlyn Hill. Edinburgh: T. and T. Clark, 1894.

Written about A.D. 160, this is the oldest attempt to reconstruct the life of Christ from the four gospels. Enhanced with a historical and critical introduction, notes, and appendices. 226.1.T53

Wieand, Albert Cassel. *A New Harmony of the Gospels.* Grand Rapids: Wm. B. Eerdmans Publishing Co., 1947.

Based upon the RSV, includes an

analytical outline and is replete with sketch maps, index, and footnotes. 226.1.W63

SYNOPTIC PROBLEM

Butler, Basil Christopher. The Originality of St. Matthew: A Critique of the Two-Document Hypothesis. Cambridge: At the University Press, 1951.

A careful and exacting critique of the Synoptic Problem, and one that exposes the inadequacies of the theories of Streeter and Burney. Roman Catholic. 226.11.B97

Campbell, D. B. J. *The Synoptic Gospels.* New York: Seabury Press, 1969.

Compiled to ease the task of the teacher and the student, and to summarize biblical scholarship in the area of the synoptic gospels. 226.11.C15

Farmer, William Reuben. The Synoptic Problem: A Critical Analysis. New York: Macmillan Co., 1964.

A scholarly defense of the priority of Matthew. 226.11.F22

Grant, Frederick Clifton. *The Gospels: Their Origin and Their Growth.* New York: Harper and Row, 1957.

†A standard, easy-to-read work. An extensive study of the Synoptic Problem based on form-criticism. 226.11.G76

Harnack, Karl Gustav Adolf von. *The Sayings of Jesus.* New Testament Studies. Translated by J. R. Wilkinson. London: Williams and Norgate, 1908.

†An endeavor to find the second source of Matthew's and Luke's gospels. 226.11.H22

Hawkins, John Caesar. Horae Synopticae. 2d rev. ed. Grand Rapids: Baker Book House, 1968.

An excellent contribution to the study of the Synoptic Problem, but of use only to those students who have attained a mastery of Greek. From the edition first published in 1909. 226.11.H31 1968

Knox, Wilfred Lawrence. *The Sources*

of the Synoptic Gospels. 2 vols. Cambridge: At the University Press, 1953.

A painstaking source-critical work. Many of the writer's conclusions have been called in question as a result of recent research. 226.11.K77

Montefiore, Claude Joseph Goldsmid. *The Synoptic Gospels.* 2 vols. New York: Ktav Publishing House, 1967.

†Attempts to distinguish between the authentic teachings of Jesus in the gospels and the later accretions the writer claims have been added to it. First published in 1927. 226.11.M76

Nineham, Dennis Eric, ed. *Studies in the Gospels: Essays in Memory of R. H. Lightfoot.* Oxford: Basil Blackwell, 1955.

A festschrift containing essays on gospel origins, criticism, and theology. 226.1'08.N62

Sanders, E. P. *The Tendencies of the Synoptic Tradition.* New York: Cambridge University Press, 1969.

A helpful analysis of the continuing debate surrounding the Synoptic Problem. 226.11.SA5

Stonehouse, Ned Bernard. Origins of the Synoptic Gospels. Grand Rapids: Wm. B. Eerdmans Publishing Co., 1963.

An evangelical treatment favoring the priority of Mark. 226.11.ST7

Streeter, Burnett Hillman. *The Four Gospels.* London: Macmillan Co., 1964.

†First published in 1924, this treatment of the manuscript tradition, sources, authorship, and dates of writing has been looked upon as a standard treatment for many years. Because the writer tends to include only the materials from the gospels that harmonize with his preconceived ideas, this work has been largely set aside by modern students of the Synoptic Problem. 226.11.ST8 1964

MATTHEW

Allen, Willoughby Charles. *The Gospel According to St. Matthew.* International

Critical Commentary. Edinburgh: T. and T. Clark, 1907.

†The most helpful part of this work is the introduction. The rest of the comments on the Greek text reflect the writer's liberal theology. 226.2'07.AL5

Alexander, Joseph Addison. *Matthew Explained.* London: James Nisbet and Co., 1870.

The author died before this volume was completed. His treatment of the first 16 chapters is of the utmost value. 226.2'07.1—16.AL21

Arco, William P. *As Matthew Saw the Master.* Westwood, N.J.: Fleming H. Revell Co., 1964.

Messages on selected passages. Good for illustrations. 226.2'08.AR2

Armerding, Carl Edwin. *The Olivet Discourse.* Findlay, Ohio: Dunham Publishing Co., 1955.

A premillennial treatment. 226.2'07.24—25.AR5

*Boice, James Montgomery. *The Sermon on the Mount.* Grand Rapids: Zondervan Publishing Co., 1972.

An exposition unfolding the dimensions of the sermon and relating its message to modern living. 226.2'07.5—7.B63

Boreham, Frank William. *The Heavenly Octave.* New York: Abingdon Press, 1936.

Eight messages on the beatitudes. Colorful and eloquent. 226.2'07.5:1-12.B64

*Broadus, John Albert. *Commentary on the Gospel of Matthew.* Philadelphia: American Baptist Publication Society, 1886.

A singularly helpful exposition based upon careful exegesis and containing practical applications of the text that will be of help to preachers. Amillennial. 226.2'07.B78

Carr, Arthur. *The Gospel According to St.*

Matthew. Cambridge Greek Testament for Schools and Colleges. Cambridge: At the University Press, 1906.

Still of value for its theological and grammatical annotations. 226.2'07.C23

Criswell, Wallie Amos. *Expository Notes on the Gospel of Matthew.* Grand Rapids: Zondervan Publishing House, 1970.

Helpful devotional messages on Christ's earthly life and ministry. 226.2'07.C86

Davis, William David. *The Setting of the Sermon on the Mount.* Cambridge: At the University Press, 1964.

†Provides valuable summaries of the different methods of interpretation, probes their weaknesses, and concludes that chapters 5-7 "span the arch of grace and law" and form a Christian *Mishnah.* 226.2'06.5—7.D29

Davis, Wiliam Hersey. *Notes on Matthew.* Nashville: Broadman Press, 1962.

A "thematic" approach to Matthew's gospel that stresses the messianic character of Christ. However, Davis fails to organize his treatment around Matthew's thematic outline. 226.2'07.D29

English, Eugene Schuyler. *Studies in the Gospel According to Matthew.* New York: Loizeaux Brothers, 1960.

A helpful premillennial treatment in which the writer appears to draw heavily upon the earlier work of Pettingill. 226.2'07.EN3

*Erdman, Charles Rosenbury. *The Gospel of Matthew.* Philadelphia: Westminster Press, 1920.

A brief, conservative exposition that adequately explains the thematic development of the gospel. 226.2'07.ER2

Filson, Floyd Vivian. *Commentary on the Gospel According to St. Matthew.* Harper's New Testament Commentaries. New York: Harper and Brothers, 1960.

†While denying the Matthean authorship, the writer provides a good

treatment of Matthew's theology in his section on "Prominent Themes." The exposition is weak. 226.2'07.F48

Findlay, James Alexander. *Jesus in the First Gospel.* London: Hodder and Stoughton, n.d.

†A series of perceptive sermons that follow the sequence of chapters in Matthew's gospel. 226.2'07.F49

Fitch, William. *The Beatitudes of Jesus.* Grand Rapids: Wm. B. Eerdmans Publishing Co., 1961.

Weak in interpretation and strongly antidispensational, but ably applies this passage to the needs of people today. Lacks a proper hermeneutical foundation. 226.2'07.5:1-12.F55

Franzmann, Martin H. *Follow Me: Discipleship According to St. Matthew.* St. Louis: Concordia Publishing House, 1961.

A devout study designed to show how the Lord prepared His disciples for their future ministry. 226.2'08.F85

*Gaebelein, Arno Clemens. *The Gospel of Matthew.* New York: Loizeaux Brothers, 1910.

A very thorough premillennial exposition. Weak in handling chapters 13 and 24-25. 226.2'07.G11

Glover, Richard. *A Teacher's Commentary on the Gospel of Matthew.* Grand Rapids: Zondervan Publishing House, 1956.

A reprint of an old (1889), conservative treatment. Devotional and practical. Contains some good expository ideas for preachers, but is inferior to other works. 226.2'07.G51 1956

Goodspeed, Edgar Johnson. *Matthew, Apostle and Evangelist.* Philadelphia: John C. Winston Co., 1959.

In attempting to solve the critical problem of authorship, Goodspeed concludes that the gospel was indeed written by Matthew. Valuable for background infor-

mation. 226.2'061.G62

Graham, William Franklin. *The Secret of Happiness.* Garden City: Doubleday and Co., 1955.

Sermons on the Beatitudes. A popular treatment. Contains good illustrations. 226.2'07.5:1-12.G76

*Gundry, Robert Horton. *The Use of the Old Testament in St. Matthew's Gospel.* Leiden: E. J. Brill, 1967.

A work of exceptional scholarship in which the author examines each quotation as it appears in the text, evaluates the theories of writers who have preceded him, and offers his own view of the fulfillment of messianic prophecy. 226.2'08.G95.

Hargrove, Hubbard Hoyt. *At the Master's Feet.* Grand Rapids: Baker Book House. 1963.

Conservative messages on the Sermon on the Mount. 226.2'07.5—7.H22

Hobbs, Herschel H. *An Exposition of the Gospel of Matthew.* Grand Rapids: Baker Book House, 1965.

Echoes the thoughts of Broadus, Robertson, and other Baptist writers and follows Broadus's amillennial explanation of the Olivet discourse. 226.2'07.H65

Howard, Fred D. *The Gospel of Matthew.* Grand Rapids: Baker Book house, 1961.

A brief, elementary survey. 226.2'07.H83

Hunter, Archibald Macbride. *A Pattern for Life.* Philadelphia: Westminster Press, 1953.

†Mildly evangelical, but advocates the documentary sources for Matthew and provides an ineffectual commentary on the text. 226.2'07.5—7.H91

Kelly, William. *Lectures on the Gospel of Matthew.* New York: Loizeaux Brothers, 1959.

Valuable because the writer does not willingly avoid any interpretative prob-

lem. First published in London in 1868.
226.2'07.K29 1959

Kik, Jacob Marcellus. *Matthew 24: An Exposition.* Philadelphia: Presbyterian and Reformed Publishing Co., 1948.

An amillennial approach to the problems of the Olivet discourse.
226.2'07.24.K55

Kilpatrick, George Dunbar. *The Origins of the Gospel According to St. Matthew.* New York: Oxford University Press, 1946.

An imaginative attempt to explain the way in which this gospel may have come into being. 226.2'06.K55

King, Guy Hope. *The New Order.* London: Marshall, Morgan and Scott, 1954.

A devotional exposition of real merit.
226.2'07.5—7.K58

Laurenson, L. *Messiah the Prince.* New York: Loizeaux Brothers, 1924.

An interesting and, in many respects, original outline and exposition of Matthew's gospel. Long out of print, this devotional book will richly repay the reader. Plymouth Brethren.
226.2'07.L36

*Lenski, Richard Charles Henry. *The Interpretation of St. Matthew's Gospel.* Minneapolis: Augsburg Press, 1943.

A thorough, strongly conservative Lutheran exposition. Amillennial.
226.2'07.L54

*Lloyd-Jones, David Martyn. *Studies in the Sermon on the Mount.* 2 vols. Grand Rapids: Wm B. Eerdmans Publishing Co., 1959-60.

Careful and thorough expository messages. Weak on interpretation. Helpful for its application. Preachers will find this set helpful. 226.2'07.5—7.L77

McLaren, Alexander. *A Garland of Gladness.* Grand Rapids: Wm. B. Eerdmans Publishing Co., 1945.

Devotional messages on the Beatitudes, originally published in the latter part of the nineteenth century.
226.2'07.5:1-12.M22 1945

*M'Neile, Alan Hugh. *The Gospel According to St. Matthew.* London: Macmillan Co., 1915.

†A critical commentary in which the author denies the Matthean authorship and discounts the virgin birth as being "imaginative." Helpful, however, in unfolding the theme of the gospel.
226.2'07.M23

Meyer, Frederick Brotherton. *The Directory of the Devout Life.* Grand Rapids: Baker Book House, 1954.

An old, devotional, and somewhat simplistic study of the Sermon on the Mount. Suggests enlightening applications of spiritual truths. First published in 1904. 226.2'07.5—7.M57 1954

Morgan, Edward J. *No Thoughts for Tomorrow.* Grand Rapids: Wm. B. Eerdmans Publishing Co., 1961.

A psychological approach to the Sermon on the Mount. 226.2'07.5—7.M82

*Morgan, George Campbell. *The Gospel According to Matthew.* New York: Fleming H. Revell Co., 1929.

An able expository treatment with numerous practical observations. Particularly helpful on the Sermon on the Mount. Includes some novel ideas on the parables of chapter 25. 226.2'07.M82

*Morison, James. *A Practical Commentary on the Gospel According to St. Matthew.* Revised ed. Boston: N. J. Bartlett and Co., 1884.

A practical and devotional, phrase-byphrase commentary. In many instances, provides helpful comments on textual problems. Although the interpretation of the Greek nuances is not always accurate, this work should be purchased if found. 226.2'07.M82

Pink, Arthur Walkington. *An Exposition of the Sermon on the Mount.* Grand Rapids: Baker Book House, 1951.

A thorough exposition containing an abundance of practical material. 226.2'07.5—7.P65

*Plummer, Alfred. *The Gospel According to St. Matthew.* Grand Rapids: Wm. B. Eerdmans Publishing Co., 1956.

†A most helpful technical and critical commentary. Plummer denies Matthew's authorship and believes that there are inaccuracies in Scripture; yet he defends the virgin birth and the reality of miracles. In spite of the weaknesses inherent in this volume, it is one of the best expository treatments of this gospel. 226.2'07.P73 1956

Ridderbos, Herman Nicholas. *Matthew's Witness to Jesus Christ.* New York: Association Press, 1958.

A leading Reformed theologian from The Netherlands provides a brief survey of Matthew's gospel. 226.2'06.R43

Robertson, Archibald Thomas. *Commentary on the Gospel According to Matthew.* New York: Macmillan Co., 1911.

An exposition by an able exegete. 226.2'07.R54

Robinson, Theodore H. *The Gospel of Matthew.* Moffatt New Testament Commentary. New York: Harper and Brothers, 1927.

†An exceedingly inadequate treatment. 226.2'07.R56

Saphir, Adolph. *Christ and the Church.* Revised ed. London: Religious Tract Society. n.d.

Expository thoughts on the Great Commission. Originally published in 1874. 226.2'07.28:18-20.SA6

Simcox, Carroll E. *The First Gospel.* Greenwich. Conn.: Seabury Press, 1963.

†Devotional and practical studies. 226.2'07.SI4

Sockman, Ralph Washington. *The Higher Happiness.* New York: Abingdon-Cokesbury Press, 1950.

†A well-researched series of studies.

The illustrations are particularly helpful. 226.2'07.5—7.SO1

*Spurgeon, Charles Haddon. *The Gospel of the Kingdom.* Grand Rapids: Zondervan Publishing House, reprint.

First published in 1893, this devotional exposition contains fervent and practical admonitions based on the text. 226.2'07.SP9

Stonehouse, Ned Bernard. *The Witness of Matthew and Mark to Christ.* Grand Rapids: Wm. B. Eerdmans Publishing Co., 1958.

A critical evaluation of the theories surrounding the priority of the gospels. One entire section deals with Christ's use of the OT in Matthew. 226.2'06.ST7

Tasker, Randolph Vincent Greenwood. *The Gospel According to St. Matthew.* Tyndale Commentaries on the New Testament. Grand Rapids: Wm. B. Eerdmans Publishing Co., 1961.

Provides some interesting historical details that illumine the text, but shows what happens when a conservative scholar is unduly influenced by higher critical theories. Unworthy of serious consideration. 226.2'07.T18

Thielicke, Helmut. *Life Can Begin Again.* Philadelphia: Fortress Press, 1963.

†Philosophical addresses on the Sermon on the Mount. A strange mixture of liberal theology, conservative ideas, and catchy sermon titles. 226.2'07.5—7.T34

Tholuck, August. *Commentary on the Sermon on the Mount.* Edinburgh: T. and T. Clark, 1869.

An exhaustive treatment that provides a comprehensive survey of the older literature. Of little value today. 226.2'07.5—7.T35

Thomas, David. *The Gospel of St. Matthew.* Grand Rapids: Baker Book House, 1956.

A homiletical and practical exposition that overlooks many difficulties in in-

terpretation. First published in 1873.
226.2'07.T36 1956

Thomas, William Henry Griffith.
Outline Studies in the Gospel of Matthew.
Grand Rapids: Wm. B. Eerdmans Publishing Co., 1961.

This work contains nearly 500 pages of homiletical and expository outlines.
226.2'07.T36S 1961

Wirt, Sherwood Eliot. *Magnificent Promise.* Chicago: Moody Press, 1959.

Eight timely messages that abound in practical application and provide preachers with helpful illustrations.
226.2'07.5:1-12.W74

MARK

*Alexander, Joseph Addison. *The Gospel According to Mark.* London: Banner of Truth Trust, 1960.

A heartwarming study that does not adequately explain the theme of Mark's gospel, but still is worth consulting.
226.3'07.AL2

Allen, Willoughby Charles. *The Gospel According to St. Mark.* England: Rivingtons, 1915.

Particularly strong on the Aramaic background of the gospel. 226.3'07.AL5

Beasley-Murray, George Raymond. *A Commentary on Mark 13.* London: Macmillan Co., 1957.

A premillennial approach by a British Baptist theologian. 226.3'07.13.B38

Best, Ernest. *The Temptation and the Passion: The Markan Soteriology.* Cambridge: At the University Press, 1965.

†An attempt to forge a link between Markan soteriology and the *kenosis* passage in Philippians 2. Built upon an extreme view of form-criticism, this book provides an example of the kind of work being done today on the theology of the synoptic Gospels. 226.3'06.B46

*Blaiklock, Edward Musgrave. *Mark:*

The Man and His Message. Chicago: Moody Press, 1967.

Eight enlightening studies containing helpful preaching values. 226.3'092.B57

Branscomb, Bennett Harvie. *The Gospel of St. Mark.* London: Hodder and Stoughton. 1937.

†An exposition from an advanced form-critical viewpoint. Unworthy of serious consideration. 226.3'07.B73

*Cole, Robert Alan. *The Gospel According to St. Mark.* Tyndale New Testament Commentaries. Grand Rapids: Wm. B. Eerdmans Publishing Co., 1961.

Combines exegesis with exposition and provides a provocative, evangelical study of Mark's gospel. 226.3'07.C67

*Cranfield, C. E. B. *The Gospel According to St. Mark.* Cambridge: At the University Press, 1963.

A valuable exegetical study. Should be in every preacher's library. 226.3'07.C85

Earle, Ralph. *The Gospel According to Mark.* Evangelical Commentary on the Bible. Grand Rapids: Zondervan Publishing House, 1957.

Provides helpful exegetical insights, but fails to follow the theme of Mark's gospel. 226.3'07.EA7

*English, Eugene Schuyler. *Studies in the Gospel According to Mark.* New York: "Our Hope," 1943.

A comprehensive exposition emphasizing the "Servant of Jehovah" concept as the theme of this gospel.
226.3'07.EN3

Glover, Richard. *A Teacher's Commentary on the Gospel of Mark.* London: Marshall, Morgan and Scott, 1957.

A devotional work. Originally published in 1884. 226.3'07.G51 1957

Gould, Ezra Palmer. *A Critical and Exegetical Commentary on the Gospel According to St. Mark.* International Critical Commentary. Edinburgh: T. and T. Clark, 1955.

Helpful for its exegetical insights, but superseded by more recent works. First published in 1896. 226.3'07.G73 1955

Hobbs, Herschel H. *An Exposition of the Gospel of Mark.* Grand Rapids: Baker Book House, 1970.

Makes frequent references to the original Greek, but does not emphasize the overall unity of the gospel and its theme. Good for illustrations. 226.3'07.H65

Hooker, Morna Dorothy. *The Son of Man in Mark.* Montreal: McGill University, 1967.

†A work that brings new light to bear upon an old problem and, having done so, takes it place alongside the writings of H. E. Todt, P. Vielhauer, E. Schweizer, O. Cullmann, A. J. B. Higgins, and R. H. Fuller. 226.3'07.H76

Hunter, Archibald Macbride. *The Gospel According to St. Mark.* Torch Bible Commentaries. London: SCM Press, 1949.

Avoids many of the problems in Mark's gospel, and the greater majority of the comments are obvious. 226.3'07.H91

*****Kelly, William.** *An Exposition of the Gospel of Mark.* Edited by E. E. Whitfield. London: Alfred Holness, n.d.

A valuable addition to any preacher's library. Originally published in 1907. 226.3'07.K29

Luckock, Herbert Mortimer. *Footprints of the Son of Man as Traced by St. Mark.* London: Longmans, Green, and Co., 1893.

A suggestive, devotional commentary of real merit. 226.3'07.L96

Meye, Robert P. *Jesus and the Twelve.* Grand Rapids: Wm. B. Eerdmans Publishing Co., 1968.

Draws heavily upon *Redactiongeschichte* and emphasizes the fact of "discipleship" as found in Mark's gospel. Presents Jesus as a teacher, and places due emphasis on the disciples as recipients of a taught

revelation. 226.3'06.M57

Mitton, Charles Leslie. *The Gospel According to St. Mark.* Epworth Preacher's Commentaries. London: Epworth Press, 1957.

Not a commentary, but a work for preachers. Makes available the fruit of the writer's wide reading and extensive research. 226.3'07.M69

*****Morgan, George Campbell.** *The Gospel According to Mark.* Westwood, N.J.: Fleming H. Revell Co., 1927.

Emphasizes the concept of "service" as the key to understanding this gospel, and provides a fast-moving chronological exposition. Morgan's works should be in every preacher's library. 226.3'07.M82

*****Morison, James.** *A Practical Commentary on the Gospel According to St. Mark.* 4th rev. ed. London: Hodder and Stoughton, 1882.

A very full, devotional treatment. The overall strength of this exposition far outweighs its syntactical deficiencies. 226.3'07.M82 1882

Moule, Charles Francis Digby. *The Gospel According to Mark.* Cambridge: At the University Press, 1965.

A very brief exposition based on the NEB. Not as valuable as the author's other works. 226.3'07.M86

Nineham, Dennis Eric. *The Gospel of St. Mark.* London: A. and C. Black, 1968.

†A negative, form-critical study. In spite of this weakness, highlights the nuances of the Greek text and for this reason may prove useful. 226.3'07.N62

Rawlinson, Alfred Edward John. *St. Mark, with Introduction, Commentary and Additional Notes.* Westminster Commentaries. London: Methuen and Company, 1925.

†A moderately critical commentary that has now been superseded. 226.3'07.R19

Robertson, Archibald Thomas. *Studies in Mark's Gospel.* Revised and edited by Herber F. Peacock. Nashville: Broadman Press. 1958.

First published in 1919 under the title *Making Good in the Ministry.* Does not follow a verse-by-verse exposition, but deals with introductory problems before discussing such items as miracles, parables, the teaching of Christ, Aramaic and Latin terms, and the disputed ending of the gospel. 226.3'08.R54 1958

Robinson, James McConkey. *The Problem of History in Mark.* Studies in Biblical Theology. London: SCM Press, 1957.

Building upon an extensive survey of various approaches to and treatments of Mark's gospel. Robinson provides an assessment of the many and varied views regarding the historicity of Mark. The writer has been deeply influenced by form criticism, which minimizes the value of the "*kerygmatic* history" Robinson sees underlying Mark's theological convictions. 226.3'095.R54

*Swete, Henry Barclay. *The Gospel According to St. Mark.* Grand Rapids: Wm. B. Eerdmans Publishing Co., 1956.

Long regarded as one of the finest exegetical treatments available. Not as up-to-date as Vincent, but more conservative and should be consulted. First published in 1898. 226.3'07.SW4 1956

*Taylor, Vincent. *The Gospel According to St. Mark.* London: Macmillan Co., 1963.

†A very full commentary with a detailed discussion of all the critical problems, and a complete résumé of all the conflicting points of view. 226.3'07.T21

LUKE

*Arndt, William F. *Gospel According to St. Luke.* St. Louis: Concordia Publishing House, 1956.

A thorough exposition by a conservative Lutheran scholar. 226.4'07.AR6

Barclay, William. *The Gospel of Luke.* Philadelphia: Westminster Press, 1953.

†A series of popular studies on this gospel. Barclay provides helpful word studies, good illustrations, and colorful historical data. Liberal leanings are evident in several places. 226.4'07.B23

Barrett, Charles Kingsley. *Luke the Historian in Recent Study.* London: Epworth Press, 1961.

A modern evaluation of the contributions of the different schools of thought, with the writer's own assessment of Luke as a historian and theologian. 226.4'08.B27

Barth, Karl. *The Great Promise.* New York: Philosophical Library, 1963.

A devotional exposition of Luke 1. Rich and full. 226.4'07.1.B28

Browning, Wilfred Robert Francis. *The Gospel According to St. Luke.* The Torch Commentaries. New York: Macmillan Co., 1960.

†Brief comments based on the use of form-criticism, but endeavoring to avoid the negative results often accompanying this approach to God's Word. 226.4'07.B82

Burnside, W. F. *The Gospel According to St. Luke.* Cambridge: Cambridge University Press, 1913.

A critical and, in many respects, reliable commentary. Its chief value, however, lies in the writer's interesting comments on the usage of Greek words and his comparison of Luke with other synoptic gospels. 226.4'07.B93

Caird, George Bradford. *The Gospel of St. Luke.* New York: Seabury Press, 1963.

†A most unsatisfactory commentary that rejects the virgin birth, explains away many of the miracles, denies the fact that Christ claimed to be God, and so on. Disappointing, for Caird has written

some fine expositions. 226.4'07.C12

Creed, John Martin. *The Gospel According to St. Luke.* London: Macmillan and Co., 1930.

†A highly critical work that claims Luke abounds in historical and technical discrepancies, the virgin birth narrative is full of errors, Christ's healing of the demoniac is nothing more than a folk tale, and so on. 226.4'07.C86

Ellis, Edward Earl. *The Gospel of Luke.* New Century Bible. New York: Thomas Nelson and Sons, 1966.

A critical work based upon the RSV. While generally sound and containing some helpful thoughts based on the original, Ellis's work does not attempt to grapple with the purpose of Luke's gospel or to expound its theme. 226.4'07.EL5

*Erdman, Charles Rosenbury. *Gospel of Luke.* Philadelphia: Westminster Press, 1956.

A devotional and practical exposition of the theme of Luke's gospel. Excellent as a study guide. 226.4'07.ER2

Geldenhuys, Johannes Norval. *Commentary on the Gospel of Luke.* New International Commentary of the New Testament. Wm. B. Eerdmans Publishing Co., 1951.

A disappointing, blithe exposition that inadequately explains the argument of this gospel and does not provide enough helpful data for the expository preacher. 226.4'07.G28

*Godet, Frederic Louis. *A Commentary on the Gospel of St. Luke.* Grand Rapids: Zondervan Publishing House, 1957.

Originally published in two volumes in 1870. An exhaustive, technical commentary that ably defends the cardinal doctrines of the Christian faith while expounding the text. Deserves a place on the shelf of every pastor. 226.4'07.G54 1957

Gettys, Joseph M. *How to Study Luke.* Richmond: John Knox Press, 1962.

A valuable synthetic survey. 226.4'007.G33S

———. *How to Teach Luke.* Richmond: John Knox Press, 1958.

A study manual that leaders of Bible discussion groups will find helpful. 226.4'007.G33T

Harnack, Karl Gustav Adolf von. *Luke the Physician.* London: Williams and Norgate, 1909.

†An original study linking the vocabulary and style of Luke and Acts and supporting the Lukan authorship of both. 226.4'06.H22

Hobart, William Kirk. *Medical Language of St. Luke.* Grand Rapids: Baker Book House, 1954.

A technical comparison of the vocabulary of Luke and Acts with the vocabulary of the Greek medical writers. Interesting and helpful, and in some ways held in balance by Harnack's *Luke the Physician.* 226.4'06.H65

Hobbs, Herschel H. *An Exposition of the Gospel of Luke.* Grand Rapids: Baker Book House, 1966.

An exposition of brief sections of Luke's gospel. Not thorough enough to make a lasting contribution. 226.4'07.H65

Kelly, William. *An Exposition of the Gospel of Luke.* London: Pickering and Inglis, n.d.

An exposition based upon sound exegesis. See under *Matthew.* 226.4'07.K29

Leaney, Alfred Robert Clare. *A Commentary on the Gospel According to St. Luke.* Harper New Testament Commentary. New York: Harper and Brothers, 1958.

†Denies the virgin birth, derides Luke's knowledge of Palestinian geography, and provides only poor comments on the text. 226.4'07.L47

*Liddon, Henry Parry. *The Magnificat.*

3d ed. London: Longman's, Green and Co., 1898.

Sermons preached in St. Paul's Cathedral. Excellent. 226.4'07.1:46-56.L61 1898

Manson, William. *The Gospel of Luke.* New York: Harper and Brothers, 1930.

A consistently liberal exposition that denies the cardinal doctrines of the Bible. 226.4'07.M31

Marshall, F. *The Gospel of St. Luke.* London: George Gill and Sons, 1921.

Brief expository notes following a particularly thorough introduction. Presents a helpful defense of the Lukan authorship, the deity of Christ, and miracles. Includes biographical sketches of persons mentioned in the gospel. Of particular value to preachers. 226.4'07.M35

Martin, Hugh. *Luke's Portrait of Jesus.* London: SCM Press, 1949.

Adherence to the tenets of higher criticism leads the author to attack some miracles while defending othes. Upholds the deity of Christ. Inconsistency mars this work and deprives it of any lasting usefulness. 226.4'07.M36

Moorman, John Richard Humpidge. *The Path to Glory.* London: SPCK, 1960.

†Devotional studies. Discounts the miraculous elements in the gospel, denies the deity of Christ, and does not expect a second advent. 226.4'07.M78

*****Morgan, George Campbell.** *The Gospel According to Luke.* New York: Fleming H. Revell Co., 1931.

A carefully reasoned exposition that adheres quite closely to Luke's argument and provides an example of expository preaching at its best. Morgan follows the premillennial approach here but, toward the end of his life, he rejected this method of interpretation. 226.4'07.M82.

*****Plummer, Alfred.** *A Critical and Exegetical Commentary on the Gospel According to St. Luke.* International Critical Commentary. Edinburgh: T. and T. Clark, 1896.

†A most exhaustive and helpful treatment of the Greek text. 226.4'07.P73

Reiling, J. and **J. L. Swellengrebel.** *A Translator's Handbook on the Gospel of Luke.* Leiden: E. J. Brill, 1971.

An invaluable work for cross-cultural translators. 226.4'05.R27

Robertson, Archibald Thomas. *Luke the Historian in the Light of Research.* New York: Charles Scribner's Sons, 1936.

A formal, scholarly defense of the accuracy of Luke's gospel. Includes a discussion of Luke's use of "medical terms," the account of Christ's birth, miracles, and so on. 226.4'06.R54

Schweizer, Eduard. *The Good News According to Mark.* Translated by Donald H. Madvig. Richmond: John Knox Press, 1970.

†A comprehensive, thematic exposition accompanied by the text of *Good News for Modern Man.* Schweizer's exegesis is of considerable value. 226.3'07.SCH9

*****Scroggie, William Graham.** *The Gospel of Mark.* London: Marshall, Morgan and Scott, n.d.

A rich, rewarding devotional exposition. 226.3'07.SCR5

Selwyn, Edward Carus. *St. Luke the Prophet.* London: Macmillan and Co., 1901.

Attempts to identify Luke with Silas and contends that the "we" sections in Acts are patterned after the book of Joshua. Presents some very unusual ideas. 226.4'06.SE4

*****Stonehouse, Ned Bernard.** *The Witness of Luke to Christ.* Grand Rapids: Wm. B. Eerdmans Publishing Co., 1951.

A formal defense of the historical and theological accuracy of Luke's gospel. 226.4'06.ST7

Thomas, William Henry Griffith. *Outline Studies in the Gospel of Luke.* Grand

Rapids: Wm. B. Eerdmans Publishing Co., 1950.

A collection of sermon outlines. Incomplete. 226.4'07.T36

JOHN

*Barrett, Charles Kingsley. *The Gospel According to St. John.* London: SPCK, 1962.

†A combination of solid learning and balanced judgment. For serious students of the NT who have a thorough knowledge of Greek. 266.5'07.B27G

*Bernard, Thomas Dehany. *Central Teaching of Jesus Christ.* London: Macmillan and Co., 1892.

An exposition of the upper room discourse and the prayer of Christ. Makes for rich, rewarding reading. 226.5'07.13—17.B45

*Brown, Raymond. *The Anchor Bible: The Gospel According to John.* Garden City: Doubleday and Co., 1966.

†An important, modern treatment by a Roman Catholic writer. Of particular value to serious and discerning students of the NT. Brown's moderate historiography ably complements Barrett's scholarly volume. One of the better volumes in this series. 226.5'07.B81

Dodd, Charles Harold. *The Interpretation of the Fourth Gospel.* Cambridge: At the University Press, 1965.

†In reaction to the overly critical position of German scholarship, the writer pleads for an independent line of tradition that he claims represents an early strain of Christian tradition. 226.5'06.D66

Gaebelein, Arno Clemens. *The Gospel of John.* Wheaton: Van Kampen Press, 1936.

A complete analytical exposition by a great Bible teacher of the generation past. 226.5'07.G11

Gettys, Joseph M. *How to Study John.*

Richmond: John Knox Press, 1960.

A manual the pastor may well use to encourage others to study the Scriptures for themselves. 226.5'007.G33S

_____. *How to Teach John.* Richmond: John Knox Press, 1960.

An excellent aid to the teacher of an adult Bible study class. 226.5'007.G33T

*Godet, Frederic Louis. *Commentary on the Gospel of John.* Translated by Timothy Dwight. 2 vols. Grand Rapids: Zondervan Publishing House, reprint.

Based upon the third French edition; first published in English in 1893. A monumental work by a great theologian and an able defender of the faith. Thorough and exhaustive without being elaborate and verbose. 266.5'07.G54

*Harrison, Everett Falconer. *Meditations on the Gospel of John.* Boston: W. A. Wilde Co., 1949.

Meditations centering on the personalities in John's gospel and showing the uniqueness of our Lord's ministry as He met the deepest needs of the human heart. First published as *The Son of God among the Sons of Men.* 226.5'092.H24

*Hendriksen, William. *A Commentary on the Gospel of John.* New Testament Commentary. 2 vols. Grand Rapids: Baker Book House, 1953.

A thorough treatment based on the original text and representative of the finest evangelical scholarship. Reformed. 226.5'07.H38

*Hengstenberg, Ernst Wilhelm. *Commentary on the Gospel of St. John.* 2 vols. Edinburgh: T. and T. Clark, 1865.

This study, by the same person who gave us his now-famous *Christology of the Old Testament,* is rich in insights and treats with rare piety the life and labors of Christ. Recommended. 226.5'07.H38

Hobbs, Herschel H. *An Exposition of the Gospel of John.* Grand Rapids: Baker Book House, 1968.

Expounds the gospel of John from a

conservative viewpoint. Devotional. 226.5'07.H65

Hoskyns, Edwyn Clement. *The Fourth Gospel.* Edited by Francis Noel Davey. London: Faber and Faber, 1947.

A masterful study, but not in the conservative tradition of Westcott, Godet, and Luthardt. 226.5'07.H97

Howard, Wilbert Francis. *Christianity According to St. John.* London: Duckworth Co., 1943.

A helpful survey of Johannine theology. 226.5'082.H83

————. *The Fourth Gospel in Recent Criticism and Interpretation.* London: Epworth Press, 1935.

Scholarly, critical studies. 226.5'06.H83

Hunter, Archibald Macbride. *According to John.* Philadelphia: Westminster Press, 1968.

†A work of unquestioned scholarship that, while basically evangelical, follows a critical approach to the Scriptures, leading to some unreliable conclusions. 226.5'06.H91

Hutcheson, George. *An Exposition of the Gospel According to John.* Grand Rapids: Kregel Publications, 1959.

Vast in scope, rich in background information, and warm in devotional emphasis. May well be described as a pastor's commentary on this gospel. 226.5'07.H97 1959

Ironside, Henry Allan. *Addresses on the Gospel of John.* New York: Loizeaux Brothers, 1942.

Enriching comments first delivered in the form of addresses at the Moody Memorial Church in Chicago. Of great value to laypeople. 226.5'07.IR6

Kelly, William. *An Exposition of the Gospel of John.* London: T. Weston, 1898.

Working from the text of the RV of 1881, and supplementing this with his own translation, Kelly provides an informative and satisfying exposition. He is

always worth reading. 226.5'07.K29

Luthardt, Christoph Ernst. *St. John the Author of the Fourth Gospel.* Revised and translated by Casper Rene Gregory. Edinburgh: T. and T. Clark, 1875.

An extensive treatment of the authorship of John's gospel. 226.5'06.L97

*————. *St. John's Gospel, Described and Explained According to Its Peculiar Character.* Translated by Casper Rene Gregory. 3 vols. Edinburgh: T. and T. Clark, 1876-78.

An informative and thorough study. While not as scintillating as Godet, Luthardt's treatment should be purchased if found. 226.5'07.L97

Macaulay, Joseph Cordner. *Devotional Studies in St. John's Gospel.* Grand Rapids: Wm. B. Eerdmans Publishing Co., 1954.

Brief expository studies stressing the experiential aspects of this gospel. 226.5'07.M11

MacDuff, John Ross. *Noontide at Sychar.* London: James Nisbet and Co., 1877.

An extensive devotional treatment of John 4. A rare example of exemplary exposition and fine application of spiritual truth. 226.5'07.4.M14

MacGregor, Geddes H. C. *The Gospel of John.* Moffatt New Testament Commentary. New York: Harper and Brothers, 1928.

A critical work. Not as helpful as many other works available to pastors today. 226.5'07.M17

Maclaren, Alexander. *The Holy of Holies.* London: Alexander and Shephard, 1890.

Expository sermons on John 14-16. 226.5'07.14—16.M22

***Manton, Thomas.** *An Exposition of John 17.* Evansville, Ind.: Sovereign Grace Book Club, 1958.

A deep, rich, and full exposition by a Puritan divine. 226.5'07.17.M31 1958

***Morgan, George Campbell.** *The Gos-*

pel According to John. Westwood, N.J.: Fleming H. Revell Co., 1933.

An expository treatment intelligible to the ordinary layman and of value to the preacher. 226.5'07.M82

Morris, Leon L. *Studies in the Fourth Gospel.* Grand Rapids: Wm. B. Eerdmans Publishing Co., 1969.

In-depth studies on introductory topics in keeping with the scholarly tradition of the Cambridge triumvirate of Lightfoot, Westcott, and Hort. All the writings of Morris are of the utmost value. 226.5'06.M83

Moule, Handley Carr Glyn. *The High Priestly Prayer.* London: The Religious Tract Society, 1907.

A devotional commentary on John 17. 226.5'07.17.M86

*_____. *Jesus and the Resurrection.* 3d ed. London: Seeley and Co., 1898.

Satisfying expository studies on John 20-21. 226.5'07.21—22.M86 1898

Odeberg, H. *The Fourth Gospel Interpreted in Its Relation to Contemporaneous Religious Currents.* Uppsala, Sweden: Almquist and Wiksell, 1929.

†A work for the scholar. 226.5'08.OD2

Pink, Arthur Walkington. *Exposition of the Gospel of John.* 3 vols. Grand Rapids: Zondervan Publishing House, 1945.

An extensive, enriching devotional study. Ideal for those who intend to preach a series of sermons on this gospel. 226.5'07.P65

Plummer, Alfred. *The Gospel According to St. John.* Cambridge Bible for Schools and Colleges. Cambridge: At the University Press, 1889.

Brief expository notes. "Covers the bases" adequately. 226.5'07.P73

Rainsford, Marcus. *Our Lord Prays for His Own.* Chicago: Moody Press, 1950.

Timely, relevant devotional thoughts on John 17. 226.5'07.17.R13 1950

Robertson, Archibald Thomas. *The Divinity of Christ in the Gospel of John.* New York: Fleming H. Revell Co., 1916.

Thematic studies that survey the manifestation of the Messiah to His people, the growing hatred of the Jews for Jesus, the teaching of Christ in the upper room, the scorn of Christ's enemies, and His vindication. 226.5'08.R54

Ross, Charles. *The Inner Sanctuary.* London: Banner of Truth Trust, 1967.

This exposition of John 13-17 may well be regarded as a classic. First published in 1888. 226.5'07.13—17.R73 1967

Sanders, J. N. *The Gospel According to St. John.* Harper's New Testament Commentaries. New York: Harper and Row, 1969.

†An important work that is fully abreast of current NT study. 226.5'07.SA5

Scroggie, William Graham. *St. John, Introduction and Notes.* Study Hours Series. New York: Harper and Brothers, 1931.

Brief suggestive studies. Devotional. 226.5'07.SCR5

Smith, Jonathan Ritchie. *The Teaching of the Gospel of John.* New York: Macmillan Co., 1903.

A worthwhile treatment, but one now out of print for many years. 226.5'07.SM6

Speer, Robert E. *John's Gospel: The Greatest Book in the World.* New York: Fleming H. Revell Co., 1915.

Brief suggestions for individual study. 226.5'07.SP3

Strachan, Robert Harvey. *The Fourth Gospel: Its Significance and Environment.* London: SCM Press, 1941.

†A highly critical work of interest, even if only to note how the writer abandons his earlier attempt to distinguish gospel passages that he claimed were due to the work of a redactor, and also how he now rejects the theory that the text has been rearranged. 226.5'06.ST8

Swete, Henry Barclay. *The Last Discourse and Prayer of Our Lord.* London:

Macmillan Co., 1914.

A careful study of John 14-17. As with Swete's other works, this one is worthy of serious consideration. 226.5'07.14—17.SW4

Tasker, Randolph Vincent Greenwood. *The Gospel According to St. John, an Introduction and Commentary.* Tyndale New Testament Commentary. Grand Rapids: Wm. B. Eerdmans Publishing Co., 1960.

More reliable than his work on Matthew. Handles the gospel in sections (rather than verse-by-verse), and includes additional notes on points of particular interest and importance. 226.5'07.T18

*Tenney, Merrill Chapin. *John: The Gospel of Belief.* Grand Rapids: Wm. B. Eerdmans Publishing Co., 1948.

Says Wilbur M. Smith: "This volume is for those who really wish to make a study of John's Gospel, to know the deeper veins of its great message, and to understand more thoroughly the conflict between belief and unbelief." 226.5'07.T25

Thomas, William Henry Griffith. *The Apostle John: Studies in His Life and Writings.* Grand Rapids: Wm. B. Eerdmans Publishing Co., 1953.

A lucid study of the Johannine writings that includes a biographical sketch of the apostle and an extensive analysis of the gospel, epistles, and Revelation. 226'092.T36

Turner, George Allen and **Julius R. Mantey.** *The Gospel According to John.* The Evangelical Commentary on the Bible. Grand Rapids: Wm. B. Eerdmans Publishing Co., 1964.

Divided into two sections: part I deals with exegesis; part II, with exposition. This should result in an ideal commentary for the preacher. Not one of the better commentaries on John's gospel. Arminian. 226.5'07.T85

*Westcott, Brooke Foss. *The Gospel Ac-cording to St. John.* Grand Rapids: Wm. B. Eerdmans Publishing Co., 1950.

Part of the *Speaker's Commentary,* but later issued separately because it made a unique contribution to the study of this gospel. Remains one of the best exegetical studies. Originally published in 1882. 226.5'07.W52 1950

————. *The Revelation of the Father.* London: Macmillan Co., 1887.

Studies covering the titles of the Lord Jesus Christ in John's gospel. 226.5'082.W52

ACTS

*Alexander, Joseph Addison. *Commentary on the Acts of the Apostles.* Grand Rapids: Zondervan Publishing House, 1956.

Reprinted from the 1857 edition. An exhaustive, thorough exposition that gives valuable help on the meaning of Greek words, defends Stephen's accuracy of chronology in Acts 7, and provides preachers with an abundance of usable material. Reformed. 226.6'07.AL2 1956

Allen, Frank Emmett. *The Acts of the Apostles.* Boston: Christopher Publishing House, 1931.

An exhaustive, practical exposition containing numerous illustrations and anecdotes by great preachers of the past. Not as timeless as Alexander. 226.6'07.AL5

Andrews, Herbert Tom. *The Acts of the Apostles.* Westminster Commentaries. London: Andrew Melrose, 1908.

†Brief notes that defend the Lukan authorship of Acts but deny the reality of miracles, the deity of the Holy Spirit, and the inerrancy of the Scriptures. 226.6'07.AN2

Autrey, C. E. *Evangelism in the Acts.* Grand Rapids: Zondervan Publishing House, 1964.

A devotional and practical study of evangelism based upon the book of Acts. Shallow. 226.6'08.AU8

Barclay, William. *The Acts of the Apostles.* Philadelphia: Westminster Press, 1953.

Valuable for the fine literary quotations and helpful Greek word studies scattered throughout the book. Denies miracles, looks upon Paul's conversion as the result of an electrical storm, and bypasses many problems in the text. 226.6'07.B23

Bartlett, J. Vernon. *The Acts.* The Century Bible. Edinburgh: T. C. and E. C. Jack, 1901.

†At times defends the accuracy and integrity of the Scriptures, and at other times denies it. Only valuable for exegesis. Arminian. 226.6'07.B28

Barton, George Aaron. *The Apostolic Age.* Philadelphia: University of Pennsylvania Press, 1936.

An interpretative introduction to the NT, and a history of the apostolic age. 225.7'09.B28

*Baumgarten, Michael. *The Acts of the Apostles or the History of the Church in the Apostolic Age.* Clark's Foreign Theological Library. Translated by A. J. W. Morrison. 3 vols. Edinburgh: T. and T. Clark, 1854.

Technical and helpful. Adds depth to an understanding of the church in the first century A.D. 226.6'07.B23A

Blaiklock, Edward Musgrave. *The Acts of the Apostles.* Tyndale New Testament Commentary. Grand Rapids: Wm. B. Eerdmans Publishing Co., 1959.

A work that ably concentrates on the historicity of the Acts, but fails to deal adequately with the text. 226.6'07.B57

Blunt, Alfred Walter Frank. *The Acts of the Apostles.* The Clarendon Bible. Oxford: At the Clarendon Press, 1922.

Among other things, disallows verbal inspiration in his treatment of the text, claims that many of the miracles would

have a more normal interpretation today, "trembles on the verge of ascribing personality" to the Holy spirit (p. 145), and feels that Paul's phrase "Son of God" does not ascribe deity to Christ. 226.6'07.B62

Brown, John. *Discourses the Sayings of Our Lord Jesus Christ.* 3 vols. London: Banner of Truth Trust, 1967.

Based upon the revised and enlarged edition of 1852. Rich in thought. Pastors will appreciate the writer's application of spiritual truths to the needs of men and women. 226.07.B81 1967

Bruce, Frederick Fyvie. *The Acts of the Apostles.* Grand Rapids: Wm. B. Eerdmans Publishing Co., 1965.

First published in 1951. An exegetical work not to be confused with the author's exposition in the NICNT. Takes into account the most recent research into all questions of authorship, sources, style, and so on, and then sets forth a commentary based solely upon the Greek text. 226.6'07.B83

*———. *Commentary on the Book of Acts.* New International Commentary on the New Testament. Grand Rapids: Wm. B. Eerdmans Publishing Co., 1954.

Perhaps the best expository work for the pastor. Sound exposition based upon careful exegesis and a thorough knowledge of the historical background. 226.6'07.B83N

Cadbury, Henry Joel. *The Book of Acts in History.* New York: Harper and Brothers, 1955.

†Concentrates on studying the historical sidelights in the book of Acts. Charges Luke with writing speeches that were never delivered, claims that Pentecost is not historical, denies that medical language of Luke is significant, and thinks there is an error in the census. These are only a few of Cadbury's abberations. 226.6'06.C11

Carter, Charles W., and **Ralph Earle.** *The Acts of the Apostles.* The Evangelical

Commentary. Grand Rapids: Zondervan Publishing House, 1959.

While the exegetical portion is valuable, the exposition of the text fails to grasp the significance of the transition that is taking place. Surprisingly allows for the possibility of errors in Stephen's speech. Arminian. 226.6'07.C24

Carver, William Owen. *The Acts of the Apostles.* Nashville: Sunday School Board, Southern Baptist Convention, 1916.

†A popular exposition, but one that fails to defend apparent contradictions in the text. 226.6'07.C25

Dibelius, Martin. *Studies in the Acts of the Apostles.* New York: Charles Scribner's Sons, 1956.

†A series of essays based on a form-critical study of Acts. 226.6'06.D54

***Erdman, Charles Rosenbury.** *The Acts.* Philadelphia: Westminster Press, 1919.

A devotional and practical commentary of great help to preachers. 226.6'07.ER2

Findlay, James Alexander. *The Acts of the Apostles.* London: SCM Press, 1934.

†Brief comments on the text of the RV of 1881. 226.6'07.F49

Foakes-Jackson, Frederick John. *The Acts of the Apostles.* Moffatt New Testament Commentary. New York: Harper and Brothers, 1931.

†Of little value as a result of the author's theological position, denial of the miraculous, and rejection of the inerrancy and authority of the Scripture. 226.6'07.F68

*_____ and **Kirsopp Lake.** *The Beginnings of Christianity.* 5 vols. London: Macmillan Co., 1920-33.

†A technical, theologically liberal work that does contain valuable information on the background of the first century A.D. in volumes 1 and 2, a reconstruction of the text in volume 3, and a commentary with notes in volumes 4 and 5. 226.6'07.F68

Gaebelein, Arno Clemens. *The Acts of the Apostles.* New York: Loizeaux Brothers, 1961.

A capable exposition that dates the origin of the church from Acts 2, maintains that the "tongues" at Pentecost were known languages, and claims that James gives God's plan for the church age in Acts 15. 266.6'07.G11

Gettys, Joseph Miller. *How to Study Acts.* Richmond: John Knox Press, 1959.

A *must* for those studying Acts for the first time. 226.6'007.G33S

***Gloag, Paton James.** *A Critical and Exegetical Commentary on the Acts of the Apostles.* 2 vols. Edinburgh: T. and T. Clark, 1870.

A thorough exposition based on careful exegesis. Particularly praiseworthy is the writer's handling of critical problems. Deserves reprinting. 266.6'07.G51

***Hackett, Horacio Balch.** *A Commentary on the Acts of the Apostles.* Philadelphia: American Baptist Publication Society, 1851.

A valuable verse-by-verse treatment. Calvinistic. 226.6'07.H11

Hanson, Richard Patrick Crosland. *The Acts.* The New Clarendon Bible. Oxford: At the Clarendon Press, 1967.

†A revision of Blunt's volume that retains the liberal leanings of its predecessor. 226.6'07.H19

***Hastings, James, ed.** *Dictionary of the Apostolic Church.* 2 vols. New York: Charles Scribner's Sons, 1963.

†Supplements *HDCG* and carries the history of Christianity through the period covered by the book of Acts to the close of the first century. Even though there is a greater representation of articles by American scholars, British contributors still predominate. Each book of the New Testament (the gospels ex-

cepted) is carefully outlined, introduced, and commented on in such a way as to bring out its primary purpose and message. Perhaps the greatest single asset of this set is the manner in which historical events are used to highlight biblical teachings (e.g., adoption, emperor worship, the development of the law, and so on). In addition, the correlation of historical references with people and places, cities and events (e.g., Paul and Tarsus, John and Patmos, and the cities referred to in Revelation 2-3) all add richness to the study of different New Testament passages. 226.6'03.H27 1963

Ironside, Henry Allan. *Lectures on the Book of Acts.* New York: Loizeaux Brothers, 1965.

Expository messages that encourage the systematic study of the Scripture. Devotional 226.6'07.IR6

*Jensen, Irving Lester. *Acts: An Inductive Study.* Chicago: Moody Press, 1968.

A helpful study manual that stresses the importance of making charts as an aid in Bible study. 226.6'007.J45

Kelly, William. *An Exposition of the Acts of the Apostles.* London: C. A. Hammond, 1952.

A devotional commentary that evaluates all the problems and provides helpful comments on the text. First published in 1895. 226.6'07.K29 1952

Knox, Wilfred Lawrence. *The Acts of the Apostles.* Cambridge: At the University Press, 1948.

A critical work that raises more problems than it solves. 226.6'07.K77

Laurin, Roy Leonard. *Acts: Life in Action.* Findlay, Ohio: Dunham Publishing Co., 1962.

Popular but superficial sermons. Contains some interesting illustrations, but unfortunately lacks those qualities that would make a lasting contribution. 226.6'07.L36

Lindsay, Thomas M. *The Acts of the Apostles.* 2 vols. Edinburgh: T. and T. Clark, 1884.

An introduction with brief expository notes. Reformed. 226.6'07.L64

Luccock, Halford Edward. *The Acts of the Apostles in Present-Day Preaching.* 2 vols. New York: Willett, Clark and Co., 1938-39.

†Follows in the footsteps of Fosdick. Attacks Christ's deity, charges orthodoxy with naivete, cries out for social reform, and defends communism. 226.6'07.L96

Lumby, Joseph Rawson. *The Acts of the Apostles.* Cambridge Bible for Schools and Colleges. Cambridge: At the University Press, 1893.

See below.
226.6'07.L97

*_____. *The Acts of the Apostles.* Cambridge Greek Testament. Cambridge: At the University Press, 1899.

Two works of great value that obviously contain many similarities in content. The latter volume is of particular importance for its handling of syntactical problems. For those who lack a knowledge of Greek, the former work still is helpful. 226.6'07.L97G

Macaulay, Joseph Cordner. *A Devotional Commentary on the Acts of the Apostles.* Grand Rapids: Wm. B. Eerdmans Publishing Co., 1946.

A homiletic commentary. Possesses little of intrinsic worth. 226.6'07.M11

*Morgan, George Campbell. *The Acts of the Apostles.* New York: Fleming H. Revell Co., 1924.

Regarded by many as *the* most important single expository work for the pastor. 226.6'07.M82

_____. *The Birth of the Church.* Old Tappan, N.J.: Fleming H. Revell Co., 1968.

Deals with the events that took place on the day of Pentecost. Devotional. 226.6'07.2.M82 1968

Moule, Charles Francis Digby. *Christ's Messengers.* New York: Association Press, 1957.

Brief studies on the subject of "witness." Contains helpful material on Peter's sermon at Pentecost, Stephen's speech, and Paul's address at the Areopagus, together with an excellent discussion of the etymology of Greek words. 226.6'08.M86

Munck, Johannes. *The Anchor Bible. The Acts of the Apostles.* Garden City: Doubleday and Co., 1967.

†A modern introduction and translation with brief, insightful, and generally helpful comments on the text. 226.6'07.M92

*Ogg, George. *The Odyssey of Paul.* Old Tappan, N.J.: Fleming H. Revell Co., 1968.

An invaluable study of the chronology of the life of Paul. Corrects the chronological deficiencies found in Conybeare and Howson and the attempts of others to correlate Paul's itinerant ministry. 226.6'012.OG3

Olson, Arnold Theodore. *The Pacemakers.* Minneapolis: Board of Publications Evangelical Free Church of America, 1957.

A devotional study of six conversions in the book of Acts. 226.6'092.OL8

Pierson, Arthur Tappan. *The Acts of the Holy Spirit.* New York: Fleming H. Revell Co., 1895.

A devotional book that rightly stresses the ministry of the Holy Spirit in the work of the early church. 226.6'07.P31

*Rackham, Richard Belward. *The Acts of the Apostles.* Grand Rapids: Baker Book House, 1964.

A helpful exposition tending to overemphasize the sacraments and church offices, but compensates for this by providing a brilliantly perceptive study of the text. Deserves to be regarded as a

classic. Originally published in 1901. 226.6'07.R11 1964

Ramsay, William Mitchell. *Pictures of the Apostolic Church: Studies in the Book of Acts.* Grand Rapids: Baker Book House, 1959.

Studies highlighting important facets in the history and growth of the early church. First published in 1910. 226.6'07.R14 1959

Ridderbos, Herman Nicholas. *The Speeches of Peter in the Acts of the Apostles.* London: Tyndale Press, 1962.

Composed of the Tyndale New Testament Lecture for 1961. Provides a scholarly exposition of Peter's speeches. 226.6'08.R43

Ryrie, Charles Caldwell. *The Acts of the Apostles.* Chicago: Moody Press, 1961.

A brief, popular, and genuinely helpful exposition. Ideal for home Bible classes and Bible study groups. 226.6'07.R99

*Scroggie, William Graham. *The Acts of the Apostles.* London: Marshall, Morgan and Scott, 1931.

Abounds in helpful outlines, wholesome exposition, and usable illustrations. 226.6'07.SCR5

Smith, James. *The Voyage and Shipwreck of St. Paul.* 4th ed. revised by W. E. Smith. London: Longmans, Green and Company, 1880.

Contains an important discussion of the chronology of Paul's life, the climate of the times, and the terminology used by ancient seamen to describe certain of the conditions that either made possible or hindered travel by sea. 227.SM6

Stagg, Frank. *The Book of Acts.* Nashville: Broadman Press, 1955.

†De-emphasizes the deity and role of the Holy Spirit, and provides relatively few insights into the text and theme of the book. 226.6'07.ST1

Stier, Ewald Rudolph. *The Words of the*

Apostles. Clark's Foreign Theological Library. Translated by G. H. Venables. Edinburgh: T. and T. Clark, 1869.

A comprehensive analysis of the speeches and sermons of the book of Acts. Deserves a place in every expository preacher's library. 226.6'04.ST5

Stifler, James Madison. *An Introduction to the Study of Acts of the Apostles.* New York: Fleming H. Revell Co., 1892.

A helpful introduction to and an interpretive analysis of the book of Acts. 226.6'07.ST5

Thomas, David. *Acts of the Apostles.* Grand Rapids: Baker Book House, 1956.

A homiletic commentary that gives 111 sermons on different paragraphs in the book of Acts. First published in 1870. 226.6'07.T36 1956

Thomas, William Henry Griffith. *Outline Studies in the Acts of the Apostles.* Grand Rapids: Wm. B. Eerdmans Publishing Co., 1956.

An extensive series of homiletical outlines. 226.6'07.T36S

Vaughan, Charles John. *The Church of the First Days: Lectures on the Acts of the Apostles.* 3 vols. London: Macmillan Co., 1864.

A series of sermons accompanied by a paraphrase of the Greek text and providing some penetrating insights into the Scriptures. Excellent as examples of exposition. 226.6'07.V46

Veil, Carolus M. du. *A Commentary on the Acts of the Apostles.* London: J. Haddon, 1851.

Reprinted from the first edition, which appeared in 1685. Lengthy exposition by a man whose theological pilgrimage took him from Judaism to Roman Catholicism to Anglicanism and finally to the Baptists. Supports all the cardinal doctrines of the faith. Argues for immersion. 226.6'07.V53 1851

Walker, Thomas. *The Acts of the Apostles.* Chicago: Moody Press, 1965.

Warm and fervent in style, but provides little connection between one verse and the next. First published in 1910. 226.6'07.W15 1965

Williams, Charles Steven Conway. *A Commentary on the Acts of the Apostles.* Harper's New Testament Commentaries. New York: Harper and Brothers, 1957.

†While denying inspiration, the writer does provide a perceptive exposition of the text. Helpful for the discerning reader. 226.6'07.W67

MIRACLES

*Bruce, Alexander Balmain. *The Miraculous Element in the Gospels.* London: Hodder and Stoughton, 1886.

A valuable apologetic treatment. Contains much original material. Of real help to expository preachers. 226.7'06.B83

Habershon, Ada Ruth. *The Study of the Miracles.* Grand Rapids: Kregel Publications, 1957.

A helpful supplement to Trench's masterly treatment. Premillennial. 226.7'07.H11 1957

*Laidlaw, John. *The Miracles of Our Lord.* Grand Rapids: Baker Book House, 1956.

Reprinted from the edition published in 1900. An unusually complete and satisfying exposition. 226.7'07.L14 1956

Lang, Cosmo Gordon. *The Miracles of Jesus as Marks on the Way of Life.* London: Isaac Pitman and Sons, 1906.

A companion volume to the *Parables of Jesus.* Devotional. 226.7'07.L25

Richardson, Alan. *Miracle Stories of the Gospels.* 2d ed. London: SCM Press, 1942.

†While avoiding the skepticism of some critics, this work attempts to bring out the significance of miracles. 226.7'07.R39 1942

Taylor, William Mackergo. The Miracles of Our Saviour. London: Hodder and Stoughton, 1891.

A series of moving messages by one of the great preachers of a generation past. 226.7'07.T21

*Trench, Richard Chenevix. *Notes on the Miracles of Our Lord.* London: Pickering and Inglis, 1953.

A scholarly study of the thirty-three miracles of Christ recorded in the gospel narratives. Originally published in 1846, but still valuable. 226.7'07.T72 1953

Wallace, Ronald S. *Many Things in Parables,* and *The Gospel Miracles.* Grand Rapids: Wm. B. Eerdmans Publishing Co., 1963.

†Expounds the parables and miracles of the gospels with forcefulness, clarity, and persuasive eloquence. 226.7'07.W14

PARABLES

Arnot, William. *The Parables of Our Lord.* London: Thomas Nelson and Sons, 1893.

These devotional studies are rewarding. Preachers will find them helpful. 226.8'07.AR6

———. *The Lesser Parables of Our Lord.* London: Thomas Nelson and Sons, 1884.

Contains only ten chapters on the lesser parables of our Lord, and then proceeds to discuss different theological and biblical concepts. Includes twenty-four chapters on I Peter, and concludes with a discussion of the life of Christ. Valuable in spite of its vintage. 226.8'07.AR6L

Barclay, William. *And Jesus Said: A Handbook on the Parables of Jesus.* Philadelphia: Westminster Press, 1970.

A moderately evangelical, historical, and theological approach to the parables. Should be read with discernment. 226.8'06.B23

*Bruce, Alexander Balmain. *The Par-*

abolic Teaching of Christ. New York: A. C. Armstrong, 1908.

A systematic, critical study of the parables of Christ that includes in its treatment similies and other forms of speech. Will richly reward the careful reader. 226.8'06.B83

Dodd, Charles Harold. *The Parables of the Kingdom.* Welwyn Herts, England: James Nisbet and Co., 1935.

†An approach to the parables from a form-critical eschatological point of view. 226.8'06.D66

Dods, Marcus. *The Parables of Our Lord.* London: Hodder and Stoughton, 1902.

Limited to the parables found in Matthew's gospel. Experiences difficulty in the parable of the ten virgins, but provides helpful material on the "laborers in the vineyard," and "the unforgiving debtor." 226.8'07.D66

Fraser, Donald. *Metaphors in the Gospels.* London: James Nisbet and Co., 1885.

Thirty-six chapters that illuminate the metaphors and figures of speech found in the gospels. Ideal for preachers. 226.8'07.F86

Habershon, Ada Ruth. *The Study of the Parables.* Grand Rapids: Kregel Publications, 1957.

A perceptive treatment by a capable Hebrew Christian writer. 226.8'07.H11 1957

*Hunter, Archibald Macbride. *Interpreting the Parables.* Philadelphia: Westminster Press, 1960.

A valuable contribution. 226.8'06.H91

*Jeremias, Joachim. *The Parables of Jesus.* Revised ed. Translated by S. H. Hooke. New York: Charles Scribner's Sons, 1963.

†A standard, form-critical work that seeks to recover the original form and meaning of the parables. At once enlightening and helpful. 226.8'07.J47 1963

———. *Rediscovering the Parables.* New

York: Charles Scribner's Sons, 1966.

†A revised version of the *Parables of Jesus*. Less technical than the writer's earlier work, and abridged to make the material helpful to laymen. Adherence to *Redactiongeschichte* still evident. 226.8'06.J47

Lang, Cosmo Gordon. *The Parables of Jesus*. London: Isaac Pitman and Sons, 1906.

Expository messages that still are of value today. Evangelical. 226.8'07.L25

*****Lang, George Henry.** *Pictures and Parables*. London: Paternoster Press, 1955.

A series of perceptive studies on the parabolic teaching of the Scripture. Abounds in usable material. 226.8'07.L25P

Lunnemann, A. *The Parables of Jesus*. London: SPCK, 1966.

†A mediating work from a moderately liberal point of view. Does not deal with all parables, but selects those best suited to his purpose. 226.8'07.L97

Morgan, George Campbell. *The Parable of the Father's Heart*. New York: Fleming H. Revell Co., 1949.

A touching and reverent exposition of Luke 15 that concentrates on the prodigal son, but also includes material on the lost sheep and the lost coin. The climax is an appeal to service and provides an example of expository preaching. 226.4'07.15.M82

_____. *The Parables of the Kingdom*. London: Hodder and Stoughton, 1907.

Good preaching values may be gleaned from a study of these expository messages on the parables of Matthew 13. 226.2'07.13.M82

*_____. *The Parables and Metaphors of Our Lord*. Westwood, N.J.: Fleming H. Revell Co., 1943.

A provocative, stimulating work. Should have an honored place in every preacher's library. 226.8'07.M82

Swete, Henry Barclay. *The Parables of the Kingdom*. London: Macmillan Co., 1920.

A scholarly study including the Greek text, with exegesis and notes. Amillennial. 226.8'07.SW4

*****Trench, Richard Chenevix.** *Notes on the Parables of Our Lord*. London: Pickering and Inglis, 1953.

A standard work. The preacher should consult Jeremias, Morgan, and other more recent writers to update Trench's treatment. First published in 1841. 226.8'07.T72

THE LORD'S PRAYER

Allen, Charles Livingstone. *The Lord's Prayer*. Westwood, N.J.: Fleming H. Revell Co., 1963.

A brief treatment that is not as valuable as some of the author's other works. 226.9'06.AL5

Dods, Marcus. *The Prayer that Teaches to Pray*. Cincinnati: Cranston and Curts, 1893.

A fervent, eloquent exposition of the Lord's Prayer. While not all will agree with the writer, his devotional emphasis and inspirational thoughts will prove helpful to many. 226.9'07.D66

Macartney, Clarence Edward Noble. *The Lord's Prayer*. New York: Fleming H. Revell Co., 1942.

A phrase-by-phrase exposition. Popular, with excellent illustrations. 226.9'07.M11

Macaulay, Joseph Cordner. *After This Manner*. Grand Rapids: Wm. B. Eerdmans Publishing Co., 1952.

A brief devotional meditation on the Lord's Prayer. Provides excellent outlines and good illustrations. 226.9'07.M11A

Redpath, Alan. *Victorious Praying*. Westwood, N.J.: Fleming H. Revell Co., 1957.

A helpful study of the Lord's Prayer. 226.9'07.R24

Saphir, Adolph. *The Lord's Prayer*. London: James Nisbet and Co., 1870.

Fervent messages that expound the

text and edify the reader. Frequent digressions into matters of theological importance make fascinating reading. 226.9'07.SA6

Thielicke, Helmut. *Our Heavenly Father.* Translated by John W. Doberstein. New York: Harper and Brothers, 1960.

†A series of sermons on the Lord's Prayer first delivered in Stuttgart in 1944. The historical setting that gave rise to these messages also gives them extraordinary force. 226.9'06.T34

Thompson, J. G. S. S. *The Praying Christ.* London: Tyndale Press, 1959.

An exceedingly valuable study on Christ's pattern of and teaching on prayer. 226.96.T37

Watson, Thomas. *The Lord's Prayer.* London: Banner of Truth Trust, 1960.

A part of the writer's famous *Body of Divinity.* An excellent exposition combining sound doctrine with practical application. Reprinted from the 1890 edition. 226.9'07.W33 1960

THE PAULINE EPISTLES

Barclay, William. *The Mind of St. Paul.* New York: Harper and Row, 1959.

†A popular treatment that follows the old British tradition of psychoanalyzing Paul. Ephemeral. 227'.06.B23

Barrett, Charles Kingsley. *From First Adam to Last: A Study in Pauline Theology.* New York: Charles Scribner's Sons, 1962.

Builds upon the theology of form-criticism and, by ignoring the theme of the epistle, treats parts of the letter as a running debate. The reconstruction of the historic setting of the first century A.D. is helpful. 227'.082.B27F

*Barth, Karl. *Christ and Adam: Man and Humanity in Romans 5.* Translated by T. A. Smail. New York: Harper and Row, 1956.

†Adequately examines Romans 5, but falls short of a thorough representation of Paul's thought by its failure to explain justification *by faith,* and by making universalism implicit in the atonement. 227'.082.B28C

Best, Ernest. *One Body in Christ.* London: SPCK, 1955.

†A study in Pauline ecclesiology. Very full. 227'.082.B46

Bruce, Alexander Balmain. *St. Paul's Conception of Christianity.* Edinburgh: T. and T. Clark, 1894.

After tracing Paul's religious history, the writer concentrates on the doctrines

expounded in Paul's letters to Galatia, Corinth, and Rome. He discourses on the doctrine of sin, the righteousness of God, the death of Christ, adoption, and so on. Provides interesting studies on different topics. 227'.082.B83

Caird, George Bradsford. *Principalities and Powers: A Study in Pauline Theology.* Oxford: The Clarendon Press, 1956.

†A recent critical study of the theology of the apostolic age. 227'.082.C12

*Davies, William David. *Paul and Rabbinic Judaism.* New York: Harper and Row, 1948.

A fascinating and thorough study of some rabbinic elements in Pauline theology. Bears evidence of the author's thorough acquaintance with the subject matter. 227'.082.D28

Dodd, Charles Harold. *The Meaning of Paul for Today.* London: Allen and Unwin, 1920.

†A scholarly endeavor to give Paul his place in the history of religion. 227'.082.D66

Ellis, Edward Earle. *Paul and His Recent Interpreters.* Grand Rapids: Wm. B. Eerdmans Publishing Co., 1961.

Aims at equipping the student of the Pauline epistles with information by which he can better evaluate his exegesis in the light of current critical concerns. Neither comprehensive nor the first of its kind. 227'.06.EL5

Findlay, George Gillanders. *The Epistles of Paul the Apostle.* New York: Wilbur B. Ketcham, n.d.

A brief introduction and outline of the Pauline epistles. Too old to be of lasting value. 227'.061.F49

Gloag, Paton James. *Introduction to the Pauline Epistles.* Edinburgh: T. and T. Clark, 1874.

Old, but full of valuable information. 227'.061.G51

Hamilton, Neill Quinn. *The Holy Spirit and Eschatology in Paul.* Edinburgh: Oliver and Boyd, 1957.

A critical inquiry into the role of the Spirit as the revealer of Christ, His place in the eschatological program of God, and ministry to the redeemed. 227'.082.H18

Hatch, William Henry Paine. *The Pauline Idea of Faith in Its Relation to Jewish and Hellenistic Religions.* Cambridge: Harvard University Press, 1917.

Belongs to the old *religionsgeschichtliche Schule,* which attempts to prove that Paul's theology was a Hellenistic mystery religion carried over into the NT. 227'.082.H28

Hayes, Doremus Almy. *Paul and His Epistles.* Grand Rapids: Baker Book House, 1969.

Provides a helpful analysis of Paul's life and thought. Also contains a mine of homiletic information for pastors. Originally published in 1915. 227'.06.H32 1969

Headlam, Arthur Cayley. *St. Paul and Christianity.* London: John Murray, 1913.

A quasi-evangelical approach to Pauline theology. 227'.082.H34

*Hiebert, David Edmond. *An Introduction to the Pauline Epistles.* Chicago: Moody Press, 1954.

Among the best introductory studies available. Thoroughly conservative, fully abreast of the latest advances in scholarship, and contains comprehensive outlines based upon an analysis of the Greek text. 227'.061.H53

Howson, John Saul. *The Character of St. Paul.* London: Hodder and Stoughton, 1885.

Composed of the Hulsean Lectures, Cambridge University, 1862, these strikingly original studies shed much light on the personality of the apostle and readily reveal the motivating force of his life. A welcome addition to any preacher's library. 225.92.P28.H83

*_____. *The Metaphors of St. Paul.* London: Strahan and Co., n.d.

Four studies based upon the NT Scriptures and centering in the metaphors used of or about Roman soldiers, classical architecture, ancient agriculture, and the Grecian games. Originally published in 1868. 227'.08.H84

Hunter, Archibald Macbride. *Interpreting Paul's Gospel.* Philadelphia: Westminster Press, 1955.

Reflects theological vacillation, but deserves to be read. 227'.06.H91

*_____. *Paul and His Predecessors.* Philadelphia: Westminster Press, 1961.

†Attempts to prove that Paul originated the theology he expounds in his epistles with little regard for the life and teachings of Christ. Contains a capable analysis of contemporary European scholarship. 227'.082.H91

Kennedy, Henry Angus Alexander. *St. Paul and the Mystery-Religions.* London: Hodder and Stoughton, 1913.

A standard study that reacts against those who interpret Pauline theology solely against the background of the mystery religions. 227'.08.K38

_____. *The Theology of the Epistles.* London: Gerald Duckworth, 1919.

A brief survey stressing the unity of thought in the epistles. 227'.082.K38T

Knowling, Richard John. The Testimony of St. Paul to Christ. 3d ed. London: Hodder and Stoughton, 1911.

Based upon the Boyle Lectures for 1903-5. Deals with the Pauline epistles, Paul's conversion and testimony to the veracity of the gospel records, and his teaching on the life and function of the church. A scholarly study. 227'.082.K76 1911

*_____. The Witness of the Epistles: A Study in Modern Criticism. London: Longmans, Green and Co., 1892.

Establishes the origin of Pauline theology, discourses on Paul's Christology and the incarnation, provides an interesting chapter on the resurrection of Christ, and a discussion of His ascension and second coming. A final chapter evaluates Paul as an evangelist. 227'.082.K76W

Lake, Kirsopp. The Earlier Epistles of St. Paul. London: Rivington's, 1911.

The value of this work lies in the reconstruction of the historical setting of Paul's early epistles. Later in his life the author reversed a number of positions he advocated in this study. 277'.061.L14

Lightfoot, Joseph Barber. Notes on the Epistles of St. Paul. Grand Rapids: Zondervan Publishing House, 1957.

Contains exegetical notes on I and II Thessalonians, I Corinthians 1-7, Romans 1-7, and Ephesians 1:1-14. Exceedingly helpful. Indexed. 227'.07.L62 1957

The Letters of St. Paul and Hebrews. Translated by Arthur S. Way. Grand Rapids: Kregel Publications, 1951.

A unique translation, with many of the portions written in poetic form. Easy to understand, and true to the meaning of Scripture, even when the author indulges in a brief paraphrase of the text. 227'.052.W36

Longenecker, Richard Norman. Paul, Apostle of Liberty. New York: Harper and Row, 1964.

An exacting study of the origin and nature of Paul's message. Holds that the "key to Pauline Christianity is found in the creative tension between law and liberty that runs throughout his thought." 227'.082.L86

Machen, John Gresham. The Origin of Paul's Religion. Grand Rapids: Wm. B. Eerdmans Publishing Co., 1925.

Consists of the James Sprunt Lectures, Union Theological Seminary, Virginia. Surveys the early years of Paul's life, his Jewish environment, religious training, and the development of his doctrine. A valuable treatment. Amillennial. 227'.082.M13

Matheson, George. Spiritual Development of St. Paul. 3d ed. Edinburgh: Wm. Blackwood and Sons, 1892.

Confining himself to a consideration of Paul's life *after* his conversion, Matheson studies Paul's reminiscences, struggles, accomplishments, and abiding legacy. 225.92.P28.M41

Moe, Olaf Edvard. The Apostle Paul: His Message and Doctrine. Translated by L. A. Vigness. Minneapolis: Augsburg Publishing House, 1954.

Based upon the German edition published in 1928. Centers on the doctrinal concepts of the apostle to the Gentiles. Lutheran. 227'.082.M72

Moffat, James. Paul and Paulinism. London: J. Constable, 1910.

A short but important study. 227'.082.M72P

Peake, Arthur Samuel. Paul and the Jewish Christians. Manchester: University Press, 1929.

A capable work, but now superseded by more recent studies. 227.082.P31

_____. The Quintessence of Paulinism. Manchester: University Press, 1918.

A brief, seminal lecture. 227'.082.P31Q

Pink, Arthur Walkington. Gleanings from Paul: Studies in the Prayers of the Apostle. Chicago: Moody Press, 1967.

Concentrates on the prayers and notes of praise of the apostle Paul. Expounds the Scriptures so as to give a better understanding of Paul himself. 227'.06.P65

*Ramsay, William Mitchell. *Pauline and Other Studies in Early Christian History.* Grand Rapids: Baker Book House, 1970.

Reprinted from the 1906 edition, these essays deal with a wide variety of NT themes. Of particular interest are his chapters on "The Statesmanship of Paul," "The Worship of the Virgin Mary at Ephesus," "The Authorship of the Acts," and "Pauline Chronology." 227'.08.R14 1970

*_____. *The Teaching of Paul in Terms of the Present Day.* 2d ed. London: Hodder and Stoughton, 1914.

Deals with the thought of the apostle, his Areopagus address, his relationship to the mystery religions, his conversion and imprisonment, and the date of the Galatian letter. 227'.082.R14 1914

Ridderbos, Herman Nicholas. *Paul and Jesus.* Translated by D. H. Freeman. Philadelphia: Presbyterian and Reformed Publishing Co., 1958.

A scholarly study of Paul's preaching of Christ. Reformed. 227'.082.R43

Robertson, Archibald Thomas. *Paul the Interpreter of Christ.* London: Hodder and Stoughton, 1921.

Offers a series of studies of different aspects of Paul's ministry and teaching. 227'.082.R54

Robinson, John Arthur Thomas. *The Body: A Study of Pauline Theology.* Studies in Biblical theology. London: SCM Press, 1966.

†A selection of scholarly essays. Of value if read with discernment. 227'.082.R54B

Sabatier, Auguste. *The Apostle Paul.* Translated by A. M. Hellier. London: Hodder and Stoughton, 1906.

Reacts against the Tübingen school and, in contrast to their rationalistic approach, stresses the need for and significance of the development of Paul's theology. 227'.082.SA1

Sandmel, Samuel. *The Genius of Paul.* New York: Farrar, Straus and Cudahy, 1958.

A Jewish comparative religionist of liberal persuasion attributes the genius of Paul to his ability to recast Christianity into a Christ-Savior cult. 227'.082.SA5

Schoeps, Hans Joachim. *Paul: The Theology of the Apostle in the Light of Jewish Religious History.* Translated by H. Knight. Philadelphia: Westminster Press, 1961.

An impartial study by a renowned Jewish historian. Evaluates the Jewish influences in the life and thought of the apostle to the Gentiles. 227'.082.SCH6

Schweitzer, Albert. *The Mysticism of Paul the Apostle.* Translated by W. Montgomery. London: A. and C. Black, 1931.

A sequel to *Paul and His Interpreters.* Seeks to prove that Paul was not responsible for the Hellenization of Christianity, but that he adhered closely to his Judaistic heritage and the teaching of Jesus. 227'.08.SCH9M

_____. *Paul and His Interpreters.* Translated by W. Montgomery. London: A. and C. Black, 1912.

†The result of a study of the relationship between the teaching of Jesus and the apparent discrepancies in the theology of Paul. 227'.08.SCH9P

Scott, Charles Archibald Anderson. *Christianity According to St. Paul.* Cambridge: At the University Press, 1966.

†Seeks to show that the influence of Hellenism upon the thought-pattern of the apostle was negligible, but that his teaching was derived almost entirely from Judaism. Scholarly and readable, but needs to be read with discretion. 227'.082.SCO8

Stevens, George Barker. *The Messages of Paul.* New York: Charles Scribner's Sons, 1900.

An able evaluation of the setting, content, and structure of Paul's discourses. 227'.08.ST4

_____. *The Pauline Theology.* New York: Charles Scribner's Sons, 1918.

Draws heavily upon the epistle to the Romans. Makes a valuable contribution to a study of Paul's theology. All will not agree with the writer. 227'.082.ST4

*****Stewart, James Stuart.** *A Man in Christ: The Vital Elements in St. Paul's Religion.* New York: Harper and Row, 1935.

A treatment of Pauline thought that ranks high among the very best contributions in the field. 227'.082.ST4M

Thomas, William Henry Griffith. *The Prayers of St. Paul.* Edinburgh: T. and T. Clark, 1914.

A devotional gem that makes rewarding reading and contains numerous seed thoughts for preachers. 227'.08.T36

Vos, Gerhardus. *Pauline Eschatology.* Grand Rapids: Wm. B. Eerdmans Publishing Co., 1961.

A unique and helpful study from an amillennial point of view. 227'.082.V92

White, Reginald Ernest Oscar. *Prayer Is the Secret.* Evesham, England: James, 1958.

A study of apostolic prayer experience. 227'.08.W58

Whiteley, Denys Edward Hugh. *The Theology of Paul.* Philadelphia: Fortress Press, 1964.

†A serious attempt to describe Paul's theology in its entirety. Minimizes the Hellenistic element of Paul's thought, follows a mild form of Tübingenism in tracing his relationship to the theology of apostolic Christianity, and then discusses the development of Paul's thought topically and chronologically. 227'.082.W58

ROMANS

Archer, Gleason Leonard, Jr. *The Epistle to the Romans.* Grand Rapids: Baker Book House, 1959.

A brief outline giving the main argument of the book. Evangelical. 227.1'07.AR2

Barnhouse, Donald Grey. *Exposition of Bible Doctrine Taking the Epistle to the Romans as the Point of Departure.* 10 vols. Grand Rapids: Wm. B. Eerdmans Publishing Co., 1952-63.

An exposition of Bible doctrine that is very full, well illustrated, and appropriately applied. 227.1'07.B26

Barrett, Charles Kingsley. *A Commentary on the Epistle to the Romans.* Harper's New Testament Commentary. New York: Harper and Brothers, 1957.

†A helpful work in which the writer manifests a precision of thought that is highly commendable but seems to express a Pelagian view of sin, and appears to have an inadequate view of the deity of Christ. 227.1'07.B27C

Barth, Karl. *The Epistle to the Romans.* Translated by E. C. Hoskyns. London: Oxford University Press, 1933.

This landmark book first appeared in German after World War I. In it Barth showed the failure of liberalism and used the epistle as a platform from which to launch his own "new orthodoxy." Not a good exposition, but an epochal work of historical significance in the study of theology. 227.1'07.B28

Beet, Joseph Agar. *Commentary on St. Paul's Epistle to the Romans.* London: Hodder and Stoughton, 1902.

†An Arminian commentary that manifests a weakness when handling the doctrine of the deity of Christ, but contains many valuable exegetical insights. 227.1'07.B39

*****Bruce, Frederick Fyvie.** *The Epistle of*

Paul to the Romans. Tyndale New Testament Commentaries. Grand Rapids: Wm. B. Eerdmans Publishing Co., 1963.

Draws upon a wide knowledge of literature, frequently cites theological writers, and provides an understandable and, in many ways, significant exposition of this epistle. Occasionally the comments are too brief to be of help to the pastor, and at other times exceptionally full. 227.1'07.B83

Brunner, Heinrich Emil. *The Letter to the Romans.* Philadelphia: Westminster Press, 1959.

†A Neoorthodox treatment that minimizes the deity of Christ and comes close to denying the doctrine of original sin. 227.1'07.B83L

Chadwick, Henry. *The Enigma of St. Paul.* London: Athlone Press, 1969.

These Ethel Wood Lectures, delivered at the University of London, focus on Paul's pastoral and pedagogical methodology, particularly as shown in his dealings with the converts at Corinth. 227.1'08.C34

Dodd, Charles Harold. *The Epistle of Paul to the Romans.* Moffat New Testament Commentary. New York: Harper and Brothers, 1932.

†Based upon a psychological approach to Paul and his theology, this work, at its best, is a study of Dodd's own exegetical method. Dodd does not hesitate to take issue with Paul whenever he feels his logic is faulty. Does not deserve to be ranked among the better commentaries on this epistle. 227.1'07.D66

Ellison, Henry Leopold. *The Mystery of Israel—An Exposition of Romans 9-11.* Grand Rapids: Wm. B. Eerdmans Publishing Co., 1966.

Brings to bear upon the subject of Israel a background of practical experience, as well as an extensive knowledge of Hebrew and rabbinic sources on the biblical text. While some statements require clarification, the general treatment is commendable. Amillennial. 227.1'07.9-11.EL5

*Erdman, Charles Rosenbury. *The Epistle to the Romans.* Philadelphia: Westminster Press, 1925.

A devotional and practical commentary on the theme of this epistle. 227.1'07.ER2

*Gifford, Edwin Hamilton. *The Epistle of St. Paul to the Romans.* The Speaker's Bible. London: John Murray, 1886.

A very thorough, amillennial exposition based upon the Greek text. Should be purchased if found because of its helpful exegetical insights. 227.1'07.G36

*Godet, Frederic Louis. *Commentary on St. Paul's Epistle to the Romans.* Grand Rapids: Zondervan Publishing House, n.d.

This exhaustive and technical commentary provides an excellent treatment of the argument of the epistle. The author surveys the varying theories, refutes theological liberals who differ with him on important points of doctrine, and adequately defends his views. A valuable addition to a pastor's library. Originally printed in 1883. 227.1'07.G54

Gore, Charles. *St. Paul's Epistle to the Romans.* 2 vols. New York: Charles Scribner's Sons, 1899.

†Denies imputed sin and man's total depravity. 227.1'07.G66

*Haldane, Robert. *Exposition of the Epistle to the Romans.* London: Banner of Truth Trust, reprint.

First published between 1835-39, this Reformed commentary by a Christian layman has enjoyed a wide-spread ministry since its first appearance. The lectures were delivered in Geneva and brought about a genuine movement of the Spirit among theologues who heard them. 227.1'07.H12

Hamilton, Floyd Eugene. *The Epistle to the Romans.* Grand Rapids: Baker Book House, 1958.

A strongly conservative, Reformed exposition. 227.1'07.H18

Harrison, Norman Baldwin. *His Salvation.* Minneapolis: The Harrison Service, 1926.

An expository gem. Warmly devotional, and ideal for use with laymen's groups. 227.1'07.H24

*Hodge, Charles. *Commentary on the Epistle to the Romans.* Grand Rapids: Wm. B. Eerdmans Publishing Co., reprint 1950.

Not easy reading, but provides a detailed exposition of the doctrine of the epistle. Strongly Calvinistic. Originally published in 1835. 227.1'07.H66 1950

Hort, Fenton John Anthony. *Prolegomena of St. Paul's Epistles to the Romans and the Ephesians.* London: Macmillan Co., 1895.

Brief and to the point. Focuses on the founding of the church of Rome and the purpose of the epistles. Includes a helpful analysis of Paul's letters. 227.1'06.H78

Hoyt, Herman Arthur. *The Gospel: God's Way of Saving Men.* Winona Lake, Ind.: Brethren Missionary Herald Co., n.d.

A brief analysis of the theme of the epistle. 227.1'07.H85

Hunter, Archibald Macbride. *The Epistle to the Romans.* London: SCM Press, 1955.

†The chief value of this study lies in the etymology of the Greek words and an occasional illuminating comment on Paul's thought. 227.1'07.H91

Ironside, Henry Allan. *Lectures on the Epistle to the Romans.* New York: Loizeaux Brothers, 1951.

A clear, direct exposition. Recommended to new Christians and lay discussion groups. 227.1'07.IR6

*Lenski, Richard Charles Henry. *The Interpretation of St. Paul's Epistle to the Romans.* Minneapolis: Augsburg Publishing House, 1936.

A conservative Lutheran exposition based upon the Greek text. Lenski manifests a rigidity in handling the original that at times mars his treatment; however, his strengths far outweigh his weaknesses. Amillennial. 227.1'07.L54

*Liddon, Henry Parry. *Explanatory Analysis of St. Paul's Epistle to the Romans.* Grand Rapids: Zondervan Publishing House, 1961.

A thorough, technical commentary providing preachers with a comprehensive outline of the epistle. Frequently serves to give readers useful insights into the trend of Paul's thought. First printed in 1892. 227.1'07.L61 1961

Lloyd-Jones, David Martyn. *The Plight of Man and the Power of God.* Grand Rapids: Wm. B. Eerdmans Publishing Co., 1966.

Five messages based on selected verses in Romans 1. 227.1'07.1.L77

_____. *Romans: Exposition of Chapters 3:20 to 4:25.* Grand Rapids: Zondervan Publishing House, 1971.

A superb exposition of the doctrines of the atonement and justification. Here is expository preaching at its best. 227.1'07.3:20—4:25.L77

_____. *Romans: Assurance.* London: Banner of Truth Trust, 1971.

An important companion volume to the writer's study on justification and the atonement. Expounds Paul's teaching on sin and grace, hope and faith, redemption and glory. The heartwarming application of the Word of God to the needs of people today will edify preachers and laymen alike. 227.1'07.5.L77

*Loane, Marcus Lawrence. *The Hope of Glory.* London: Hodder and Stoughton, 1968.

Provides a rare combination of accu-

rate exegesis, capable biblical exposition, and conservative scholarship. 227.1'07.8.L78

Luther, Martin. *Lectures on Romans.* Translated by Wilhelm Pauck. Philadelphia: Westminster Press, 1961.

This indispensable work contains lectures first delivered to his students in 1515-16. Shows the process through which Luther went as he grappled with the problems of Catholic dogma versus justification by faith. 227.1'07.L97

MacDuff, John Ross. *St. Paul's Song of Songs.* London: James Nisbet and Co., 1891.

With his characteristic verbosity, this great Scottish preacher expounds Romans 8. Richly devotional. 227.1'07.8.M14

McGee, John Vernon. *Reasoning Through Romans.* 2 vols. Los Angeles: Church of the Open Door, n.d.

Plain, practical studies by a famous pastor and Bible teacher. 227.1'07.M17

Morison, James. *Exposition of the 9th Chapter of the Epistle to the Romans.* London: Hodder and Stoughton, 1888.

A revision of the writer's earlier treatment of this chapter, with an exposition of chapter 10 appended to it. Very thorough. Advocates the universal atonement of Christ, and abounds in practical application. 227.1'07.9.M82

————. *St. Paul's Teaching on Sanctification.* London: Hodder and Stoughton, 1886.

A practical exposition based upon the original text and applying the message of this portion with skill and insight into the life and experience of the believer. 227.1'07.6.M82

Moule, Handley Carr Glyn. *Romans.* Cambridge Bible for Schools and Colleges. Cambridge: At the University Press, 1879.

A capable exegetical study that contains notes on the text by a leading Calvinistic theologian of the last century. Not as valuable as the author's exposition in the *Expositor's Bible.* 227.1'07.M86

*————. *Romans.* The Expositor's Bible. Grand Rapids: Zondervan Publishing House, n.d.

One of the finest and most helpful expositions available today. Deeply devotional, based upon a very careful exegesis of the text, and abounding in practical truths. Originally printed in 1896. 227.1'07.M86E

*Murray, John.** *The Epistle to the Romans.* 2 vols. New International Commentary on the New Testament. Grand Rapids: Wm. B. Eerdmans Publishing Co., 1959-65.

Based upon a thorough knowledge of the original. Strongly Reformed in doctrine, but advocates a postmillennial interpretation of chapters 9-11. 227.1'07.M96

Nee, Watchman [pseud.]. *The Normal Christian Life.* Fort Washington, Penn.: Christian Literature Crusade, 1961.

Expository messages on certain key passages in the epistle by a Chinese Christian, Nee To-Sheng. Vividly portray the essential steps in the life of faith. 227.1'08.N28

Newell, William Reed. *Romans, Verse-by-Verse.* Chicago: Moody Press, 1938.

A practical, devotional treatment containing many digressions. Usable illustrations. Of value to the expositor. 227.1'07.N44

Nygren, Anders. *Commentary on Romans.* Philadelphia: Muhlenberg Press, 1949.

†A scholarly Lutheran commentary. 227.1'07.N98

Olshausen, Hermann. *Biblical Commentary on St. Paul's Epistle to the Romans.* Clark's Foreign Theological Library. Edinburgh: T. and T. Clark, 1846.

A staunch evangelical, Olshausen died before he could complete his projected series on the NT. This detailed study of Romans bears testimony to his erudition. Recommended. 227.1'07.OL8

Pierson, Arthur Tappan. *Vital Union With Christ.* Grand Rapids: Zondervan Publishing House, 1961.

Formerly published under the title of *Shall We Continue in Sin?* Covers Romans 6-8, and deals with the duty and privilege of Christians and the liberty they have in Christ. 227.1'07.6—8.P61

Rainsford, Marcus. *No Condemnation—No Separation.* London: Hodder and Stoughton, 1885.

Devotional lectures on Romans 8. 227.1'07.8.R13

Sanday, William and **Arthur C. Headlam.** *A Critical and Exegetical Commentary on the Epistle to the Romans.* International Critical Commentary. Edinburgh: T. and T. Clark, 1895.

A thorough commentary on the Greek text. Arminian in doctrine, but generally quite sound theologically. Long ranked as one of the better exegetical treatments of the text. 227.1'07.SA5

Shedd, William Greenough Thayer. *A Critical and Doctrinal Commentary on the Epistle of St. Paul to the Romans.* Grand Rapids: Zondervan Publishing House, 1967.

Designed for the theologian, it provides an exhaustive exegetical study of the epistle. Reformed. First published in 1879. 227.1'07.SH3 1967

Steele, David N. and **Curtis C. Thomas.** *Romans: An Interpretive Outline.* Philadelphia: Presbyterian and Reformed Publishing Co., 1963.

A brief outline of the main teaching of the epistle from a strongly Calvinistic viewpoint. Not always clear on the teaching of those branded as "Arminian." Maintains an unswerving allegiance to the inerrancy of the Word of God. 227.1'07.ST3

Stifler, James Madison. *The Epistle to the Romans.* Chicago: Moody Press, 1960.

A brief, premillenial, devotional, verse-by-verse treatment that richly repays close study. 227.1'07.ST5

Stott, John Robert Walmsey. *Men Made New.* London: Inter-Varsity Fellowship, 1966.

An expanded version of the author's 1965 Keswick Convention Bible readings. They cover Romans 5-8 and are based upon solid exegesis. Stott is always challenging and rates as one of the finest living expositors today. 227.1'07.5—8.ST7

Taylor, Vincent. *The Epistle to the Romans.* Epworth Preacher's Commentaries. London: Epworth Press, 1955.

†A brief analysis with some rather obvious comments. Arminian. 227.1'07.T21

Thomas, William Henry Griffith. *St. Paul's Epistle to the Romans.* Grand Rapids: Wm. B. Eerdmans Publishing Co., 1946.

A practical and devotional commentary is of particular value to pastors for its excellent outlines and illustrations. 227.1'07.T36

Vaughan, Charles John. *St. Paul's Epistle to the Romans.* London: Macmillan Co., 1890.

A helpful commentary on the Greek text. Of particular value to expositors. Worthy of consultation. 227.1'07.V46

Wilson, Jeffrey B. *Romans.* London: Banner of Truth Trust, 1969.

A brief, Reformed treatment that is thoroughly abreast of the latest literature. 227.1'07.W69

Wood, Arthur Skevington. *Life by the Spirit.* Grand Rapids: Zondervan Publishing House, 1963.

Published in England under the title of *Paul's Pentecost,* these messages on Romans 8 combine scholarship with spirituality into a provocative study. 227.1'07.8.W85

Wuest, Kenneth Samuel. *Romans in the Greek New Testament.* Grand Rapids: Wm. B. Eerdmans Publishing Co., 1956.

Of value to those who lack a knowledge of Greek. 227.1'07.W95

FIRST CORINTHIANS

Barclay, William. *The Letters to the Corinthians.* 2d ed. Philadelphia: Westminster Press, 1956.

†Of value for the light cast on the historical background of the Corinthian church and the milieu of the Grecian world in the first century A.D. 227.2'07.B23 1956

*Barrett, Charles Kingsley. *A Commentary on the First Epistle to the Corinthians.* Harper's New Testament Commentaries. New York: Harper and Row, 1968.

†A modern treatment that makes a vital contribution to the study of this epistle. The writer does not believe in inspiration and has a weak theological system. However, he is a capable exegete, and his handling of this letter deserves attention. 227.2'07.B27C

Barth, Karl. *The Resurrection of the Dead.* Translated by H. J. Steuning. London: Hodder and Stoughton, 1933.

Concentrates on I Corinthians 15, but contains an illuminating exposition of the entire epistle. 227.2'07.15.B28

Beet, Joseph Agar. *A Commentary on St. Paul's Epistles to the Corinthians.* 6th ed. London: Hodder and Stoughton, 1895.

†A careful study based upon the Greek text. Now superceded by more recent treatments. 227.2'07.B39 1895

Boyer, James L. *For a World Like Ours: Studies in I Corinthians.* Grand Rapids: Baker Book House, 1972.

Encourages readers to study the biblical text for themselves. Each lesson is followed by a series of thought- and discussion-provoking questions. An elucidating treatment. 227.2'07.B69

*Brown, John. *The Resurrection of Life: An Exposition of First Corinthians 15.* Edinburgh: William Oliphant and Sons, 1852.

A rich, full expository treatment that includes a lengthy essay on our Lord's resurrection. To be purchased if found. 227.2'07.15.B81

Bruce, Frederick Fyvie. *I and II Corinthians.* New Century Bible. London: Oliphants Ltd., 1971.

A brief, perceptive study. 227.2'07.B83

Candlish, Robert Smith. *Life In a Risen Saviour.* Edinburgh: Adam and Charles Black, 1863.

Contains sermons preached by Candlish at the Church of Saint George, Edinburgh. Gives evidence of having drawn heavily upon the writings of his colleague, John Brown, and other great expositors. 227.2'07.15.C16

Cox, Samuel. *The Resurrection.* London: Daldy, Isbister and Co., 1879.

A series of twelve expository messages. Well organized and ably presented. 227.2'07.15.C83

*Edwards, Thomas Charles. *A Commentary on the First Epistle to the Corinthians.* London: Hodder and Stoughton, 1885.

One of the truly great commentaries on the Greek text. Of inestimable value. Should be in the library of every seminarian and pastor. 227.2'07.ED9

Gettys, Joseph Miller. *How to Study I Corinthians.* Richmond: John Knox Press, 1960.

An aid in personal Bible study. Recommended. 227.2'007.G33S

————. *How to Teach I Corinthians.* Richmond: John Knox Press, 1956.

Valuable to teachers of adult Bible study groups. 227.2'007.G33T

*Godet, Frederic Louis. *Commentary on the First Epistle of St. Paul to the Corinthians.* Translated by A. Cousins. Grand Rapids: Zondervan Publishing House, 1957.

Reprinted from the 1886 edition. Scholarly, exegetical comments on the text and theme of the epistle make this work one of the outstanding treatments of all time. 227.2'07.G54 1957

Grosheide, Frederick Willem. *Commentary on the First Epistle to the Corinthians.* New International Commentary on the New Testament. Grand Rapids: Wm. B. Eerdmans Publishing Co., 1953.

Does not measure up to the stature of the other volumes in this series. Weak in virtually every dimension. 227.2'07.G89

*Hodge, Charles. *An Exposition of the First Epistle to the Corinthians.* Grand Rapids: Wm. B. Eerdmans Publishing Co., 1965.

Helpful for its doctrinal emphasis. Ably deals with the problems at Corinth, and pastors will profit from a careful consideration of the issues involved. First published in 1857. 227.2'07.H66 1965

*Ironside, Henry Allan. *Addresses on the First Epistle to the Corinthians.* New York: Loizeaux Brothers, 1952.

Expository messages that are informative and stimulating. Shows how each believer should live in order that he might bring glory to Christ. Illustrations are pertinent and timely. 227.2'07.IR6

Jones, John David. *The Greatest of These: An Exposition of First Corinthians 13.* London: Hodder and Stoughton, 1925.

Expository messages revealing the writer's intellectual force, illustrative ability, and relevant application of truth to life. 227.2'07.13.J71

Luck, G. Coleman. *First Corinthians.* Chicago: Moody Press, 1958.

A clear, nontechnical exposition. Of particular value to those who teach home Bible classes or other adult study groups. 227.2'07.L96

Moffat, James. *Commentary on I Corinthians.* Moffat New Testament Commentary. New York: Harper and Brothers, 1938.

†A critical and in some respects helpful testament of the problems arising directly from a study of the text. 227.2'07.M72

Morgan, George Campbell. *The Corinthian Letters of Paul.* Westwood, N.J.: Fleming H. Revell Co., 1956.

A renowned pulpiteer addresses himself to the problems that plague the church. His statements are timely and show a mastery of the subject matter. 227.2'07.M82

Morris, Leon. *The First Epistle of Paul to the Corinthians.* Tyndale New Testament Commentary. Grand Rapids: Wm. B. Eerdmans Publishing Co., 1958.

A compact, serviceable commentary that will prove valuable to those who teach through this epistle. 227.2'07.M83

Olshausen, Hermann. *A Biblical Commentary on St. Paul's First and Second Epistles to the Corinthians.* Edinburgh: T. and T. Clark, 1855.

Said W. Lindsay Alexander, "Highly esteemed for his happy combinations of grammatico-historical exegesis, with spiritual insight into the meaning of the sacred writings." 227.2'07.OL8

Redpath, Alan. *The Royal Route to Heaven: Studies in I Corinthians.* London: Pickering and Inglis, 1960.

Messages delivered at the Moody Memorial Church, Chicago. They rebuke shallowness and ineffectiveness in the church, expose the tragedy of living in sinfulness and worldliness, and vigorously apply the message of this epistle to the lives of believers today. 227.2'07.R24

*Robertson, Archibald and **Alfred Plummer.** *A Critical and Exegetical Commentary on the First Epistle of St. Paul to the Corinthians.* 2d ed. Edinburgh: T. and T. Clark, 1914.

A monumental work that has earned for itself a deserved place on the Bible teacher's bookshelf. 227.2'07.R54 1914

Robertson, Frederick William. *Expository Lectures on St. Paul's Epistles to the Corinthians.* London: Kegan Paul, Trench and Co., 1885.

Devotional and practical studies by an

outstanding Anglican preacher of the last century. Out-of-print. Should be purchased if a copy can be located. 227.2'07.R54

Scroggie, William Graham. *The Love Life: A Study of I Corinthians 13.* London: Pickering and Inglis, n.d.

A valuable, devotional work. Its major weakness lies in its brevity. 227.2'07.13.SC5

Stanley, Arthur Penrhyn. *The Epistles of St. Paul to the Corinthians.* 2d ed. London: John Murray, 1876.

A scholarly, critical study with numerous digressions on the theme of the epistle, paraphrases of the text, and dissertations on thoughts that have arisen in the writer's mind as a result of this study. 227.2'07.ST2 1876

Thrall, Margaret Eleanor. *The First and Second Letters of Paul to the Corinthians.* Cambridge Bible Commentary. Cambridge: At the University Press, 1965.

Brief expository notes based on the NEB. 227.2'07.T41

SECOND CORINTHIANS

*Hodge, Charles. *An Exposition of the Second Epistle to the Corinthians.* Grand Rapids: Wm. B. Eerdmans Publishing Co., n.d.

A doctrinal commentary of considerable merit. First published in 1860. 227.3'07.H66

*Hughes, Philip Edgcombe. *Paul's Second Epistle to the Corinthians.* New International Commentary on the New Testament. Grand Rapids: Wm. B. Eerdmans Publishing Co., 1962.

May well be regarded as the finest conservative exposition of this epistle. 227.3'07.H87

Ironside, Henry Allan. *Addresses on the Second Epistle to the Corinthians.* Neptune, N.J.: Loizeaux Brothers, 1954.

Messages delivered at the Moody Memorial Church, Chicago. A clear, con-

cise, practical expository treatment. 227.3'07.IR6

Luck, G. Coleman, *Second Corinthians.* Chicago: Moody Press, 1959.

An ideal work for laypeople in adult discussion groups. 227.3'07.L96

*Plummer, Alfred. *A Critical and Exegetical Commentary on the Second Epistle of St. Paul to the Corinthians.* International Critical Commentary. Edinburgh: T. and T. Clark, 1956.

†One of the best commentaries on the Greek text. However, the writer's approach to the introductory matters of this epistle leaves much to be desired. 227.3'07.P73

Tasker, Randolph Vincent Greenough. *The Second Epistle of Paul to the Corinthians.* Tyndale New Testament Commentaries. Grand Rapids: Wm. B. Eerdmans Publishing Co., 1960.

A very brief and not very satisfactory treatment. 227.3'07.T18

GALATIANS

*Barclay, William. *Flesh and Spirit: An Examination of Galatians 5:19-23.* Nashville: Abingdon Press, 1962.

A valuable series of word studies ably contrasting the works of the flesh with the fruit of the Spirit. 227.4'07.5:19-23.B23F

Beet, Joseph Agar. *A Commentary on St. Paul's Epistle to the Galatians.* London: Hodder and Stoughton, 1888.

A technical treatment superseded by more recent works and containing little material of lasting value. 227.4'07.B39

*Brown, John. *An Exposition of the Epistle of Paul the Apostle to the Galatians.* Evansville, Ind.: Sovereign Grace Book Club, 1957.

Perhaps one of the most satisfactory commentaries for the expository preacher. Unfortunately, the introduction has been omitted from this edition. 227.4'07.B81

*Burton, Ernest DeWitt. *A Critical and Exegetical Commentary on the Epistle to the Galatians.* International Critical Commentary. Edinburgh: T. and T. Clark, 1962.

A most extensive, satisfactory exegetical commentary. 227.4'07.B95

*Cole, Robert Alan. *The Epistle of Paul to the Galatians.* Tyndale New Testament Commentaries. Grand Rapids: Wm. B. Eerdmans Publishing Co., 1865.

Readable, informative, and suggestive. A valuable discussion that should be in every church library. 227.4'07.C67

*Eadie, John. *Commentary on the Epistle of Paul to the Galatians.* Grand Rapids: Zondervan Publishing House, n.d.

Based upon the 1894 edition. Scholarly, practical, and designed for those with a knowledge of Greek. 227.4'07.EA2

Ellicott, Charles John. *St. Paul's Epistle to the Galatians.* 3d ed. London: Longman, Robert and Green, 1863.

A critical and grammatical handling of the text that retains its value and can be used by preachers who are able to work from the original text. 227.4'07.EL5 1863

Findlay, George Gillanders. *The Epistle to the Galatians.* The Expositor's Bible. London: Hodder and Stoughton, 1900.

A scholarly, succinct, and relevant exposition that may well be regarded as one of the more important treatments. 227.4'07.F49

Girdlestone, Robert Baker. *St. Paul's Epistle to the Galatians.* London: Religious Tract Society, 1912.

A devotional exposition. 227.4'07.G44

Hamilton, Floyd E. *The Epistle to the Galatians.* Grand Rapids: Baker Book House, 1954.

A helpful, brief study manual. 227.4'07.H18

Harrison, Norman B. *His Side versus Our Side: Galatians—God's Great Antithesis.* Minneapolis: Harrison Service, 1940.

A brief, devotional exposition. 227.4'07.H24

*Hendriksen, William. *Exposition of Galatians.* New Testament Commentary. Grand Rapids: Baker Book House, 1968.

Prefaced with an extensive introduction giving the arguments for both the North and the South Galatian theories. As always, the writer's exposition is very complete and applies the text in a meaningful and practical manner. Not all will agree with the "two covenants" of Galatians 4:24. Conservative. Deserves a place on every pastor's bookshelf. Reformed. 227.4'07.H38

Hogg, C. F. and William Edwy Vine. *The Epistle to the Galatians.* London: Pickering and Inglis, 1959.

A doctrinal commentary that continues the development of Paul's thought begun in his epistle to the Romans. Holds to a late date for the writing of this letter, deals quite ably with the chronological problems, and provides a practical exposition. 227.4'07.H67

*Lightfoot, Joseph Barber. *The Epistle of St. Paul to the Galatians.* Grand Rapids: Zondervan Publishing House, 1966.

An important study that cannot be overlooked or ignored. Without question one of the greatest commentaries on the Greek text of this epistle. The essays included in each work are always important. Originally published in 1865. 227.4'07.L62 1966

Luther, Martin. *Lectures on Galatians.* Vols. 26-27: *Luther's Works.* St. Louis: Concordia Publishing House, 1963-64.

Contains lectures given by the Reformer to his students in 1519 and 1539. Makes up the most complete and exhaustive study of Luther's teaching of this epistle available today. 227.4'07.L97

*Ramsay, William Mitchell. *A Historical Commentary on St. Paul's Epistle to the Galatians.* Grand Rapids: Baker Book House, 1965.

Surprisingly rich in background material, and deals expertly with the geography, culture, and history of the times. Champions the South Galatia theory and, as such, deserves careful consideration. Originally published in 1899. 227.4'07.R14 1965

*Stott, John Robert Walmsey. *The Message of Galatians.* London: Inter-Varsity Press, 1968.

A brilliant series of expository messages. Each serves as a model of what a good sermon should be like. 227.4'07.ST6

*Strauss, Lehman. *Devotional Studies in Galatians and Ephesians.* Neptune, N.J.: Loizeaux Brothers, 1957.

Well-outlined devotional messages aimed at expounding the text and edifying believers. Practical, evangelical, and Christ-centered. 227.4'07.ST8

Tenney, Merrill Chapin. *Galatians: The Charter of Christian Liberty.* Grand Rapids: Wm. B. Eerdmans Publishing Co., 1954.

Designed to help students of the Word grapple with the text firsthand. Approaches the epistle from synthetic, critical, biographical, and devotional points of view. Excellent. 227.4'07.T25

Vos, Howard F. *Galatians: A Call to Christian Liberty.* Chicago: Moody Press, 1971.

Emphasizing the need for biblical "freedom," the writer expounds Paul's teaching in an understandable manner. 227.4'07.V92

Williams, A. Lukyn. *The Epistle of Paul the Apostle to the Galatians.* Cambridge: At the University Press, 1910.

A handy, helpful, exegetical study. 227.4'07.W67

EPHESIANS

Abbott, Thomas Kingmill. *A Critical and Exegetical Commentary on the Epistles to the Ephesians and the Colossians.* International Critical Commentary. Edinburgh:

T. and T. Clark, 1964.

Of help exegetically, but not always reliable. 227.5'07.AB2

Beet, Joseph Agar. *A Commentary on St. Paul's Epistles to the Ephesians, Philippians, Colossians, and to Philemon.* London: Hodder and Stoughton, 1890.

A practical exposition. Now suffers from the limitations of age. 227.5'07.B39

Bruce, Frederick Fyvie. *The Epistle to the Ephesians.* Westwood, N.J.: Fleming H. Revell Co., 1961.

Following a careful introduction to the epistle, Bruce deals with the contents under two main headings: The new community in the purpose of God, and the new community in the life of the believers. The exposition is clear and nontechnical. 227.5'07.B83

Dale, Robert William. *The Epistle to the Ephesians: Its Doctrine and Ethics.* 3d ed. London: Hodder and Stoughton, 1887.

Expository messages abounding in practical insights into, and meaningful applications of, the text. 227.5'07.D15 1887

Duncan, George Simpson. *St. Paul's Ephesian Ministry.* London: Hodder and Stoughton, 1929.

†An epochal work advocating three Ephesian imprisonments and claiming that the "Prison Epistles" were written, not from Rome, but from Ephesus. 227.5'06.D91

Eadie, John. *Commentary on the Epistle to the Ephesians.* Grand Rapids: Zondervan Publishing House, n.d.

Based on the edition published in 1883. A very full exposition that deals with all the exegetical problems, pays careful attention to the development of Paul's theme, and provides important digressions on the theological truths of the epistle. 227.5'07.EA2

Ellicott, Charles John. *St. Paul's Epistle to the Ephesians.* 4th ed. London: Longmans, Green, Reader and Dyer, 1868.

A critical work based on a new translation of the text. Still of value to the expositor, even though this work has been superseded by more recent treatments. 227.5'07.EL5 1868

Findlay, George Gillanders. *The Epistle to the Ephesians.* The Expositor's Bible. New York: A. C. Armstrong and Son, 1908.

A handy, generally reliable treatment. Arminian. 227.5'07.F47

*Foulkes, Francis. *The Epistle of Paul to the Ephesians.* Tyndale New Testament Commentaries. Grand Rapids: Wm. B. Eerdmans Publishing Co., 1963.

A perceptive interpretation successfully combining sound scholarship with a clear understanding of the scope and import of the epistle. 227.5'07.F82

Gerstner, John H. *The Epistle to the Ephesians.* Grand Rapids: Baker Book House, 1958.

A helpful study manual. 227.5'07.G32

Gettys, Joseph Miller. *How to Study Ephesians.* Richmond: John Knox Press, 1960.

An introductory study worthy of careful attention. 227.5'007.G33S

Gurnall, William. *The Christian in Complete Armor.* London: Banner of Truth Trust, 1964.

This exhaustive exposition by a Puritan writer ably treats the spiritual warfare of the saints and the equipment given them by God to assure victory. First published in 1655. 227.5'07.6:10-18.G96

Harrison, Norman Baldwin. *His Very Own: Paul's Epistle to Ephesians.* Chicago: Moody Press, 1930.

This devotional gem makes rewarding reading. 227.5'07.H24

*Hendriksen, William. *Exposition of Ephesians.* New Testament Commentary. Grand Rapids: Baker Book House, 1967.

A well-written commentary that is both scholarly and practical—and of great value to preachers. Reformed. 227.5'07.H39

*Hodge, Charles. *A Commentary on the Epistle to the Ephesians.* Grand Rapids: Wm. B. Eerdmans Publishing Co., 1966.

A practical and doctrinal exposition. Should be in every pastor's library. 227.5'07.H66

*Ironside, Henry Allan. *In the Heavenlies: Practical Expository Addresses on the Epistle to the Ephesians.* Neptune, N.J.: Loizeaux Brothers, 1955.

One of Ironside's best studies. Recommended. 227.5'07.IR6

*Kent, Homer A., Jr. *Ephesians: The Glory of the Church.* Chicago: Moody Press, 1971.

An evangelical commentary that ably expounds the theme of this epistle and clearly defines the nature and function of the church. 227.5'07.K41

Kirby, John C. *Ephesians: Baptism and Pentecost.* London: SPCK, 1968.

An inquiry into the structure and purpose of the epistle. 227.5'07.K63

Miller, Herbert Sumner. *The Book of Ephesians.* Houghton, N.Y.: Word-Bearer Press, 1931.

A well-outlined, nontechnical exposition based upon a careful examination of the text. 227.5'07.M61

Moody, Dale. *Christ in the Church.* Grand Rapids: Wm. B. Eerdmans Publishing Co., 1963.

An exposition of Ephesians, with special application to some problems within the Southern Baptist Convention. 227.5'06.M77

*Moule, Handley Carr Glyn. *Ephesian Studies: Lessons in Faith and Walk.* 2d ed. Grand Rapids: Zondervan Publishing House, n.d.

A devotional masterpiece full of comfort and exhortation. Originally published in 1900. 227.5'07.M86

Nee, Watchman [pseud.] *Sit, Walk,*

Stand. 4th ed. Fort Washington, Penn.: Christian Literature Crusade, 1966.

Messages by Nee To-Sheng designed to stir the hearts of readers with their practical emphasis. 227.5'07.N28 1966

*Pattison, Robert Everett. *A Commentary, Explanatory, Doctrinal, and Practical, on the Epistle to the Ephesians.* Boston: Gould and Lincoln, 1859.

Charles Haddon Spurgeon said of this work, "A book to instruct intelligent, experienced believers." Recommended. 227.5'07.P27

Paxson, Ruth. *The Wealth, Walk and Warfare of the Christian.* Westwood, N.J.: Fleming H. Revell Co., 1939.

An excellent exposition with helpful application of biblical truth. 227.5'07.P28

*Robinson, Joseph Armitage. *St. Paul's Epistle to the Ephesians.* 2d ed. London: James Clarke and Co., 1903.

Really two commentaries in one. Part I contains the introduction, translation, and exposition with notes on critical problems. Part II provides one of the finest exegetical treatments to be found anywhere. The writer's paraphrase of the Greek text is particularly valuable. 227.5'07.R56 1903

Simpson, Edmund Kidley and **Frederick Fyvie Bruce.** *Commentary on the Epistles to the Ephesians and Colossians.* New International Commentary on the New Testament. Grand Rapids: Wm. B. Eerdmans Publishing Co., 1965.

These commentaries, while not the last word on the subjects they treat, nevertheless deserve to be consulted. 227.5'07.SI5

*Westcott, Brooke Foss. *St. Paul's Epistle to the Ephesians.* Grand Rapids: Wm. B. Eerdmans Publishing Co., 1958.

Exegetical studies by the late bishop of Durham, England. Deserving of the same attention given his other works.

First edition published in 1906. 227.5'07.W52 1958

PHILIPPIANS

Anderson, Henry E. *Outline Studies in Philippians.* London: Marshall, Morgan and Scott, n.d.

Fervent, practical messages drawing heavily on Scofield, Scroggie, James Gray, and others. Reveals a lack of awareness of the scope and purpose of the epistle, but illumines the text with illustrations from the author's ministry in China. 227.6'07.AN2

Barth, Karl. *The Epistle to the Philippians.* Richmond: John Knox Press, 1962.

A brief but valuable exegetical commentary. 227.6'07.B28

Beare, Francis Wright. *A Commentary on the Epistle to the Philippians.* London: Adam and Charles Black, 1959.

†Working from the premise that this epistle is a compilation of three different letters pieced together, the writer provides a critical explanation of the text. He looks upon Philippians 2:5-11 as an early hymn based on pre-Christian myths. Disappointing. 227.6'07.B38

Blair, J. Allen. *Living Victoriously.* Grand Rapids: Wm. B. Eerdmans Publishing Co., 1956.

Twelve "victorious life" messages. The illustrations are of real value. 227.6'07.B57

*Eadie, John. *Commentary on the Greek Text of the Epistle of Paul to the Philippians.* Grand Rapids: Zondervan Publishing House, reprint.

Gives excellent definitions of Greek words, contains a very comprehensive discussion of the *kenosis* passage, and presents the writings of leading men of all schools of thought. First published in 1859. 227.6'07.EA2

*Erdman, Charles Rosenbury. *The*

Epistle of Paul to the Philippians. Philadelphia: Westminster Press, 1932.

A devotional exposition of the theme of the epistle, with good outlines based upon a grammatical analysis of text. 227.6'07.ER2

Gettys, Joseph Miller. *How to Study Philippians, Colossians, and Philemon.* Richmond: John Knox Press, 1964.

An important tool for gaining a synthetic view of the content and purpose of these epistles. 227.6'007.G33S

Harrison, Norman Baldwin. *His in Joyous Experience.* Minneapolis: Harrison Service, 1926.

A study guide based on a chart and containing outlines and comments, with a digression on the names of Christ in Scripture. 227.6'07.H24

*Hendriksen, William. *A Commentary on the Epistle to the Philippians.* New Testament Commentary. Grand Rapids: Baker Book House, 1962.

A verse-by-verse exposition in which the grammatical nuances are clearly presented. Reformed. 227.6'07.H38

Herklots, Hugh Gerard Gibson. *The Epistle of St. Paul to the Philippians.* London: Lutterworth Press, 1946.

A devotional commentary that emphasizes the cardinal tenets of the Christian faith, exalts the deity of Christ, and defends the Pauline authorship and unity of the epistle. Anglican. 227.6'07.H42

Ironside, Henry Allan. *Notes on Philippians.* New York: Loizeaux Brothers, 1922.

A brief exposition with apt illustrations and thought-provoking comments. 227.6'07.IR6

*Johnstone, Robert. *Lectures Exegetical and Practical on the Epistle of Paul to the Philippians.* Grand Rapids: Baker Book House, 1955.

First printed in 1875. A thorough, practical, and homiletical exposition that warns against the fallacies of church-ianity, strongly defends the preexistence and deity of Christ, and remains one of the leading expository works on the subject. 227.6'07.J65 1955

Jones, Maurice. *The Epistle to the Philippians.* London: Methuen and Co., 1918.

An exhaustive introduction, followed by brief comments on the text. The discussion of the Christology of the epistle is perhaps this work's greatest contribution. 227.6'07.J72

Jowett, John Henry. *The High Calling: Meditations on St. Paul's Letter to the Philippians.* London: Andrew Melrose, 1909.

Meditations that contain excellent preaching values for the expositor. 227.6'07.J83

King, Guy Hope. *Joy Way.* London: Marshall, Morgan and Scott, 1954.

A devotional exposition of real merit. Brief and to-the-point. 227.6'07.K58

*Lightfoot, Joseph Barber. *St. Paul's Epistle to the Philippians.* Grand Rapids: Zondervan Publishing House, n.d.

A thorough exposition discussing every grammatical and interpretive problem imaginable. Particularly noteworthy essays on "The Christian Ministry" and "St. Paul and Seneca" are included. First published in 1868. 227.6'07.L62

Martin, Ralph Philip. *Carmen Christi.* New York: Cambridge University Press, 1967.

An exacting study of Philippians 2:5-11 in recent interpretation and in early Christian worship. Martin regards this as a baptismal hymn and the early Christian's answer to the problems of meaninglessness and subjection to the tyranny of astro powers. This manifests a change in thinking since the author's earlier work, *An Early Christian Confession* (1960). 227.6'07.2:5-11.M36C

————. *An Early Christian Confession.* London: Tyndale Press, 1960.

A historical and exegetical study. 227.6'07.2:5-11.M36E

_____. *The Epistle of Paul to the Philippians.* Tyndale New Testament Commentaries. Grand Rapids: Wm. B. Eerdmans Publishing Co., 1959.

Shows that Paul's letter, written from a Roman prison, spreads warmth, cordiality, and joy. An exposition particularly well adapted to Christians living under tension and facing the pressures of life. 227.6'07.M36

Meyer, Frederick Brotherton. *The Epistle to the Philippians.* Grand Rapids: Baker Book House, 1952.

Textual messages, devotional and edifying. Reprinted from the 1905 edition. 227.6'07.M57 1952

***Motyer, J. A.** Philippian Studies: The Richness of Christ.* Chicago: Inter-Varsity Press, 1966.

An expository treatment that opens up the Scriptures and discourses on the "surpassing worth of knowing Christ Jesus" as Lord. Reformed. 227.6'07.M85

***Moule, Handley Carr Glyn.** Philippian Studies: Lessons in Faith and Love.* Grand Rapids: Zondervan Publishing House, n.d.

A beautifully written, deeply devotional treatment expounding the affectionate character of this epistle and relating its message to the lives of believers. Printed from the original publication. 227.6'07.M86

Müller, Jacobus Johannes. *The Epistle of Paul to the Philippians.* New International Commentary on the New Testament. Grand Rapids: Wm. B. Eerdmans Publishing Co., 1955.

Concise and helpful. Defends the unity of the epistle and the preexistence and deity of Christ. A praiseworthy treatment of the Greek text. Pedantic in style. 227.6'07.M91

Plummer, Alfred. *A Commentary on St. Paul's Epistle to the Philippians.* London: Robert Scott, 1919.

Important for its word studies based on the papyri, and still helpful from a grammatical point of view. 227.6'07.P73

Rees, Paul Stromberg. *The Adequate Man.* Westwood, N.J.: Fleming H. Revell Co., 1959.

A series of well-illustrated messages. Popular and lacking in substance. 227.6'07.R25

Robertson, Archibald Thomas. *Paul's Joy in Christ: Studies in Philippians.* Revised and edited by W. C. Strickland. Nashville: Broadman Press, 1959.

Brings to the study of this passage ripe scholarship and a mature understanding of the personality of the apostle. 227.6'07.R54 1959

Simcox, Carroll Eugene. *They Met at Philippi.* New York: Oxford University Press, 1958.

†Denies the unity of the letter, holds to a theory that makes Paul the "father of all heresies," supports his wide reading and scholarship with numerous literary allusions and quotations, and out of the confusion he has created tries to provide some edifying material. 227.6'07.SI4

***Strauss, Lehman.** Devotional Studies in Philippians.* New York: Loizeaux Brothers, 1959.

A delightful, well-outlined series of meditations. 227.6'07.ST8

Tenney, Merrill C. *Philippians: The Gospel at Work.* Grand Rapids: Wm. B. Eerdmans Publishing Co., 1956.

A comprehensive introduction is followed by a popular exposition that combines loyalty to the Scriptures with an application of the text to the needs of the human heart. 227.6'07.T25

Vaughan, Charles John. *Lectures on St. Paul's Epistle to the Philippians.* London: Macmillan Co., 1864.

Twenty-one messages based upon a detailed exegesis of the text and containing some valuable expository thoughts. 227.6'07.V46

Vincent, Marvin R. *A Critical and Ex-*

egetical Commentary on the Epistles to the Philippians and to Philemon. International Critical Commentary. New York: Charles Scribner's Sons, 1897.

An important, generally conservative commentary with word studies and exegetical notes. 227.6'07.V74

Walvoord, John Flipse. *Philippians: Triumph in Christ.* Chicago: Moody Press, 1971.

A brief exposition. Theologically accurate. 227.6'07.W17

COLOSSIANS

*Eadie, John. *Commentary on the Epistle of Paul to the Colossians.* Grand Rapids: Zondervan Publishing House, 1957.

First published over a century ago, this rich and inspiring exposition is one that preachers who have a knowledge of Greek will appreciate for its insights and detailed explanations. 227.7'07.EA2 1957

English, Eugene Schuyler. *Studies in the Epistle to the Colossians.* New York: "Our Hope," 1944.

A devotional and practical study combining doctrinal orthodoxy with loyalty to the Word. The exposition unfolds the meaning and theme of the epistle. 227.7'07.EN3

Guthrie, Thomas. *Christ and the Inheritance of the Saints.* Grand Rapids: Zondervan Publishing House, n.d.

A Presbyterian preacher of the last century, Guthrie pastored the Edinburgh Church of Old Greyfriars for nearly thirty years. These expository discourses cover Colossians 1:12-20. First published in 1858. 227.7'07.1:12-20.G98

Harrison, Everett Falconer. *Colossians: Christ All-Sufficient.* Chicago: Moody Press, 1971.

Good things frequently come in small packages. This is one of them. 227.7'07.H24

*Hendriksen, William. *Exposition of Colossians and Philemon.* New Testament Commentary. Grand Rapids: Baker Book House, 1964.

Contains an extensive introduction, a new translation of the text, an informative commentary, a valuable summary of the data covered in the book, and a series of critical notes dealing with problems of a more specialized nature. 227.7'07.H38

*Ironside, Henry Allan. *Lectures on the Epistle to the Colossians.* Neptune, N.J.: Loizeaux Brothers, 1955.

Points out that old errors are being paraded under the guise of new terms and by modern sects. Concentrates on illumining the meaning of the biblical text. A most helpful work. 227.7'07.IR6

King, Guy Hope. *Crossing the Border: An Expositional Study of Colossians.* London: Marshall, Morgan and Scott, 1957.

A lucid study that emphasizes the spiritual truths of a believer's position in Christ and shows how the reality of this truth affects everyday living. 227.7'07.K58

*Lightfoot, Joseph Barber. *St. Paul's Epistles to the Colossians and to Philemon.* Grand Rapids: Zondervan Publishing House, 1959.

First published nearly a century ago, this volume contains valuable studies that admirably illuminate the text of both epistles. Of particular interest are the essays on the epistle from Laodicea, the origin and affinities of the Essenes, and the Essenes and Christianity. 227.7'07.L62 1959

*Moule, Handley Carr Glyn. *Colossian and Philemon Studies: Lessons in Faith and Holiness.* Grand Rapids: Zondervan Publishing House, n.d.

Moule was known for his saintliness and evangelical fervor. These studies bear testimony to his ability as an expositor. They deal adequately with the text and deftly apply the message of

these epistles. First published in 1877.
227.7'07.M86

*Moule, Charles Francis Digby. *The Epistles of Paul the Apostle to the Colossians and to Philemon.* Cambridge Greek Testament. Cambridge: At the University Press, 1958.

Part of the new edition of the Cambridge Greek Testament. An exegetical commentary particularly valuable for its treatment of theological terms and linguistic points of interest.
227.7'07.M86C

*Nicholson, William Rufus. *Popular Studies in Colossians.* Edited by James M. Gray. Grand Rapids: Kregel Publications, reprint.

Formerly published under the title of *Oneness in Christ,* this study combines outstanding scholarship with a deeply devotional spirit. 227.7'07.N52

Robertson, Archibald Thomas. *Paul and the Intellectuals: The Epistle to the Colossians.* Revised and edited by W. C. Strickland. Nashville: Broadman Press, 1959.

A verse-by-verse treatment of the letter expounded in the light of its historic setting and the emergence of an incipient form of Gnosticism. 227.7'07.R54 1959

Westcott, Frederick Brooke. *A Letter to Asia.* London: Macmillan Co., 1914.

The son of the renowned B. F. Westcott provides his readers with an informative paraphrase and a brief exposition of Paul's letter to the believers at Colossae. Deserving of reissue.
227.7'07.W52

THESSALONIAN EPISTLES

Askwith, Edward Harrison. *An Introduction to the Thessalonian Epistles.* London: Macmillan Co., 1902.

An effective vindication of the Pauline authorship of both letters, with a treatise

on II Thessalonians 2. 227.81'06.AS4

Denney, James. *The Epistles to the Thessalonians.* The Expositor's Bible. New York: A. C. Armstrong and Son, 1908.

Contains some useful expository ideas, but it is generally inferior to Milligan and cannot hope to compete with Hiebert's masterful study on *The Thessalonian Epistles.* 227.81'07.D41

*Eadie, John. *A Commentary on the Greek Text of the Epistles of Paul to the Thessalonians.* Edited by William Young. London: Macmillan Co., 1877.

Characterized by Eadie's usual thoroughness. Readers may not always agree with his exegesis, but he does provide a helpful evaluation of all the different points of view, with an assessment of the strengths and weaknesses. An essay on "The Man of Sin" is appended.
227.81'07.EA2

Ellicott, Charles John. *Commentary on the Epistle of St. Paul to the Thessalonians.* Grand Rapids: Zondervan Publishing House, 1957.

An exegetical study first published in 1861. Highly technical. Ranked as one of the most scholarly treatments of these letters. 227.81'07.EL5 1957

Findlay, George Gillanders. *The Epistles of Paul the Apostle to the Thessalonians.* Cambridge Greek Testament. Cambridge: At the University Press, 1911.

A brief, helpful, technical treatment.
227.81'07.F49

Frame, James Everett. *A Critical and Exegetical Commentary on the Epistles of St. Paul to the Thessalonians.* International Critical Commentary. Edinburgh: T. and T. Clark, 1960.

An important grammatical study. Weak because the writer sidesteps theological issues and fails to deal adequately with the eschatological passages.
227.81'07.F84

*Hendriksen, William. *Exposition of I and II Thessalonians.* New Testament

Commentary. Grand Rapids: Baker Book House, 1964.

Hendriksen, abreast of the latest philological, archaeological, and patristic scholarship, combines the information from each of these disciplines with his exposition of the text. Amillennial. 227.81'07.H38

Hiebert, David Edmond. The Thessalonian Epistles. Chicago: Moody Press, 1971.

An outstanding exposition based upon unusually comprehensive and complete exegesis. A leader among commentaries for accuracy and reliability. Premillennial. 227.81'07.H53

Hogg, Charles Frederick and **William Edwy Vine.** *The Epistles to the Thessalonians.* London: Pickering and Inglis, 1959.

Sound and clear exposition. While the writers' other works advocate a pretribulation return of Christ, this exposition appears to leave the matter open. As a consequence, some have concluded that Hogg and Vine believed in a posttribulation rapture. 227.81'07.H67

Lineberry, John. *Vital Word Studies in I Thessalonians.* Grand Rapids: Zondervan Publishing House, 1960.

Elementary studies that, while based on the Greek text, are frequently unreliable. 227.81'07.L63

————. *Vital Word Studies in II Thessalonians.* Grand Rapids: Zondervan Publishing House, 1961.

Similar to the writer's earlier studies on I Thessalonians. Emphasizes the meaning of NT words, but is full of inaccuracies. 227.82'07.L63

Milligan, George. *St. Paul's Epistles to the Thessalonians.* London: Macmillan Co., 1908.

A brilliantly written, critical study that must of necessity take second place to more recent works. However, it is worth consulting. 227.81'07.M62

Morris, Leon. *The First and Second Epistles to the Thessalonians.* New International Commentary on the New Testament. Grand Rapids: Wm. B. Eerdmans Publishing Co., 1959.

Does not manifest the same maturity characterizing Morris's later writings, but does contain a wealth of learning. Amillennial. 227.81'07.M83N

————. *The Epistles of Paul to the Thessalonians.* Tyndale New Testament Commentaries. Grand Rapids: Wm. B. Eerdmans Publishing Co., 1960.

Brief, to the point, clear, relevant, and generally helpful. Amillennial. 227.81'07.M83T

Neil, William. *The Epistle of Paul to the Thessalonians.* Moffat New Testament Commentary. New York: Harper and Brothers, 1950.

Contains worthwhile exegetical insights, but manifests a distinct weakness in handling the eschatological passages. 227.81'07.N31

Ockenga, Harold John. *The Church in God.* Westwood, N.J.: Fleming H. Revell Co., 1956.

Expository sermons of marginal value. 227.81'07.OC4

Plummer, Alfred. *A Commentary on St. Paul's First Epistle to the Thessalonians.* London: Robert Scott, 1908.

While not as helpful as some of the writer's other excellent studies, this exegetical work may, nevertheless, be read with profit. 227.81'07.P73

————. *A Commentary on Paul's Second Epistle to the Thessalonians.* London: Robert Scott, 1908.

See above. 227.82'07.P73

PASTORAL EPISTLES

Barrett, Charles Kingsley. *The Pastoral Epistles.* The New Clarendon Bible. Oxford: At the Clarendon Press, 1963.

†A critical study based upon the NEB.

Barrett attempts to provide solutions to the problems of date, authorship, and historical background of these epistles. He believes that the epistles contain fragments of Paul's letters and expounds them with little thought of any unifying theme. 227.83'07.B27

Bernard, John Henry. *The Pastoral Epistles.* Cambridge Greek Testament. Cambridge: At the University Press, 1922.

Provides helpful exegetical studies on all three epistles. Thorough. 227.83'07.B45

*Fairbairn, Patrick. *Commentary on the Pastoral Epistles.* Grand Rapids: Zondervan Publishing Co., 1956.

Based on the 1874 edition, this old standard treatment shows how pastors may use the Greek text to aid their exposition. A fine work in spite of its age. More recent works, of course, benefit from material unknown to Fairbairn. 227.83'07.F15 1956

Guthrie, Donald. *The Pastoral Epistles in the Mind of Paul.* London: Tyndale Press, 1955.

A Tyndale New Testament Lecture. 227.83'06.G98

Harrison, Percy Neale. *Paulines and Pastorals.* London: Villiers Publications, 1964.

†A sequel to *The Problem of the Pastoral Epistles,* in which the writer still rejects the Pauline authorship of these epistles. Harrison has been ably answered by Hendriksen, Kent, and others. 227.83'06.H24P 1964

_____. *The Problem of the Pastoral Epistles.* Oxford: University Press, 1921.

†A critical work. The precursor of *Paulines and Pastorals.* 227.83'06.H24 1921

*Hendriksen, William. *Exposition of the Pastoral Epistles.* New Testament Commentary. Grand Rapids: Baker Book House, 1968.

Firmly establishes the credibility of the Pauline authorship of the epistles, ably refutes the critical theories of men like P. N. Harrison, and provides a satisfying exposition of the text. 227.83'07.H38

*Hiebert, David Edmond. *First Timothy.* Chicago: Moody Press, 1957.

A balanced exposition, true to the original text and fully abreast of the most recent scholarship. 227.83'07.H53

*_____. *Second Timothy.* Chicago: Moody Press, 1958.

Combines evangelical zeal with a devotional appeal. Deals with the historical and critical problems, emphasizes the need for two imprisonments, and expounds the text in the light of Paul's impending death. 227.84'07.H53

*_____. *Titus and Philemon.* Chicago: Moody Press, 1957.

A careful blending of exegesis with a capable exposition of the text. 227.85'07.H53

Ironside, Henry Allan. *Timothy, Titus and Philemon.* Neptune, N.J.: Loizeaux Brothers, 1955.

An adequate explanation of the scope and import of these personal letters. Ideal for new converts. 227.83'07.IR6

*Kelly, John Norman Davidson. *The Pastoral Epistles.* Harper's New Testament Commentaries. New York: Harper and Row Publishers, 1963.

Able defense of the Pauline authorship. Presents a vivid picture of first-century church life. Thorough. 227.83'07.K29

Kelly, William. *An Exposition of the Two Epistles to Timothy.* 3d ed. London: C. A. Hammond, 1948.

An able exposition by a Plymouth Brethren writer. Originally published in 1889. 226.83'07.K29 1948

*Kent, Homer Austin, Jr. *The Pastoral Epistles: Studies in I and II Timothy and Titus.* Chicago: Moody Press, 1958.

A work of quality and reliability. Admirably bridges the gap between a laborious, technical treatment and a superficial, popular one. 227.83'07.K41

*Liddon, Henry Parry. *Explanatory Analysis of St. Paul's First Epistle to Timothy.* London: Longmans, Green and Co., 1897.

A competent treatment based upon a grammatical analysis of the Greek text. Excellent. Serves as a model of good expository preparation. 227.83'07.L61

Moule, Charles Francis Digby. *The Problem of the Pastoral Epistles: A Reappraisal.* Manchester: John Rylands Library, 1965.

The Manson Memorial Lecture for 1965, reprinted from the "Bulletin of the John Rylands Library." Rejects the Pauline authorship and follows in large measure Harrison's *Problem of the Pastorals.* 227.83'06.M86

*Moule, Handley Carr Glyn. *The Second Epistle to Timothy.* London: Religious Tract Society, 1905.

A short devotional study of Paul's last letter. 227.84'07.M86

Plummer, Alfred. *The Pastoral Epistles.* The Expositor's Bible. New York: A. C. Armstrong and Son, 1908.

Worth consulting, but there are better treatments of these epistles. 227.83'07.P73

*Simpson, Edmund Kidley. *The Pastoral Epistles.* London: Tyndale Press, 1954.

Ably defends the Pauline authorship, carefully examines the external and internal evidence that bears on the authenticity of these letters, draws on an extensive knowledge of classical literature, and

expounds the text in a scholarly, satisfying way. 227.83'07.S15

Vine, William Edwy. *The Epistles to Timothy and Titus: Faith and Conduct.* Grand Rapids: Zondervan Publishing House, 1965.

Basing his studies upon the premise that the epistles were written in order that men might know how to behave themselves in the house of God. Vine expounds them in the light of the needs of the local church or assembly. 227.83'07.V75

PHILEMON

*Cox, Samuel. *The Private Letters of St. Paul and St. John.* London: Miall Publishing Company, 1867.

Of this work, Spurgeon said, *"Such exposition as this adds interest to the epistles* [to Philemon, and of II and III John], *and makes their writers live again before our eyes."* 227.86'07.C83

*Gaebelein, Frank Ely. *Philemon: The Gospel of Emancipation.* Wheaton: Van Kampen Press, 1939.

A brief, sympathetic exposition. 227.86'07.G11

*Scroggie, William Graham. *A Note to a Friend: Paul to Philemon.* London: Hulbert Publishing Co., n.d.

A rewarding and in-depth study. One of the best ever produced on this epistle. 227.86'07.SCR5

(Note: For other commentaries on Philemon *see under* Colossians *and the* Prison Epistles. *The works of Hiebert, Lightfoot, and Moule are worth consulting.)*

GENERAL EPISTLES

Beasley-Murray, George Raymond. *The General Epistles.* Bible Guides. New York: Abingdon Press, 1965.

Brief introductory studies on the epis-

tles of James, Peter, and Jude. Limited in scope. 227.9'06.B35

Calvin, John. *Commentaries on the Catholic Epistles.* Grand Rapids: Wm. B.

Eerdmans Publishing Co., 1959.

Reprinted from the 1551 edition, these old but helpful comments are enlightening and edifying. 227.9'07.C13 1959

*Erdman, Charles Rosenbury. *The General Epistles.* Philadelphia: Westminster Press, 1918.

Practical and devotional comments defending the Johannine authorship, upholding the deity of Christ, maintaining a belief in a personal anti-Christ, and furnishing the reader with a clear exposition of each epistle. Commendable. 227.9'07.ER2

Gloag, Paton James. *Introduction to the Catholic Epistles.* Edinburgh: T. and T. Clark, 1887.

A detailed introductory work containing a series of informative essays on such topics as "the anointing of the sick," "Pauline and Jacobean views of justification," "Peter's residence in Rome," "Petrine theology," and a very scholarly treatment of the "Relation Between II Peter and Jude." 227.9'06.G51

*Hiebert, David Edmond. *An Introduction to the Non-Pauline Epistles.* Chicago: Moody Press, 1962.

A lucid, accurate, and reliable introduction to the background and content of the general epistles. 227.9'061.H53

HEBREWS

Archer, Gleason Leonard, Jr. *The Epistle to the Hebrews.* Grand Rapids: Baker Book House, 1957.

A conservative exposition. Suitable for Bible study groups. 227.87'07.AR2

Barclay, William. *The Letter to the Hebrews.* Philadelphia: Westminster Press. 1957.

†Good for word studies, and abounds with quotations from sacred and secular writers. 227.87'07.B23

*Brown, John. *An Exposition of the Epistle of the Apostle Paul to the Hebrews.* Lon-

don: Banner of Truth Trust, reprint.

A devout, Reformed exposition that is true to the text and edifying to the believer. First published in 1862. 227.87'07.B81

Bruce, Alexander Balmain. *The Epistle to the Hebrews.* Edinburgh: T. and T. Clark, 1899.

An exhaustive interpretation of the epistle based on the premise that it is a formal defense of the Christian faith. Readers will not always agree with Bruce, but they will find that he has made a valuable contribution to the overall study of this epistle. 227.87'07.B83

*Bruce, Frederick Fyvie. *The Epistle to the Hebrews.* New International Commentary on the New Testament. Grand Rapids: Wm. B. Eerdmans Publishing Co., 1964.

A thorough, reverent exposition. The footnotes are helpful and give evidence of the author's vast learning. 227.87'07.B82N

Bullinger, Ethelbert William. *A Great Cloud of Witnesses.* London: Lamp Press, 1956.

A series of studies on Hebrews 11 by the "father" of modern ultradispensationalism. An extensive expository treatment that frequently provides discerning explanations of Greek words and their origin. Preachers will find these studies helpful. 227.87'07.11.B87

Dale, Robert William. *The Jewish Temple and the Christian Church.* London: Hodder and Stoughton, 1870.

Eloquent, sophisticated sermons covering almost every facet of Hebrews. 226.87'07.D15

Davidson, Andrew Bruce. *The Epistle to the Hebrews.* Grand Rapids: Zondervan Publishing House, 1950.

Small in size, but contains many valuable insights into the truths contained in this epistle. The additional notes are most helpful. Originally published in

1882. 227.87'07.D28 1950

Davies, John Howard. *A Letter to the Hebrews.* Cambridge: At the University Press, 1967.

†A commentary based on the text of the NEB. The writer thinks that Apollos was probably the author. His comments amount to little more than theologically biased paraphrase. 227.87'07.D36

DeHaan, Martin Ralph. *Hebrews.* Grand Rapids: Zondervan Publishing House, 1959.

A collection of radio messages. Ideal for the layman. 227.87'07.D36

Delitzsch, Franz. *Commentary on the Epistle to the Hebrews.* 2 vols. Edinburgh: T. and T. Clark, 1868-1870.

An exhaustive treatment of the Greek text in which the writer deals with many of the critical problems and draws heavily upon rabbinic and Talmudic literature for many of his ideas. 227.87'07.D37

Ebrard, John H. A. *Biblical Commentary on the Epistle to the Hebrews in Continuation of the Work of Olshausen.* Translated by J. Fulton. 3d ed. Edinburgh: T. and T. Clark, 1868.

A clear and perceptive study that pays particular attention to the problematical (or warning) passages of the epistle and succeeds in ably analyzing the theme of the writer, at the same time challenging each reader with the need for and importance of personal spiritual growth. 227.87'07.EB3 1868

Edwards, Thomas Charles. *The Epistle to the Hebrews.* The Expositor's Bible. London: Hodder and Stoughton, 1911.

An excellent, easy-to-follow discussion of the purpose of the epistle. 227.87'07.ED9

*English, Eugene Schuyler. *Studies in the Epistle to the Hebrews.* Travelers Rest, S.C.: Southern Bible Book House, 1955.

A capable exposition of the theme

of this epistle. Recommended. 227.87'07.EN3

*Erdman, Charles Rosenbury. *The Epistle to the Hebrews.* Philadelphia: Westminster Press, 1934.

A devotional and practical commentary that can be used to real profit in adult Bible study groups. 227.87'07.ER2

Filson, Floyd Vivian. *Yesterday.* Studies in Biblical Theology. Naperville, Ill.: Alec. R. Allenson, 1967.

†An assessment of the teaching of the epistle in the light of chapter 13. Argues cogently for the unity and consistency of the book. 227.87'06.F48 13

Goodspeed, Edgar Johnson. *The Epistle to the Hebrews.* New York: Macmillan Co., 1908.

A brief exposition. Of little value to preachers today. 227.87'07.G62

Hewitt, Thomas. *The Epistle to the Hebrews.* Tyndale New Testament Commentary. Grand Rapids: Wm. B. Eerdmans Publishing Co., 1960.

A strongly conservative, Reformed treatment. Silas is looked upon as being the most likely author. The writer has some novel interpretations on the "apostasy" passages and has not reasoned through some of the historic and interpretative problems. 227.87'07.H49

Hoyt, Herman Arthur. *Christ: God's Final Word to Man.* Winona Lake, Ind.: Brethren Missionary Herald Co., n.d.

A brief analysis and exposition. 227.87'07.H85

Lindsay, William. *Lectures on the Epistle to the Hebrews.* Edinburgh: William Oliphant and Co., 1867.

An exhaustive commentary on the Greek text. 227.87'07.L64

Macaulay, Joseph Cordner. *Devotional Studies in the Epistle to the Hebrews.* Grand Rapids: Wm. B. Eerdmans Publishing Co., 1948.

A homiletic commentary. Good for its

illustrations. Of limited value as an exposition. 227.87'07.M11

Manson, William. *The Epistle to the Hebrews.* London: Hodder and Stoughton, 1951.

†A polemic in which the writer holds that the recipients of the letter were not Jews. In attempting to prove his point, he cites almost every paragraph in Hebrews and, in doing so, provides many interesting comments on the text. This is not a work for the expositor. 227.87'06.M32

Milligan, Robert. *The Epistle to the Hebrews.* Des Moines, Iowa: Eugene S. Smith, 1875.

An able work by an early leader of the Disciples of Christ. Supports the Pauline authorship of the epistle, and expounds the text in keeping with the doctrine of his denomination. 227.87'07.M62

Moffatt, James. *The Epistle to the Hebrews.* International Critical Commentary. New York: Charles Scribner's Sons, 1924.

Exposes the non-Jewish character of the recipients of this letter. A critical work that provides a helpful section on the rhythmic cadences. One of the better commentaries on the *theme* of Hebrews. 227.87'07.M72

Montefiore, Hugh. *The Epistle to the Hebrews.* Harper New Testament Commentaries. New York: Harper and Row, 1964.

Brief, critical, perceptive comments based on the original text. Provides twelve arguments for Apollos's authorship of the epistle. Scholarly. 227.87'07.M76

Morgan, George Campbell. *God's Last Word to Man.* New York: Fleming H. Revell Co., 1936.

Not a verse-by-verse commentary, but sixteen expository studies based on selected texts in the epistle. Warm and practical. Often overlooks difficulties in interpretation. Not Morgan's best work. 227.87'07.M82

***Murray, Andrew.** *The Holiest of All.* New York: Fleming H. Revell Co., 1965.

First published in the latter part of the nineteenth century. Devotional, Reformed, and applies the truths of the text in a pleasing, practical way. 227.87'07.M96

Nairne, Alexander. *The Epistle of Priesthood.* Edinburgh: T. and T. Clark, 1913.

†Sacramentarian in outlook. Provides valuable essays on the incarnation, the priesthood, the sacrifices of the OT, and so on. 227.87'07.N14

***Newell, William Reed.** *Hebrews, Verse by Verse.* Chicago: Moody Press, 1947.

A popular commentary preachers will find helpful. Conservative. 227.87'07.N44

Owen, John. *An Exposition of the Epistle to the Hebrews.* 4 vols. Wilmington: Sovereign Grace Publishers, n.d.

An exhaustive, Puritan work first published between 1668-84. An abridged edition has been issued by Kregel Publications entitled *Hebrews: The Epistle of Warning.* 227.87'07.OW2

Peake, Arthur Samuels. *Hebrews.* New Century Bible. New York: Henry Frowde, n.d.

†The introduction is very careful and full; the comments on the text are brief and uninspiring. 227.87'07.P31

Pfeiffer, Charles Franklin. *The Epistle to the Hebrews.* Chicago: Moody Press, 1962.

A brief exposition. Of value to laypeople. 227.87'07.P48

Pink, Arthur Walkington. *An Exposition of Hebrews.* 3 vols. Grand Rapids: Baker Book House, 1954.

An exhaustive exposition that, in spite of its verbosity, contains helpful expository values. 227.87'07.P65

Robinson, Theodore Henry. *The Epistle to the Hebrews.* Moffatt New Testament Commentary. New York: Harper and Brothers, 1933.

†Replete with illuminating comments on the text. Doctrinally unreliable, and not on a par with the works by Brown, Bruce, English, and Westcott. 227.87'07.R56

Sauer, Erich Ernst. *In the Arena.* Grand Rapids: Wm. B. Eerdmans Publishing Co., 1955.

Written with verve and insight. Provides a handy exposition of the Christian wayfarer as seen in Hebrews 12. 227.87'07.12.SA8

*Saphir, Adolph. *The Epistle to the Hebrews.* 2 vols. New York: Gospel Publishing House, n.d.

Fervent expository studies by a converted Jew. Originally published 1874-76. 227.87'07.SA6

Schneider, Johannes. *The Letter to the Hebrews.* Grand Rapids: Wm. B. Eerdmans Publishing Co., 1957.

A helpful commentary by a European Baptist theologian. Generally conservative and of value to the expositor. 227.87'07.SCH5

Scott, Ernest Findlay. *The Epistle to the Hebrews.* Edinburgh: T. and T. Clark, 1922.

†A study of the background and teaching of the epistle that denies the Jewish character of the letter, questions the authenticity of Stephen's speech in Acts, ridicules the inerrancy of the Scriptures, and has little to contribute to the expository preacher. 227.87'07.SCO8

Seiss, Joseph Augustus. *Lectures on Hebrews.* Grand Rapids: Baker Book House, 1954.

Thirty-six eloquent sermons that exalt the deity of Christ, stress the necessity of studying the Word, expound the fundamental doctrines of the Christian faith, and exhort believers to a closer walk with Christ. 227.87'07.SE4

Stibbs, Alan Marshall. *So Great Salvation: The Meaning and Message of the Letter to the Hebrews.* Exeter, England: Paternoster Press, 1970.

A capable expository study of the theme of Hebrews that admirably links precept with practice. 227.87'07.ST5

Stuart, Moses. *A Commentary on the Epistle to the Hebrews.* Andover: Warren F. Draper, 1860.

A concise, conservative commentary based on the Greek text. Its main strength lies in its extensive introduction. 227.87'07.ST9

*Thomas, William Henry Griffith. *Hebrews: A Devotional Commentary.* Grand Rapids: Wm. B. Eerdmans Publishing Co., 1962.

Forty-one devotional messages based on the theme of the epistle and stressing the need for spiritual progress in the Christian life. Excellent for laypeople. Recommended. 227.87'07.T36

Vaughan, Charles John. *The Epistle to the Hebrews.* London: Macmillan Co., 1891.

A thorough study by a theologian and pastor. Illuminating and helpful. 227.87'07.V29.

Vos, Geerhardus. *The Teaching of the Epistle to the Hebrews.* Grand Rapids: Wm. B. Eerdmans Publishing Co., 1956.

A series of lectures portraying the central theme of the epistle. 227.87'06.V92

*Wescott, Brooke Foss. *The Epistle to the Hebrews.* Grand Rapids: Wm. B. Eerdmans Co., reprint.

One of the best treatments of the Greek text. The notes on Melchizedek, the Tabernacle, the Christology of the epistle, the use of OT quotations by the writer of Hebrews, and so on, are worth the price of the book. First published in 1889. 227.87'07.W52

JAMES

Barkman, Paul Friesen. *Man in Con-*

flict. Grand Rapids: Zondervan Publishing House, 1965.

Tries to relate the scientific theory of knowledge to man's condition and environment. Freudian. 227.91'08.B24

*Gaebelein, Frank Ely. *Practical Epistle of James: Studies in Applied Christianity.* Greatneck, N.Y.: Doniger and Raughley, 1955.

Abounds in illustrative values and contains a helpful application of the text to situations prevailing in the present day. A biblically sound commentary. 227.91'07.G11

*Johnstone, Robert. *Lectures, Exegetical and Practical, on the Epistle of James.* Grand Rapids: Baker Book House, 1954.

A classic in the field. Published originally in 1871. A *must* for the expository preacher. Buy it! 227.91'07.J65 1954

Knowling, Richard John. *The Epistle of James.* Westminster Commentaries. London: Methuen and Co., 1904.

One of the better works in this series, but long out of print. 227.91'07.K76

Manton, Thomas. *An Exposition of the Epistle of James.* London: Banner of Truth Trust, 1962.

First published in 1693, these exhaustive studies highlight the special relevance of this epistle in the situations facing the church. 227.91'07.M31 1962

Mayor, Joseph Bickersteth. *The Epistle of James.* Grand Rapids: Zondervan Publishing House, 1954.

An encyclopedic work on the Greek text. Regarded by many as the most important critical commentary on this portion of God's Word. Technical. First published in 1892. 227.91'07.M45 1954

*Mitton, Charles Leslie. *The Epistle of James.* Grand Rapids: Wm. B. Eerdmans Publishing Co., 1966.

Provides a scholarly exposition of the meaning and message of James and its outworking in human relationships. The product of mature scholarship. 227.91'07.M69

Motyer, J. A. *The Test of Life.* London: Inter-Varsity Press, 1970.

A short, readable commentary by an evangelical. 227.91'07.M85

Plummer, Alfred. *The General Epistles of St. James and St. Jude.* The Expositor's Bible. New York: A. C. Armstrong and Son, 1908.

Worth consulting, but does not deserve to be placed high on the preacher's priority list. 227.91'07.P73

Robertson, Archibald Thomas. *Studies in the Epistle of James.* Revised and edited by Heber F. Peacock. Nashville: Broadman Press, 1959.

The contents of this volume grew out of lectures delivered at Northfield, Chautauqua, and Winona Lake. Practical and unsophisticated. 227.91'07.R54 1959

Ross, Alexander. *The Epistles of James and John.* New International Commentary on the New Testament. Grand Rapids: Wm. B. Eerdmans Publishing Co., 1954.

A helpful, practical exposition refuting the theories of C. H. Dodd and defending the Johannine authorship of John's epistles. Interprets the epistles in the light of their first-century setting. 227.91'07.R73

Stevenson, Herbert F. *James Speaks for Today.* Westwood, N.J.: Fleming H. Revell Co., 1966.

Lucid exposition of the practical and corporate relationships of the message of James. 227.91'07.ST4

*Strauss, Lehman. *James, Your Brother: Studies in the Epistle James.* New York: Loizeaux Brothers, 1956.

A well-outlined, carefully reasoned exposition. 227.91'07.ST8

*Tasker, Randolph Vincent Greenwood. *The General Epistle of James.* Tyndale New Testament Commentaries. Grand Rapids: Wm. B. Eerdmans Publishing Co., 1960.

Far superior to the author's expositions on Matthew and John. Introductory data is carefully outlined, and verse-by-verse exposition is practical and helpful. 227.91'07.T18

Zodhiates, Spiros. The Behavior of Belief. Grand Rapids: Wm. B. Eerdmans Publishing Co., 1970.

Formerly published in three volumes, these well-illustrated expository messages emphasize with simplicity, clarity, freshness, and zeal the practical lessons to be learned from a study of this letter. 227.9'07.Z7

PETER'S EPISTLES

Best, Ernest. *I Peter.* New Century Bible. London: Oliphants Ltd., 1971.

†This scholarly study by a leading NT exegete denies the Petrine authorship. By building upon a careful examination of the original text, Best presents the theme of the letter as containing encouragement to Christians who are undergoing persecution. The value of his work is undermined by his theology. 227.92'07.B46

Bigg, Carl. *A Critical and Exegetical Commentary on the Epistles of St. Peter and St. Jude.* International Critical Commentary. Edinburgh: T. and T. Clark, 1961.

The introductory material is helpful and informative. Second Peter is dated after the closing of the canon and, while looked upon as having practical value, is not regarded as authentic. The exposition of the Greek text has been well done. First published in 1901. 227.92'07.B48 1961

Blair, J. Allen. *Living Faithfully.* New York: Loizeaux Brothers, 1961.

A devotional study of Second Peter. 227.93'07.B58

Brown, John. Expository Discourses in the First Epistle of the Apostle Peter. 3 vols. Marshalltown. Del.: National Foundation for Christian Education, n.d.

Has stood the test of time. Full and complete. Indispensible to the expositor. First published in 1848. 227.92'07.B81

Clark, Gordon Haddon. *Peter Speaks Today.* Philadelphia: Presbyterian and Reformed Publishing Co., 1967.

A devotional study of I Peter. Clear and concise. 227.92'07.C54

Cramer, George H. *First and Second Peter.* Chicago: Moody Press, 1967.

Brief studies suitable for adult groups. 227.92'07.C84

Cranfield, C. E. B. *First Epistle of Peter.* London: SCM Press, 1950.

A meritorious critical study, but too brief for the expository preacher. 227.92'07.C85

Green, Edward Michael Bankes. Second Epistle General of Peter and the General Epistle of Jude. Tyndale New Testament Commentary. Grand Rapids: Wm. B. Eerdmans Publishing Co., 1968.

Written by a leading conservative theologian in England, this work is a valuable companion volume to Stibbs's fine treatment of First Peter. Green handles the matters of textual criticism and the problems of authorship with rare ability. His exposition of the text is based upon a detailed exegesis, and he ably applies the teaching of these epistles to the needs of the present. 227.93'07.G82

Hort, Fenton John Anthony. *The First Epistle of St. Peter, 1:1-2:17.* London: Macmillan Co., 1898.

A critical and exegetical study. Long out of print and hard to obtain. 227.92'07.H78 1:1-2:17

Jowett, John Henry. *The Epistles of St. Peter.* Grand Rapids: Kregel Publications, 1970.

A practical and devotional exposition. Reprinted from the 1904 edition. 227.92'07.J83 1970

Kelly, John Norman Davidson. *A Commentary on the Epistles of Peter and of Jude.* Harper New Testament Commentaries. New York: Harper and Row, 1969.

A scholarly, comprehensive treatment. Does not adhere to the Petrine authorship of the second epistle, and lacks the dynamic conviction so evident in Kelly's treatment of the pastoral epistles. 227.92'07.K29

*Leighton, Robert. *A Practical Commentary upon the First Epistle General of Peter.* London: Thomas Tegg, 1831.

One of the best expository works on I Peter. Leighton provides his reader with the results of his vast learning without ostentation; his theology is accurate and his eloquence unmatched. Devotional. 227.92'07.L53

Lumby, Joseph Rawson. *The Epistles of St. Peter.* The Expositor's Bible. New York: A. C. Armstrong and Sons, 1908.

Like Lumby's other writings, this one is worth consulting. 227.92'07.L97

Meyer, Frederick Brotherton. *Tried by Fire.* London: Marshall, Morgan and Scott, 1955.

A devotional exposition of First Peter. Edifying and thoroughly evangelical. Reprinted from the edition published in 1890. 227.92'07.M57 1955

*Selwyn, Edward Gordon. *First Epistle of St. Peter.* London: Macmillan Co., 1961.

A brilliant work regarded by many as the finest treatment of the Greek text extant. 227.92'07.SE4

*Stibbs, Alan Marshall. *The First Epistle General of Peter.* Tyndale New Testament Commentaries. Grand Rapids: Wm. B. Eerdmans Publishing Co., 1960.

Prefaced with a brilliant introduction by Andrew F. Walls. The exposition is representative of the finest evangelical scholarship. A work of real value. 227.92'07.ST5

JOHN'S EPISTLES

Alexander, Neil. *The Epistles of John: Introduction and Commentary.* New York: Macmillan Co., 1962.

†A brief, critical exposition in which the writer repudiates the Johannine authorship and attributes the letter to "John the Elder." Alexander frequently takes issue with the biblical author and openly denies the authority of the Scriptures. 227.94'07.AL2

Barker, Charles Joseph. *The Johannine Epistles.* London: Lutterworth Press, 1948.

†A brief commentary based on the RV. Rejects the apostolic authorship of the letter and holds that both John's gospel and his epistles were written by "John the Elder." Overly critical of the writer, and lacking in practical value. 227.94'07.B24

Blaiklock, Edward Musgrave. *Faith Is the Victory.* Grand Rapids: Wm. B. Eerdmans Publishing Co., 1959.

Brief devotional comments by a layman. Evangelical. 227.94'04.B57

*Brooke, Alan England. *A Critical and Exegetical Commentary on the Johannine Epistles.* International Critical Commentary. New York: Charles Scribner's Sons, 1928.

†A commentary that deprecates the deity of Christ, rejects as "legend" the teaching regarding the Antichrist, and minimizes the efficacy of Christ's death on the cross. Exegetically valuable; theologically unreliable. 227.94'07.B79

Bruce, Frederick Fyvie. *The Epistles of John.* London: Pickering and Inglis, 1970.

A verse-by-verse treatment emphasizing the need for Christians to guard against the temptation to make the gospel conform to current trends of thought and modes of theology. Hits hard against materialism, and stresses the practical lessons to be learned from these letters. 227.94'07.B83

Burdick, Donald W. *The Epistles of John.* Chicago: Moody Press, 1970.

A careful exposition of the argument of the first epistle, with an analysis of the ascending stages, or spiral, in John's thought. The writer sees John's basic purpose in writing as being to develop a correct view of Christ that will result in a life of love and righteousness. Good for Bible study classes. 227.94'07.B89

*Candlish, Robert Smith. *The First Epistle of John.* Grand Rapids: Zondervan Publishing House, n.d.

Expository messages presenting a moving portrait of Christ and the believer's relationship to Him. A product of the times, these studies vigorously attack Roman Catholicism and warn against apostasy. First published in 1866. 227.94'07.C16

Conner, Walter Thomas. *The Epistles of John.* Nashville: Broadman Press, 1957.

These expository thoughts defend the Johannine authorship, attack liberal tendencies, contain appropriate illustrations, and warn against false teachers. Originally published in 1929. 227.94'07.C76 1957

Cotton, John. *An Exposition of First John.* Evansville, Ind.: Sovereign Grace Publishers, 1962.

A Puritan work first published in 1657. So extensive that the reader can virtually develop a systematic theology from its contents. 227.94'07.C83 1962

Dodd, Charles Harold. *The Johannine Epistles.* Moffat New Testament Commentary. New York: Harper and Brothers, 1946.

†A brief, radical exposition in which the writer takes issue with John for his crude view of sin, argues for expiation not propitiation, and advances some of his views concerning "realized eschatology" rather than what he chooses to call "crude mythology." Also denies the possibility of a future judgment. 227.94'07.D66

Ebrard, Johannes Heinrich August. *Biblical Commentary on the Epistles of St. John.* Edinburgh: T. and T. Clark, 1860.

An exhaustive, technical commentary that defends the genuineness of the epistles and provides some novel interpretations of material in the text. 227.94'07.EB7

*Findlay, George G. *Fellowship in the Life Eternal.* Grand Rapids: Wm. B. Eerdmans Publishing Co., 1955.

An outstanding exposition since its first appearance in 1909. Dedicated scholarship is combined with rare spiritual insight, making this a first-rate work. 27.94'07.F49 1955

Gloag, Paton James. *Introduction to the Johannine Writings.* London: James Nisbet and Co., 1891.

A scholarly introduction that may profitably be consulted even by those who have access to the more recent works by Guthrie and Harrison. 227.94'06.G51

Gore, Charles. *The Epistles of St. John.* London: John Murray, 1920.

†A popular exposition advancing the teachings of baptismal regeneration and other errors. 227.94'07.G66

*Ironside, Henry Allan. *Addresses on the Epistles of John and an Exposition on the Epistle of Jude.* 2d ed. New York: Loizeaux Brothers, 1954.

One of Ironside's best works. Plain and practical, clear and concise. 227.94'07.IR6 1954.

Kelly, William. *An Exposition of the Epistles of John the Apostle.* London: T. Weston, 1905.

These lectures by a Plymouth Brethren writer defend the deity of Christ, uphold the divine inspiration of the Scriptures, attack Pelagianism and liberalism in churches, and provide an important study of the text. Recommended. 227.94'07.K29

*King, Guy Hope. *The Fellowship.* London: Marshall, Morgan and Scott, 1954.

A devotional and practical exposition of I John. 227.94'07.K58

*Law, Robert. *The Tests of Life. A Study of*

the First Epistle of St. John. 3d ed. Grand Rapids: Baker Book House, 1968.

Out of print and unobtainable for nearly sixty years, this unique contribution covers a major portion of the first epistle, provides timely discussion on theological and Christological themes, and includes the doctrine of sin, the account of propitiation, and the tests of righteousness, love, and belief. 227.94'07.L41 1968

Lewis, Greville P. *The Johannine Epistles.* London: Epworth Press, 1961.

†It is surprising to come across an attempted exposition of these epistles by a writer who claims that it is "impossible to discover a clear scheme of thought" in the first epistle. Lenski, Stott, and Findlay have adequately expounded the theme of John's letters. 227.04'07.L58

Lias, John James. *The First Epistle of St. John.* London: James Nisbet and Co., 1887.

A conservative and scholarly exposition defending the genuineness of the epistle and containing some valuable exegetical insights. 227.94'07.L61

*Morgan, James. *Exposition of the First Epistle of John.* Edinburgh: T. and T. Clark, 1865.

Active in both evangelism and church planting, Morgan was also a capable expositor. This work gives evidence of his expertise and is worthy of purchase by all who are in the ministry. 227.94'07.M82

Plummer, Alfred. *The Epistles of St. John.* Cambridge Greek Testament. Cambridge: At the University Press, 1894.

Critical notes on the Greek text. 227.94'07.P73

*Stott, John Robert Walmsey. *The Epistles of John.* Tyndale New Testament Commentaries. Grand Rapids: Wm. B. Eerdmans Publishing Co., 1964.

Combines an understanding of exegesis with a knowledge of the local church situation that lies behind these epistles, and expounds their theme in the light of the work of the ministry. A beautiful blending of Bible teaching and practical theology. Evangelical. 227.94'07.ST6

Strauss, Lehman. *The Epistles of John.* New York: Loizeaux Brothers, Inc., 1962.

A slender volume containing alliterated messages covering almost all the text. Contains usable illustrations, and abounds in appropriate application. 227.94'07.ST8

Vine, William Edwy. *The Epistles of John.* Grand Rapids: Zondervan Publishing House, reprint.

A strongly conservative development of the theory that John wrote to defend Christianity against the false teachings of the Ebionites, Docetists, and Cerinthians. Based upon a thorough knowledge of the Greek text. 227.94'07.V75

*Westcott, Brooke Foss. *The Epistles of St. John.* Edited with an introduction by F. F. Bruce. Grand Rapids: Wm. B. Eerdmans Publishing Co., 1966.

Long recognized as one of the most thorough, complete commentaries on the Greek text. Bruce has updated the introductory material and provided a summary of the significant discoveries and commentaries since Westcott's time. First published in 1883. Excellent. 227.94'07.W52 1966

White, Reginald Ernest Oscar. *An Open Letter to Evangelicals; A Devotional and Homiletic Commentary on the First Epistle of John.* Grand Rapids: Wm. B. Eerdmans Publishing Co., 1964.

Adheres to many of the form-critical views of C. H. Dodd, and claims that the believer's authority lies not in the words of Scripture, but in Christ. Helpful for its illustrations; disappointing because of its weak theology. Not as helpful as Findlay, Law, Lenski, or Stott. 227.94'07.W58

William, Ronald Ralph. *The Letters of*

John and James. Cambridge: At the University Press, 1965.

†Brief comments based upon the text of the NEB. The writer's knowledge of Greek leaves much to be desired, and he does not hesitate to contradict the apostle where he thinks fit. States that the Bible contains half-truths and exaggerations. 227.94'07.W67

JUDE

*Coder, S. Maxwell.** *Jude: The Acts of the Apostates.* Chicago: Moody Press, 1958.

An adequate unfolding of the message of Jude. 227.97'07.C64

Jaeger, Harry. *Hidden Rocks.* Boston: Fellowship Press, 1949.

A devout approach to the theme of this epistle. 227.97'07.J17

*Jenkyn, William.** *An Exposition Upon the Epistle of Jude.* Revised by James Sherman. London: Henry G. Bohn, 1653.

This work preceded Manton's monumental treatment. Manton regarded this exposition with such awe that he purposely avoided duplicating any of its material in his own work. Should be purchased if found. 227.97'07.J41

*Manton, Thomas.** *An Exposition of the Epistle of Jude.* London: Banner of Truth Trust, 1958.

Manton died in 1677, and this expository study has been reprinted from his works. He is very extensive, as can be seen from the fact that this exposition covers 375 pages. 227.97'07.M31 1958

Mayor, Joseph Bickersteth. *The Epistle of St. Jude and the Second Epistle of St. Peter.* Grand Rapids: Baker Book House, 1965.

A brilliant, technical treatment. Denies the Petrine authorship of II Peter, but is inclined to accept its canonicity and fully appreciates its intrinsic spiritual value and practical worth. 227.97'07.M45

Wolff, Richard. *A Commentary on the Epistle of Jude.* Grand Rapids: Zondervan Publishing Co., 1960.

After carefully dealing with the problems of authorship, the writer provides his readers with a helpful exposition. Lack of a knowledge of Greek diminishes the value of this study. 227.97'07.W83

REVELATION

*Barclay, William.** *Letters to the Seven Churches.* New York: Abingdon Press, 1958.

A historical treatment based upon a careful re-creation of the historic setting of the first century A.D. Includes a description of the pagan religions and customs, Caesar worship, persecution, the slander of the Jews, internal heresy, and apathy—all of which faced the early church. 228'.07.2—3.B23L

*_____. *The Revelation of John.* 2 vols. Philadelphia: Westminster Press, 1961.

Volume 1 is devoted entirely to chapters 1-5 and provides an extensive study of the seven letters to the churches of Asia. It in no way duplicates material contained in the writer's *Letters to the Seven Churches.* The chief value of this set lies in the historical data and interesting Greek word studies. Apart from these notable features, the exposition is uninspiring. 228'.07.B23

*Beckwith, Isbon Thaddaeus.** *The Apocalypse of John.* Grand Rapids: Baker Book House, 1967.

A critical and exegetical commentary by a priest in the Protestant Episcopal Church. First published in 1919. Extensive introductory material, followed by over 400 pages of commentary. A work of impeccable scholarship. Amillenial. 228'.07.B38 1967

Blaiklock, Edward Musgrave. *The Seven Churches.* London: Marshall, Morgan and Scott, 1950.

An up-to-date historical and geographical treatment. 228'.07.2—3.B58

Caird, George Bradford. *The Revelation of St. John the Divine.* Harper's New Testament Commentaries. New York: Harper and Row, 1966.

A scholarly commentary reflecting a determined effort to follow a consistent hermeneutic. One of the major strengths of this work is the reconstruction of the first-century A.D. setting with continuous emphasis upon a present understanding of what the Spirit might be saying to churches in our own day. 228'.07.C12

*Charles, Robert Henry. *A Critical and Exegetical Commentary on the Revelation of St. John.* International Critical Commentary. 2 vols. Edinburgh: T. and T. Clark, 1920.

This work and Swete's exemplary treatment vie for supremacy. Exegetical. Amillenial. 228'.07.C38

Criswell, Wallie Amos. *Expository Sermons on Revelation.* Grand Rapids: Zondervan Publishing House, 1961-66.

These expositions cover both the prophetic and practical aspects of Revelation, explain many of the events, symbols, and prophecies in the light of their future fulfillments, and provide encouragement and edification to believers, with a warning to the unsaved. 228'.07.C86

DeHaan, Martin Ralph. *Revelation.* Grand Rapids: Zondervan Publishing House, 1967.

A series of studies on the major themes in the book of Revelation. Premillenial. 228'.07.D36

Gaebelein, Arno Clemens. *The Revela-*

tion: An Analysis and Exposition of the Last Book of the Bible. New York: Loizeaux Brothers, 1961.

A premillennial interpretation. 228'.07.G11

Gettys, Joseph Miller. *How to Study the Revelation.* Richmond: John Knox Press, 1963.

A study manual that attempts to guide readers through the maze of symbols to an interpretation of the book of Revelation. 228'.007.G33S

————. *How to Teach the Revelation.* Richmond: John Knox Press, 1964.

A valuable reference work for Bible class teachers. 228'.007.G33T

Hadjiantoniou, George A. *The Postman of Patmos.* Grand Rapids: Zondervan Publishing House, 1961.

This work by Geōrgios A. Chatzeautoniou denies any prophetic significance in these letters, expounds the meaning of the message as it applied to the early church addressed by Christ, and interprets the timeless truths in the light of the "postscripts" appended to each letter. 228'.07.H11 2-3

Hendriksen, William. *More Than Conquerors: An Interpretation of the Book of Revelation.* Grand Rapids: Baker Book House, 1939.

This work ably sets forth the amillennial interpretation of this prophecy. 228'.07.H38

Hobbs, Herschel H. *The Cosmic Drama: An Exposition of the Book of Revelation.* Waco: Word Books, 1971.

An amillennial interpretation. 228'.07.H65

Hoeksema, Herman. *Behold He Cometh! An Exposition of the Book of Revelation.* Grand Rapids: Reformed Free Publishing Association, 1969.

A carefully worded, amillennial exposition. 228'.07.H67

Ironside, Henry Allan. *Lectures on the*

Book of Revelation. New York: Loizeaux Brothers, 1955.

A strongly typological, premillennial interpretation. 228'.07.IR6

Kelly, William. *Lectures on the Book of Revelation.* London: G. Morrish, n.d.

A premillennial approach based upon a literal interpretation of the text. Does not avoid problems, and uses Scripture passages to explain the types and symbols encountered in the book. An important contribution. 228'.07.K29

Kiddle, Martin. *The Revelation of St. John.* Moffat New Testament Commentary. New York: Harper and Brothers, 1940.

†Based upon *The New Translation* of the late James Moffat. Begins with an extensive introduction and then treats the text in ways that provide interesting homiletic insights. Fails to provide the kind of exposition that contributes to the development of a consistent biblical eschatology. 228'.07.K53

Kik, Jacob Marcellus. *Revelation 20: An Exposition.* Philadelphia: Presbyterian and Reformed Publishing Co., 1948.

Following the Augustinian interpretation of Revelation, Kik presents a clear, cogent defense of his views. 228'.07.20.K55

*Morgan, George Campbell. *The Letters of Our Lord: A First Century Message to Twentieth Century Christians.* London: Pickering and Inglis, 1961.

A series of simple, devout messages revealing the conditions of church life to be found continuously in the Christian church. Of value to laypeople. 228'.07.1—3.M82

Newell, William R. *The Book of Revelation.* Chicago: Moody Press, 1935.

A careful unfolding of the theme and purpose of the Revelation of John. Premillennial. 228'.07.N44

Ottman, Ford Cyrinde. *The Unfolding of the Ages in the Revelation of John.* Fincas-

tle, Va.: Scripture Truth Book Co., 1967.

This work follows a premillennial interpretation colored by the dominant thoughts of the era in which Ottman lived. First published in 1905. 228'.07.OT8 1967

*Ramsay, William Mitchell. *Letters to the Seven Churches of Asia.* Grand Rapids: Baker Book House, 1963.

A brilliant study of the historical and archaeological material relating to these churches. Reprinted from the 1904 edition. 228'.06.2—3.R14 1963

*Ryrie, Charles Caldwell. *Revelation.* Chicago: Moody Press, 1968.

A premillennial approach. Ideally suited for laypeople's study groups. 228'.07.R99

Scott, Walter. *Exposition of the Revelation of Jesus Christ.* 4th ed. London: Pickering and Inglis, n.d.

This work gives evidence of intensive research, careful exposition, and an awareness of God's plan for the future. Strongly typological. 228'.07.SCO8

*Scroggie, William Graham. *The Great Unveiling.* Edinburgh: The author, 1920.

A study guide of the different views of interpretation. For brevity, clarity, and accuracy, it is hard to duplicate. 228'.07.SCR7

Seiss, Joseph Augustus. *The Apocalypse.* Grand Rapids: Zondervan Publishing House, 1964.

An exhaustive, premillennial exposition by a well-known Lutheran writer of the past century. 228'.07.SE4 1964

*_____. *Letters to the Seven Churches.* Grand Rapids: Baker Book House, 1956.

A series of practical studies designed to "impress the heart, awaken spiritual consciousness, animate our hopes, and further us in the way of Christian improvement." First published in 1889. 228'.07.1—3.SE4 1956

*Smith, Jacob Brubaker. *A Revelation of Jesus Christ.* Edited by J. Otis Yoder.

Scottdale, Penn.: Herald Press, 1961.

A premillennial treatment based on careful exegesis and providing rich source material. Well-substantiated conclusions. 228'.07.SM6

*Stott, John Robert Walmsey. *What Christ Thinks of the Church.* Grand Rapids: Wm. B. Eerdmans Publishing Co., 1958.

Characteristic of the writer's penetrating insight and usual brilliant exposition, these messages on Revelation 2-3 set forth the ideal qualities of the church. 228'.07.2—3.ST6

*Strauss, Lehman. *The Book of the Revelation.* Neptune, N.J.: Loizeaux Brothers, 1965.

Expository messages. Helpful in elucidating the text. 228'.07.ST8

*Swete, Henry Barclay. *The Apocalypse of St. John.* Grand Rapids: Wm. B. Eerdmans Publishing Co., n.d.

A masterful exposition of the Greek text. First published in 1906. Amillennial. 228'.07.SW4

*Tatford, Frederick Albert. *The Patmos Letters.* Grand Rapids: Kregel Publications, 1969.

A scholarly investigation into the historic setting of the Asian churches in the first century A.D., together with a careful exposition of the text of Scripture. 228'.07.T18 2-3

————. *Prophecy's Last Word.* Grand Rapids: Kregel Publications, 1969.

This remarkable study seeks to unveil God's prophetic program by combining the historical data with a premillennial interpretation. The author's research is extensive; his investigation into the meaning of the text is meticulous. Adherence to a consistent hermeneutic makes this a valuable reference work. 228'.07.T18

Tenney, Merrill Chapin. *Interpreting Revelation.* Grand Rapids: Wm. B. Eerdmans Publishing Co., 1958.

An introduction to the various methods of interpretation. Advocates a premillennial, post-tribulation return of Christ. 228'.06.T25

*Trench, Richard Chenevix. *Commentary on the Epistles to the Seven Churches in Asia.* 6th ed. London: Kegan Paul, Trench, Trubner and Co., 1897.

An important exegetical exposition. 228'.07.2—3.T72

*Walvoord, John Flipse. *The Revelation of Jesus Christ.* Chicago: Moody Press, 1966.

The writer is consistently literal in his interpretation, thoroughly abreast of the latest scholarly research, and builds his exposition upon a detailed exegesis of the text. Premillennial. 228'.07.W17

APOCRYPHA AND PSEUDEPIGRAPHA

Andrews, Herbert Tom. *An Introduction to the Apocryphal Books of the Old and New Testament.* Revised and edited by Charles F. Pfeiffer. Grand Rapids: Baker Book House, 1964.

Concentrates on the historic value and literary importance of these non-canonical books. 229.06.AN2

The Apocrypha of the Old Testament. Revised Standard Version. New York: Thomas Nelson and Sons, 1957.

A readable translation. 229.04.AP4

The Apocryphal New Testament. Translated by Montague Rhodes James. Oxford: At the Clarendon Press, 1955.

An ideal, compact edition of the Gnostic texts for those who cannot afford the more expensive versions. 229.9.J23

Charles, Robert Henry. *The Apocrypha and Pseudepigrapha.* 2 vols. Oxford: At the Clarendon Press, 1963.

The standard, critical work. 229.C38

Grand, Robert McQueen and **David Noel Freedman.** *The Secret Sayings of Jesus.* Garden City: Doubleday and Co., 1960.

Includes an English translation of the *Gospel of Thomas,* by William R. Schoedel. Provides an authoritative interpretation of the manuscripts. 229.951.G76

Hennecke, Edgar. *New Testament Apocrypha.* Edited by Wilhelm Schneenelcher. Translated by Robert McL. Wilson. 2 vols. Philadelphia: Westminster Press, 1963-65.

Scholarly introductory articles on the canon of the New Testament, the origin of the Apocrypha, nonbiblical material about Jesus, the Gnostic writings, studies of work and sufferings of Jesus, a scholarly series of articles on the apostles and apostolic pseudepigrapha, and so on. A work for the scholar. 229.H39

Jewish Apocryphal Literature. Edited by Solomon Zeitlin, et al. Philadelphia: Dropsie College of Hebrew and Cognate Learning.

An important series for those who desire to study the apocryphal and pseudepigraphal literature of the intertestamental period. Complete with English translation and commentary. Faithfully records the influence of the literature upon later rabbinic Judaism and early Christianity. 229'.07.J55

Jones, M. J. *The Apocryphal New Testament, Being the Apocryphal Gospels, Acts, The Epistles, and Apocalypse.* Oxford: At the Clarendon Press, 1924.

Together with the studies by R. H. Charles, this work has been used as primary source material for the study of the noncanonical writings. 229.J72

*Metzger, Bruce Manning. *An Introduction to the Apocrypha.* New York: Oxford University Press, 1957.

A comprehensive examination of the books of the Apocrypha, together with an evaluation of their history and significance. 229.06.M56

Oesterley, William Oscar Emil. *An Introduction to the Books of the Apocrypha.* London: SPCK, 1946.

Now superseded by Metzger's *Introduction to the Apocrypha.* 229.06.OE8

*Russell, David Syme. *Between the Testaments.* London: SCM Press, 1960.

Adequate sections on "The Cultural and Literary Background" and "The Apocalyptists." Contains a treatment of the Messiah as the Son of Man. An excellent synthesis. 229.R91

Summers, Ray. *The Secret Sayings of the Living Jesus.* Waco: Word Books, 1968.

A concise evaluation of the fourth-century library discovered at Nag Hammadi, Egypt. 229'.8.SU6

7

Doctrinal Theology

Theology has been called the "queen of the sciences." Other disciplines contribute to our knowledge of theology, but they never rise to the sublime height of the study of doctrine in value or importance. Unfortunately, few pastors study theology after graduating from seminary. This neglect has its effect upon themselves and upon their ministry. A proper grasp of doctrine—based squarely upon the Scriptures as the inspired revelation of God to man—lies at the very heart of our preaching ministry. The neglect of this area of study results in preaching that is characterized by uncertainties, inaccuracies, and immaturity.

One writer said: "While it is true that the Bible is the source of the material which enters into Systematic Theology, *it is equally true that the function of Systematic Theology is to unfold the Bible*" (italics added). A thorough knowledge of doctrine gives the preacher a consistent, harmonious view of God, man, the world we live in, God's plan of salvation, His program for the world, and man's place in that program.

As ministers of God, our duty is to expound the Scriptures so that Jesus Christ is presented in all the beauty and glory of His mediatorial character. Too frequently our messages become an exposition of our own views on the subject at hand. A study of systematic theology awakens us to a realization of the authority of the Bible and the relevancy of its message. It adds precision and clarity, authority and unction, breadth and depth to our preaching, and edifies those who sit under our ministry.

As with Paul, we should be equipped to declare to our congregations "the whole counsel of God" (Acts 20:27). Nothing less will do.

REFERENCE WORKS

Allmen, Jean-Jacques von, ed. *Vocabulary of the Bible*. Translated by P. J. All- cock. London: Lutterworth Press, 1958.
†An English translation of a French

work published in the U.S. under the title *A Companion to the Bible* and containing in dictionary form short articles on the major theological terms and ideas found in the Bible. 230'.03.AL5

Baker's Dictionary of Theology. Edited by E. F. Harrison. Grand Rapids: Baker Book House, 1960.

Containing articles by 138 evangelical scholars, this work is ideal for laypeople who desire an easy-to-use compendium on a wide variety of theological issues. It is also a handy reference tool for the busy pastor. The articles are generally fairly short, yet they serve to alert readers to the main viewpoints held by different branches of Christendom. 203.B17H

Leon-DuFour, Xavier, ed. *Dictionary of Biblical Theology.* London: G. Chapman, 1967.

†Similar in scope to von Allmen's *Vocabulary of the Bible* and produced entirely by Roman Catholic scholars, this work is generally more helpful than other European works of a similar nature. Conservative and liberal articles often stand side by side, necessitating discernment on the part of the user. 230'.03.L55

***Ramm, Bernard Lawrence.** A Handbook of Contemporary Theology.* Grand Rapids: Wm. B. Eerdmans Publishing Co., 1966.

A practical explanation of theological terminology. Very helpful. 230'.09'03.R14

Richardson, Alan, ed. *Dictionary of Christian Theology.* Philadelphia: Westminster Press, 1969.

†A comprehensive work aiming at a clear definition of theological terms. At times the articles are very illuminating, but many of them are too brief to be of any value. 203'.03.R39

SYSTEMATIC THEOLOGY

Alexander, William Lindsey. *A System of Biblical Theology.* 2 vols. Edinburgh: T. and T. Clark, 1888.

An evangelical theological work by a British Congregationalist. Unconventional. 230'.58.AL2

***Barth, Karl.** Church Dogmatics.* Edited by G. W. Bromiley and T. F. Torrance. Edinburgh: T. and T. Clark, 1936-.

†This epochal work by a great neo-orthodox theologian records the stages through which Barth's theology went during his long and fruitful lifetime. The areas covered focus on "The Doctrine of the Word of God," "The Doctrine of Creation," and "The Doctrine of Reconciliation." Those who do not have the time to spend in mastering this erudite study can turn to Come's *An Introduction to Barth's Dogmatics* (1963). 230'.41.B28C

***Berkhof, Louis.** Systematic Theology.*

2d rev. ed. Grand Rapids: Wm. B. Eerdmans Publishing Co., 1941.

This particularly capable treatment is perhaps the best one-volume theology available. Reformed, evangelical. 230'.51.B45 1941

Boettner, Loraine. *Studies in Theology.* 7th ed. Philadelphia: Presbyterian and Reformed Publishing Co., 1965.

Contains a series of articles reprinted from *Christianity Today* and *The Evangelical Quarterly* dealing with "The Inspiration of the Scriptures," "Christian Supernaturalism," "The Trinity," "The Person of Christ," and "The Atonement." Reformed. 230'.51.B63 1965

Brown, William Adams. *Christian Theology in Outline.* New York: Charles Scribner's Sons, 1906.

†A clear statement of nineteenth-century radical theology. 230'.51.B81

Brunner, Heinrich Emil. *Dogmatics.* 3

vols. Philadelphia: Westminster Press, 1950.

†Volume 1 covers the Christian doctrine of God, volume 2 the Christian doctrine of creation and redemption, and volume 3 the Christian doctrine of the church, faith, and consummation. This work is very readable and presents the neoorthodox point of view. 230'.41.B83D

_____. *Our Faith.* Translated by John W. Rilling. New York: Charles Scribner's Sons, 1936.

Published before World War II, these simple studies attempt to grapple with the realities of the Christian faith. 230'.41.B83F

*Buswell, James Oliver, Jr. *A Systematic Theology of the Christian Religion.* 2 vols. Grand Rapids: Zondervan Publishing House, 1962.

Gives evidence of a thorough knowledge of Greek and Hebrew. Frequently shows how this kind of information may be used to good advantage. Reformed. Premillennial. 230'.51.B85

Calvin, John. *The Institutes of the Christian Religion.* Translated by Henry Beveridge. 2 vols. Grand Rapids: Wm. B. Eerdmans Publishing Co., 1953.

A complete translation based upon the original Latin and French editions. Lacks a good index. 230'.42.C13B

*_____. *Institutes of the Christian Religion.* Library of Christian Classics. Translated by Ford Lewis Battles. Edited by John T. McNeill. 2 vols. Philadelphia: Westminster Press, 1960.

Working from Latin, French, German, and English manuscripts, the translator and his associates have produced what must be the most accurate modern English edition of Calvin's famous *Institutes.* Contains chapter divisions, symbols indicating the growth of the *Institutes* from the outline of faith of 1536 to the systematic treatise of 1559, and provides notes

on the background and development of Calvin's thought. The Scripture, author, and subject indexes are invaluable. 230'.42.C13L

_____. *Instruction in Christianity.* Translated by Joseph Pitts Wiles. Stamford, England: Dolby Brothers, 1920.

An abridged edition of the *Institutes* that is designed for use by nontheological students. 230.42.C13I

*Chafer, Lewis Sperry. *Major Bible Themes.* Grand Rapids: Zondervan Publishing House, 1926.

A comprehensive manual of Christian doctrine. Remarkable for its clarity, brevity, and accuracy. Ideal for individual use or adult study groups. 230'.51.C34M

*_____. *Systematic Theology.* 8 vols. Dallas: Dallas Seminary Press, 1948.

An evangelical, premillennial work. Reliable and worthy of repeated use. 230'.51.C34S

*Evans, William. *The Great Doctrines of the Bible.* Rev. ed. Chicago: Moody Press, 1964.

A handy manual on basic Bible doctrine. Ideal for laypeople's discussion groups. 230'.51.EV1

Finney, Charles. *Lectures on Systematic Theology.* Grand Rapids: Wm. B. Eerdmans Publishing Co., 1951.

An unabridged edition of Finney's theology lectures delivered at Oberlin College. Arminian. 230'.58.F49

Hodge, Archibald Alexander. *Evangelical Theology.* London: Thomas Nelson and Sons, 1890.

Nineteen theological studies ranging from providence to predestination, the Godhead to man's state after death, and the inspiration of the Scriptures to the sacraments. Reformed. 230'.51.H66E

_____. *Outlines of Theology.* New York: R. Carter and Brothers, 1860.

A concise work by the son of Charles Hodge. One of the best treatments of the bearing of history, and the creeds and confessions, on the main points of theology. 230'.51.H66T

*Hodge, Charles. *Systematic Theology.* 3 vols. Grand Rapids: Wm. B. Eerdmans Publishing Co., 1960.

A comprehensive theological treatment by one of the greatest nineteenth-century Princeton theologians. Originally published 1871-73. Reformed. 230'.51.H66 1960

———. *The Way of Life.* London: Banner of Truth Trust, 1959.

Reprinted from the 1841 edition. Studies suited to the needs of laypeople. 230'.51.H66W 1959

Hoeksema, Herman. *Reformed Dogmatics.* Grand Rapids: Kregel Publications, 1966.

A theology built on the antithesis between election and reprobation. Contends that whatever God brings into the life of the reprobate is brought in for the purpose of damnation. In spite of this extreme view, Hoeksema's work does contain a considerable amount of sound theology. 230'.51.H67

*Kuyper, Abraham. *Principles of Sacred Theology.* Translated by J. Hendrik DeVries. Grand Rapids: Wm. B. Eerdmans Publishing Co., 1954.

Containing part of the author's *Encyclopedia of Sacred Theology* (1898), this work deals with the science of theology, its methodology, history, and distinctive principles. Reformed. 230'.42.K96

*Litton, Edward Arthur. *Introduction to Dogmatic Theology.* New ed. Edited by Phillip E. Hughes. London: James Clarke and Company, 1960.

A comprehensive, well-balanced treatment of dogmatic theology. Reformed. 230'.3.L73

Miley, John. *Systematic Theology.* 2 vols. New York: Hunt and Eaton, 1892.

A complete, thorough study of theology by an American Methodist Episcopal theologian. Arminian. 230'.71.M59

*Mueller, John Theodore. *Christian Dogmatics.* St. Louis, Mo.: Concordia Publishing House, 1934.

A one-volume work by an orthodox Lutheran. Evangelical. 230'.41.M88

Mullins, Edgar Young. *Christian Religion in its Doctrinal Expression.* Philadelphia: Judson Press, 1949.

Presents a fresh and original apologetic approach to theology. First published in 1917. 230'.6.M91 1949

Pentecost, John Dwight. *Things Which Become Sound Doctrine.* Westwood, N.J.: Fleming H. Revell Co., 1965.

A devout study of the doctrines of grace, regeneration, imputation, substitution, repentance, redemption, reconciliation, propitiation, and so on. 230'.51.P38

Pieper, Franz August Otto. *Christian Dogmatics.* 4 vols. St. Louis: Concordia Publishing House, 1950-57.

A monumental work setting forth the doctrines of Christianity as taught by the Lutheran Church Missouri Synod. 230'.41.P59

*Shedd, William Greenough Thayer. *Dogmatic Theology.* 3 vols. Grand Rapids: Zondervan Publishing House, 1969.

An eminently readable, thoroughly biblical work containing a most extensive and satisfactory treatment of the doctrine of endless punishment. Lacks a good index. First published between 1888-94. 230'.51.SH3 1969

Stevens, William Wilson. *The Doctrines of the Christian Religion.* Grand Rapids: Wm. B. Eerdmans Publishing Co., 1967.

A biblically oriented, well-outlined, college level text. Uncritical of the views of Tillich, Barth, and Brunner. Provides a good discussion of the person and work of Christ, but manifests a weakness in dealing with anthropology. Merges Israel and the church in unfolding God's program past, present, and future. Southern Baptist. 230'.6.ST4

*Strong, Augustus Hopkins. *Systematic Theology.* Valley Forge, Penn.: Judson Press, 1907.

In spite of its age and well-known weaknesses, this work is still esteemed as one of the best in the field for the general coverage of the whole scope of systematic theology. 230'.6.ST8

Thiessen, Henry Clarence. *Introductory Lectures in Systematic Theology.* Grand Rapids: Wm. B. Eerdmans Publishing Co., 1949.

A lucid, nontechnical, readable work explaining all the essentials of theology. 230'.51.T34

Tillich, Paul. *Systematic Theology.* 3 vols. Chicago: University of Chicago Press, 1951-63.

†In his apologetic, Tillich constantly tries to relate theology to philosophy. He occupies a position in the far left-wing of theologians and has very little to contribute to pastors engaged in preaching the Word. 230'.41.T46

Wardlaw, Ralph. *Unitarianism, Incapable of Vindication.* London: Longman, Hurst, Rees, Orme and Brown, 1816.

A valuable defense of true orthodoxy, with a vigorous and powerful refutation of every tenet upon which Unitarianism rests. Vindicates the deity of Christ from the limbo to which these deceivers had relegated it. An excellent discussion. 230.8.UN3.W21

Watson, Richard. *Theological Institutes: Or a View of the Evidences, Doctrines, Morals and Institutions of Christianity.* 2 vols. New York: G. Lane and P. B. Sandford, 1843.

Widely respected as an apologist, Watson provides a polemic for Christianity. Not as radical as some Arminian theologians. 230.71.W33

Watson, Thomas. *A Body of Divinity.* London: Banner of Truth Trust, 1965.

A series of sermons based on the Westminster Assembly's Shorter Catechism. Less extensive than the edition published in 1890 because it lacks the author's treatment on the Ten Commandments and the Lord's Prayer. 230.42.W33 1965

Wiley, Henry Orton. *Christian Theology.* 3 vols. Kansas City, Mo.: Nazarene Publishing House, 1940.

A standard Wesleyan theology from the Nazarene perspective. 230.71.W64

Wolf, Lotan Harold de. *Theology of the Living Church.* New York: Harper and Brothers, 1953.

†Useful as a compendium of liberal theology. 230.7.W83

FUNDAMENTALISM

Bass, Clarence B. *Backgrounds to Dispensationalism.* Grand Rapids: Wm. B. Eerdmans Publishing Co., 1960.

†As a critique of J. N. Darby this is biased, though not without merit for its historical data. It manifests, however, an appalling ignorance of dispensationalism as a theological discipline. 230'.082.B29

Feinberg, Charles Lee, ed. *The Fundamentals for Today.* 2 vols. Grand Rapids: Kregel Publications, 1958.

The famous *Fundamentals* that first appeared in 1909 are here revised and edited for republication. 230'.082.F32 1958

Henry, Carl Ferdinand Howard, ed. *Basic Christian Doctrines.* Contemporary Evangelical Thought. New York: Holt, Rinehart and Winston, 1962.

Contains forty-three chapters on as many different theological themes. Contemporary, but not necessarily reliable. 230'.082.H39B

————, ed. *Fundamentals of the Faith.*

Contemporary Evangelical Thought. Grand Rapids: Zondervan Publishing House, 1969.

A series of articles contributed to *Christianity Today* by leading evangelical scholars in the United States and Australia. Of varying quality. 230'.082.H39F

Ironside, Henry Allan. *Wrongly Dividing the Word of Truth*. Neptune, N.J.: Loizeaux Brothers, n.d.

An examination of ultradispensationalism. Should be read by all informed Christians, and particularly those who tend to place all dispensationalists in the same camp. 230'.082.IR6

Kraus, Clyde Norman. *Dispensationalism in America: Its Rise and Development*. Richmond: John Knox Press, 1958.

Fails to provide a definitive critique of dispensationalism. Does not cite sources later than the 1930s. Erratic and unreliable. 230'.082.K86

*Packer, James Innell. *"Fundamentalism" and the Word of God*. Grand Rapids: Wm. B. Eerdmans Publishing Co., 1958.

A reply to Hebert's *Fundamentalism and the Church* in which Packer seeks to show that by rejecting the so-called fundamentalist view of Scripture, theologians are, in fact, rejecting the traditional view of inspiration. 230'.082.P12

*Patton, Francis L. *Fundamental Christianity*. New York: Macmillan Co., 1928.

Lectures originally delivered in 1924 at Union Theological Seminary, Va. Provides a definitive analysis of theism, the seat of authority in religion, an analysis of the new "Christianity," the person of Christ, and Pauline theology. 230'.082.P27

*Ryrie, Charles Caldwell. *Dispensationalism Today*. Chicago: Moody Press, 1965.

Written to correct misconceptions about dispensationalism and, at the same time, to give a positive presentation of dispensationalism as it is taught today. Defines, describes, and defends this system of interpretation. 230'.082.R99

Sandeen, Ernest R. *The Roots of Fundamentalism*. Chicago: University of Chicago Press, 1970.

Generally fair and objective. Evaluates the rise of fundamentalism in the 1920s, and traces its origin to British millennarianism. One chapter is devoted to a comparison of the millennarianism of fundamentalists and the old Princeton theological school. The common denominator is shown to be a biblical literalism and a belief in the plenary verbal inspiration of the Scriptures. While frequently out of sympathy with premillennialism, the writer nevertheless provides a much better presentation of the history of fundamentalism than do predecessors such as Furniss, Cole, and Gasper. 230'.082.SA5

Stam, Cornelius Richard. *Fundamentals of Dispensationalism*. Chicago: Berean Searchlight, 1954.

An ultradispensational work. Unreliable. 230'.082.ST2

Historical Theology

*Berkhof, Louis. *The History of Christian Doctrine*. London: Banner of Truth Trust, 1969.

Reprinted from the 1937 edition. A valuable supplement to the author's *Systematic Theology*. 230'.09.B45 1969

Cunningham, William. *The Reformers and the Theology of the Reformation*. Stu-

dents Reformed Theological Library. London: Banner of Truth Trust, 1967.

First published over one hundred years ago. Traces the spiritual revival and theological controversies of the sixteenth century. A clear, evangelical discussion. Recommended. 230'.09.C91 1967

Fisher, George Park. *History of Chris-*

tian Doctrine. International Theological Library. 2d ed. Edinburgh: T. and T. Clark, 1949.

An informative survey that, because of its age and limitations, must take second place to the work by Seeberg. 230'.09.F53 1949

Harnack, Karl Gustav Adolf von. *History of Dogma.* Translated by Neil Buchanan. 5 vols. New York: Dover Publications, 1961.

†In spite of its obvious liberalism, this work is of immense value. Contains perceptive thoughts on the movements within Christendom, and treats the events and circumstances in a generally objective manner. 230'.09.H22 1961

*Heick, Otto William. *A History of Christian Thought.* 2 vols. Philadelphia: Fortress Press, 1965.

A complete revision and updating of the standard treatment by J. L. Neve. Provides a comprehensive treatment of historical theology. 230'.09.H36

*Hughes, Philip Edgcumbe. *Theology of the English Reformers.* London: Hodder and Stoughton, 1965.

A brilliant treatment of the doctrines of Scripture, justification, sanctification, preaching and worship, the ministry, sacraments, and church and state, as taught by Tyndale, Cranmer, Latimer, Ridley, Jewel, and others. 230'.0922.H87

*Kelly, John Norman Davidson. *Early Christian Doctrines.* 2d ed. New York: Harper and Row, 1960.

In the study of the history of early Christian doctrines from the apostolic era to the Council of Chalcedon, few works can compete with this one. A vast amount of material has been presented in a skillful, readable manner. 230'.09.K29 1960

Neve, Juergen Ludwig. *A History of Christian Thought.* 2 vols. Philadelphia: Fortress Press, 1946.

This important, conservative study has now been replaced by Heick's *History of*

Christian Thought. See above. 230'.09.N41

*Orr, James. *The Progress of Dogma.* Grand Rapids: Wm. B. Eerdmans Publishing Co., n.d.

Shows that the church's doctrine developed through a series of crises. Establishes the fact that the church's theology rests upon the criterion of Scripture, and that the periods of controversy within the church have brought to the fore doctrines that otherwise might have been neglected. First published in 1901. Excellent. 230'.09.OR7

*Seeberg, Reinhold. *Text-Book of the History of Doctrines.* Translated by Charles E. Hay. 2 vols. Grand Rapids: Baker Book House, 1961.

A monumental work combining theological acumen with a readable style. Remains an indispensable aid in the study of historical theology. Originally published in German in 1895-98. 230'.09.SE3 1961

Torrance, Thomas Forsyth. *Kingdom and Church: A Study in the Theology of the Reformation.* Edinburgh: Oliver and Boyd, 1956.

†A learned series of essays that students of historical theology will need to study. Torrance does not do justice to Luther's thought, manifests an eagerness to include Bucer in the Reformed tradition, and expounds Calvin's "eschatology of hope" in contrast to Luther's emphasis on faith and Bucer's stress on love. 230'.09.T63

CATHOLIC THEOLOGY

Aquinas, Thomas. *Nature and Grace.* Library of Christian Classics. Translated and edited by A. M. Fairweather. Philadelphia: Westminster Press, 1954.

This important volume contains translations of sections of *Summa Theologica* and will be of particular interest to students of church history. The passages selected cover all five parts of Aquinas's writings, demonstrate his method, and set forth the crucial areas of his system of doctrine. 230'.2.AQ5

Berkouwer, Gerrit Cornelis. *Conflict with Rome.* Grand Rapids: Baker Book House, 1958.

A thorough, scholarly critique in which the tenets of Roman Catholic dogma are examined in the light of the Scripture. 230'.2.B45

Carson, Herbert M. *Roman Catholicism Today.* Grand Rapids: Wm. B. Eerdmans Publishing Co., 1965.

Written in the light of Vatican II, this work evaluates the entire scope of Roman Catholic belief and doctrine. 230'2.C23

Catholic Dictionary of Theology. Edited by H. F. Davis, et al. 4 vols. Appleton, Wis.: C. C. Nelson, 1962-.

Three volumes in print and a fourth in preparation. Aims at providing a connected account of Roman Catholic theology in a series of scholarly, signed articles. Fully abreast of the developments in the Catholic church since Vatican II. 230.2'03.C28

Daniélou, Jean. *The Theology of Jewish Christianity: A History of Christian Doctrine Before the Council of Nicea.* London: Darton, Longman and Todd, 1964.

While regarded by many as avantgarde, this work aims at explaining the primitive Jewish Christian framework of thought that, the author claims, antedates both the orthodoxy and the heresy of the early Catholic era. 230'.2.D22

Davis, Charles. *A Question of Conscience.* New York: Harper and Row, 1967.

Having seen no change in the attitude of the Roman See since Vatican II, this British Catholic theologian gives his reasons for leaving Romanism. 230'.2.D29

Denzinger, Heinrich Joseph Dominik. *The Sources of Catholic Dogma.* St. Louis: B. Herder Co., 1957.

A comprehensive book containing an extensive array of official pronouncements by popes and councils. 230'.2.D43

Kavanaugh, James. *A Modern Priest Looks at His Outdated Church.* New York: Trident Press, 1967.

A frank assessment by a Roman Catholic priest of trends within the church of Rome, coupled with an appeal to lay aside the old legalism for a new humanism. 230'.2.K17

Küng, Hans. *The Council in Action.* New York: Sheed and Ward, 1963.

A Roman Catholic theologian's interpretation of the deliberations of Vatican II. 230'.2.K96

Lindbeck, George A. *The Future of Roman Catholic Theology.* Philadelphia: Fortress Press, 1969.

†This book, by an official observer at the Second Vatican Council, is the outgrowth of lectures delivered at Concordia Theological Seminary in 1966. Its immediate purpose is to explain the significance of Vatican II to Protestants. 230'.2.L64

Ott, Ludwig. *Fundamentals of Catholic Dogma.* Translated by Patrick Lynch. New York: Herder and Herder, 1955.

A presentation of Catholic doctrine by a German theologian. In need of revision. 230'.2.OT8

Rahner, Karl. *The Teaching of the Catholic Church.* Staten Island, N.Y.: Alba House, 1967.

A compilation of documents on the essential doctrines of Romanism, with an introduction and exposition of each doctrine. 230'.2.R12

*Sacramentum Mundi: An Encyclopedia of Theology. Edited by Karl A. Rahner, Cornelius Ernst and Kevin Smyth. New York: Herder and Herder, 1968-70.

†A serious attempt on the part of Catholic scholars to restate their theological beliefs in the light of the decisions reached at the Second Vatican Council. Published simultaneously in English, Dutch, French, German, Italian, and

Spanish, and containing articles by authorities in many countries, this work manifests a marked trend to update the scholastic phraseology of the older manuals on theology. Where biblical topics are concerned, the writers almost uniformly accept the conclusions of modern higher criticism. They adopt a modified Wellhausean approach to the sources of the Pentateuch, adhere to three distinct periods of the composition of the prophecies of Isaiah, hold to a Maccabean date for Daniel, and reject as pseudepigraphal several New Testament books. Interesting and informative. 230'.2.SA1

ANGLICAN THEOLOGY

Gore, Charles. *Lux Mundi.* London: John Murray, 1899.

†A series of doctrinal studies by a liberal bishop with Anglo-Catholic leanings. 230'.3.G66

Hammond, Thomas Chatherton. *In Understanding Be Men.* 4th ed. Chicago: Inter-Varsity Press, 1960.

An elementary handbook on Christian doctrine for nontheological students. 230'.3.H18 1960

Stott, John Robert Walmsey. *Basic Christianity.* Rev. ed. Grand Rapids: Wm. B. Eerdmans Publishing Co., 1957.

Written specifically for those seeking to know the truth about Christianity. 230'.3.ST7

*Thomas, William Henry Griffith. *The Principles of Theology: An Introduction to the Thirty-nine Articles.* London: Longmans, Green and Company, 1930.

An exposition of the Anglican articles of faith. Evangelical and scholarly. Recommended. 230'.3.T36

LUTHERAN THEOLOGY

Kerr, Hugh Thompson. *A Compend of Luther's Theology.* Philadelphia: Westminster Press, 1943.

Valuable for its arrangement of the appropriate material from Luther's voluminous writings. 230'.41.K46

*Montgomery, John Warwick. *Crisis in Lutheran Theology.* Vol. 1. Grand Rapids: Baker Book House, 1967.

230'.41.M76 v. 1

*_____. *Crisis in Lutheran Theology.* Vol. 2. Grand Rapids: Baker Book House, 1967.

A series of articles on inspiration and hermeneutics that focus on the erosion of these biblical distinctives in American Lutheranism. 230'.41.M76 v. 2

_____. *In Defense of Martin Luther.* Milwaukee: Northwestern Publishing House, 1970.

A series of essays vindicating Luther from criticism directed against him by liberal Lutheran theologians. 230'.41.L97.M76

Preus, Robert D. *The Theology of Post-Reformation Lutheranism.* St. Louis: Concordia Publishing House, 1970.

A comprehensive study of the entire era of Lutheran orthodoxy. 230'.41.P92

Watson, Phillip Saville. *Let God Be God!* London: Epworth Press, 1960.

A modern interpretation of Luther's theology. 230'.41.W33

CALVINISTIC THEOLOGY

Bavinck, Herman. *Our Reasonable Faith.* Grand Rapids: Wm. B. Eerdmans Publishing Co., 1956.

A condensation of the author's three-volume study of Reformed dogmatics, which is available only in Dutch. 230'.42.B32

Bube, Richard H. *To Every Man an Answer.* Chicago: Moody Press, 1955.

A clear, systematic study of basic Bible doctrine. 230'.51.B85

Dabney, Robert Lewis. *Discussions: Evangelical and Theological.* 2 vols. London: Banner of Truth Trust, 1967.

This collection of papers retains some

value for students of theology today. The author's vigorous literary style makes these lectures interesting reading. Includes a censure of non-Presbyterian groups. Thought-provoking. First published in 1890-91. 230'.51.D11 1967

Jocz, Jakob. *The Covenant.* Grand Rapids: Wm. B. Eerdmans Publishing Co., 1968.

Rather than being a restatement of traditional covenant theology, this book defends special revelation and supernatural redemption. However, the author adheres to the documentary hypothesis and a second Isaiah, and he appears to accept evolution as a fact. Also, he leans towards the doctrine of universal salvation. 230'.51.J58

*__Kuyper, Abraham.__ *Lectures on Calvinism.* New ed. Grand Rapids: Wm. B. Eerdmans Publishing Co., 1931.

The Stone Lectures for 1898. Deals with Calvinism as a life-system and its influence upon religion, politics, science, art, and the future. 230'.42.K96 1931

*__Steele, David N.__ and **Curtis C. Thomas.** *The Five Points of Calvinism.* Philadelphia: Presbyterian and Reformed Publishing Co., 1963.

A vigorous defense of Calvinism. 230'.42.ST3

*__Til, Cornelius van.__ *The Case for Calvinism.* Philadelphia: Presbyterian and Reformed Publishing Co., 1964.

A critical analysis of three contemporary theological viewpoints regarded by many as being established upon the foundation of historic Protestant Christianity. From this premise van Til discusses Calvinism—biblically, historically, and practically. 230'.42.V45

_____. *The Defense of the Faith.* Philadelphia: Presbyterian and Reformed Publishing Co., 1955.

A defense of the Reformed position, often amounting to a personal defense of van Til's beliefs in light of the criticisms leveled against his system of thought. 230'.51.T45

Wallace, Ronald S. *Calvin's Doctrine of the Word and Sacrament.* Grand Rapids: Wm. B. Eerdmans Publishing Co., 1957.

A work for the scholar. Well executed. Recommended. 230'.42.W15

Warfield, Benjamin Breckenridge. *Biblical Foundations.* London: Tyndale Press, 1958.

Selected theological studies taken from Warfield's other collected writings. 230'.51.W23B

_____. *Calvin and Augustine.* Edited by Samuel G. Craig. Philadelphia: Presbyterian and Reformed Publishing Co., 1956.

Important scholarly articles on the theology of Augustine and Calvin. Reformed. 230'.42.W23

Wendel, Francois. *Calvin: The Origins and Development of His Religious Thought.* New York: Harper and Row, 1963.

A valuable summary of Calvin's life and thought. 230'.42.W48

WESLEYAN THEOLOGY

Burtner, Robert W., and **Robert E. Chiles, ed.** *A Compend of Wesley's Theology.* New York: Abingdon Press, 1954.

A scholarly reevaluation of Wesley's teaching. Appropriate quotations from the writings of John Wesley make this volume an exceedingly helpful, handy reference tool. 230'.71.B95

Cannon, William Ragsdale. *The Theology of John Wesley.* Nashville: Abingdon Press, 1946.

A readable presentation of Wesley's entire theological system containing numerous insights into the ways in which Wesley's thought developed and the emphasis he placed upon "the economy of grace." 230'.7.W51C

Williams, W. *John Wesley's Theology Today.* New York: Abingdon Press, 1960.

A contemporary examination of the historic theological roots of Methodism. 230'.71.W67

OTHER THEOLOGICAL SYSTEMS

Mikolaski, Samuel J., ed. *The Creative Theology of P. T. Forsyth.* Grand Rapids: Wm. B. Eerdmans Publishing Co., 1969.

These studies center in the theology of the atonement and stress an experiential relationship with God in contrast to a dead, formal orthodoxy. 230'.58.M58

Olson, Arnold Theodore. *This We Believe.* 2d ed. Minneapolis: Free Church Publications, 1961.

A definitive exposition of the doctrinal statement of the Evangelical Free Church of America. 230'.49.OL8 1961

Seventh-Day Adventists Answer Questions on Doctrine. Washington, D.C.: Review and Herald Publishing Association, 1957.

An explanation by Seventh-Day Adventists of certain major aspects of their belief. 230'.67.SE8

MODERN THEOLOGY

Berkouwer, Gerrit Cornelis. *The Triumph of Grace in the Theology of Karl Barth.* Translated by Harry R. Boer. Grand Rapids: Wm. B. Eerdmans Publishing Co., 1956.

Long regarded as one of the best evaluations of Barth's theology. 230'.09.B28.B45

Brunner, Heinrich Emil. *Scandal of Christianity.* Richmond: John Knox Press, 1965.

A volume of sermons that raises more problems than answers. Focuses attention on the degree of "otherness" the household of faith should maintain in its relation to the world. Doubt is engendered in the areas of common grace, the meaning of history, and the place of ethics in church life. Ecumenical. 230'.08.B83

Bultmann, Rudolf Karl. *Existence and Faith.* London: Hodder and Stoughton, 1961.

†A selection of sermons providing some insight into Bultmann's polemical methodology. 230'.08.B87

Buren, Paul Matthew van. *The Secular Meaning of the Gospel.* New York: Macmillan Co., 1963.

†In attempting to combine Christianity with philosophical linguistic analysis,

the writer comes to the conclusion that he does not believe there is a God, that Jesus Christ was only a man who did not survive the crucifixion, and that, while there is no God to pray to, prayer can lead to appropriate action. 230'.08.B89

Carnell, Edward John. *A Case for Orthodox Theology.* Philadelphia: Westminster Press, 1959.

While purporting to present evidence to support the conservative view of theology, Carnell does more to tear it down than do the critics. 230'.09.C21

_____. *The Theology of Reinhold Niebuhr.* Rev. ed. Grand Rapids: Wm. B. Eerdmans Publishing Co., 1960.

†A clear presentation of the salient features of Niebuhr's thought. 230'.09.N55.C21 1960

Cauthen, Wilfred Kenneth. *The Impact of American Religious Liberalism.* New York: Harper and Row, 1962.

Exceptional for the way it traces the history of theological liberalism in the U.S. Attributes the demise of theological orthodoxy to its failure to seek reconciliation between Christ and culture, and identifies the central theological issue of the day—the historical character of revelation. 230'.09.C31

Clark, Gordon Haddon. *Karl Barth's*

Theological Method. Philadelphia: Presbyterian Publishing Co., 1963.

Emphasizes Barth's biblical foundation, but points out that his thought is frequently molded by presuppositions outside of the evangelical, biblical tradition. 230'.09.B28.C54

Collins, James. *The Existentialists.* Chicago: Regnery Press, 1959.

A thorough examination by a Roman Catholic philosopher. 111.C69

Erickson, Millard. *The New Evangelical Theology.* Westwood, N.J.: Fleming H. Revell Co., 1968.

A defense of neoevangelicalism and of the teachings and doctrinal position of its founders and adherents. Lacks thoroughness and builds upon a faulty apologetic. Shows that the system has no commitment toward the infallibility of the Scriptures, and reveals that members of this new movement are, at best, "thin ice conservatives." 230'.09.ER4

Fletcher, William Catherwood. *The Moderns.* Grand Rapids: Zondervan Publishing House, 1962.

†A superficial (though generally conservative) approach to contemporary theologians and their systems of thought. Unreliable. 230'.0922.F63

Hamilton, Kenneth. *Life in One's Stride.* Grand Rapids: Wm. B. Eerdmans Publishing Co., 1968.

A short study of the theology and contribution of Dietrich Bonhoeffer. 230'.09.B64.H18

_____. *Revolt Against Heaven.* Grand Rapids: Wm. B. Eerdmans Publishing Co., 1965.

A systematic inquiry into the contemporary manifestations of antisupernaturalism in the demythologizing of Bultmann, the ground of being doctrine of Tillich, the secularization of the gospel of van Buren, and so on. A final chapter is devoted to a sympathetic study of Bonhoeffer. 230'.0922.H18R

_____. *The System and the Gospel.*

Grand Rapids: Wm. B. Eerdmans Publishing Co., 1963.

A definitive critique of Tillich's theology. 230'.09.T46.H18

_____. *What's New in Religion?* Grand Rapids: Wm. B. Eerdmans Publishing Co., 1968.

A critical study of new theology, new morality, and secular Christianity. 230'.0922.H18W

Hamilton, William. *The New Essence of Christianity.* Rev. ed. New York: Association Press, 1966.

†A book in which the writer explains his reasons for moving toward a "Christian atheism." Written before he espoused the death-of-God theology. 230'.0924.H18N

Harnack, Karl Gustav Adolf von. *What Is Christianity?* Translated by Baily Saunders. 5th ed. London: Ernest Benn, 1958.

†A landmark volume that represents a crystalization of the writer's views of Christianity. Defines the gospel in terms of the love of the Father, and omits its Christological emphasis. 230'.08.H22 1958

Henry, Carl Ferdinand Howard. *Frontiers in Modern Theology.* Chicago: Moody Press, 1965.

A serious evaluation of trends in European theology today, together with an appraisal of evangelical attitudes and opportunities in America. 230'.01.H39

_____, ed. *Christian Faith and Modern Theology.* Contemporary Evangelical Thought. New York: Channel Press, 1964.

A series of twenty articles by contemporary theologians in which they seek to answer the new interpretations and revolutionary ideas facing Christendom today. 230'.092.H39

_____, ed. *Contemporary Evangelical Thought.* Grand Rapids: Baker Book House, 1968.

Contains essays by leading conservative theologians on such topics as the Old and New Testaments, ethics, apologetics, education, philosophy, science and religion, and evangelism and preaching. Originally published in 1957. 230.0922.H39C

Hordern, William. *The Case for a New Reformation Theology.* Philadelphia: Westminster Press, 1959.

An assessment of and an apologetic for Neoorthodox theology. 230'.09.H78

————. *A Layman's Guide to Protestant Theology.* Rev. ed. New York: Macmillan Co., 1962.

†A clear, simply written exposition of liberal trends in theology. 230'.09.H78L

Horton, Walter Marshall. *Christian Theology, An Ecumenical Approach.* New York: Harper and Brothers, 1958.

An attempt at theological ecumenism. 230'.09.H78C

Jewett, Paul King. *Emil Brunner: An Introduction to the Man and His Thought.* Chicago: Inter-Varsity Press, 1961.

A clear analysis of Brunner's contribution to theology. Also lays bare the weaknesses inherent in the Swiss theologian's doctrine. 230'.09.B83.J54

Kegley, Charles W., ed. *The Theology of Rudolf Bultmann.* New York: Harper and Row, 1966.

An analysis of the ideas that have thrust Bultmann into the forefront of today's radical theologians. 230'.09.B87.K24

Ladd, George Eldon. *Rudolf Bultmann.* Chicago: Inter-Varsity Press, 1964.

Grapples with Bultmann's contention that the real Jesus of history can never be known. Provides a brief but comprehensive analysis of Bultmann's main thesis, and positively answers his contentions. 230'.09.B87.L12

Lightner, Robert Paul. *Neo-Evangelicalism.* Des Plaines, Ill.: Regular Baptist Press, 1965.

A limited critique of the origin, history, and foundation of neoevangelicalism. 230'.09.L62E

————. *Neo-Liberalism.* Des Plaines, Ill.: Regular Baptist Press, 1959.

An evaluation of the old liberalism and its present unreconstructed counterpart. 230'.09.L62L

*Mackintosh, Hugh Ross. *Types of Modern Theology.* New York: Charles Scribner's Sons, 1937.

A capable survey of the main movements in Protestant theology from Schleiermacher to Barth. 230'.0922.M21

Macquarrie, John. *Principles of Christian Theology.* New York: Charles Scribner's Sons, 1966.

†This work by a left-wing theologian presents the major themes of systematic theology in the light of contemporary thought and the challenges of contemporary philosophy. He advocates a response on the part of Protestants to the ecumenical outreach of Roman Catholicism. 230'.08.M24

McKelway, Alexander J. *The Systematic Theology of Paul Tillich.* Richmond: John Knox Press, 1964.

A clear and concise section-by-section explanation of Tillich's theology. Evaluates its strength and weaknesses from a philosophical point of view. 230'.09.T46.M19

*Machen, John Gresham. *Christianity and Liberalism.* Grand Rapids: Wm. B. Eerdmans Publishing Co., 1923.

A brilliant presentation of the differences between biblical Christianity and modernism. 230'.09.M18

Mascall, Eric Lionel. *The Secularization of Christianity.* New York: Holt, Rinehart and Winston, 1965.

An exposé of the false presuppositions of John Robinson's *Honest to God* and van Buren's *The Secular Meaning of the Gospel.* Shows that doubt is not the key to the understanding of the Scriptures, that a false premise cannot lead to a correct solution, and that these clergymen have robbed the gospel of its efficacy and substituted something foreign for Christianity. 230'.08.M37

Michalson, Carl, ed. *Christianity and the Existentialists.* New York: Charles Scribner's Sons, 1956.

Contains a series of articles on existentialists and existentialism by modern philosophers. 111.M58

Nash, Ronald H. *The New Evangelicalism.* Grand Rapids: Zondervan Publishing House, 1963.

Called a "dispassioned and unbiased examination of the writings of the New Evangelicals." Does not answer many of the charges brought against the new movement, and fails to provide a thorough biblical apologetic for their beliefs. 230'.09.N17

*Packer, James Innell. *Keep Yourselves from Idols.* Grand Rapids: Wm. B. Eerdmans Publishing Co., 1964.

Challenges Bishop Robinson's anti-supernaturalistic assumptions contained in *Honest To God.* 230'.09.R56.P12

Parker, Thomas H. L. *Karl Barth.* Grand Rapids: Wm. B. Eerdmans Publishing Co., 1970.

An account of Barth's life, writings, and theology. For theological students. 230'.09.B28.P22

Ramm, Bernard Lawrence. *Pattern of Authority.* Grand Rapids: Wm. B. Eerdmans Publishing Co., 1957.

A carefully researched treatment of the far-reaching issues confronting evangelical Christians holding to a conservative position of biblical authority. Makes a distinction between the "grounds of accepting an authority" and "the right of authority," and claims that reason, or intuition, or inclination are modes of perceiving or receiving an authority, but do not constitute the right of the authority received. 230'.01.R14

Roberts, David Everett. *Existentialism and Religious Belief.* New York: Oxford University Press, 1957.

A critical evaluation of the struggle

between contemporary Christianity and secularism. Not as incisive as Collins's *The Existentialists.* 111.R54

Schmithals, Walter. *An Introduction to the Theology of Rudolf Bultmann.* Translated by John Bowden. Minneapolis: Augsburg Publishing House, 1967.

†Lectures delivered at the University of Marburg, Germany. Pays homage to Bultmann as a great scholar, emphasizes the dialectical background out of which he came, and stresses the importance of Bultmannian studies in the development of a "biblical" theology. 230'.09.B87.SCH5

Spier, J. M. *Christianity and Existentialism.* Translated by David Hugh Freeman. Philadelphia: Presbyterian and Reformed Publishing Co., 1953.

A critical introduction to, and a mature assessment of, existentialism. 111.SP4

Thielicke, Helmut. *A Little Exercise for Young Theologians.* Grand Rapids: Wm. B. Eerdmans Publishing Co., 1962.

A sane, sensible appeal for fruitful communication between the theologically trained pastor and the common people of his church. 230'.08.T513

Wolf, Lotan Harold de. *The Case for Theology in Liberal Perspective.* Philadelphia: Westminster Press, 1959.

†A rational approach to faith that takes into account modern man's view of himself and his world. 230.09.W83

"GOD IS DEAD" THEOLOGY

Altizer, Thomas J. J., ed. *Toward a New Christianity: Readings in the Death of God Theology.* New York: Harcourt, Brace and World, 1967.

†An anthology of sources of the radical elements in theology during the past two hundred years. 231.08.AL7

The Altizer-Montgomery Dialogue: A Chapter in the God Is Dead Controversy.

Downers Grove, Ill.: Inter-Varsity Press, 1967.

Presents the papers read by "God Is Dead" theologian Altizer and John Warwick Montgomery when the two met in debate at Rockefeller Chapel, University of Chicago. 231.08.AL7M

Cobb, John B., ed. *Theology of Altizer: Critique and Response.* Philadelphia: Westminster Press, 1970.

A critical study that includes a bibliography of the works of Thomas Altizer. 231'.09.AL7C

Is God Dead? Grand Rapids: Zondervan Publishing House, 1966.

A symposium by Vernon Grounds, Billy Graham, Bernard Ramm, and David Hubbard. 231.08.G91

Montgomery, John Warwick. *The "Is God Dead?" Controversy.* Grand Rapids: Zondervan Publishing House, 1966.

A succinct refutation of the philosophical system that threatened to sweep all before it in the 1960s. 231.08.M76

***Wolff, Richard.** *Is God Dead?* Wheaton: Tyndale House Publishers, 1966.

A brilliantly written, carefully researched book representing the revolutionary ideas and ideals of "God-Is-Dead" theologians. A scathing rebuttal. 231.08.W83

THE GODHEAD

Baillie, John. *Our Knowledge of God.* New York: Charles Scribner's Sons, 1939.

A moderately evangelical treatment focusing upon religious experience and epistemology. 231.B15

Bavinck, Herman. *The Doctrine of God.* Grand Rapids: Wm. B. Eerdmans Publishing Co., 1951.

A scholarly exposition. Reformed. Makes rewarding reading. 231.B32

***Bickersteth, Edward Henry.** *The Trinity.* Grand Rapids: Kregel Publications, 1965.

Formerly published under the title of *The Rock of Ages* in 1859. Deals with the biblical evidence for belief in the one eternal Godhead of the Father, Son, and Holy Spirit. An important contribution. 231.B47 1965

Jukes, Andrew. *The Names of God in Holy Scripture.* Grand Rapids: Kregel Publications, 1967.

Reproduced from the 1888 edition, these devotional studies center in the Old Testament. Though they are less complete than Stone's *Names of God* and are very pedantic, they are edifying to read. 231.J93 1967

Motyer, J. A. *The Revelation of the Divine Name.* London: Tyndale Press, 1959.

The Tyndale Old Testament lecture for 1956. 231.M85

***Phillips, John Bertram.** *Your God Is Too Small.* New York: Macmillan Co., 1967.

A fresh approach to biblical teaching about God, with an exposé of common erroneous concepts of Him. 231.P54

Pieters, Albertus. *The Seed of Abraham.* Grand Rapids: Wm. B. Eerdmans Publishing Co., 1950.

A brilliantly written, though at times misleading, statement of the Abrahamic covenant. Pieters defines "seed" in such a way as to practically eliminate the racial concept, and his discussion soon focuses upon the seed as a *spiritual* entity. Amillennial. 231.P61

Stevenson, Herbert F. *Titles of the Triune God.* London: Marshall, Morgan and Scott, 1965.

A series of studies on the divine self-revelation of God in Scripture. 231.ST3

Stone, Nathan J. *Names of God in the Old Testament.* Chicago: Moody Press, 1944.

This work by a Hebrew Christian

focuses upon the names of God in the OT and shows them to be rich in meaning and of great significance. 231.ST7

GOD THE FATHER

Candlish, Robert Smith. *The Fatherhood of God.* 3d ed. Edinburgh: Adam and Charles Black, 1866.

An old work by a Presbyterian theologian. Aroused a storm of controversy when first published because Candlish extended the concept of God's "Fatherhood" further than was permitted in theological circles of his day. 231.1.C16 1866

Strauss, Lehman. *The First Person.* Neptune, N.J.: Loizeaux Brothers, 1967.

A series of devotional studies. 231.1.ST8

GOD THE HOLY SPIRIT

Barclay, William. *The Promise of the Spirit.* London: Epworth Press, 1960.

†Not in the same category as the treatments by Ryrie and Walvoord, and at times very misleading. Needs to be read with caution. 231.3.B23

*Bickersteth, Edward Henry. *The Holy Spirit: His Person and Work.* Grand Rapids: Kregel Publications, 1959.

A complete study of the personality of the Godhead and the divine work of the Holy Spirit. 231.3.B47 1959

Bruner, Frederick Dale. *A Theology of the Holy Spirit.* Grand Rapids: Wm. B. Eerdmans Publishing Co., 1970.

†Focuses attention on the Pentecostal experience of Acts and the new movement within Pentecostalism. Grounds his work in the theological development of the twentieth century and the dramatic turning to a charismatic experience. Divided into two parts: (1) the Pentecostal experience, its significance, background, and teaching; and (2) the biblical and

exegetical material found in Acts and the Pauline epistles. A documentary section probes the teaching of Wesley on perfection, Finney on justification, Torrey on the baptism of the Holy Spirit, and Andrew Murray on absolute surrender. Concludes with a brief critique of A. J. Gordon and F. B. Meyer. 231.3.B83

*Buchanan, James. *The Office and Work of the Holy Spirit.* Student's Reformed Theological Library. London: Banner of Truth Trust, 1966.

These studies adequately expound the role of the Holy Spirit in the conversion of sinners and the edification of saints. First published in 1843. 231.3.B85 1966

*Criswell, Wallie Amos. *The Holy Spirit in Today's World.* Grand Rapids: Zondervan Publishing House, 1966.

An inspirational series of studies. Ably illustrated. 231.3.C86

Cumming, James Elder. *"Through the Eternal Spirit." A Biblical Study on the Holy Spirit.* Minneapolis: Bethany Fellowship, 1965.

A devotional masterpiece. 231.3.C91 1965

Hendry, George Stuart. *The Holy Spirit in Christian Theology.* Philadelphia: Westminster Press, 1956.

†An introductory text. Neoorthodox. 231.3.H38

*Kuyper, Abraham. *The Work of the Holy Spirit.* Translated by Henri de Vries. Grand Rapids: Wm. B. Eerdmans Publishing Co., n.d.

This extensive, scholarly, and exhaustive study gives the Holy Spirit His rightful place in Christian theology. Reformed. First published in 1900. 231.3.K96

Macaulay, Joseph Cordner. *Life in the Spirit.* Grand Rapids: Wm. B. Eerdmans Publishing Co., 1955.

A study of the place and work of the Holy Spirit in the life and labors of the apostles. Not as inspirational or as edifying as the title of the book might suggest. 231.3'08.M11

Marsh, Frederick Edward. *Emblems of the Holy Spirit.* Grand Rapids: Kregel Publications, 1963.

An old, typological work. 231.3.M35

*****Morris, Leon.** *Spirit of the Living God.* Downers Grove, Ill.: Inter-Varsity Press, 1960.

A nontechnical treatment of the biblical teaching on the doctrine of the Holy Spirit. 231.3.M83

*****Moule, Handley Carr Glyn.** *Veni Creator.* London: Hodder and Stoughton, 1895.

A deeply reverent, scholarly treatment. Will abundantly repay careful consideration. Anglican. 231.3.M86

Murray, Andrew. *The Spirit of Christ.* Fort Washington, Penn.: Christian Literature Crusade, 1964.

These studies focus on the indwelling of the Holy Spirit in the believer and the church. Each chapter edifies and enriches the life and experience of the believer. 231.3.M96 1964

*****Owen, John.** *The Holy Spirit, His Gifts and Power.* Grand Rapids: Kregel Publications, 1960.

One of the outstanding books of all time. Presents a learned and spiritual analysis of the names and titles of the Spirit, His nature and personality, and His varied works and influence. 231.3.OW2 1960

*****Pache, René.** *The Person and Work of the Holy Spirit.* Chicago: Moody Press, 1954.

An able treatment by an evangelical European scholar. 231.3.P11

Pentecost, John Dwight. *The Divine Comforter.* Westwood, N.J.: Fleming H. Revell Co., 1963.

Doctrinal sermons dealing with the Holy Spirit's character, ministry, gifts, and work in the believer. 231.3.P38

Pink, Arthur Walkington. *The Holy Spirit.* Grand Rapids: Baker Book House, 1970.

Lamenting the fact that genuine spirituality in Christendom is waning, Pink writes to restore the Holy Spirit to His place in the church. He hopes that a knowledge of the teaching of Scripture will encourage Christians to avail themselves of His power. 231.3.P65 1970

Ramm, Bernard Lawrence. *The Witness of the Spirit.* Grand Rapids: Wm. B. Eerdmans Publishing Co., 1959.

This historic study emphasizes the contemporary relevance of the doctrine. Manifests a strong appreciation for the writings of existentialists. 231.3.R14

Ridout, Samuel. *The Person and Work of the Holy Spirit.* New York: Loizeaux Brothers, n.d.

A helpful though pedantic study. Plymouth Brethren. 231.3.R43

*****Ryrie, Charles Caldwell.** *The Holy Spirit.* Chicago: Moody Press, 1965.

A brilliantly written, brief, complete study of pneumatology. Ideal for Bible study groups. 231.3.R99

*****Smeaton, George.** *The Doctrine of the Holy Spirit.* London: Banner of Truth Trust, 1958.

Combining theological accuracy with practical teaching, Smeaton expounds the biblical data concerning the Trinity, the person and work of the Holy Spirit, and the development of pneumatology in the Christian church. Reformed. 231.3.SM3 1958

Stott, John Robert Walmsey. *The Baptism and Fullness of the Holy Spirit.* Chicago: Inter-Varsity Press, 1964.

A message delivered at the Clerical Conference, Islington, England, in January 1964. Keeps distinct the *baptism* and the *fullness* of the Spirit. 231.3.ST7

Swete, Henry Barclay. *The Holy Spirit*

in the Ancient Church. Grand Rapids: Baker Book House, 1966.

This work was prepared as a sequel to *The Work of the Holy Spirit in the New Testament.* Ably presents the teaching of the church Fathers on the subject. Thorough. Reprinted from the 1912 edition. 231.3'09.SW4 1966

————. *The Holy Spirit in the New Testament.* Grand Rapids: Baker Book House, 1964.

Reprinted from the 1910 edition. Studies surveying the NT teaching on pneumatology. For the scholar. 231.3.SW4 1964

*Thomas, William Henry Griffith. *The Holy Spirit of God.* Grand Rapids: Wm. B. Eerdmans Publishing Co., 1950.

First delivered as lectures at Princeton Theological Seminary in 1913. Since their first appearance they have won the admiration of theologians in all parts of the English-speaking world. These lectures survey the work of the Spirit in biblical revelation, historical interpretation, theological formulation, and modern application. 231.3.T36

Torrey, Reuben Archer. *The Person and Work of the Holy Spirit.* Grand Rapids: Zondervan Publishing Co., 1968.

Superseded by more recent treatments. Confuses the *baptism* of the Spirit with filling of the Spirit. Also tends to build his doctrine on experience rather than the teaching of Scripture. Pastors should consult the writings of Kuyper, Pache, Thomas, and Walvoord in preference to this work. The writer's confusion over terminology will mislead the uninstructed. Reprinted from the 1910 edition. 231.3.T63

*Unger, Merrill Frederick. *The Baptizing Work of the Holy Spirit.* Wheaton: Scripture Press, 1953.

An important, reliable study of a much misunderstood subject. 231.3.UN3

*Walvoord, John Flipse. *The Holy Spirit.* 3d ed. Findlay, Ohio: Dunham Publishing Co., 1965.

Based on the author's classroom lectures at Dallas Seminary, these definitive studies focus upon the person and work of the Holy Spirit. A concluding section deals with the eschatology of the Holy Spirit, a survey of the doctrine of pneumatology in the history of the church, and an appraisal of pneumatology in liberal and Neoorthodox theologians. Recommended. 231.3.W17 1965

ATTRIBUTES

*Charnock, Stephen. *The Existence and Attributes of God.* Grand Rapids: Kregel Publications, n.d.

A classic work. First published in 1797. 231.4.C38

*Tozer, Aiden Wilson. *The Knowledge of the Holy.* New York: Harper and Brothers, 1961.

May well be regarded as one of the most wholesome and inspiring expositions of the attributes of God and the relationship of this knowledge to the Christian life. 231.4.T66

PROVIDENCE

*Berkouwer, Gerrit Cornelis. *The Providence of God.* Studies in Dogmatics. Translated by Lewis Smedes. Grand Rapids: Wm. B. Eerdmans Publishing Co., 1952.

A work to place alongside John Flavel's standard treatment. Considers the doctrine of God's providence in relation to knowledge, sustenance, government, concurrence, history, and miracles. Concludes with a discussion of the problem of theodicy. 231.5.B45

LOVE AND WISDOM

Faber, Frederick William. *The Creator and the Creature.* Philadelphia: P. Reilly Co., 1961.

A Roman Catholic mystic, Faber writes
with evangelical warmth and zeal. First
published in 1859. 231.6.F11 1961

*Flavel, John. *The Mystery of Providence.*
London: Banner of Truth Trust, 1963.

Has gone through many editions and
expounds the teaching of the Bible on
the subject of God's providence. Shows
how it affects every aspect of a believer's
life. First published in 1678. 231.5.F61
1963

Lewis, Clive Staples. *Till We Have
Faces.* Grand Rapids: Wm. B. Eerdmans
Publishing Co., 1964.

Retells the ancient story of Cupid and
Psyche, and builds up an allegory of human and divine love upon it. 231.6.L58

Nygren, Anders T. S. *Agape and Eros.*
London: SPCK, 1953.

An extensive discussion and interpretation of love as the basic Christian
motif. Foundational in Christian ethics.
231.6.N98

SOVEREIGNTY

Berkhof, Louis. *The Kingdom of God.*
Grand Rapids: Wm. B. Eerdmans Publishing Co., 1951.

An analysis of the kingdom concept in
the liberal, social, and Neoorthodox theological systems. Reformed. 231.7.B45

Bright, John. *The Kingdom of God in
Bible and Church.* London: Lutterworth
Press, 1955.

†A mediating work that respects the
trustworthiness of the OT narratives.
231.72.B76

Buber, Martin. *Kingship of God.* New
York: Harper and Row, 1967.

†Deals with the history of Yahweh's
kingship over Israel. It contains many
new and controversial ideas. Unreliable.
Jewish. 231.7.B85

*Fairbairn, Patrick. *The Revelation of
Law in Scripture.* Grand Rapids: Zondervan Publishing House, 1957.

Reprinted from the 1869 edition.

These studies stress the sanctity of God's
law, which "without the gospel of grace is
meaningless." The law is considered with
respect both to its own nature and to its
relative place in successive dispensations.
231.7.F15 1957

Kevan, Ernest Frederick. *The Evangelical Doctrine of Law.* London: Tyndale
Press, 1956.

The Tyndale Biblical Research Lecture for 1955. 231.7.K51

_____. *The Grace of Law: A Study of
Puritan Theology.* Grand Rapids: Baker
Book House, 1965.

Outlines the Reformed view of the law
of God and its relationship to the Christian in his daily life. The historical treatment of the doctrine in the OT is clear
and helpful. Makes no distinction between Israel and the church. The treatment of the NT data lacks cohesion.
231.7.K51G

Lewis, Clive Staples. *Miracles, a Preliminary Study.* New York: Macmillan Co.,
1947.

A lucid Christian apologetic.
231.73.L58

Moule, Charles Francis Digby, ed.
Miracles. London: A. R. Mowbray, 1965.

Specific studies on the philosophy and
history of miracles. 231.73.M86

Orr, James. *The Christian View of God
and the World.* Grand Rapids: Wm. B.
Eerdmans Publishing Co., 1947.

In spite of its age, this work is still
relevant and useful. Now out-of-print.
Should be purchased if found. First published in 1902. 231.7.OR7 1947

*Packer, James Innell. *Evangelism and
the Sovereignty of God.* London: Inter-Varsity Fellowship, 1961.

A popular, conservative presentation
of the relationship between these two
areas of theology. Emphasis is placed
upon the effect of Christian witness.
231.7.P12

Pink, Arthur Walkington. *The Sovereignty of God.* Grand Rapids: Baker

Book House, 1959.

Handles the intricacies of the doctrine with the skill of an accomplished theologian. Calvinistic. 231.7.P65

Van der Loos, H. *The Miracles, a Preliminary Study.* New York: Macmillan Co., 1947.

A detailed, scholarly treatment. Valuable. 231.73.V87

*Warfield, Benjamin Breckenridge. *Miracles: Yesterday and Today.* Grand Rapids: Wm. B. Eerdmans Publishing Co., 1953.

First published in 1918 under the title of *Counterfeit Miracles,* these chapters survey alleged miracles down through the ages and provide a fascinating study of those who have claimed to possess miraculous powers. 231.73.W23 1953

REVELATION

*Berkouwer, Gerrit Cornelis. *General Revelation.* Studies in Dogmatics. Grand Rapids: Wm. B. Eerdmans Publishing Co., 1955.

A biblical and theological study of the extent and meaning of general revelation and the nature of man's responsibility. 231.74.B45

Brunner, Heinrich Emil. *Revelation and Reason.* Philadelphia: Westminster Press, 1956.

†A definitive presentation of Brunner's appraisal of the character of revelation in Neoorthodoxy. 231.74.B83

McDonald, Hugh Dermot. *Ideas of Revelation.* New York: St. Martin's Press, 1959.

This companion volume to and predecessor of *Theories of Revelation (1860-1960)* contains an excellent discussion of the history of the doctrine. 231.74.M14

Ramm, Bernard Lawrence. *Special Revelation and the Word of God.* Grand Rapids: Wm. B. Eerdmans Publishing Co., 1961.

A valiant attempt to stress the reality of God's self-revelation. 231.74.R14

JUSTICE AND GOODNESS

*Fitch, William. *God and Evil: Studies in the Mystery of Suffering and Pain.* London: Pickering and Inglis, 1969.

A contemporary presentation of theodicy. 231.8.F55

Lewis, Clive Staples. *The Problem of Pain.* New York: Macmillan Co., 1965.

Discusses the perennial problem of pain and why there must be suffering and illness in the world today. 231.8.L58

*Wilder-Smith, A. E. *The Paradox of Pain.* Wheaton: Harold Shaw Publishers, 1971.

A detailed consideration of the problem of suffering, good and evil, and the providence of God. 231.8.W64

CHRISTOLOGY

PERSON AND WORK OF CHRIST

Anderson, Robert. *The Lord from Heaven.* Grand Rapids: Kregel Publications, 1965.

A study of the deity of Christ, with particular emphasis on His messiahship and His role as "King of kings and Lord of lords." First published in 1910. 232.1.AN2 1965

Athanasius. *The Incarnation of the Word of God.* London: A. R. Mowbray and Co., 1963.

A classic treatment by one of the great leaders of the early Christian church. 232.1.AT3

Baillie, Donald Macpherson. *God Was in Christ: An Essay on Incarnation and Atonement.* New York: Charles Scribner's Sons, 1948.

†An incisive investigation of the historical Jesus, with a reconstruction of the message of Christ interwoven into the NT teaching on the incarnation and atonement. An appendix deals with Christology and mythology. 231.1.B15

*****Barndollar, W. W.** *Jesus' Title to the Throne of David: A Study in Biblical Eschatology.* Findlay, Ohio: Dunham Publishing Co., 1963.

A fresh, illuminating contribution that builds upon a hermeneutical approach to the Scriptures to demonstrate that the promises made to David are to be fulfilled literally. 232.1.B25

Barrett, Charles Kingsley. *Jesus and the Gospel Tradition.* London: SPCK, 1967.

†Attempts rather unconvincingly to define the relationship of Jesus to Christian tradition. 232.1.B27

*****Berkouwer, Gerrit Cornelis.** *The Person of Christ.* Studies in Dogmatics. Translated by John Vriend. Grand Rapids: Wm. B. Eerdmans Publishing Co., 1954.

By a theologians' theologian whose writings are all of utmost importance. Examines the historical pronouncements of the ecumenical councils and the Christian confessions, the nature, unity, and sinlessness of Christ, together with a consideration of the other teachings centering in a study of His person. Reformed. 232.B45P

*****_____.** *The Work of Christ.* Studies in Dogmatics. Translated by Cornelius Lambregtse. Grand Rapids: Wm. B. Eerdmans Publishing Co., 1965.

An in-depth discussion of the biblical teaching on the theological development of the doctrine of Christ as seen in His birth, suffering, resurrection, ascension, heavenly session, and second advent.

Fully abreast of the latest theological literature. Reformed. 232.1.B45W

Bruce, Alexander Balmain. *The Humiliation of Christ.* 2d ed. New York: George H. Doran Co., n.d.

A historic study of Christ's state of humiliation based upon a careful explanation of the *kenosis* passage, as well as other passages that bear on the subject. The survey of the history of the interpretation of this doctrine from the Council of Chalcedon through to Schleiermacher and Beyschlag is exceedingly helpful. First published in 1876. 232.1.B83

Brunner, Heinrich Emil. *The Mediator.* Translated by Olive Wyon. Philadelphia: Westminster Press, 1934.

†An extensive and information treatment of the person and work of Christ. Adheres to a belief in the deity of Christ and His substitutionary death, but rejects His virgin conception. 232.1.B83M

Cerfaux, Lucien. *Christ in the Theology of St. Paul.* Translated by G. Webb and A. Walker. New York: Herder and Herder, 1959.

Traces the development of Pauline Christology by following the chronology of the NT writings. Roman Catholic. 232.1.C33

Dodd, Charles Harold. *The Founder of Christianity.* New York: Macmillan Co., 1970.

†Drawing heavily upon his past research, Dodd gives his readers a general overview of Jesus and the movement that arose about Him. 232.1.D66

Fairbairn, Andrew Martin. *Place of Christ in Modern Theology.* New York: Charles Scribner's Sons, 1894.

A survey of Christological study to the end of the last century. 232.09.F15

Farrar, Frederic William. *The Witness of History to Christ.* London: Macmillan Co., 1906.

These Hulsean lectures for 1870 contain an evaluation of the credibility of the miraculous, the adequacy of the gospel records, the triumph of Christianity, Christianity and racism, and so on. 232.09.F24

Franks, Robert Sleightholme. *A History of the Doctrine of the Work of Christ.* 2 vols. London: Hodder and Stoughton, 1918.

A standard historical survey. 232.09.F85

Fuller, Reginald Horace. *The Foundations of New Testament Christology.* New York: Charles Scribner's Sons, 1965.

†Builds his thesis upon a belief that the church's response to Jesus of Nazareth as the Christ began with the resurrection. Ignores Peter's confession at Caesarea Phillippi and the other incidents in the gospels that indicate the disciples believed in Christ's deity before the resurrection. Prefers to build his theory upon extrabiblical data. 232.1.F95

Guthrie, Donald. *Jesus the Messiah.* Grand Rapids: Zondervan Publishing House, 1972.

A basic, nontechnical introduction to the life of Christ. Emphasizes Christ's deeds and words as evidence of the truth of His claims. 232.1.G98

Hahn, Ferdinand. *The Titles of Jesus in Christology: Their History in Early Christianity.* Translated by H. Knight and G. Ogg. London: Lutterworth Press, 1969.

†A detailed discussion of the terms "Son of Man," *"Kyrios," "Christos,"* "Son of David," and "Son of God." 232.1.H12

*Hengstenberg, Ernst Wilhelm. *Christology of the Old Testament.* 4 vols. Grand Rapids: Kregel Publications, 1956.

A first-rate study of Christ as He appears in type and prophecy in the OT. Of great value to preachers. Now available in an abridged edition. Originally published 1872-78. 232.12.H38 1956

Henry, Carl Ferdinand Howard, ed. *Jesus of Nazareth, Savior and Lord.* Grand Rapids: Wm. B. Eerdmans Publishing Co., 1966.

Essays examining the presuppositions of form-criticism and exposing the weaknesses of this method of investigation. 232.1.H39

Jeremias, Joachim. *New Testament Theology.* Vol. 1. New York: Charles Scribner's Sons, 1971.

A detailed study of the teaching of the gospels on the place and importance of Jesus Christ in theology. 232.1.J47

Kirkpatrick, Dow, ed. *The Finality of Christ.* Nashville: Abingdon Press, 1966.

Papers representing the effort of Methodist theologians to portray the significance of Christ in terms of present-day needs. 232.1.K63

*Longenecker, Richard Norman. *The Christology of Early Jewish Christianity.* London: SCM Press, 1970.

Provides a brilliant delineation of Jewish messianic expectation during the intertestamental period and first century A.D. A work of impeccable scholarship. 232.1.L85

MacDonald, Hugh Dermot. *Jesus, Human and Divine.* Grand Rapids: Zondervan Publishing House, 1968.

A brief introduction to Christology. Conservative. 232.1.M14

*Mackintosh, Hugh Ross. *The Doctrine of the Person of Christ.* 3d ed. Edinburgh: T. and T. Clark, 1914.

A standard work. Exhibits true erudition. Of importance to all evangelicals. 232.1.M19 1914

*Owen, John. *The Glory of Christ.* Chicago: Moody Press, 1949.

The last work by this great Puritan preacher. No one can read this treatise and remain unmoved. First published in 1696. 232.1.OW2 1949

Rawlinson, Alfred Edward John. *The New Testament Doctrine of Christ.* London:

Longmans, Green Co., 1926.

†A standard, moderately liberal treatment of NT Christology. 232.1.R19

Taylor, Vincent. *The Person of Christ in New Testament Teaching.* London: Macmillan Co., 1958.

†Deals with the exegetical, historical, and theological data relating to Christ's Person. Cites the different theories held by writers who have preceded him. Deals with the divine consciousness of Jesus. Mature in scholarship. 232.1.T21

*Walvoord, John Flipse. *Jesus Christ Our Lord.* Chicago: Moody Press, 1969.

A recent, scholarly, evangelical presentation of Christology. An indispensable contribution to this aspect of biblical theology. 232.1.W17

*Warfield, Benjamin Breckenridge. *The Person and Work of Christ.* Philadelphia: Presbyterian and Reformed Publishing Co., 1950.

A work of massive scholarship. Ably combines exegetical skills with polemic ability. 232.1.W23 1950

Wood, Nathan E. *The Person and Work of Jesus Christ.* Philadelphia: American Baptist Publication Society, 1908.

A standard work. Evangelical. 232.1.W85

Woods, Ralph Louis. *Behold the Man: An Anthology of Jesus Christ.* New York: Macmillan Co., 1944.

A well-documented treatise containing numerous testimonies about Christ with full bibliographical references. 232.082.W85

ATONEMENT

Cave, Sydney. *The Doctrine of the Work of Christ.* Nashville: Cokesbury Press, 1937.

A companion volume to *The Doctrine of the Person of Christ.* Helpful for its historic survey of the doctrine. 232.3.C31

Crawford, Thomas Jackson. *The Doctrine of Holy Scripture Respecting the Atonement.* Grand Rapids: Baker Book House, 1954.

An outstanding nineteenth-century treatment. Reformed. 232.3.C85

Dale, Robert William. *The Atonement.* London: Congregational Union of England and Wales, 1905.

Dale's most influential work. Advocates the penal doctrine of the atonement, and as such is misleading. 232.3.D15

Denney, James. *The Death of Christ.* Rev. ed. London: Hodder and Stoughton, 1911.

A definitive study that, in this new edition, includes the writer's work on *The Atonement and the Modern Mind.* Superior to the abridged edition by R. V. G. Tasker. 232.3.D41 1911

*Forsyth, Peter Taylor. *The Cruciality of the Cross.* Grand Rapids: Wm. B. Eerdmans Publishing Co., 1966.

A vigorous defense of the centrality of the atonement in NT teaching and Christian experience. 232.3.F77

*_____. *The Work of Christ.* Naperville, Ill.: Alec R. Allenson, 1958.

Writing from a moderately conservative point of view, the writer stresses the holiness of God in the atonement of Christ. 232.3.F77W

Grant, F. W. *The Atonement.* New York: Loizeaux Brothers, 1956.

A study of the atonement in type, prophecy, and accomplishment. 232.3.G76

Guillebaud, H. E. *Why the Cross?* London: Inter-Varsity Fellowship, 1964.

A candid, unvarnished statement of the necessity of the atonement. 232.3.G94

*Hodge, Archibald Alexander. *The Atonement.* Edited by William H. Goold. London: Thomas Nelson and Sons, 1868.

A careful presentation of the doctrine. Reformed. 232.3.H66

Kuiper, Rienk Bouke. *For Whom Did Christ Die?* Grand Rapids: Wm. B. Eerdmans Publishing Co., 1959.

A study in the divine design of the atonement. Reformed. 232.3.K95

Lang, George Henry. *Atoning Blood, What It Does and What It Does Not Do: An Exposition of the Truth of Atonement as Taught in the Holy Scripture.* Wimborne, England: The Author, 1955.

An important study abounding in preaching values. Deserves reprinting. 232.3.L25

*Lightner, Robert Paul. *The Death Christ Died: A Case for Unlimited Atonement.* Des Plaines, Ill.: Regular Baptist Press, 1967.

A thorough examination of the problems associated with both the limited and unlimited views of Christ's atonement. 232.3.L62

Marsh, Frederick Edward. *Why Did Christ Die?* Grand Rapids: Zondervan Publishing House, n.d.

A Christ-centered, scriptural exposition of the atonement. Reprinted from the 1921 edition. 232.3.M35

Marshall, I. Howard, *Work of Christ.* Grand Rapids: Zondervan Publishing House, 1970.

A remarkable synthesis of a vast amount of material. Focuses on the death of Christ (not His resurrection) as being the locus of NT Christology. Moderately conservative. 232.3.M35W

*Morris, Leon. *The Cross in the New Testament.* Grand Rapids: Wm. B. Eerdmans Publishing Co., 1964.

An extensive discussion of the NT teaching about the cross of Christ. Interprets the death of Christ against the teaching of the OT, traces rabbinic instruction through the centuries immediately preceding the death of Christ, and demonstrates from the NT the essential unity and considerable variety of this teaching. Excellent. 232.3.M83 (Alt. DDC 225.823)

————. *Glory in the Cross.* London: Hodder and Stoughton, 1966.

A brief work ably supplementing the author's *Cross in the New Testament.* 232.3.M83G

Owen, John. *The Death of Death in the Death of Christ.* London: Banner of Truth Trust, 1963.

A thorough treatment, even if the author does appear to go round and round certain problems before coming to the point. Combines in one volume two of Owen's previous works. Originally published in 1852. 232.3.OW2 1963

*Smeaton, George. *The Apostle's Doctrine of the Atonement.* Grand Rapids: Zondervan Publishing House, 1957.

First published in 1870 under the title *The Doctrine of the Atonement as Taught by the Apostles.* Provides a most helpful and thorough exposition of the biblical teaching of the atonement. Reformed. 232.3.SM3A 1957

*————. *The Doctrine of the Atonement as Taught by Jesus Christ Himself.* Grand Rapids: Zondervan Publishing House, 1957.

Is, in many respects, one of the greatest works on the subject. Reformed. Reprinted from the 1871 edition. 232.3.SM3C 1957

Stibbs, Alan Marshall. *The Finished Work of Christ.* 2d ed. London: Tyndale Press, 1964.

A scholarly refutation of the theory that Christ is continuously offering Himself to God in order to secure our acceptance. 232.3.ST5 1964

Taylor, Vincent. *The Cross of Christ.* London: Macmillan Co., 1956.

†Eight studies evaluating the biblical and historical restatements of the atonement. 232.3.T21

RESURRECTION OF CHRIST

Fuller, Daniel P. *Easter Faith and History.* Grand Rapids: Wm. B. Eerdmans

Publishing Co., 1965.

A survey of the critical approaches to the resurrection of Jesus Christ. 232.5.F95

*Orr, James. *The Resurrection of Jesus.* Grand Rapids: Zondervan Publishing House, 1965.

A penetrating examination and re-statement of the basis for belief in the bodily resurrection of Christ. The author's last literary work. Published in 1908. 232.5.OR7 1965

Ramsey, Arthur Michael. *The Resurrection of Christ.* 2d ed. London: Geoffrey Bles, 1962.

A new defense of the traditional position. 232'.5.R14 1962

Simpson, William John Sparrow. *Our Lord's Resurrection.* Grand Rapids: Zondervan Publishing House, 1964.

Based on the second edition published in 1909. Provides a powerful apologetic for the bodily resurrection of Christ, deals with Paul's personal evidence of the resurrection, and explains the theological significance of these events for believers today. 232'.5.SI5 1964

*_____. *The Resurrection and the Christian Faith.* Grand Rapids: Zondervan Publishing House, 1968.

Originally published in 1911 under the title *The Resurrection and Modern Thought.* Has long been regarded as a classic in its field. Adequately evaluates the doctrinal implications stemming from Christ's resurrection. A most important treatment. 232'.5.SI5R 1968

SECOND COMING

Ladd, George Eldon. *Jesus Christ and History.* Chicago: Inter-Varsity Press, 1963.

A brief, scholarly study. 232.6.L12

Minear, Paul Sevier. *Christian Hope and the Second Coming.* Philadelphia: Westminster Press, 1954.

†Attempts to deal with eschatology apart from the Scriptures. Characterized by lack of clarity. 232.6.M66

NATURES OF CHRIST

Cave, Sydney. *The Doctrine of the Person of Christ.* London: Gerald Duckworth, 1925.

Of value as a historical study of Christology. 232.8.C31

Forsyth, Peter Taylor. *The Person and Place of Jesus Christ.* Grand Rapids: Wm. B. Eerdmans Publishing Co., 1964.

A vigorous vindication of the fact that the Christian gospel rests upon the witness of the apostles to Christ, and that believers today are to communicate the gospel to others by means of their words and works. Reprinted from the fourth edition, 1930. 232.8.F77 1964

*Liddon, Henry Parry. *The Divinity of Our Lord.* London: Pickering and Inglis, reprint.

Has been a standard treatment on the subject for more than a century. First published in 1866. 232.8.L61

*Morris, Leon. *The Lord From Heaven.* London: Inter-Varsity Press, 1958.

In his own inimitable way, Morris presents the clear biblical teaching on the deity and humanity of Christ. A vital study of these aspects of Christology. 232.8.M83

Perowne, Edward Henry. *The Godhead of Jesus.* Cambridge: Deighton, Bell and Co., 1967.

Comprising the Hulsean Lectures for 1866, these chapters survey the biblical teaching on the Godhead and the sinlessness, divinity, and power of Christ. 232.8.P42

Rimmer, Harry. *The Magnificence of Jesus.* Grand Rapids: Wm. B. Eerdmans Publishing Co., 1943.

An informative discussion of the origin, nature, incarnation, and office of Christ. Of particular significance is the chapter on "The Psychology of the Virgin Birth." 232.8.R46

Schaff, Philip. *The Person of Christ: The Perfection of His Humanity Viewed as a Proof of His Divinity.* 2d ed. New York: American Tract Society, 1882.

One of the many excellencies of this work is the numerous testimonies of people, both pagan and Christian, to the greatness of Jesus Christ. 232.8.SCH1 1882

Sellers, Robert Victor. *Two Ancient Christologies.* London: SPCK, 1940.

A definitive discussion on the "Antioch versus Alexandria" argument. 232.8.SE4T

Smith, Wilbur Moorehead. *The Supernaturalness of Christ: Can We Still Believe in It?* Boston: W. A. Wilde Co., 1954.

An apologetic vindicating the trustworthiness of the gospel records and dealing with the supernatural elements surrounding Christ's birth, miraculous works, transfiguration, and bodily resurrection. 232.8.SM6

Soltau, Theodore Stanley. *Jesus: Man or God?* Fort Washington, Penn.: Christian Literature Crusade, reprint.

This booklet on the deity of Christ discusses the doctrine cogently and with remarkable completeness. 232.8.SO4J

Turner, Henry Ernest William. *Jesus, Master and Lord.* Oxford: A. R. Mowbray and Co., 1953.

A modern, positive assessment of the problems surrounding the study of the historical Jesus. 232.9'08.T85

*Warfield, Benjamin Breckenridge. *The Lord of Glory.* London: Hodder and Stoughton, 1907.

A scholarly examination of the biblical evidence for the deity of Christ. 232.8.W23

Wyngaarden, Martin J. *The Glory of Christ.* Grand Rapids: Baker Book House, 1969.

A biblical study of the glory of Christ as presented in the Word of God. 232.8.W99

LIFE OF CHRIST

*Anderson, James Norman Dalrymple. *Christianity: The Witness of History.* London: Tyndale Press, 1969.

An investigation of the evidence for the historicity of Jesus, His death by Roman execution, and His supernatural resurrection. Finds that the laws of evidence support the biblical records and confirm the evangelical belief in the bodily resurrection of Christ. 232.971.AN2

Barclay, William. *The Mind of Jesus.* New York: Harper and Row, 1961.

†A cogent but unorthodox work. 232.95.B23M

Benoit, Pierre. *The Passion and Resurrection of Jesus Christ.* London: Darton, Longman and Todd, 1969.

†A treatment of the accounts of the resurrection from a historical and nontechnical point of view. Roman Catholic. 232.96.B44

Bishop, James Alonzo. *The Day Christ Died.* New York: Harper and Row, 1957.

An examination of the events and circumstances that led up to the crucifixion of Christ. 232.963.B54

————. *The Day Christ Was Born.* New York: Harper and Row, 1960.

Recounts the circumstances of the virgin conception of Christ and the events in Bethlehem at the time of His birth. Roman Catholic. 232.92.B54

Boslooper, Thomas David. *The Virgin Birth.* Philadelphia: Westminster Press, 1962.

†Asserts that theologians must affirm a belief in the virgin birth, but treats the subject matter as a doctrine and not as an event. Approaches the virgin conception of Christ on the basis of a Christian myth.

This failure to integrate history and doctrine destroys any lasting value this book might have had. 232.921.B65

Brandon, Samuel George Frederick. *The Trial of Jesus of Nazareth.* New York: Stein and Day Publishers, 1968.

†A scholarly study built upon the form-critical method of investigation. Seeks to separate fact from faith in an endeavor to provide a rationale that would support the theory that Jesus was executed for sedition. 232.962.B73

Broadus, John Albert. *Jesus of Nazareth.* Grand Rapids: Baker Book House, 1962.

A brief presentation of the personal character of Christ, together with His ethical teachings and supernatural works. First published in 1890. 232.9'01.B78 1962

*Bruce, Alexander Balmain. *The Training of the Twelve.* Grand Rapids: Zondervan Publishing House, 1963.

Unequalled in its field. Shows how Christ disciplined and trained His disciples for the position of apostleship. A most rewarding study. First published in 1871. 232.953.B83 1963

————. *With Open Face or, Jesus Mirrored in Matthew, Mark and Luke.* London: Hodder and Stoughton, 1896.

Popular sketches on the spirit and teaching of Christ as exhibited in the synoptic gospels. 232.954.B83

Bultmann, Rudolf Karl. *Jesus and the Word.* Translated by Louise Pettibone Smith and Erminie Huntress. New York: Charles Scribner's Sons, 1934.

†A radical treatment probing the ministry of Jesus and attempting to present His teachings in the light of His times. 232.9'01.B97

Burton, Ernest DeWitt and **Shailer Matthews.** *The Life of Christ.* Rev. ed. Chicago: University of Chicago Press, 1927.

A geographic presentation of the ministry of Christ. 232.9'07.B95

Butterworth, G. W. *Jesus, Leader of Men.* Wallington, Surrey: Religious Education Press, 1952.

†A study of the claims Jesus made upon man and society. 232.9'01.B97

Calkins, Raymond. *How Jesus Dealt With Men.* New York: Abingdon-Cokesbury Press, 1942.

Informative studies on the strategy Christ used in dealing with different types of personalities. 232.953.C12

Cartledge, Samuel Antione. *Jesus of Fact and Faith.* Grand Rapids: Wm. B. Eerdmans Publishing Co., 1968.

An attempt to face squarely the criticisms that deny Christ's deity, and to provide students with a guide supporting Christ's claim to being one with the Father. 232.95.C24

Charnock, Stephen. *Christ Our Passover.* Evansville, Ind.: Sovereign Grace Book Club, 1959.

Devotional messages centering in the events of the Last Supper and Christ's voluntary death. 232.957.C37

Clow, William Maccallum. *The Day of the Cross.* Rev. ed. Grand Rapids: Baker Book House, 1954.

Sermons on the men and women, events and circumstances of the day of the crucifixion. Helpful. Reprinted from the 1909 edition. 232.96.C62 1954

————. *The Secret of the Lord.* London: Hodder and Stoughton, 1910.

Penetrating, practical sermons focusing on the disclosure of Christ's person, the cross and its issues, Christ's glory and its significance, and so on. 232.9'01.C62

Cohn, Haim. *The Trial and Death of Jesus.* New York: Harper and Row, 1971.

†A justice of the Israeli Supreme Court, Cohn brings his legal training to bear upon the problem of the trial and death of Christ. Attempts to vindicate

the Sanhedrin for meeting at night on the grounds that they were not trying to prosecute or even examine Jesus, but rather trying to save Him from the Romans. Fails to provide a worthwhile contribution to the subject. 232.962.C66

*Craig, Samuel G. *Jesus of Yesterday and Today.* Philadelphia: Presbyterian and Reformed Publishing Co., 1956.

Portrays with skill and acumen the historical Christ, and shows him to be not only Savior and Lord, example, and friend, but also teacher and judge. 232.9'01.C84

Cramer, Raymond L. *The Psychology of Jesus and Mental Health.* Grand Rapids: Zondervan Publishing House, 1965.

A careful review of the way in which the teaching and ministry of Christ met the needs of the human heart. Takes pains to show the integration between true education and the behavioral sciences. Based on Matthew 5:1-12. 232.954.C84

*Dalman, Gustaf Hermann. *Jesus-Jeshua, Studies in the Gospels.* Translated by Paul T. Levertoff. New York: Ktav Publishing House, 1971.

Reprinted from the 1929 edition, this exemplary study illumines the Jewish background and environment of Jesus. 232.95.D16 1971

*_____. *The Words of Jesus.* Translated by D. M. Kay. Edinburgh: T. and T. Clark, 1902.

A series of studies on a wide variety of themes ranging from a consideration of God's theocracy to the evasive modes postexilic Jews used in referring to God. Includes Jewish eschatologic belief and essays dealing with "Son of Man," "Son of God," "Christ," and the Semitic idea of kingship inherent in the "Son of David." 232.9'01.D16

Dibelius, Martin. *Jesus.* Philadelphia: Westminster Press, 1949.

†A form-critical work. Lacking in vir-

tually every way. 232.95.D54

Dodd, Charles Harold. *The Leader: A Vivid Portrayal of the Last Years of the Life of Jesus.* 2d ed. London: Independent Press, 1958.

†A critical study. Of value to the discerning theologian. 232.92.D66 1958

*Edersheim, Alfred. *The Life and Times of Jesus the Messiah.* 2 vols. Grand Rapids: Wm. B. Eerdmans Publishing Co., 1962.

The classic work to which all modern treatments are indebted. No pastor should be without this magisterial work. 232.95.ED2 1962

Ellicott, Charles John. *Historical Lectures on the Life of Our Lord Jesus Christ.* Andover: Warren F. Draper, 1877.

These Hulsean Lectures for 1859 are geographic in their presentation of Christ's life rather than thematic. Largely superseded by more recent treatments. 232.9'01.EL5

Fairbairn, Andrew Martin. *Studies in the Life of Christ.* New York: D. Appleton and Co., 1880.

A discussion of the problems relating to the person and work of Jesus Christ at the end of the nineteenth century. 232.95.F15

*Farrar, Frederic William. *The Life of Christ.* Portland, Ore.: Fountain Publications, 1964.

A reverent treatment. The literary excellence of this work, as well as its historic reliability, place this study only slightly behind Edersheim for overall value and reliability. First published in 1874. 232.95.F24 1964

*Feinberg, Charles Lee. *Is the Virgin Birth in the Old Testament?* Whittier, Calif.: Emeth Publications, 1967.

A devout series of studies on Genesis 3:14, 15; Isaiah 7:14; and Jeremiah 31:22. 232.91.F32

Finlayson, R. A. *The Cross in the Experience of Our Lord.* London: Perry, Jackman, 1955.

Messages on the doctrine of redemption. 232.96.F49

*Foster, Rupert Clinton. *Studies in the Life of Christ.* 3 vols. Grand Rapids: Baker Book House, 1966.

A modern, scholarly study that rivals Edersheim for thoroughness and informative background material. 232.9'01.F81

Fuller, Reginald Horace. *The Mission and Achievement of Jesus.* 2d ed. London: SCM Press, 1956.

†A form-critical study that has very little to offer the pastor. 232.95.F95 1956

Geikie, John Cunningham. *The Life and Words of Christ.* 2 vols. London: Strahan and Co., 1879.

Studies based on a careful exegesis and highlighted with information from the writer's own visits to the Holy Land. Devotional. 232.95.G27

Glover, Terrot Reaveley. *The Jesus of History.* London: SCM Press, 1920.

While not a radical treatment of the historical Jesus, this work leaves much to be desired. A classical scholar, Glover sees the NT against the background of the times. Worth reading for the incisive comments scattered throughout the work. 232.95.G51

Goodspeed, Edgar Johnson. *A Life of Jesus.* New York: Harper and Brothers, 1950.

†Builds upon critical scholarship in vogue at the time. Extensively researched. Readable. 232.95.G62

*Green, Edward Michael Bankes. *Man Alive!* London: Inter-Varsity Fellowship, 1968.

This fascinating, dynamic book examines the resurrection of Christ and shows that the resurrection is relevant to our situation, powerful enough to change men's lives, and provides a basis for a meaningful life. 232.97.G82

Guthrie, Donald. *A Shorter Life of Christ.* Grand Rapids: Zondervan Pub-

lishing House, 1970.

Part of the forthcoming Zondervan *Pictorial Encyclopedia of the Bible.* Presents a guide to the main periods of Christ's life on earth. 232.9'01.G98

*Hanke, Howard A. *The Validity of the Virgin Birth.* Grand Rapids: Zondervan Publishing House, 1963.

Deserves an honored place alongside Machen's timely treatment. 232.821.H19

Hanna, William. *Our Lord's Life on Earth.* 5 vols. London: Religious Tract Society, 1882.

Superseded by more recent treatments. 232.95.H19

Harrison, Everett Falconer. *A Short Life of Christ.* Grand Rapids: Wm. B. Eerdmans Publishing Co., 1968.

Views the life of Christ geographically rather than thematically, ably traces the major events of His preaching ministry, interprets these events in the light of Jewish thought and culture, and provides the general reader with an able treatment of Christ's teaching and work on the cross. 232.9'01.H24

*Horne, Herman Harrell. *Jesus: The Master Teacher.* Grand Rapids: Kregel Publications, 1964.

Pastors today need to learn from the teaching techniques of Jesus Christ. This book is designed to stimulate such a study and deserves a place on every pastor's desk. First published in 1920. 232.954.H78 1964

Hunter, Archibald Macbride. *Work and Words of Jesus.* Philadelphia: Westminster Press, 1950.

†A concise, readable treatment of the main events and discourses in the life of Christ. Based upon a popular interpretation of source critical material. 232.9'01.H91

*Jeremias, Joachim. *The Eucharistic Words of Jesus.* Translated by A. Ehrhardt. New York: Macmillan Co., 1955.

†A forceful presentation of the Eu-

charist, with a discussion of the chronological and textual problems involved. Of great help in understanding what transpired in the upper room. Marred by adherence to form-criticism. 232.957.J48

Jervell, Jacob. *The Continuing Search for the Historical Jesus.* Minneapolis: Augsburg Publishing House, 1965.

Believing that the Christian has direct access to the historical Jesus through the "picture" of Jesus in the Scripture and the church, Jervell claims that there is no great difference between the historical Jesus and the picture of faith. A wordy, unsatisfactory study. 232.9'08.J48

Kennedy, John. *The Resurrection of Jesus.* London: Religious Tract Society, 1881.

A scholarly vindication of the historical fact of the resurrection, with an examination of the naturalistic hypothesis. 232.97.K38

King, Geoffrey R. *The Forty Days.* Grand Rapids: Wm. B. Eerdmans Publishing Co., 1962.

Refreshing exposition that draws attention to the last six weeks of Christ's earthly life and centers on the resurrection appearances of the Master from Easter to His ascension. 232.97.K58

Klausner, Joseph. *Jesus of Nazareth.* 2d ed. London: Allen and Unwin, 1929.

A hostile, inconsistent approach to the life of Christ that rejects the validity and reliability of the gospel records. 232.9'01.K66 1929

*Kuyper, Abraham. *The Death and Resurrection of Christ.* Translated by Henry Zylstra. Grand Rapids: Zondervan Publishing House, 1960.

An engaging study of Christ's humiliation and exaltation. First published in 1888. 232.96.K96 1960

*Lange, John Peter. *The Life of the Lord Jesus Christ.* 4 vols. Grand Rapids: Zondervan Publishing House, n.d.

The author's insights are profound, his theological treatment is generally very reliable, and his writings abound with information that will delight the heart of the pastor. Based on the German edition that was published 1844-47; ET, 1864. 232.9'01.L26

*Latham, Henry. *Pastor Pastorum.* Cambridge: Deighton Bell & Co., 1908.

Similar to Bruce's *The Training of the Twelve.* Centers in the schooling of the apostles by Jesus Christ. A work of unusual excellence. 232.954.L34

*———. *The Risen Master.* Cambridge: Deighton Bell and Co., 1901.

Designed as a sequel to the writer's *Pastor Pastorum,* these brilliant messages deal in depth and detail with the facts attending Christ's bodily resurrection. 232.97.L34

*Loane, Marcus Lawrence. *Life Through the Cross.* Grand Rapids: Zondervan Publishing House, 1966.

A stimulating study of the events that immediately preceded the crucifixion, with an analysis of Christ's suffering, death, and burial. An extensive treatment of the resurrection appearances completes this excellent work. 232.96.L78

———. *Our Risen Lord.* Grand Rapids: Zondervan Publishing House, 1965.

These messages are thoroughly evangelical and evaluate the importance of the resurrection in Christian life and service. 232.97.L78

———. *The Voice of the Cross.* Grand Rapids: Zondervan Publishing House, 1963.

A careful study of Christ's words from the cross. Evangelical. 232.963'5.L78

Ludwig, Emil. *The Son of Man, the Story of Jesus.* Translated by Eden and Cedar Paul. London: Ernest Benn, 1950.

Attempts to trace the events of the life of Christ without entering into theological controversy. Contains some rare insights into the characters and events contained in the biblical record and presents the human side of Christ's character. Fails to grasp the significance of His atoning death, and thereby misses the true message of the gospel records. First published in 1928. 232.95.L96 1960

Macartney, Clarence Edward Noble. *Twelve Great Questions about Christ.* Grand Rapids: Baker Book House, 1956.

Expository messages on questions found in the gospels and their relevance to today. 232.95.M11

Macaulay, Alexander Beith. *The Death of Jesus in Three Aspects.* London: Hodder and Stoughton, 1938.

These studies, based on lectures delivered in Auburn Theological Seminary, New York, approach the death of Christ from historical, psychological, and theological perspectives. 232.96.M11

Maclaren, Alexander. *After the Resurrection.* London: Hodder and Stoughton, 1902.

Sermonic studies covering Christ's postresurrection ministry. 232.97.M22

*M'Intosh, Hugh. *Is Christ Infallible and the Bible True?* Edinburgh: T. and T. Clark, 1902.

This work has long been buried in oblivion because the author dared to expose (through their own writings!) some of the leading scholars of his day: George Adam Smith, William Robertson Smith, John Watson, et al. Nor does he hesitate to take on the different European schools of thought whose views, in modified form, still are being taught today. What remains is a powerful, well-reasoned apologetic for a belief in the inspiration and inerrancy of Scripture. 232.954.M18

*Machen, John Gresham. *Virgin Birth of Christ.* Grand Rapids: Baker Book House, 1967.

A scholarly defense of the supernatural conception of Christ. First published

in 1930. 232.921.M18 1967

Manson, Thomas Walter. *Ethics in the Gospel.* New York: Charles Scribner's Sons, 1961.

Emphasizes the need for moral responsibility in Christian living. 232.954.M31

Miegge, Giovanni. *The Virgin Mary.* Philadelphia: Westminster Press, 1956.

Having been alarmed at the extraordinary growth of Mariolatry in the Roman Catholic church, Miegge writes to expose its character and trends. 232.91.M58

*Milligan, William. *The Ascension and Heavenly Priesthood of Our Lord.* London: Macmillan Co., 1908.

The Baird lectures for 1891, these studies focus upon Christ's postresurrection ministry on earth and present ministry in heaven. Excellent. 232.973.M62

*_____. *The Resurrection of Our Lord.* 2d ed. London: Macmillan Co., 1884.

Helpful studies substantiating the doctrine of the bodily resurrection of Christ. 232.971.M62 1884

*Morgan, George Campbell. *The Crises of the Christ.* London: Pickering and Inglis, 1963.

A timely series of studies on the birth, baptism, temptation, transfiguration, crucifixion, resurrection, and ascension of Christ. Should be read at frequent intervals. 232.95.M82

*_____. *The Great Physician.* Westwood, N.J.: Fleming H. Revell Co., 1963.

Covers most of the personalities and leading incidents in the gospels and Acts. Shows the method Jesus used in dealing with different types of people and reveals His understanding of human nature. Also shows how the message of the gospel is suited to the needs of each personality. A valuable work. First published in 1937. 232.95.M82G

_____. *The Teaching of Christ.* London: Pickering and Inglis, n.d.

A serious study of Christ's teaching

concerning the Trinity, angelic beings and man, sin and salvation, His saving mission and human responsibility, the redemptive processes, and so on. Not the last word on the subject, but deserves frequent reading. 232.954.M82

*Morison, Frank [pseud.]** Who Moved the Stone?* New ed. London: Faber and Faber, 1958.

First published in 1930, this work by Albert Henry Ross, an attorney, has been looked upon as a standard apologetic ever since. Ross waited until he retired before bringing his legal training to bear upon what he regarded as the myth of Christ's resurrection. It is the result of his very exacting investigation. 232.971.R73

*Morris, Leon.** The Story of the Christ Child.* Grand Rapids: Wm. B. Eerdmans Publishing Co., 1960.

Combines scholarship with a devotional emphasis in an exposition of the nativity stories in Matthew and Luke. 232.921.M83

*_____.** The Story of the Cross.* Grand Rapids: Wm. B. Eerdmans Publishing Co., 1957.

A brilliant, evangelical study of the passion narrative in Matthew 26-28. 232.96.M83

*Ogg, George A.** A Chronology of the Public Ministry of Jesus.* Cambridge: At the University Press, 1940.

†A detailed discussion of the problem of chronology, but one that concludes John's account of Christ's life and ministry is essentially irreconcilable with the accounts presented by the synoptics. 232.95.OG3

*Orr, James.** The Virgin Birth of Christ.* New York: Charles Scribner's Sons, 1927.

These studies contain lectures delivered at the chapel of the Fifth Avenue Presbyterian Church, New York, in 1907. They evaluate the criticisms leveled against the virgin conception of Christ and provide a scholarly rebuttal to these antisupernaturalistic theories. 232.921.OR7

Papini, Giovanni. *The Story of Christ.* Translated by Mary Pritchard Agnetti. 8th ed. London: Hodder and Stoughton, 1923.

An interesting treatment by an Italian theologian. 232.9'01.P19 1923

Perrin, Norman. *Rediscovering the Teaching of Jesus.* New York: Harper and Row, 1967.

†A form-critical study that seeks to establish criteria to determine the genuineness of the sayings attributed to Jesus. 232.95'4.P42

Peter, James F. *Finding the Historical Jesus.* New York: Harper and Row, 1966.

Continues Schweitzer's *Quest for the Historical Jesus.* Contains little that will be of value to expositors. 232.9'08.P44

Powell, Frank John. *The Trial of Jesus Christ.* Grand Rapids: Wm. B. Eerdmans Publishing Co., 1945.

A British barrister evaluates the trial of Christ in the light of Jewish and Roman law—and comes up with some startling conclusions. 232.962.P87

Price, John Milburn. *Jesus the Teacher.* Nashville: Southern Baptist Sunday School Board, 1946.

A study of the teaching methods used by the master teacher. 232.95.P93

*Ramsay, William Mitchell.** Was Christ Born at Bethlehem?* London: Hodder and Stoughton, 1898.

A formal defense of the accuracy of Luke's gospel. Concentrating on the enrollment of Quirinius, Ramsay shows that enrollment went back to 8 B.C. and that Christ was probably born in 6 B.C. 232.921.R14

_____. *The Education of Christ.* London: Hodder and Stoughton, 1909.

An informative, historical study that makes a unique contribution to our knowledge of the time. 232.927.R14

Robertson, Archibald Thomas. *Ep-*

ochs in the Life of Jesus. New York: Charles Scribner's Sons, 1913.

Begins with an evaluation of the messianic consciousness of Jesus. Traces the development of His ministry and reaction to opposition through to His death. Culminates in His resurrection. 232.95.R54

———. *The Mother of Jesus: Her Problems and Her Glory.* Grand Rapids: Baker Book House, 1963.

Reprinted from the 1925 edition, these studies attempt to give Mary her rightful place in Protestant thought. 232.931.R54

Sanday, William. *The Life of Christ in Recent Research.* Oxford: At the Clarendon Press, 1907.

A useful survey of Christological discussions at the close of the nineteenth century. 232.9'009.SA5

———. *Outlines of the Life of Jesus.* Edinburgh: T. and T. Clark, 1925.

†Based on the author's article in Hasting's *Dictionary of the Bible.* 232.95.SA5

Sanders, John Oswald. *The Incomparable Christ.* Chicago: Moody Press, 1971.

A devotional study of the person, work, and leadership qualities of Christ. First published in 1952. 232.95.SA5I

Sangster, William Edwin Robert. *They Met at Calvary: Were You There . . .?* London: Epworth Press, 1956.

Lenten sermons by a famous Methodist preacher. 232.96.SA5

Saphir, Adloph. *The Good Shepherd Finding His Sheep.* Glasgow: Pickering and Inglis, n.d.

Seven studies centering, for the most part, in John's gospel and providng rewarding devotional insights into Christ's methods of dealing with people. 232.953.SA6

*Schilder, Klaas. *Christ Crucified.* Translated by Henry Zylstra, Grand Rapids: Wm. B. Eerdmans Publishing Co., 1940.

First appeared in 1940 and completes the trilogy of Christ's suffering and death. Theologically accurate, abounds in suggestive insights, and provides exegetical illumination for a score of Easter sermons. 232.963.SCH3

*———. *Christ in His Suffering.* Translated by Henry Zylstra. Grand Rapids: Wm. B. Eerdmans Publishing Co., 1938.

A classic treatment on the passion of Christ. Deserves a place in every pastor's library. First published in 1937. 232.961.SCH3

*———. *Christ on Trial.* Translated by Henry Zylstra. Grand Rapids: Wm. B. Eerdmans Publishing Co., 1939.

Reprinted from the 1939 edition, and a sequel to *Christ in His Suffering.* Covers the events of the night of His betrayal to His condemnation. A learned, accurate treatment. 232.962.SCH3

Schonfield, Hugh Joseph. *The Passover Plot.* New York: Barnard Geis Associates, 1965.

†The author admits that Christ thought He was the Messiah, but believes that He was deluded. As a fraud He went about misleading the people. 232.9'01.SCH6

Shepard, John Watson. *The Christ of the Gospels: An Exegetical Study.* Grand Rapids: Wm. B. Eerdmans Publishing Co., 1939.

Builds upon grammatical exegesis and historical data. Provides a vivid picture of the personality of the Master. 232.9'01.SH4

Smith, Wilbur Moorehead. *A Treasury of Great Sermons on the Death of Christ.* Grand Rapids: Baker Book House, 1970.

In this handy, inexpensive paperback volume, pastors may read messages on the death of Christ by great men of the past and present. For those who find preaching on special occasions difficult, this work contains a mine of information. 232.963.SM6

_____. *A Treasury of Great Sermons on the Resurrection*. Grand Rapids: Baker Book House, 1970.

Contains important expository and apologetic sermons by men like G. Campbell Morgan, G. G. Findley, F. B. Meyer, and C. H. Spurgeon. 232.97.SM6

*Spurgeon, Charles Haddon. *Christ's Words from the Cross*. Grand Rapids: Zondervan Publishing House, 1965.

An exceptional collection culled from a lifetime of preaching. 232.963'5.SP9

*Stalker, James. *Christ Our Example*. Grand Rapids: Zondervan Publishing House, 1960.

First published in 1908 under the title *Imago Christi*, this work provides a thought-provoking treatise on the teaching of Christ. 232.9'04.ST1 1960

*_____. *The Life of Jesus Christ*. Westwood, N.J.: Fleming H. Revell Co., 1949.

An ideal work for laymen. Clear and direct. Uncluttered by supposedly scholarly approaches to the text. Recommended. 232.95.ST1 1949

*_____. *The Trial and Death of Jesus Christ*. Grand Rapids: Zondervan Publishing House, 1966.

An exceptional work that every pastor should read. 232.962.ST1 1966

Stauffer, E. *Jesus and His Story*. London: SCM Press, 1960.

An attempt on the part of a German scholar to reinstate a study of the "historical Jesus" to some degree of respectability. 232.9'08.ST2

Stevenson, Herbert F. *The Road to the Cross*. Westwood, N.J.: Fleming H. Revell Co., 1962.

Devotional studies on the passion of Christ that ably unfold the plan of salvation. 232.96.ST4

*Stewart, James Stuart. *The Life and Teaching of Jesus Christ*. New York: Abingdon Press, n.d.

Contains twenty-one topical studies on the life and ministry of Christ. 232.95.ST4

*Stier, Ewald Rudolph. *The Words of the Lord Jesus*. Translated by William B. Pope. 8 vols. Edinburgh: T. and T. Clark, 1855.

An extensive study revealing the author's mystical leanings, thorough familiarity with ascetic literature, and unique ability to present Greek concepts and word studies in a pleasing manner. 232.954.ST5

*_____. *The Words of the Risen Savior, and Commentary on the Epistle of St. James*. Clark's Foreign Theological Library. Translated by William B. Pope. Edinburgh: T. and T. Clark, 1871.

See comments under *The Words of the Lord Jesus*. 232.97.ST5

Strauss, David Friedrich. *The Life of Jesus Critically Examined*. Edited with an Introduction by P. C. Hodgson. London: SCM Press, 1970.

†A work of rare but misguided genius. Strauss's extreme views have all been refuted. This work is of value primarily for the sources Strauss cites. His opinions reflect his radical theology. 232.9.ST8 1970

Strauss, Lehman. *The Day God Died*. Grand Rapids: Zondervan Publishing House, 1965.

Meaningful messages on Christ's last words from the cross. 232.963'5.ST8

Swete, Henry Barclay. *The Appearances of Our Lord After His Passion: A Study in the Earliest Christian Tradition*. London: Macmillan Co., 1912.

A perceptive evaluation of the objections to Christ's bodily resurrection. 232.972.SW4

_____. *The Ascended Christ: A Study in the Earliest Christian Teaching*. London: Macmillan Co., 1913.

Designed as a sequel to the author's *Appearances of Our Lord After His Passion*, this work stresses Christ's role as king, priest, prophet, head of His church; and His ministry as mediator, intercessor, advocate, and so on. 232.973.SW4A

Taylor, Vincent. *Jesus and His Sacrifice: A Study of the Passion-Sayings in the Gospels.* London: Macmillan Co., 1937.

†Part of the writer's trilogy. While there is much to commend in this treatment, it needs to be read with discernment. 232.96.T21

_____. *The Life and Ministry of Jesus.* Nashville: Abingdon Press, 1955.

†Attempts to reconcile two opposing schools of thought. Points out that "we cannot see the Jesus of history if we close our eyes to the Christ of faith; we do not see the Christ of faith except in the light of the Jesus of history." 232.95.T21

Tenney, Merrill Chapin. *The Reality of the Resurrection.* New York: Harper and Row, 1963.

A scholarly study, but one that does not apply the doctrine of the resurrection to the major areas of systematic theology. 232.971.T25

_____. *The Vital Heart of Christianity.* Grand Rapids: Zondervan Publishing House, 1964.

A succinct, concise work on the relationship of the resurrection of Christ to everyday living. 232.97.T25

Thielicke, Helmut. *Between God and Satan.* Grand Rapids: Wm. B. Eerdmans Publishing Co., 1959.

†An exegetical study of the temptation of Christ. 232.952.T34

Vallings, James Frederick. *Jesus Christ the Divine Man: His Life and Times.* London: James Nisbet and Co., 1889.

In spite of its age, this work contains a helpful introduction to the biblical era and the messianic hope of the Jews. Concentrates more on the historic incidents in Christ's ministry than on the theological truths contained in the gos-

pels. Concludes with an interesting chapter on "the Character of Christ." 232.9'01.V24

*Vos, Howard Frederick. *The Life of Our Divine Lord.* Grand Rapids: Zondervan Publishing House, 1958.

Emphasizes the divinity of Christ in a series of thematic studies that include a discussion of the history of the times, the nature of Christ's person, His message, parables, and miracles, the prophecies fulfilled during His lifetime, and so on. 232.95.V92

Watson, John. *The Mind of the Master.* 3d ed. London: Hodder and Stoughton, 1897.

Watson frequently wrote under the name of Ian Maclaren. While not always reliable, this book does provide interesting insights as it deals with the personality of Christ. Moderately liberal. 232.95.W33 1897

Weatherhead, Leslie Dixon. *Over His Own Signature.* London: Epworth Press, 1955.

†A devotional study of Christ's ministry and its relevancy to our lives. 232.9'01.W37

Westcott, Brooke Foss. *Christus Consumator.* London: Macmillan Co., 1886.

A brief survey of the person and work of Christ in relation to modern thought. 232.9'01.W52

_____. *The Revelation of the Risen Lord.* London: Macmillan Co., 1902.

A scholarly assessment of the resurrection of Christ and His postresurrection appearances. 232.97.W52

White, Reginald Ernest Oscar. *The Stranger of Galilee.* Grand Rapids: Wm. B. Eerdmans Publishing Co., 1960.

Scholarship is blended with devotional zeal as the writer unfolds the prophetic mission of the life of Christ. 232.95.W58

Whyte, Alexander. *The Walk, Conversation and Character of Jesus Christ Our Lord.*

Grand Rapids: Zondervan Publishing House, [1953?].

A classic. First published in 1905. 232.95.W62 1953

Wilson, William Riley. *The Execution of Jesus: A Judicial, Literary and Historical Investigation.* New York: Charles Scribner's Sons, 1970.

†Built on the results of form-criticism and *Redactiongeschichte.* Presents a carefully reasoned, penetrating analysis of the events that led up to Christ's execution. A concluding postscript deals with the legality and responsibility of those involved. 232.96.W69

Winter, Paul. *On the Trial of Jesus.* Berlin: Walter de Gruyter and Co., 1961.

†An astute, prodigious study that builds upon Wilhelm Brandt's nineteenth-century concepts, denies the authenticity of the gospel records, and claims that Jesus was executed for political reasons. 232.962.W73

ANTHROPOLOGY

Berkouwer, Gerrit Cornelis. *Man: The Image of God.* Studies in Dogmatics. Grand Rapids: Wm. B. Eerdmans Publishing Co., 1962.

More a discussion of contemporary views of man than a systematic theological treatment. 233.B45

_____. *Sin.* Studies in Dogmatics. Translated by Phillip C. Holtrop. Grand Rapids: Wm. B. Eerdmans Publishing Co., 1971.

Stresses the fact of guilt, and shows that only through true confession can man be forgiven. Destined to take its place as one of the most authoritative works of its kind. 233.2.B45

*Boston, Thomas. *Human Nature in Its Fulfilled State.* London: Banner of Truth Trust, 1964.

First published in 1720, this book exerted considerable influence on the life and thought of Jonathan Edwards. It concentrates on man's state of innocence, sinful nature after the fall, the grace of God, and the inheritance of the righteous. 233.B65 1964

*Cairns, David. *The Image of God in Man.* New York: Philosophical Library, 1953.

†One of the best treatments of its kind. Deals with the OT and NT on the *imago Dei* before tracing the history of belief through Aquinas, Luther, Calvin, Brunner, Barth, Marx, and Freud. Provides helpful evaluations en route. 233.C12

Cave, Sydney. *The Christian Estimate of Man.* London: Duckworth, 1944.

Follows the pattern established in the author's other works, *The Doctrine of the Person of Christ* and *The Doctrine of the Work of Christ.* Traces the history of the doctrine through church history. 233.C31

Chambers, Oswald. *The Philosophy of Sin.* London: Marshall, Morgan and Scott, 1960.

Pertinent studies by a former army chaplain. 233.2.C35

Darling, Harold W. *Man in Triumph.* Grand Rapids: Zondervan Publishing House, 1969.

An attempt to integrate psychology and Christianity. Analyzes and deals with such matters as guilt, motivation, and mental health; cites the leading psychoanalytic writers and existential and humanistic thinkers; and concludes with a biblically oriented assessment. 233.2.D24

*Edwards, Jonathan. *Original Sin.* The Works of Jonathan Edwards. New Haven: Yale University Press, 1970.

Pastors of this present generation need to familiarize themselves with this treatment if they are to correct the moral and theological drift prevalent today. First published in 1758. 233.14.ED9

Griffith, Gwilym O. *Interpreters of Man: A Review of Secular and Religious Thought From Hegel to Barth.* London: Lutterworth Press, 1943.

While written at about the same time as S. Cave's work, this present study fleshes out the last century and a half and provides a penetrating analysis of anthropological theory in the existentialist writers of this period. 233.G87

*Harris, Robert Laird. *Man: God's Eternal Creation.* Chicago: Moody Press, 1971.

Explores man's culture during OT times. Emphasizes the uniqueness of the divinely appointed worship patterns, stresses the importance of the divinely appointed social controls, and explains the military struggles of God's people. A very thorough, *biblical* study. 233.H24

*Laidlaw, John. *The Bible Doctrine of Man.* 3d ed. Edinburgh: T. and T. Clark, 1895.

The Cunningham Lectures, New College, Edinburgh, 1880. Provides one of the ablest introductions to biblical anthropology ever written. Excellent. 233.L14 1895

McDonald, Hugh Dermot. *I and He.* London: Epworth Press, 1966.

A well-written presentation of the old moral argument for the existence of God. 233.M14

*Machen, John Gresham. *The Christian View of Man.* London: Banner of Truth Trust, 1965.

Provides an excellent introduction to Christian anthropology. First published in 1937. 233.M18 1965

Mascall, Eric Lionel. *The Importance of Being Human: Some Aspects of the Christian Doctrine of Man.* London: Oxford University Press, 1959.

†A philosophical approach to biblical anthropology. Originally delivered as the Bampton Lectures, Oxford, 1958, and in a series of addresses at Columbia University, New York City. 233.M37

*Morgan, George Campbell. *The Voice of the Devil.* London: Pickering and Inglis, n.d.

Sermons that analyze Satan's methodology in the temptation of Eve, Job, and Christ, and the application of these truths to believers today. 233.2.M82

*Murray, John. *The Imputation of Adam's Sin.* Grand Rapids: Wm. B. Eerdmans Publishing Co., 1959.

A classic statement of the Reformed teaching of Romans 5. Refutes the Pelagian and Roman Catholic views of original sin; prefers to use the term "imputed sin." Clarifies the *realistic* approach of Shedd and Strong, and pleads for the representative view. A thorough theological treatise. 233.14.M96

Niebuhr, Reinhold. *The Nature and Destiny of Man.* 2 vols. New York: Charles Scribner's Sons, 1949.

†The text of the Gifford Lectures, these studies show that only a "Christian" view of human nature and human destiny can offer a meaningful interpretation of history. Sociological in orientation. Neoorthodox. 233.N55

*Orr, James. *God's Image in Man and Its Defacement in the Light of Modern Denials.* Grand Rapids: Wm. B. Eerdmans Publishing Co., 1948.

Based on the Stone Lectures at Princeton Theological Seminary, 1903, this valuable apologetic carefully distinguishes between the biblical teaching, the theories of men, and movements throughout church history. 233.OR7

Pink, Arthur Walkington. *Gleanings from the Scriptures: Man's Total Depravity.* Chicago: Moody Press, 1969.

A strongly Calvinistic treatment. 233.2.P65

Robinson, Henry Wheeler. *The Chris-*

tian Doctrine of Man. 3d ed. Edinburgh: T. and T. Clark, 1926.

†A biblical and psychological assessment. Readers will find Machen's *The Christian View of Man* to be superior. 233.R56 1926

*Sauer, Erich Ernst. *The King of the Earth: The Nobility of Man According to the Bible and Science.* Grand Rapids: Wm. B. Eerdmans Publishing Co., 1962.

This intriguing study traces man from his beginnings as the crown of God's creation through his fall and redemption, and back to his rightful kingship. 233.SA8

Smith, Charles Ryder. *The Bible Doctrine of Man.* London: Epworth Press, 1951.

A learned work that abounds in insights drawn from the text of the MT, LXX, and NT. Sees man wholistically. 233.SM5

Tournier, Paul. *The Whole Person in a Broken World.* Translated by John and Helen Doberstein. New York: Harper and Row, 1964.

A helpful book on a greatly misunderstood subject. Provides a diagnosis of the illness of our age, and prescribes the only message of help and healing, namely, the gospel. 233.T64

*Tozer, Aiden Wilson. *Man: The Dwelling Place of God.* Harrisburg, Penn.: Christian Publications, 1966.

An unusual series of essays that penetrate beneath the surface and expose the carnality of religious externals as opposed to "the union of the spirit of man with the Spirit of God." 233.T66

Verduin, Leonard. *Somewhat Less Than God: The Biblical View of Man.* Grand Rapids: Wm. B. Eerdmans Publishing Co., 1970.

A systematic approach to Christian anthropology. 233.V58

White, William Luther. *The Images of Man in C. S. Lewis.* Nashville: Abingdon Press, 1969.

While some see Lewis as a "defender of the faith," White sees him in the role of an imaginative and poetic remythologizer of Christian truth. 233.W58

*Wright, John Stafford. *Man in the Process of Time.* Grand Rapids: Wm. B. Eerdmans Publishing Co., 1956.

An evangelical approach to the powers and functions of the human personality. 233.W93

———. *What Is Man? A Christian Assessment of the Powers and Functions of Human Personality.* Fort Washington, Penn.: Christian Literature Crusade, [1955].

Expounds the scriptural teaching on man and all that he can be when mastered by God's grace and empowered by His Spirit. 233.W93W

SALVATION

Anderson, Robert. *The Gospel and Its Ministry: A Handbook of Evangelical Truth.* Grand Rapids: Kregel Publications, 1956.

A complete survey of Bible doctrine. Contains a clear definition of terms, with excellent illustrations. Ideal for Bible study groups. 234.AN2

Baillie, Donald Macpherson. *Faith in God and Its Christian Consummation.* New ed. London: Faber and Faber, 1964.

†Examines the nature of *faith* in the

NT, and concludes that its usage and meaning have no exact parallel in any other literature. Scholarly, but not without devotional application. First published in 1927. 234.2.B15 1964

Barabas, Steven. *So Great Salvation: The History and Message of the Keswick Convention.* London: Marshall, Morgan and Scott, 1957.

A critical study of the theological development of "Keswick teaching." 234.8'08.B23

*Baxter, James Sidlow. *God So Loved.* Grand Rapids: Zondervan Publishing House, 1960.

An expository study on John 3:16. 234.B33

_____. *His Part and Ours.* Grand Rapids: Zondervan Publishing House, 1964.

A valuable devotional study emphasizing God's promises and our responsibilities. 234.8.B33

Berkouwer, Gerrit Cornelis. *Divine Election.* Studies in Dogmatics. Translated by Hugo Bekker. Grand Rapids: Wm. B. Eerdmans Publishing Co., 1960.

Traces the historic development of the doctrine, and recovers the Reformed position from the limbo to which other writers have relegated it. 234.9.B45

*_____. *Faith and Justification.* Studies in Dogmatics. Translated by Lewis B. Smedes. Grand Rapids: Wm. B. Eerdmans Publishing Co., 1954.

A much-needed discussion of justification and the historical development of the doctrine. 234.7.B45

*_____. *Faith and Perseverance.* Studies in Dogmatics. Translated by Robert D. Knudsen, Grand Rapids: Wm. B. Eerdmans Publishing Co., 1958.

Provides a penetrating study of the biblical teaching on perseverance from the perspective of the historical Reformed tradition. Does not confine itself to statements about the doctrine drawn from the early era of the Christian church, but ably evaluates the teaching of Ritschl, Schleiermacher, Schlink, and Barth. Gives helpful assurance to believers in the midst of a world caught up in the tides of change and transition. 234.9.B45P

*_____. *Faith and Sanctification.* Studies in Dogmatics. Translated by John Vriend. Grand Rapids: Wm. B. Eerdmans Publishing Co., 1952.

A thorough study of sanctification and its relationship to theology and Christian living. Reformed. 234.8.B45

Bloesch, Donald G. *The Christian Life and Salvation.* Grand Rapids: Wm. B. Eerdmans Publishing Co., 1967.

Comes to grips with the problem of salvation and whether or not it involves the lordship of Christ. Bloesch has deficient views of sin and flirts with the doctrine of universalism. 234.B62

Boettner, Loraine. *The Reformed Doctrine of Predestination.* Philadelphia: Presbyterian and Reformed Publishing Co., 1968.

A presentation of the distinctive doctrine of Calvinism. First published in 1932. 234.9.B63 1968

*Buchanan, James. *The Doctrine of Justification.* Grand Rapids: Baker Book House, 1955.

This work has a clear evangelical emphasis. It is thoroughly grounded in the Scriptures and stresses the imputation of the righteousness of Christ to the believer. Reformed. First published in 1867. 234.7.B85

Cell, George Croft. *The Rediscovery of John Wesley.* New York: Henry Holt and Co., 1935.

This historic introduction to Wesley's thought shows him to be closer to Calvin in the doctrine of sanctification than many of his successors. Provides an informative chapter on Wesley's teaching of sin, and defends him against the charge of Pelagianism. 234.8.C33

*Chafer, Lewis Sperry. *Grace.* Grand Rapids: Zondervan Publishing House, 1965.

Represents the distinctions between law and grace, and emphasizes the supernatural salvation that God has made available in Christ. 234.1.C34

*_____. *He That Is Spiritual.* Grand Rapids: Zondervan Publishing House, 1965.

A definitive exposition of true Christian living based on a clear exposition of selected biblical passages. 234.8.C34

*_____. *Salvation.* Grand Rapids: Zondervan Publishing House, 1965.

A forthright presentation of the doctrine of salvation based upon a clear exposition of the Scriptures. 234.C34

Chamberlain, W. D. *The Meaning of Repentance.* Philadelphia: Westminster Press, 1943.

A biblically oriented, theologically conservative study of a greatly neglected doctrine. 234.5.C35

Chambers, Oswald. *The Psychology of Redemption.* Fort Washington, Penn.: Christian Literature Crusade, 1955.

An example of effective doctrinal preaching. 234.3.C35

Colquhoun, John. *Repentance.* London: Banner of Truth Trust, 1965.

First published in 1826, this Reformed treatment deals with the sources of true repentance, their nature and import, how to distinguish between true and counterfeit repentance, and the fruit and evidences of true repentance. 234.5.C71

Conner, Walter Thomas. *Faith of the New Testament.* Nashville: Broadman Press, 1940.

Of particular significance to Baptists because it goes to the very heart of Baptist doctrine and practice. Builds upon experiences in the lives of Christ, Paul, and John. 234.2.C76

_____. *The Gospel of Redemption.* Nashville: Broadman Press, 1945.

A discussion of sin, election, the redemptive work of Christ, and Christian living in the light of Christ's second coming. 234.3.C76

Cullman, Oscar. *Salvation in History.* Translated by Sydney G. Sowers. New York: Harper and Row, 1967.

†This defense of *Heilsgeschichte* is also a reply to Cullman's critics. In this book he makes a stronger and more comprehensive statement of his own position. 234.C89

*Denney, James. *The Christian Doctrine of Reconciliation.* London: James Clarke and Co., 1959.

Alexander Whyte wrote of this work: "Read it again and again, and then preach its doctrine all your days," and "I do not know any modern book that has so much preaching power in it." 234.7.D41

Edwards, Jonathan. *Charity and Its Fruits: Christian Love as Manifested in the Heart and Life.* Edited by Tyron Edwards. London: Banner of Truth Trust, 1969.

First published in 1852, this work has long been regarded as a classic. 234.1.ED9 1969

*_____. *Freedom of the Will.* Edited by Paul Ramsey. New Haven: Yale University Press, 1957.

Contains a detailed inquiry into the prevailing theory regarding the freedom of the will and human determinism. First published in 1754. 234.9.ED9 1957

*_____. *The History of Redemption.* Evansville, Ind.: Sovereign Grace Book Club, 1959.

A carefully worded discussion of the teaching of redemption in the OT and NT. First published in 1722. 234.3.ED9 1959

Finney, Charles Grandison. *Sanctification.* Fort Washington, Penn.: Christian Literature Crusade, 1963.

Brief and challenging. Covers fifty-four relationships of Christ to Christians. 234.8.F49

*Fletcher, John. *Christ Manifested.* Fort Washington, Penn.: Christian Literature Crusade, 1968.

When speaking of this book, Martyn Lloyd-Jones said: "I shall never forget my first reading of these Letters and the benediction to my soul that they proved to be. They are undoubtedly a spiritual classic." 234.8.F63 1968

Flew, Robert Newton. *The Idea of Perfection in Christian Theology.* New York:

Humanities Press, 1968.

This historical study begins with an analysis of the teaching of Jesus and Paul, then surveys the development of the doctrine from the early church Fathers to Francois de Sales and Ritschl. His handling of the Reformation period leaves much to be desired. First published in 1934. 234.8.F63 1968

Gordon, Adoniram Judson. *The Two-Fold Life.* New York: Fleming H. Revell Co., 1883.

Focuses on Christ's work for us and His work in us. Devotional. 234.G65

*Green, Edward Michael Bankes. *The Meaning of Salvation.* London: Hodder and Stoughton, 1965.

A recent, helpful work on "salvation-history" that relates the biblical material to Christian doctrine as well as evangelism. 234.G82

Holliday, John Francis. *Life From Above: The Need for Emphasis on Biblical Regeneration.* London: Marshall, Morgan and Scott, 1957.

Lays bare the doctrine of redemption, and explains the nature of and need for the new birth, as well as how those who are regenerated receive a new dynamic for Christian living. 234.4.H71

Horne, Charles M. *Salvation.* Chicago: Moody Press, 1971.

An excellent treatise of the basis, nature, application, results, assurance, and climax of salvation. Reformed. 234.H78

*Hoyt, Herman Arthur. *Expository Messages on the New Birth.* Grand Rapids: Baker Book House, 1961.

A revision of the book originally published under the title *The New Birth.* Eloquent and persuasive studies grounded upon the Word and dealing fully and completely with the new birth. 234.H85

*Hughes, Philip Edgcumbe. *But For the Grace of God . . .* Philadelphia: Westminster Press, 1965.

These studies on man's need and the divine initiative deal with grace in its relationship to faith, works, law, the covenant, sacraments, and election. 234.1.H87

Hulme, William Edward. *The Dynamics of Sanctification.* Minneapolis: Augsburg Publishing House, 1966.

A discussion of the doctrine of sanctification from a pastoral viewpoint. Draws a clear line between biblical sanctification and the cheap imitations of the present day. 234.8.H87

Ironside, Henry Allan. *Except Ye Repent.* Grand Rapids: Baker Book House, 1970.

The writer lays his finger upon a neglected aspect of present-day preaching and expounds the Bible's teaching on this theme. 234.5.IR6 1970

Kevan, Ernest Frederick. *Salvation.* Grand Rapids: Baker Book House, 1963.

This careful study inquires into man's need of salvation, explains God's grace in salvation, and enlarges on His saving purpose. 234.K51

Knox, David Broughton. *Justification by Faith.* London: Church Book Room Press, 1959.

The first annual lecture of the Inter-Varsity Fellowship in Australia. 234.7.K77

Lindstrom, Harold Gustaf. *Wesley and Sanctification: A Study in the Doctrine of Salvation.* London: Epworth Press, 1950.

Significantly more Arminian than Wesley's teachings, and carries to a logical conclusion many of Wesley's seminal ideas. 234.8.L64

*Luther, Martin. *The Bondage of the Will.* Translated by J. I. Packer and O. R. Johnston, Westwood, N.J.: Fleming H. Revell Co., 1957.

A modern, accurate translation of Luther's reply to the diatribe of Erasmus, *De Servo Arbitrio.* Expounds the theme that Luther believed lay at the very heart of the gospel. 234.9.L97 1957

Luther and Erasmus on Free Will. Translated and edited by E. Gordon Rupp and Philip S. Watson. Library of Christian Classics. Philadelphia: Westminster Press, 1969.

An excellent translation of these primary documents. 234.9.R87

*Machen, John Gresham. *What Is Faith?* Grand Rapids: Wm. B. Eerdmans Publishing Co., 1962.

A vital, persuasive apologetic presenting biblical Christianity as the only antidote for the modern drift toward skepticism. First published in 1925. 234.2.M18

Marshall, I. Howard. *Kept by the Power of God: A Study of Perseverance and Falling Away.* London: Epworth Press, 1969.

An exacting study of the historical development of the doctrine of perseverance. Wesleyan. 234.9.M35

Marshall, Walter. *The Gospel-Mystery of Sanctification.* London: Oliphants Press, 1956.

Makes the doctrine of a believer's union with Christ the focal point of his treatise, and builds a strong case for practical holiness in everyday living. Includes the writer's famous sermon on "The Doctrine of Justification Opened and Applied." First published in 1692. 234.8.M35 1956

Moule, Handley Carr Glynn. *Faith: Its Nature and Work.* New York: Cassell and Co., 1909.

Messages dealing with the relationship between faith and Christian living. 234.2.M86

Murray, Andrew. *Holy in Christ.* Grand Rapids: Zondervan Publishing House, 1962.

A discourse on the true meaning of "holiness." 234.8.M96 1962

*Murray, John. *Redemption: Accomplished and Applied.* Grand Rapids: Wm. B. Eerdmans Publishing Co., 1955.

With his characteristic precision, Mur-

ray writes on and defends the doctrine of limited atonement. It is a pity that he omits from his treatment passages of Scripture that do not appear to support his thesis. 234.3.M96

Orr, James Edwin. *Full Surrender.* London: Marshall, Morgan and Scott, 1964.

A full discussion of the doctrine of sanctification. 234.8.OR7

*Owen John. *The Doctrine of Justification by Faith.* London: Banner of Truth Trust, 1959.

A scholarly exposition of this vital doctrine. First published in 1677. 234.7.OW2 1959

*Romaine, William. *The Life, Walk and Triumph of Faith.* Edited by Peter Toon. Cambridge: James Clarke, 1970.

Stresses the divinity of Christ and the need for believers to walk in subjection to the teaching of the Word. A new edition of an old classic published in 1856 as three separate works. Makes inspirational reading. 234.2.R66 1970

*Ryle, John Charles. *Holiness: Its Nature, Hinderances, Difficulties, and Roots.* Grand Rapids: Kregel Publications, 1956.

Recommended by Martyn Lloyd-Jones: "Ryle, like his great masters, has no easy way to holiness to offer us, and no 'patent' method by which it can be obtained; but he invariably produces that 'hunger and thirst after righteousness' which is the only indispensable condition to being 'filled.'" First published in 1879. 234.8.R98 1956

*Ryrie, Charles Caldwell. *The Grace of God.* Chicago: Moody Press, 1963.

Begins with a survey of the words for grace in biblical and nonbiblical literature. Considers what grace meant in the OT before the coming of Christ, and enlarges upon the doctrines of grace as displayed in the NT, particularly as personified in the life and ministry of Christ. Two informative essays conclude this treatment: "What Is Legalism?" and "What Is Liberty?" A valuable volume. 234.1.R99

Sangster, William Edwin Robert. *The Path to Perfection.* London: Hodder and Stoughton, 1943.

A challenging study. Interprets and defends Wesley's views. 234.8.SA5

*Sauer, Erich Ernst. *The Dawn of World Redemption.* Translated by G. H. Lang. Grand Rapids: Wm. B. Eerdmans Publishing Co., 1951.

The first of a trilogy. Surveys the divine purposes in the history of salvation. One of the ablest studies of salvation in the OT available today. All of Sauer's works are of the utmost value. 234.SA8D

*_____. *The Triumph of the Crucified.* Translated by G. H. Lang. Grand Rapids: Wm. B. Eerdmans Publishing Co., 1951.

A companion volume to *The Dawn of World Redemption.* Focuses on the doctrine of salvation in the NT. It centers in the redemptive work of Christ, includes a study of the Antichrist, and culminates in the final triumph of Christ. 234.SA8T

Schaeffer, Francis A. *True Spirituality.* Wheaton: Tyndale House Publishers, 1971.

Comes to grips with the problem of reality and the all-sufficiency of Christ, and presents the gospel as the only message to meet the needs of men and women today. 234.8.SCH1

Shank, Robert. *Elect in the Son: A Study of the Doctrine of Election.* Springfield, Mo.: Westcott Publishers, 1971.

A sequel to *Life in the Son.* Attempts to demonstrate that Calvin's doctrine of unconditional election and reprobation is without foundation in the Scriptures. Arminian. 234.9.SH1E

_____. *Life in the Son: A Study of the Doctrine of Perseverance.* 2d ed. Springfield, Miss.: Westcott Publishers, 1961.

A frank, comprehensive discussion that seeks to devastate Calvin's teaching regarding perseverance. Fails to demolish the doctrine of eternal security. 234.9.SH1P 1961

*Smedes, Louis B. *All Things Made New.* Grand Rapids: Wm. B. Eerdmans Publishing Co., 1970.

The author writes with insight and skill on "union with Christ." He makes a determined effort to avoid the pantheistic and mystical tendencies to which this theme often leads, but he is not as successful in handling the doctrines of baptism of the Spirit and of the Body of Christ. He deals at great length with the evolutionary pantheism of Teilhard de Chardin, and his advocacy of amillennialism is shown by his adherence to the "realized eschatology" of C. H. Dodd. In spite of these shortcomings, this work makes a valuable contribution to the study of Pauline theology. 234.SM3

Smith, Charles Ryder. *The Bible Doctrine of Grace and Related Doctrines.* London: Epworth Press, 1956.

A very full study that lacks any distinctive characteristics. 234.1.SM5

Stevens, George Barker. *The Christian Doctrine of Salvation.* International Theological Library. New York: Charles Scribner's Sons, 1905.

An extensive treatment of the doctrine of salvation, including its biblical basis, the principle forms of its development in the history of the church, and an extensive section on the theological ramifications. 234.ST4

Stibbs, Alan Marshall. *Obeying God's Word.* London: Inter-Varsity Fellowship, 1955.

An important devotional study. 234.6.ST5

*Strombeck, John Frederick. *Shall Never Perish.* 9th ed. Moline, Ill.: Strombeck Foundation, 1964.

A logical refutation of the Arminian

teaching on perseverance. 234.9.ST8 1964

Taylor, Vincent. *Forgiveness and Reconciliation: A Study in New Testament Theology.* London: Macmillan and Company, 1941.

†This sequel to *Jesus and His Sacrifice* treats with admirable scholarship the atonement of Christ, but disavows any belief in His substitutionary death. 234.T21F

Thomas, W. Ian. *The Mystery of Godliness.* Grand Rapids: Zondervan Publishing House, 1964.

Persuasive chapters on God's capacity to reproduce Himself in the lives of believers. 234.8.T36

Torrance, Thomas Forsyth. *The Doctrine of Grace in the Apostolic Fathers.* Grand Rapids: Wm. B. Eerdmans Publishing Co., 1960.

A Barthian presentation designed to show that the true teaching of the doctrine of grace disappeared from the Christian church in the second and third centuries and was recovered only in part, and then by the Reformers. Discerning and informative. 234.1.T63

Watson, John. *The Doctrines of Grace.* London: Hodder and Stoughton, 1900.

Relates the doctrines of grace to salvation and service. A capable treatment. 234.1.W33

Warfield, Benjamin Breckenridge.

Perfectionism. New York: Oxford University Press, 1931.

Essays defending the Reformed doctrine of sanctification against the claims of those who adhere to a second work of grace. 234.8.W23

———. *The Plan of Salvation.* Grand Rapids: Wm. B. Eerdmans Publishing Co., 1935.

A sound, sane discussion. Reformed. 234.W23

Wesley, John. *A Plain Account of Christian Perfection.* London: Epworth Press, 1960.

A concise statement of Wesley's concept of sanctification. Arminian. 234.8

Whitley, William Thomas, ed. *The Doctrine of Grace.* New York: Macmillan Co., 1931.

A symposium by European, British, and American scholars. Surveys the history of the doctrine in the NT and patristic periods through the Reformation and post-Reformation periods. 234.1.W78

*****Woychuk, N. A.** *The Incomparable Salvation.* St. Louis, Mo.: Miracle Press, 1967.

For clarity, simplicity, and accuracy, this book cannot be equalled. Ideal for young people's discussion groups. 234.W91

SPIRIT BEINGS

*****Barnhouse, Donald Grey.** *The Invisible War.* Grand Rapids: Zondervan Publishing House, 1965.

An important, biblically oriented study of the continuing conflict between good and evil in the spiritual realm. 235.4.B26

*****Bounds, Edward McKendree.** *Satan: His Personality, Power and Overthrow.* Grand Rapids: Baker Book House, 1963.

Has much in common with the book by Jennings. Both reliable. 235.47.B66

*****Chafer, Lewis Sperry.** *Satan: His Motives and Methods.* Grand Rapids: Zondervan Publishing House, 1964.

A comprehensive study of Satan's origin, sin, purpose, and end. 235.47.C34 1964

Gaebelein, Arno Clemens. *The Angels of God.* Grand Rapids: Zondervan Publishing House, 1969.

A fascinating book. Complete in coverage and not without its devotional emphasis. 235.3.G11 1969

Jennings, Frederick Charles. *Satan: His Person, Work, Place and Destiny.* New York: "Our Hope," n.d.

A biblical treatise ably fulfilling the subtitle of the book. 235.47.J44

Koch, Kurt E. *The Devil's Alphabet.* Grand Rapids: Kregel Publications, 1969.

A review of forty-seven forms of superstition, fortune-telling, magic, and spiritism. 133.3.K81

Lockyer, Herbert. *The Mystery and Ministry of Angels.* Grand Rapids: Wm. B. Eerdmans Publishing Co., 1958.

Angelology here receives a singularly complete interpretation. A well-presented account of the Bible's teaching on this neglected topic. 235.3.L81

Parrinder, Edward Geoffrey. *Witchcraft: European and African.* New York: Barnes and Noble, 1963.

A valuable probe into the history and origin of witchcraft. 133.9.P24

*Pentecost, John Dwight. *Your Adversary the Devil.* Grand Rapids: Zondervan Publishing House, 1969.

Based solidly upon the Scriptures, these messages follow the chronological sequence of Satan's origin, life and ministry, and future punishment. Helpful in providing guidelines for a series of sermons on the subject. 235'47.P38

*Pink, Arthur Walkington. *The Antichrist.* Swengel, Penn.; Bible Truth Depot, 1923.

A very capable synthesis of the biblical evidence surrounding the person and work of the Antichrist. A work of exceptional merit. 235.48.P65

Thompson, Charles John Samuel. *The Mystery and Romance of Astrology.* Detroit: Singing Tree Press, 1969.

This historical survey covers one of the oldest forms of the occult sciences from the star worship of the earliest civilizations, through the Middle Ages to its decline in the eighteenth century. Particularly significant in the light of the present resurgence of interest in the occult. First published in 1929. 133.5'09.T37 1969

ESCHATOLOGY

Adams, Jay Edward. *I Tell You the Mystery.* Lookout Mountain, Tenn.: Prospective Press, 1966.

A vigorous defense of the amillennial system of interpretation. Commendable for its positive statement of the Reformed position. 236.AD1

Brunner, Heinrich Emil. *Eternal Hope.* Translated by Harold Knight. Philadelphia: Westminster Press, 1954.

†Manifests a marked degree of uncertainty regarding the future, flirts with universalism, and fails to make any lasting contribution to the study of eschatology. 236.B83

Gaebelein, Arno Clemens. *The Conflict of the Ages.* London: Pickering and Inglis, 1933.

An evaluation of the mystery of lawlessness, with an assessment of its origin, historic development, continuing conflict, and coming defeat. A sorely needed discussion, but one that is now in need of revision. 236.G11

Hoyt, Herman Arthur. *The End Times.* Chicago: Moody Press, 1969.

An instructive introduction to biblical eschatology. Premillennial. 236.H85

Kennedy, Harry Angus Alexander. *St. Paul's Conceptions of the Last Things.* London: Hodder and Stoughton, 1904.

A study in the history of early Christian thought, particularly as this relates to the church's concept of life and death, the coming of Christ, and the resurrection of the righteous and unrighteous. The text of the Cunningham Lectures, New College, Edinburgh, 1904. 236.K38

Ludwigson, C. R. *Biblical Prophecy Notes.* 3d ed. Grand Rapids: Zondervan Publishing House, 1951.

An excellent summary of the different views of prophetic interpretation. 236.L96 1951

Mauro, Philip. *The Seventy Weeks and the Great Tribulation.* Rev. ed. Swengel, Penn.: Bible Truth Depot, 1944.

A study of the last two visions of Daniel and the Olivet discourse of Matthew 24-25. Amillennial. 236.M44

Moltmann, Jurgen. *Theology of Hope.* New York: Harper and Row, 1967.

†Devoted to the establishment of eschatological and historical categories essential to theology. Highly critical in its approach to the NT, and at best of marginal value. 236.M73

Murray, Iain Hamish. *The Puritan Hope: A Study in Renewal and the Interpretation of Prophecy.* London: Banner of Truth Trust, 1971.

A significant study of the eschatology of those Puritans who expected many revivals before Christ came to bring in the eternal state. 236.M96

*Pentecost, John Dwight. *Things to Come.* Grand Rapids: Zondervan Publishing House, 1958.

An exhaustive, well-outlined, clear, comprehensive presentation of premillennial eschatology. 236.P38

*Peters, George Nathaniel Henry. *The Theocratic Kingdom of Our Lord Jesus, the Christ.* 3 vols. Grand Rapids: Kregel Publications, 1957.

Discourses at length on the theocratic kingdom concept contained in the Scrip-

tures. Sometimes laborious, but no one can claim to have a thorough grasp of this subject until he has interacted with this treatise. Espouses a midtribulation rapture. 236.P44 1957

Ryrie, Charles Caldwell. *The Basis of the Premillennial Faith.* New York: Loizeaux Brothers, 1953.

A scholarly defense based upon a consistently literal interpretation of the Scriptures. 236.R99

Weiss, Johannes. *Paul and Jesus.* Translated by H. J. Chaytor. New York: Harper and Brothers, 1909.

A moderate *Religionsgeschichte* that strives after a consistent eschatology. 236.W43

*West, Nathaniel. *The Thousand Years in Both Testaments.* Grand Rapids: Kregel Publications, n.d.

A learned treatment of the subject of the Millennium. 236.W52

Smith, Wilbur Moorehead. *World Crises and the Prophetic Scriptures.* Chicago: Moody Press, 1952.

Views contemporary world affairs in the light of the Word of God. Premillennial. 236.08.SM6

OLD TESTAMENT PROPHECY

DeHaan, Martin Ralph. *The Jew and Palestine in Prophecy.* Grand Rapids: Zondervan Publishing House, 1950.

Discourses on the return of the Jews to Palestine and the emergence of the nation in the light of the Scriptures, and uses these events to highlight prophetic teaching. 236.1.D36

*Pember, George Hawkins. *The Great Prophecies of the Centuries Concerning Israel and the Gentiles.* London: Hodder and Stoughton, 1895.

Pember's espousal of the "gap theory" in his earlier work, *Earth's Earliest Ages,* has caused some Bible students to neglect his later writings. The present work contains excellent chapters on the Abrahamic and Palestinian covenants, the prophecies of Balaam and Daniel, with appendices on "The Desire Of Women," "The Worship of Satan," and so on. A later edition with slightly different content appeared under the title *The Great Prophecies of the Centuries Concerning Israel, the Gentiles, and the Church of God* (1942). 236.1.P36

Walvoord, John Flipse. *Israel in Prophecy.* Grand Rapids: Zondervan Publishing House, 1962.

An important study. Distinguishes between Israel and the church. Expounds the biblical teaching regarding God's earthly people with simplicity and clarity. 236.1.W17

NEW TESTAMENT PROPHECY

Walvoord, John Flipse. *The Church in Prophecy.* Grand Rapids: Zondervan Publishing House, 1964.

A specific treatise on the place, role, and destiny of the church in God's program. 236.2.W17

END OF THE CHURCH AGE,
SIGNS OF THE TIMES

Darms, Anton. *The Jew Returns to Israel.* Grand Rapids: Zondervan Publishing House, 1965.

A presentation of the Jew in the plan of God from the time of Abraham to the present, with several chapters on Israel's future in the light of God's Word and world events. 236.3.D25

Hamilton, Floyd Eugene. *The Basis of Millennial Faith.* Grand Rapids: Wm. B. Eerdmans Publishing Co., 1942.

A popular, amillennial treatment. Unconvincing in that it fails to explain the Scriptures in a consistent fashion. 236.3.H17

Kellogg, Samuel Henry. *The Jews; or*

Prediction and Fulfillment, and Argument for the Times. New York: Anson D.F. Randolph and Company, 1883.

Now almost forgotten, this book serves both a prophetic and an apologetic purpose. It describes God's plan for His ancient people and shows how many of these predictions have been literally fulfilled. 236.3.K48

Walvoord, John Flipse. *The Nations in Prophecy.* Grand Rapids: Zondervan Publishing House, 1967.

This study is true to its title, includes Bible teaching from Genesis to Revelation, and completes the author's trilogy. 236.3.W17

SECOND ADVENT, RAPTURE

Allis, Oswald Thompson. *Prophecy and the Church.* Philadelphia: Presbyterian and Reformed Publishing Co., 1964.

This examination of the claims of dispensationalists regarding Israel and the church, and of the fulfillment of the OT kingdom prophecies to Israel, is based on Reese's *The Approaching Advent of Christ.* It is not abreast of more recent developments in dispensational theology and eschatology, and even those of an amillennial persuasion have found it an unreliable guide. 236.4.AL5 1964

Berkhof, Louis. *The Second Coming of Christ.* Grand Rapids: Wm. B. Eerdmans Publishing Co., 1953.

Writes to support the amillennial position. Uses a special hermeneutic that makes his approach subjective and his conclusions untrustworthy. 236.4.B45S

Berkouwer, Gerrit Cornelis. *The Return of Christ.* Translated by James Van Oosterom. Edited by Marlin J. Van Elderen. Studies in Dogmatics. Grand Rapids: Wm. B. Eerdmans Publishing Co., 1972.

A learned treatise on the doctrine of the second advent. Valuable for the thorough way the writer presents the teaching and position of contemporary theologians. Amillennial. 236.4.B45

Blackstone, William E. *Jesus Is Coming.* Westwood, N.J.: Fleming H. Revell Co., 1908.

An old classic presenting the imminent return of Christ from a premillennial point of view. Many of "W.E.B.'s" observations are unique. 236.4.B56

DeHaan, Martin Ralph. *Coming Events in Prophecy.* Grand Rapids: Zondervan Publishing House, 1962.

Popular messages on the second advent. Makes stimulating reading. Should be in church libraries. 236.4.D36

Derham, Arthur Morgan. *Shall These Things Be?* London: Inter-Varsity Press, 1956.

A brief book in which the writer stresses the definite, personal return of Christ and ably applies the implications of this doctrine to Christian living. 236.4.D44

Harrison, William K. *Hope Triumphant: Studies on the Rapture of the Church.* Chicago: Moody Press, 1966.

Provides data on the rapture of the church that the writer has not found in any other book on the subject. 236.4.H24

Hughes, Archibald. *A New Heaven and a New Earth.* London: Marshall, Morgan and Scott, 1958.

An introductory study of the coming of Christ and the believer's eternal inheritance. Amillennial. 236.4.H87

*Ironside, Henry Allan. *The Mystery of Daniel's Prophecy.* Grand Rapids: Zondervan Publishing House, 1962.

First published in 1943 under the title *The Great Parenthesis,* this work surveys the interval between the sixty-ninth and seventieth weeks of Daniel's prophecy and other "gaps" between events predicted in God's Word. A valuable treatise. 236.4.IR6 1962

Ladd, George Eldon. *The Blessed Hope.* Grand Rapids: Wm. B. Eerdmans Publishing Co., 1956.

The central thesis of this book is that the church will go through the tribulation. The writer vacillates between amillennialism and posttribulationism and only comes out on the side of the latter on account of Revelation 20. 236.4.L12

Manley, George Thomas. *The Return of Jesus Christ.* London: Inter-Varsity Press, 1960.

Written with the intention of helping young people understand the promise of Christ's second coming, this work avoids interpretive problems and skirts difficult areas of study. 236.4.M31

*Pache, René. *The Return of Jesus Christ.* Translated by William Sanford LaSor. Chicago: Moody Press, 1955.

A standard work on the subject. 236.4.P11

Payne, John Barton. *The Imminent Appearing of Christ.* Grand Rapids: Wm. B. Eerdmans Publishing Co., 1962.

Advocates a form of posttribulationism that attempts to retain "imminency" while spiritualizing prophetic concepts relating to the tribulation. Denies the future fulfillment of Daniel 9:24-27. 236.4.P29

Reese, Alexander. *The Approaching Advent of Christ.* London: Marshall, Morgan and Scott, reprint.

A critical, posttribulation examination of the teachings of J. N. Darby. At those points where his argument is weak, Reese becomes vitriolic and caustic. 236.4.R25

Stanton, Gerald B. *Kept From the Hour.* Grand Rapids: Zondervan Publishing House, 1956.

Answers the objections leveled against pretribulationism, and defends the doctrine of Christ's imminent return. 236.4.ST2

Strombeck, John Frederick. *First the Rapture.* 5th ed. Moline, Ill.: Strombeck Foundation, 1964.

A layman writes with clarity and discernment of the events that will begin the "Day of the Lord." 236.4.ST8 1964

Tregelles, Samuel Prideaux. *The Hope of Christ's Second Coming.* London: Sovereign Grace Advent Testimony, n.d.

This work first appeared in 1864. While it has been superseded by more systematic treatments, it is not without its abiding significance. 236.4.T71

Walvoord, John Flipse. *The Return of the Lord.* Grand Rapids: Zondervan Publishing House, 1955.

Popular studies designed to establish the doctrine of the premillennial return of Christ upon a solid biblical and theological foundation. 236.4.W17

MILLENNIUM, KINGDOM AGE

Boettner, Loraine. *The Millennium.* 4th ed. Philadelphia: Presbyterian and Reformed Publishing Co., 1958.

A vigorous defense of postmillennialism. 236.6.B63 1958

Feinberg, Charles Lee. *Premillennialism or Amillennialism?* 2d ed. New York: American Board of Missions to the Jews, 1961.

An assessment of premillennial and amillennial systems of biblical interpretation, with specific application to the present time. 236.6.F32 1961

Kromminga, Diedrich Hinrich. *The Millennium in the Church: Studies in the History of Christian Chiliasm.* Grand Rapids: Wm. B. Eerdmans Publishing Co., 1945.

Evaluates the teachings of the apostolic church and early church Fathers regarding the second coming of Christ, and propounds his own theory for a "Covenental Millennialism" as distinct from the amillennialism of the church to which he belongs. 236.6.K92

Ladd, George Eldon. *Crucial Questions About the Kingdom of God.* 3d ed. Grand Rapids: Wm. B. Eerdmans Publishing Co., 1952.

Begins with brief survey of the data, and then proceeds to evaluate the kingdom concept in relation to time, the linguistic problems, and objections to premillennialism. 236.6.L12 1952

————. *Gospel of the Kingdom.* Grand Rapids: Wm. B. Eerdmans Publishing Co., 1959.

Stresses the fact that the kingdom of God has invaded the present. Accepts the fact that the kingdom concept is deeply rooted in the OT, but does not discuss this in his development of the NT teaching. Interprets "the mystery of the Kingdom" in Matthew 13 as applying to a hidden kingdom in the hearts of men, sees no distinction between Israel and the church, and insists upon a premillennial return of Christ solely on the basis of the teaching of the book of Revelation. 236.6.L12

*McClain, Alva J. *The Greatness of the Kingdom.* Grand Rapids: Zondervan Publishing House, 1959.

A rich and satisfying study from which theologians, regardless of their view of eschatology, will profit. Combines exegetical insights with refreshing literary excellence. One of the best works of its kind. 236.6.M13

Marshall, I. Howard. *Eschatology and the Parables.* London: Tyndale Press, 1963.

In spite of its brevity, provides a valuable examination of the eschatological significance of the parables. 236.8.M368

Ottman, Ford C. *God's Oath: A Study of an Unfulfilled Promise of God.* New York: "Our Hope," 1911.

Draws together the biblical data in support of a belief in a future, literal, Davidic (millennial) kingdom. Builds upon a careful, consistent, literal interpretation of Scripture. 236.6.OT8

Ridderbos, Herman Nicholas. *The Coming of the Kingdom.* Philadelphia: Presbyterian and Reformed Publishing Co., 1962.

A thorough treatment of the teaching pertaining to the Kingdom. Amillennial.

236.6.R43

***Walvoord, John Flipse.** *The Millennial Kingdom.* Rev. ed. Findlay, Ohio: Dunham Publishing Co., 1965.

An exceptionally fine, biblical evaluation of the various schools of thought. Premillennial. Should be in every preacher's library. 236.6.W17 1965

FUTURE STATE

***Pache, René.** *The Future Life.* Translated by Helen I. Needham. Chicago: Moody Press, 1962.

A companion volume to *The Return of Jesus Christ,* this extensive and thorough treatment covers the entire biblical teaching on man and his destiny, death, the world of spirits, the resurrection, eternal perdition, and heaven. Excellent. 237.P11

DEATH

Holden, Douglas T. *Death Shall Have No Dominion.* St. Louis: Bethany Press, 1971.

A study of the concept of death as found in the synoptic gospels, the Pauline letters, and the Johannine writings. 237.1.H71

Motyer, J. A. *After Death: A Sure and Certain Hope?* Philadelphia: Westminster Press, 1966.

Explores the biblical doctrine of life after death. Evangelical. 237.1.M85

Summers, Ray. *The Life Beyond.* Nashville: Broadman Press, 1959.

A study of the NT teaching about death, disembodied spirits, resurrection, the second coming, judgment, and eternal destiny. Amillennial. 237.1.SU6

Thielicke, Helmut. *Death and Life.* Translated by Edward H. Schroeder. Philadelphia: Fortress Press, 1970.

†Studies in Christian anthropology. Good is intermingled with lack of clarity

on some essential issues, which mars this otherwise fine treatment. 237.1.T34

IMMORTALITY

***Boettner, Loraine.** *Immortality.* 7th ed. Philadelphia: Presbyterian and Reformed Publishing Co., 1958.

A clear-cut evangelical presentation of physical death, immortality, and the intermediate state. Includes a discussion of soul sleep, annihilation, purgatory, spiritism, prayers for the dead, cremation, and so on. A valuable work. 237.2.B63 1958

Martin-Achard, Robert. *From Death to Life: A Study of the Development of the Doctrine of the Resurrection in the Old Testament.* Translated by J. P. Smith. Edinburgh: Oliver and Boyd, 1960.

†A recent, full-scale treatment of the doctrine of the resurrection of OT theology. The discussion is based on the Wellhausen reconstruction of Israel's religion. 237.3.M36

RESURRECTION, GENERAL
DISCUSSION

Schep, J. A. *The Nature of the Resurrection Body.* Grand Rapids: Wm. B. Eerdmans Publishing Co., 1964.

Makes a significant contribution to the discussion of the concepts regarding flesh and body in the OT and NT and, by building upon known data regarding

Christ's resurrection body, draws parallels to explain the nature of the believer's resurrection. 237.3.SCH2

*Morris, Leon. *The Biblical Doctrine of Judgment.* London: Tyndale Press, 1960.

An analysis of the teaching contained in the OT and NT on the present reality and future certainty of judgment. 237.4.M83

Wolff, Richard. *The Final Destiny of the Heathen.* Richfield Park, N.J.: Interdenominational Foreign Mission Association, 1961.

A short but cogent discussion of a difficult subject. Conservative, with ample scriptural documentation. 237.4.W83

HEAVEN

Bounds, Edward McKendree. *Heaven: A Place, A City, A Home.* Grand Rapids: Baker Book House, 1966.

A vital survey of the scriptural teaching regarding heaven. 237.6.B66

Baxter, Richard. *The Saint's Everlasting Rest.* Grand Rapids: Zondervan Publishing House, 1962.

A classical treatment of the final destiny of believers. 237.6.B33 1962

*Smith, Wilbur Moorehead. *The Biblical Doctrine of Heaven.* Chicago: Moody Press, 1968.

Fills a very real need in the study of biblical eschatology. 237.6.SM6

APOLOGETICS

Augustine, Aurelius. *The City of God.* New York: Oxford University Press, 1964.

Looked upon as being the first philosophy of history, this work emphasizes religious and secular knowledge, asserts that paganism bears within itself the seeds of its own destruction, and vindicates God's dealings with the world. Abridged. 239.3.AU4

*Bruce, Alexander Balmain. *Apologetics: or Christianity Defensively Stated.* International Theological Library. 3d ed. Edinburgh: T. and T. Clark, 1927.

A standard defense of biblical Christianity. Makes stimulating reading. 239.B83 1927

*Bruce, Frederick Fyvie. *The Defense of the Gospel in the New Testament.* Grand Rapids: Wm. B. Eerdmans Publishing Co., 1959.

These lectures were first delivered at Calvin College and Seminary, Grand Rapids, in 1958. They ably defend the integrity of the NT message and the impact it had on the Jewish, pagan, and Roman cultures. 239.B83

Carnell, Edward John. *Christian Commitment: An Apologetic.* Grand Rapids: Wm. B. Eerdmans Publishing Co., 1957.

Attempts to make Christianity intellectually respectable. Shows that only in Christ's atonement can man's moral need be met. 239.C21C

──────. *An Introduction to Christian Apologetics.* Grand Rapids: Wm. B. Eerdmans Publishing Co., 1948.

†A thought-provoking but disappointing work. Makes many concessions to science, and persistently detracts from or stretches the intent of Scripture in an attempt to satisfy the present-day claims of scientists. 239.C21

Clark, Gordon Haddon. *A Christian View of Men and Things.* Grand Rapids: Wm. B. Eerdmans Publishing Co., 1952.

A definitive study showing how a correct philosophy supports faith and aids in the development of a biblical view of anthropology. 239.C54

*Craig, Samuel G. *Christianity Rightly So Called.* Philadelphia: Presbyterian and Reformed Publishing Co., 1953.

This apologetic treatment distinguishes between the geniune and the spurious religious beliefs, and provides a solid scriptural foundation upon which readers may base their beliefs. 239.C84

Fisher, George Park. *Essays on the Supernatural Origin of Christianity.* New ed. New York: Charles Scribner's Sons, n.d.

An old work that has been superseded by more recent treatments. 239.8.F53

*Gerstner, John H. *Reasons for Faith.* Grand Rapids: Baker Book House, 1966.

A popular account of the traditional approach to apologetics. Conservative. 239.G32

*Green, Edward Michael Bankes. *Runaway World.* London: Inter-Varsity Fellowship, 1968.

Examines the historical evidence for Christianity; ably defends it against the accusations of Freud, Marx, other humanists, and the developers of a scientific Utopia; and shows Christianity to be unique among the religions of the world and the only true basis for a meaningful existence. 239.G82

Hamilton, Floyd Eugene. *The Basis of Christian Faith.* Rev. ed. New York: Harper and Row, 1964.

A well-written apologetic for the Christian religion. 239.H18 1964

Holmes, Arthur Frank. *Christianity and Philosophy.* Chicago: Inter-Varsity Press, 1960.

A brief introduction that explores the relationship between philosophy and the Christian faith. 239.H73

Keyser, Leander S. *A System of Christian Evidence.* 10th ed., revised. Burlington, Iowa: Lutheran Literary Board, 1953.

An important evangelical work. Lutheran. 239.K52 1953

*Lewis, Clive Staples. *Mere Christianity.* London: Macmillan Co., 1952.

A defense of Christianity and Christian behavior. 239.L58

*Little, Paul E. *Know Why You Believe.* Wheaton, Ill.: Scripture Press Publications, 1967.

Designed specifically for collegiates. Handles such thorny problems as "Is Christianity rational?" "Is there a God?" "Did Christ rise from the dead?" "Are miracles possible?" "Why does God allow suffering and evil?" and "Does Christianity differ from other religions?" 239'.009.L72

Luthardt, Christoph Ernst. *Apologetic Lectures on the Saving Truths of Christianity.* Translated by Sophia Taylor. 2d ed. Edinburgh: T. and T. Clark, 1872.

Composed of lectures delivered at Leipzig in 1866, these studies seek to provide a rational and biblical basis for belief. They include a consideration of the nature of Christianity, sin and grace, the person and work of Christ, and Holy Scripture. 239.L97 1872

*Machen, John Gresham. *Christian Faith in the Modern World.* Grand Rapids: Wm. B. Eerdmans Publishing Co., 1967.

A masterful Christian apologetic that seeks to answer such questions as "How may God be known?" "Has God spoken?" and "Is the Bible the Word of God?" 239.M18

Mullins, Edgar Young. *Why Is Christianity True?* Philadelphia: Judson Press, 1905.

An old, standard defense. 239.M91

Orr, James Edwin. *Faith That Makes Sense.* Valley Forge, Penn.: Judson Press, 1965.

A popularly written book. Ideal for use with college groups. 239.OR7

Ramm, Bernard Lawrence. *Protestant Christian Evidences.* Chicago: Moody Press, 1953.

An intelligent, philosophically based defense of the Christian faith. Widely used as a college text. 239.R14

———. *Varieties of Christian Apologetics.* Grand Rapids: Baker Book House, 1961.

This volume supersedes the writer's *Types of Apologetic Systems* (1953). It differs from the earlier edition in that it contains chapters on the apologetic systems of

John Calvin and Abraham Kuyper. 239'08.R14 1961

Reid, John Kelman Sutherland. *Christian Apologetics.* Grand Rapids: Wm. B. Eerdmans Publishing Co., 1970.

A historical account of how the Christian faith has been defended and explained from NT times to the present. 239'.009.R27

Short, A. Rendle. *Why Believe?* Downers Grove, Ill.: Inter-Varsity Press, 1958.

A medical doctor answers questions about God, Christ, the Bible, man's relationship to God, the death of Christ, and so on. 239.SH8

Smith, Wilbur Moorehead. *Therefore Stand.* Boston: W. A. Wilde Co., 1945.

An apologetic for biblical Christianity that was one of the best works available when it first appeared. Now superseded by more recent works. 239.SM6

*Thomas, William Henry Griffith. *Christianity Is Christ.* London: Longmans, Green and Co., 1925.

Centers in the person and work of Christ, vindicates the uniqueness of His character and mission, establishes the credibility of the gospel records, and deals convincingly with the meaning of and need for His bodily resurrection. A most important volume. 239.T36

8

Devotional Literature

The reading of well-chosen books is one of the best ways pastors can add depth to their own lives and bring spiritual vigor to their ministry. The influence of good books cannot be measured. The sage counsel of one writer fires the imagination of another and stirs the heart of a third, and through their multiplied ministry countless thousands are blessed. For example, a devotional work by Richard Sibbes was read by Richard Baxter who, as a result, wrote his famous *Call to the Unconverted*. This book deeply influenced Philip Doddridge, who in turn wrote *The Rise and Progress of Religion in the Soul*. The celebrated British prime minister, William Wilberforce, was keenly exercised as a result of reading Doddridge's book and, following his conversion, penned his famous work on *Practical Christianity*. Wilberforce's treatise was read by Leigh Richmond, who wrote *The Dairyman's Daughter*—a book that brought thousands to the Lord, including Thomas Chalmers, a man destined to become a great preacher and teacher.

The books listed in this chapter are broad in their scope. Some are old, and some are new. Some focus on contemporary issues, while others have a timeless appeal. Whether the needs of the pastorate cause you to read in the area of moral theology in order to expound the teaching of the Scriptures in keeping with the trend of the times; or to read books on personal Christianity, evangelism, religious drama, prayer, or daily living; or if you feel that you ought to have a series of messages on the place and importance of the Christian home in today's society, you will find suggestions in this chapter.

A statement made by the late J. C. Penney is worth remembering. He said: *"There is nothing that will strengthen the mind, broaden the vision, and enrich the soul more than the reading of good books."*

Edwards, Jonathan. *The Nature of True Virtue*. Ann Arbor: University of Michigan Press, 1960.

A systematic treatise on the nature of

true ethics. Modern writers have much to learn from this reprint from Edwards's works. 170.ED9

Kempis, Thomas á. *The Imitation of Christ.* Grand Rapids: Zondervan Publishing House, 1969.

A large number of editions of this classic treatment are available, all based upon the writer's work first published in 1441. A Kempis is ascetic in his approach to and exposition of the life of Christ. He explores the nature of spirituality with clarity, and he writes of the beauty of Christ's life with enriching simplicity. 242.1.K32

Lewis, Clive Staples. *The Four Loves.* New York: Harcourt, Brace, and World, 1960.

In his own inimitable way, the author discourses on the different types of love and affection experienced in life for things, animals, the opposite sex, and God. A most valuable volume. 241.L58

*Murray, John. *Principles of Conduct.* Grand Rapids: Wm. B. Eerdmans Publishing Co., 1957.

A serious, scholarly attempt to build a Christian ethic squarely upon the Scriptures. Recommended. 241.M96

Phillips, John Bertram. *New Testament Christianity.* London: Hodder and Stoughton, 1956.

Penetrating studies on faith, the ground of hope, love, peace, and Christian service. 240.P54

Unger, Merrill Frederick. *The God-Filled Life.* Grand Rapids: Zondervan Publishing House, 1959.

Focuses upon the believer's thought life, example, worship, and service. Unfolds the scriptural teaching on Christian living. 242.UN3

MORAL THEOLOGY

MacQuarrie, John, ed. *Dictionary of Christian Ethics.* Philadelphia: Westminster Press, 1967.

†Compendious and complete. Avoids rigid norms, exposes the problem in each area, deals with philosophical systems of thought, and evaluates their attempted solution. But the treatment of the major issues lacks a solid theological foundation and fails to provide a biblical philosophy for life. 241.03.M24

GENERAL WORKS

Bell, L. Nelson. *While Men Slept.* Garden City: Doubleday and Co., 1970.

Calls the church back to its primary function as a spiritual rather than a political or social power. Valuable. 242.B41

Breasted, James Henry. *The Dawn of Conscience.* New York: Charles Scribner's Sons, 1933.

Discloses the origins of social idealism in ancient Egypt, records the emergence of moral ideas from nature worship, and shows how these culminated in the effort of Pharaoh Ikhnaton to bring in a new age of brotherly kindness in 2000 B.C. Of historical value. 170.932.B74

Bushnell, Horace. *Christian Nurture.* New Haven, Conn.: Yale University Press, 1947.

†Attempts to show that radical conversionism is not the biblical pattern of salvation, but that Christ intends a child to grow into a life of righteousness through Christian nurture. 240.B96

Fletcher, Joseph Francis. *Situation Ethics.* Philadelphia: Westminster Press, 1966.

†A rejection of biblical standards of morality in favor of a "contextual" ethic based upon a love motif. 170.F63

_____. *Moral Responsibility.* Philadelphia: Westminster Press, 1967.

†A companion volume to *Situation Ethics*. Applies more fully the principles laid down in the earlier treatises. 241.F63M

Geisler, Norman L. *Ethics: Alternatives and Issues.* Grand Rapids: Zondervan Publishing House, 1971.

Contains a complete introduction and analysis of the theories and issues involved in ethics. Advocates a reactive rather than a proactive approach. Instead, stresses a hierarchialism that many see as similar to Fletcher's situationalism. 241.G27

Gustafson, James Moody. *Christ and the Moral Life.* New York: Harper and Row, 1968.

A clear, precise assessment of the influence of Christology upon ethical principles. 241.G97

Henry, Carl Ferdinand Howard. *Christian Personal Ethics.* Grand Rapids: Wm. B. Eerdmans Publishing Co., 1957.

A learned treatise on speculative philosophy, the moral quest, and the application of redemption to the moral issues. 171.1.H39

Kevan, Ernest Frederick. *The Moral Law.* Jenkintown, Penn.: Sovereign Grace Publishers, 1963.

A scholarly, Reformed treatment stressing the place of the Decalogue in the life of believers today. Does not distinguish between Israel and the church. An essay by Lancelot Andrews on Exodus 20:17 is appended. 241.K51

Niebuhr, Reinhold. *Moral Man and Immoral Society: A Study in Ethics and Politics.* New York: Charles Scribner's Sons, 1932.

†Deals with the distinction between the morality of individuals and the idealogies of social groups. Sociological in orientation. 241.N55

Ramsey, Paul. *Deeds and Rules in Christian Ethics.* New York: Charles Scribner's Sons, 1967.

A philosophical analysis of and reply to Robinson's *Honest to God* and Fletcher's *Situation Ethics.* 241.R14D

Redding, David A. *The New Immorality.* Westwood, N.J.: Fleming H. Revell Co., 1967.

Sermon-like essays that stress the priority of the first commandment and assert that love is made subservient to the law in contrast to the "situation ethics" of Fletcher. 241.R24

Robinson, John Arthur Thomas. *Christian Morals Today.* Philadelphia: Westminster Press, 1964.

†Seeks to clarify the position adopted in *Honest to God,* then moves from a consideration of individual needs as the only basis for making ethical decisions to one involving corporate and social action. 241.R56

Thielicke, Helmut. *Theological Ethics.* Edited by William H. Lazareth. 2 vols. Philadelphia: Fortress Press, 1966.

†By making justification central to ethics, Thielicke establishes a challenging debate with Catholics and offers his readers "models" of Christian behavior. 241.T34

SPECIFIC MONOGRAPHS

Cornils, Stanley P. *Managing Grief Wisely.* Grand Rapids: Baker Book House, 1967.

A valiant attempt to come to grips with the meaning and purpose of grief—and the best therapeutic way to handle it. 242.4.C81

Drakeford, John W. *The Great Sex Swindle.* Nashville: Broadman Press, 1966.

A vigorous attack upon present-day, Freudian-based permissiveness, coupled with an attempt to establish a biblical norm for sexual conduct. 176.D78

*Fleece, Isabel. *Not by Accident.* Chicago: Moody Press, 1964.

Written out of the author's own experiences of loss. Stresses God's overruling sovereignty and a mother's submission to His will. An ideal book to give to those who have been bereaved. 242.4.F62

Genne, Elizabeth and **William Genne.** *Christians and the Crisis in Sex Morality.* Baltimore: Penguin Books, 1962.

This material grew out of a conference on family life sponsored by the Canadian and National (USA) Councils of Churches. Only in the broadest sense of the word can the material in this book be regarded as "Christian." The writers do make an honest attempt to answer questions objectively and, in this respect, the book is helpful. 176.G28

Gockel, Herman William. *Answer to Anxiety.* St. Louis: Concordia Publishing House, 1961.

Comes to grips with questions asked by thousands of sincere people, and points out that the Christian religion is not a "bargain salvation" system or a "heavenly cash register" to which people can go for handouts. Rather, it is a battle, with all the tensions and anxieties of war. 242.G53

Graham, William Franklin. *World Aflame.* Garden City: Doubleday and Co., 1965.

A series of well-illustrated evangelistic messages analyzing the reasons behind a world filled with riots and demonstrations, wars and rebellions. Sees the only remedy in the gospel of Christ. 243.G76

Harrison, Norman Baldwin. *Suffering: Why and How.* Minneapolis: Harrison Service, 1945.

An explanation of the reason for suffering and how it is used in the life of the believer. 242.4.H24

Haselden, Kyle. *Morality and the Mass Media.* Nashville: Broadman Press, 1968.

An important, revealing study of the effect of radio, TV, newspapers, and novels on the moral climate. 176.H27 (Alt. DDC 301.16)

Hiltner, Seward. *Self-Understanding through Psychology and Religion.* New York: Charles Scribner's Sons, 1951.

†An evaluation of the physical and emotional reactions to crises in one's experience, social perception, conscience, sex, personal freedom, failure, and so on. 158.1.H56

Klausler, Alfred P. *Censorship, Obscenity, and Sex.* St. Louis: Concordia Publishing House, 1967.

A realistic attempt to grapple with the problems of censorship and pornography, and to develop a balanced approach to these issues that avoids prudishness as well as moral torpor. 323.44.K66

Lewis, Clive Staples. *A Grief Observed.* New York: Seabury Press, 1961.

Writing soon after his wife's death, Lewis examines his own grief, continuing doubts, awareness of human frailty, and faith. 242.4.L58

————. *The Screwtape Letters* [and] *Screwtape Proposes a Toast.* New York: Macmillan Co., 1961.

Two excellent books containing wit, wisdom, and practical counsel on temptation. Of value to Christians in all walks of life. 244.L58

Scanzoni, Letha. *Sex and the Single Eye.* Grand Rapids: Zondervan Publishing House, 1968.

In developing a Christian philosophy of sex, the writer points out that the Christian is not his own, because he has been bought with a price. The implications of this are far-reaching. Commendable. 176.SC6

Schlink, Basilea. *And None Would Believe It: An Answer to the New Morality.* Translated by M. D. Rogers and Larry Christenson. Grand Rapids: Zondervan Publishing House, 1967.

Warns of the spiritual and moral decay facing the western world. Presents sufficient factual evidence to convince her readers of the depth of her research, and offers a vital, biblically sound, and effective solution to the problem of morality. 176.SCH3

Thielicke, Helmut. *The Ethics of Sex.* Translated by John W. Doberstein. New York: Harper and Row, 1964.

Thielicke takes issue with the apostle Paul over his supposed insensitivity to *eros*, and, in a new hermeneutical endeavor, attempts to separate the *kerygmatic* "kernel" from the original "husk." Has much to commend it, but lacks a biblical foundation. 176.T34

*Tournier, Paul. *Escape from Loneliness.* Translated by John S. Gilmore. Philadelphia: Westminster Press, 1961.

Working from the premise that loneliness is a product of the age, Tournier shows that only the church (functioning effectively!) has the answer to the tremendous need of people in the world today. 242.6.T64

_____. A Place for You. New York: Harper and Row, 1968.

Facing squarely the problems of loneliness and insecurity, the author exposes man's basic need to belong. He points out that only by being in the place of God's appointing can a person find true fulfillment and satisfaction in life. 242.64.T64

Walker, Brooks R. *The New Immorality.* Garden City: Doubleday and Co., 1967.

Based upon the author's pastoral and counseling experiences. Describes such cultural phenomena as spouse-swap-

ping, premarital and extramarital intercourse, the "Playboy" philosophy, and pornography. The case histories are illuminating, but the author does little to establish biblical norms in the midst of the moral interregnum. 176.W15

Weatherhead, Leslie Dixon. *Mastery of Sex.* New York: Abingdon Press, 1962.

Attempts to bridge the gap between the psychology and theology of sex. The chief value of this book lies in the guidance given for the control of sex impulses. 176.W37

_____. *Salute to a Sufferer.* London: Epworth Press, 1962.

An attempt to offer to plain people a Christian philosophy of suffering. 242.4.W37

Wesley, Suzanna. *The Prayers of Suzanna Wesley.* Edited and arranged by W. L. Doughty. London: Epworth Press, 1956.

An inspirational volume. 242.1.W51

Wood, Frederic C., Jr. *Sex and the New Morality.* New York: Association Press, 1968.

†Tries to unravel some of the confusion surrounding sex and sexuality. Views morality as based entirely upon philosophical presuppositions, an erroneous view of history, and an ignorance of the teaching of Scripture. Provides a platform for permissiveness. 176.1.W85

HYMNOLOGY

Bailey, Albert Edward. *The Gospel in Hymns.* New York: Charles Scribner's Sons, 1950.

A comprehensive study of 313 hymns and their composers. 245.2.B15

Benson, Louis Fitzgerald. *The Hymnody of the Christian Church.* Richmond: John Knox Press, 1956.

An informative treatment of the value

and purpose of hymnody. One of the few works providing solid scriptural foundation for hymns used in Christian worship. 245'.09.B44

_____. *The English Hymn.* Richmond: John Knox Press, 1962.

A work of exceptional value. Investigates the history of hymns and metrical psalms from the earliest times. The documentation is thorough, the information provided is concise and valuable, and the literary style is excellent. 245'.0924.B44E

Foote, Henry Wilder. *Three Centuries of American Hymnody.* Cambridge, Mass.: Harvard University Press, 1961.

A definitive study tracing American congregational singing from the days of the Pilgrims to the twentieth century. 245.2.F73

Julian, John, ed. *A Dictionary of Hymnology Setting Forth the Origin and History of Christian Hymns of All Ages and Nations.* Rev. ed. London: John Murray, 1925.

First published in 1892, this alphabetically arranged dictionary to hymns, hymn writers and compilers, hymn books, and tunes and translators provides in one volume a vast amount of information (estimated at more than 10,000 entries) that pastors and choir directors will find useful. An index cross references the information and makes it easy for the user to locate specific data. Appendix I lists various psalters in use at the time of compilation, and Appendix II makes accessible information included in the supplement that was added to the first edition. 783'.03.J94 1925

Lovelace, Austin Cole. *The Anatomy of Hymnody.* Nashville: Abingdon Press, 1965.

An analysis of Christianity's greatest hymns, with an explanation of the metrical structure of poetry. 245.L94

*McDormand, Thomas Bruce and **Frederic S. Crossman.** *Judson Concordance to Hymns.* Valley Forge: Judson Press, 1965.

Provides access to the individual lines of 2,343 hymns arranged in two very extensive indexes. Designed to help ministers who wish to use quotations from hymns to illustrate their sermons. Indispensable to choir directors as well. 245.2'03.M14

Manning, Bernard. *The Hymns of Wesley and Watts.* 7th ed. London: Epworth Press, 1960.

Captures the passion and evangelical fire of Wesley and Watts. Informative and well presented. 245.9.M31 1960

Noss, Luther, ed. *Christian Hymns.* Cleveland: Meridian Books, 1962.

An important study of the historical value and music of 118 hymns. The editor's notes about each hymn are enlightening and make this work a pleasure to use. 245.9.N84

Parks, Bob. *Music—Does it Make Any Difference?* Grand Rapids: Grand Rapids School of the Bible and Music, 1970.

A highly readable, sensible, and scriptural study of music and the Christian's enjoyment of it. 245.P23

Routley, Erik. *Hymns and Human Life.* 2d ed. Grand Rapids: Wm. B. Eerdmans Publishing Co., 1966.

An acknowledged authority on hymnody covers the origin and development of hymns from a historical perspective. 245.R76 1966

Sheppard, W. J. Limmer. *Great Hymns and Their Stories.* Fort Washington, Penn.: Christian Literature Crusade, 1957.

A popular treatment of the events leading up to the writing of some of Christendom's best-loved hymns. 245.SH4

RELIGIOUS DRAMA

Ehrensperger, Harold Adam. *Religious Drama: Ends and Means.* Nashville: Abingdon Press, 1962.

A comprehensive manual covering such items as dramatic form and content and the history of contemporary religious drama. 792.EH8

Halverson, Marvin, ed. *Religious*

Drama. 3 vols. Gloucester, Mass.: Peter Smith, 1959.

A collection of the best medieval and modern religious plays. 246.7.H16

Moseley, Joseph Edward. *Using Drama in the Church.* St. Louis: Bethany Press, n.d.

A basic work. 246.7.M85

PERSONAL RELIGION

Drummond, Henry. *The Greatest Thing in the World.* London: Hodder and Stoughton, 1959.

Contains several famous addresses, the most important of which is based upon I Corinthians 13. 248.D84

Fenelon, Francois de. *Christian Perfection.* New York: Harper and Row, 1947.

A spiritual classic that ably presents the laws of the spiritual life and the conflicts of the human heart. 248.F35

Jabay, Earl. *Search for Identity.* Grand Rapids: Zondervan Publishing House, 1967.

Focuses on the problem of finding meaning and identity in today's society. Moderately evangelical. 248.J11

Oates, Wayne Edward. *Religious Dimensions of Personality.* New York: Association Press, 1957.

A scholarly treatment of personality from both psychological and theological points of view. 248.OA8

Petry, Ray C., ed. *Late Medieval Mysticism.* Library of Christian Classics. Philadelphia: Westminster Press, 1957.

A collection of mystical and contemplative literature from the eleventh to the sixteenth centuries. Designed to help students of medieval and pre-Reformation history understand the lives and thoughts of the leaders of the period. Space devoted to the seventeenth and eighteenth centuries is inadequate. Helpful biographical sketches and bibliographies. 248.P44

Strombeck, John Frederick. *Disciplined by Grace: Studies in Christian Conduct.* Chicago: Moody Press, 1946.

Contains observations and expositions of selected NT passages. Makes *uncomfortable* reading. 248.ST8

Torrey, Reuben Archer. *How to Obtain Fullness of Power in Christian Life and Service.* New ed. London: Oliphants Ltd., 1955.

Devotional messages. Of help to laymen. 248.T63

*Tournier, Paul. *The Person Reborn.* Translated by Edwin Hudson. New York: Harper and Row, 1966.

By carefully distinguishing between man's physical and spiritual natures, moralism and morality, the genuineness of conversion as opposed to counterfeit experience, faith and the "spirit of adventure." Tournier helps the Christian understand himself more fully in order that he may "grow in grace." 248.T64

Tozer, Aiden Wilson. *The Divine Conquest.* New York: Fleming H. Revell Co., 1950.

A vigorous protest against formality in religion, combined with a stirring call for genuine spiritual renewal. 248.T66D

*_____. *The Pursuit of God.* Harrisburg, Penn.: Christian Publications, 1948.

The writer exhorts believers to spend time in the presence of God, speaks out against the activism of his day, and implores Christians to accomplish spiritual ends by spiritual means. 248.T66P

RELIGIOUS EXPERIENCE,
CONVERSION

Augustine, Aurelius. *The Confessions of St. Augustine.* Rev. ed. Garden City: Doubleday and Co., 1960.

The autobiography of this great North African churchman traces his life from childhood, through his libertine years, to his conversion. Shows how a life of self-denial and devotion to Christ can be very rewarding. A spiritual classic. 248.2.AU4

Bull, Geoffrey T. *The Sky Is Red.* Chicago: Moody Press, 1966.

The author recounts incidents drawn from his experiences in Communist China. 248.2.B87

Bunyan, John. *Grace Abounding to the Chief of Sinners.* New York: Oxford University Press, 1966.

Similar to Augustine's *Confessions.* Traces Bunyan's spiritual pilgrimage from his youth, through several crises, to his conversion, and through many trials and difficulties, temptations and sorrows, until he came to rely solely on Christ for his every need. Another spiritual classic. Originally published in 1666. 248.2.B88 1966

_____. *The Pilgrim's Progress.* Grand Rapids: Zondervan Publishing House, reprint.

A vivid allegory describing the experiences of a soul from the time when he is first awakened to his need of Christ until he reaches the heavenly city at the end of his earthly pilgrimage. First published in 1678. 248.2.B88P

Cailliet, Emile. *Journey into Light.* Grand Rapids: Zondervan Publishing House, 1968.

This spiritual autobiography traces the author's spiritual journey from intellectual atheism to childlike faith in Christ. 248.2.C12

Cook, Robert A. *Now That I Believe.* Chicago: Moody Press, 1945.

The finest work of its kind. A *must* for new converts. 248.2.C77

Edman, Victor Raymond. *The Disciplines of Life.* Wheaton: Scripture Press, 1948.

Chapel talks emphasizing the need for discipline in Christian life and service. 248.2.ED5

_____. *They Found the Secret.* Grand Rapids: Zondervan Publishing House, 1960.

An examination of the lives of twenty people with diverse personalities and backgrounds who came under the control of the Holy Spirit. 248.2.ED5T

Herman, Nicolas. *The Practice of the Presence of God.* Westwood, N.J.: Fleming H. Revell Co., 1958.

As Brother Lawrence, the writer served as a lay monk in the kitchen of a monastery. He grumbled continuously until he realized that he could serve God as effectively in a kitchen as anywhere else. He made continuous communication with God a habitual practice. This book is the result. 248.2.H42

King, Guy H. *Brought In.* London: Marshall, Morgan and Scott, 1953.

Expository studies dealing with the positive aspect of Christian experience. 248.2.K58

Lewis, Clive Staples. *Surprised by Joy.* New York: Harcourt, Brace, and World, 1956.

Describes Lewis's search for joy in childhood and adulthood, until he found it in Christ. 248.2.L58

Mavis, W. Curry. *The Psychology of Christian Experience.* Grand Rapids: Zondervan Publishing House, 1963.

A helpful contribution to the study of repentance, conversion, commitment, and assurance. 248.2.M44

*Murray, Andrew. *Abide in Christ.* Three Hills, Alberta: Prairie Book Room, n.d.

A deeply devotional study. Reprinted from the 1883 edition. 248.2.M96

*Nelson, Marion H. *How to Know God's Will.* Chicago: Moody Press, 1962.

A physician and theologian presents a sound, biblical, and genuinely practical approach to the problem of making decisions. Pinpoints a plan for discerning the will of God. 248.2.N33

Pink, Arthur Walkington. *Spiritual Growth.* Grand Rapids: Baker Book House, 1971.

Biblical teaching on growth in grace. Reformed. 248.2.P65

Taylor, Frederick Howard and **G. Taylor.** *Hudson Taylor's Spiritual Secret.* Chicago: Moody Press, 1950.

Deserves a place in every pastor's library. 248.2.T21

White, Ernest. *Christian Life and the Unconscious.* New York: Harper and Row, 1955.

Demonstrates that religion and psychology, far from being mutually antagonistic disciplines, are both necessary in the attainment of mental and spiritual health. 248.2.W58

PRIVATE WORSHIP, PRAYER

Bounds, Edward Mckendree. *Power Through Prayer.* Grand Rapids: Zondervan Publishing House, 1965.

A book every pastor and Christian worker should read. 248.32.B66

*Hallesby, Ole Christian. *Prayer.* London: Tyndale Press, 1956.

An excellent study on the doctrine of prayer, with an analysis of its difficulties, misuse, and varying forms. Practical and devotional. 248.3.H15

Henry, Matthew. *The Secret of Communion with God.* Westwood, N.J.: Fleming H. Revell Co., 1963.

Writes about maintaining unbroken fellowship with the Lord throughout the day. Simple and practical, and based solidly on the Word. 248.22.H39

Houghton, Frank. *Faith's Unclaimed Inheritance.* London: Inter-Varsity Fellowship, 1964.

Brief devotional messages on the place and importance of prayer in the Christian life. 248.3.H81

King, Guy Hope. *Prayer Secrets.* London: Marshall, Morgan and Scott, 1953.

Emphasizes the goal of prayer as being the glorification of God. Shows the tremendous force prayer can exercise in the experience of the individual and in the affairs of the world. 248.3.K58

Laubach, Frank Charles. *Letters of a Modern Mystic.* Westwood, N.J.: Fleming H. Revell Co., 1958.

An inspirational classic. 248.22.L36

Law, William. *The Spirit of Prayer,* [and] *The Spirit of Love.* Edited by Sidney Spencer. Cambridge: James Clarke, 1969.

Originally published in two volumes in London in 1749-50 and 1750-54, this unabridged edition contains the riches of Law's insights into the Scriptures and an experiential understanding of prayer. 248.3.L41 1969

*Murray, Andrew. *The Inner Chamber* [and] *The Inner Life.* Grand Rapids: Zondervan Publishing House, 1958.

These books strike out against the feebleness of many Christians and their inability to resist the world, and they emphasize the need for earnest prayer if the believer is to be fruitful in his service. Reprinted from the 1905 edition. 248.3.M96I 1958

*_____. *The Ministry of Intercession.* Westwood, N.J.: Fleming H. Revell Co., 1966.

The style may be old, but the message is pertinent and timely and emphasizes the two great prayer promises of Christ. 248.3.M96M 1966

*_____. *With Christ in the School of Prayer.* Westwood, N.J.: Fleming H. Revell Co., 1953.

A devotional classic on the ministry of intercession. First published in 1886. 248.3.M96W 1953

Thompson, James G. S. S. *The Praying Christ.* Grand Rapids: Wm. B. Eerdmans Publishing Co., 1959.

A survey of Christ's teaching on prayer. Includes an exposition of John 17, the "Lord's Prayer," Christ as our high priest, and the need for waiting upon the Lord. 248.37.T37

Torrey, Reuben Archer. *How to Pray.* New ed. London: Oliphants Ltd., 1955.

A reprint of the 1900 edition. Devotional. 248.3.T63

_____. *The Power of Prayer, and The Prayer of Power.* Grand Rapids: Zondervan Publishing House, 1955.

These messages cover the whole subject of prayer and are designed to awaken Christians to the need for and importance of prayer in daily living. First published in 1924. 248.3.T63P

CHRISTIAN CONDUCT

Anderson, John B. *Between Two Worlds: A Congressman's Choice.* Grand Rapids: Zondervan Publishing House, 1970.

Analyzes the problems confronting America today, and makes a plea for the relevant application of biblical principles to the solution of the nation's needs. 248.4.AN2

Blaiklock, Edward Musgrave. *The Way of Excellence.* London: Pickering and Inglis, 1968.

Emphasizes the fact that it is no accident that a "new morality" follows a "new theology." Expounds I Corinthians 13 and Romans 12 as a spiritual and moral corrective to the present disintegration in our society. 248.4.B57

*_____ **Bonhoeffer, Dietrich.** *The Cost of Discipleship.* New York: Macmillan Co., 1949.

†Condemns cheap grace [i.e., grace which he feels requires only an intellectual assent] and stresses the fact that true discipleship means following Christ into the world to minister and show His love to it. 248.4.B64

Briscoe, D. Stuart. *The Fullness of Christ.* Grand Rapids: Zondervan Publishing House, 1968.

Messages that confront Christians with the fact that they may be living carnal lives. Challenges them to a new commitment to Christ. 248.4.B77

Brooks, Thomas. *Precious Remedies Against Satan's Devices.* London: Banner of Truth Trust, reprint.

A skillfully written, readable guide to experiential religion. Reprinted from the writer's works. 248.4.B79

Bunyan, John. *The Holy War.* Chicago: Moody Press, 1948.

A description of the spiritual warfare between Christ and Satan for the "town of Mansoul." A spiritual classic, first published in 1682. 248.4.B88H

Culbertson, William. *God's Provision for Holy Living.* Chicago: Moody Press, 1970.

Highlights the believer's responsibility, and stresses the need for obedience to the revealed will of God. 248.4.C89

*****Gibbs, Alfred Perks.** *A Dreamer and His Dream.* 4th ed. Kansas City, Kan.: Walterick Publishers, 1944.

An "exposition" of *Pilgrim's Progress* that brings out the full message of Bunyan's allegory. 248.2.G35D

*_____. *The Marvelous City of Mansoul.* St. Louis: Faithful Words Publishing Co., 1949.

A devotional study of Bunyan's *Holy War.* 248.4.G35M

*****Griffiths, Michael C.** *Consistent Christianity.* London: Inter-Varsity Fellowship, 1960.

An analysis of common human failings, coupled with a clear explanation of Christian duty. 248.42.G87

_____. *Take My Life.* Chicago: Inter-Varsity Press, 1967.

A vigorous plea for practical, everyday Christian living. Designed specifically for collegiates. 248.42.G87T

*****Hopkins, Evan Henry.** *The Law of Liberty in the Spiritual Life.* Fort Washington, Penn.: Christian Literature Crusade, 1952.

A classic in the field, these messages

are as timely today as when they were first delivered. 248.4.H77

LaHaye, Tim F. *Transformed Temperaments.* Wheaton: Tyndale House Publishers, 1971.

Building upon his earlier book *Spirit-Controlled Temperaments,* this work deals successively with Peter the *sanguine,* Paul the *choleric,* Moses the *melancholy,* and Abraham the *phlegmatic.* Exposes the strengths and weaknesses of each temperament, and shows how God worked in the life of each individual. 248.4.L52

*Lloyd-Jones, David Martyn. *Spiritual Depression: Its Causes and Cure.* Grand Rapids: Wm. B. Eerdmans Publishing Co., 1965.

A physician turned preacher deals with the scriptural causes of spiritual depression and shows how it may be cured. Aims at developing an effective, healthy Christian life. 248.42.L77

Larson, Bruce. *Living on the Growing Edge.* Grand Rapids: Zondervan Publishing House, 1968.

Shows how believers may achieve a right relationship with God and live in harmony with others. Part of the literature supporting the "relational theology" movement. 248.4.L32

*Law, William. *A Serious Call to a Devout and Holy Life.* Grand Rapids: Wm. B. Eerdmans Publishing Co., 1966.

Devotional thoughts dealing with the pattern for serving God in daily life and the nurture of the inner life. First published in 1729. 248.4.L41 1966

Meyer, Frederick Brotherton. *The Soul's Pure Intention.* 3d ed. London: Samuel Baxter and Sons, 1906.

Reverent, devotional messages based upon select Scripture passages. 248.4.M57 1906

Miller, Keith. *The Taste of New Wine.* Waco: Word Books, 1965.

A vigorous call for personal renewal among laymen in the church. *The* work that gave rise to the relational movement

in America. 248.4.M61

_____. *Habitation of Dragons.* Waco: Word Books, 1965.

Calls upon believers to face honestly the weaknesses in their daily lives. The writing is popular but lacks theological perception. 248.4.M61H

*Murray, Andrew. *The Master's Indwelling.* Grand Rapids: Zondervan Publishing House, n.d.

Thirteen addresses originally delivered at the Northfield Conference in 1895 stress the need for complete dependence upon the enabling and sustaining ministry of the Holy Spirit. Reprinted from the 1896 edition. 248.42.M96

*Pentecost, John Dwight. *Pattern for Maturity.* Chicago: Moody Press, 1966.

A definitive study that provides a very capable summary of the NT teaching on the doctrine of sanctification. 248.4'2.P38 (Alt. DDC 234.8.P38)

Redpath, Alan. *Learning to Live.* Grand Rapids: Wm. B. Eerdmans Publishing Co., 1961.

An eloquent plea for a return to the NT standards of Christian living. 248.4.R24

*Ryle, John Charles. *Practical Religion.* Edited by J. I. Packer. Cambridge: James Clarke and Co., 1970.

A concise guide to the daily duties, experiences and dangers, privileges and responsibilities of professing Christians. Based upon the third edition published in 1883. 248.4.R98 1970

Ryrie, Charles Caldwell. *Balancing the Christian Life.* Chicago: Moody Press, 1969.

Expounds the Scriptures after first developing a theology based upon exegesis. Then discusses such issues as the filling of the Holy Spirit, confession of sin, speaking in tongues, the ever present problem of legalism, and the lordship of Christ. 248.4.R99

_____. *Pattern for Christian Youth.* Chicago: Moody Press, 1966.

Pointed discussions dealing specifically with the problems faced by young people today. 248.4'2.R99P

Shelley, Bruce, ed. *A Call to Christian Character.* Grand Rapids: Zondervan Publishing House, 1970.

Essays analyzing the contemporary crisis of piety and offering positive suggestions for developing true Christian character. 248.4.SH4

Spring, Gardiner. *The Distinguishing Traits of Christian Character.* Philadelphia: Presbyterian and Reformed Publishing Co., 1967.

A disquieting series of studies adapted from *Essays on the Distinguishing Traits of Christian Character,* published in 1829. The chapters are brief, and the material contained in them is particularly pertinent to the needs of the present day. 248.4.SP8 1967

Taylor, Jeremy. *Holy Living.* New York: Harper and Row, 1961.

An abridgment of the classic *Rules and Exercises for Holy Living,* by Jeremy Taylor, first published in 1650. Spells out the entire duty of man, with emphasis on the fact that holiness in life is a condition of wholeness. 248.4.T21 1961

*Tournier, Paul. *The Adventure of Living.* Translated by Edwin Hudson. New York: Harper and Row, 1965.

Written specifically for those who go on indefinitely preparing for life instead of living it. Shows how those who are frustrated may find fulfillment in life. 248.4.T64

Trumbull, Charles Gaullaudet. *Victory in Christ.* Fort Washington, Penn.: Christian Literature Crusade, 1970.

Portrays the reality of victory in Christ with insight and understanding. 248.4.T77

Whyte, Alexander. *The Spiritual Life: The Teaching of Thomas Goodwin.* 2 vols. London: Oliphants and Co., 1918.

Essays highlighting Goodwin's theological position, method of interpretation, and teaching on sanctification. 248.4.W62

WITNESSING

*Chafer, Lewis Sperry. *True Evangelism: or, Winning Souls by Prayer.* Grand Rapids: Zondervan Publishing House, 1965.

Deals with some of the common difficulties involved in personal evangelism. Emphasizes the basic need for spiritual power and the need for earnest prayer if witnessing is to be effective. Reprinted from the 1911 edition. 248.5.C34 1965

Dobbins, Gaines Stanley. *Evangelism According to Christ.* Nashville: Broadman Press, 1949.

Studies centering in the gospel of John, explaining the original method of Christ's evangelism and its application to the church today. 248.5.D65

Kuiper, Rienk Bouke. *God-Centered Evangelism: A Presentation of the Scriptural Theology of Evangelism.* London: Banner of Truth Trust, 1966.

A logical presentation of the theology of evangelism showing that God is its author and establishing its rationale in His unchanging love, the doctrine of election, the covenant of grace, and Christ's commission. Reformed. 248.5.K95

*Kunz, Marilyn and **Catherine Shell.** *How to Start a Neighborhood Bible Study.* Dobbs Ferry, N.Y.: Neighborhood Bible Studies, 1966.

A brief, informative guide dealing with the promotion and leadership of home discussion groups. 248.5.K96

*Little, Paul E. *How to Give Away Your Faith.* Chicago: Inter-Varsity Press, 1966.

May well be regarded as one of the most important treatments on personal evangelism available today. 248.5.L72

Macaulay, Joseph Cordner and **Robert H. Belton.** *Personal Evangelism.* Chicago: Moody Press, 1956.

A thorough explanation of the prerequisites and training needed for effective evangelism. 248.5.M11

*Strachan, Kenneth R. *The Inescapable Calling.* Grand Rapids: Wm. B. Eerdmans Publishing Co., 1968.

A thought-provoking study of the implications of Christ's missionary imperative contained in Matthew 28. 248.5.ST8

Trumbull, Charles Gallaudet. *Taking Men Alive.* New ed. Westwood, N.J.: Fleming H. Revell Co., 1938.

An old, standard treatment. 248.5.T77

*Wollen, Albert J. *How to Conduct Home Bible Classes.* Wheaton: Scripture Press, 1969.

An up-to-date study guide for organizing and leading informal study groups in the home. 248.5.W83

CHRISTIAN HOME

*Adams, Theodore Floyd. *Making Your Marriage Succeed.* New York: Harper and Row, 1952.

Explains how problems may be prevented, and what to do when things go wrong. Combines practical wisdom with youthful idealism. 241.1.AD1

Allmen, Jean-Jacques von. *Pauline Teaching on Marriage.* London: Faith Press, 1963.

A scholarly study containing a fresh approach to marriage and an interpretation of older material. 241.1.AL5

*Andelin, Helen B. *Fascinating Womanhood.* Santa Barbara: Pacific Press, 1965.

A simple, clear explanation of *how* women may find fulfillment in marriage. A must. 306.4.AN3

*Anderson, Wayne J. *Design for Family Living.* Minneapolis: T. S. Denison and Co., 1964.

A practical discussion. Explores the needs of each member of the family, and shows how they may be met. Written from a wealth of practical experience. 249.AN2

*_____. *How to Explain Sex to Children.* Minneapolis: T. D. Denison and Co., 1971.

Will give parents some needed guidelines and practical answers to youth's questions about sex. 306.7.AN2

_____. *How to Understand Sex: Guidelines for Students.* Minneapolis: T. D. Denison and Co., 1966.

A frank discussion of sex decisions facing college students today, with suggested guidelines for resolving them. 306.72.AN2.

*Barclay, William. *Train Up a Child.* Philadelphia: Westminster Press, 1960.

Focuses on the educational ideas of the ancient world, deals with the educational methods of the God-centered Jewish people, the brutality of the totalitarian Spartan state, the cultural genius of the Athenians, and the stalwart, lofty ideals of the Romans. Provides insights into the educational processes of pagan cultures, but also emphasizes the rich heritage of Christianity and the respected tradition of the early church. Readable and well illustrated. 370.93.B23

Baruch, Dorothy (Walter). *How to Live with Your Teen-ager.* New York: McGraw-Hill Book Co., 1953.

Imparts understanding to parents puzzled by the attitude and conduct of their teenagers. 155.5.B28

_____. *New Ways in Sex Education.* New York: McGraw-Hill Book Co., 1959.

A careful analysis of problems common to teenagers. Illustrated with case histories. Offers sane suggestions for dealing with these situations. 612.6.B28N

*Berne, Eric. *Games People Play: The Psychology of Human Relationships.* New York: Grove Press, 1964.

A best seller on Transactional Analysis (TA). A handy technique to know about when dealing with people who either have been reared in or otherwise come from authoritarian settings. 301.15.B45

Bovet, Theodore. *A Handbook to Marriage.* Garden City: Doubleday and Co., 1958.

Discusses marital problems from the nature of love and the selection of a mate to handling crises in marriage. A popular, wholesome, well-balanced approach. 306.8.B66

*Bower, Robert K. *Solving Problems in Marriage: Guidelines for Christian Couples.* Grand Rapids: Wm. B. Eerdmans Publishing Co., 1971.

Spells out ways in which husbands and wives can find solutions to the problems arising in the normal course of everyday living. Practical. 306.8.B67

*Bowman, George M. *Here's How to Succeed with Your Money.* Chicago: Moody Press, 1960.

Provides some down-to-earth advice on how to live within your budget, succeed with investment goals, provide for the future, and honor the Lord with your income. 332.094.B68

*Brandt, Henry R. and **Homer E. Dowdy.** *Building a Christian Home.* Wheaton: Scripture Press, 1960.

An eminently readable book on the roles and responsibilities of parents and children in the Christian home. 249.B73

Burton, Rulon T. *How To Get Out of Debt—And Stay Out.* Salt Lake City: Brigham Street House, 1970.

Contains counsel about the problems and perplexities of debt. Helpful for use in counseling situations. 301.5.B95

Butterfield, Oliver McKinley. *Sex Life in Marriage.* Rev. ed. New York: Emerson Books, 1965.

An unusually successful attempt at information about how love may be nourished and strengthened. Abreast of modern sociological, psychological, and medical research. 306.8.B98 1965

_____. *Sexual Harmony in Marriage.* New York: Emerson Books, 1960.

A frank, wise discussion. 306.8.B98S

Capper, William Melville and **Hugh Morgan Williams.** *Heirs Together.* 3d ed. London: Inter-Varsity Fellowship, 1956.

A Christian approach to the privileges and responsibilities of sex and marriage. 306.8.C17 1956

_____. *Towards Christian Marriage.* Chicago: Inter-Varsity Press, 1958.

An elementary book on privileges and responsibilities of sex in Christian marriage. 306.7.C17

Cleaver, Nancy. *The Treasury of Family Fun.* Westwood, N.J.: Fleming H. Revell Co., 1960.

A manual on indoor and outdoor activities, with ideas and projects for every month of the year. 790.19.C623

Clinebell, Howard John, Jr. and **Charlotte H. Clinebell.** *The Intimate Marriage.* New York: Harper and Row, 1970.

A factual work that deals with the nature of intimacy, the barriers to its achievement, and the ways in which it may enhance a marriage. Worthwhile. 306.8.C61

Cole, William Graham. *Sex in Christianity and Psychoanalysis.* London: Allen and Unwin, 1956.

†An analysis of the Christian attitude toward sex, marriage, and divorce, accompanied by a summary of the psychoanalytical positions held by Freud, Horney, Alexander, and others. 306.7.C67

Coleman, James Samuel. *The Adolescent Society.* New York: Free Press of Glencoe, 1962.

An assessment of the outstanding features in adolescent society, with an evaluation of the variations produced by school and community. 305.23.C67

Cook, Robert. *It's Tough to Be a Teenager.* Wheaton: Scripture Press, 1955.

Written by one who is cognizant of and sympathetic with the problems of youth. 155.5.C77

Dehoney, Wayne. *Homemade Happiness.* Nashville: Broadman Press, 1963.

Provides some lively and constructive counsel about love overcoming obstacles and the blessings of the Christian faith in the modern home. 306.8.D36

Denton, Wallace. *What's Happening to Our Families?* Philadelphia: Westminster Press, 1963.

A constructive discussion on the structure and changing patterns of family life today. Evaluates the emasculated man and the unfulfilled woman, anxious parents, accelerated living, retirement, the demise of religious belief, and family isolation. A final section considers the new role of churches in rebuilding family life. 306.8.D43

Dobson, James. *Dare to Discipline.* Wheaton: Tyndale House Publishers, 1970.

Written specifically for parents and teachers who are charged with the responsibility of molding the "now" generation. 649.6.D65

Drakeford, John W. *Games Husbands and Wives Play.* Nashville: Broadman Press, 1970.

Describes fourteen games and the "ground rules" governing each. The diagnosis and suggestions will go a long way toward making marriages happier. 306.8.D78

————. *The Home: Laboratory of Life.* Nashville: Broadman Press, 1965.

Exposes the erosion taking place in family life today, and offers counsel to parents on the best way to prepare their children for the future. 306.8.D78H

*Dreikurs, Rudolf. *The Challenge of Marriage.* New York: Duell, Cloan and Pearce, 1946.

A remarkably helpful treatment designed to build a strong, constructive relationship between a husband and wife. 306.8.D81

————. *The Challenge of Parenthood.* New York: Duell, Sloan and Pearce, 1958.

Informative and helpful. Contains a wealth of usable material. Pastors will find Dreikurs' material helpful whenever they preach on the home and the family. 649.1.D81

*Drucker, Peter Ferdinand. *The Age of Discontinuity: Guidelines to Our Changing Society.* New York: Harper and Row, 1969.

A brilliant study. As up-to-date as Reich's *Greening of America,* and more reliable than Toffler's *Future Shock.* 309.104.D84

*Duvall, Evelyn Ruth (Millis). *Family Development.* Philadelphia: J. B. Lippincott Co., 1962.

Assesses the functional factors relating to family relationships. Includes additions to the family, as well as the contractions that take place when children leave the nest. 306.8.D95

————. *In-Laws, Pro and Con.* New York: Association Press, 1954.

Contains constructive advice to both the younger and the older generations. Nothing has been written to date that equals it. 306.87.D95

————. *Love and the Facts of Life.* New York: Association Press, 1963.

Not the usual love-and-marriage guidebook. Takes for granted a greater degree of sophistication among modern teenagers, and counsels them toward wholesome and mature relationships. 176.D95L

*————. *Today's Teen-agers.* New York: Association Press, 1967.

Written for today's baffled and bewildered parents. Also of value to teachers who are not sure of, and do not know what to do with, their adolescent students. Ably evaluates the trends and mores among teenagers; explains why some drop out; how, when, and why to date, and with whom; and concludes with a study of "what teen-agers need from adults." 305.23.D95

_____. *When You Marry.* New York: Association Press, 1962.

A helpful guide for use in counseling young people. Provides much-needed guideposts for insuring happiness, and discusses at length the emotional, psychological, economic, and social aspects of marriage. Overlooks the spiritual dimension. 306.8.D95W

*_____. *Why Wait Till Marriage?* New York: Associated Press, 1965.

A candid discussion of the reasons for premarital chastity. Recommended. 176.D95

_____ and **Reuben Hill.** *Being Married.* New York: Association Press, 1960.

Beginning with dating and friendship-making, this book continues with an appraisal of choosing mates. Contains chapters on sex, manners, morals, home building, in-laws, finance, facing crises, having children, and avoiding the cul-de-sac of divorce. 306.8.D95B

Duvall, Sylvanus M. *Before You Marry.* New rev. ed. New York: Association Press, 1962.

Helps couples prepare for happier, more enduring marriages. Full of excellent ideas, and incorporates recent sociological and psychological research. 306.82.D95B

*__Eichenlaub, John B.__ *The Marriage Art.* New York: Lyle Stewart, 1961.

Takes the burden of individual responsibility for technique off the husband's shoulders and the burden of responsiveness from the wife. Shows how the problems of marriage should be solved by a unified approach of husband and wife. Dispells much of the myth surrounding sex in marriage. Secular. 306.8.EI2

Erb, Alta Mae. *Christian Nurture of Children.* Rev. ed. Scottdale, Penn.: Herald Press, 1955.

A plain, practical presentation of the responsibility of parents, and their relationship to their children, God, the church, others, and themselves. 305.23.ER1 1955

Ellul, Jacques. *The Meaning of the City.* Grand Rapids: Wm. B. Eerdmans Publishing Co., 1970.

Shows that the Bible contains a complete, sophisticated, coherent teaching about cities and city life. A remarkable treatise. 301.364.EL5

Ellzey, William Clark. *Preparing Your Children for Marriage.* Baltimore, Md.: Penguin Books, Inc., 1964.

A practical guide containing ideas and counsel designed to help parents achieve maturity in marriage so that they, in turn, will be able to influence their children's future marital relationship. 306.7.EL5

Fairchild, Roy W., and **John C. Wynn.** *Families in the Church.* New York: Association Press, 1961.

A well-structured book incorporating the findings of psychology and sociology into the church's ministry to families. 249.F16

Fallow, Wesner. *The Modern Parent and the Teaching Church.* New York: Macmillan Co., 1957.

While readers will disagree with the writer's theological presuppositions, they should not discount his work, for it discusses the problems between the church and the home. In fact, it sounded a warning long before others were aware of the problem and was well ahead of its time. 249.F19

*__Feucht, Oscar E., ed.__ *Helping Families Through the Church: A Symposium on Family*

Life Education. St. Louis: Concordia Publishing House, 1957.

Aims at the development of the Christian family with the love of Christ as its basis. Lutheran. 249.F43

―――. *Ministry to Families.* St. Louis: Concordia Publishing House, 1963.

A handbook for Christian congregations. Packed with practical information. Serves well as a model for all denominations. 249.F43M

―――, ed. *Sex and the Church.* Marriage and Family Research. St. Louis: Concordia Publishing House, 1961.

A sociological, historical, and theological investigation of sex attitudes in the OT, the apostolic Fathers, and the history of the church. 306.7.F95

*Fields, Wilbert J. *Unity in Marriage.* St. Louis: Concordia Publishing House, 1961.

A delightful blending of Christian altruism with "other-directed" Christian love and its contributions to a lifelong process of working out the incompatibilities of marriage. 249.F46

Fitch, William. *Christian Perspectives on Sex and Marriage.* Grand Rapids: Wm. B. Eerdmans Publishing Co., 1971.

Lifts the subject of sex out of the morass of contemporary literature, exalts it as God's gift to man, and enlarges upon the unifying and perfecting aspects of sex in the strengthening of the marriage bond. 241.1.F55

Fromme, Allan. *The Ability to Love.* New York: Farrar, Strauss and Giroux, 1963.

A companion volume to *The Art of Loving.* Practical and helpful. 157.3.F92

*Gangel, Kenneth O. *The Family First.* Minneapolis: His International Service, 1972.

A particularly thorough, biblical treatment of the various aspects of family living. Perhaps one of the finest works of its kind. 249.G15

Gesell, Arnold Lucius, et al. *The First Five Years of Life.* New York: Harper and Row, 1940.

A seminal study. In need of revision, but still very helpful. 155.42.G33F

―――. *The Child from Five to Ten.* New York: Harper and Row, 1946.

A carefully presented evaluation of the distinctive behavior characteristics of each period of the child's life. Of obvious benefit to parents and teachers. 155.424.G33

―――. and **Frances L. Ilg.** *Child Development: An Introduction to the Study of Human Growth.* New York: Harper and Row, 1949.

A valuable work reflecting the influence of culture on the personality of the child and providing guidelines for physical and emotional growth. 155.4.G33C

―――. and **Louise Bates Ames.** *Youth: The Years from Ten to Sixteen.* New York: Harper and Row, 1956.

Surveys the behavior characteristics of adolescents in the home, at school, and among their friends. Makes the problems of this age group more understandable. 155.5.G33Y

Ginott, Haim G. *Between Parent and Child.* New York: Macmillan Co., 1965.

Attempts to minimize the irritation that frequently exists between parent and child, and aims at making family life more rewarding. 649.1.G43

Gordon, Ira J. *Human Development from Birth through Adolescence.* New York: Harper and Row, 1962.

Explains how transitions from one phase of development to another can be made without trauma. Thought-provoking. 155.4.G65

Granberg, Lars I. *For Adults Only.* Grand Rapids: Zondervan Publishing House, 1970.

A psychologist places his finger on the reason for breakdown in family relationships. Calls on people willingly to return to the biblical blueprint for marriage, in which the wife freely accepts her husband's leadership. 249.G76

*Greenblatt, Bernard R. *A Doctor's Marital Guide for Patients.* Chicago: Budlong Press, 1959.

An informative guide to meaningful sexual relationships in marriage. Sold only to M.D.'s and ministers of religion. Ideal to give to young couples in premarital counseling sessions. 306.8.G56

Griffith, Leonard. *Illusions of Our Culture.* Waco: Word Books, 1971.

Analyzes the "appearance of reality" of our present culture, and shows how these illusions degenerate into the "leafy trees of a desert mirage." Among the topics considered are affluence, security, independence, happiness, and freedom. 301.44.G87

Grimm, Robert. *Love and Sexuality.* New York: Association Press, 1964.

A biblically sound view of sex and marriage. 306.8.G88

Harris, Thomas Anthony. *I'm OK, You're OK.* New York: Harper and Row, 1969.

Focuses on helping people change through group processes. Popularizes the principles of Transactional Analysis (TA). Well written. 616.89'1.H24

Havard, Allen and **Margaret Havard.** *Death and Rebirth of a Marriage.* Wheaton: Tyndale House Publishers, 1970.

A true-to-life story about a marriage on the rocks . . . until God stepped in. 249.H29

Havemann, Ernest. *Men, Women and Marriage.* Garden City: Doubleday and Co., 1962.

A practical approach to the problems of human relationships in marriage. Secular. 306.8.H29

Havighurst, Robert James and **Hilda Taba.** *Adolescent Character and Personality.* New York: John Wiley and Sons, 1949.

An investigation into the influence of the social environment on the character development of youth. Conclusions emphasize areas where social adjustment is needed. Of interest to all who work with teen-agers. 155.5.H29

Hiltner, Seward. *Sex and Christian Life.* New York: Association Press, 1957.

Draws attention to certain guidelines that should control Christian conduct. Brief and to the point. 306.7.H56

*Hopkins, Hugh Alexander Evan. *The Mystery of Suffering.* Chicago: Inter-Varsity Press, 1961.

Without expecting to receive or daring to offer any facile solution to the problem of suffering, the writer expounds the biblical teaching and provides sane counsel for those who face pain and misfortune. 248.86.H77

*Hulme, William Edward. *Building a Christian Marriage.* Englewood Cliffs, N.J.: Prentice-Hall, 1965.

A welcome discussion of the reciprocal duties and responsibilities of husbands and wives. Includes a treatment of the identity of each partner, outlines the respective sphere of each, and makes a strong plea for the biblical pattern to be maintained by Christian couples today. 249.H87

*_____. *God, Sex and Youth.* Englewood Cliffs, N.J.: Prentice-Hall, 1965.

A thorough coverage of the many problems that perplex teenagers today. Discusses dating, going steady, and sexual deviations in a frank, mature, and reverent manner. 248.83.H87G

Hunt, Morton. *Her Infinite Variety: The American Woman as Lover, Mate and Rival.* New York: Harper and Row, 1962.

A contemporary analysis of the seven disconnected ages of woman. Provocative. 306.4.H91

Ilg, Frances L., and **Louise Bates Ames.** *Child Behavior: Advice on Bringing up Children.* New York: Harper and Row, 1955.

Definitive studies reflecting years of intensive research on the part of the Yale Clinic of Child Development. Of particular value to parents. 155.2.IL4C

_____. *Parents Ask: Child Care Guidance.* New York: Harper and Row, 1962.

An important sequel to *Child Behavior.* Gives practical answers to parental questions on all phases of child rearing. 155.2.IL4P

Jacobsen, Margaret Bailey. *The Child in the Christian Home.* Wheaton: Scripture Press, 1959.

A practical guidebook for Christian parents and church workers. Well illustrated, easy to read, and biblically oriented. 249.J15

Jaeck, Gordon and **Dorothea Jaeck.** *I Take Thee . . . : The Art of Successful Marriage.* Grand Rapids: Zondervan Publishing House, 1967.

The authors share, from their own experience, lessons they hope will be of value and of practical help to other married couples. 249.J15

*Janeway, Eliot. *What Shall I Do with My Money?* New York: David McKay, 1970.

Deals with a problem facing many Americans today. Secular, but the advice on investments is sound. 332.6.J25

Jepson, Sarah Anne. *For the Love of Singles.* Carol Stream, Ill.: Creation House, 1970.

Discusses the problems of loneliness, depression, and pressure, and draws comfort and consolation from biblical characters like Elijah, Dorcas, and Barnabas. 306.7.J46

Jersild, Arthur Thomas. *Child Psychology.* 5th ed. Englewood Cliffs, N.J.: Prentice-Hall, 1960.

Provides a systematic study of the developments that shape a child's ideas and attitudes regarding himself and his parents. Analyzes the parent-child relationship, and explains the concepts of a healthy self-acceptance and the interplay

between thought and feeling. Also focuses on the interaction between heredity and environment. An excellent work. 155.4.J48 1960

*_____. *The Psychology of Adolescence.* 2d ed. New York: Macmillan Co., 1963.

A practical treatment. Contains a veritable gold mine of information that will handsomely repay the time parents and youth workers spend reading it. 155.5.J48 1963

Johnson, Eric W. *How to Live Through Junior High School.* Philadelphia: J. B. Lippincott Co., 1959.

Helpful in understanding how a public school educator looks at the total picture of junior high school life. Practical, nontechnical. 155.5.J63

Kirkpatrick, Clifford. *The Family as Process and Institution.* 2d ed. New York: Ronald Press, 1963.

A sociological approach embracing every facet of family life. Impressive documentation. 306.8.K63 1963

Knox, David. *Marriage Happiness: A Behavioral Approach to Counseling.* Champaign, Ill.: Research Press Co., 1971.

An analysis of the cause and cure of marital problems. Of value in premarital and postmarital counseling. Secular in its orientation. 306.8.K77

Koehler, George and **Nikki Koehler.** *My Family, How Shall I Live With It?* Chicago: Rand McNally and Co., 1968.

A very practical book by a father-daughter team. Written for the young person, but also of value to adults. 170.202'23.K81

Kooiman, Gladys. *When Death Takes a Father.* Grand Rapids: Baker Book House, 1968.

Relives the shattering experience the author faced when her husband and the father of her eight children was suddenly taken from her. A record of triumph in the face of overwhelming difficulties. 306.88.K83

LaHaye, Tim F. *How to Be Happy Though Married.* Wheaton: Tyndale House Publishers, 1968.

Discusses how the dream of happiness may become a reality. The author shares some of the techniques and ideas he has used in his counseling ministry. 306.8.L43

*Landis, Judson T., and **Mary G. Landis.** *Building a Successful Marriage.* 6th ed. Englewood Cliffs, N.J.: Prentice-Hall, 1973.

An informative volume containing detailed information on courtship, dating, sexual attitudes, behavior, and engagements as reported by more than three thousand students in American colleges and universities. Pertinent information relating to the problem of adjustment in marriage has been taken from 581 happily married couples, 155 troubled couples who have received counsel, and 164 divorced people. No one seriously interested in counseling can afford to neglect this well-balanced book. 306.8.L23 1968

Lee, Mark W. *Our Children Are Our Best Friends.* Grand Rapids: Zondervan Publishing House, 1972.

Draws material from the Bible, and shows how a family can be established as a unit and develop a haven in the midst of a chaotic, restless world. 306.87.L51

Levinsohn, Florence, ed. *What Teenagers Want to Know.* Chicago: Budlong Press, 1962.

Written by M.D.s, this helpful book is designed to explain sex to those in their adolescent years. 305.23.L57

*Lewin, Samuel Aaron and **John Gilmore.** *Sex withour Fear.* New York: Medical Research Press, 1957.

One of the best introductory manuals available today. A work that pastors could easily loan to those whom they counsel before marriage. 612.6.L58

Lobsenz, Norman N. and **Clark W.**

Blackburn. *How to Stay Married.* New York: Carrolls Book Co., 1969.

A modern approach to sex, money, and emotional problems in marriage, coupled with a penetrating analysis of the illusory and romantic expectations of married couples. 306.8.L78

Lowell, C. Stanley. *Protestant-Catholic Marriage.* Nashville: Broadman Press, 1962.

This book grew out of the alarming divorce rate in Protestant-Catholic marriages in the pre-Vatican II era. 306.8.L95

*_____. *Marriage: The Art of Lasting Happiness.* London: Hodder and Stoughton, 1952.

This work is plain and practical and aims at the education and maturity of the marriage partners. 306.8.M15M

McFarland, Robert L., and **John David Burton.** *Learning for Loving: The Importance of Communication in the Marriage Relationship.* Grand Rapids: Zondervan Publishing House, 1969.

Focusing on couples in suburbia, this book highlights many of the pressures facing upper middle-class people today. Provides valuable suggestions for keeping the lines of communication open. 306.8.M16

*McGinnis, Tom. *Your First Year of Marriage.* Garden City: Doubleday and Co., 1967.

One of the most helpful books on the market. Will help pastors engaged in a counseling ministry prepare young people for the major adjustments that take place in the first year of marriage. Secular. 306.8.M17

*Mace, David Robert. *Success in Marriage.* Nashville: Abingdon Press, 1958.

Shows the need for adequate preparation before marriage, proper adjustment to the new relationship, a willingness to share, and a recognition of a gradual need for maturity and development. Easy to read, factual, and sound. 306.8.M15

Maves, Paul B. *Understanding Ourselves as Adults.* Nashville: Abingdon Press, 1959.

A careful examination of the nature of personality development, education, and change in adulthood. 155.6.M44

May, Rollo. *Love and Will.* New York: W. W. Norton and Co., 1969.

A thoughtful and sympathetic approach to the problems of modern married couples, with a definitive analysis of the pressures that have arisen in today's transitional period between the old world and the new. 152.4.M45

*Miles, Herbert J. *Sexual Happiness in Marriage.* Grand Rapids: Zondervan Publishing House, 1967.

Ranks as one of the most practical and helpful treatments on the subject. Examines attitudes and techniques essential to sexual harmony and happiness in marriage, and provides needful correctives to some of the abuses of marriage. 306.8.M59

_____. *Sexual Understanding Before Marriage.* Grand Rapids: Zondervan Publishing House, 1967.

A realistic approach providing a solid moral foundation for young unmarried people. 306.7.M59

Mow, Anna B. *Your Child From Birth to Rebirth.* Grand Rapids: Zondervan Publishing House, 1963.

Exposes the inadequacies of nurture in the home, and provides practical, down-to-earth counsel on how to influence children for Christ. 249.M87

Mullins, David and **Mary Mullins.** *This Year, Next Year, Sometime . . . ?* London: Inter-Varsity Fellowship, 1960.

A booklet setting forth a Christian philosophy of friendship and marriage. 249.M95T

Narramore, Stanley Bruce. *Help! I'm a Parent.* Grand Rapids: Zondervan Publishing House, 1972.

An important psychological study designed to acquaint parents with the complex problems associated with the rearing of children and the shaping of their individual personalities. A study manual, *A Guide to Child Rearing,* is also available. Designed for study groups. Neo-Freudian. 249.N16

Nelson, Martha. *The Christian Woman in the Working World.* Nashville: Broadman Press, 1970.

Pastors will find this book helpful, and church members should read it in order better to understand the tensions and frustrations of Christian women caught up in the turmoil of commerce and industry. 305.43.N33

Overton, Grace Sloan. *Living with Parents.* Nashville: Broadman Press, 1954.

Written specifically for teenagers. Outlines *why* they have trouble with their parents and also explains *what* they can do about it. Of value to counselors and parents, as well as to teenagers. 306.87.OV2

_____. *Living with Teen-agers.* Nashville: Broadman Press, 1950.

Contains practical, though dated, pointers for parents, and emphasizes principles for helping teenagers. 155.5.OV2

Patterson, Gerald R. *Families: Applications of Social Learning to Family Life.* Champaign, Ill.: Research Press Co., 1971.

A behavioristic approach to family life and its problems, with particular emphasis being placed on the rearing of children. 306.8.P27

Peale, Ruth (Stafford). *The Adventure of Being a Wife.* Englewood Cliffs, N.J.: Prentice-Hall, 1971.

A scintillating book. Provides a helpful

and healthy approach to the frequently misunderstood role of a wife in today's culture. 170.202.P31

Pearson, Gerald Hamilton Jeffrey. *Adolescence and the Conflict of the Generations.* New York: W. W. Norton & Co., 1958.

An introduction to the psychoanalysis of adolescence. 155.5.P31

Peterson, James Alfred. *Married Love in the Middle Years.* New York: Association Press, 1968.

The author assists couples to understand what happens in a home when children mature and leave for college or get married, and how they can control their emotions and attitudes. 306.8.P44

———. *Toward a Successful Marriage.* New York: Charles Scribner's Sons, 1960.

A functional approach. Includes all aspects of marriage, from courtship to old age. 306.8.P44T

Pink, Arthur Walkington. *Comfort for Christians.* Swengel, Penn.: Reiner Publications, 1952.

A timely work full of consolation. A valuable addition to the other books treating suffering. Should be in every church library. 248.86.P65

Piper, Otto A. *The Biblical View of Sex and Marriage.* New York: Charles Scribner's Sons, 1960.

After discussing the biblical view of sex, the writer proceeds to elaborate on the standards he deems to be necessary for an adequate sexual life. He then discusses the objectives of marriage in the light of the Scriptures. 176.P66

*Popenoe, Paul Bowman. *Preparing for Marriage.* Los Angeles: American Institute of Family Relations, 1961.

A very helpful booklet designed to help couples make the most of their marriage relationship. 306.8.P81

*——— and **Dorothy Cameron Disney.** *Can This Marriage Be Saved?* New York: Macmillan Co., 1960.

Contains twenty typical cases, each illustrating a problem area of marriage. In each instance provides the step-by-step process by which the marriage may be saved. 306.8.P81C

*———. *Marriage Is What You Make It.* New York: Macmillan Co., 1965.

Shows the difficulties in marriage are not disastrous, but should be expected; and the couple should be encouraged to work through their difficulties toward a stronger and more wholesome relationship. 306.8.P81M

Pre-Marital Counseling Manual. 2d ed. Dallas: Christian Education Department, Dallas Theological Seminary, 1966.

A reference volume outlining the successive steps in the premarital counseling interviews. 306.7.P91 1966 (Alt. DDC 253.5.P91)

Reich, Charles A. *The Greening of America.* New York: Random House, 1970.

A popular work that attempts to analyze the youth culture of present-day America. 309.1'73.R27

*Riesman, David. *The Lonely Crowd: A Study of the Changing American Character.* New Haven: Yale University Press, 1950.

A definitive study that calls attention to the changing character-pattern of middle class, urban Americans. A book every pastor should read. 301.2.R44

Rosenberg, Morris. *Society and the Adolescent Self-Image.* Princeton: Princeton University Press, 1965.

In spite of its obvious value, this work suffers from a basic flaw: the writer works from the premise that he can isolate and meaningfully analyze a single causal chain in a network of complicated reactions. This is particularly noticeable in his attempts to measure self-esteem. 155.5.R72

Scudder, C. W. *The Family in Christian Perspective.* Nashville: Broadman Press, 1962.

A frank discussion of the responsibilities facing couples as they marry, rear a family, take care of the elderly, and work in their church. 249.SCR9

Seifert, Harvey and **Howard J. Clinebell, Jr.** *Personal Growth and Social Change: A Guide for Ministers and Laymen as Change Agents.* Philadelphia: Westminster Press, 1969.

Recognizing the need for adaptation in today's counseling, teaching, and social setting, the writers provide an informative guide for ministers and laymen in their role as agents of change. 253.5.SE4

Shedd, Charlie W. *Letters to Karen.* Nashville, Abingdon Press, 1965.

Focuses on keeping love in marriage. Ideal for young people. Should be in every church library. 306.7.SH3

Shultz, Gladys Denny. *The Successful Teenage Girl.* Philadelphia: J. B. Lippincott Co., 1968.

A secular guide for the teenage girl in junior or senior high school. 305.23.SH9

Skousen, Willard Cleon. *So You Want To Raise A Boy?* Garden City: Doubleday and Co., 1962.

The father of eight children is well equipped to discuss the subject of rearing children—a role frequently shirked by fathers. Practical, informative, helpful. 155.2.SK5

*Small, Dwight Harvey. *Design for Christian Marriage.* Westwood, N.J.: Fleming H. Revell Co., 1959.

A perceptive treatment of the spiritual, sociological, and psychological factors in the growth and development of a strong and abiding relationship between husband and wife. 306.8.SM1

*_____. After You've Said "I Do." Old Tappan, N.J.: Fleming H. Revell Co., 1968.

Thoroughly oriented to our game-playing, mask-wearing, and role-expectation society. Shows how a marriage may be strengthened at the possible points of breakdown, and stresses the need for listening as part of the communication. 306.8.SM1A

Smith, Leona Jones. *Guiding the Character Development of the Pre-School Child.* New York: Association Press, 1968.

Contains in a brief, easily understood form the findings of the Union College Character Research Project. Of value to parents and teachers alike. 155.423.SM6

Snyder, Ross. *Young People and Their Culture.* Nashville: Abingdon Press, 1969.

A definitive portrayal of the life-style of young people today. 170.202'23.SN9

Steward, Verne. *Are They Qualified for Marriage?* Minneapolis: T. S. Denison Co., 1964.

A guidebook for parents, pastors, and counselors. Of specific value in outlining the dangers facing those who are too young to have good judgment in appraising their prospective mates. 306.7.ST4

Stewart, Charles William. *Adolescent Religion: A Developmental Study of the Religion of Youth.* Nashville: Abingdon Press, 1967.

A careful analysis of the total development of young people, with an examination of the psychological factors that bring about their individualistic religious attitudes. 248.83.ST4

Stith, Marjorie. *Understanding Children.* Nashville: Convention Press, 1969.

A study of the development, relationships, thinking, and feelings of children. 155.424.ST5

Strecker, Edward Adam. *Their Mother's Daughters.* Philadelphia: J. B. Lippincott Co., 1956.

See below. 616.85.ST914

_____. Their Mother's Sons. Philadelphia: J. B. Lippincott Co., 1951.

Two books exposing the devastating influence of a matriarchal society upon children. No parent can afford to avoid interacting with these vital works. 616.85.ST8

Terkelsen, Helen E. *Counseling the Unwed Mother.* Englewood Cliffs, N.J.: Prentice-Hall, 1964.

Acquaints the minister and counselor with cultural, socio-economic, and psychological factors involved in prewedlock pregnancies. 253.5.T27

*****Tournier, Paul.** *To Resist or to Surrender?* Translated by John S. Gilmore. Richmond: John Knox Press, 1964.

A helpful book on human relations. 158.2.T64

*———. *To Understand Each Other.* Translated by John S. Gilmore. Richmond: John Knox Press, 1967.

A well-balanced, provocative discussion of the problems encountered by husbands and wives, their need for self-expression, and the ways in which each may be better understood. 306.8.T64

Toynbee, Arnold. *Surviving the Future.* New York: Oxford University Press, 1971.

Toynbee gives his views on the world's most pressing problems and tells how history may help contemporary man solve them. 301.6.T66

Trueblood, David Elton and **Pauline Trueblood.** *The Recovery of Family Life.* New York: Harper and Row, 1953.

The error of our times is adequately exposed by the authors, who analyze the trends and lay down principles for meaningful family life. 306.8.T76

*****Van de Velde, Th. H.** *Ideal Marriage.* Rev. ed. Translated by Stella Brawne. New York: Random House, 1968.

A book that has stood the test of time. Provides an analysis of the physical problems of marriage for which the medical profession and the lay public have long been waiting. 306.8.V54

Vermes, Hal G. *Helping Youth Avoid Four Great Dangers.* New York: Association Press, 1965.

Discusses the dangers of smoking,

drinking, VD, and drug addiction. 178.V59

Westberg, Granger E. *Premarital Counseling.* New York: Division of Christian Education, National Council of Churches of Christ in the U.S.A., 1958.

Good in methodology; weak in theology. 253.5.P91.W52

White, Ernest. *Marriage and the Bible.* Nashville: Broadman Press, 1965.

Surveys the biblical teaching on marriage. Includes an examination of the secondary purposes of marriage, discusses the roles of husbands and wives, deals with the varieties of conflicts in marriage, and provides material on the problems associated with divorce and remarriage. 306.8.W58

*****Wilder-Smith, A. E.** *The Drug Users.* Wheaton: Harold Shaw Publishers, 1969.

A pharmacologist writes with authority on LSD, marijuana, hashish, tranquilizers, amphetamines, and morphine. His material is relevant, timely, and greatly needed. 615.78.W64

Williamson, Robert Clifford. *Marriage and Family Relations.* New York: John Wiley and Sons, 1966.

An extensive, technical treatment covering all the major facets of family life and development. Ideal for the counselor or pastor. 306.87.W67

Winter, Gibson. *Love and Conflict.* Garden City: Doubleday and Co., 1958.

Discusses the new patterns in family relationships that the writer sees developing in our changing society, including the abdication of the father as head of the family, the lack of intimate unity, and the alienation of the rising generation. 306.8.W73

Wittenberg, Rudolph M. *The Troubled Generation.* New York: Association Press, 1967.

Calls attention to the post-adolescent period, where teen-agers face new and difficult problems. Analyzes the causes behind drug addiction, violence, and crime, and offers counsel that pastors will find particularly helpful. 155.5.W78

Wright, Helena. *The Sex Factor in Marriage.* London: Williams and Norgate, 1937.

One of the best books on the subject. 306.8.W93

Wynn, John Charles. *How Christian Parents Face Family Problems.* Philadelphia: Westminster Press, 1955.

Contains sane counsel for troubled parents, and includes a Christian approach to child-rearing. Nontechnical. 249.W99

9

Pastoral Theology

What has happened to the image of the pastor in the community? To what extent is he fulfilling his calling, and is this compatible with what people have come to expect of him?

Some churches expect their pastors to be good administrators, possess a knowledge of accounting procedures, be able to raise money, and have Roberts *Rules of Order* at their fingertips. Other churches require their ministers to be competent counselors with expertise in the use of the different techniques, and with the ability to fit into all kinds of situations. Still others expect their pastors to be eloquent pulpiteers, though surprisingly little place is given to the exposition of the Word of God.

A knowledge of administration, the ability to counsel, and oratorical gift are important, but they should never take the place of the preaching of the gospel. Unfortunately, the image of the pastor has changed. To be sure, the change did not come about overnight. The inroads of liberal theology that caused many to abdicate their role as messengers of the Lord began by depriving them of their belief in the authoritative, inerrant Word of God. The result is plain to see.

The pastor's new image has been appropriately described by a homiletics professor who satirically remarked that the teacher of biblical truth has become "the congregation's congenial, ever-faithful, ever-helpful 'boy scout,' who is the darling of old ladies and the epitome of circumspect behavior with the younger ones; the father image for the young men, and the congenial companion of the aged; and the affable raconteur at church socials and civic luncheons."

But what of the minister as the man of God? What of his place in the community as the prophet of the Lord? Why has his calling to preach been so sadly sidelined? Some are prone to blame modern methods of communication, but these can never replace a Spirit-controlled personality imparting to spiritually hungry people the truths of the Scriptures.

Some people feel that pastors are no longer in touch with what is going on about them. They feel that with the knowledge explosion, pastors and preaching have become obsolete. Forgetting the fact that man is more than the material, they claim that preachers are seldom abreast of social trends, psychological progress, and economic developments. However, these critics have forgotten that man has a spiritual nature as well, and that the pastor's primary responsibility is to minister to man's spiritual needs.

The Bible, however, contains the revelation of God for the whole man—his material and immaterial natures, and his mind, emotions, and will as well. To be successful, the pastor needs to know how to apply the truths of the Word of God to the many and varied needs of man. In order to be able to do this, he needs to be widely read. The following list of books aims at being qualitative rather than quantitative. It makes an honest attempt to touch all bases and include titles that will contribute directly to the work of the ministry.

Considerable space could have been devoted to books of sermons and sermon illustrations. In the first place, only a few representative works of sermons have been included. Nothing can replace the personal exposure of the preacher to the Word of God, and the sermons of others should only be studied for the ideas that can be gleaned from them.

Secondly, where illustrations are concerned, I have included several entries to works that will lead you to contemporary information and the kind of human interest stories or factual data found in newspapers and authoritative sources of information. Beginning with the entry *Annual Register of World Events,* you will find several reference volumes that will lead you to an abundance of illustrative material on every imaginable topic. All you will need to do is cull the information from the sources you consult.

Many pastors of my acquaintance overlook the value of dictionaries, contemporary literature, humor, quotations, and poetry as sources of illustrations. A few suggestions have been made in this regard as well. *All of these works will be found in public and institutional libraries, and so it will not be necessary for you to purchase or subscribe to these reference volumes.*

Finally, recognizing the value of sound counsel, considerable space has been devoted to books in the area of pastoral counseling. The books selected include elementary and introductory titles, as well as studies for those who are more advanced. In addition, several worthy volumes of books in the area of church administration and leadership have been included for those who feel that they may need to become better informed in these areas of practical work.

A well-selected reading program will assist you in keeping abreast of the latest developments in each of these different areas of responsibility and will contribute significantly to the overall value and scope of your ministry.

*Baker's Dictionary of Practical The-
ology. Edited by Ralph G. Turnbull.

Grand Rapids: Baker Book House, 1967. A comprehensive reference book covering virtually every aspect of practical theology. Helpful bibliographies are included at the end of each division. 250'.03.T84B

Blackwood, Andrew Watterson. *Pastoral Leadership.* Nashville: Abingdon-Cokesbury Press, 1949.

A thorough treatment covering the executive and administrative duties of pastors. 250.B56

_____. *Pastoral Work.* Grand Rapids: Baker Book House, 1954.

A helpful, inspiring treatise on *how* the pastor can meet the demands of his office. 250.B56P

Calkins, Raymond. *The Romance of the Ministry.* Boston: Pilgrim Press, 1944.

Geared to the personal life of the pastor. 250.C12

Carpenter, Edmund Snow and **Marshall McLuhan,** eds. *Explorations in Communication: An Anthology.*

A significant compendium of articles from *Explorations,* a journal on communication. 006.082.C22

Colton, Clarence Eugene. *The Minister's Mission.* Grand Rapids: Zondervan Publishing House, 1961.

Focuses on ministerial responsibilities and relationships. 250.C72

Dobbins, Gaines Stanley. *Building Better Churches: A Guide to Pastoral Ministry.* Nashville: Broadman Press, 1947.

An extensive treatment of pastoral theology. 250.D65

Fallaw, Wesner. *The Case Method in Pastoral and Lay Education.* Philadelphia: Westminster Press, 1963.

An existential approach to religious education. A provocative work. 250.F19

Goulooze, William. *The Christian Worker's Handbook.* Grand Rapids: Baker Book House, 1953.

Contains a compendium of passages of Scripture that may be used whenever problem situations are encountered, or when the pastor is dealing with Chris-tians facing different crises. Included are ceremonies for a Christian marriage and a commital of the dead. 250.G72

Jefferson, Charles Edward. *The Building of the Church.* Grand Rapids: Baker Book House, 1969.

Reprinted from the first edition of 1910, these Lyman Beecher Lectures stress the NT foundation of the church and its pattern for building the church. 250.J35 1969

***Kent, Homer Austin, Sr.** *The Pastor and His Work.* Chicago: Moody Press, 1963.

A realistic approach to the pastoral ministry. Provides numerous important and practical ideas for those occupying the pastoral office. 250.K41

Lightfoot, Joseph Barber. *The Christian Ministry.* London: Macmillan Co., 1903.

A definitive essay reprinted from the writer's *Commentary on the Epistle to the Philippians,* and afterward published in *Dissertations on the Apostolic Age.* May be read with profit by everyone entering the ministry. Anglican. 250.L62

***Morgan, George Campbell.** *The Ministry of the Word.* Grand Rapids: Baker Book House, 1970.

This valuable tool defines the biblically prescribed task of the pastor. May well serve to restore the preaching of the Word to its rightful place. Originally published in 1919. 250.M82 1970

Morison, James. *Sheaves of Ministry.* London: Hodder and Stoughton, 1890.

A Scottish preacher shares his experiences with ministerial candidates. 250.M82

***Robertson, Archibald Thomas.** *The Glory of the Ministry: Paul's Exaltation in Preaching.* Grand Rapids: Baker Book House, 1967.

This expository treatment covers II Corinthians 2:12—6:10 and includes a wealth of practical, edifying, and usable material. Geared to human needs. Of particular value to those who have become discouraged in the ministry. Originally published in 1911. 250.R54 1967

Shedd, William Greenough Thayer. *Homiletics and Pastoral Theology.* London: Banner of Truth Trust, 1965.

These studies focus on the preparation and delivery of biblical messages and conclude with an assessment of pastoral theology. Reprinted from the 1873 edition. 250.SH3 1965

***Spurgeon, Charles Haddon.** Lectures to My Students.* Grand Rapids: Zondervan Publishing House, 1955.

This indispensable work covers every facet of the pastor's life, including his calling, preparation for the ministry, visitation program, private and public prayer life, methods of preaching, use of illustrations, and so on. Deserves careful reading once a year. Based on three series of lectures, and published 1874-94. 250.SP9 1955

***Stott, John Robert Walmsey.** The Preacher's Portrait.* Grand Rapids: Wm. B. Eerdmans Publishing Co., 1964.

A penetrating analysis of the biblical qualifications of the preacher. Views the man and his mission in the light of the scriptural teaching on the preacher as a steward, a herald, a witness, a father, and a servant. 250.ST7

Thielicke, Helmut. *The Trouble with the Church.* Translated by John W. Doberstein. New York: Harper and Row, 1965.

A candid appraisal of the contemporary church, with a condemnation of its busyness for busyness' sake, coupled with a clear-cut call for renewal. An evaluation of the character of the pastor and the quality of his preaching. 250.T34

Thiessen, John C. *Pastoring the Smaller Church.* Grand Rapids: Zondervan Publishing House, 1962.

A guide for those preparing for the ministry. 250.T34P

Thomas, William Henry Griffith. *Ministerial Life and Work.* Chicago: Bible Institute Colportage, 1927.

An abridgment of *The Work of the Ministry.* 250.T36

———. *The Work of the Ministry.* London: Hodder and Stoughton, 1911.

A valuable treatise covering different aspects of ministerial life and service. Anglican. 250.T36W

***Turnbull, Ralph G.** The Preacher's Heritage, Task and Resources.* Grand Rapids: Baker Book House, 1968.

Invaluable for preachers and those preparing for the ministry. Well researched. 250.T84

Vanderbilt, Amy. *New Complete Book of Etiquette.* Garden City: Doubleday and Co., 1963.

A complete guide covering every conceivable situation and occasion. 395.V26

Vinet, Alexander Rodolphe. *Pastoral Theology, or The Theory of the Evangelical Ministry.* New York: Ivison, Phinney, Blakeman and Co., 1866.

An exhaustive study regarded by many as one of the most satisfactory and complete works on the subject. 250.V75

PREACHING, HOMILETICS

Bartlett, Gene E. *The Audacity of Preaching.* New York: Harper and Brothers, 1962.

An encouraging volume for those ministers who have, at one time or another, questioned their own identity or wondered whether their messages are relevant to the needs of their parishioners. 251'.01.B28

Blackwood, Andrew Watterson. *Biographical Preaching for Today.* New York: Abingdon Press, 1953.

Replete with information on sermon strategy and how to adapt the principles of biographical preaching to pastoral situations. 251'.01.B56

————. *Expository Preaching for Today.* New York: Abingdon Press, 1953.

A presentation of the aims and methods of expository preaching. 251'.8.B56

————. *The Fine Art of Preaching.* New York: Macmillan Co., 1937.

A guide to the use of biblical materials in the construction of a sermon. 251'.01.B56F

*————. *Planning a Year's Pulpit Work.* New York: Abingdon Press, 1942.

An indispensable work geared to helping the minister with the task of long-range planning. 251.01.B56P

————. *The Preparation of Sermons.* New York: Abingdon Press, 1948.

Emphasizes the need for preparing for the pulpit rather than relying on the personality of the preacher. 251.01.B56S

Bowie, Walter Russell. *Preaching.* New York: Abingdon Press, 1954.

Help to young ministers who desire to develop good habits for sermon preparation. 251'.01.B67

Booth, John Nicholls. *The Quest for Preaching Power.* New York: Macmillan Co., 1943.

An approach to sermon construction based on a study of the techniques of great men of the past. 251'.01.B64

Broadus, John Albert. *Lectures on the History of Preaching.* New York: Sheldon and Co., 1876.

A standard work. 251'.009.B78

*————. *On the Preparation and Delivery of Sermons.* Rev. ed. by Jesse Burton Weatherspoon. New York: Harper and Row, 1943.

This work has been a standard treatment on the fundamentals of homiletics for over a century. First published in 1870. 251'.01.B78 1943

Brooks, Phillips. *Lectures on Preaching.*

Grand Rapids: Zondervan Publishing House, n.d.

Contains eight lectures on preaching that were delivered at Yale University as part of the Lyman Beecher Lectures, 1877. 251'.01.B79

Brown, Henry Clifton, Jr., H. Gordon Clanard and **Jessie J. Northcutt.** *Steps to the Sermon: A Plan for Sermon Preparation.* Nashville: Broadman Press, 1963.

Spells out how to write a sermon. Methodological. 251'.01.B81

Buttrick, George Arthur. *Jesus Came Preaching.* New York: Charles Scribner's Sons, 1931.

Based on lectures delivered at Yale University, these messages stress the place of the preacher in the world and seek to recover his lost authority. Dated. 251'.01.B98

Caemmerer, Richard Rudolph. *Preaching for the Church.* St. Louis: Concordia Publishing House, 1959.

A textbook on homiletics that is especially helpful for its information on preaching through the Christian calendar. 251'.01.C11

Calkins, Harold L. *Master Preachers, Their Study and Devotional Habits.* Washington, D.C.: Review and Herald Publishing Association, 1960.

A helpful study of British and American preachers. 251'.09.C12

Cleland, James T. *Preaching to Be Understood.* Nashville: Abingdon Press, 1965.

Based on the Warrack Lectures for 1964, this readable discussion of the problems of contemporary preaching describes the source of the preacher's authority, the message he proclaims, and the principles of sound interpretation. 251'.01.C58

*Clowney, Edmund P.** *Preaching and Biblical Theology.* Grand Rapids: Wm. B. Eerdmans Publishing Co., 1961.

A scholarly, biblically oriented contribution to the continuing debate over the nature and method of biblical theology. 251'.01.C62

Coffin, Henry Sloane. *Communion Through Preaching: The Monstrance of the Gospel.* New York: Charles Scribner's Sons, 1952.

†Containing lectures delivered at Seabury-Western Theological Seminary, Evanston, these studies survey the field from a distinctly liberal point of view. 251'.01.C65

Dale, Robert William. *Nine Lectures on Preaching.* London: Hodder and Stoughton, 1898.

Of historical value. 251'01.D15

Dargan, Edwin Charles. *The Art of Preaching in the Light of Its History.* 2 vols. New York: George H. Doran Co., 1922.

A history of homiletics. Unique in its field. 251'.009.D24

———. *The History of Preaching.* 2 vols. Grand Rapids: Baker Book House, 1968.

Surveys the history of preaching from apostolic times to 1900. Possibly the most complete and authoritative work of its kind. First published in 1905. 251'.009.D24H 1968

*Davis, Henry Grady. *Design for Preaching.* Philadelphia: Fortress Press, 1958.

Emphasizes the growth-process of a sermon from a single idea into the substance of the message itself. Clear and comprehensive. Will be of great help to preachers who wish to become better expositors. 251'.01.D29

Farmer, Herbert Henry. *The Servant of the Word.* New York: Charles Scribner's Sons, 1942.

Emphasizes the fact that effective communication can only take place when minister and hearer understand the place of preaching in the life of the church. 251'.01.F22

Faw, Chalmer E. *A Guide to Biblical*

Preaching. Nashville: Broadman Press, 1962.

A systematic approach to the preparation of sermons that can lead to a lifetime of profitable biblical preaching. 251'01.F28

Forsyth, Peter Taylor. *Positive Preaching and the Modern Mind.* Grand Rapids: Wm. B. Eerdmans Publishing Co., 1964.

Emphasizes the need for including the element of judgment and the element of love in preaching, coupled with an ethical reform in doctrine, a practical holiness of life, and a conviction that faith has a basis in history. First published in 1907. 251'.01.F77

Garvie, Alfred Ernest. *The Christian Preacher.* New York: Charles Scribner's Sons, 1921.

A survey of the history of preaching, with a discussion of the preacher and his homiletic methodology. 251'.01.G19

Gammie, Alexander. *Preachers I Have Heard.* London: Pickering and Inglis, 1945.

Personal impressions of great preachers of a generation past. 251'.09.G14

Garrison, Webb B. *Creative Imagination in Preaching.* Nashville: Abingdon Press, 1960.

One of the few books of its kind. Should be read in conjunction with Osborn's *Applied Imagination.* 251'.001.G19

———. *The Preacher and His Audience.* Old Tappen, N.J.: Fleming H. Revell Co., 1954.

A clear explanation of the methods by which a preacher communicates with his congregation. Psychological. 251'.01.G19P

Jackson, Edgar Newman. *A Psychology for Preaching.* Great Neck, N.Y.: Channel Press, 1961.

An attempt on the part of a Methodist preacher to bring the "insights" of modern psychology to the aid of pastoral preaching. 251'.01.J13

Jones, Edgar DeWitt. *The Royalty of the Pulpit.* New York: Harper and Brothers, 1951.

Focuses on the men who delivered the Lyman Beecher Lectures on preaching at Yale University. Thematic. 251'.09.J71

Kemp, Charles F. *Life-Situation Preaching.* St. Louis: Bethany Press, 1956.

A rationale for gearing one's preaching to life's problems. Replete with model messages and biographies. 251'.01.K32

_____. *Pastoral Preaching.* St. Louis: Bethany Press, 1963.

A book designed to help pastors meet the personal needs of their people. 251'.01.K32P

Killinger, John. *The Centrality of Preaching in the Total Task of the Ministry.* Waco: World Books, 1969.

Rejects the slogan that preaching is "the bogus currency of a bankrupt ministry," and redefines the place of preaching in the ministry today. 251'.01.K55

Koller, Charles W. *Expository Preaching without Notes.* Grand Rapids: Baker Book House, 1962.

This book has also been bound with *Sermons Preached without Notes.* The work has grown out of many years of teaching homiletics. 251'.01.K83

Linn, Edmond Holt. *Preaching as Counselling.* Valley Forge: Judson Press, 1966.

An analysis of Harry Emerson Fosdick's method of preaching. 251'.01.L64

Liske, Thomas V. *Effective Preaching.* Rev. ed. New York: Macmillan Co., 1962.

A popular Catholic work emphasizing the techniques of public speaking. 251'.01.L68 1962

MacGregor, William Malcolm. *The Making of a Preacher.* Philadelphia: Westminster Press, 1946.

Draws parallels from Christ's ministry, and blends these into a discussion of the role of the preacher and his ministry. 251'.01.M17

MacLennan, David Alexander. *Entrusted with the Gospel.* Philadelphia: Westminster Press, 1956.

Contains the Warrack Lectures for 1955. Discusses the preacher's personal duties and pastoral responsibilities. 251'.01.M22

Macpherson, Ian. *The Burden of the Lord.* New York: Abingdon Press, 1955.

A careful, succinct discussion of sermon construction and delivery. 251'.01.M24

McCracken, Robert James. *The Making of the Sermon.* New York: Harper and Brothers, 1956.

A practical treatise stressing the need for long-range preparation and the careful selection of texts and themes. 251'.01.M13

McNeil, Jesse Jai. *The Preacher-Prophet in Mass Society.* Grand Rapids: Wm. B. Eerdmans Publishing Co., 1961.

An analysis of the problems of communication that frequently exist between preachers and their congregations. 251.03.M23

Mark, Harry Clayton. *Patterns for Preaching.* Grand Rapids: Zondervan Publishing House, 1959.

A survey of forty different ways to organize material for sermons. 251'.027.M34

Marsh, Patrick O. *Persuasive Speaking: Theory, Models, Practice.* Scranton: Harper and Row, 1967.

An informative introductory text. 808.51.M35

Meyer, Frederick Brotherton. *Expository Preaching—Plans and Methods.* New York: George H. Doran and Co., 1912.

A practical guidebook. Ideal for lay preachers. Now very difficult to obtain. 251'.8.M57

Miller, Donald G. *Fire in Thy Mouth.* New York: Abingdon Press, 1954.

An analysis of biblical preaching as a redemptive event. Deals with the place of the Bible in preaching, the preacher as an interpreter, and the values of biblical preaching. 251'.01.M61

————. *The Way to Biblical Preaching.* Nashville: Abingdon Press, 1957.

A discussion on how to communicate the gospel in depth. A sequel to *Fire in Thy Mouth.* 251'.01.M61W

Morgan, George Campbell. *Preaching.* Westwood, N.J.: Fleming H. Revell Co., 1937.

A classic—but by no means his best work. 251'.01.M82

Mounce, Robert H. *The Essential Nature of New Testament Preaching.* Grand Rapids. Wm. B. Eerdmans Publishing Co., 1960.

A valuable description of the NT *kerygma.* 251'.01.M86

*****Osborn, Alexander Faickney.** *Applied Imagination.* 3d rev. ed. New York: Charles Scribner's Sons, 1963.

Shows how innate creativity can be harnessed and applied to all aspects of personal and vocational life. A valuable work for preachers. 155.3.OS1 1963

Pearce, J. Winston. *Planning Your Preaching.* Nashville: Broadman Press, 1967.

To be preferred over Blackwood for its contemporaneous quality. 251'.01.P31

Perry, Lloyd Merle. *Biblical Sermon Guide.* Grand Rapids: Baker Book House, 1970.

Deals with the total process of sermon preparation. Contains a wealth of bibliographical and reference material, and makes a practical contribution to the biblical preacher's library. 251'.01.P42

————. *Manual for Biblical Preaching.* Grand Rapids: Baker Book House, 1965.

In a clear and logical way, the author sets forth the methodology of sermon preparation from the conception of the idea to the delivery of the message. He includes chapters on planning biblical preaching programs and presenting biblical messages for different occasions. Of the utmost importance. 251'.01.P42M

————. and **Faris Daniel Whitesell.** *Variety in Your Preaching.* Westwood, N.J.: Fleming H. Revell Co., 1954.

Explains the need for variety in preaching, and shows *how* it may be achieved. 251'.01.P42V

Phelps, Arthur Stevens. *Speaking in Public.* Revised by Lester R. DeKoster. Grand Rapids: Baker Book House, 1958.

A practical volume illustrating the principles of effective public speaking. 808.5.P51

Pickell, Charles N. *Preaching to Meet Men's Needs.* New York: Exposition Press, 1958.

A preaching guide based on a study of the meaning of the *Acts of the Apostles.* 251'.01.P58

Pierson, Arthur Tappan. *The Making of a Sermon.* New York: Gospel Publishing House, 1907.

A practical study that will be of particular help to lay preachers. 251'.01.P61

Ray, Jefferson Davis. *Expository Preaching.* Grand Rapids: Zondervan Publishing House, 1965.

A popular treatment. 251'.8.R21

*****Reu, Johann Michael.** *Homiletics: A Manual of the Theory and Practice of Preaching.* Translated by Albert Steinhaeuser. Grand Rapids: Baker Book House, 1967.

Pleads for a thorough analysis of the text in order to discover the intended meaning and message of a particular passage. Lutheran. First published in 1924. 251'.01.R31 1967

*****Roberts, Richard.** *The Preacher as a Man of Letters.* Nashville: Abingdon Press, 1931.

An important study that, while dated, may be read with profit. 251'.01.R54

Roddy, Clarence Stonelynn, ed. *We Prepare and Preach.* Chicago: Moody Press, 1959.

Eleven preachers write about their own individual method of preparation and provide an example of the type of sermons they preach. 251'.082.R61

Sangster, William Edwin Robert. *The Approach to Preaching.* Philadelphia: Westminster Press, 1952.

A brief, useful book. 251'.01.SA5

*_____. *The Craft of Sermon Construction.* Philadelphia: Westminster Press, 1951.

Preachers will welcome the reissuing of this highly regarded, practical homiletical treatise. Contains informative guidelines for building strong and effective sermons. 251'.01.SA5C

*_____. *Doctrinal Preaching: Its Neglect and Recovery.* Birmingham, England: Berean Press, 1953.

A very brief presentation of contemporary doctrinal preaching. 251'.01.SA5D

_____. *Power in Preaching.* Nashville: Abingdon Press, 1958.

These lectures were delivered at Perkins School of Theology, Dallas, and abound in practical counsel to preachers. 251'.01.SA5P

Scherer, Paul. *For We Have This Treasure.* New York: Harper and Row, 1965.

Lyman Beecher Lectures for 1943. Contains a stimulating survey of the need for challenging preaching. 251'.01.SCH2 1965

Sleeth, Ronald Eugene. *Persuasive Preaching.* New York: Harper and Row, 1956.

A definitive study of the place of persuasion in preaching. 251'.03.SL2

Stalker, James. *The Preacher and His Models.* Grand Rapids: Baker Book House, 1967.

Taking the prophet Isaiah and the apostle Paul as his models, the author

discourses on the dynamics of preaching. First published in 1891. 251'.01.ST1 1967

Stamm, Frederick Keller. *So You Want to Preach.* Nashville: Abingdon Press, 1958.

†Contains sage counsel for young preachers. 251'.01.ST2

Stevenson, Dwight Eshelman. *In the Biblical Preacher's Workshop.* Nashville: Abingdon Press, 1967.

A recent work containing an abundance of worthwhile material. Marred by the writer's inadequate view of Scripture. 251'.01.ST4

_____ and **Charles F. Diehl.** *Reaching People from the Pulpit.* New York: Harper and Brothers, 1958.

A practical study of the physiological, psychological, and methodological characteristics of effective communication. 251'.01.ST4R

Stewart, James Stuart. *Exposition and Encounter: Preaching in the Context of Worship.* Birmingham, Eng.: Berean Press, 1956.

A brief lecture outlining the essential purpose of exposition, namely, to bring men into an encounter with God in Christ. 251'.01.ST4

_____. *A Faith to Proclaim.* New York: Charles Scribner's Sons, 1953.

An author with the ability to expound the Scriptures in a fresh, revitalizing way here stresses the *content* of preaching. Timely, helpful. 251'.01.ST4F

*_____. *Heralds of God.* New York: Charles Scribner's Sons, 1946.

Offers practical advice to those engaged in the ministry, describes the aims and objectives of sermon preparation, and warns against the dangers facing the minister. Invaluable. 251'.01.ST4H

Stibbs, Alan Marshall. *Words of Faith Which We Preach.* London: Westminster Chapel, 1957.

The Campbell Morgan Lectures for 1957. Brief, pointed. 251'.01.ST5

Wagner, Don M. *The Expository Method of G. Campbell Morgan.* Westwood, N.J.: Fleming H. Revell Co., 1957.

An analysis of the methodology of a renowned and skillful Bible expositor. 251'.01.W12

Weatherspoon, Jesse Burton. *Sent Forth to Preach.* New York: Harper and Brothers, 1954.

Designed specifically for pastors, this study stresses the apostolic heritage of present-day preachers. 251'.01.W37

Webber, Frederick Roth. *A History of Preaching in Britain and America.* 3 vols. Milwaukee: Northwestern Publishing House, 1957.

A short biographical sketch, with an analysis of the preaching styles of masters of the pulpit. 251'.09.W38

Whitesell, Faris Daniel. *The Art of Biblical Preaching.* Grand Rapids: Zondervan Publishing House, 1950.

A vigorous defense of biblical preaching. 251'.01.W58

———. *Power in Expository Preaching.* Westwood, N.J.: Fleming H. Revell Co., 1963.

A manual setting forth the rationale and methodology of expository preaching. 251'.8.W58

*———. *Preaching on Bible Characters.* Grand Rapids: Baker Book House, 1955.

An important, practical work listing the advantages of Bible character preaching and containing chapters on "how-to" organize Bible character sermons, prepare them, develop a series, and so on. An extensive bibliography concludes this practical treatment. 251'.01.W58C

*Wood, Arthur Skevington.** *The Art of Preaching: Message, Method and Motive in Preaching.* Grand Rapids: Zondervan Publishing House, 1964.

Exhibits a knack for coming to grips with the central issues of the preacher's task, and emphasizes the important details of sermon preparation. 251'.01.W85

Yohn, David Waite. *The Contemporary Preacher and His Task.* Grand Rapids: Wm. B. Eerdmans Publishing Co., 1969.

Attempts to discover a way by which expository preaching can become a profound joy and an exciting adventure for both preacher and parishioners. Contains helpful insights into the task of expository preaching, but is marred by the writer's theological presuppositions. 251'.01.Y7

SERMON ILLUSTRATIONS

Boreham, Frank William. *A Bunch of Everlastings.* Philadelphia: Judson Press, 1920.

Sermons based on the favorite texts of outstanding men and women showing the relationship between the text and their lives. A companion volume to *A Faggot of Torches, A Casket of Cameos,* and *A Handful of Stars.* Excellent for biographical illustrations. 251'.08.B64

Doan, Eleanor. *The Speaker's Source Book.* Grand Rapids: Zondervan Publishing House, 1960.

A collection of more than four thousand illustrations, anecdotes, maxims, axioms, poems, and one-sentence sermons. Arranged alphabetically by subject. 251'.08.D65S

———. *The New Speaker's Source Book.* Grand Rapids: Zondervan Publishing House, 1968.

A companion volume to the *Speaker's Source Book.* 251'.08.D65 (Alt. DDC 808.88)

Guthrie, William Dameron. *Magna Carta and Other Addresses.* Freeport, N.Y.: Books for Libraries Press, 1969.

Abounds with usable homiletical material. Treats the Magna Carta, the Mayflower Compact, and similar documents. Ably relates historic precedents to the vital issues of life. 342.73.G98

Kippax, John Robert. *Churchyard Literature: A Choice Collection of American Epi-*

taphs, . . . Detroit: Singing Tree Press, 1969.

Epitaphs classified according to their nature and type, whether admonitory, devotional, adulatory, laudatory, ludicrous, eccentric, satirical, and so on. Taken from epitaphs on the tombs of men such as Washington, John Harvard, Lincoln, Elihu Yale, Daniel Webster, and many others. Reprinted from the 1876 edition. 929.5.K62

Lockyer, Herbert. *Last Words of Saints and Sinners.* Grand Rapids: Kregel Publications, 1969.

Recounts the testimonies of those whose simple faith in Christ was sufficient for the crises confronting them. Also contains the testimony of those who turned to Christ in their final hours. Provides source material and illustrations for sermons. 808.88.L81

Prochnow, Herbert Victor. *The Successful Speaker's Handbook.* New York: Prentice-Hall, 1951.

A very effective, stimulating study that analyzes every facet of delivery, including the voice, breathing, articulation, pronunciation, and bodily actions and provides helpful insights into each of these areas. 808.5.P94

————. *The Speaker's Book of Illustrations.* Grand Rapids: Baker Book House, 1960.

A book containing hundreds of epigrams, quotations, anecdotes, humorous stories, and usable quotations. 251'.08.P94S (Alt. DDC 808.8)

————. *A Treasury of Stories, Illustrations, Epigrams, and Quotations for Ministers and Teachers.* Grand Rapids: Baker Book House, 1957.

The contents of this book will add spice to many a sermon. 251'.08.P94T (Alt. DDC 808.8)

NOTE: *All preachers, at one time or another, have experienced the frustration of searching for a contemporary incident with which to illustrate a sermon. The following entries are designed to place within your reach an abundance of current information on a wide variety of topics. These "reference tools" are to be found in almost every public and institutional library. They will give you access to the kind of data with which John Layman can identify.*

Annual Register of World Events. New York: St. Martin's Press, 1961-.

Formerly published under the title *Annual Register: A Review of Public Events at Home and Abroad.* Places strong emphasis on biographical information and obituaries. Includes a survey of articles on significant developments in the United Kingdom, Commonwealth, and other countries during the course of the year, and has special chapters devoted to religion, science, law, and so on. Supplies pastors with important information they can use to illustrate and apply biblical truth. 313.AN7

Facts about the Presidents: A Compilation of Biblical and Historical Data. Edited by Joseph Nathan Kane. 2d ed. New York: H. W. Wilson Co., 1964.

Contains a wealth of illustrative material, focuses on the private and public lives of the presidents, lists their significant achievements and terms of office, and provides pertinent information about their families. 923.173.K13 1964

Facts on File. New York: Facts on File. 1960-.

A weekly four-to-eight page paper that offers precise information on important facts in the news from metropolitan newspapers in the U.S. and abroad. Accumulative index appears monthly, with quarterly and annual cumulations. Pastors will find this excellent survey of standard news items to contain a wealth of illustrative material. *Facts on File* serves as a type of "encyclopedia" of current events, and its brief summary of affairs affecting the man in the street will provide an abundance of illustrative sermon material. 323.4'0973.F11

Famous First Facts. Edited by Joseph Nathan Kane. 3d ed. New York: H. W. Wilson Co., 1964.

A greatly enlarged edition giving information on the first happenings, discoveries, and inventions in America. Well indexed by years, days of the month, personal names, and geographical location. 031.K13 1964

Market Guide. New York: The Editor and Publisher Co., 1924-.

A detailed survey of over 1500 daily newspaper markets. Pastors will find information relating to population trends, principal sources of trade and industry, average income and housing, and so on, particularly helpful whenever they are considering a ministry in a new area. 330.03.M4

Information Please Almanac, Atlas and Yearbook. New York: Simon and Schuster, 1947-.

Published annually, these volumes contain miscellaneous information on books, sports, the theater, fiction, screen, music, statistical and historical descriptions of different countries, social, geographical, economic, religious, educational, biographical information on "celebrated persons," and other kinds of information. More readable but less comprehensive than *World Almanac*. Particularly useful to pastors for its factual data. Supplies a wide range of illustrative material for sermons and addresses. 317.3.IN3

Monthly Labor Review. Washington, D.C.: Bureau of Labor Statistics, 1915-.

This monthly reviews current events in labor and management and provides numerous tables of statistics. It will be of particular interest to pastors who are seeking a change in their ministry, for it provides information on consumer prices of goods and services purchased by families and single workers, with data

on housing, clothing, health, recreation, and so on. Its primary function is economic, but pastors who know how to cull information will find that it contains a wealth of material. See also *Consumer Reports* and *Consumer Bulletin*. 331.7.M76

Public Affairs Information Service, Bulletin. New York: Public Affairs Information Service, 1915-.

These weekly bulletins cumulate five times a year. The fifth cumulation becomes the permanent annual volume. *PAIS* is an important index to current books and periodical articles, government documents and pamphlets, and other useful material relating to public affairs. Its coverage extends to "all English-speaking countries," as well as English publications in foreign countries. This work and many of the sources cited are available in larger public libraries. 350'.0003.P96

New York Times Biographical Index. New York: New York Times Company, 1970-.

Published weekly, this work contains articles exactly as they appear in the *New York Times.* Each issue is accompanied by an alphabetic index cumulated every fourth and twelfth week. In January of each year, all indices for the previous year are merged into a single annual cumulation. This annual index makes it easy to trace biographical essays since the inception of the *NYBI*. All reported accounts are factual and replete with stories of human interest. They record the hopes and fears, trials, disappointments, and eventual triumphs of people from virtually every walk of life: athletes and musicians, politicians and industrialists, judges and preachers, criminals, writers and entertainers, academicians and ethnic leaders, Nobel and Pulitzer Prize winners, and so on. Preachers in search of relevant material for sermon illustration will find in these pages information on the beliefs, philosophies for success, and highpoints in the careers of notables such as Marion Anderson, Billy Graham, Howard Hughes, Henry Jackson, Henry Kissinger, Charles Manson, Laurence Olivier, Baron von Rothschild, Jim Ryun, Arthur Rubenstein, Jessica Savitch, Peter Sellers, B. F. Skinner, Mark Spitz, Barbara Walters, and Earl Warren, to name just a few. As a resource, this work has been neglected for too long. Its value increases the more it is used. It is available in all large public and college libraries. 920'.02.N42

The New York Times Index. New York: The New York Times Co., 1913-.

Regarded as a master-key to the news since 1851, this index to newspaper items records, interprets (when necessary), and communicates information in all areas of human knowledge. By using the carefully made subject index, the pastor can gain exact reference to the date, page, and column of any topic or incident he wishes to use to illustrate his sermons. 071.016.N42

Index to THE TIMES. London: 'The Times' Office, 1906-.

The British counter-part of *The New York Times Index,* this work contains a detailed alphabetic index referring to the date, page, and column referred to in the final edition of *The Times.* Its value to American users is limited to public libraries subscribing to British newspapers. 072.016.IN2

Statesmen's Year-Book. New York: St. Martin's Press, 1864-.

Contains well-written paragraphs and statistical charts with precise and accurate information on political, economic, social, historical, educational, religious, and military aspects of every country in the world. Its usefulness lies in its comprehensiveness. 320.03.ST2

World Almanac. New York: The New York World-Telegram, 1868-.

Published annually, this important book of facts and statistical information is rated as the most comprehensive almanac published in the U.S. Pastors will find the statistical data particularly helpful. 317.3.W83

SPECIAL OCCASIONS

Chambers, Robert, ed. *The Book of Days: A Miscellany of Popular Antiquities in Connection with the Calendar, . . .* 2 vols. Detroit: Gale Research Co., 1967.

These volumes contain an abundance of material on the history of holy days, lore, fasts and feasts, phenomena connected with the seasonal changes, notable events, biographies and anecdotes. Most public libraries have copies. Should be read in conjunction with Hone's *The Every-Day Book.* 902'.02.C35

Douglas, George William. *The American Book of Days.* 2d ed. Revised by Helen Douglas Compton. New York: H. W. Wilson Co., 1948.

A handy guide to national and state holidays, local celebrations, and birthdays of famous Americans, with data pertaining to church feast and fast days, and notable anniversaries. Arranged in chronological order. 394.26'973.D74 1948

Ford, James Lauren and **Mark K. Ford.** *Everyday in the Year.* New York: Dodd, Mead and Co., 1902.

This collection of poems commemorates many of the most striking events in history and the men and women who have left their imprint on their own day and generation. Preachers will find it full of illustrative material. 808.81'9.F75

Hone, William. *The Every-Day Book.* 2 vols. Detroit: Gale Research Co., 1967.

Contains an extensive calendar of popular amusements and sports, pastimes and ceremonies, manners and customs, and events and incidents for each of the 365 days of the year. Provides an abundance of material to account for changes in the weather, rules for health and conduct, and miscellany of diverse information on natural history, art, science, literature, biography, facts, and legends. Use the public library copy. 032'.02.H75

CHRISTIAN POETRY

Bryant, Thomas Alvin. *Source Book of Poetry.* Grand Rapids: Zondervan Publishing House, 1968.

A comprehensive source book of more than four thousand poems arranged according to subject matter. Well indexed. 808.1.B84

Clarkson, Edith Margaret. *Clear Shining after Rain.* Grand Rapids: Wm. B. Eerdmans Publishing Co., 1962.

A commendable volume that those who like religious verse will find rewarding. 808.1.C56

Flint, Annie Johnson. *Best-Loved Poems.* Grand Rapids: Zondervan Publishing House, 1962.

Some of the best religious verse to be written in our time. 808.1.F64

Masterpieces of Religious Verse. Edited by James Dalton Morrison. New York: Harper and Row, 1948.

Divided topically, with poems arranged under God, Jesus, Man, Christian Life, Kingdom, The Nation, Death, and Immortality. Of real value to pastors who use poems to illustrate sermons. 808.1.M39

Smith, Oswald J. *Poems of a Lifetime.* London: Marshall, Morgan and Scott, 1962.

Ably portrays the life and duties of believers in the devotional gems that make up this book. 808.1.SM6

Strong, Augustus Hopkins. *The Great Poets and Their Theology.* Philadelphia: American Baptist Publication Society, 1899.

Discusses the writings of Homer, Virgil, Dante, Shakespeare, Milton, Goethe, Wordsworth, Browning, and Tennyson. Each treatment is full and readily shows how preachers may use the writings of these great literary figures for sermon illustrations. 928.ST8

Tozer, Aiden Wilson. *The Christian Book of Mystical Verse.* Harrisburg, Penn.: Christian Publications, 1963.

A fascinating book containing poems on all aspects of the Christian life. 808.1.T66

DICTIONARIES

Funk and Wagnalls New Standard Dictionary of the English Language. New York: Funk and Wagnalls, 1961.

The publishers follow the policy of continuous revision, but, for every piece of information that is added, something must be omitted in order to keep the dictionary within the existing pagination. This dictionary, therefore, stands in need of complete revision. It contains 45,000 word entries and a section on foreign words and phrases. The most modern meaning of the word is listed first, together with definitions and concise etymologies. The quotations used to illustrate the usage of words are frequently longer than those found in Webster's, and many prefer these because they are chosen from a wider range of sources and include popular authors as well as the classics. 423.F96 1961

Harbottle, Thomas Benfield. *Dictionary of Battles from the Earliest Date to the Present Time.* New York: E. P. Dutton, 1966.

Includes battles that parallel the biblical record and the history of the church. Arranged alphabetically according to campaign, participants, dates, outcome, and so on. Use the copy in your public library. First published in 1905. 903.H21

Oxford Classical Dictionary. Edited by M. Cary, et al. Oxford: Clarendon Press, 1949.

A convenient, one-volume source book that facilitates speedy reference to Greek and Roman names, subjects, customs, terms, art, mythology, philosophy, science, and geography. Only prominent Christians are included. Contains an abundance of illustrative material. 913.38.OX2

The Random House Dictionary of the English Language. New York: Random House, 1966.

An unabridged dictionary containing foreign words and phrases, abbreviations and symbols, an atlas, and four concise, bilingual foreign language dictionaries, viz., French, Spanish, Italian, and German. It is the most recent work of its kind. The inclusion of "A Directory of Colleges and Universities," "Basic Manual of Style," and list of "Major Dates in World History" enhances its overall usefulness. 423.R15

Shorter Oxford English Dictionary on Historical Principles. Edited by J. A. H. Murray. 3d ed. Revised. Oxford: Clarendon Press, 1955.

This official abridgment of the *OED* was first published in 1933. It contains more than two-thirds of the vocabulary of the *OED,* concentrates on new words too recent to have been included in the older, more extensive work, follows the same basic arrangement as the *OED,* and, while definitions and quotations are fewer, they are generally quite adequate. 423.OX2S 1955

Webster's Geographical Dictionary: A Dictionary of Names of Places with Geographical and Historical Information and Pronunciations. Rev. ed. Springfield, Mass.: G. and C. Merriam Co., 1962.

This pronouncing dictionary includes geographical places and historical names from biblical times, the ancient Grecian and Roman world, medieval Europe, and two world wars. Alternate spellings are included, and a gazetteer contains information regarding the location, area, population, altitudes of mountains, and largest cities of each of the U.S. states and important countries around the world. 910.3.W39

Webster's New International Dictionary of the English Language. 2d ed. Unabridged. Springfield, Mass.: G. and C. Merriam Co., 1960.

The publication of this dictionary in 1934 represented the work of over 250 scholars. It was designed to provide an accurate, clear, comprehensive record of the English language for adult education. Words obsolete before 1500 were omitted. Contains over 600,000 entries and is of value for its phonetic spelling, detailed etymology, and definitions, synonyms and antonyms, and the way in which word definitions are often illustrated by quotations from other sources. The supplementary material is extensive. Ministers will find the usage of the words and illustrations from literature to be particularly helpful. 423.W38 1934

Webster's Third New International Dictionary of the English Language. Springfield, Mass.: G. and C. Merriam Co., 1961.

The publication of the third edition is the work of over 200 consultants. It covers the current vocabulary of written and spoken English and omits obsolete and obscure words from before 1755. Particularly comprehensive for words since 1900, and contains a biographical dictionary and gazetteer. Biblical information contained in the second edition has been omitted. Etymological quotations have been taken from contemporary sources. The greatest criticism leveled against it is its colloquialism, inclusion of slang, and tendency toward vulgarity. 423.W38 1961

HUMOR

Hefley, James C. *Source Book of Humor.* Grand Rapids: Zondervan Publishing House, 1968.

Helpful for the pastor when he is called upon to speak at a banquet or needs something humorous for a special address. 817.008.H36

Prochnow, Herbert Victor. *The New Speaker's Treasury of Wit and Wisdom.* New York: Harper and Row, 1958.

Even veteran speakers will find usable material between the covers of this book. 808.8.P94N

———. *Speaker's Handbook of Epigrams and Witticisms.* New York: Harper and Row, 1955.

A mine of material for use by public speakers and ministers is included. 808.88.P94W

———. *The Successful Toastmaster.* New York: Harper and Row, 1966.

A treasury of introductory remarks, epigrams, and humorous quotations ideal for use in preparing for church socials and banquets. 808.51.P94S

——— and **Herbert V. Prochnow, Jr.** *The Public Speaker's Treasure Chest.* Rev. ed. New York: Harper and Row, 1964.

A handy compendium of source material to make speeches and public addresses alive and interesting. 808.88.P94P

Shriner, Charles Anthony [comp.] *Wit, Wisdom, and Foibles of the Great.* New York: Funk and Wagnalls, 1918.

These anecdotes and biographical sidelights provide entertaining reading and furnish public speakers with informative anecdotes. 808.88'2.SH8

Williams, Leewin B. *Encyclopedia of Wit, Humor and Wisdom.* Nashville:

Abingdon Press, 1949.

A practical work containing 4100 witticisms designed to help speakers regain lost attention, win agreement, or apply important truths. 808.87.W67

LITERATURE

Babbage, Stuart Barton. *The Mark of Cain.* Grand Rapids: Wm. B. Eerdmans Publishing Co., 1966.

Finds significance in the persistent recurrence of the mark of Cain in contemporary literature. A most enlightening and provocative study. 809.933.B11M

Barnett, James Harwood. *Divorce and the American Divorce Novel, 1858-1937.* New York: Russell and Russell, 1968.

This study is a literary reflection on social influences and the way in which divorce novels have been influenced by and have themselves influenced American culture. First published in 1939. 813.409.B26

Buxton, Charles Roden. *Prophets of Heaven and Hell.* Edited by Dorothy F. Buxton. New York: Russell and Russell, 1969.

A helpful introductory work to the writings of Virgil, Dante, Milton, and Goethe. 809.193.B98

Divine Comedy of Dante Alighieri. Translated by Jefferson Butler Fletcher. New York: Columbia University Press, 1967.

An imaginative account of the circles of punishment (including "hell" and "purgatory") and the dazzling glories of heaven ("paradise"). 851.1.D64F

Davies, Horton. *A Mirror of the Ministry in Modern Novels.* New York: Oxford University Press, 1959.

Attempts to define the role that religion has played and continues to play in the development of Western civilization. Surveys a vast amount of literature, skillfully draws the needed material from the writings of many authors, and ably blends this information into a ministerial profile. 820.993.D28

Hammarskjold, Dag. *Markings.* New York: Alfred A. Knopf, 1964.

Reveals the fear, loneliness, and heart-searching Hammarskjold underwent while in public office. Discloses his commitment to the things he believed to be right. 839.7874.H18

Kafka, Franz. *The Trial.* Rev. ed. New York: Alfred A. Knopf, 1957.

Describes in a masterful way the predicament of fallen man and the nightmare world in which he finds himself. He is declared guilty, but can never face his accuser, obtain a hearing, or learn what charges have been brought against him. 833.91.K11

Kilby, Clyde S. *The Christian World of C. S. Lewis.* Grand Rapids: Wm. B. Eerdmans Publishing Co., 1964.

A profound and informative study of Lewis's religion and literary expression. 823.912.K55

Lewis, Clive Staples. *Perelandra.* New York: Collier-Macmillan, 1962.

A brilliantly written novel that describes the attempts of evil to gain a foothold on Venus by adopting a strategy similar to Satan's temptation of Eve. Preachers should be familiar with all of Lewis's writings. 823.L58

———. *The Pilgrim's Regress.* Grand Rapids: Wm. B. Eerdmans Publishing Co., 1958.

An allegorical apologetic for Christianity. 823.912.L58P

Lewis, Henry. *Modern Rationalism as Seen in Its Biographies.* London: SPCK, 1913.

A well-documented study outlining the consequences of rationalism in the lives of men such as Voltaire, Thomas Paine, John Stuart Mill, Joseph Ernest Renan, Herbert Spencer, and Fredrich Wilhelm Nietzsche. 149.7.L58

Scott, Nathan A., Jr. *The Broken Center: Studies in the Theological Horizon of Modern Literature.* New Haven: Yale University Press, 1966.

A collection of essays dealing with faith and literature. 809.933.SCO8B

———. *Modern Literature and the Religious Frontier.* New York: Harper and Brothers, 1958.

Points out that the literature of our times is "the richest mine of confessional experience and spiritual exploration" available since the Renaissance. 809.04.SCO8M

Stewart, Randall. *American Literature and Christian Doctrine.* Baton Rouge: Louisiana State University Press, 1958.

A distinctive study emphasizing the place of Christian doctrine in its lessening impact on American literature. 810.9.ST4

Wallis, Charles Langworthy, ed. *Speaker's Resources from Contemporary Literature.* New York: Harper and Row Publishers, 1965.

Draws from a wide source of literature to provide preachers with resources for their sermons. 808.882.W15

Wilder, Amos Niven. *Theology and Modern Literature.* Cambridge: Harvard University Press, 1958.

A sympathetic and helpful discussion of the relationship between theology and aesthetic judgment as seen in contemporary literature. 809.W64

BIOGRAPHY

International Who's Who. London: Europa Publications, 1935-.

This annual is continuously revised and contains brief biographical sketches of eminent living persons of all nationalities. Facts are minimal. 920.01.IN8

New Century Cyclopedia of Names. Edited by Clarence L. Barnhart and William D. Halsey. 3 vols. New York: Appleton-Century-Crofts, Inc., 1954.

Provides access to more than 100,000 proper names of persons, places, historical events, plays and operas, works of fiction, literary characters, works of art, mythology, legendary persons and places, and so on. In need of updating. Its usefulness lies in the ease and rapidity with which the preacher can verify important data. 929.4.N42

Webster's Biographical Dictionary. Springfield, Mass.: G. and C. Merriam, 1962.

This pronouncing biographical dictionary is not restricted by period, nationality, race, religion, or occupation, but contains over 40,000 names including those of living persons, and provides a condensed biographical sketch of each. Of particular value for its contemporaneity and inclusiveness. First published in 1943. 920.02.W39

Who's Who. New York: St. Martin's Press, 1849-.

Published annually, this biographical dictionary deals with living men and women and, while principally British, contains more than 20,000 character sketches of notable people, with their accomplishments and official positions. Brief. 920.042.W62

Who's Who in America: A Biographical Dictionary of Notable Living Men and Women. Chicago: Marquis-Who's Who, 1899-.

A standard dictionary of approximately 66,000 contemporary biographical sketches. Issued biennially, and constantly expanded to meet the demands of researchers. Contains the names of outstanding persons of other countries, together with the representatives of these countries to the United Nations. 920.073.W62A

QUOTATIONS

Bartlett, John. *Familiar Quotations.* 14th ed. Boston: Little, Brown and Co., 1968.

The most popular book of quotations available today. Well indexed. 808.88.B28 1968

Oxford Dictionary of Quotations. 2d ed. New York: Oxford University Press, 1955.

First published in 1941, this work has been regarded as one of the most valuable reference works of its kind for more than three decades. 808.8.OX2 1955

Simpson, James Beasley, comp. *Contemporary Quotations.* New York: Thomas Y. Crowell Co., 1964.

Provides quotations uttered or written since 1950. Includes statements by educators and entertainers, writers and religious leaders, social critics and people from all walks of life. Subject and source indexes make this work easy to use. 808.88.SI5

*Stevenson, Burton Egbert. *The Home Book of Quotations, Classical and Modern.* 10th ed. New York: Dodd, Mead and Co., 1967.

This mammoth work of 2816 pages and 75,000 quotations is arranged by subject, with a complete index of authors and a complete concordance to the quotations. Approximately 100,000 cross references. 808.88'2.ST4 1967

Wale, William, ed. *What Great Men Have Said About Great Men: A Dictionary of Quotations.* Detroit: Gale Research Co., 1968.

Of particular value for its allusions and witty quotations by friends and enemies of over five hundred people from all times and places. Each citation includes the work from which the quotation is taken. 808.88'2.W14

BOOKS OF SERMONS

NOTE: The late William Graham Scroggie, writing in the Life of Faith *(England) magazine, said:* "Other people's sermons should be studied, not with a view to preaching their material but of learning the art of sermon construction and delivery." *His words are most apropos. The following works are suggestive of the kind of study Dr. Scroggie advocated in his article. They are also illustrative of the kind of diversity preachers will encounter as they begin to learn the secrets of greatness from the great men of the past.*

Alexander, Archibald. *The Stuff of Life.* 4th ed. London: H. R. Allenson, n.d.

Brief talks on the responsibility of Christians to God, the church, and their fellowman. 252'.051.AL2

Allen, R. Earl. *Memorial Messages.* Nashville: Broadman Press, 1964.

Timely, comforting messages. 252'.1.AL2

Blackwood, Andrew Watterson, ed. *The Protestant Pulpit: An Anthology of Master Sermons from the Reformation to Our Own Day.* Nashville: Abingdon Press, 1947.

An attempt to make the contributions of Luther, Wesley, Whitefield, Edwards, Maclaren, Brooks, and others available to students of homiletics for in-depth study. 252'.051.B56

Chappell, Clovis Gillham. *Surprises in the Bible.* Nashville: Abingdon Press, 1967.

A series of sermons about amazing people and unexpected events. 252'.076.C36

Clow, William MacCallus. *The Cross in Christian Experience.* London: Hodder and Stoughton, 1908.

Sermons on the Atonement and the application of doctrine to Christian living. 252'.042.C62

Criswell, Wallie Amos. *In Defense of the Faith.* Grand Rapids: Zondervan Publishing House, 1967.

Popular messages delivered from the pulpit of the First Baptist Church, Dallas. 252'.06.C86

Dixon, Amzi Clarence. *The Glories of the Cross.* Grand Rapids: Wm. B. Eerdmans Publishing Co., 1962.

When called on to preach at Spurgeon's Metropolitan Tabernacle, London, Dixon presented the expository messages comprised in this book. It distills in a simple, adequate measure the riches of divine grace that so powerfully moved him and those who heard him. 252'.06'1.D64

Engstrom, Theodore Wilhelm. *Great Sermons from Master Preachers of All Ages.* Grand Rapids: Zondervan Publishing House, 1951.

A sample of great preaching. Of marginal value. 252'.0082.EN3

Fant, Clyde E. Jr. and **William M. Pinson, Jr.** *Twenty Centuries of Great Preaching: An Encyclopedia of Preaching.* 13 vols. Waco: Word Books, 1971.

Contains sermons of men of all denominations and periods of history. Extensive, but contains little of help to expositors. 252'.008.F21

Finney, Charles Grandison. *Charles G. Finney Memorial Sermon Library.* 7 vols. Grand Rapids: Kregel Publications, 1967.

A collection of sermons by a great revival preacher. These messages speak to the conditions within the church, and also relate to the world in general. Arminian. 252'.058.F49

Gibson, George. *The Story of the Christian Year.* New York: Abingdon Press, 1955.

An aid in developing a vigorous preaching program, with specific material on the origin of special days. 252.6.G35

Grounds, Vernon Carl. *The Reason for Our Hope.* Chicago: Moody Press, 1945.

Eloquent radio messages. 252'.06'1.G91

Hodge, Charles. *Princeton Sermons.* London: Banner of Truth Trust, 1958.

Originally published in 1879, these doctrinal and practical discourses were first delivered at Princeton Theological Seminary and later published in book form. 252'.051.H66 1958

Kleiser, Grenville. *Christ, the Master Speaker.* New York: Funk and Wagnalls, 1920.

A study of Christ's discourses. Insightful and worthy of careful study. 252'.008.K67

*****Macartney, Clarence Edward Noble.** *Great Interviews of Jesus.* New York: Abingdon Press, 1944.

While Jesus preached to the multitudes, He dealt with individuals ranging in social status from the thief on the cross to Pontius Pilate. These interviews are studied in depth. 252'.051.M11C

———. *The Greatest Texts of the Bible.* Nashville: Abingdon Press, 1947.

An example of textual preaching. 252'.051.M11C

———. *You Can Conquer.* Nashville: Abingdon Press, 1954.

Contains Bible messages on personal problems. 252'.051.M12Y

MacBeath, John. *The Face of Christ.* London: Marshall, Morgan and Scott, 1954.

Devotional messages by a leading Scottish theologian. 252'.042.M12

McLaren, Alexander. *Paul's Prayers.* Rev. ed. London: Alexander and Shepherd, 1893.

Containing 30 sermons in all, this volume covers Paul's prayers in depth and provides other studies on personalities such as Zacchaeus, "the lowliness and loftiness of Jesus" in John 4, and Rhoda. 252'.06.M22

*****Morgan, George Campbell.** *The Westminster Pulpit.* 10 vols. London: Pickering and Inglis, 1955-56.

A reprint containing the cream of Morgan's exemplary expositions. 252'.058.M82W

*———. *Great Chapters of the Bible.* London: Marshall, Morgan and Scott, 1963.

Masterly addresses on forty-five chapters of the Bible. 252'.058.M82G

Moyer, Elgin Sylvester. *The Pastor and His Library.* Chicago: Moody Press, 1953.

An important work that needs to be updated. 025.M87

Ockenga, Harold John. *Power through Pentecost.* Preaching for Today. Grand Rapids: Wm. B. Eerdmans Publishing Co., 1959.

An example of biblical preaching, but lacking in anything of lasting significance. 252'.058.OC4

———. *Protestant Preaching in Lent.* Grand Rapids: Wm. B. Eerdmans Publishing Co., 1957.

Writing from a wealth of experience, Ockenga reveals an understanding of the needs of men and the power of God. 252'.058.OC4P

Parker, Joseph. *Preaching Through the Bible.* 28 vols. Grand Rapids: Baker Book House, reprint, 1956-61.

First published in 1896-1907 under the title *The People's Bible,* these expository studies by the renowned pastor of the City Temple, London, sparkle with brilliance, revealing Parker's rare insight into the meaning of the text and the needs of the human heart. The prayers accompanying each meditation center in the passage to be expounded and are at once suggestive and helpful. 252'.58.P22

Robertson, Frederick William. *Sermons Preached at Brighton.* New ed. London: Keagan Paul Trench, and Co., 1890.

All the power and pathos, warmth of feeling and beautiful expression of language for which Robertson was renowned are contained in these messages. 252'.03.R54

———. *Sermons.* 5 vols. New York: E. P. Dutton and Co., 1906-9.

Published posthumously, these sermons focus on religion and life, Christian doctrine, and Bible subjects. These are eloquent expositions of Scripture and abound in practical application of biblical truth. 252'.3.R545

*Ryle, John Charles. *The Upper Room.* London: Banner of Truth Trust, 1970.

Messages on NT Christianity. Combines doctrine with exposition. Challenges and edifies his readers. First published in 1888. 252'.3.R98

Simeon, Charles. *Expository Outlines on the Whole Bible.* 21 vols. Grand Rapids: Zondervan Publishing House, n.d.

Reprinted from the eighth edition published in 1847, these studies by a leading Anglican clergyman cover each chapter of the Bible, contain extensive quotations from writers of the past, and aim at elucidating the text. 252'.3.SI14

Smith, Wilbur Moorehead. *Chats from a Minister's Library.* Grand Rapids: Baker Book House, 1969.

Contains a mine of information on "Where to Find the Best Printed Sermons on any Given Text," a "Discussion of the Reliability of the Gospels by a Famous Legal Authority," and a chapter "On Finding Books and the Books We Might Try to Find." First published in 1951. 016.2.SM6 1969.

The Speaker's Bible. Edited by James Hastings and Edward Hastings. Incomplete. Grand Rapids: Baker Book House, 1961.

This series is designed to provide preachers with homiletical material on the different passages and verses of the Bible. Some of this material is exceptionally good, but it reflects its age. Portions of the Scripture were never completed. These include Leviticus, Numbers, Samuel, Kings, Chronicles, Ezra, Nehemiah, Esther, Proverbs, Ecclesiastes, Song of Solomon, Ezekiel, Daniel, and Revelation. Originally published in 1923-41. 252.SP3 1961

*Spurgeon, Charles Haddon. *The New Park Street Pulpit.* 6 vols. London: Banner of Truth Trust, 1963-64.

Spurgeon's sermons became some of the most widely read literature of the Victorian era. Completed in 1917. Special interest attaches to this series because of the revival which broke out under Spurgeon's ministry in 1855-60. 252'.6.SP9

*―――. *Metropolitan Tabernacle Pulpit.* In process. London: Banner of Truth Trust, 1965-.

Continues the tradition begun in the *New Park Street Pulpit.* These messages make available to a new generation of preachers the essential characteristics of Spurgeon's preaching. Unlike the "Kelvendon" edition, these are unabridged. 252'.6.SP9M

――――. *New Library of Spurgeon's Sermons.* 24 vols. Grand Rapids: Zondervan Publishing House, reprint.

Now issued in twelve double volumes. This publication of the Kelvedon edition has been edited in such a way that the sermons lack Spurgeon's characteristic zeal, forthright application, and unfailing allegiance to the truth of the Word of God. 252'.6.SP9N

*――――. *Treasury of the Bible.* 8 vols. Grand Rapids: Zondervan Publishing House, 1962.

Contains more than 2600 sermons, and provides an example of pastoral preaching at its best. 252'.6.SP9T 1962

Stevenson, Herbert F., ed. *Keswick's Authentic Voice.* Grand Rapids: Zondervan Publishing House, 1959.

Following the usual thematic presentation common to Keswick Conventions, these addresses deal with "Sin and the Believer," "God's Remedy for Sin," "Consecration," and "The Spirit-filled Life." Devotional. 252'.03.ST4A

――――. *Keswick's Triumphant Voice.*

Grand Rapids: Zondervan Publishing House, 1963.

Choice Bible readings delivered at the Keswick Convention through the years. Some of them, particularly the older ones, are allegorical in their interpretation of Scriptures. 252'.03.ST4T

Stalker, James. *Seven Cardinal Virtues.* Grand Rapids: Kregel Publications, 1961.

Dealing with wisdom, courage, temperance, justice, faith, hope, and love, these messages ably demonstrate the characteristics that should adorn the Christian's character. 252'.042.ST1 1961

*Stott, John Robert Walmsey. *Christ the Controversialist: A Study in Some Essentials of Evangelical Religion.* Downers Grove, Ill.: Inter-Varsity Press, 1970.

A brilliant, informative series of doctrinal and practical messages based on the conversations of Christ. Stott shows the implications of these discussions on morality, worship, authority, and social responsibility. 252'.03.ST7

Thielicke, Helmut. *Out of the Depths.* Grand Rapids: Wm. B. Eerdmans Publishing Co., 1962.

†These sermons, delivered toward the end of World War II and in the postwar years, grapple with the reality of what defeat and occupation meant to Christians and endeavor to find a sure footing for faith in the midst of doubt and uncertainty. Read in this light, they show the relevancy of the Word of God to the deepest needs of the human heart. 252.041.T34D

————. *The Silence of God.* Grand Rapids: Wm. B. Eerdmans Publishing Co., 1962.

†These sermons are relevant to an age of anxiety and uncertainty. 252'.041.T34S

*Wesley's Standard Sermons. Edited by Edward H. Sugden. 2 vols. London: Epworth Press, 1951.

The first annotated edition of these sermons was published in 1921. Contains not only the forty-four discourses published during the middle of the eighteenth century, but also nine additional sermons taken from his collected writings and published in 1771. 252'.7.W51 1951

*Whitefield, George. *Select Sermons of George Whitefield.* London: Banner of Truth Trust, 1964.

D. Martyn Lloyd-Jones says: "Of few men can it be said that their preaching was 'apostolic' in character, but it certainly can be said of Whitefield." These six sermons deserve to be studied by all who are engaged in preaching the Word. 252'.7.W58 1964

NOTE: How can you continue to keep pace with new books and other materials that are published annually? The following suggested reference volumes—most of which will be found in your public library—will prove helpful.

American Book Publishing Record. New York: R. R. Bowker, 1960-.

Published monthly and arranged according to the Dewey Decimal Classification system with author and title indexes. Contains the same information found in *Publisher's Weekly.* Annual cumulations have been published since 1965, with five-year cumulations. The chief value of *BPR* lies in the cataloging and classification material (including the DDC number) it contains. Of particular value to pastors and church librarians. 015.AM3

Besterman, Theodore. *A World Bibliography of Bibliographies and of Bibliographic Catalogs, Calendars, Abstracts, Digests, Indexes, and the Like.* 4th ed. Rev. and enl. ed. 5 vols. Lausanne, Switzerland: Societas Bibliographica, 1965-66.

This monumental set includes material about and references to 117,000 separately published bibliographies, with pertinent information about each. The material is arranged alphabetically. It omits bibliographies that appear as part of books or articles. 016.01.B46 1966

Bibliographic Index: A Cumulative Bibliography of Bibliographies, 1937-. New York: H. W. Wilson, 1938-.

Published quarterly with annual and other permanent cumulations issued at varying intervals, this subject index gives extensive coverage to articles containing bibliographies in some 1,500 periodicals, together with books and pamphlets. Differs from Besterman's *World Bibliography of Bibliographies* in that it contains entries leading to bibliographies that are part of larger works. 016.016.B47

Book Review Index. Detroit: Gale Research Co., 1956-.

Published monthly with quarterly and annual cumulations. Provides a relatively up-to-date guide to current reviews of books found in approximately 220 periodicals. Arranged alphabetically by author, with an alphabetical listing of the magazines in which the review appears. Pastors and researchers will profit from consulting this reference tool because of the critical evaluation given each book. 028.1B64

Books in Print: An Author-Title-Series Index to Publisher's Trade List Annual. New York: R. R. Bowker, 1948-.

Annual volumes based on active lists and forthcoming publications in *Publisher's Trade List Annual (PTLA)*. Volume 1 has an author and editor index, and volume 2 contains the title and series index, plus addresses of publishers in the United States. The value of *BIP* lies in the fact that it lists books presently *in print* and, therefore, available. It also contains information pertaining to the publisher and price of the book. 015.73.P96

British Books in Print: The Reference Catalog of Current Literature . . . , 1965-. London: J. Whitaker and Sons, 1956-.

This annual contains information about books in print and available in the United Kingdom. Its value is similar to *Books in Print*, mentioned above. 015.42.B77

Cumulative Book Index: A World List of Books in the English Language. New York: H. W. Wilson Co., 1898-.

Catalogers and church librarians will find this set particularly helpful inasmuch as it contains extensive bibliographic data on the author (his full name and date of birth, etc.), title, edition, series, paging, illustrations, price, date of publication, publisher or publishers, and Library of Congress card numbers. While focusing on English language literature, it records a vast number of books and scholarly pamphlets, proceedings, and selected periodicals that have been published by University presses, religious denominations, societies, scientific institutions, conferences, and councils in all countries. 015.73.C91

Publisher's Trade List Annual. New York: R. R. Bowker, 1873-.

Contains active trade lists and forthcoming publications from about 2,000 American publishing companies. Arranged alphabetically by the name of the larger publishers. Volume 1, however, includes the catalogs of smaller publishers at the beginning of the volume. Its value lies in its comprehensiveness and up-to-date information of prices and publishing trends. 015.73.P96

Subject Guide to Books in Print: An Index to Publisher's Trade List Annual. New York: R. R. Bowker, 1957-.

Includes approximately 70 percent of the titles listed in *Books in Print (BIP)*. Arranged alphabetically by Library of Congress subject headings, with minor variations. 015.73.SU2

PASTORAL DUTIES

*Baxter, Richard. *The Reformed Pastor.* Revised and edited by Hugh Martin. Richmond: John Knox Press, 1956.

A classic treatment that has been a blessing to pastors since its first appearance in 1656. Deserves to be studied in depth. 253.1.B33

*Bedsole, Adolph. *The Pastor in Profile.* Grand Rapids: Baker Book House, 1958.

Combines humor with pathos as it portrays the contemporary pastor and evaluates his preaching and education, tendencies towards laziness, and involvement in ecclesiastical politics. Should be read at frequent intervals. 253.2.B39

Blackwood, Andrew Watterson. *The Growing Minister.* Nashville: Abingdon Press, 1960.

A frank discussion of the opportunities for, and the obstacles to, growth that can either "make or break" the pastor. 253.B56

Bowers, Margaretta K. *Conflicts of the Clergy.* New York: Thomas Nelson and Sons, 1963.

Concentrates more on the therapist and the therapy than on the clergymen, but does provide information that will help some ministers understand themselves and their tension. 131.34.B67

Flynn, Leslie B. *How to Save Time in the Ministry.* Nashville: Broadman Press, 1966.

An inexpensive volume designed to help the pastor "work smarter, not harder." 253.1.F67

Gardner, John William. *Recovery of Confidence.* New York: W. W. Norton and Co., 1970.

An objective approach to the problems of peace, discrimination, poverty, and pollution. Recommended. 309.1'73.G17

―――. *Self-Renewal.* New York: Harper and Row, 1964.

An examination of the basic dilemma of how a good society can protect its members without stifling their creativity or crushing their individuality. 301.24.G17

*Hiltner, Seward. *Ferment in the Ministry.* Nashville: Abingdon Press, 1969.

†After dispensing with the negative charges against the ministry, the writer studies the Christian pastoral tradition from the second century onward in an endeavor to find a "model" for ministers. His material is practical but lacks a solid biblical foundation. 253.H56

Hungerford, Kenneth G. II. *Federal Income Tax Handbook for Clergy.* Grand Rapids: Baker Book House, published annually.

A valuable and informative handbook by a CPA. 343.05.H89

Lee, Mark W. *The Minister and His Ministry.* Grand Rapids: Zondervan Publishing House, 1960.

An assessment of the many and varied facets of pastoral theology, including ethics and general ministerial problems. 253.L51

*Oates, Wayne Edward. *The Christian Pastor.* Rev. ed. Philadelphia: Westminster Press, 1963.

An extensive discussion of the historical role and function of the pastor as a counselor, with an evaluation of the theological context of Christian counseling and a reconsideration of the work of the pastor in the light of present-day trends in psychiatry, psychology, and psychoanalysis. 253.1.OA8

―――. *New Dimensions in Pastoral Care.* Philadelphia: Fortress Press, 1970.

Highlights the importance of counselors' reaching people where they are, and attempts to redefine the role of the pastor in the social milieu of the 70s. 253.OA8

Perry, Lloyd Merle and Edward J.

Lias. *A Manual of Pastoral Problems and Procedures.* Grand Rapids: Baker Book House, 1962.

Comprehensive and practical. Includes a detailed discussion of just about every pastoral problem the minister will face as he discharges his duties. 253'.02.P42

Spurgeon, Charles Haddon. *An All-Round Ministry.* London: Banner of Truth Trust, 1960.

Contains Spurgeon's addresses to ministers and students on the nature and function of the ministry. Cannot fail to revive the weary, encourage the dispirited, and rekindle hope in the downcast. An inspiration. Based on the 1900 edition. 253.1.SP9A

***Turnbull, Ralph G.** A Minister's Obstacles.* Westwood, N.J.: Fleming H. Revell Co., 1964.

A valuable, informative, and sympathetic study dealing with the inner struggles and external problems pastors face in discharging their duties. A must. 253.T84

PERSONAL LIFE

***Blackwood, Carolyn Philips.** The Pastor's Wife.* Philadelphia: Westminster Press, 1951.

Remains the finest work of its kind. Written in a happy, optimistic style, it shows without any varnish or gloss the trials and tensions facing pastors' wives. Helpful suggestions come from years of experience in the pastorate. 253.22.B56

Denton, Wallace. *The Minister's Wife as a Counselor.* Philadelphia: Westminster Press, 1966.

Provides the necessary guidance that will enable the pastor's wife to recognize and respond constructively to people in need. 253.22.D43M

———. *The Role of the Minister's Wife.* Philadelphia: Westminster Press, 1962.

Not an idealistic manual on pastoral ethics and etiquette, but a frank, thorough discussion of the attitude of a pastor's wife toward her husband's work, her family life, and her role in the church and the community. Focuses on the emotions of a pastor's wife and explains *why* she feels and acts the way she does. 253.22.D43R

Hartman, Olov. *Holy Masquerade.* Translated by Karl A. Olsson. Grand Rapids: Wm. B. Eerdmans Publishing Co., 1964.

The dramatic story of a pastor's wife who seeks to find reality instead of living a life of pretense. 253.2.H25

***Hulme, William Edward.** Your Pastor's Problems: A Guide for Ministers and Laymen.* Garden City: Doubleday and Co., 1966.

A frank discussion of the dilemma facing men in the ministry today. Should be read by pastors as well as laymen. 253.2.H87

Jowett, John Henry. *The Preacher: His Life and Work.* Grand Rapids: Baker Book House, 1968.

Practical lectures designed for those who seek to be more effective and influential in their ministry. First published in 1912. 253.2.J83 1968

Oates, Wayne Edward, ed. *The Minister's Own Mental Health.* New York: Channel Press, 1961.

Possessing a clear and full grasp of the pastor's unique role in the community, Oates is able to evaluate the privileges and problems of ministers. He prescribes what precautions the pastor should take in order to perserve his own mental health. 253.2.OA8

Parrott, Lora Lee. *How to Be a Preacher's Wife and Like It.* Grand Rapids: Zondervan Publishing House, 1956.

A discussion of the role of the pastor's

wife that covers virtually every facet of her life, from evaluating her husband's sermons to preparing for a church supper. 253.22.P24

Shoemaker, Samuel Moor. *Beginning Your Ministry.* New York: Harper and Row, 1963.

A practical book containing wise counsel to those entering the ministry. Episcopalian. 253.2.SH7

PASTORAL COUNSELING

Ard, Ben N., Jr., and **Constance C. Ard, eds.** *Handbook of Marriage Counseling.* Palo Alto: Science and Behavior Books, 1969.

A professional approach to marriage counseling. Scholarly and secular. Helpful. 301.42.AR2

Bell, Arthur Donald. *How to Get Along with People in the Church.* Grand Rapids: Zondervan Publishing House, 1960.

A unique book designed to help church members increase their effectiveness in the work of the local church. 253.B41

Berne, Eric. *A Layman's Guide to Psychiatry and Psychoanalysis.* 3d ed. New York: Simon and Schuster, 1957.

First published in 1947 under the title *The Mind in Action.* Contains a lucid explanation of normal and abnormal development, together with an evaluation of recent developments in psychotherapy, Transactional Analysis, and related fields. 616.89.B45

Brand, Norton F., and **V. N. Ingram.** *The Pastor's Legal Advisor.* Nashville: Abingdon-Cokesbury Press, 1942.

An informative volume, but one that needs to be updated. 253.534.B73

Clark, Homer H., Jr. *The Law of Domestic Relations in the United States.* St. Paul: West Publishing Co., 1968.

Focuses on marital problems, and provides a comprehensive, nontechnical discussion of breach of promise suits, annulments, obligations to support the family, the legal status of women, tort liability, protection for rights of consortium, divorce, alimony and custody, and so on.

Wherever the laws of a state differ from the general norm these variations appear in the footnotes. Pastors and counselors will find this an invaluable treatment. 346.016

***Clinebell, Howard John, Jr.** *Basic Types of Pastoral Counseling.* Nashville: Abingdon Press, 1966.

†Discusses how the pastor may minister to people who are faced with the frustrations, disappointments, and tensions of our present-day society. Presents a revised model for the pastoral counselor and a valuable study in the typology of counseling. 253.5.K68

————. *Understanding and counseling the Alcoholic.* Rev. ed. New York: Abingdon Press, 1968.

A helpful book providing important psychological principles for use in counseling alcoholics. 616.861.C62

Come, Arnold B. *Drinking, A Christian Position.* Philadelphia: Westminster Press, 1964.

An attempt to present a balanced approach to the problem of social drinking. Not all readers will agree with this author's conclusions. 178.1.C73

Drakeford, John W. *The Awesome Power of the Listening Ear.* Waco: Word Books, 1967.

A useful discussion that includes in its treatment the improvement of sick marriages, the rearing of children, interpersonal relationships, and so on. 158'.2.D78

***Dunn, Jerry G.** *God Is for the Alcoholic.* Chicago: Moody Press, 1965.

The author, a former alcoholic, furnishes helpful information on understanding alcoholism and the ways in which alcoholics may be helped. Full of sane suggestions. 362.292.D92

Farnsworth, Dana L., and **Francis J. Braceland.** *Psychiatry, The Clergy and Pastoral Counseling.* Collegeville, Minn.: Institute for Mental Health. St. John's University Press, 1969.

Designed to furnish orientation, information, and practical methods of dealing with emotionally disturbed people. Intended for men with little or no background in mental health. 253.5.F23

Glasser, William. *Mental Health or Mental Illness?: Psychiatry for Practical Action.* New York: Harper and Row, 1961.

A treatise designed to help people face life's situation realisitically. The pastor will find *Reality Therapy* to be more helpful. 616.89.G46

_____. *Reality Therapy: A New Approach to Psychiatry.* New York: Harper and Row, 1965.

A landmark book destined to bring about a revolution in psychology. 616.89.G46R

Haas, Harold I. *Mental Illness.* St. Louis: Concordia Publishing Co., 1966.

A brief evaluation of the causes leading to mental disorders. 618.89.H11

Howe, Reuell L. *The Miracle of Dialogue.* Greenwich, Conn.: Seabury Press, 1963.

An important book for pastors. Explains the benefits of catharsis, sharing, and self-disclosure. 253.5.H83

*Hulme, William Edward. *How to Start Counseling: Building the Counseling Program in the Local Church.* New York: Abingdon Press, 1955.

A practical guidebook for ministerial students. 253.5.H87

_____. *Counseling and Theology.* Philadelphia: Fortress Press, 1956.

Shows what will happen when the right kind of psychotherapy is blended

with the right kind of theology. Makes a valuable contribution to the overall study of the pastor as a counselor. 253.5.H87C

*_____. *Pastoral Care of Families: Its Theology and Practice.* New York: Abingdon Press, 1962.

A practical presentation covering every facet of family life and designed to *prevent* (rather than remedy) crises. Helpful for its emphasis on developing the family in the church. 253.5.H87P

Hudson, Robert Lofton. *Marital Counseling.* Englewood Cliffs, N.J.: Prentice-Hall, 1966.

†Contains information on the professional techniques and procedures for couples troubled by marital difficulties. 301.426.H86

Johnson, Dean. *Marriage Counseling, Theory and Practice.* Englewood Cliffs, N.J.: Prentice-Hall, 1961.

Sets forth the basic techniques for effective marital counseling. Good for definitions, theoretical formulations, and practical illustrations. Secular. 301.426.J63

Johnson, Paul Emanuel. *Psychology of Pastoral Care.* Nashville: Abingdon Press, 1953.

†A systematic treatment of each phase of pastoral psychology, with stress upon the needs of the individual, the pastor's own personality, and the relationship between psychology and religion. 253.5.J63

Joslin, G. Stanley. *The Minister's Law Handbook.* New York: Channel Press, 1962.

Alerts the pastor or counselor about possible legal complications. Not sufficiently detailed to be of lasting value. 340.0973.J78 (Alt. DDC 253.534)

London, Perry. *The Modes and Morals of Psychotherapy.* New York: Holt, Rinehart, and Winston, 1964.

A brief, informative volume. Secular in orientation, but contains a valuable analysis of the different kinds of therapy used by psychotherapists today. 616.8916.L84

McKenzie, John Grant. *Guilt: Its Meaning and Significance.* Nashville: Abingdon Press, 1963.

†A British psychologist presents an in-depth study of man's conscience from both psychological and theological points of view. 171.6.M19

May, Rollo. *The Art of Counseling.* New York: Abingdon Press, 1939.

A study of the factors involved in the guidance of young people. Deserves careful reading. 159.913.M45

*Morris, James Kenneth. *Marriage Counseling: A Manual for Ministers.* Englewood Cliffs, N.J.: Prentice-Hall, 1965.

A helpful manual containing the tried and tested methods used when counseling couples in conflict. Covers the entire counseling process in detail, from the first interview to intermittent follow-ups. Of inestimable value. 301.42.M83

*_____. *Premarital Counseling: A Manual for Ministers.* Englewood Cliffs, N.J.: Prentice-Hall, 1960.

A prescriptive book that will help ministers detect trouble in future marriages before it occurs. Provides technical data on counseling before marriage. 301.41.M83

Mowrer, Orval Hobart. *The New Group Therapy.* New York: Van Nostrand Reinhold Co., 1964.

A sequel to *The Crisis in Psychiatry and Religion.* Portrays the new kind of interpersonal therapy being used by clinical psychologists today. 616.891'5.M87

*Murray, John. *Divorce.* Grand Rapids: Baker Book House, 1961.

An attempt to resolve the questions and difficulties surrounding divorce. Provides a biblical approach. Discusses the complications arising within the church as a result of divorce. 306.89.M96

*Oates, Wayne E. *Premarital Pastoral*

Care and Counseling. Nashville: Broadman Press, 1958.

An introductory handbook. 301.41.OA8

*_____ and Andrew D. Lester, eds. *Pastoral Care in Crucial Human Situations.* Valley Forge: Judson Press, 1969.

Of particular value because each chapter deals with a different type of crisis in life. The suggestions offered by the different writers are practical and geared toward ministering to those people who are facing seemingly unbearable problems. No biblical rationale is provided to justify the different approaches to the problems discussed. 253.5.OA8S

Phillips, Clinton E., and Irma Pixley. *A Guide for Pre-marriage Counseling.* Los Angeles: American Institute of Family Relations, 1963.

A valuable booklet that outlines the different steps to be taken in each interview and how to meet the specific needs of individual couples. Helpful. 301.414.P54

Sarano, Jacques. *The Hidden Face of Pain.* Translated by Dennis Pardee. Valley Forge: Judson Press, 1970.

Gives the reader a deeper understanding of the universal problem of pain by pointing out the difference between a biological study of pain and a philosophical inquiry into suffering. Of help to counselors. 111.84.SA7

Smith, Ethel Sabin. *The Dynamics of Aging.* New York: W. W. Norton and Co., 1956.

A discussion of the psychological factors involved in growing old gracefully—and enjoying one's retirement. 301.43.SM5

Southard, Samuel. *Counseling for Church Vocations.* Nashville: Broadman Press, 1958.

A handy volume for the pastor who counsels young people regarding their future areas of service. There are very few books of its kind. 253.5.SO8

*Stewart, Charles William.** *The Minister as a Marriage Counselor.* New York: Abingdon Press, 1961.

†Covers the areas of premarital, marital, and family counseling. By providing this manual that stresses the "role-playing" technique, the pastor allows counselees to develop their own solutions to the problems they face. 301.426.ST4

Tournier, Paul. *A Doctor's Case Book in the Light of the Bible.* Translated by Edwin Hudson. New York: Harper and Row, 1960.

First published as *Bible et Medicine,* this book is filled with significant insights about the interrelationship of biblical faith and the problems encountered in the practice of medicine. It will give doctors a Christian perspective on the problems of their practice, and ministers will find in it helpful material for pastoral counseling. 616.89.T64

_____. *Guilt and Grace: A Psychological Study.* Translated by Arthur W. Heathcote. New York: Harper and Row, 1962.

Explains how God's grace encompasses man's guilt, and that man needs to accept God's forgiveness. 171.6.T64

_____. *The Healing of Persons.* Translated by Edwin Hudson. New York: Harper and Row, 1965.

Interesting chapters deal with different physical and emotional diseases and disturbances, man's temperaments and conflicts, the problem of suffering, the laws of life, choosing a vocation, and facing life realistically. Stresses the need for man to have a vital relationship with God. The writer's existentialism is in evidence. 616.08.T64

_____. *The Meaning of Persons.* Translated by Edwin Hudson. New York: Harper and Row, 1957.

Accepting the findings of Freud, Jung, and other psychiatrists, the author proceeds to stress the need for a meaningful relationship between man and man, and man and God. 137.T64

_____. *The Strong and the Weak.* Translated by Edwin Hudson. Philadelphia: Westminster Press, 1963.

Shows that the psychological roots of anxiety lie in a misunderstanding of the real nature of strength and weakness. Attributes the pervading spiritual recession of our times to this basic misunderstanding, and demonstrates how fears may be resolved and a wholesome life enjoyed. 131.3.T64

*Tweedie, Donald Ferguson, Jr.** *The Christian and the Couch.* Grand Rapids: Baker Book House., 1963.

A Christian approach to psychotherapy, with an evaluation of the problems of anxiety, the understanding of human behavior, and the different types of mental disorders. 131.32.T91

_____. *Logotherapy and the Christian Faith.* Grand Rapids: Baker Book House, 1961.

Explores the field of mental health while analyzing and evaluating Frankl's approach to psychotherapy. 131.32.T91

Weatherhead, Leslie Dixon. *Why Do Men Suffer?* Nashville: Abingdon Press, 1936.

Attempts to answer one of the world's most persistent problems. Combines a philosophical approach to religion with a practical concern for those who suffer. 214.W362

Westberg, Granger E. *Minister and Doctor Meet.* New York: Harper and Brothers, 1961.

An informative treatise ministers should read before engaging in a hospital ministry. 253.5.W52

*White, Ernest.** *The Way of Release.* Fort Washington, Penn.: Christian Literature Crusade, 1963.

Blends the teaching of the gospel with modern medical research in an endeavor to provide an answer to the dilemmas facing man today. 616.89.W58

Young, Richard K. *Pastor's Hospital Ministry.* Nashville: Broadman Press, 1954.

Emphasizing the fact that the pastor's visitation in the hospital should be as carefully planned as the ministry of the physician to the body, or the psychiatrist to the mind, Young outlines the pastor's place in the "healing team." 253.5.Y8

CHURCH LEADERSHIP AND ADMINISTRATION

*Boyd, Malcolm. *Crisis in Communication.* Garden City: Doubleday and Co., 1957.

An examination of the problems and use of mass media. 254.3.B69

Buchanan, Paul C., and **Warren H. Schmidt.** *Techniques That Produce Teamwork.* New London, Conn.: A. C. Croft Publications, 1954.

A basic work dealing with leadership techniques. 301.155.B85

*Cartwright, Dorwin and Alvin Zander, eds. *Group Dynamics: Research and Theory.* 2d ed. New York: Harper and Row, 1960.

Evaluates the factors that contribute toward group cohesiveness, standards, goals, and performance. Includes a consideration of the place and importance of individual motives in setting up group objectives, and the need for adequate leadership in the structure of a group. 301.15.C24 1960.

Claassen, Willard. *Learning to Lead.* Scottsdale, Penn.: Herald Press, 1963.

Contains helpful principles of leadership. 301.155.C51

*Gordon, Thomas. *Group-Centered Leadership.* New York: Macmillan Co., 1966.

By using case studies, the author furnishes his readers with a perceptive analysis of group leadership and outlines the ways in which the creative power of groups may be released. 301.155.G66

Hodnett, Edward. *The Art of Working with People.* New York: Harper and Row, 1959.

Candid advice on the understanding of people and their problems, along with better methods of communication and negotiation. 150.13.H66

*Knowles, Malcolm Shephard and Hulda Knowles. *Introduction to Group Dynamics.* New York: Association Press, 1959.

A basic work that serves as an admirable introduction for those who have had little or no training in group dynamics. 301.152.K76

Leach, William H. *Putting It Across.* Nashville: Cokesbury Press, 1925.

Discusses the rules of leadership, provides guidance on what will and will not work, and shows how to turn possible failure into success. 254.1.L46

Leadership Pamphlets. Adult Education Association of the U.S.A. Washington, D.C.

These pamphlets are non-sectarian, aimed at developing leadership in adult communities. Contain helpful discussions on the formation of better programs, understanding how groups work, different ways to teach adults, the training of group leaders, working with volunteers, enlisting and keeping members, effective public relations, how to develop better boards and committees, how to train people in human relations, education for the aging, and so on. They are inexpensive. 301.155.L46

McLuhan, Herbert Marshall. *Understanding Media: The Extensions of Man.* New York: McGraw-Hill Book Co., 1964.

A candid evaluation of mass media by the "philosopher of the electronic age." 301.243.M22

Milhouse, Paul W. *Enlisting and Developing Church Leaders.* Anderson, Ind.: Warner Press, 1946.

Containing helpful suggestions on topics frequently overlooked by pastors. 254.1.M59

*Montgomery, Bernard Law. *The Path to Leadership.* London: Collins Press, 1961.

An indispensable study of the essentials of leadership by a Christian military leader. A most important study. 301.155.M76

Thelen, Herbert Arnold. *The Dynamics of Groups at Work.* Chicago: University of Chicago Press, 1963.

A "manual" of suggestions for the organizer or leader of a group. 301.4.T34

*Trecker, Harleigh Bradley and **Audrey R. Trecker.** *How to Work with Groups.* New York: Association Press, 1952.

This how-to-do-it book contains helpful ideas for adult discussion groups. 301.155.T71

Whyte, William Hollingsworth, Jr. *The Organization Man.* Garden City: Doubleday and Co., 1957.

Does not deal specifically with group dynamics, but does contain invaluable information about group structure and what happens to an individual who loses his identity. Warns against overstructuring groups. Christian leaders should take its sane counsel seriously. 301.15.W62

CHURCH MANAGEMENT

Allen, Lewis A. *The Management Profession.* New York: McGraw-Hill Book Co., 1964.

Divides management into four functions, and establishes nineteen separate areas of management activity. 658.3.AL5

Anderson, Martin. *A Guide to Church Building and Fund Raising.* Minneapolis: Augsburg Press, 1959.

While not including the latest techniques, this book contains some valuable ideas for those involved in building and fund raising. 254.8.AN2

Appley, Lawrence Asa. *Management in Action.* New York: American Management Association, 1957.

A series of brief essays taken from "The President's Scratch Pad," in *The Management News.* 658.04.AP5

*Argyris, Chris. *Integrating the Individual and the Organization.* New York: John Wiley and Sons, 1964.

Discusses at length the continuing problems of management and the ways of resolving individual differences and merging individual goals with corporate objectives. 658.018.AR2

Atkinson, Charles Harry. *How to Finance Your Church Building Program.* Westwood, N.J.: Fleming H. Revell Co., 1963.

A handbook containing information on successful fund raising, relating the individual to the goal, procuring church building loans, and finishing the job. 254.8.AT5

Barrows, William J., Jr. *How to Publicize Church Activities.* Westwood, N.J.: Fleming H. Revell Co., 1962.

Deals with the many and varied facets of church publicity. Includes information on radio and television as media for publicizing the activities of the church. 254.4.B27

*Batten, Joe D. *Tough-Minded Management.* New York: American Management Association, 1963.

An appraisal of management's growing need for tough-minded executives who can "make things happen." 658.B32

Bow, Russell. *The Integrity of Church Membership.* Waco: Word Books, 1968.

Evaluates the problems related to "easy" membership and the lack of a vital NT ministry, and suggests ways for correcting the situation. Urges church boards to aim at a regenerated membership coupled with an active involvement of all members in the life of the church. 254'.5.B67

Bramer, John C., Jr. *Efficient Church Business Management.* Philadelphia: Westminster Press, 1960.

An informative guide that should be read in conjunction with the books by Peter Drucker. 254.B73

Cashman, Robert. *The Business Administration of a Church.* New York: Harper and Brothers, 1937.

A guide to efficiency in church administration. 254.C26

Dale, Ernest. *Organization.* New York: American Management Association, 1967.

A helpful manual covering all aspects of organization, reorganization, and administration. The pastor will find this treatment too technical for his needs, but he can derive help from the perusal of selected chapters. 658.D15

Davis, Keith. *The Dynamics of Organizational Behavior.* 3d ed. New York: McGraw-Hill Co., 1967.

Focuses on the leader's role in developing a sound behavioral climate in the organization (or church), and gives numerous practical examples of how leaders may improve their working relationships. 658.3.D29 1967

Ditzen, Lowell R. *Handbook of Church Administration.* New York: Macmillan Co., 1962.

Designed for metropolitan churches.

However, much of the information can be used to good advantage by the average pastor in suburbia. 254.D63

Dobbins, Gaines Stanley. *A Ministering Church.* Nashville: Broadman Press, 1960.

Deals with the administration and function of the church. 254.D65

Dolloff, Eugene D. *The Efficient Church Officer: His Responsibilities and Problems.* Westwood, N.J.: Fleming H. Revell Co., 1949.

Has considerable common sense advice on the many and varied tasks and duties of church officers. Chapters include planning evangelistic meetings and procedures to be followed by nominating and pulpit committees. 254.1.D69

Douglas, Mack R. *How to Succeed in Your Life's Work.* Anderson, S.C.: Droke House, 1970.

Believes that success in life is success in your life's work. Outlines principles of success that have helped others through the years. 158.1.D74

*Drucker, Peter Ferdinand. *The Effective Executive.* New York: Harper and Row, 1967.

A wise, practical guide to the problems of administration. Ministers will profit from its careful perusal. 658.4.D84E

*_____. *Managing for Results.* New York: Harper and Row, 1964.

Cuts across conventional management strategy, shows executives how decisions may be made and efficiency preserved, cites examples of creative and effective leadership, and provides practical counsel for all who are in positions of responsibility. 658.D84M

*_____. *The Practice of Management.* New York: Harper and Row, 1954.

An authoritative and penetrating analysis of the principles of management. Help to the pastor who lacks business training. 658.D84P

*Dubin, Robert, ed. *Human Relations in Administration.* Englewood Cliffs, N.J.: Prentice-Hall, 1961.

A well-organized, selective collection of the best thinking and research on human behavior in organizations. 658.3.D85

Engstrom, Theodore Wilhelm and **Alec Mackenzie.** *Managing Your Time.* Grand Rapids: Zondervan Publishing House, 1968.

Shows how a pastor can better manage himself in order to conserve his time. 658.EN3

Ewing, David W. *The Human Side of Planning.* New York: Macmillan Co., 1969.

One of the few books dealing with the problems associated with good planning. Pastors will find it particularly helpful. 309.2.EW5

*_____, ed. *Long-Range Planning for Management.* New York: Harper and Row, 1964.

A book for top-level managers stressing the need for long-range planning and ably evaluating the problems associated with management today. 658.EW5

Feldman, Julian. *Church Purchasing Procedure.* Englewood Cliffs, N.J.: Prentice-Hall, 1964.

Few writers have addressed themselves to this theme. Worth consulting. 254.F33

*Gellerman, Saul W. *Management by Motivation.* New York: American Management Association, 1968.

Aimed at the staff man, middle manager, or top manager and designed to help him improve his skills. Psychological in orientation. Pastors who must deal with committees and people from all walks of life will find the principles of motivation particularly helpful. 658.001.G28

Graves, Allen Willis. *Using and Main-*

taining Church Property. Englewood Cliffs, N.J.: Prentice-Hall, Inc., 1965.

A manual for church custodians. 254.8.G78

*Greenewalt, Crawford H. *The Uncommon Man: The Individual in the Organization.* New York: McGraw-Hill Book Co., 1959.

Stresses the need for providing proper incentives to draw men into positions of heavy responsibility. Helpful for the pastor faced with the problem of seeking out a new chairman of the board, a youth sponsor, or someone to head up a new program. 658.04.G83

Harral, Stewart. *Public Relations for Churches.* Nashville: Abingdon-Cokesbury Press, 1945.

A usable volume containing suggestions to those who have had little training in public relations. 254.4.H23

Holck, Manfred. *Accounting Methods for the Small Church.* Minneapolis: Augsburg Publishing House, 1961.

Seminarians without a business background will find this an indispensable asset. 254.8.H69

Holt, David R. *Handbook of Church Finances.* New York: Macmillan Co., 1960.

Designed to help churches—whether large or small—administer their finances. Timely and practical. 254.8.H74

*Hughes, Charles L. *Goal Setting: Key to Organizational Effectiveness.* New York: American Management Association, 1965.

Describes how overall objectives can be broken down into subgoals for managers and employees. Meets the needs of people at all levels. 658.38.H87

Jones, G. Curtis. *Handbook of Church Correspondence.* New York: Macmillan Co., 1962.

A handy volume emphazing the importance of good letter writing and the ministry letters can have. 254.J71

Johnson, Frederick Ernest. *The Church as Employer, Money Raiser, and Investor.* New York: Harper and Brothers, 1959.

A useful manual for administrators. 254.8.J63

Kerfoot, Franklin Howard. *Parliamentary Law.* Nashville: Broadman Press, 1899.

A manual on parliamentary procedure. Indispensable. 328.1.K39

Kloetzli, Walter. *The Church and the Urban Challenge.* Philadelphia: Muhlenberg Press, 1961.

A sociological and statistical examination of Lutheran churches that raises more questions than it answers and contributes little toward an analysis of the problems facing urban churches today. 254.22.K69

Knowles, Malcolm Shepherd and **Hulda F. Knowles.** *How to Develop Better Leaders.* New York: Association Press, 1955.

Outlines the basic steps that must be taken in the training of potential leadership. 374.24.K76

Laird, Donald Anderson and **Eleanor C. Laird.** *The Techniques of Delegating.* New York: McGraw-Hill Publishing Co., 1957.

A practical work on how to accomplish tasks through others. 658.3.L14

Leach, William H. *Toward a More Efficient Church.* New York: Fleming H. Revell Co., 1948.

Helpful pointers on efficient church administration. 254.L46

―――. *Handbook of Church Management.* Englewood Cliffs, N.J.: Prentice Hall, 1958.

Covers virtually every conceivable area of church management, with suggestive information on what to do when faced with different situations. 254.L46H

Leavitt, Harold J. *Managerial Psychology.* Chicago: University of Chicago Press, 1964.

Based on the behavioral sciences, this book systematically discusses the major categories of personnel problems in modern businesses. The pointers given are valid to pastors of churches. 658.L48

Levine, Howard and **Carol Levine.** *Effective Public Relations for Community Groups.* New York: Association Press, 1965.

Designed for nonprofessionals in public relations. Offers sane counsel on the techniques to be employed. Includes a section on problem solving. 659.2.L57 (Alt. DDC 254.4)

Lifton, Walter M. *Working with Groups: Group Process and Individual Growth.* 2d ed. New York: John Wiley and Son, Inc., 1966.

An able evaluation of the political problems involved in group work. 301.152.L62 1966

Linamen, Harold F. *Business Handbook for Churches.* Rev. ed. Anderson, Ind.: Warner Press, 1957.

Well outlined, practical, and designed for those who lack business training. There are very few of its kind. 254.L63 1957

*Lindgren, Alvin J. *Foundations for Purposeful Church Administration.* Nashville: Abingdon Press, 1965.

Deals with *what* jobs should be undertaken and what guiding principles are required in order to achieve them. 254.L64

*Longenecker, Harold. *The Village Church: Its Pastor and Program.* Chicago: Moody Press, 1961.

A full and complete treatment of the problems facing the local church in a small rural area. 254.2.L86

McCartt, Clara Annis. *How to Organize Your Church Office.* Westwood, N.J.: Fleming H. Revell Co., 1962.

A booklet designed to help pastors and

their secretaries "get the work done" speedily and efficiently. 254.M12

*McLaughlin, Raymond W. *Communication for the Church*. Grand Rapids: Zondervan Publishing House, 1968.

A basic work in which the failure of the church to communicate is effectively analyzed and a knowledge of the communication process and techniques is adequately presented. 254.4.M22

Odeirne, George S. *Management by Objective*. New York: Pitman, 1965.

Holds that if managers organize themselves and their employees around certain goals and objectives, management functions will find their proper place. 658.4'02.OD2

*Peter, Laurence J., and Raymond Hull. *The Peter Principle*. New York: Morrow and Co., 1969.

This indispensable, well-written satire exposes the science of "hierarchiology" and vividly describes how people rise in the hierarchy until they reach the level of incompetence. Pastors, as well as administrators, have much to learn from this book. 658'.007.P44

Prince, George M. *The Practice of Creativity*. New York: Harper and Row, 1970.

A manual on the dynamics of group problem solving. While secular in orientation, this book will still be of help to all who are faced with the problems of committee work. 658.45.P93

Richardson, Lovella Stoll. *Handbook for the Church Office*. Cincinnati, Ohio: Standard Publishing Co., 1972.

A modern, up-to-date manual. 651'.374.R39

Spaan, Howard B. *Christian Reformed Church Government*. Grand Rapids: Kregel Publications, 1971.

A volume on the government of the Christian Reformed Church. 254.057.SP1

Stevenson, Fred Gray. *Pocket Primer of Parliamentary Procedure*, 4th ed. Boston: Houghton Mifflin Co., 1952.

Supplies simple, quickly available, correct answers to the problems confronting those who conduct meetings. Well outlined. 328.1.ST4 1952

Stoody, Ralph. *A Handbook of Church Public Relations*. Nashville: Abingdon Press, 1959.

Contains ideas that will keep the church before the public and help to create a favorable image. Comprehensive. 254.4.ST7

*Sutherland, Sidney Samson. *When You Preside*. Danville, Ill.: The Interstate Printers and Publishers, 1962.

An informative guide on how to plan and conduct informal round-table discussions, formal business meetings, service club meetings, panel discussions, symposiums and forums, conferences, workshops, business conferences, and staff meetings. 301.1583.SU8

*Sweet, Herman J. *The Multiple Staff in the Local Church*. Philadelphia: Westminster Press, 1963.

A fresh, creative approach to one of the major problems confronting pastors and churches of all denominations. Deals adequately with staff relationships, and examines the different "philosophies" of administration, with an evaluation of their respective strengths and weaknesses. 254.1.SW3

Three Steps to More Skillful Management. 3d ed. Washington, D.C.: Nation's Business, n.d.

Three booklets the pastor will find helpful as he appraises himself, his people, and the work of the church. 658.N21

Wedel, Leonard E. *Building and Maintaining a Church Staff*. Nashville: Broadman Press, 1966.

A step-by-step approach to the varied facets involved in securing, training, and supervising church employees. 254.W48

Winter, Gibson. *The Suburban Captivity of the Churches, An Analysis of Protestant Responsibility in the Expanding Metropolis.* New York: Doubleday and Co., 1961.

An attempt to trace a pattern of development of the American church that has grown in a central area, but whose members with increasing prosperity are moving to the suburbs. 254.23.W73

STEWARDSHIP

*Salstrand, George A. E. *The Grace of Giving.* Grand Rapids: Baker Book House, 1964.

Stewardship talks by a professional fund raiser. 254.8.SA3

―――. *The Good Steward.* Grand Rapids: Baker Book House, 1965.

Surveys the biblical teaching on stewardship, and emphasizes the the tithe as being the basis of NT giving. 254.8.SA3G

―――. *Tithe: The Minimum Standard for Christian Giving.* Grand Rapids: Baker Book House, 1952.

Does not distinguish between the teaching in the OT and NT. Includes a chapter on the teachings of the church Fathers regarding tithing, and emphasizes its place in the Christian church today. 254.8.SA3T

Thompson, David Walter. *How to Increase Memorial Giving.* Westwood, N.J.: Fleming H. Revell Co., 1963.

Deals with ways to encourage giving. 254.8.T37

CHURCH ARCHITECTURE

Bruggink, Donald J., and **C. H. Droppers.** *Christ and Architecture.* Grand Rapids: Wm. B. Eerdmans Publishing Co., 1965.

An expensive, superbly produced, and beautifully illustrated book about building new churches. While the emphasis is on Presbyterian churches, the ideas may easily be applied to the erection of other churches as well. 726.5855.B83

Drummond, Andrew Landale. *The Church Architecture of Protestantism.* Edinburgh: T. and T. Clark, 1934.

Too old to be of value today. 726.D84

Hammond, Peter, ed. *Towards a Church Architecture.* New York: Columbia University Press, 1962.

Essays by theologians and architects resulting from the the the discussions held by the New Churches Research Group. 726.5.H18

Harrell, William Asa. *Planning Better Church Buildings.* Nashville: Convention Press, 1957.

A book for those contemplating building a new church. Baptist. 726.5.H23

Maguire, Robert and **Keith Murray.** *Modern Churches of the World.* London: Studia Vista, 1968.

A lavishly illustrated paperback. The authors are professional architects and demonstrate clearly that the architectural design of a contemporary church building should be geared toward usefulness at all levels of activity. 726.5.M27

Scotford, John Ryland. *When You Build Your Church.* Great Neck, N.Y.: Channel Press, 1958.

There are relatively few works of this kind, and this book is worth consulting. 726.5.SCO8

Smalley, Stephen. *Building for Worship: Biblical Principles in Church Design.* Christian Foundations. London: Hodder and Stoughton, 1967.

Geared toward the needs of evangelical Anglicans and Presbyterians. Attempts to determine the biblical principles of worship and the type of church architecture that will contribute most toward this end. 726'.5.SM1

White, James F. *Protestant Worship and Church Architecture.* New York: Oxford University Press, 1964.

A comprehensive study of the principles of architecture for liturgical worship. 726.584.W58

CHURCH MUSIC

Douglas, Winfred. *Church Music in History and Practice: Studies in the Praise of God.* New York: Charles Scribner's Sons, 1961.

An informative volume that traces the relationship between worship and music from the beginnings of the Christian era to the present. Includes the development of liturgical worship and hymnology. 783.9.D74

Ellinwood, Leonard Webster. *The History of American Church Music.* New York: Morehouse-Gorham Co., 1953.

While somewhat out of date, this book provides a complete account of the origin and development of church music in the U.S. 783.09.EL5

Harman, Alec, et al. *Man and His Music, The Story of Musical Experience in the West.* New York: Oxford University Press, 1962.

A comprehensive history by specialists in the field. 780.9.H22

Hoffelt, Robert O. *How to Lead Informal Singing.* Nashville: Abingdon Press, 1963.

A practical guide book for amateur or expert, with diagrams on conducting and advice on meeting unforeseen situations. 784.96.H67

Jackson, George Pullen. *The Spiritual Folk Songs of Early America.* Gloucester, Mass.: Peter Smith Publications, 1964.

An extensive introduction to early American music, followed by 250 religious ballads, folk hymns, and revival songs with their texts and tunes. 784.406.J13

Jacobs, Ruth Krehbial. *The Children's Choir.* Rock Island: Augustana Book Concern, 1958.

A useful tool for those who work with children. 784.96.J15

Kettring, Donald D. *Steps Toward a Singing Church.* Philadelphia: Westminster Press, 1958.

A capable, practical work. 783.8.K51

*Larson, Bob. *Rock and Roll: The Devil's Diversion.* McCook, Neb.: The author, 1970.

Writing from experience as a guitarist-singer, radio announcer, and disc jockey, Larson tells about the effect of modern music. 781.57.L32

Lovelace, Austin Cole and **William Carroll Rice.** *Music and Worship in the Church.* Nashville: Abingdon Press, 1960.

An assessment of the relationship between music appropriate for worship services and music that "tugs at the heartstrings." Ministers, organists, and choir directors can learn much from this book. 783.L94

Mathis, William Stephan. *The Pianist and Church Music.* New York: Abingdon Press, 1962.

A specialized treatment. Ideal for musicians as well as those who aspire to the position of church pianist. 786.3.M42

Osbeck, Kenneth W. *Choir Responses.* Grand Rapids: Kregel Publications, 1962.

An ideal selection of responses for all occasions. 783.8.OS1

————. *The Ministry of Music.* Grand Rapids: Zondervan Publishing House, 1961.

A basic work. 783.0264.OS1

————. *My Choir Workbook.* Grand Rapids: Kregel Publications, 1972.

Prepared especially for junior-age choir members, this material can readily be adapted to any teen-age choir. Carefully graded, and aimed at developing vocal techniques, tone, diction, and interpretation. 783.8.OS1M

———. *Choral Praises.* Grand Rapids: Kregel Publications, 1962.

Sixteen adult choir arrangements. 783.3.OS1C

———. *Teenage Praise.* Grand Rapids: Kregel Publications, 1962.

Fifteen attractive, easy arrangements based on well-known gospel hymns. 783.8.OS1T

Reynolds, William Jensen. *A Survey of Christian Hymnody.* New York: Holt, Rinehart and Winston, 1963.

A survey followed by 160 hymns, with the text and music as the songs appear in many American hymnals. Well documented. 783.9.R33

Routley, Erik. *The Music of Christian Hymnody.* London: Independent Press, 1957.

Concentrates on the subject of hymn tunes, and uses them in their historical and critical perspective. 783.9.R76

Smith, Augustine. *Lyric Religion: The Romance of Immortal Hymns.* New York: Fleming H. Revell Co., 1931.

Contains the history of 150 hymns with the text of the hymn and, in many cases, the hymn tune. Includes the biblical passage on which the hymn is based, a glimpse of the author's life, and the circumstances under which the hymn was written. Well indexed. 783.9.SM5

Steere, Dwight. *Music in Protestant Worship.* Richmond: John Knox Press, 1960.

A valuable contribution to the role of music in worship. Devout, reverent, practical. 783.ST4

Thayer, Lynn W. *The Church Music Handbook.* Grand Rapids: Zondervan Publishing House, 1971.

A complete and exhaustive treatment that includes a discussion of the duties of the music director, the music committee and its responsibilities, and an examination of the various problems and situations that must be faced if the church is to have a well-balanced musical program. 783.026.T33

Thomas, Edith Lovell. *Music in Christian Education.* Nashville: Abingdon Press, 1953.

A study guide planned by the NCC. Emphasizes congregational participation. 783.T36

Urang, Gunnar. *Church Music for the Glory of God.* Moline, Ill.: Christian Service Foundation, 1956.

Admirably fulfills its title. 783.UR1

Wienandt, Elwyn Arthur. *Choral Music of the Church.* New York: The Free Press, 1965.

A discussion of functional choral music from early times to the middle of the twentieth century. 783.09.W63

OTHER CHURCH MINISTRIES

Beach, Waldo. *Conscience on Campus.* New York: Association Press, 1958.

An analysis of the trends that have led to the morality crisis on American campuses. Dated, but provides a helpful analysis of recent trends. Written from a Christian viewpoint. 259.B35

*Blackwood, Carolyn Philips. *How to Be an Effective Church Woman.* Philadelphia: Westminster Press, 1955.

A valuable manual for all women engaged in active service in the church. 259.B56

Bockelman, Eleanor. *The Stewardess.* Minneapolis: Augsburg Publishing House, 1956.

Explains the *why* and *how* of a woman's stewardship responsibilities: in her home, to her family, and among her friends. 259.B63

Chamberlin, John Gordon. *Churches and the Campus.* Philadelphia: Westminster Press, 1963.

Of great value to anyone interested in college work. Thorough piece of research. 259.C35

Crossland, Weldon Frank. *Better Leaders for Your Church.* Nashville: Abingdon Press, 1955.

A compact, practical treatment. 259.C88

Douglass, Paul Franklin. *The Group Workshop Way in the Church.* New York: Association Press, 1956.

One of the very few works that attempts to view the educational program of the church in the light of good management procedures. 259.D74

Evans, David M. *Shaping the Church's Ministry with Youth.* Valley Forge: Judson Press, 1965.

An attempt honestly to reappraise the youth program of a typical local church, analyze the reasons for its ineffectiveness, and integrate the youth group into the work of the church. 259.EV1

Gable, Lee J. *Christian Nurture Through the Church.* New York: National Council of the Churches of Christ in U.S.A., 1955.

A valuable contribution to this field of study. 259.G11

*Gray, Robert M., and **David O. Moberg.** *The Church and the Older Person.* Grand Rapids: Wm. B. Eerdmans Publishing Co., 1962.

The writers have undertaken an important task but do not achieve their objectives. They fail to deal with the relevant literature, omit a consideration of the problems of "adjustment," and show little awareness of the problems of the aged. 259.G79

Hatner, Nevin C. *The Educational Work of the Church.* New York: Abingdon-Cokesbury Press, 1952.

An older work with some provocative ideas. 259.H28

*Hugen, Melvin D. *The Church's Ministry to the Older Unmarried.* Grand Rapids: Wm. B. Eerdmans Publishing Co., 1960.

A significant contribution to an area of study receiving considerable attention today. 259.H87

Kuhn, Margaret E. *You Can't Be Human Alone.* New York: National Council of Churches of Christ in U.S.A., 1956.

The handbook on group procedures for the local church. 259.K95

Maves, Paul B., and **J. Lennart Cedarleaf.** *Older People and the Church.* Nashville: Abingdon Press, 1949.

Assesses the unique problems of "senior citizens," and explains how these may be relieved. 259.M44

Nystrom, Gertrude. *Middle Age: The Challenging Years.* Chicago: Moody Press, 1956.

A book on the untapped resources of the church. 259.N99

Person, Peter P. *The Church and Modern Youth.* Grand Rapids: Zondervan Publishing House, 1963.

A basic work that lacks lasting significance. 259.P43

*Ryrie, Charles Caldwell. *The Place of Woman in the Church.* New York: Macmillan Co., 1958.

This biblical and historical study of the position of women in the church is one of the most definitive and reliable treatments available. 259.R99

Wilkerson, David. *The Cross and The Switchblade.* New York: B. Geis Associates, 1963.

Written in collaboration with John and Elizabeth Sherrill, this book recounts Wilkerson's fight against teen-age crime. 258.W65

———— with **Leonard Ravenhill.** *Twelve Angels from Hell.* Old Tappan, N.J.: Fleming H. Revell, 1965.

Recounts the captivating story of twelve people who came from backgrounds of filth, drugs, crime, and immorality to Christ. 258.W65T

————— and **Don Wilkerson.** *The Gutter and the Ghetto.* Waco: Word Books, 1969.

The story of Teen Challenge. 258.W65C

10

Social and Ecclesiastical Theology

This section presents books about the church. It is a challenging list. Some books raise probing questions on how the church relates to the world: to the cultures surrounding her; to the conflicting ideologies that threaten her; and to the various social problems that challenge the authenticity and relevance of her ministry.

Other books in this section explore the nature of the church, unity within the church, and the polity of the church. In addition, other good books are included that explore the how and why of church worship, the administration of the ordinances, the meaning of Sunday and Sabbath, the conducting of funerals, and the performing of marriages.

You will find in this section a good balance of theory and practice.

THE CHURCH IN THE WORLD

Benson, Clarence Herbert. *Techniques of a Working Church.* Chicago: Moody Press, 1946.

A practical book used extensively by evangelicals since its first appearance over a quarter of a century ago. 260.B44

Dobbins, Gaines Stanley. *The Church Book: A Treasury of Materials and Methods.* Nashville: Broadman Press, 1951.

An encyclopedic work. 260.D65

Lee, Robert. *The Church and the Exploding Metropolis.* Richmond, Va.: John Knox Press, 1965.

†Essays dealing with theological, biblical, and sociological aspects of urban American life and culture. 260.83.L51

MacGregor, Geddes. *Corpus Christi.* Philadelphia: Westminster Press, 1958.

†Sketches the main viewpoints within Protestantism concerning the nature of the church, and presents a thorough, scholarly, thought-provoking contribution that can be read with profit by theologians of all persuasions. Ecumenical in orientation. 260.M17

Marty, Martin E. *The Search for a Usable Future.* New York: Harper and Row, 1969.

†Observes the current search for a usable past among various groups within the church. Proposes a series of responses that he hopes will bring Chris-

tian resources to play in social and political struggles. 260.M36

Poling, David. *The Last Years of the Church.* Garden City: Doubleday and Co., 1969.

†The writer directs his thrusts against the complacency of our modern-day, self-centered church, whose end, he predicts, will come about because of its failure to challenge the goals of a welfare society. By failing to build his thesis upon scriptural grounds, Poling makes the mistake of emphasizing sociological factors rather than spiritual ones. Pessimistic. 260'.09'04.P75

Richards, Lawrence O. *A New Face for the Church.* Grand Rapids: Zondervan Publishing House, 1970.

By reexamining the nature of the church as revealed in the Scriptures, the author highlights directions for congregations and groups of Christians in order that they may effectively provide "a new face" for their churches' educational programs. A revolutionary work. 260.R39

Robinson, John Arthur Thomas. *Honest To God.* Philadelphia: Westminster Pres, 1963.

†A controversial work spelling out the radical views of the author. 260.R54

———. *The New Reformation?* Philadelphia: Westminster Press, 1965.

This sequel to *Honest to God* seeks to answer some of Robinson's critics and clarify some of the obscure facets of his antisupernaturalistic, unorthodox theology. 260.R56N

Your Church–Their Target. Compiled by Kenneth W. Ingwalson. Arlington, Va.: Better Books, 1966.

This symposium tells what is happening in Protestant churches and how political and socialistic forces are arraigned against them. 260.IN4

SOCIAL THEOLOGY

Armerding, Hudson T., ed. *Christianity and the World of Thought.* Chicago: Moody Press, 1968.

A scholarly assessment of the contemporary milieu. 261.AR5

Bainton, Roland Herbert. *Christian Attitudes Toward War and Peace.* Nashville: Abingdon Press, 1960.

A full discussion of the origins and adaptations of the various Christian responses to the problem of war and peace. Includes a discussion of the ethic of the just war and the crusade. 261.63.B16C

———. *The Travail of Religious Liberty.* Hamden, Conn.: Shoestring Press, 1951.

Biographical studies of Thomas R. Torquemada, John Calvin, Miguel Servetus, Sebastian Castellio, David Joris, Bernardino Ochino, John Milton, Roger Williams, and John Locke. First published in 1951. 261.7'2.B16T

***Bales, James D.** *Communism, Its Faith and Fallacies.* Grand Rapids: Baker Book House, 1962.

An intelligent assessment of Marxist beliefs, with an analysis of the claims of Lenin and an exposition and critique of the system that threatens to engulf all mankind. 335.43.B21

Bea, Augustin. *The Church and the Jewish People.* New York: Harper and Row, 1966.

An examination of the Roman Catholic Church's attitude toward the Jewish people. 261.2.B35

Bennett, John Coleman. *Christianity and Communism Today.* New York: Association Press, 1960.

A small but excellent treatment of the major issues of conflict between Christianity and Communism. 335.4382.B43

Blake, Eugene Carson. *The Church in the Next Decade.* New York: Macmillan Co., 1966.

†Contains a collection of essays on the problems of poverty, civil liberty, extreme rightists, prayer in public schools, and taxation of church property that the writer feels will face the church in the next decade. 261.8.B58

Boer, Cecil de. *Responsible Protestantism.* Grand Rapids: Wm. B. Eerdmans Publishing Co., 1957.

A philosophical discussion of the relevancy of the Christian faith in a secular society. 261.8.B63

Brink, William and **Louis Harris.** *Black and White.* New York: Simon and Schuster, 1966.

A careful study of racial attitudes in the U.S. today. The writers include a series of revealing profiles, as well as the questions used in their poll. They omit the very dimension of man stressed so strongly by Robert Fife in *Teeth on Edge.* 301.451.B77

Brisbane, Robert H. *The Black Vanguard.* Valley Forge: Judson Press, 1970.

A detailed account of the origins of the Negro social revolution from 1900 to 1960. 301.451'96.B77

Broomhall, Alfred James. *Time for Action: Christian Responsibility to a Non-Christian World.* Chicago: Inter-Varsity Press, 1965.

A portrayal of the social, economic, and spiritual needs of the masses, and an assessment of the church's responsibilities. 261.83.B79

Brown, Harold O. J. *Christianity and the Class Struggle.* Grand Rapids: Zondervan Publishing House, 1970.

A thorough exposé of the fallacies and evils of the class struggle. Calls for reformation instead of revolution in Christendom today, and laments the tendency of professing Christian leaders to hold to the Bible's inspiration but reject its authority. Passes judgment upon those who adhere to a materialistic and secularistic philosophy instead of developing a sound biblical theology. 261.83.B81

Brown, Ina Corinne. *Understanding Other Cultures.* Englewood Cliffs, N.J.: Prentice-Hall, 1963.

A good, basic introductory work to cultural anthropology and cross-cultural communication. Designed for the non-specialist. 301.2.B81

Brunner, Heinrich Emil. *Christianity and Civilization.* New York: Charles Scribner's Sons, 1948.

†Warns against the severing of civilization and culture from their traditional Christian heritage. 261.B83

_____. *Justice and Social Order.* New York: Harper and Row, 1945.

†Evaluates the problem of justice as seen in Western culture, and compares it to the Scriptures. Abounds with poignant, practical information. 323.4.B83

Buswell, James Oliver III. *Slavery, Segregation and Scripture.* Grand Rapids: Wm. B. Eerdmans Publishing Co., 1964.

Attempts to use the teaching of Scripture and the study of anthropology to put an end to the social evil of radical discrimination. 301.451.B96

Cailliet, Emile. *The Christian Approach to Culture.* New York: Abingdon-Cokesbury Press, 1952.

Views culture from a biblical perspective, and shows that to divorce Christianity and culture ultimately involves the impoverishment and demise of both. 261.5.C12

*Cairns, Earle Edwin. *Saints and Society.* Chicago: Moody Press, 1960.

Recounts the social impact of the eighteenth-century English revivals and their contemporary relevance. 261.83.C12

*Carson, Herbert Moore. *The Christian and the State.* London: Tyndale Press, 1957.

A brief, informative study. Evangelical. 261.7.C23

Catherwood, Henry Frederick Ross. *The Christian in Industrial Society.* Downers

Grove, Ill.: Inter-Varsity Press, 1966.

A detailed analysis of the implications of Christianity in economics, politics, and industry. 261.85.C28

Daniels, Robert Vincent. *The Nature of Communism.* New York: Random House, 1962.

A historical and topical survey of the rise of Communism as a revolutionary movement. 335.43.D22

Davis, Allen T. *Anti-Semitism and the Christian Mind.* New York: Herder and Herder, 1969.

Davis believes that Christians have sinned against the Jews and that they should repent and make reparations. These should include the support of the State of Israel. His work manifests the influence of Reinhold Niebuhr and is a present-day example of "situation ethics" dictating the pace to theology. In spite of these weaknesses, Davis's work has much to commend it. 301.451.D29

Davis, John Preston. *The American Negro Reference Book.* Englewood Cliffs, N.J.: Prentice-Hall, 1966.

Provides ready access to material on black history, with information about essays, lectures, and addresses on black studies. 301.451.D29

DeKoster, Lester. *Communism and Christian Faith.* Grand Rapids: Wm. B. Eerdmans Publishing Co., 1956.

A concise guide to the fundamentals of Communism, with a painstaking apologetic for genuine Christianity. 335.43.D36

Delavignette, Robert Louis. *Christianity and Colonialism.* Translated by J. R. Foster, New York: Hawthorn Press, 1964.

A vivid portrayal of the rising influence of the Roman Catholic Church in emerging nations. 261.6.D37

Drakeford, John W. *Red Blueprint for the World.* Grand Rapids: Wm. B. Eerdmans Publishing Co., 1962.

An examination of communist proposals, plans, and techniques. 335.43.D78

Eliot, Thomas Stearns. *Christianity and Culture.* New York: Harcourt, Brace and World, 1949.

†Building upon his thesis that a people's culture is the incarnation of its religion, Eliot provides a stimulating and provocative discussion of Christian and secular education. 261.5.EL4

Ellul, Jacques. *Violence: Reflections from a Christian Perspective.* Translated by Cecilia Gaul Kings. New York: Seabury Press, 1969.

A clear and decisive analysis of the trend that downgrades virtue and values. Probes the complex issues that have resulted in violence and disorder and rejection of authority. 261.8'3.EL5

Fisher-Hunter, W. *The Divorce Problem.* Waynesboro, Penn.: MacNeish Publishers, 1952.

A forthright statement of the biblical teaching regarding divorce, with an inflexible attitude toward remarriage. 261.834.F53

Franklin, John Hope. *From Slavery to Freedom.* 3d ed. New York: Alfred A. Knopf, 1967.

A substantial discussion of the history, ethnic origin, and role of the Negro in America. Includes an analysis of the character of slavery and the struggle for freedom. 261.83.F85 1967

Fuller, Reginald Horace and **Brian K. Rice.** *Christianity and the Affluent Society.* Grand Rapids: Wm. B. Eerdmans Publishing Co., 1967.

†An assessment of a Christian's attitude toward wealth in the light of present world need. The value of this work for the Christian is minimized because of the writer's faulty hermeneutics and exegesis. 261.85.F95

Gordon, M. S., ed. *Conference on Poverty*

in America. San Francisco: Chandler Publishing Co., 1965.

In certain respects this work is similar to Dunne's *Poverty in Plenty.* 301.5.G65

Haselden, Kyle. *Mandate for White Christians.* Richmond, Va.: John Knox Press, 1966.

In clarifying the historic quandary facing black and white Christians, Haselden illuminates the present dilemma and provides a stimulating guide for Christian action. 261.83.H25

———. *Racial Problem in Christian Perspective.* New York: Harper and Row, 1959.

The editor of *Christian Century* writes on racism from the perspective of one who, coming from the South, has had an extensive exposure to the problem. 301.451.H27

Henry, Carl Ferdinand Howard. *Aspects of Christian Social Ethics.* Grand Rapids: Wm. B. Eerdmans Publishing Co., 1965.

Pleads for vigorous social action. 261.H39

Hershberger, Guy Franklin. *War, Peace and Nonresistance.* Rev. ed. Scottsdale, Penn.: Herald Press, 1953.

A comprehensive discussion of the problem of military involvement from a Mennonite Brethren point of view. 261.6.H43

*Hoover, John Edgar. *A Study of Communism.* New York: Holt, Rinehart and Winston, 1962.

The late director of the FBI was eminently qualified to write on this subject. He was also the author of *Masters of Deceit.* Both of these books deserve careful reading. 335.43.H76

Hutten, Jurt. *Iron Curtain Christians: The Church in Communist Countries Today.* Minneapolis: Augsburg Publishing House, 1967.

A timely, well-balanced discussion of the trials through which the churches in communist countries are passing, with an analysis of their struggle against Communism. 322'.1'0947.H97

Jackson, Edgar Newman. *How to Preach to People's Needs.* New York: Abingdon Press, 1956.

Brings the techniques of modern psychology to aid the preacher in his ministry to people. 261.J13

Kay, Thomas O. *The Christian Answer to Communism.* Grand Rapids: Zondervan Publishing House, 1961.

A practical assessment of the dogmas of Communism and the life-and-death struggle that exists between Christianity and those who espouse these atheistic beliefs. 335.43.K18

Kelsey, George D. *Racism and the Christian Understanding of Man.* New York: Charles Scribner's Sons, 1965.

Provides a definitive analysis of the theological assumptions of racism, and exposes the idolatrous character of racial pride and prejudice. 261.83.K29

*Kik, Jacob Marcellus. *Church and State in the New Testament.* Philadelphia: Presbyterian and Reformed Publishing Co., 1962.

A brief evaluation of the contemporary problem, distinct spheres of operation, and the teaching of Christ, with a historic survey of the results of "mergers." 261.7.K55

Kitagawa, Daisuke. *Race Relations and Christian Mission.* New York: Friendship Press, 1964.

Contends that racial prejudice has been a millstone around the necks of missionaries. Analyzes the situation, especially as it relates to the emerging churches. 261.88.K64

Lee, Francis Nigel. *Communism versus Creation.* Grand Rapids: Baker Book House, 1967.

A Reformed theologian provides a

thorough exposé of the origin and development of communistic doctrine regarding the creation of the universe, the nature of God, life, and religion. 335.43.L51

*Loane, Marcus Lawrence. *Makers of Religious Freedom in the Seventeenth Century.* Grand Rapids: Wm. B. Eerdmans Publishing Co., 1961.

Students of church and state will appreciate this book because it narrates the vigorous struggle for religious freedom on the part of Alexander Henderson and Samuel Rutherford in Scotland, and John Bunyan and Richard Baxter in England. 261.7'2.L78

Luzbetak, Louis J. *The Church and Cultures: An Applied Anthropology for the Religious Worker.* Techny, Ill.: Divine Word Publications, 1970.

This practical book is indispensable for missionaries involved in cross-cultural communication (at home or abroad). Is concerned with the effective introduction and establishment of churches within cultures and subcultures different from their own. Roman Catholic. 301.24.L97

*Mace, David Robert. *The Christian Response to the Sexual Revolution.* Nashville: Abingdon Press, 1970.

Surveys Hebrew customs and the teaching of the early church regarding the training of children, and draws principles that correct many of the misconceptions about sex that have been accepted as "Christian" principles in Western culture. 261.83.M15

Marshall, John. *Catholics, Marriage, and Contraception.* Baltimore: Helicon Press, 1965.

Building upon the premise of the absolute necessity of population control, the author, a Roman Catholic, describes the importance of love in Christian marriage and the need for sexual intimacy without procreation. 261.83.M35

Mayo, Henry Bertram. *Introduction to Marxist Theory.* New York: Oxford University Press, 1960.

Originally published in 1955 under the title *Democracy and Marxism.* Provides a capable exposition of Marxist doctrine. 335.43.M45

Miller, Elizabeth W. *The Negro in America: A Bibliography.* Cambridge: Harvard University Press, 1966.

For those who are interested in work in the inner city, this bibliography provides ready access to an abundance of important material on intergroup relations, urban problems, employment, education, and political rights of Negroes. The emphasis falls upon works published in 1954-65. 016.3014.M61

*Moberg, David O. *Inasmuch: Christian Social Responsibility in the Twentieth-Century.* Grand Rapids: Wm. B. Eerdmans Publishing Co., 1965.

An extensive coverage of all the major aspects of Christian social concern. Designed for use in study groups. 261.83.M71

Montagu, Ashley. *Man's Most Dangerous Myth: The Fallacy of Race.* 4th rev. ed. Cleveland, Ohio: World Publishing Co., 1965.

A comprehensive analysis of the concept of race by the man who drafted the UNESCO statement on racialism. 572.M758.M76 1965

Morgan, George Campbell. *Peter and the Church.* London: Pickering and Inglis, 1937.

A careful consideration of the description of the church based on I Peter 2:9. 261.M82

*Nederhood, Joel H. *The Holy Triangle.* Grand Rapids: Baker Book House, 1970.

This fine book deals with such subjects as family planning, birth control, and abortion. The writer believes that God's

Word can guide families into a meaningful experience with one another so that they will bring glory to Him. 261.83.N28

Newbigin, James Edward Lesslie. *The Finality of Christ.* Richmond, Va.: John Knox Press, 1969.

†The influential leader of the WCC writes of the gospel, not as a religion, but as an occurrence in secular history that contains a clue to all history and the place of ecumenism in man's historic framework. 261.2.N42

———. *Household of God: Lectures on the Nature of the Church.* New York: Friendship Press, 1964.

†An influential work containing lectures delivered at Trinity College, Glasgow, in 1952. Deals with the constitution of the church from an ecumenical point of view. 261.001.N42 1964

Nida, Eugene Albert. *Customs and Cultures.* New York: Harper and Row, 1954.

An introduction to anthropology for Christian missionaries. 301.2.N54

———. *Religion across Culture.* New York: Harper and Row, 1967.

Distinguishes between natural and supernatural communication, and compares the leading religious systems to Christianity in an endeavor to show the different kinds of communication involved. 261.N54

Niebuhr, Helmut Richard. *Christ and Culture.* New York: Harper and Row, 1951.

†A clear assessment of Christ as the "Transformer of culture." Society is viewed as the realm in which divine activity takes place and where "Christians" show forth their conversion in the transforming of culture according to their conception of Christ and His standards. A landmark book. Marred by the author's neoorthodox theology and so-

ciological tendencies. 261.6.N55

———. *The Kingdom of God in America.* Hamden, Conn.: Shoestring Press, 1956.

†A classic in Christian social criticism. 261.N55

Niebuhr, Reinhold. *Man's Nature and His Communities.* New York: Charles Scribner's Sons, 1956.

†In this work the author modifies some of his earlier political theories as he reexplores the moral nature of man, reevaluates idealistic and realistic social philosophies, and analyzes afresh tribalism as a pervasive quality of human society. 301.2.N55

Nygren, Anders. *Christ and His Church.* Philadelphia: Westminster Press, 1956.

†A critical study of the central issues facing those who strive for unity in the church today. 261.N98

O'Mahony, Patrick J., ed. *Catholics and Divorce.* London: Thomas Nelson and Sons, 1959.

A symposium by seven British Catholics on the church's attitude toward divorce. 261.41.OM1

Oates, Wayne Edward. *Alcohol In and Out of the Church.* Nashville: Broadman Press, 1966.

While minimizing the sinfulness of alcoholism, the author provides psychological, sociological, and religious information about alcoholics. 261.83.OA8

***Pannell, William E.** My Friend, The Enemy.* Waco: Word Books, 1967.

A charitable, forthright discussion of racism. 261.83.P19

Parker, Thomas Maynard. *Christianity and the State in the Light of History.* London: A. and C. Black, 1955.

An introduction to the subject, with a definitive treatment of persecution in the church. 322.1.P22

***Phillips, John Bertram.** Plain Christianity.* New York: Macmillan Co., 1956.

A vigorous rebuttal to all who think

that Christianity is out-of-date.
261.04.P54

Pike, Kenneth. *With Heart and Mind.* Grand Rapids: Wm. B. Eerdmans Publishing Co., 1962.

Represents the writer's personal attempt to synthesize scholarship and devotion. Encourages Christians to exercise a degree of responsibility in this increasingly complex social and cultural milieu. 261.5.P63

Pinson, William M., Jr. *How to Deal with Controversial Issues.* Nashville: Broadman Press, 1966.

One of the few books of its kind. Abounds in sage counsel. 261.P65

Ploski, Harry A., and **Roscoe C. Brown.** *The Negro Almanac.* New York: Bellwether Publishing Co., 1967.

This comprehensive volume provides extensive coverage of a wide range of topics in the social sciences and includes in its treatment numerous statistical tables and charts illustrating various aspects of Negro life, history, and culture. Those who work in metropolitan areas or with Blacks in the ghettos will find it helpful. Other helpful works are: Welsch's *The Negro in the United States* (Bloomington: Indiana University Press, 1965); and *The Negro in Print* (Washington: Negro Bibliographic and Research Center. 1965-). 973.P72 (Alt. DDC Z185.P55)

Price, Francis Wilson. *Marx Meets Christ.* Philadelphia: Westminster Press, 1957.

An extensive analysis of the comparisons and contrasts between Christianity and communism. Attempts to relate the theological teaching of the church to the actualities of the world situation. 335.4.P93

Rahtjen, Bruce D. *Scripture and Social Action.* Nashville: Abingdon Press, 1966.

The writer's thesis is that evangelism

and social action are not alternatives for Christians today to choose from, but that both are necessary for effective Christian witness. 261.83.R12

Ramsey, Paul. *Who Speaks for the Church?* Philadelphia: Westminster Press, 1968.

†A critical evaluation of ecumenical social thought today. Confuses Christian social ethics with the formation of public policy and thereby obscures the distinction between church and state. 261.R14

Rauschenbusch, Walter. *Christianity and the Social Crisis.* New York: Harper and Row, 1964.

†The reprinting of this work indicates to what extent the teachings of the writer are still being studied today. An exponent of the "social gospel," Rauschenbusch makes a passionate plea for a reconstruction of society in order to cope with social crises. First published in 1907. 261.8.R19

Regan, Richard J. *Conflict and Consensus: Religious Freedom and the Second Vatican Council.* New York: Macmillan Co., 1967.

Records and evaluates the principal events surrounding the framing of the Declaration of Religious Freedom of Vatican II. 261.7'2.R26

Schaeffer, Francis August. *The Church at the End of the Twentieth Century.* Downers Grove, Ill.: Inter-Varsity Press, 1970.

The author sees the ecumenical and denominational churches increasing in size but diminishing in spiritual vigor. He expects that by the end of the twentieth century, evangelicals will again be suffering persecution from both the ecumenical and denominational groups. He calls for a reform that will produce revolutionary Christianity. 261.8.SCH1

————. *Escape from Reason.* Downers Grove, Ill.: Inter-Varsity Press, 1968.

Confronts the nonrational fantasy that

seeks expression in absurd experiences, and challenges those who are "hooked" on drugs. Includes an evaluation of the trends that have led to the present saturation of society with pornographic literature, and the means by which art, music, movies, television, and the theater are undermining the resistance of people at large. 261.8.SCH1E

_____. *Pollution and the Death of Man: The Christian View of Ecology.* Wheaton, Ill.: Tyndale House Publishers, 1970.

Sets forth some biblical guidelines for the Christian's attitude toward and response to his environment. 261.8.SCH1P

Schwartz, Gary. *Sect Ideologies and Social Status.* Chicago: University of Chicago Press, 1970.

A penetrating study of urban religion, with an examination of the nature of the relationship between religious belief and social order. Includes an appraisal of the socio-economic status of those who affiliated themselves with different sects. 261.8.SCH9

Scudder, C. W., ed. *Crises in Morality.* Nashville: Broadman Press, 1964.

A frank discussion of moral problems encountered by every pastor in counseling situations. 261.83.SCR2

_____. *Danger Ahead!* Nashville: Broadman Press, 1961.

The writer contends that Christian parents unwittingly aid crime and delinquency by either their ignorance or indifference. He tries to warn parents of the prevalency of alcoholism, delinquency, syndicated crime, and moral corruption. His suggestions and "remedies" are not sugar-coated but based upon Scripture, and they are frequently in marked conflict with modern trends in sociology. 261.83.SCR9D

*Skinner, Tom. *Black and Free.* Grand Rapids: Zondervan Publishing House, 1970.

For the Christian worker whose ministry has not taken him into the ghetto. Excellent. 269.'2.SK3

_____. *How Black Is the Gospel?* Philadelphia: J. B. Lippincott Co., 1970.

Deals with the crises facing black people in America today, explores the myth of the Anglo-Saxon Protestant image of Christianity, and presents the need of Christ as the only solution to the problems of black Americans. 261.83.SK3H

_____. *Words of Revolution: A Call to Involvement in the Real Revolution.* Grand Rapids: Zondervan Publishing Co., 1970.

In contrast to *How Black Is the Gospel,* this work is addressed to the "evangelical world" and "the establishment." It seeks to apprise them of the problems facing Blacks today. The vigorous presentation of the gospel disassociates Christ from the white image Blacks have of Him. 261.8.SK3W

Social Sciences and Humanities Index. New York: H. W. Wilson, Co., 1965.

This work continues the *Reader's Guide to Periodical Literature* (1909-19) and *International Index* (1920-64). Indexes approximately 175 scholarly periodicals. Provides the minister with access to the most authoritative literature for the past sixty years, and covers a wide variety of themes. 301.03.SO1

Stroup, Herbert Hewitt. *Church and State in Confrontation.* New York: Seabury Press, 1967.

A comprehensive examination of church-state relations from ancient and biblical times to the present. 261.7.ST8

Tucker, Robert C. *Philosophy and Myth in Karl Marx.* Cambridge: At the University Press, 1961.

A reinterpretation of Marxism showing how Marx was influenced by the idealism of Kant and Hegel; how he came to see man as alienated from his primal creative self through historical economic processes; and how, by means of revolution, he sought to destroy capitalism and liberate man to his original role. 193.T79

Tucker, Sterling. *Black Reflections on White Power.* Grand Rapids: Wm. B. Eerdmans Publishing Co., 1969.

A sobering assessment of white power. 323.1'19.T79

Washington, Joseph R., Jr. *Black Religion: The Negro and Christianity in the United States.* Boston: Beacon Press, 1964.

A scathing denunciation of Christianity as found in black churches in America today. 261.83.W27

Wilkerson, David and **Phyllis Murphy.** *The Little People.* Old Tappan, N.J.: Fleming H. Revell, 1969.

Aptly describes the plight of the ne-

glected, filthy, and unwanted, who are locked in lonely tenement rooms or cast out to roam the streets of the city. Born to muggers, prostitutes, alcoholics, addicts, and pushers, they face a world filled with hate. Discusses what can be done about them. 261.83.W65

Wirt, Sherwood Eliot. *The Social Consciences of the Evangelical.* New York: Harper and Row, 1968.

A biblically oriented approach to the social problems of the day. 261.8.W74

*Woolley, Paul. *Family, State and Church–God's Institutions.* Grand Rapids: Baker Book House, 1965.

Four lectures delivered at the Conservative Baptist Seminary. Denver, that focus attention on the origin, purpose, function, and boundaries of each institution. 261.7.W88

ECCLESIOLOGY

*Bannerman, James. *The Church of Christ.* 2 vols. London: Banner of Truth Trust, 1960.

This extensive treatise deals with the nature, powers, ordinances, discipline, and government of the church. Reformed. First published in 1869. 262.B22C

Cole, Robert Alan. *The Body of Christ: A New Testament Image of the Church.* Philadelphia: Westminster Press, 1965.

A brief examination of the significance of the metaphor that pictures the church as the Body of Christ. Anglican. 262.C67

Dana, Harvey Eugene. *Christ's Ecclesia.* Nashville: Sunday School Board of the Southern Baptist Convention, 1956.

Defends the thesis that the *universal* church (i.e., the Body of Christ) is not to be found in the NT and that the only church of the NT is a local one. 262.D19

————. *A Manual of Ecclesiology.* 2d ed. Revised by L. M. Sipes, Kansa City, Kan.:

Central Seminary Press, 1944.

A summary of Baptist polity. 262.D19 1944

*Gangel, Kenneth O. *Leadership for Church Education.* Chicago: Moody Press, 1970.

Focuses on two deficiencies in the church, namely, the lack of a proper program of Christian education and the absence of leadership in the church, and sets out to explain how these deficiencies may be rectified. 262.G15

*Hay, Alexander Rattray. *New Testament Order for Church and Missionary.* Audubon, N.J.: New Testament Missionary Union, n.d.

An exceptionally fine presentation of ecclesiology. 262.J32

*Hort, Fenton John Anthony. *Christian Ecclesia.* London: Macmillan Co., 1900.

There are those who feel that this work detracts from the doctrine of the church as the Body of Christ. The author's exegesis and thorough treatment of the material commends itself to many. Anglican. 262.H78

*Kuen, Alfred F. *I Will Build My Church.* Chicago: Moody Press, 1971.

A frank discussion of God's plan for the church. Tackles the problems facing the established church, and seeks to find answers for them in the pages of biblical revelation. 262.K95

*Kuiper, Rienk Bouke. *The Glorious Body of Christ.* Grand Rapids: Wm. B. Eerdmans Publishing Co., 1955.

A masterful treatment of the nature and function of the church. Reformed. 262.K96

Lang, George Henry. *The Church of God: A Treatise for the Times.* London: Paternoster Press, 1959.

Comments on the constitution, government, discipline, and ministry of the church. Plymouth Brethren. 262.L25

MacDonald, William. *"Christ Loved the Church": An Outline of New Testament Church Principles.* Oak Park, Ill.: Midwest Christian Publishers, 1956.

A definitive study of NT church principles. 262.M14

McBrien, Richard P. *The Church in the Thought of Bishop John Robinson.* Philadelphia: Westminster Press, 1966.

This careful analysis of Robinson's theological presuppositions finds him following in the footsteps of Cullmann, Bonhoeffer, and other radical theologians. 262.M12

Minear, Paul Sevier. *Images of the Church in the New Testament.* Philadelphia: Westminster Press, 1960.

A scholarly study of ecclesiology. 262.M66

*Ryle, John Charles. *Warnings to the Churches.* London: Banner of Truth Trust, 1967.

Formerly published in 1877 as part of *Knots Untied,* these studies deal with the

dangers facing the church and what may be done about them. 262.R98 1967

Stibbs, Alan Marshall. *God's Church.* London: Inter-Varsity Press, 1959.

A capable presentation. Anglican. 262.ST5

CHURCH UNITY, ECUMENISM

Beaver, Robert Pierce. *Ecumenical Beginnings in Protestant World Mission: A History of Comity.* New York: Thomas Nelson and Sons, 1962.

A scholarly work by a missiologist. Extremely valuable as a research tool in the study of the origins of the ecumenical movement on the mission field. 262'.001.B38

Bloesch, Donald G. *The Reform of the Church.* Grand Rapids: Wm. B. Eerdmans Publishing Co., 1970.

By focusing on preaching, the sacraments, charismatic gifts, and the social relevancy of Christianity, the writer seeks to show the changes taking place within the church and what should be done about them. 262'.008.B62

Bromiley, Geoffrey William. *The Unity and Disunity of the Church.* Grand Rapids: Wm. B. Eerdmans Publishing Co., 1958.

A mediating work. 262'.001.B78

*The Coming World Church. Lincoln, Neb.: Back to the Bible Broadcast, 1963.

Four contemporary writers provide essays in which they analyze the biblical data regarding the ecumenical movement, the NCC and WCC, and trends within Christendom today. 262'.001.C73

Douglas, James Dixon, ed. *Evangelicals and Unity.* Abingdon, Berks, Eng.: Marcham Manor Press, 1965.

An evangelical assessment of the problems of ecumenism. 262'.001.D74

Estep, William Roscoe. *Baptists and Christian Unity.* Nashville: Broadman Press, 1966.

Focuses attention on the doctrinal, ecclesiastical, and practical reasons for the refusal on the part of the Baptists to join the World Council of Churches. 262'.001.ES8

*Fey, Harold Edward, ed. *A History of the Ecumenical Movement, 1948-1968.* Philadelphia: Westminster Press, 1970.

†Designed as a companion volume to the work by Rouse and Neill, this treatment brings the earlier history up to date. 262'.001.F43

*Gillies, Donald. *Unity in the Dark.* London: Banner of Truth Trust, 1964.

An objective appraisal of ecumenism. 262'.001.G41

*Green, Edward Michael Bankes. *Called to Serve: Ministry and Ministers in the Church.* Philadelphia: Westminster Press, 1965.

Expresses sharp disagreement with current ecumenical opinion, offers different interpretations of the doctrine of the ministry, and boldly calls for a return to NT principles. 262'.001.G82

*Hedegard, David. *Ecumenism and the Bible.* 2d rev. ed. London: Banner of Truth Trust, 1964.

Examines the history and teachings, political maneuverings and open compromise of ecumenism. 262'.001.H35 1964

Horton, Walter Marshall. *Christian Theology, An Ecumenical Approach.* New York: Harper and Brothers Publishers, 1955.

An attempt at theological ecumenism. Will not appeal to evangelicals. 262'.001.H78

*Kromminga, John H. *All One Body We: The Doctrine of the Church in Ecumenical Perspective.* Grand Rapids: Wm. B. Eerdmans Publishing Co., 1970.

A candid analysis and critique of the ecumenical movement as seen in the development and present position of the WCC. Exposes the tensions that prevail,

and evaluates the weaknesses and lack of unity within its structure. 262'.001.K92

*Lloyd-Jones, David Martyn. *The Basis of Christian Unity.* Grand Rapids: Wm. B. Eerdmans Publishing Co., 1963.

In the light of uncertainty over the true basis for Christian unity and the lack of a satisfactory solution for ecumenical unity, it is refreshing to turn to this work and study the scriptural basis for Christian unity. 262'.001.L77

*Lowell, C. Stanley. *The Ecumenical Mirage.* Grand Rapids: Baker Book House, 1967.

A sharp attack on the basic assumptions and observable effects of the current movement toward church union. 262'.001.L95

McBrien, Richard P. *Do We Need the Church?* New York: Harper and Row, 1969.

A Roman Catholic theologian grapples with the problems of ecumenism, authority in the church, the relationship between Christianity and secular humanism, and between Catholicism and various non-Catholic expressions of Christianity. 262'.001.M12

Montgomery, John Warwick. *Ecumenicity, Evangelicals, and Rome.* Grand Rapids: Zondervan Publishing House, 1969.

An evaluation of basic developments in contemporary ecumenical thinking, together with an assessment of present-day theological trends in Protestant, Roman Catholic, and Eastern Orthodox churches. 262'.001.M76

Mooneyham, Walter Stanley, ed. *The Dynamics of Christian Unity: A Symposium on the Ecumenical Movement.* Grand Rapids: Zondervan Publishing House, 1963.

Six men from different denominations and walks of life write on the genius of Christian unity and the problems of ecumenism. 262'.001.M77

Neill, Stephen Charles. *Brothers of the Faith.* New York: Abingdon Press, 1960.

A collection of short biographical sketches of missionary statesmen who played an important role in the ecumenical movement in the first half of the twentieth century. 262'.001.N31

_____. *Church and Christian Union.* London: Oxford University Press, 1968.

†The Bampton Lectures for 1964, these studies survey the theological and ecumenical climate between 1920 and 1960. 262'.001.N31C

Niles, Daniel Thambyrajan. *Upon the Earth: The Mission of God and the Missionary Enterprise of the Churches.* New York: McGraw-Hill Publishing Co., 1962.

†An ecumenical approach to the theology of missions. While interestingly written and containing important insights, the author espouses universalism and speaks of *all* men as being in Christ, with or without believing in the message of the gospel. 262'.001.N59

Wilson, Talmage. *Freeway to Babylon.* 2d ed. Seattle: The author, 1966.

A satire on the United Presbyterian Church's new statement of faith and the ecumenical pressures being brought to bear upon conservative pastors and their churches. 262'.001.W69 1966

CHURCH POLITY

*Hodge, Charles. *Church and Its Polity.* London: Thomas Nelson and Sons, 1879.

A masterful presentation of the evangelical doctrine of ecclesiology. Not a part of the author's systematic theology. Reformed. 262'.051.H66

*Jackson, Paul Rainey. *The Doctrine and Administration of the Church.* Des Plaines, Ill.: Regular Baptist Press, 1968.

A practical treatise for Baptist and independent churches. 262'.061.J13

Kidd, Beresford James. *Roman Primacy*

to A.D. 461. London: SPCK, 1936.

A leading authority in patristic studies exposes the fallacies of the papal claims by appealing to early church history and the writings of the church Fathers. 262.13.K53

Küng, Hans. *Infallible? An Inquiry.* Garden City: Doubleday and Co., 1970.

A critique of infallibility, not only of the pope, but also of bishops, the council, the church, and the Bible when treated as a "paper pope." 262.131.K96

Lindsay, Thomas Martin. *Church and the Ministry in the Early Centuries.* New York: George H. Doran Co. [1902].

One of the most frequently quoted books on church polity. Reformed. A most valuable treatise. 262.009.L64

Littell, Franklin Hamlin. *Anabaptist View of the Church.* Boston: Star King Press, 1958.

A significant work on the history of Anabaptist ecclesiology and polity today. 262.0843.L777

Norbie, Donald L. *New Testament Church Organization.* Chicago: Interest, 1955.

Gives evidence of considerable study, and carefully compares the biblical data relating to the church with movements within history and the emergence of the major ecclesiastical systems. Plymouth Brethren. 262.065.N75

*Rouse, Ruth and **Stephen Charles Neill.** *A History of the Ecumenical Movement, 1517-1948.* 2d ed. Philadelphia: Westminster Press, 1967.

†Possibly the best modern history of ecumenism during this period. 262'.001.R75 1967

Rowell, J. B. *Papal Infallibility.* Grand Rapids: Kregel Publications, 1963.

Updated after Vatican II, this book examines the foundations and claims on which the Roman Catholic church is founded. 262.131.R79

*Salmon, George. *Infallibility of the*

Church: A Refutation. Grand Rapids: Baker Book House, 1959.

This historical study should be read with Hans Küng's *Infallible? An Inquiry.* Remarkably relevant. First published in 1888. 262.131.SA3

Schmithals, Walter. *The Office of Apostle in the Early Church.* Nashville: Abingdon Press, 1969.

Manifests a tendency to depend upon the research of W. Bauer and trace Paul's views on the apostolate to early Syrian thought. 262'.1.SCH5

Schweizer, Eduard. *Church Order in the New Testament.* Naperville, Ill.: Alec R. Allenson, 1961.

†A plea to give Christ His place as head of the church. Contains many valid and valuable concepts. Neoorthodox. 262.9.SCH9

CHURCH OFFICERS

***Bromiley, Geoffrey William.** *The Christian Ministry.* Grand Rapids: Wm. B. Eerdmans Publishing Co., 1960.

An incisive study into the nature and purpose of the Christian ministry; the power available to those who minister; the importance of the Word; and form, scope, validity, and unity of the ministry. 262.14.B78

Jumper, Andrew A. *Chosen to Serve: The Deacon.* Richmond: John Knox Press, 1961.

A descriptive training manual containing data that is applicable to all who hold the office. 262.15.J95

―――. *The Noble Task: The Elder.* Richmond, Va.: John Knox Press, 1961.

A manual prepared for use in the Southern Presbyterian Church. Contains material on the role and responsibilities of elders in the church. 262.14.J95

Küng, Hans. *The Church.* Translated by Ray and Rosaleen Ockenden. New York: Sheed and Ward, 1968.

Basing his argument on the theory that the church's essence cannot be separated from her initial form, Küng surveys the history of the Protestant and Roman Catholic churches, reveals some of the inadequacies of Roman ecclesiology, and charts a course for future ecumenical mergers. 262.7.K96

***Morris, Leon.** *Ministers of God.* London: Inter-Varsity Press, 1964.

After drawing principles from the ministry of Christ, the writer applies them to present-day ministers of the gospel. An invaluable study. Anglican. 262.14.M83

Naylor, Robert E. *The Baptist Deacon.* Nashville: Broadman Press, 1955.

Writing after extensive experience in church administration, the author highlights the need for well-trained deacons in the church. 262.15.N23

Paul, Robert S. *Ministry.* Grand Rapids: Wm. B. Eerdmans Publishing Co., 1965.

†This thorough discussion provides many insights into the problems confronting ministers today. Ecumenical. 262.14.P28

SABBATH AND SUNDAY

***Feinberg, Charles Lee.** *The Sabbath and the Lord's Day.* 3d ed. Wheaton: Van Kampen Press, 1952.

A brief monograph that ably distinguishes between the Jewish and Christian observance of a holy day. 263.1.F32 1952

Jewett, Paul King. *The Lord's Day: A Theological Guide to the Christian Day of Worship.* Grand Rapids: Wm. B. Eerdmans Publishing Co., 1971.

A responsible and valuable discussion of the Lord's day. Builds upon a thorough biblical and historical foundation,

and provides a survey of redemptive history and the change that took place

between the Jewish Sabbath and Sunday as the day of worship. 263.3.J55

PUBLIC WORSHIP

Blackwood, Andrew Watterson. *The Fine Art of Public Worship.* Nashville: Abingdon-Cokesbury Press, 1939.

An old work containing practical suggestions for improving public worship. 264.B56

————. *Prayers for All Occasions.* Grand Rapids: Baker Book House, 1960.

A valuable work providing information on prayers for inspiration, encouragement, and guidance. 264.1.B56

Common Worship. Philadelphia: Presbyterian Board of Christian Education, 1962.

A standard book for Presbyterian pastors. 264.05.C73

Cully, Iris V. *Christian Worship and Church Education.* Philadelphia: Westminster Press, 1967.

†The writer, long an advocate of the existential wing of Protestant Christian education, presents a persuasive plea for a new type of congregational involvement in liturgy and communal worship. 264.C89

*Forsyth, Peter Taylor. *The Soul of Prayer.* Grand Rapids: Wm. B. Eerdmans Publishing Co., 1949.

By emphasizing a life of continuous prayer, Forsyth provides needed guidelines to insure that prayer is not wrongly directed. He then deals with the naturalness of prayer, moral reactions to prayer, and other related topics. 264.F77

Koenker, Ernest Benjamin. *Liturgical*

Renaissance in the Roman Catholic Church. Chicago: University of Chicago Press, 1954.

†The first major study in English of the world-wide movement toward the participation of laity in the liturgy and worship of the church. 264.02.K81

Lamar, Nedra N. *How to Speak the Written Word.* New York: Fleming H. Revell Co., 1959.

This timely work aims at achieving naturalness in reading from the pulpit. 264.1.L16

*Martin, Ralph Philip. *Worship in the Early Church.* Westwood, N.J.: Fleming H. Revell Co., 1964.

Studies the Jewish inheritance of the early church, prayers and praise, hymns, creeds and confessions, the ministry of the Word, stewardship, baptism, the Lord's Supper, and later developments in Christian worship. Baptist. 264.009.M36

Maxwell, William Delbert. *Outline of Christian Worship.* New York: Oxford University Press, 1936.

†An excellent introduction to the history of public worship in the church. 264.M45

Morsch, Vivian Sharp. *The Use of Music in Christian Education.* Philadelphia: Westminster Press, 1956.

An informative, down-to-earth blueprint for integrating music into the whole program of Christian education and worship. 264.04.M83

CEREMONIES AND ORDINANCES

Baillie, Donald McPherson. *The Theology of the Sacraments.* London: Faber and Faber, 1957.

This book of essays attempts to relate

the relevance of the sacraments to the needs of the church and the edification of believers. 265.B15

Berkouwer, Gerrit Cornelis. *The Sac-*

raments. Vol. 10 of Studies in Dogmatics. Translated by Hugo Bekker, Grand Rapids: Wm. B. Eerdmans Publishing, 1969.

In the process of discussing the place of the sacraments in the Christian church, Berkouwer evaluates the teaching of Romanism and Lutheranism, as well as various contemporary views of the sacraments. Reformed. 265.B45

*Christensen, James L. *The Minister's Service Handbook.* Westwood, N.J.: Fleming H. Revell Co., 1960.

A complete anthology of materials for a large number of different services. 264.C46

Forsyth, Peter Taylor. *The Church and the Sacraments.* Naperville, Ill.: Alec R. Allenson, 1955.

An outstanding volume highlighting the need for and importance of the sacraments. First published in 1917. Congregational. 265.F77 1955

*Hiscox, Edward Thurston. *The Star Book for Ministers.* Philadelphia: Judson Press, 1953.

This work first appeared in 1878 and since that time has been eagerly sought after for its material on special observances, functions, and services. 265.H62 1953

*Hutton, Samuel Ward. *Minister's Service Manual.* Grand Rapids: Baker Book House, 1965.

A helpful manual containing orders of service for all the different types of functions ministers are called upon to perform. 265.H97

Leach, William Herman, ed. *The Minister's Handbook of Dedications.* Nashville: Abingdon Press, 1961.

A compendium of information on thirty-five different occasions that require dedication services. 265.9.L46

McCall, Duke K., ed. *What Is the Church?* Nashville: Broadman Press, 1958.

Baptist professors and ministers express their views on various aspects of the church and its ordinances. 265.M12

McNeil, Jesse Jai. *Minister's Service Book for Pulpit and Parish.* Grand Rapids: Wm. B. Eerdmans Publishing Co., 1961.

A comprehensive manual covering a wide variety of ministerial services. Ecumenical. 265.M23

Murch, James DeForest, ed. *Christian Minister's Manual.* Cincinnati: Standard Publishing Foundation, 1937.

Covers virtually every facet of ministerial service, and includes material dealing with ordinations, installations, ground-breaking ceremonies, the laying of corner stones, dedications, and so on. 265.M93

Palmer, Gordon. *A Manual of Church Services.* Westwood, N.J.: Fleming H. Revell Co., 1947.

Includes a summary of the state laws governing marriage. 265.P18

Stott, John Robert Walmsey. *Confess Your Sins.* Philadelphia: Westminster Press, 1964.

An examination of the biblical teaching on confession as the way of reconciliation. 265.62.ST7C

Underhill, Evelyn. *Worship.* New York: Harper and Brothers, 1936.

A study of the nature and principles of worship by a "Christian mystic." 264.UN2

Weiser, Francis Xavier. *Handbook of Christian Feasts and Customs.* New York: Harcourt, Brace and World, 1958.

Combining three of the author's earlier books into one, this work contains a readable introduction to the feasts, customs, and holy days of the church based upon folklore and tradition. Roman Catholic. 265.9.W43

Williamson, Robert L. *Effective Public Prayer.* Nashville: Broadman Press, 1960.

Companion volume to Blackwood's *Leading in Public Prayer.* Focuses on the part prayer plays in public worship, and stresses the need for proper preparation. 264.1.W67

BAPTISM

Aland, Kurt. *Did the Early Church Baptize Infants?* Library of History and Doctrine. Translated by A. R. Beasley-Murray. Philadelphia: Westminster Press, 1963.

A discussion of documentary evidence surrounding baptism in the first four centuries, with a rationale for the introduction of infant baptism into the early church. 265.1.AL1

Barth, Karl. *The Teaching of the Church Regarding Baptism.* Translated by Ernest A. Payne. London: SCM Press, 1965.

Aims at stating precisely what the author believed to be the true doctrine of the Reformed church on the subject of baptism. First published in 1948. 265.1.B28 1965

*Beasley-Murray, George Raymond. *Baptism in the New Testament.* London: Macmillan Co., 1963.

A learned treatment of the antecedents of Christian baptism. Beasley-Murray feels it necessary to interact with contemporary European theologians and, while this makes his treatment of baptism highly significant, it loses its value for the pastor who wishes only to learn the teaching of Scripture on the matter. Exhaustive. 265.13.B38

Brown, Henry F. *Baptism through the Centuries.* Mountain View, Calif.: Pacific Press Publishing Association, 1965.

Beginning with the archaeology of baptism, the writer traces the history of the rite through the church Fathers, Reformers, historians, and other witnesses to the present time. 265.1'09.B81

*Carson, Alexander. *Baptism, Its Mode and Its Subjects.* Grand Rapids: Baker Book House, 1957.

A full discussion on the proper subjects of baptism, as well as a vigorous plea for the immersion of believers. First published in 1831. 265.1.C23

*Conant, Thomas J. *The Meaning and Use of BAPTIZEIN.* Philadelphia: American Baptist Publication Society, 1860.

A thorough treatment of the usage of the work *baptizein* in Greek literature from classical to koinē times, with an investigation of both pagan and religious sources. Written originally to alleviate denominational controversy, this work has long been out of print. 265.14.C74

Cullman, Oscar. *Baptism in the New Testament.* Translated by J. K. S. Reid. Chicago: Regnery Press, 1950.

A polemic for infant baptism. 265.12.C89

Gilmore, Alec, ed. *Christian Baptism.* London: Lutterworth Press, 1960.

Written by Reformed Baptist theologians, this work attempts to understand the rite of baptism in the light of the Scriptures, history, and theology. 265.13.G42

*Howard, James Keir. *New Testament Baptism.* London: Pickering and Inglis, 1970.

A careful review of the NT teaching on baptism that concludes it is not an effecting agent *ex opere operato* but an effective sign requiring a responsible act by a mature person who "gets himself baptized." The writer also stresses the fact that immersion was the "normal mode." 265.13.H83

Jeremias, Joachim. *Infant Baptism in the First Four Centuries.* Translated by David Cairns. Philadelphia: Westminster Press, 1962.

A work that caused Kurt Aland to investigate the same material and come to a different conclusion. Pedo-baptist. 265.12.J48

Kline, Meredith G. *By Oath Consigned: A Reinterpretation of the Covenant Signs of*

Circumcision and Baptism. Grand Rapids: Wm. B. Eerdmans Publishing Co., 1968.

A scholarly study by a Reformed theologian. 265.1.K68

Murray, John. *Christian Baptism.* Grand Rapids: Baker Book House, 1952.

Contains the best argument for pedobaptism extant. It presents in a clear, well-reasoned manner the arguments upon which the affusionist doctrine rests. 265.12.M96

*****Newman, Albert Henry.** *A History of Anti-Pedobaptism: From the Rise of Pedobaptism to A.D. 1609.* Philadelphia: American Baptist Publication Society, 1897.

A scholarly, well-researched volume dealing with the history of the immersionist-affusionist controversy. Particularly valuable for its historical references to persecution that arose over the mode and recipients of baptism. 265.1'09.N46

*****Warns, Johannes.** *Baptism.* Translated by G. H. Lang. London: Paternoster Press, 1957.

Contains an additional chapter on the form of the original Christian baptism by N. Rudnitsky. The entire work on the origin and history of believer's baptism is well done. 265.13.W24

Watson, T. E. *Baptism Not for Infants.* Ribchester, Lancs., Eng.: The author, 1962.

A scholarly study of the history of pedo-baptism, with a vigorous defense of believer's baptism. 265.13.W33

White, Reginald Ernest Oscar. *The Biblical Doctrine of Initiation.* Grand Rapids: Wm. B. Eerdmans Publishing Co., 1960.

A systematic study of the theology of baptism and evangelism. 265.1.W58

LORD'S SUPPER, EUCHARIST

*****Jeremias, Joachim.** *The Eucharistic Words of Jesus.* Translated by Arnold Ehrhardt. Oxford: Basil Blackwell, 1955.

†An epochal work. 265.3.J47

Kevan, Ernest Frederick. *The Lord's Supper.* London: Evangelical Press, 1966.

A nontechnical treatment emphasizing the aspects of remembrance, covenant, fellowship, and hope as part of the Lord's Supper. 265.3.K51

Murray, Andrew. *The Lord's Table.* Fort Washington, Penn.: Christian Literature Crusade, 1962.

Designed to prepare the hearts and minds of communicants for effective, meaningful participation in the Lord's Supper. A valuable booklet. Reformed. 265.3.M96

Phillips, John Bertram. *Appointment with God.* New York: Macmillan Co., 1967.

Devotional meditations on the Lord's Table. 265.3.P54

Kidd, Beresford James. *The Later Medieval Doctrine of the Eucharistic Sacrifice.* London: SPCK, 1958.

An analysis of the background against which the Eucharistic doctrine of the Reformers was formed. 265.3'09.K53

MARRIAGE

Bainton, Roland Herbert. *What Christianity Says about Sex, Love and Marriage.* Baltimore: Penguin Books, 1957.

Deals with the church's attitude toward sex, love, and marriage from the first century of the Christian era to the present day. Explains many of the conflicts, misunderstandings, and misinterpretations of Scripture, and also describes sacramental, romantic, and companionable views regarding marriage. 265.5.B16

Emerson, James Gordon, Jr. *Divorce, The Church and Remarriage.* Philadelphia: Westminster Press, 1961.

While lacking in biblical content, this study does focus attention upon the contemporary problems surrounding divorce and remarriage. 265.5.EM3

*Christensen, James L. *The Minister's Marriage Handbook*. Westwood, N.J.: Fleming H. Revell Co., 1966.

A comprehensive guide to matters relating to wedding etiquette, laws, music, procedure, decorations, and so on, together with suggested ceremonies for different church groups. 265.5.C46

*Hutton, Samuel Ward. *Minister's Marriage Manual*. Grand Rapids: Baker Book House, 1968.

A modern manual on preparation for and the performance of weddings. Includes Baptist, Christian Church, Episcopal, Lutheran, Methodist, Presbyterian, Catholic, and Jewish marriage ceremonies. 265.5.H97

Leach, William Herman, ed. *The Cokesbury Marriage Manual*. Nashville: Abingdon-Cokesbury Press, 1945.

Following the eight different types of wedding services, the editor provides a summary of the state laws on marriage and divorce, as well as a bibliography for further study. 265.5.L46

*Swadley, Elizabeth. *Your Christian Wedding*. Nashville: Broadman Press, 1966.

A minister's daughter and now a minister's wife writes on what makes a wedding distinctively Christian. 395.22.SW971

Weston, Elizabeth S., ed. *Good Housekeeping's Complete Wedding Guide*. Garden City: Hanover House, 1957.

A complete, secular discussion of the subject of weddings, with emphasis on the arrangements that must be made before the ceremony. An excellent sourcebook for pastors. 392.5.W52

FUNERALS

Christensen, James L. *Funeral Services*. Westwood, N.J.: Fleming H. Revell Co., 1959.

A complete series of funeral services. 265.85.C46

*Criswell, Wallie Amos. *Our Home in Heaven*. Grand Rapids: Zondervan Publishing House, 1965.

Contains Scripture passages that will be of comfort and encouragement to the bereaved, a sermon preached on numerous occasions, and choice poems to encourage the hearts of those who mourn. 265.8.C86

Lauterbach, William Albert. *Ministering to the Sick*. St. Louis: Concordia Publishing House, 1955.

A handy manual containing appropriate prayers and devotions for thirty-five different situations, including the excommunicated, parents of a stillborn child, the shut-in, the suicidal, those injured in accidents, prayers for recovery, and so on. Of particular value are the Scripture texts accompanying each topic. 265.8.L37

Leach, William Herman. *The Improved Funeral Manual*. Grand Rapids: Baker Book House, 1956.

A compendium of suggestions. 265.8.L46

Lockyer, Herbert. *The Funeral Source Book*. Grand Rapids: Zondervan Publishing House, 1967.

A unique and useful tool for those who are called upon to minister to bereaved and sorrowing. 265.85.L81

Mitford, Jessica. *The American Way of Death*. New York: Simon and Schuster, 1963.

A critical evaluation of the American funeral trade, with an examination of the customs and practices that make up this multimillion dollar industry. 393.0973.M69

Puckle, Bertram S. *Funeral Customs, Their Origin and Development*. Detroit: Singing Tree Press, 1968.

Examines the ceremonies and superstitions, prayers, rites, and practices used by different peoples through the ages in connection with burying the dead. A veritable storehouse of information readily revealing the origin of superstitious practices, cremation, embalming, memorials, epitaphs, rings, and mourning cards. First published in 1926. 393.P96 1968

Wallis, Charles Langworthy, ed. *The Funeral Encyclopedia.* New York: Harper and Row, 1953.

Designed to help pastors handle one of the most trying situations of life. Contains typical funeral services for different types of people, a treasury of funeral sermons, an anthology of funeral peoms, a series of prayers suitable for use at funerals, and a section on professional conduct. Well indexed. 252.9.W15

11

Missions and Evangelism

Missions is more than an interesting discussion topic, Kodak slides from Timbuktu, or an occasional conference. In the New Testament it is a life-pervading attitude, a total way of thinking and acting. Today it is (or should be) vitally related to every phase of church life—local evangelism, Bible teaching, youth work, retreats, and even the tiny tots class. The church belongs to Jesus Christ, and one of the primary reasons for its existence is to make Jesus Christ known to the world, thereby accomplishing the mission Christ Himself came to achieve. A local church fulfills its mission in part by means of its testimony to the surrounding community. It fulfills its mission in full when it goes beyond "Jerusalem and Judea" to "Samaria"—the inner city—and the rest of the world.

It has been suggested that one reason for the apparent indifference of many Christians to the spiritual plight of those around them is that they have never been shown *how* to be anything else. It is pointed out that we (the leadership), not they (the membership), are to blame. However, every member of the church must be involved in the mission of the church. This cannot be done unless the inspiration of the missionary conference and the challenge of the special speaker is accompanied by weekly instruction and daily involvement with the spiritual needs of others. The pastor is the key to the mobilization of his congregation. He must instruct them and lead them. To do so means that he must first be instructed and led. Then he can lead. The reading of some of the books mentioned in this bibliography may well be the first step towards making missions a way of life for you and your church, instead of a week in the church calendar.

MISSIONS

*Adeney, David Howard. *The Unchanging Commission*. Chicago: Inter-Varsity Press, 1955.

A cogent discussion of some of the

most pressing concerns in modern missions. 266'.01.AD3

Adolph, Paul Ernest. *Missionary Health Manual.* Rev. ed. Chicago: Moody Press, 1970.

Should be placed in the hands of every foreign missionary. First published in 1954. 614.AD7 1970

*****Allen, Roland.** *Missionary Methods: St. Paul's or Ours?* Grand Rapids: Wm. B. Eerdmans Publishing Co., 1962.

A stimulating and provocative study. Deserves careful attention. First published in 1912. 266'01.AL5M 1962

————. *Missionary Principles.* Grand Rapids: Wm. B. Eerdmans Publishing Co., 1964.

A clear, compelling presentation which combines a knowledge of the Word with practical experience. A valuable treatise on missionary principles. Reprinted from the 1913 edition. 266'.01.AL5 1964

*————. *The Spontaneous Expansion of the Church and the Causes Which Hinder It.* Grand Rapids: Wm. B. Eerdmans Publishing Co., 1962.

A forthright challenge to the complacency which characterizes the church. Originally printed in 1927. 266'.01.AL55 1962

Bavinck, Johan Herman. *The Impact of Christianity on the Non-Christian World.* Grand Rapids: Wm. B. Eerdmans Publishing Co., 1948.

A discussion of the problems faced by the Christian missionary in a cross-cultural, trans-religious situation. 266'.01.B32

————. *An Introduction to the Science of Missions.* Philadelphia: Presbyterian and Reformed Publishing Co., 1964.

A scholarly work dealing with the Christian mission as a science. 266'.01.B32S

Beaver, Robert Pierce. *All Loves Excelling.* Grand Rapids: Wm. B. Eerdmans Publishing Co., 1968.

One of a kind! An excellent book which discusses the conditions under which single lady missionaries were first permitted to join the missionary movement of the nineteenth century. 266'.01.B38

————. *Envoys of Peace.* Grand Rapids: Wm. B. Eerdmans Publishing Co., 1964.

Not as valuable as *Pioneers in Mission,* nor as important as *All Loves Excelling.* Misinterprets the role of the church and, with a strong ecumenical emphasis, stresses its social mission to the world. 266'.01.B38E

————. *The Missionary Between the Times.* Garden City, New York: Doubleday and Co., Inc., 1968.

Focuses on the contemporary missionary situation. Attacks what the author regards as cultural arrogance and religious bigotry. Ecumenical. 266'.001.B38

*****Beyerhaus, Peter** and **Henry Lefever.** *The Responsible Church and the Foreign Mission.* Grand Rapids: Wm. B. Eerdmans Publishing Co., 1964.

Attempts to bridge the gap between the responsibilities of the local church to missions, and the responsibilities of missions to their church. 266'.023.B46

Blauw, Johannes. *The Missionary Nature of the Church: A Survey of the Biblical Theology of Mission.* New York: McGraw-Hill Publishing Co., 1962.

†The result of an extensive study of the theology of missions instituted by the Division of Missionary Studies of the WCC. 266'.01.B61

Boer, Harry. *Pentecost and Missions.* Grand Rapids: Wm. B. Eerdmans Publishing Co., 1961.

One of the finest books on the theology of the Christian mission. Places special emphasis on the dynamic of the Holy Spirit rather than on the demand of the Great Commission. 266'.01.B63

Bridston, Keith R. *Mission, Myth and Reality.* New York: Friendship Press, 1965.

†The four myths are geographical, cultural, ecclesiological, and vocational. The "reality," according to the author, is ecumenism. 266.B76

Brown, Arthur Judson. *The Foreign Missionary.* New York: Fleming H. Revell Co., 1950.

Remains the finest book ever written on the subject. The insights are still helpful and relevant today. First published in 1907. 266'.01.B81 1950

Bull, Geoffrey T. *Forbidden Land: A Saga of Tibet.* Chicago: Moody Press, 1966.

Records the transforming power of the gospel in the forbidden land of Tibet during the period immediately preceding the Communist invasion. 266.65.B87

*Cannon, Joseph L. *For Missionaries Only.* Grand Rapids: Baker Book House, 1969.

Referred to as a "must" for missionaries, these reflections apply equally as well to churches who send out missionaries. Should be read by every pastor and have a place in every church library. 266'.01.C16

Carver, William Owen. *Missions in the Plan of the Ages.* Nashville: Broadman Press, 1951.

A biblical study of the place and importance of missions in the plan of God. 266'.01.C25

Chambers, Oswald. *So Send I You.* Philadelphia: Christian Literature Crusade, 1960.

A vigorous challenge to Christians to consider seriously the work of foreign missions. 266'.01.C35

*Cook, Harold R. *Missionary Life and Work: A Discussion of Principles and Practices of Missions.* Chicago: Moody Press, 1959.

The best text on missionary principles and practice. Biblical as well as practical, this work should be read by every missionary candidate. 266'.069.C77M

———. *Strategy of Missions: An Evangelical View.* Chicago: Moody Press, 1963.

A symposium by members of the IFMA that reflects on the end of colonialism and on the inappropriateness of paternalistic missionary methods. Charts a course for conservative missions in the remaining decades of the twentieth century. 266'.01.C77

Daniels, George M. *This Is the Church in New Nations.* New York: Friendship Press, 1964.

A treatment of the problems and prospects of the Christian church in the Third World. Ecumenical. 266'.01.D22

Davies, John Gordon. *Worship and Missions.* New York: Associated Press, 1967.

A technical, ecumenical study. 266.001.D28

Davis, John Merle. *New Buildings on Old Foundations.* New York: International Missionary Council Press, 1947.

A handbook on stabilizing the younger churches in their environment. 266'.01.D29

Dodge, Ralph Edward. *The Unpopular Missionary.* Westwood, N.J.: Fleming H. Revell Co., 1964.

A candid evaluation of the charges leveled against the church in general and missionaries in particular. Contains an appraisal of missions which perpetuate colonialism, practice segregation, destroy culture, condone hypocrisy, encourage division, and preach an incomplete gospel. 266.023.D66

The Encyclopedia of Modern Christian Missions. Edited by Burton L. Goddard. Camden, N.J.: Thomas Nelson and Sons, 1967.

A historical résumé of 1437 sending and supporting missionary agencies located in all parts of the so-called Christian world. The most comprehensive encyclopedia of its kind. Amazingly accurate. 266'.003.EN1G

Fife, Eric S. *Man's Peace, God's Glory.* Chicago: Inter-Varsity Press, 1961.

Written for college students for whom the Christian mission is a live option. Discusses God's purpose for the world along with missionary service, prayer, money, and so on. 266'.023.F46

_____ and **Arthur F. Glasser.** *Missions in Crisis.* Chicago: Inter-Varsity Press, 1961.

Evaluates the position of the church in the world today and shows that the church is on the defensive and is also facing a revolutionary world which is clamoring for self-expression. Appraises the trends which have given rise to the present demands for unity and outlines the task of the church in its struggle against racism, the needs of the inner city, and the turmoil caused by student unrest. 266'.01.F46

Forman, Charles W. *The Nation and the Kingdom: Christian Missions in the New Nations.* New York: Friendship Press, 1964.

A thoughtful discussion of missions of the modern milieu and the dilemma which faces both church and mission as a result of the coming of independence. 266'.001.F76

***Glover, Robert Hall.** *The Bible Basis of Missions.* Chicago: Moody Press, 1964.

A simple, classic treatment of the major themes usually associated with the theology of the Christian mission. Conservative. 266'.01.G51

***Griffiths, Michael C.** *Give Up Your Small Ambitions.* Chicago: Moody Press, 1972.

This work is hard hitting, appeals to thinking Christians, answers questions about the short-term or career ministries, and evaluates the differences between formal training and practical experience. 266'.01.G87

Harr, Wilber Christian. *Frontiers of the Christian World Mission.* New York: Harper and Row, 1962.

Deals with the state of church and mission in various parts of the world between 1938 and 1962. The last two chapters on K. S. Latourette are extremely valuable. 266'.01.H23

Harris, Walter Stuart, ed. *Eyes on Europe.* Chicago: Moody Press, 1970.

A short, factual, country-by-country account of missionary work in Europe in recent years. 266.0094.H24

Hogg, William Richey. *Ecumenical Foundations: A History of the International Missionary Council.* New York: Harper and Row, 1952.

A historical study of the world-wide missionary movement of the last century. 266'.0631.H67

Horner, Norman A., ed. *Protestant Crosscurrents in Mission: The Ecumenical-Conservative Encounter.* Nashville: Abingdon Press, 1968.

An ecumenical-conservative encounter which purports to represent the opposing viewpoints on the motivation and strategy of mission in the modern world. 266'.001.H78

Houghton, Alfred Thomas. *Preparing to Be a Missionary.* Chicago: Inter-Varsity Press, 1956.

Deals with the practical problems facing every person preparing for missionary service. 266.007.H81

Isais, Juan, comp. *The Other Revolution: The Dramatic Story of Another Revolution in the Dominican Republic.* Waco: Word Books, 1970.

An amazing story of a year-long Evangelism-in-Depth crusade which coincided with the political revolution in the Dominican Republic. For naked faith and sheer heroism, this book is hard to beat. 266'.023.IS1

Kane, J. Herbert. *Faith Mighty Faith: A Handbook of the Interdenominational For-*

eign Mission Association. New York: Interdenominational Foreign Mission Association, 1956.

A brief sketch of thirty-six missions which are members of the IFMA. Includes their origin, historical development, and present outreach. 266'.0621.K13

Kraemer, Hendrik. *The Christian Message in a Non-Christian World.* 3d ed. Grand Rapids: Kregel Publication, 1966.

A landmark book written in 1938 at the request of the International Missionary Council for use in connection with the world missionary conference held at Tambaram, Madras, India. Remains a superlative exposition of evangelical missionary theory and technique. 266'.01.K85 1936

Lamott, Willis. *Revolution in Missions: From Foreign Missions to the World Mission of the Church.* New York: Macmillan Co., 1954.

Not as revolutionary as its title might suggest. Updates missionary methods to conform to the demands of the postcolonial era. 266'.01.L19

Latourette, Kenneth Scott. *These Sought a Country.* New York: Harper and Row, 1950.

Brief biographical sketches of five Protestant missionaries to the Orient. 266'.023.L35

Lindsell, Harold. *A Christian Philosophy of Missions.* Wheaton, Ill.: Van Kampen Press, 1949.

A biblical and practical discussion of the principles and practices of the Christian mission. 266'.01.L751

———, ed. *The Church's World-Wide Mission.* Waco: Word Books, 1966.

The report of the proceedings of the Congress of the Church's World-Wide Mission, held at Wheaton College, on April 9, 1966. Includes the "Wheaton Declaration." 266.008.L64

*———. An Evangelical Theology of Mis-*sions. Grand Rapids: Zondervan Publishing House, 1970.

Presents a theology of the Christian mission from an evangelical rather than an ecumenical point of view. First published in 1949. 266.001.L64 1970

———. *Missionary Principles and Practice.* New York: Fleming H. Revell Co., 1955.

An evangelical treatise. Theoretical. 266'.01.L64

Lovering, Kerry. *Missions Idea Notebook: Promoting Missions in the Local Church.* New York: Sudan Interior Mission, 1969.

A brief volume containing a potpourri of information, ideas, and suggestions. Includes such topics as atmosphere, equipment, giving, organization, missionary conference programs, and handicrafts. Also chapters on "holding interest" and "information sources." 266'.002.L94

Lyall, Leslie T. *Missionary Opportunity Today: A Brief World Survey.* Chicago: Inter-Varsity Press, 1963.

A brief but comprehensive survey of over 100 countries of the world where the Christian church is at work. Accurate and reliable. 266'.023.L98

McGavran, Donald Anderson. *The Bridges of God: A Study in the Strategy of Missions.* New York: Friendship Press, 1955.

Laments the fact that, while considerable effort has been expended on missionary work, the results have been relatively small. Proposes means for reaching individuals in their communities by means of "a Peoples Movement." 266'.01.M17

———, et al. *Church Growth and Christian Missions.* New York: Harper and Row, 1965.

A presentation of the "Church Growth Principle" as applied to theology, sociology, methodology, and administration. 266'.023.M17

_____. *How Churches Grow: The New Frontiers of Mission.* New York: Friendship Press, 1955.

One of the earliest books by the "father of the church growth movement" in modern missions. Contains a powerful plea for an examination of conventional methods of missionary work in the light of NT principles of growth. 266'.01.M17H

_____. *Understanding Church Growth.* Grand Rapids: Wm. B. Eerdmans Publishing Co., 1969.

Focuses on the theological basis of church growth, assesses the difficulties facing missions today, deals with their complexities, and examines the social and anthropological milieus in which churches multiply and grow. Many of the conclusions are highly controversial, but they deserve careful consideration. 266'.01.M17U

Mathews, Winifred. *Dauntless Women: Stories on Pioneer Wives.* Freeport, N.Y.: Books for Libraries Press, 1970.

A stirring account of the lives of Ann Judson, Mary Moffatt, Mary Livingstone, Christina Coillard, Mary Williams, Agnes Watt, and Lillias Underwood. 266'.023.M42

Neill, Stephen Charles. *Call to Mission.* Philadelphia: Fortress Press, 1970.

An honest appraisal of the mistakes of the nineteenth century together with a strong appeal for the continued proclamation of the gospel based on biblical truth and the appalling spiritual needs of twentieth-century man. 266'.01.N31

_____. *Colonialism and Christian Missions.* New York: McGraw-Hill Publishing Co., 1966.

By admirably compressing his work, the author has been able to deal comprehensibly with a vast amount of information centering in modern missions. 266'.01.N31C

_____. *A History of Christian Missions.* Grand Rapids: Wm. B. Eerdmans Publishing Co., 1964.

†A brilliantly-written treatise of the events of missions during the first seventeen centuries of the Christian era, including an analysis of modern missions since the time of William Carey. Ecumenically oriented. Virtually ignores independent "faith missions." 266.009.N31

Pearson, Dick. *Missionary Education Helps for the Local Church.* Palo Alto: Overseas Crusades, 1966.

A valuable aid in preparing the church for a missions conference. A little volume packed with ideas. 266.002.P31

*****Peters, George W.** *Saturation Evangelism.* Grand Rapids: Zondervan Publishing House, 1970.

A study of evangelism-in-depth with the formulation of six basic principles for effective evangelism. 266'.01.P44

Phillips, John Bertram. *The Church Under the Cross.* New York: Macmillan Co., 1956.

The personal testimonies of Anglican missionaries who have tried to live the "crucified life" on the mission field. 266'.01.P54

Sargent, Douglas N. *The Making of a Missionary.* London: Hodder and Stoughton, 1960.

A clear delineation of the changed role of missionaries, together with an assessment of their place of service in the national church. 266'.01.SA7

Scherer, James A. *Missionary, Go Home!* Englewood Cliffs, N.J.: Prentice-Hall Press, 1964.

Surveys the history of modern missionary methods and motives, and provides a serious reevaluation and reinterpretation of the role of missions today. 266'.01.SCH2

Soltau, Theodore Stanley. *Facing the Field: The Foreign Missionary and His Prob-*

lems. Grand Rapids: Baker Book House, 1959.

A lively discussion of what every young missionary ought to know before he leaves for the mission field. 266'.023.SO4 1959

Speer, Robert Elliott. *Missionary Principles and Practices.* New York: Fleming H. Revell Publishers, 1902.

A classic discussion and defense of Christian missions at the turn of the century. 266'.023.SP3

Street, T. Watson. *On the Growing Edge of the Church: New Dimensions in World Missions.* Richmond: John Knox Press, 1965.

A lively discussion of old and new procedures in world missions. Also a warm plea for sound theology coupled with evangelistic zeal. Both ecumenical and evangelical. 266'.023.ST8

Thiessen, John Caldwell. *A Survey of World Missions.* Rev. ed. Chicago: Moody Press, 1961.

A detailed survey of the different mission fields of the world, reflecting the political, economic, social, and religious changes. 266'.01.T34 1961

Tippett, Alan Richard. *Church Growth and the Word of God.* Grand Rapids: Wm. B. Eerdmans Publishing Co., 1970.

Attempts to provide a biblical basis for church growth. 266'.01.T46

Wallis, Ethel Emily and **Mary Angela Bennett.** *Two Thousand Tongues to Go.* London: Hodder and Stoughton, 1959.

The captivating story of Cameron Townsend and the dauntless volunteers who make up the Wycliffe Bible Translators. 266'.023.W16

Warren, Max Alexander Cunningham. *Social History and Christian Mission.* London: SCM Press, 1967.

Discusses the social, economic, and educational factors which helped shape missionary policy in the nineteenth century. Breaks new ground. 266'.009.W25

Williamson, Mabel. *Have We No Rights?* Chicago: Moody Press, 1957.

Claims that the Christian missionary has only one right—to please his Lord. A forthright discussion peppered with delightful illustrations from the author's experiences in China. 266'.01.W67

Winter, Ralph D. *The Twenty-Five Unbelievable Years, 1945 to 1969.* South Pasadena: William Carey Library, 1970.

A delightfully optimistic record of mission work in all parts of the world in this postwar period. Traces the demise of colonialism and the trials and triumphs of the gospel in the Third World. 266.009.W73

BIOGRAPHIES

*Anderson, Courtney. *To The Golden Shore: The Life of Adoniram Judson.* Boston: Little, Brown and Co., 1956.

A moving and colorful account of the life and spiritual struggles, unremitting zeal and extraordinary success of the first American to establish a mission in the East. 275.91.J92A

Campbell, Reginald John. *Livingstone.* London: Ernest Benn, 1929.

By availing himself of all the recent research the writer provided a new and different approach to the study of the missionary doctor's explorations and ministry. 276.72.L75C

Christian, Carol and **Gladys Plummer.** *God and One Redhead: Mary Slessor of Calabar.* London: Hodder and Stoughton, 1970.

A vivid reconstruction of the life of an outstanding missionary. 276.9.SL2

*Davis, Raymond J. *Fire on the Mountains.* Grand Rapids: Zondervan Publishing House, 1966.

A graphic presentation of the work of God being done among the Wallamo tribe of southern Ethiopia. 276.3.D29

*Dowdy, Homer E. *The Bamboo Cross: Christian Witness in the Jungles of Vietnam.* New York: Harper and Row, 1964.

A gripping story of missionary work among the people of Vietnam. 275.97.D75

*———. *Christ's Witch Doctor.* New York: Harper and Row, 1963.

A witch doctor converted to faith in Christ? Impossible! But it happened, and readers will be held entranced as they learn of the power of the gospel and the work being done in South America. 278.7.D75

*———. *Out of the Jaws of the Lion.* New York: Harper and Row, 1965.

The Congolese uprising, the Stanleyville massacre, and a heroic doctor's last journey to his burial place at Karawa, a mission station in Zaire, are only a part of this amazing reconstruction of events. Reads like the twenty-ninth chapter of the book of Acts. 276.724.D75

*Elliot, Elizabeth. *Shadow of the Almighty.* New York: Harper and Row, 1958.

Provides readers with insight into the spiritual nature of Jim Elliot. Traces the events leading up to his martyrdom by the Auca Indians in Ecuador in 1955. 278.66.EL5S

*———. *Through the Gates of Splendor.* New York: Harper and Row, 1957.

One of the greatest missionary stories of this or any other era. 278.66.EL5T

———. *Who Shall Ascend? The Life of R. Kenneth Strachan.* New York: Harper and Row, 1968.

Presents Strachan as a man besieged by feelings of inadequacy. Succeeds in revealing his inner nature, but fails to pass on any concept of his greatness or of the work that he did. 277.286.ST8E

Epp, Margaret. *This Mountain Is Mine.* Chicago: Moody Press, 1972.

A true-to-life drama of a man and his wife who left all to spearhead missionary work in the rigorous mountain area of western China. Fascinating! 275.1.EB1

Forsberg, Malcolm. *Land Beyond the Nile.* New York: Harper and Brothers, 1958.

A brilliantly written account of the drama surrounding the lives of two dedicated missionaries who brought the gospel to primitive tribes in Ethiopia and the Sudan. 276.24.F77

*———. *Last Days on the Nile.* Philadelphia: J. B. Lippincott, 1966.

A sequel to *Land Beyond the Nile.* Recounts the story of evangelism and church planting in the southern Sudan and how people individually came to a saving knowledge of Christ. Records the predicament of the church when caught between the political and ideological tensions of East Africa, the murder of Christians, and the expulsion of missionaries. 276.24.F77L

Grubb, Norman Percy. *C. T. Studd: Cricketer and Pioneer.* Fort Washington, Penn.: Christian Literature Crusade, reprint.

Recounts how this outstanding leader in the history of missions renounced his wealth and position to take the gospel first to China, then to India, and finally to the very heart of Africa. 276.4.ST9

———. *Once Caught, No Escape.* Fort Washington, Penn.: Christian Literature Crusade, n.d.

The autobiography of a man who led the World Evangelization Crusade following the death of C. T. Studd. 276.72.G92W

Hayes, Margaret. *Captive of the Simbas.* New York: Harper and Row, 1966.

Published in England under the title of *Missing—Believed Killed,* this autobiographical sketch focuses on the hardships of a missionary nurse at Banjwdi during the Congo uprising. 276.24.H32

*Hitt, Russell T. *Cannibal Valley.* Grand Rapids: Zondervan Publishing House, 1963.

The thrilling saga of intrepid missionaries who risked their lives to bring the gospel to the stone-age Dani tribesmen in West Irian. 278.8.H63

*_____. *Jungle Pilot.* Rev. ed. New York: Harper and Row, 1964.

Subtitled "The Life and Witness of Nate Saint—The Inventive Genius of Operations Auca," this biography records the events which led up to the martyrdom of the five missionaries. Makes captivating reading. 278.66.H63

_____. *Sensei.* New York: Harper and Row, 1965.

The captivating story of Irene Webster-Smith and the home which she created for eighty-seven young Japanese girls. 275.2.H63

Holme, Leonard Ralph. *The Extinction of the Christian Churches in North Africa.* New York: Burt Franklin, 1969.

This Hulsean prize-winning essay provides an important historical survey of the events which led up to the overthrow of the churches in North Africa. Originally published in 1898. 276.1.H73

Houghton, Frank. *Amy Carmichael of Dohnavur.* Fort Washington, Penn.: Christian Literature Crusade, 1953.

Amy Carmichael taught unwanted children in India to love God and one another. This biography portrays her self-sacrifice and service. 275.4.C21

Howard, David M. *Hammered as Gold.* New York: Harper and Row, 1969.

A graphic account of missionary work in Colombia. Emphasizes how God uses men and women to accomplish His will and, though they "pass through the fire," He brings them forth as gold. 278.61.H83

Hunter, James Hogg. *A Flame of Fire:*

The Life and Work of R. V. Bingham. Grand Rapids: Zondervan Publishing House, 1961.

The epochal work of Roland Bingham continues through the Sudan Interior Mission which he founded. This study records his heroic endeavors, but does not fully portray the personality of the man behind the mission. 276.69.B51

Kuhn, Isobel S. *Ascent to the Tribes.* Chicago: Moody Press, 1956.

The author writes of pioneer missionary work in North Thailand after the bamboo curtain descended on China. 275.93.K95A

_____. *By Searching.* Chicago: Moody Press, 1963.

A spiritual autobiography in which the author tells of her early agnostic beliefs, conversion, and call to the mission field. 275.1.K95

_____. *Greenleaf in Drought-Time.* Chicago: Moody Press, 1957.

The dramatic saga of the escape of the last China Inland Mission missionaries from Communist China is recounted in detail and with an excellent blending of events and circumstances which finally brought about their release. 275.1.K95G

_____. *In the Arena.* Chicago: Moody Press, 1958.

An intensely personal biographical sketch in which the writer records God's dealings with her and how, as a missionary first to China and then to Thailand, she was convinced that she was "in an arena" and a spectacle to those about her. 275.93.K95

_____. *Stones of Fire.* Chicago: Moody Press, 1960.

A fascinating study of Lisu peasant life in China. Written against a background of communistic intrigue and sedition. 275.9.K95

Lord, Donald C. *Mo Bradley in Thailand.* Grand Rapids: Wm. B. Eerdmans Publishing Co., 1969.

An exciting biography of the most famous medical missionary to Thailand in the nineteenth century. 275.93.B72

Lovestrand, Harold. *Hostage in Djakarta.* Chicago: Moody Press, 1969.

This record of missionary work in Indonesia covers the period of impending communist takeover, the abortive *coup,* and the bloody days which followed. 275.98.L94

Lyall, Leslie T. *Come Wind, Come Weather.* Chicago: Moody Press, 1960.

Tells the story of the Protestant church from the time of the communist takeover in 1950 until the last missionary left China in 1959. Of particular interest is the Red Chinese government's methods of handling different religious groups. 275.1.L98

Miller, William McElwee. *Ten Muslims Meet Christ.* Grand Rapids: Wm. B. Eerdmans Publishing Co., 1969.

The intriguing story of how ten Muslims came to faith in Jesus Christ. Provides vivid insight into the enormous problems faced by Iranian converts to Christianity. 248.2'46.M61

Moffat, John S. *The Lives of Robert and Mary Moffat.* 12th ed. London: T. Fisher Unwin, n.d.

Written by the son of these pioneer missionaries. This eyewitness account of much of their labors is authentic and recaptures the zeal which led to the conversion of the Hottentot chief, Africaner, the work of translation which the Moffats carried on so diligently, and the establishment of a mission station with the Matabele tribe. 276.8.M72

Nilson, Maria. *Malla Moe.* Chicago: Moody Press, 1956.

A well-written account of a unique, tireless, and unforgettable soul-winner in southern Africa and her service with The Evangelical Alliance Mission. 276.8.N72M

Paton, James. *John G. Paton: Missionary to the New Hebrides.* London: Banner of Truth Trust, 1965.

A missionary classic! Based on the 1889 edition. 279.34.P27

*Petersen, William John. *Another Hand on Mine: The Story of Dr. Karl K. Becker of the Africa Inland Mission.* New York: McGraw-Hill Book Co., 1967.

The revealing record of a missionary doctor who spent his life ministering to lepers in Zaire. 276.724.B38

Pollock, John Charles. *Hudson Taylor and Maria.* New York: McGraw Hill, 1962.

Exhibits Hudson Taylor's remarkable spirituality, yet shows him as "a man of like passions as we are." 275.1.T21P

*Reed, David. *111 Days in Stanleyville.* New York: Harper and Row, 1965.

Recounts the apalling saga which began with the burning of code books by the American Consulate in Stanleyville. Traces the dramatic events of the Simba uprising to their climax when Paul Carlson and some of the other missionaries lost their lives. 276.724.R25

Seaver, George. *Albert Schweitzer: The Man and His Mind.* London: Adam and Charles Black, 1947.

A well-written account which concentrates on the doctor's Lambaréné ministry and, in five concluding chapters, discusses his theology. 276.721.SCH9S

————. *David Livingstone: His Life and Letters.* New York: Harper and Brothers, 1957.

An assessment of a great missionary pioneer. 276.72.L75S

Stull, Ruth. *Sand and Stars.* New York: Fleming H. Revell Co., 1951.

A fascinating and absorbing story of two Christian and Missionary Alliance missionaries and their work in the forests of Peru. 278.5.ST9

Taylor, Frederick Howard and **Mary**

Geraldine Taylor. *J. Hudson Taylor.* Chicago: Moody Press, 1965.

A revision and abridgement of their famous two-volume work. 275.1.T21T

Taylor, Mary Geraldine. *Behind the Ranges.* Chicago: Moody Press, 1964.

An account of the life of J. O. Frazer, a pioneer missionary to the mountain people of China. 275.1.F86

_____. *The Triumph of John and Betty Stam.* Philadelphia: China Inland Mission, 1935.

The captivating story of two CIM missionaries who were killed by the Chinese during the communist guerilla activities in the 1930's. 275.1.ST2T

Walker, Frank Deaville. *William Carey: Missionary Pioneer and Statesman.* Chicago: Moody Press, 1951.

A well-written account of the shoemaker and scholar, linguist and missionary statesman who became the "father of modern missions." 275.4.C18W

Wall, Martha. *Splinters from an African Log.* Chicago: Moody Press, 1960.

Differs from other missionary biographies in that it does not deal with a tale of heroic accomplishment, but rather the ordinary routine of daily life. Paints the portrait of a life committed to God regardless of the monotonous, mundane hardships of the mission field. 276.9.W15

*Wallis, Ethel Emily. *The Dayuma Story.* New York: Harper and Row, 1965.

A valuable sequel to *Through Gates of Splendor,* this record of Rachel Saint's ministry among the Auca Indians, and of her meeting with Dayuma, deserves a place in the annals of missionary endeavor. 278.66.W15

Woodward, David B. *Aflame for God: Biography of Fredrik Franson.* Chicago: Moody Press, 1966.

A biographical sketch of the founder of The Evangelical Alliance Mission. 276.8.F85

Zwemer, Samuel Marinus. *Raymond Lull: First Missionary to the Moslems.* New York: Funk and Wagnalls Co., 1902.

In spite of its age, this work and the era with which it deals are of great importance in the study of Christian mission. The book reads well and traces Lull's life and ministry, philosophy, and literary works through to his martyrdom in Algeria. 276.11.L96

EVANGELISM

Archibald, Arthur C. *New Testament Evangelism: How It Works Today.* Philadelphia: Judson Press, 1946.

A challenging work. Dated. 253.7.AR2

Autrey, C. E. *Basic Evangelism.* Grand Rapids: Zondervan Publishing House, 1959.

A lucid presentation of evangelism. 253.7.AU8

_____. *Evangelism in the Acts.* Grand Rapids: Zondervan Publishing House, 1964.

The essence of evangelism as revealed in the book of Acts. 269.2.AU8

Campbell, Duncan. *God's Answer.* Fort Washington, Penn.: Christian Literature Crusade, n.d.

A factual account of the famous revival in the Hebrides, Scotland, 1949-50. 269.2.C15

_____. *The Price and Power of Revival.* Fort Washington, Penn.: Christian Literature Crusade, 1962.

An account of the events which led up to the revival on the Island of Lewis off the coast of Scotland. 269.2.C15P

*Coleman, Robert E. *The Master Plan of Evangelism.* Westwood, N.J.: Fleming

H. Revell Co., 1964.

Emphasizes the need for every Christian to witness for Christ. Sets forth clearly and concisely the principles which are the very essence of "perpetuated evangelism." 269.2.C67

*Conant, Judson E. *Every-Member Evangelism.* Rev. ed. New York: Harper and Row, 1922.

Exposes the fallacy of "leaving it all to the preacher." Should be read by every church elder and deacon taking office. Points out the need of involving church members in the work of the church and of bringing the knowledge of Christ to every man. 269.2.C74 1922

*_____. *Soul-Winning Evangelism.* Grand Rapids: Zondervan Publishing House, 1963.

Ably combines the teachings of the Word of God on redemption with a knowledge of human nature. Provides preachers with a handy reference volume on the theology, dynamics, and practical aspects of evangelism. 253.7.C74

Finney, Charles Grandison. *Lectures on Revivals of Religions.* London: Milner and Co., 1838.

A collection of famous messages. 269.2.F49

Ford, Leighton. *The Christian Persuader.* New York: Harper and Row, 1966.

Dynamic messages on evangelistic principles and practices. 253.7.F75

Goforth, Jonathan. *By My Spirit.* Grand Rapids: Zondervan Publishing House, 1942.

A brilliantly told eyewitness account of the movement of the Spirit in China. 269.2.G55

*Green, Edward Michael Bankes. *Evangelism in the Early Church.* Grand Rapids: Wm. B. Eerdmans Publishing Co., 1970.

Basing his treatment primarily upon the writings of the NT, and secondarily upon the teachings of the Fathers, the author provides a vivid and highly stimulating account of the kind of evangelism that created the fast-growing church described in the NT. An excellent work. 253.7.G82 (Alt. DDC 269'.2)

Henry, Carl Ferdinand Howard and **W. Stanley Mooneyham.** *One Race, One Gospel, One Task: World Congress on Evangelism, Berlin, 1966.* 2 vols. Minneapolis: World-wide Publications, 1967.

The official report of the largest, most representative, and most influential gathering of evangelicals. Provides a mine of information on the Christian church in all the major areas of the world. 269.2.H39

Howard, Walden. *Nine Roads to Renewal.* Waco: Word Books, 1967.

Stories of nine different groups who sought spiritual renewal. Provides an analysis of the dissatisfaction which produces a yearning on the part of Christians for something better. Practical. 269.H83

Jauncey, James H. *Psychology for Successful Evangelism.* Chicago: Moody Press, 1972.

A foundational treatment of the psychological drives that are met in the gospel message. 253.7.J32

Marsh, Frederick Edward. *Fully Furnished.* Grand Rapids: Kregel Publications, reprint 1969.

A popular work but one which does not lend itself to the outlook of the present day. 253.7.M35

Massey, Craig W. *How to Do Effective Visitation.* Wheaton, Ill.: Scripture Press, n.d.

An informative, inexpensive booklet explaining the "how-to" of visitation. 253.7.M38

Munro, Harry Clyde. *Fellowship Evangelism Through Church Groups.* St. Louis: Bethany Press, 1951.

An old work which has some important, workable ideas. 269.2.M92

Perry, John D. *The Coffee House Ministry.* Richmond, Va.: John Knox Press, 1966.

Discusses the place of the coffee-house ministry as an evangelical arm of the Christian church. 253.7.P42

*Roberts, W. Dayton. *Revolution in Evangelism: The Story of Evangelism-in-Depth.* Chicago: Moody Press, 1967.

The unique record of the mobilization of Christian men and women to witness to their faith in Christ in Nicaragua. 269.2.R54

Rowell, J. B. *How to Lead Roman Catholics to Christ.* Grand Rapids: Kregel Publications, 1966.

Shares with his readers ideas that have helped him in dealing with Roman Catholics. 253.7.R79

Shelley, Bruce Leon. *Evangelicalism in America.* Grand Rapids: Wm. B. Eerdmans Publishing Co., 1967.

A candid evaluation of evangelical Christianity in the U.S. Shows the continuity of witness from the Puritans to the twentieth century. Explains the emergence of the National Association of Evangelicals. 269.2.SH4

Southard, Samuel. *Pastoral Evangelism.* Nashville: Broadman Press, 1962.

A well-rounded evaluation of the challenge of pastoral evangelism. 253.7.SO8

*Spurgeon, Charles Haddon. *The Soul Winner.* Condensed and edited by David Otis Fuller, 2d ed. Grand Rapids: Zondervan Publishing House, 1948.

Emphasizes the fact that every pastor is preeminently a winner of souls, regardless of what other duties and responsibilities may be placed upon him. First published in 1895. 253.7.SP9 1948

*Stott, John Robert Walmsey. *Our Guilty Silence: The Church, the Gospel, and the World.* Grand Rapids: Wm. B. Eerdmans Publishing Co., 1969.

Realizing that the church frequently displays more enterprise in the field of theological debate, liturgical reform, and social service than in the realm of evangelism, Stott challenges the church to recover its evangelistic vision and to rededicate itself to its primary mission. 269.ST7

*Strachan, R. Kenneth. *Evangelism-in-Depth.* Chicago: Moody Press, 1961.

Recounts the impact of "evangelism-in-depth" in Latin America, evaluates what happened, and seeks to learn from the results. The value lies in the emphasis placed upon every believer's being involved. 269.2.ST8

*Towns, Elmer L. *Evangelize Through Christian Education.* Wheaton: Evangelical Teacher Training Association, 1970.

A well-illustrated and well-outlined textbook. Ideal for teacher training groups. 269.2.T66

Whitesell, Faris Daniel. *Sixty-five Ways to Give an Evangelistic Invitation.* Grand Rapids: Zondervan Publishing House, 1955.

Unique because it is the only work of its kind. 269.2.W58

Wood, Arthur Skevington. *Evangelism: Its Theology and Practice.* Grand Rapids: Zondervan Publishing House, 1966.

Carefully discerns between theology and evangelism, and evaluates the theology of evangelism. Discusses the basis, message, strategy, methods, varieties, and fruits of evangelism. 269.2.W85

12

Christian Education

Christian education is a vital arm of the church, not an "orphan child" whose presence is to be tolerated but who really is not wanted. The whole Christian education program is the means by which people, young and old, can be won to Christ and established in the faith. Unfortunately, the material available from different publishing houses is not always true to the Word of God. This has come about because, to quote D. Martyn Lloyd-Jones, "since about 1840, men have been putting philosophy in the place of revelation, and ideas before what God himself has so graciously been pleased to reveal."[1] This preference for human reason in the place of divine revelation has affected everything, even Sunday school curriculums.

Teachers need to have the freedom to study beyond the Sunday school quarterly. They should read widely in order that they may be well prepared for the task of transmitting the word of life to others. However, if they are to perform their duties well, it is imperative that they have the finest resource material close at hand. This, of course, highlights the importance of the church library. Historically, such libraries have played an important role in the advance of Christianity. For example, the church in Caesarea pastored by Eusebius (c. A.D. 260-c. 340) had over 45,000 volumes in its library. Sufficient to say that every church today *can* have a good library, particularly if it is developed around the curriculum and aimed at giving teachers the help they need.

By taking advantage of doctrinally sound commentaries, Sunday school teachers will be able to negate the influence of philosophical speculation that has been undermining the study of theology for more than a century and is distorting our view of God, the Scriptures, sin, man, and the world. Furthermore, by following a program of reading aimed at self-improvement,

1. *The Evangelical Presbyterian,* 43, no. 10 (March 1971):3. Used by permission.

teachers can also develop their skills and learn how to communicate the Word of God to those whom they teach. This present chapter contains suggestions on the administration of a Sunday school and then focuses on the development of those who have the privilege of teaching others.

Benjamin, Harold Raymond Wayne. *The Saber-Tooth Curriculum.* New York: McGraw-Hill Co., 1939.

A satire on modern methods of education. Will help give perspective to the development of a viable Christian education program. 371.3.B43

Benson, Clarence Herbert. *A Popular History of Christian Education.* Chicago: Moody Press, 1953.

A dated but popular study of Christian education. 268.09.B474

Best, John W. *Research in Education: Educational Measurement, Research and Statistics.* 2d ed. Englewood Cliffs, N.J.: Prentice-Hall, 1970.

Complete and informative, this detailed analysis of the nature and process of research is designed for graduate students in education. Contains excellent principles that theologues and students of Christian education will find helpful. 370.78.B46 1970

Brubacher, John Seiler. *Modern Philosophies of Education.* 3d ed. New York: McGraw-Hill Book Co., 1962.

A provocative discussion. Of particular interest is the evaluation of the educative process. 370.1.B83 1962

Butler, J. Donald. *Religious Education: The Foundation and Practice of Nurture.* New York: Harper and Row, 1962.

While it is difficult to relate one section of this book to the next, Butler has handled a mass of material with economy and skill. 268.01.B97

*Byrne, Herbert W. *A Christian Approach to Education.* Grand Rapids: Zondervan Publishing House, 1961.

A bibliocentric view of Christian education in which a biblical philosophy is developed and expounded in relation to the foundations and content of Christian education. 268'.01.B99

*Clark, Gordon Haddon. *A Christian Philosophy of Education.* Grand Rapids: Wm. B. Eerdmans Publishing Co., 1946.

A thorough, though difficult, work. Stands in the van Tillian tradition. Builds upon presuppositional revelation, and gears the entire educational process around the Scriptures. A similar work from an Arminian viewpoint is Byrne's *A Christian Approach to Education.* 370.1.C54

Comenius, John Amos. *The Great Didactic of John Amos Comenius.* Translated by M. W. Keatinge. New York: Russell and Russell, 1967.

Explains the educational philosophy of one of the great Christian pedagogues of all time. 370.1.C73

Cully, Kendig Brubaker, ed. *Basic Writings in Christian Education.* Philadelphia: Westminster Press, 1961.

†Articles by Christian education leaders covering the period of the church Fathers to the middle of the twentieth century. 377'.082.C89

———. *The Search for a Christian Education Since 1940.* Philadelphia: Westminster Press, 1965.

A companion volume to *Basic Writings in Christian Education.* Presents the different philosophies in Christian education since 1940. 268'.082.C89S

Dewey, John. *Experience and Education.* New York: Macmillan Co., 1952.

†A most important work in the field of education. It deserves to be read by all engaged in the ministry—even if they do not agree with everything the writer presents. 370.1.D51

*Dreikers, Rudolf. *Psychology in the Classroom.* 2d ed. New York: Harper and Row, 1968.

A manual for teachers analyzing the child's adjustment and the characteristic behavioral problems of school-age children. Although this book is secular, pastors and Sunday school teachers will find that they have much to learn from it. 370.15.D81 1968

Eavey, Charles Benton. *History of Christian Education.* Chicago: Moody Press, 1964.

There has been a long-felt need for a history of the development of Christian education. This book, in part, meets this need. 268.09.EA8

Eby, Frederick. *The Development of Modern Education.* 2d ed. Englewood Cliffs, N.J.: Prentice-Hall, 1952.

A comprehensive text on the theory, organization, and practice of modern education. Christian educators will find the discussion of methodology and some of the suggestions to be stimulating, practical, and helpful. 370.9.EB9 1952

*Edge, Findley Bartow. *A Quest for Vitality in Religion: A Theological Approach to Religious Education.* Nashville: Broadman Press, 1963.

A plea for a recovery of experiential Christianity. Calls for a radical change in our philosophy of Christian education, summons Christian leaders to vital action in order to avoid the dangers of institutionalism, and focuses attention on what Christians are to be and do in the world of which they are a part. 268'.01.ED3

*Gaebelein, Frank Ely. *The Pattern of God's Truth.* Chicago: Moody Press, 1968.

Deals with the problems of integration in Christian education. Displays a real concern for cultural values and, at the same time, is committed to communicating the gospel. First published in 1954. 268'.01.G11

Hakes, Joseph Edward, ed. *An Introduction to Evangelical Christians Education.* Chicago: Moody Press, 1964.

A comprehensive, up-to-date survey of Christian education. Constitutes a symposium on the problems, means, and needs of Christian education today. 268'.01.H12

Havighurst, Robert James. *Developmental Tasks in Education.* New York: David McKay Co., 1965.

Written before the author turned his attention to social and urban issues, this study not only describes the developmental tasks of Christian education, but also shows how they aid the learning process. 270.1.H29

Horne, Hermann Harrell. *The Democratic Philosophy of Education.* New York: Macmillan Co., 1932.

A old but extremely helpful book. Retains its relevance in spite of the passage of time. 370.1.H78

*Jaarsma, Cornelius Richard. *Fundamentals in Christian Education.* Grand Rapids: Wm. B. Eerdmans Publishing Co., 1953.

A valuable work that deserves to be reprinted. 377.857.J11

Kennedy, William Bean. *The Shaping of Protestant Education.* New York: Association Press, 1968.

Concentrates on the development of educational principles within Protestantism in the latter part of the nineteenth century. 377.K38

*LeBar, Lois Emogene. *Education That Is Christian.* Westwood, N.J.: Fleming H. Revell Co., 1958.

An excellent philosophy of Christian education that ably integrates biblical teaching with the Sunday school curriculum. 268.L49

*————. *Focus on People in Church Education.* Westwood, N.J.: Fleming H. Revell Co., 1968.

A practical and detailed handbook for those involved in Christian education. 268'.01.L49F

*Lewis, Clive Staples. *The Abolition of Man.* New York: Macmillan Co., 1947.

A thorough exposé of some of the

basic errors underlying existing pedagogical methods. 370.1.L58

Lotz, Phillip Henry, et al. *Orientation in Religious Education.* N.Y.: Abingdon Press, 1950.

An encyclopedic survey that lacks cohesion. 268.03.L91

Mason, Harold Carlton. *Abiding Values in Christian Education.* Westwood, N.J.: Fleming H. Revell Co., 1955.

Still valuable for its enunciation of the basic principles and goals of the church's educational program. 268'.01.M38

Murch, James DeForest. *Christian Education and the Local Church.* Rev. ed. Cincinnati, Ohio: Standard Publishing Co., 1958.

Too general to be of lasting significance. 268'.01.M93 1958

*————. *Teach or Perish!* Grand Rapids: Wm. B. Eerdmans Publishing Co., 1962.

A frank discussion of the present situation, potential, and need for revitalization of Christian education programs at the local church level. 268'.01.M93

***National Association of Evangelicals.** *Christian Education in a Democracy.* Edited by Frank E. Gaebelein. New York: Oxford University Press, 1951.

A cogently presented philosophy of education based upon sound scholarship. 377.1.N21

Person, Peter P. *Introduction to Christian Education.* Grand Rapids: Baker Book House, 1960.

A standard but unpretentious work. 268.01.P43

Smart, James D. *The Teaching Ministry of the Church: An Examination of the Basic Principles of Christian Education.* Philadelphia: Westminster Press, 1954.

Includes a brief historical sketch of Christian education and the need for basic doctrine in the curriculum. Shows how to develop a program of education that will lead to the maturity and growth of the people involved. 268'.01.SM2

Taylor, Marvin J., ed. *An Introduction to Christian Education.* Nashville: Abingdon Press, 1966.

A careful evaluation of the theoretical foundations, administration, programs, methods, materials, agencies, organizations, and so on, of Christian education. 268'.01.T21

Ulrich, Robert. *A History of Religious Education.* New York: New York University Press, 1968.

A definitive study of religious education based on the documents and interpretations put forward by educators who stand in the Judaeo-Christian tradition. 268'.09.UL3

***Waterink, Jan.** *Basic Concepts in Christian Pedagogy.* Grand Rapids: Wm. B. Eerdmans Publishing Co., 1954.

Develops a philosophy of Christian education within a psychological framework, and shows how the principles of this approach result in better service to God and man. 377.04.W29

Williamson, William Bedford. *Language and Concepts in Christian Education.* Philadelphia: Westminster Press, 1970.

†An evaluation of philosophical, substantive, and methodological decisions involved in Christian education. 268'.01.W67

Wyckoff, DeWitte Campbell. *The Task of Christian Education.* Philadelphia: Westminster Press, 1955.

†An approach to education that is of value for its methodology only. 268'.01.W97

ADMINISTRATION

Benson, Clarence Herbert. *The Sunday School in Action.* Chicago: Moody Press, 1948.

A standard work covering the history,

organization, extension, and training of teachers for effective Sunday school administration. Dated. 268.1.B44

Bower, Robert K. Administering Christian Education: Principles of Administration for Ministers and Christian Leaders. Grand Rapids: Wm. B. Eerdmans Publishing Co., 1964.

Borrows authenticated principles of administration from well-known authorities, and applies these to the work of the church. The result is a highly commendable study stressing the *why, what,* and *how* of effective administration. 268.1.B67

Byrne, Herbert W. Christian Education for the Local Church. Grand Rapids: Zondervan Publishing House, 1963.

A timely, evangelical, and functional approach designed to help pastors and lay workers set up and administer the Christian education program in the local church. Practical. 268.1.B995

Foster, Virgil E. How a Small Church Can Have Good Christian Education. New York: Harper and Row, 1956.

A practical "blueprint" for small churches. 268.1.F757

Glasser, William. Schools without Failure. New York: Harper and Row, 1969.

Should be read *after* mastering the writer's earlier volume, *Reality Therapy,* because in this latter work the basic principles of reality therapy are implemented in the classroom. 370'.973.G46

Heim, Ralph Daniel. Leading a Church School. Philadelphia: Fortress Press, 1968.

While avoiding technicalities, the author provides certain guidelines on how leaders may prepare for effective education in the church. 268'.1.H36

BUILDINGS AND EQUIPMENT

Adair, Thelma and **Elizabeth McCort.** How to Make Church School Equipment. Philadelphia: Westminster Press, 1955.

Of valve because there are very few works of its kind. Clear, practical, useful. 268.2.AD1

Atkinson, Charles Harry. Building and Equipping for Christian Education. New York: National Council of the Churches of Christ, 1956.

An excellent treatment. Recommended without an endorsement of the NCC being implied. 268.2.AT5

Straughan, Alice. How to Organize Your Church Library. Westwood, N.J.: Fleming H. Revell Co., 1962.

Contains helpful hints on staffing the library and processing books, but fails to provide help on the intricate problems of cataloging and classification. 027.67.ST8

White, Joyce L., and **Mary Y. Parr, eds.** Church Library Guide. Philadelphia: Drexel Institute of Technology, 1965.

An interesting booklet containing the proceedings of the third Church Library Conference. Informative; but also insufficient for most nontrained librarians' needs. 026.2.W585

LEADERSHIP TRAINING

Gwynn, Price Henderson. Leadership Education in the Local Church. Philadelphia: Westminster Press, 1952.

One of the few works to tackle the problems associated with the development of leaders in the church. Differs from Gangel's *Leadership for Church Edu-* cation in that it focuses on the church itself, whereas Gangel stresses the treatment of management concepts. 268.3.G99

Leadership Preparation Textbooks. Wheaton: Evangelical Teacher Training Association, 1968.

The fourteen booklets comprised in this series cover the OT and NT, the Sunday school, teachers, and teaching techniques. Includes a course on "The Missionary Enterprise" and a helpful volume on "Evangelize Through Christian Education." The studies also take the would-be leader through basic Bible doctrine and, after surveying the total program of the church and BBS, conclude with a study of the origin, authorship, and preservation of the Bible. These booklets are evangelical, practical, and continuously revised in order to keep them up-to-date. 268.3.L46

*Richards, Lawrence O., ed. *The Key to Sunday School Achievement.* Chicago: Moody Press, 1965.

A definitive evangelical work abounding in usable information. 268.3.R39

PERSONNEL

Benson, Clarence Herbert. *Teaching Techniques.* Wheaton: Evangelical Teacher Training Association, 1963.

A textbook for the training of evangelical teachers. 268.372.B44

Burton, Janet. *Guiding Youth.* Nashville: Convention Press, 1969.

An assessment of the various methods that can be employed in working with youth today. 268.37.B95

Eavey, Charles Benton. *The Art of Effective Teaching.* Grand Rapids: Zondervan Publishing House, 1953.

In spite of its age, this book presents principles that are still valid. Lacks lucidity. 371.3.EA8

_____. *How to Be an Effective Sunday School Teacher.* Grand Rapids: Zondervan Publishing House, 1955.

A guidebook for neophites. 268.372.EA8

Goodykoontz, Harry G. *The Persons We Teach.* Philadelphia: Westminster Press, 1965.

Describes the teaching process as centering in the students. Existential. 268.37.G63

*Gregory, John Milton. *The Seven Laws of Teaching.* Rev. ed. Grand Rapids: Baker Book House, 1960.

Contains the famous "Laws of Teaching" first thought out by this Baptist minister and educator. 268.372.G86

*Jaarsma, Cornelius Richard. *Human Development, Learning and Teaching: A Christian Approach to Educational Psychology.* Grand Rapids: Wm. B. Eerdmans Publishing Co., 1960.

Like *Fundamentals in Christian Education,* this work has been very well done and has almost achieved the status of a classic in its field. 370.15.J11

Jacobs, James Vernon. *What Makes Pupils Learn?* Grand Rapids: Zondervan Publishing House, 1961.

Contains in brief scope what Sunday school teachers should know when they *begin* to teach. 268.372.J15

Joy, Donald Marvin. *Meaningful Learning in the Church.* Winona Lake, Ind.: Light and Life Press, 1969.

Designed to help volunteer teachers communicate Christian truths, values, and attitudes. 268.37.J84

Kraft, Vernon Robert. *The Director of Christian Education in the Local Church.* Chicago: Moody Press, 1957.

A basic work. 268.32.K85

*Kuist, Howard Tillman. *Pedagogy of St. Paul.* New York: Geo. H. Doran Co., 1925.

An epochal study. Deserves careful and repeated reading. Should be available to all who teach. 268.372.K95

Leavitt, Guy P. *Superintend with Success.* Cincinnati: Standard Publishing Co., 1960.

Superintendents will find this volume

exceedingly helpful for its many practical suggestions. 268.3'33.L48

McComb, Louise. *D.C.E. A. Challenging Career in Christian Education.* Richmond, Va.: John Knox Press, 1963.

A must for would-be DCE's. Runs the gamut of all that is involved in preparing for and fulfilling this demanding and challenging task. 268.32.M13

Morse, William Charles and **G. Max Wingo.** *Psychology and Teaching.* 2d ed. New York: Scott, Foresman Co., 1962.

Poorly arranged, but contains usable material of value to *all* who teach. 370.15.M83 1962

Mursell, James Lockhart. *Successful Teaching: Its Psychological Principles.* 2d ed. New York: McGraw-Hill Book Co., 1954.

A well-written, standard treatment of the principles of communication necessary for good teacher-student relationships. 371.3.M96

————. *Developmental Teaching.* New York: McGraw-Hill Book Co., 1949.

A standard, secular work. 371.3.M96D

Person, Peter P. *The Minister in Christian Education.* Grand Rapids: Baker Book House, 1960.

Examines the various facets of Christian education, and defines the pastor's role in the light of these needs. 268.33.P43

Peterson, Houston. *Great Teachers.* New Brunswick, N.J.: Rutgers University Press, 1946.

A work with chapters written by men who studied under Professor Peterson. 923.7.P44

Rich, Bruce H. *Wanted: A Director of*

Christian Education. Forest Park, Ill.: North American Baptist General Conference, 1958.

A book setting out the need for and duties of DCE's. 268.33.R37

Spinka, Matthew. *John Amos Comenius, That Incomparable Moravian.* New York: Russell and Russell, 1967.

An excellent treatment of a great educator's life and contribution. 370'.924.SP4

*****Towns, Elmer L.** *Profitable Preparation for Teaching.* Minneapolis: Free Church Publications, 1969.

A small booklet that sets out clearly and plainly the author's thesis that "effective teaching is a blend of the Holy Spirit's power" and a willing teacher. 268.372.T66

Waterink, Jan. *Basic Concepts in Christian Pedagogy.* Grand Rapids: Wm. B. Eerdmans Publishing Co., 1954.

A thorough explanation of the basic principles of education. Reformed. 268.372.W29

Weidman, Mavis L., ed. *Charting the Course: A Handbook for Sunday School Workers.* Harrisburg: Christian Publications, 1955.

Reviews the foundations of Sunday school work. A basic study. 268.37.W42

*****Zuck, Roy B.** *The Holy Spirit in Your Teaching.* Wheaton: Scripture Press Publications, 1963.

Shows that it is the Holy Spirit who, in a very real way, becomes the Teacher in the teaching/learning process. 268.371.Z8

TEACHING DEPARTMENTS

Bartlett, Margret. *The Preschool Department.* Cincinnati: Standard Publishing Co., 1964.

A study of the basic principles involved in teaching preschool children.

268.4323.B28P

Benson, Clarence Herbert. *An Introduction to Child Study.* Chicago: Moody Press, 1942.

A vital, dated discussion of the phases

of child development from infancy to adolescence. 155.4.B44

Bergevin, Paul Emile and **John McKinley.** *Design for Adult Education in the Church.* New York: Seabury Press, 1958.

This evaluation of the needs of adults and the best principles for training should be of interest to all engaged in the task of education—church leaders and Sunday school teachers included. 268.434.B45

Bowman, Locke E., Jr. *How to Teach Senior Highs.* Philadelphia: Westminster Press, 1963.

An up-to-date book on *who* seniors are, *how* they learn, and *what* they need to know. 268.433.B68

Brunk, Ada Zimmerman and **Ethel Metzler.** *The Christian Nurture of Youth.* Scottsdale, Penn.: Herald Press, 1960.

Presents the physical, emotional, and spiritual needs of young people. 268.433.B83

Burton, Janet. *A Guidebook for Developing the Church Youth Program.* Grand Rapids: Baker Book House, 1968.

Abounds in practical suggestions for a thriving and effective youth program. 268.433.B95

Caldwell, Irene Catherine (Smith). *Adults Learn and Like it.* Anderson, Ind.: Warner Press, 1955.

A basic work for laymen. 268.434.C13A

————. *Responsible Adults in the Church School Program.* Anderson, Ind.: Warner Press, 1961.

A helpful study of lay involvement in the church. 268.434.C13R

Carter, Carlton. *A Church Training Young People.* Nashville: Convention Press, 1966.

A book youth pastors and those working with older young people will appreciate. 268.433.C24

Cheney, Ruth G. *Transition.* New York: Seabury Press, 1967.

An overview of 12-14-year-olds, their needs and place in the church. 268.433.C42

Christian Education Handbook. Cincinnati: Standard Publishing Co., 1960.

Crammed with ideas, and can be used with profit by all who work in the church, from the cradle roll to the adult departments. 268.4.C46

Cory, Bernice. *Cradle Roll Manual.* Wheaton: Scripture Press, 1959.

A basic handbook. Describes how this department may be set up, who should work in it, and those things that either *must* be done or *must* be avoided. 268.4321.C81

Doan, Eleanor. *How to Do Handcrafts for Juniors and Junior Highs: Ages 9-14.* Grand Rapids: Zondervan Publishing House, 1958.

A practical handbook. 268.4326.D65

————. *How to Plan and Conduct a Junior Church.* Grand Rapids: Zondervan Publishing House, 1954.

Contains an abundance of usable ideas. 268.4326.D65C

————. *Teaching Junior Highs Successfully.* Glendale: Gospel Light Publications, 1962.

Like the other practical booklets in this series, this work abounds in sane counsel and valuable information. 268.4331.D65

————. and **Frances Blankenbaker.** *How to Plan and Conduct a Primary Church.* Grand Rapids: Zondervan Publishing House, 1954.

A special section for kindergarten church leaders with four completely planned programs. 268.4325.D65

————. and **Lois Curley.** *Teaching Fours-n-Fives Successfully.* Glendale: Gospel Light Publications, 1963.

Packed with how-to-do-it techniques to use with kindergarten children. 268.4323.D65

Ellinghusen, Esther A. *Teaching Juniors Successfully.* Glendale: Gospel Light Publications, 1962.

An important evaluation of the needs of juniors and how to reach them for Christ. 268.4326.EL5

_____ and **Frances Blankenbaker.** *Teaching Primaries Successfully.* Edited by Eleanor L. Doan. Glendale: Gospel Light Publications, 1962.

Focuses on the concerns of the primary school teacher. 268.4325.EL5

*__**Getz, Gene A.** *The Vacation Bible School in the Local Church.* Chicago: Moody Press, 1962.

One of the best works of its kind. 268.4374.G33

Gilliland, Anne. *Understanding Preschoolers.* Nashville: Convention Press, 1969.

An assessment of the character of the child and his problems. 268.4323.G41

Gorman, Julie. *How to Have a Successful Church-time for Juniors.* Wheaton: Scripture Press, 1961.

Teachers of junior-age children will find this manual helpful. (It may also save their sanity.) 268.4326.G68

Greer, Virginia. *Give Them Their Dignity.* Richmond: John Knox Press, 1968.

A new approach to working with junior highs. 268'.433.G85

Hersey, John Richard. *Too Far to Walk.* New York: Alfred A. Knopf, 1966.

A novel in which the author investigates the aimlessness, boredom, and rebellion of collegiates in their Faustian pursuit of an illusion. Shows what Christian educators should avoid. 371.81.H43

*__**Irving, Roy G.,** and **Roy B. Zuck, eds.** *Youth and the Church: A Survey of the Church's Ministry to Youth.* Chicago: Moody Press, 1967.

Based on extensive research, this work probes the church's ministry to adolescents. 268'.433.IR8

Jacobsen, Henry. *How to Succeed with Your Home Department.* Wheaton: Scripture Press, 1956.

One of the very few books on this facet of the C. E. Program. 268.435.J15

_____. *How to Teach Adults.* Wheaton: Scripture Press, 1957.

A practical manual. 268.434.J15

Jacobs, James Vernon. *Understanding Your Pupils.* Grand Rapids: Zondervan Publishing House, 1959.

A brief introduction containing a wealth of material. 268.43.J15

Leach, Joan. *How to Vitalize Young Adult Classes.* Cincinnati: Standard Publishing Co., 1965.

Relevant and helpful. Describes the needs of young adults and how these needs may be met. While dated, much of the material still is useful, and the principles Leach presents are valid. 268.434.L46

*__**LeBar, Lois Emogene.** *Children in the Bible School: The How of Christian Education.* Westwood, N.J.: Fleming H. Revell Press, 1952.

Somewhat dated, but still a helpful book. 268.432.L49

_____. *Church Time for Four's and Five's.* Wheaton: Scripture Press, 1961.

Those who work with this age group will find this book particularly helpful. 268.432.L49

Leypoldt, Martha M. *40 Ways to Teach in Groups.* Valley Forge: Judson Press, 1967.

Ably illustrated with diagrams. Contains stimulating suggestions for teaching groups. 268'.4.L59

Little, Lawrence Calvin. *The Future Course of Christian Adult Education.* Pittsburgh: University of Pittsburgh Press, 1959.

A work for the specialist. 268.434.L72

_____, **ed.** *Wider Horizons in Christian Adult Education.* Pittsburgh: University of Pittsburgh Press, 1962.

Another work for the specialist. Not as readable as *Adult Education in the Church.* 268.434.L72W

McKinley, John. *Creative Methods for Adult Classes.* St. Louis: Bethany Press, 1960.

A manual designed to help teachers put new zest into their Sunday sessions and home Bible classes. 268.434.M21

Menninger, William C., et al. *How to Be a Successful Teenager.* Rev. ed. New York: Sterling Publishing Co., 1966.

A secular approach to success, acceptance, and the development of self-confidence. 155.5.M52

Mensing, Morella. *The Christian Kindergarten.* 2d ed. St. Louis: Concordia Publishing House, 1959.

Helpful, with many usable ideas. 372.21.M52 1959

Mohr, George J., and **Marian A. Despres.** *The Stormy Decade: Adolescence.* New York: Random House, 1958.

A fresh approach to the emotional and social life of adolescents. Interprets the drives and deviations that characterize this phase of life. 155.5.M72

Morris, Charles Eugene. *Counseling with Young People.* New York: Association Press, 1954.

Illustrates the ways in which group leaders can improve their individual counseling opportunities. 150.13.M83

***Nederhood, Joel H.** The Church's Mission to the Educated American.* Grand Rapids: Wm. B. Eerdmans Publishing Co., 1961.

The only work of its kind—now regretfully out-of-print. Speaks of "evangelical Christendom's most discriminated minority"—the educated—for whom there is little or nothing in the educational program of the church. 268.434.N28

Nelson, Lawrence Emerson. *Ways to Teach Teens.* Edited by Robert W. Schmiding. Philadelphia: Lutheran Church Press, 1965.

A practical book written from a Lutheran perspective. Enlightens and encourages those who work with this age group. 268.433.N33

Powell, William A. *How to Start New Sunday Schools.* Chicago: National Sunday School Association, 1960.

A practical guidebook. 268.422.P87

Sisemore, John T. *The Sunday School Ministry to Adults.* Nashville: Convention Press, 1959.

A vital work written from a Southern Baptist perspective. 268.434.SI8

***Soderholm, Marjorie Elaine.** The Junior.* Grand Rapids: Baker Book House, 1968.

A handy book that will be of help to those who work with juniors. Helps them understand the problems and challenges of this particular age group. 268.4326.SO1

*———. *Understanding the Pupil.* Part I: *The Preschool Child.* Grand Rapids: Baker Book House, 1957.

Designed to help Sunday school teachers understand the stages of development and needs of preschool children. Valuable. 268.4323.SO1

*———. *Understanding the Pupil.* Part II: *The Primary and Junior Child.* Grand Rapids: Baker Book House, 1957.

An informative assessment of the phases of growth and needs of these age groups. Brief but to-the-point. Recommended. 268.4325.SO1

*———. *Understanding the Pupil:* Part III: *The Adolescent.* Grand Rapids: Baker Book House, 1957.

A carefully presented study designed for those who are looking for more intimate insights into the conflicts and crises of this age group. Shows how adolescents may be won to Christ. 268.433.SO1

Swedburgh, Melva. *Nursery Class.* Cincinnati: Standard Publishing Co., 1964.

Designed to help those who work with this age group. Timely. 268.4322.SW3

Zeigler, Earl F. *Christian Education of Adults.* Philadelphia: Westminster Press, 1958.

Claims that adulthood is never fully attained but is something that necessitates continuous progress. Focuses on the grouping of "adults," with an analysis of the questions they ask. 268.434.Z3

Zuck, Roy B., and **Gene A. Getz**, eds. *Adult Education in the Church*. Chicago: Moody Press, 1970.

An exemplary work that effectively surveys the nature and needs, instructional methodology and achievements of the adult education departments in the church. 268'.434.Z8

*_____. *Christian Youth, an In-Depth Study*. Chicago: Moody Press, 1968.

Reports the results of a survey of 3,000 teen-agers regarding their attitudes and opinions about morals, values, doubts, religious practices, social characteristics, and evaluations of themselves, their families, and their churches. The results find cogent expression in this informative study guide. 268.433.Z8

CAMPING

Beker, Jerome. *Training Camp Counselors in Human Relations.* New York: Association Press, 1962.

An important handbook for those engaged in camp work. Clear, concise, practical. 796.54.B39

Dimock, Hedley Seldon, ed. *The Administration of the Modern Camp.* New York: Association Press, 1948.

A most thorough work. Still of importance in spite of its age. 796.54.D59

Doherty, John Kenneth. *Solving Camp Behavior Problems.* New York: Association Press, 1956.

Individual guidance for group work. 796.54.D68

Doty, Richard S. *The Character Dimension of Camping.* New York: Association Press, 1960.

A positive evaluation of the practical benefits of camp life. Stresses the needs of campers, and shows how many of these needs may be met by group interaction. 796.54.D74

Goodrich, Lois. *Decentralized Camping: A Handbook.* New York: Association Press, 1959.

Has grown out of more than a quarter of a century of organizing camps and camp programs. Offers an abundance of useful material on decentralizing camping. 796.54.G62

Joy, Barbara Ellen. *Annotated Bibliogra-*phy on Camping. Minneapolis: Burgess Publishing Co., 1963.

A handy reference volume for those involved in youth work. 016.79654.J88

_____. *Camp Craft.* Minneapolis: Burgess Publishing Co., 1955.

A manual for leaders responsible for organizing crafts at summer camps. 796.54.J84

Ledlie, John A. *Camping Skills for Trail Living.* New York: Association Press, 1962.

Helpful for those desiring to engage in wilderness camping. 796.54.L49

MacKay, Joy. *Creative Counseling for Christian Camps.* Wheaton: Scripture Press, 1966.

Helpful, practical, inexpensive, and an important supplement to Floyd and Pauline Todd's *Camping for Christian Youth.* 796.5422.M19

Miracle, Leonard and **Maurice H. Decker.** *Complete Book of Camping.* New York: Harper and Row, 1962.

Encyclopedic, well organized, and amply illustrated. 796.54.M67

Ott, Elmer F. *So You Want to Be a Camp Counselor.* New York: Association Press, 1946.

A secular work abounding in practical suggestions and sage counsel. 796.54.OT8

Reimann, Lewis Charles. *The Success-*

ful Camp. Ann Arbor: University of Michigan Press, 1958.

Covers virtually every facet of camp work from the selection of a suitable site to the ethics of administration. Elementary enough for neophytes; comprehensive enough for the experienced. 796.54.R363

Seger, Valerie. *Planning a Christian Day*

Camp. Chicago: Moody Press, 1961.

A practical guide. Of particular value to the novice. 268.4375.SE3

Todd, Floyd and **Pauline Todd.** *Camping for Christian Youth.* New York: Harper and Row, 1968.

A thorough, practical, introductory treatment from a Christian perspective. 268.4376.T56

METHODS OF INSTRUCTION

Anderson, Frances M. *Team Teaching in Christian Education.* Chicago: Covenant Press, 1967.

An introductory work. 268.6.AN2

Barnhouse, Donald Grey. *Teaching the Word of Truth.* Grand Rapids: Wm. B. Eerdmans Publishing Co., 1958.

An outstanding work that has been used by Sunday school teachers for many years. 268.6.B26T

Benson, Clarence Herbert. *The Christian Teacher.* Chicago: Moody Press, 1950.

Elementary in approach and thoroughly evangelical. Does not stress methodology. 268.6.B44

Bogardus, Ladonna. *Christian Education for Retarded Children and Youth.* Rev. ed. New York: Abingdon Press, 1963.

Written in cooperation with the NCC. Contains helpful hints on the learning characteristics of retarded children and the teaching procedures that will be most effective in reaching this special group. 268.6.B63 1963

Caldwell, Irene Catherine (Smith). *Teaching That Makes a Difference.* Anderson, Ind.: Warner Press, 1950.

A good work for laymen who teach in the church. 268.6.C13

Campbell, Doak Sheridan. *When Do Teachers Teach?* Nashville: Southern Baptist Sunday School Board, 1935.

A book to use in conjunction with teacher training classes. 268.6.C15

Carlson, Violet C. *The Christian Edu-*

cator's File. Minneapolis: Violet C. Carlson Press, 1953.

Contains some antiquated material, but also has some valuable ideas for DCE's and Sunday school teachers. 268.6.C19

Dobbins, Gaines Stanley. *The Improvement of Teaching in the Sunday School.* Rev. ed. Nashville: Southern Baptist Sunday School Board, 1943.

The methodology presented in this book is still sound. Lends itself to use in teacher training classes. 268.6.D65 1943

Eavey, Charles Benton. *Principles of Teaching for Christian Teachers.* Grand Rapids: Zondervan Publishing House, 1940.

An old, standard treatment. 268.6.EA8

*****Edge, Findley Bartow.** *Helping the Teacher.* Nashville: Broadman Press, 1959.

A *must* for Sunday school teachers. Provides practical suggestions on methodology. 268.6.ED34

_____. Teaching for Results. Nashville: Broadman Press, 1956.

A masterly treatment of the art of Christian teaching. 268.6.ED3T

Fulbright, Robert G. *New Dimensions in Teaching Children.* Nashville: Broadman Press, 1971.

Filled with information of value to both the lay person and the professional in the field of Christian education. The

principles and practical suggestions are designed to assist teachers to teach elementary school children in the church today. 268.6.F95

*Gangel, Kenneth O. *Understanding Teaching.* Wheaton: Evangelical Teacher Training Association, 1968.

Popularly written, up-to-date, and containing an abundance of material not normally found in books of this kind. Ideal for use by superintendents in the training of teachers. 268.6.G15

How to Use Role Playing. Washington, D.C.: Adult Education Association of the U.S.A., 1956.

An excellent guide. 268.6.AD9

Jacobsen, Henry. *The "How" of Effective Lesson Preparation.* Wheaton: Scripture Press, 1958.

A plain, practical, step-by-step presentation of lesson preparation. 268.6.J15

Knowles, Malcolm S. *Informal Adult Education.* New York: Association Press, 1950.

A guide for administrators, leaders, and teachers. 374.K76

*Leavitt, Guy P. *Teach with Success.* Cincinnati: Standard Publishing Co., 1956.

Study-type chapters on various aspects of teaching. Can be used to good effect for individual research or by Sunday school superintendents. Designed to help teachers at the "grass roots" level. 268.6.L48

Little, Sara. *Learning Together in Christian Fellowship.* Richmond: John Knox Press, 1956.

A handy introduction to the study of group dynamics. 268.6.L72

Morrison, Eleanor Shelton and **Virgil E. Foster.** *Creative Teaching in the Church.* Englewood Cliffs, N.J.: Prentice-Hall, 1962.

Covers a wide range of teaching methods, explains their use, and gives examples of each. Existential. 268.6.M83

*Nyquist, James. *Leading Bible Dis-*

cussions. Downers Grove, Ill.: Inter-Varsity Press, 1967.

A practical guide for those who are involved in preparing, leading, and evaluating Bible discussion groups. 268.6.N99

*Richards, Lawrence O. *Creative Bible Teaching.* Chicago: Moody Press, 1970.

Another timely book. Part II on "Teaching the Bible Creatively" applies theological and education principles in the development of a distinctly evangelical approach to Bible teaching. A must. 268.6.R39

Towns, Elmer L. *Successful Lesson Preparation.* Grand Rapids: Baker Book House, 1972.

Designed to assist Sunday school teachers become better communicators of the Word. 268.6.T66

Whitehouse, Elizabeth Scott. *The Children We Teach.* Valley Forge: Judson Press, 1953.

Blends the teachings of child psychology and Christian education to provide teachers with an understanding of the elements of growth, emotions, and problems of children. 268.6.W58

Wyckoff, D. Campbell. *Theory and Design of Christian Education Curriculum.* Philadelphia: Westminster Press, 1961.

†Based on the findings of the Curriculum Study Committee of the Christian Education Division of the NCC. Manifests tendency toward minimizing biblical content and stressing instead a philosophical, psychological, sociological, and anthropological thrust. Needs to be read with discernment. 268.6.W97

TEACHING AIDS AND EQUIPMENT

*Bowers, Kenneth L. *Opaque Projector.* Austin: Visual Instruction Bureau, University of Texas, 1960.

A valuable manual. 268.6352.B67

East, Marjorie. *Display for Learning:*

Making and Using Visual Materials. New York: Holt, Rinehart and Winston, 1952.

Still contains some informative ideas. 268.635.EA7

Guimarin, Spencer. *Lettering Techniques.* Austin: Visual Instruction Bureau, University of Texas, 1965.

A brief booklet dealing with the techniques of sign and poster making. Of help to all Sunday school teachers and church secretaries. 268.635.G94

Haas, Kenneth Brooks and **Harry Q. Packer.** *Preparation and Use of Audio-Visual Aids.* 3d ed. Englewood Cliffs, N.J.: Prentice-Hall, 1967.

A basic and comprehensive text on the preparation and use of audio-visual materials, including motion pictures, filmstrips and slides, opaque and overhead projectors, and so on. 371.335.H11 1967

Jackson, Benjamin Franklin Jr., ed. *Audio Visual Facilities and Equipment for Churchmen.* Nashville: Abingdon Press, 1970.

Makes available to teachers the techniques employed in modern communication. Explains how audio-visual materials may be made and used. 268.635.J13

Kemp, Jerrold E. *Planning and Producing Audio-Visual Material.* Rev. ed. San Francisco: Chandler Publishing Co., 1968.

A well-written presentation outlining the procedures for producing audiovisual material. Secular. 371.33.K32

Kinder, James Screngo. *Using Audio-Visual Materials in Education.* New York: American Book Co., 1965.

A compact manual that adequately explains the techniques involved in using audio-visual materials. 371.33.K57

*Lockridge, J. Preston. *Better Bulletin Board Displays.* Austin: Visual Instruction Bureau, University of Texas, n.d.

Part of the "Bridges for Ideas" series. Stresses the importance of teacher-pupil responsibility in designing bulletin boards and outlines, and illustrates the steps to be followed in their preparation for use. 268.635.L81

————. *Educational Displays and Exhibits.* Austin: Visual Instruction Bureau, University of Texas, 1960.

A manual on the use of visual aids in education. 268.635.L81E

*Meeks, Martin F. *Models for Teaching.* Austin: Visual Instruction Bureau, University of Texas, 1960.

Designed for the teacher (or pastor) who is interested in using AV material as part of his teaching ministry. 268.635.M47

Miller, Elfrieda. *Religious Arts and Crafts for Children.* St. Louis: Concordia Publishing House, 1966.

Those who work with this age group will appreciate the ideas contained in this book. 268.68.M61

Paulsen, Irwin Guy. *The Church School and Worship.* New York: Macmillan Co., 1940.

Not only teaches *about* worship, but guides people *into* worship. Analyzes the meaning and function of worship, and discusses how its content may be communicated. 268.73.P28

Rogers, Wm. L., and **Paul H. Vieth.** *Visual Aids in the Church.* Philadelphia: Christian Education Press, 1946.

An old work that has been replaced by more recent studies. 268.635.R63

*Ryrie, Charles Caldwell. *Easy-to-Get Object Lessons.* 4 vols. Grand Rapids: Zondervan Publishing House, 1949-58.

A fine series of booklets on object lessons. Unsophisticated, but with a real message. 268.635.R99

*Sloan, Robert, Jr. *Tape Recorder.* Austin: Visual Instruction Bureau, Univeristy of Texas, 1960.

A clear, concise guide on the use of tape recorders in teaching. 268.6352.SL5

STORY-TELLING TECHNIQUES

*Barrett, Ethel. *Story Telling—It's Easy!* Los Angeles: Cowman Publications, 1960.

Points out that everyone is a storyteller—only it's *how* we do it that makes the difference. This book explains *how* to do it better. 268.69.B27S

Emerson, Laura S. *Story Telling: The Art and the Purpose.* Grand Rapids: Zondervan Publishing House, 1959.

Written for storytellers everywhere. Aims at cultivating an appreciation for the artistic values of a good story, shows the essential steps in the preparation of a story, and concludes with the development of individual charm in story telling. 268.69.EM2

Royal, Claudia. *Story Telling.* Nashville: Broadman Press, 1955.

Designed to inspire and instruct the novice. Can also be read with profit by pastors, parents, and teachers. 268.69.R81

13

Church History

We cannot possibly understand the present without a knowledge of the past. An awareness of past mistakes helps us avoid the same pitfalls as we seek for solutions to the problems and difficulties we face today. "History repeats itself" is an old adage, but it is true whether we face the issues individually or collectively.

History provides us with an example of those who have labored before us, and a knowledge of their service encourages us to persevere in spite of obstacles. History gives us perspective and helps us understand the present as we prepare for the future. For these reasons, well-chosen books in the field of church history and historical theology, as well as biography, should be included in our reading schedule.

CREEDS AND CONFESSIONS
OF THE FAITH

Barth, Karl. *Credo.* New York: Charles Scribner's Sons, 1962.

†A statement of the faith of the church. Easier to read than Barth's other works. 238.11.B23C

———. *Dogmatics in Outline.* Translated by G. T. Thompson. New York: Harper and Brothers, 1949.

A study on the Apostles' Creed. 238.1.B28

*Bettenson, Henry Scrowcroft, ed. *Documents of the Christian Church.* 2d ed. New York: Oxford University Press, 1963.

A selection of documents pertaining to the early history of Christianity and made available to students in an English translation. An important, compact volume. 238.B46 1963

Forell, George Wolfgang. *Understanding the Nicene Creed.* Philadelphia: Fortress Press, 1965.

A liturgical approach. Of importance to those of a sacramental persuasion. 238.142.F76

*Hodge, Archibald Alexander. *The Confession of Faith.* London: Banner of Truth Trust, 1961.

A handbook on Christian doctrine based on the Westminster Confession. 238.5.H66

*Kelly, John Norman Davidson. *The Athanasian Creed.* New York: Harper and Row, 1964.

The Paddock Lectures delivered at the General Theological Seminary, New York, 1963. Handles with rare acumen the difficult problems associated with the origin and authorship of the creed, together with a clear and comprehensive treatment of it. 238.144.K29

*_____. *Early Christian Creeds.* 2d ed. New York: Harper and Row, 1960.

A learned analysis that is invaluable if we are to understand the contribution of this period of history. 238.1.K29 1960

Neufeld, Vernon H. *The Earliest Christian Confessions.* New Testament Tools and Studies. Grand Rapids: Wm. B. Eerdmans Publishing Co., 1963.

This study of primitive Christian *homologia* describes their origin and nature, considers their development and form, and emphasizes their importance and function in the life of the early church. 238.1.N39

Routley, Erik, ed. *Creeds and Confessions: From the Reformation to the Modern Church.* Philadelphia: Westminster Press, 1963.

An introductory work on the Confessions of Reformed churches. 238.R75

*Schaff, Philip. *The Creeds of Christendom.* 6th ed. Revised and enlarged. 3 vols. Grand Rapids: Baker Book House, n.d.

First published in 1877, and later reprinted in 1919. Describes the history of the creeds, and provides a critical appraisal of them. Includes the intrigue surrounding the framing of the creeds, the insights contained in the creeds, and their influence on church history. Volume 1 traces the origin of the creeds from the earliest times to the Wesleyan revival. Volume 2 deals with the creeds in their original form, and Volume 3 contains the evangelical Protestant creeds, with a translation of each. 238.SCH1

Schlink, Edmund. *Theology of the Lutheran Confessions.* Translated by Paul F. Koehneke and Herbert J. A. Bouman. Philadelphia: Fortress Press, 1961.

†A scholarly study of Lutheran theology. 238.41.SCH3

GENERAL WORKS

The American Catholic Who's Who. Edited by Walter Romig. Grosse Point, Mich.: Herder and Herder, 1934/35-.

Published biennially, this work contains an abundance of material, a geographical index, a list of men arranged alphabetically by state and then by town, and a necrology. 282.092.AM3

*The Atlas of American History. Edited by James Truslow Adams. New York: Charles Scribner's Sons, 1943.

A valuable reference tool containing 147 original maps prepared under the supervision of our nation's leading historians and designed to illustrate important geographical information. Cover-

age is from the earliest days of America's history through to the territorial expansion of the U.S. Available in most public libraries. 911.73.AD1A

Bainton, Roland Herbert. *The Church of Our Fathers.* New York: Charles Scribner's Sons, 1969.

A popular presentation of the historic drama, intrigues, rivalry, persecution, suffering, courage, and heroism displayed by Christian leaders from Paul to the establishment of the church in the New World. 270'.09.B16

The Baptist Encyclopedia. Edited by William Carthcart. Philadelphia: Louis H. Everts, 1881.

An old, dated dictionary of the doctrines, ordinances, usages, confessions of faith, sufferings, labors, successes, and general history of Baptist denominations in all lands. 286'.003.B22

Bracht, Tieleman Janszoon van. *The Bloody Theater, or Martyrs Mirror* . . . Translated by Joseph F. Sohm. Scottsdale, Penn.: Mennonite Publishing House, 1964.

This work traces the history of the suffering, persecution, and martyrdom of those who were baptized upon confession of faith. First published in 1837. 272.B72

*Broadbent, Edmund Hamer. *Pilgrim Church.* London: Pickering and Inglis, 1935.

A clear presentation of the history of the evangelical church from the apostolic age to the present. A most valuable study. 270.B78

*Burton, John Hill. *The History of Scotland.* 8 vols. plus index. Edinburgh: William Blackwood and Sons, 1897.

The work to acquire. Covers the years between A.D. 84 and 1745, and furnishes a full and faithful record of seventeen centuries of history. Also deals adequately with the events leading up to the Reformation era, as well as the people involved. Excellent. 941.1.B95

Butler's Lives of the Saints. Edited and revised by Herbert Thurston and Donald Attwater. 2d ed. 12 vols. New York: P. J. Kenedy and Sons, 1953.

Arranged chronologically by the months of the calendar year, this work treats the saints of the Western church in chronological order. A sympathetic treatment. 282'.092.B97 1953

Catholic Encyclopedia: An International Work of Reference on Constitution, Doctrine, Discipline and History of the Catholic Church. 17 vols. New York: Catholic Encyclopedia Press, 1907-22.

An authoritative work on the constitution, doctrine, discipline, and history of the Catholic church with long, signed articles by specialists, helpful bibliographies, and excellent illustrations. Particularly valuable for its coverage of medieval literature, history, philosophy, and art. Manifests a tendency to favor works by French Catholics. Volume 16 contains additional articles and an index, and volume 17 constitutes a supplement. In 1950, supplement 2 was issued in looseleaf form and recorded the events since the original publication in 1913 and the first supplement in 1922. 282.03.C28

*Cross, Frank Leslie, ed. *The Oxford Dictionary of the Christian Church.* Oxford: Clarendon Press, 1958.

†An alphabetical dictionary containing biographical, theological, and ecclesiastical articles. The articles themselves are concise, and many of them have valuable bibliographies appended to them. An indispensable reference tool. Predominantly Anglican. 270'.03.C87

*Cunningham, John. *The Church History of Scotland, From the Commencement of the Christian Era to the Present Time.* 2d ed. 2 vols. Edinburgh: James Thin, 1882.

Few people are as well qualified to write such a history as the author of these volumes. Provides a vivid recounting of the struggle for independence and religious freedom. 274.1.C91

Cyclopedia of Methodism. Edited by Matthew Simpson. Philadelphia: Everts and Stewart, 1878.

Particularly helpful in tracing the development of Methodism in the early years. Sketches its rise and progress, doctrines and practices through to the middle of the nineteenth century. 287'.003.C99

Deen, Edith. *Great Women of the Christian Faith.* New York: Harper and Row, 1959.

Records the way in which women have helped their husbands achieve great things for Christ and have stood boldly for their faith in times of persecution and crisis. 922.D36

Dictionary of American Biography. 11 vols. New York: Charles Scribner's Sons, 1928-.

Edited under the auspices of the American Council of Learned Societies, this important reference work contains authoritative life-stories of 14,870 Americans who have contributed to the growth and greatness of our country. Two supplements bring the material up to date. Available in college, seminary, university, or public libraries. 920.073.D56

Dictionary of American History. Edited by James Truslow Adams. 6 vols. New York: Charles Scribner's Sons, 1942.

Containing 6,668 articles by America's leading historians, this valuable and informative dictionary abounds with facts on our national history. The first supplement was issued in 1961 and either amplifies or replaces previous articles. Arranged alphabetically. An analytical index provides a key to people, places, events, and circumstances. 973.03.AD1D

Dictionary of Catholic Biography. Edited by J. J. Delaney and J. E. Tobin. Garden City: Doubleday and Co., 1961.

An extensive one-volume reference work containing entries about Catholics from the earliest times to the present. Includes material on saints, patrons and places, symbols in art, and a chronological chart of popes and world rulers. 282.092.D56

Dictionary of National Biography. Edited by Leslie Stephen and Sidney Lee. 22 vols. London: Smith, Elder and Co., 1938.

Constitutes one of the most important reference tools for English biography to the end of the nineteenth century. Contains signed articles written by specialists, and excellent bibliographies. Includes all noteworthy people of the British Isles and colonies, together with noteworthy

Americans of the colonial period. The details are reliable and scholarly. Two supplements update this work to the end of 1950. First published in 1908-9. 920.042.D56

Durant, Will and **Ariel Durant.** *The Lessons of History.* New York: Simon and Schuster, 1968.

The writers survey *The Story of Civilization* and glean from their research information about the motives and conduct of man, his great ideas, and their impact upon the events of history. They show how these themes can help people today to understand their own era. 901.9.D93

Encyclopedia of Southern Baptists. Edited by C. J. Allen, et al. 2 vols. Nashville: Broadman Press, 1958.

While not the official encyclopedia of Southern Baptists, this work presents the history of the expansion of the SBC, their present organization, and an evaluation of their methodology. Lacks an index. 286.1'03.EN1

Encyclopedia of the Presbyterian Church in the United States of America. Philadelphia: Presbyterian Publishing Co., 1888.

Difficult to use because the index shows only subjects and bibliographies included in this work, but does not provide any page references. A supplement at the end of the volume attempts to bring the work up to date, but it is now very deficient. 285.1'03.EN1

*Eusebius Pamphilus. *The Ecclesiastical History.* Translated by Christian Frederick Cruse. Grand Rapids: Baker Book House, 1962.

This famous work was first published in English in 1850. Contains in translation all the relevant documents pertaining to the early history of Christianity. Includes an essay on the life of Eusebius and a historical sketch of the Council of Nice. 270.1.EU7

The Fathers of the Church: A New Translation. Edited by Ludwig Schopp, et al. New York: Fathers of the Church, 1947-.

A readable Roman Catholic work. A valuable resource tool. 270.F26

*Fox's Book of Martyrs. Edited by William Byron Forbush. New York: Holt, Rinehart and Winston, 1926.

This abridgment of John Fox's monumental work on the lives, suffering, and triumphant deaths of early Christian and Protestant martyrs has long been regarded as a classic. 272.F83

Grub, George. An Ecclesiastical History of Scotland From the Introduction of Christianity to the Present Time. 4 vols. Edinburgh: Edmonston and Douglas, 1861.

Building his historic résumé upon the best source material available, Grub provides a continuous narrative of the events from the time of Ninian (A.D. 360) to 1857. A worthy acquisition. 274.1.G92

Hughes, Philip. A History of the Church. 3 vols. New York: Sheed and Ward, 1935.

A comprehensive survey from NT times to Martin Luther. Roman Catholic. 270.H87

Kidd, Beresford James. A History of the Church to A.D. 461. 3 vols. Oxford: Clarendon Press, 1922.

While far more complete than Duchesne, this work is digestible only in small helpings. Contains a vast amount of information, and remains one of the finest reference works in its field. 270.K53

*Latourette, Kenneth Scott. History of Christianity. New York: Harper and Brothers, 1953.

A superb work that embraces both Occident and Orient, treats at length the history of Eastern Christianity, is fair and objective in handling developments within Catholicism, and provides a brilliant synthesis of trends in the church for students of church history. 270.L35

*_____. Christianity Through the Ages. New York: Harper and Row, 1965.

A frank, informative survey of Christianity in the broad setting of world history. The writer maintains that only in

this way may Christianity be rightly understood and the history of the church properly evaluated. 270.L35C

*_____. A History of the Expansion of Christianity. 7 vols. Grand Rapids: Zondervan Publishing House, 1971.

Surveys the whole scope of church history, including the Eastern Orthodox church from the first century to 1914. No one can afford to ignore this monumental work. 270.L35H

Lightfoot, Joseph Barber. Historical Essays. London: Macmillan Co., 1896.

Essays dealing with different aspects of church history. Not as valuable as the writer's other works. 270.L62

Lutheran Cyclopedia. Edited by E. L. Lueker, et al. St. Louis: Concordia Publishing House, 1954.

Not restricted to Lutheranism. Covers all aspects of church life since the days of the apostles. 284.1'03.L97

Mayer, Frederick Emanuel. The Religious Bodies of America. 4th ed. St. Louis: Concordia Publishing House, 1960.

A handbook of denominations, sectarian groups, and interdenominational trends in the U.S. An important reference work. Lutheran. 280.0973.M45 1960

Mead, Frank Spencer. Handbook of Denominations in the U.S. 5th ed. Nashville: Abingdon Press, Annual.

Contains brief historical sketches of religious denominations in the U.S., and lists the principal doctrines, relations to other denominations, and present worship. Informative. 280.0973.M46 1970

Mennonite Encyclopedia. Edited by Harold S. Bender, et al. 4 vols. Hillsboro, Kan.: Mennonite Brethren Publishing House, 1955.

A comprehensive reference work on the Anabaptist-Mennonite movement. 284.3.M52B

Morison, Samuel Eliot. The Oxford History of the American People. New York: Oxford University Press, 1956.

This extensive, popular treatment surveys the history of America from the earliest times to the Kennedy administration. An excellent one-volume treatment. 973.M82

Mosheim, John Laurence von. *Institutes of Ecclesiastical History, Ancient and Modern.* Translated by J. Murdock. 2d rev. ed. 4 vols. London: Longman, Brown, Green and Longman, 1850.

This work, by a renowned German logician and historian, reflects the devotion of the Pietists but is also tainted with the doctrinal distinctives of the Deists—even though Mosheim refused to be identified with either group. In these volumes he advanced the cause of the church historian by laying a foundation for greater accuracy in interpreting historic data. 270.M85 1850

Moyer, Elgin Sylvester. *Great Leaders of the Christian Church.* Chicago: Moody Press, 1951.

Thirty well-written and well-documented chapters that survey the leading men from the time of the apostles to D. L. Moody. 270.092.M87

*———. *Who Was Who in Church History.* Rev. ed. Chicago: Moody Press, 1968.

An important reference tool containing biographical sketches of Christian and non-Christian leaders who influenced the church for better or worse. The writer has rendered all Christians valuable service by compiling this book. 270.092.M87W 1968

New Catholic Encyclopedia. Edited by William J. McDonald, et al. 15 vols. New York: McGraw-Hill Book Co., 1967.

Prepared by the editorial staff of the Catholic University of America, this compilation of authoritative articles deals with every aspect of Catholic church life and teaching, history and organization, and its activities throughout the world. Provides an indispensable

reference work on all questions of Catholic doctrine and history. 282.03.M14N

Phillips, W. A., ed. *History of the Church of Ireland From the Earliest Times to the Present Day.* 3 vols. London: Oxford University Press, 1933.

Beginning with a history of the Celtic church, the contributors to these volumes survey the various movements that have characterized the church in Ireland from the time of Patrick to its disestablishment. A far-ranging and important discussion. 274.15.P54

Religious Leaders in America. Edited by Julius Caesar Schwarz. 2d ed. New York: J. C. Schwarz, 1941.

First published under the title of *Who's Who in the Clergy* (1936). Lists all those who are connected directly or indirectly with religious work. Includes a list of divinity schools and seminaries, addenda, biographical sketches, and contains cross-referenced material to the 1936 edition. 922.SCH9 1941

Renwick, A. M. *The Story of the Church.* Grand Rapids: Wm. B. Eerdmans Publishing Co., 1960.

An absorbing account of the principal events in the history of the Christian church from Pentecost to the present. 270.R29

Schaff, Philip. *History of the Christian Church.* 8 vols. Grand Rapids: Wm. B. Eerdmans Publishing Co., 1960.

A brilliant, detailed account of the history of Christianity up to and including the continental Reformation. Well written and easy to read. One of the most informative and valuable treatments available. Based on the edition published in 1910. 270.SCH1 1960

*Smith, Hilrie Shelton, Robert T. Handy and **Lefferts A. Loetscher.** *American Christianity: A Historical Interpretation with Representative Documents.* 2 vols. New York: Charles Scribner's Sons, 1960-63.

†By dividing up the history of the

United States into major periods, the authors evaluate the events of these periods in the light of the original documents. The result is a very authoritative contribution. 277.3.SM5

Smith, James Ward and **A. Leland Jamison, eds.** *Religion in American Life.* 4 vols. Princeton: Princeton University Press, 1961-63.

†Scholarly and authoritative essays written by outstanding church historians. They cover the shaping of American religion, religious perspectives in American culture, and religious thought and economic society. 277.3.SM6R

*Smith, William and **Henry Wace, eds.** *A Dictionary of Christian Biography,* 4 vols. Boston: Little, Brown and Company, 1877.

Extensive material on the literature, sects and doctrines, people, and places connected with the early Christian church. 270092.SM6B

*_____ and S. Cheetham. *Dictionary of Christian Antiquities.* 2 vols. Hartford, Conn.: J. B. Burr, 1880.

Provides a full account of the leading persons, institutions, art, social life, and so on of the Christian church from the earliest times to Charlemagne. 271.009.SM6A

Sprague, William Buell. *Annals of the American Pulpit.* 9 vols. New York: Arno Press, 1969.

This set contains "commemorative notices of distinguished American clergymen of various denominations," with historical introductions contributed by Dr. Sprague. Surveys the Trinitarian and Congregational leaders of the past together with Presbyterians, Episcopalians, Baptists, Methodists, Unitarians, Lutheran, and Dutch Reformed clergymen. Highlights the advances and theological controversies within the denominations, and makes a valuable contribution to ecclesiastical Americana. First

published in 1856. 280.4.SP7 1969

*Stevenson, James, ed. *A New Eusebius: Documents Illustrative of Church History to A.D. 337.* London: SPCK, 1960.

Supersedes Kidd's *Documents Illustrative of the History of the Church.* Contains 319 extracts in translation from ancient Christian and pagan authors to A.D. 337. Of great help to those who do not have access to the *Anti-Nicene Church Fathers.* 270.1.ST4

Wace, Henry and **W. C. Piercy, eds.** *A Dictionary of Christian Biography and Literature to the End of the Sixth Century A.D.* Boston: Little, Brown and Company, 1911.

An abridgment of the famous work by Smith and Wace. 270.092.W11

Walker, Williston. *A History of the Christian Church.* 3d ed. New York: Charles Scribner's Sons. 1970.

This scholarly church history remains one of the most authoritative texts in its field. First edition, 1918. 270.W15 1970

Westcott, Brooke Foss. *The Two Empires: The Church and the World.* London: Macmillan and Company, 1909.

More than a discussion of the separation of church and state, this work traces the historic conflict between these rival realms of authority from A.D. 100-325. Excellent. 261.7.W52

*The Westminster Dictionary of Church History. Edited by Gerald C. Brauer, et al. Philadelphia: Westminster Press, 1971.

†Affords immediate, accurate definition and explanation of the major men, events, facts, and movements in the history of Christianity. Emphasis is on the western spread of Christianity from the eighteenth century onward. The section dealing with developments within the United States is particularly full. Includes data on art, politics, and philosophical movements within church history. Major doctrines are dealt with, biographies of Christian theologians are

given, and crises in history receive adequate coverage. The bibliographies are excellent. 270'.03.B73

*Weston, Gunnar. *Free Church Through the Ages*. Translated by Virgil A. Olson. Nashville: Broadman Press, 1958.

This work, with Broadbent's treatment, forms a solid foundation for tracing the history of the evangelical church through the ages. Indispensable. 270.W52

Who's Who in Methodism. Edited by E. T. Clark and T. A. Stafford, Chicago: Marquis Who's Who, 1952.

The chief value of this work lies in the brief biographical sketches. Some important names have been omitted, but the arrangement is helpful. 287.173.W62

World Christian Handbook. Edited by H. W. Coxill and Kenneth Grubb. London: World Dominion Press, 1949-.

Arranged alphabetically by country, this work contains extensive statistical tables, lists of ecumenical organizations, and details about other religions. Well indexed. 270.8.W89

Yearbook of American Churches: Information on All Faiths in the U.S.A. New York: National Council of Churches of Christ, 1916-.

Contains a calendar of the Christian year, directories of religious bodies, agencies, and councils together with statistical and historical information on church membership, clergy, and so on. 280'.0973.Y3

THE ANCIENT CHURCH
(APOSTOLIC ERA TO A.D. 590)

Alföldi, András. *The Conversion of Constantine and Pagan Rome*. Oxford: At the Clarendon Press, 1948.

This monograph will intrigue students of church history. Presents information in a factual manner. 270.1.C76

Altaner, Berthold. *Patrology*. Translated by Hilda C. Graef. New York: Herder and Herder, 1960.

A standard guide to the literature of the early church. 281.1.AL7

Atiya, Aziz Suryal. *A History of Eastern Christianity.* London: Methuen and Co., Ltd. 1968.

A detailed account of the development of "Christianity" in the Coptic, Jacobite, Nestorian, Armenian, and South Indian churches. 281.AT4

*Bainton, Roland Herbert. *Christendom: A Short History of Christianity and Its Impact on Western Civilization*. 2 vols. New York: Harper and Row, 1964.

A brilliantly written treatise explaining how Christianity has been the greatest single force in the shaping of Western civilization. 270.B16

Baus, Karl. *From the Apostolic Community to Constantine*. Handbook of Church History. London: Burns and Oates, 1965.

Generally reliable and thoroughly up-to-date. Particularly helpful for its evaluation of theological trends and developments within the early church. 281.3.B32

Blackman, Edwin Cyril. *Marcion and His Influence*. London: SPCK, 1948.

Provides a necessary corrective to Harnack's overly zealous study and Knox's highly speculative treatment. *Marcion and the New Testament*. 273.1.B56

Bonner, Gerald. *St. Augustine of Hippo*. Philadelphia: Westminster Press, 1963.

An accurate biography. Ably combines a devotional emphasis with the theological conflicts of the period. 282.61.AU4B

Brandon, Samuel George Frederick.

The Fall of Jerusalem and the Christian Church. 2d ed. London: SPCK, 1957.

†A study of the effect on Christianity of the Jewish overthrow of A.D. 70. 270.1'939.B73 1957

*Bruce, Frederick Fyvie. *The Spreading Flame.* Advance of Christianity through the Centuries. Grand Rapids: Wm. B. Eerdmans Publishing Co., 1958.

A clear, dramatic account of the rise and progress of Christianity from its first beginnings to the conversion of the English. 270.B83

Burleigh, John H. S., ed. *Augustine: Earlier Writings.* Library of Christian Classics. Philadelphia: Westminster Press, 1953.

A selection and translation of works written before 391. 281.4.B92

———, **ed.** *Augustine: Later Works.* Library of Christian Classics. Philadelphia: Westminster Press, 1955.

A translation of several of Augustine's shorter treatises, with an analysis of the argument of each. 281.4.B93L

Bury, John Bagnell. *A History of the Eastern Roman Empire.* New York: Russell and Russell, 1965.

This influential work traces the history of the Eastern Roman Empire from the fall of Irene to the accession of Basil I in A.D. 802-67. 949.502.B95

Cadoux, Cecil John. *The Early Church and the World.* Edinburgh: T. and T. Clark, 1925.

An extensive discussion of the attitudes of the early church toward the major social issues of the times. 270.1.C11

Campenhausen, Hans von. *Ecclesiastical Authority and Spiritual Power in the Church of the First Three Centuries.* London: A. and C. Black, 1969.

Of particular value and help to the ambitious student of church history. 281.3.C15

Carrington, Philip. *The Early Christian Church.* 2 vols. Cambridge: At the University Press, 1957.

Excellent as a survey of the literary sources, but deficient as a synthesis of the history of events. 270.1.C23

*Chadwick, Henry. *The Early Church.* Pelican History of the Church. Grand Rapids: Wm. B. Eerdmans Publishing Co., 1968.

Sketches the history of the Christian church from the first to the sixth century A.D. Includes an account of the intense persecution under Diocletian, the fanaticism of the martyrs, the bitterness of the controversies that plagued the church, the conversion of Constantine, the Edict of Theodosius, and so on. 270.C34

Cross, F. L. *The Early Christian Fathers.* Studies in Theology. London: Gerald Duckworth and Co., 1960.

Part of a trilogy on patrology, a companion volume to *The Later Greek Fathers* and *The Later Latin Fathers.* Deals individually with each church Father and summarizes the thought of each school in terms of geographic location. 270.1.C88

Duchesne, Louis Marie Oliver. *The Early History of the Christian Church.* 3 vols. London: John Murray, 1909-24.

†This study by a Roman Catholic theologian of the old school remains an important work on the early history of the church. 270.D85

*The Early Christian Fathers. Edited and translated by Henry Bettenson. London: Oxford University Press, 1963.

This companion volume to the author's *Documents of the Christian Church* contains selections from the writings of the early Fathers—from Clement of Rome to Athanasius. The topical arrangement of the material is exceedingly helpful. First published in 1956. 281.1.B46E 1963

Farrar, Frederic William. *Darkness and Dawn, or Scenes in the Days of Nero.* London: Longman's, Green, and Co., 1904.

A graphic portrayal of the impact of Christianity on paganism in the time of Emperor Nero and the apostle Paul. 270.1.F24D

———. *Gathering Clouds: A Tale of the Days of St. Chrysostom.* 2 vols. London: Longmans, Green, and Co., 1895.

A sequel to *Darkness and Dawn.* Continues to provide a picturesque portrait of life in the history of the early Christian church. 270.2.F24G

———. *Lives of the Fathers: Sketches of Church History in Biography.* 2 vols. London: Adam and Charles Black, 1907.

A popularly written, historical novel treating the life and thought, character and contribution of church Fathers from Ignatius to Chrysostom. A valuable study. 270.1.F24L

Frend, W. H. C. *The Early Church.* London: Hodder and Stoughton, 1965.

A lively, personal account of events that took place in the life of the early church. 270.1.F88

———. *Martyrdom and Persecution in the Early Church.* Oxford: Basil Blackwell, 1965.

An important treatment in spite of the author's tendency to exaggerate certain features. 272.1.F88

Gibbon, Edward. *The Decline and Fall of the Roman Empire.* Abridged by D. M. Low. New York: Harcourt, Brace and Co., 1960.

Gibbon was no lover of Christianity, but his work deserves to be read. While unreliable in certain respects, Gibbon nevertheless included an abundance of information that preachers can use. 937.06.G35

Goodspeed, Edgar Johnson. *A History of Early Christian Literature.* Rev. ed. Chicago: University of Chicago Press, 1942.

An old, standard work. 281.1.G62

Goppelet, Leon Hard. *Apostolic and Post-Apostolic Times.* Translated by Robert

A. Guelich. New York: Harper and Row, 1970.

†Deals with an era of church history that is under continual reexamination. Sees the church emerging by means of a witness that struggled with both Judaism and Hellenism from without, and with Nomism and Gnosticism from within. 270.1.G64

Grant, Robert McQueen, ed. *The Apostolic Fathers: A New Translation and Commentary.* New York: Thomas Nelson and Sons, 1965.

Originally scheduled for six volumes, this series contains a new translation and commentary. Scholarly, but very expensive. 281.1.G76

———. *Gnosticism and Early Christianity.* New York: Columbia University Press, 1959.

A generally reliable treatment. 273.1.G76

———. *Gnosticism: A Source Book of Heretical Writings from the Early Christian Period.* New York: Harper and Brothers, 1961.

Traces the emergence of Gnosticism and the collapse and disillusionment of apocalyptic Judaism. Claims that Gnosticism was influenced by Christianity. 273.1.G76G

——— and **David Noel Freedman.** *The Secret Sayings of Jesus.* Garden City: Doubleday and Co., 1960.

A study of the Gnostic sayings attributed to Christ. Of particular interest is the comparison between the canonical sayings and those found in the Gnostic writings. 273.1.G76 (Alt. DDC 229.951)

Greenslade, Stanley Lawrence, ed. *Early Latin Theology.* Library of Christian Classics. Philadelphia: Westminster Press, 1956.

A discerning selection of documents illustrating this era of church history. 281.3.G85

Haines, C. R. *Heathen Contact with*

Christianity During Its First Century and a Half. Cambridge: Deighton Bell and Co., 1923.

Contains original Greek and Latin texts, with full references and translation. An indispensable aid in the study of the apostolic church. 270.1.H12

Harnack, Karl Gustav Adolph von. *The Expansion of Christianity in the First Three Centuries.* Translated and edited by James Moffatt. 2 vols. London: Williams and Norgate, 1904-5.

†Of value for its overview. Should be read with discernment. 270.1.H22

*Helmbold, Andrew K. *The Nag Hammadi Gnostic Texts on the Bible.* Grand Rapids: Baker Book House, 1967.

This discussion of the discovery of the Gnostic texts, together with an explanation of their significance, will be sufficient to keep pastors abreast of developments within this area of scholarly pursuit. 273.1.H36

Jeremias, Joachim. *The Unknown Sayings of Jesus.* London: SPCK, 1957.

A collection of the noncanonical sayings attributed to Christ. 273.1.J47

Jonas, Hans. *The Gnostic Religion.* Boston: Beacon Press, 1963.

One of the most extensive expositions of Gnosticism extant. Provides students with a reliable guide to the study of the entire Gnostic problem. 273.1.J69

Jones, Arnold Hugh Martin. *Constantine and the Conversion of Europe.* London: Hodder and Stoughton, 1948.

A standard treatment. 281.3.J71

Kidd, Beresford James. *Documents Illustrative of the History of the Church.* 2 vols. London: SPCK, 1935-40.

These helpful volumes have now been replaced by Bettenson's *The Early Christian Fathers.* 270.1.K53

Lake, Kirsopp. *Paul: His Heritage and Legacy.* London: Christopher's, 1938.

While there is much in this book with which evangelicals will disagree, there is much in its reconstruction of events and assessment of the life of Paul that makes the study of NT history enjoyable. 270.1.L14

*The Later Christian Fathers. Edited and translated by Henry Bettenson. London: Oxford University Press, 1970.

Follows the topical format adopted in *The Christian Fathers.* Concentrates on such men as Cyril of Jerusalem, Hilary of Poitiers, Basil of Caesarea, Gregory of Nazianzus, Gregory of Nyssa, Theodore of Mopsuestia, Chrysostom, Ambrose, Jerome, and Augustine. Important excerpts draw attention to their teaching on the fall of Man, the Person and work of Christ, the doctrine of the Holy Spirit, the sacraments, discipline, the Trinity, and so on. 281.4.B46L

*Lietzmann, Hans. *A History of the Early Church.* 4 vols. London: Lutterworth Press, 1937-51.

†Now available in paperback, this scholarly treatment is particularly important for its survey of the "history of ideas." Not as reliable as other works covering the same period. 270.1.L62

*Lightfoot, Joseph Barber. *The Apostolic Fathers.* 5 vols. London: Macmillan Co., 1890.

A critical edition with extensive notes, essays, and a revised translation. Those who do not have access to this critical edition can obtain the English abridgment published by Baker Book House. 281.1.L62

MacLean, Magnus. *The Literature of the Celts.* Port Washington, N.Y.: Kennikat Press, 1970.

Traces the history of the Celts from the time of Julius Caesar to the nineteenth century. Has excellent chapters on Patrick and the mission school he founded, Columba and the work he established on the island of Iona, the famous Book of Kells, the revivals of the period, and so on. A stimulating work. 891.6.M22

McIntyre, John. *The Christian Doctrine of History.* Grand Rapids: Wm. B. Eerdmans Publishing Co., 1958.

A closely reasoned treatise. Of value to the discerning student. 901.M18

Milman, Henry Hart. *The History of Christianity, From the Birth of Christ to the Abolition of Paganism in the Roman Empire.* 3 vols. London: John Murray, 1840.

With literary aplomb, Milman sketches the main historic movements of the times. His "broad church" leanings cause him to overlook the evangelical movements within the activities of the church, and this reduces the value of his work. 270.M63

Oetting, Walter W. *The Church of the Catacombs.* St. Louis: Concordia Publishing House, 1964.

An important introductory study. Of value for the information it provides on the attitudes of believers in the early church. 270.1.OE8

Oulton, John Ernest Leonard and **Henry Chadwick, eds.** *Alexandrian Christianity.* Library of Christian Classics. Philadelphia: Westminster Press, 1954.

Contains excerpts on marriage and spiritual perfection, prayer, martyrdom, and so on, taken from the writings of Clement of Alexandria and Origen. 281.3.OU5

Prestige, George Leonard. *God in Patristic Thought.* London: SPCK, 1959.

A profound, mind-stretching treatment. 281.3.P92

Quasten, Johannes. *Patrology.* 3 vols. Westminster, Md.: Newman Press, 1950-60.

While more complete than Altaner's work, this treatment is also more obviously "Catholic." 281.1.Q2

*Ramsay, William Mitchell. *The Church in the Roman Empire.* Grand Rapids: Baker Book House, 1954.

An important book in studying the narratives in The Acts, and one that provides considerable information about the culture and times of the places from which the epistles were written and the people to whom they were addressed. First published in 1893. 270.1.R14

Richardson, Cyril Charles, ed. *Early Christian Fathers.* Library of Christian Classics. Philadelphia: Westminster Press, 1953.

A new translation of some of the basic Christian writings of the first two centuries. 270.1.R39

*Schlatter, Adolf von. *The Church in the New Testament Period.* Translated by Paul P. Levertoff. Naperville, Ill.: Alec R. Allenson, 1955.

A careful analysis of the leaders of the NT church, with an account of the development of the church up to A.D. 120. 270.1.SCH3

Sellers, Robert Victor. *The Counsel of Chalcedon.* London: SPCK, 1953.

A historical and doctrinal survey. 270.2.SE4

*Shelley, Bruce L. *The Cross and Flame.* Grand Rapids: Wm. B. Eerdmans Publishing Co., 1967.

Provides interesting chapters in the history of martyrdom. A valuable "supplement" to Fox's *Book of Martyrs.* 272.SH4

Stanley, Arthur Penrhyn. *Lectures on the History of the Eastern Church.* New ed. London: John Murray, 1884.

One of the most informative treatments of the origin, doctrine, and development of the Greek Orthodox Church. Dated. 281.9.ST2

―――. *Sermons and Essays on the Apostolic Age.* 2d ed. Oxford: John Henry Parker, 1852.

Includes an assessment of the character and position of Peter, Paul, and John in the apostolic church; evaluates the writings of the early church Fathers;

studies in depth the "apostolic office"; discourses at length on Peter and the promise of Matthew 16:17-19; and provides an interesting essay on the Judaizers of the apostolic age. 270.1.ST2 1852

Wand, John William Charles. *The Four Great Heresies.* London: A. R. Mowbray, 1955.

A scholarly discussion of the Arian, Apollinarian, Nestorian, and Eutychian heresies. 273.W18

Widengren, George. *Mani and Manichaeism.* New York: Holt, Rinehart and Winston, 1965.

A helpful book providing a fairly detailed discussion of the various aspects of Manician teaching and history. 273.23.W63

Wiles, Maurice F. *The Christian Fathers.* London: Hodder and Stoughton, 1966.

A splendid introductory work. More objective in treating the conservative elements of the early church than some of this writer's other theological works. 270.1.W64

Williams, Robert R. *A Guide to the Teachings of the Early Church Fathers.* Grand Rapids: Wm. B. Eerdmans Publishing Co., 1960.

A concise, readable guide. 281.1.W67

Wilson, Robert McLachlan. *The Gnostic Problem: A Study in the Relations between Hellenistic Judaism and the Gnostic Heresy.* London: A. R. Mowbray and Co., 1958.

This notable volume contains two rather recently discovered Gnostic documents—the *Apocryphon Johannis* and the *Gospel of Truth*—which have not been made available in an English translation prior to this time. 273.1.W69

————. *The Gospel of Philip.* London: A. R. Mowbray and Co., 1962.

The Coptic text has long been available in photographic facsimile. Now the writer has provided NT students with an English translation, accompanied by an introduction and commentary on the text. 273.1.W69P

————. *Studies in the Gospel of Thomas.* London: A. R. Mowbray and Co., 1960.

A candid, sober study of the suggestions and hypotheses that have been made regarding the significance of this Gnostic work. 273.1.W69T

MEDIEVAL CHURCH (590—1517)

Bainton, Roland Herbert. *Erasmus of Christendom.* New York: Charles Scribner's Sons, 1968.

Provides an informative introduction to the thought and writings of "the incomparable Erasmus," who here appears as a moral statesman who consistently stood for the principles of classical Christian humanism. 274.92.ER1B

Baird, Henry Martyn. *History of the Rise of the Huguenots.* 2 vols. London: Hodder and Stoughton, 1879.

A pleasing account of the history of the Huguenots from the beginning of the French reformation to the death of Charles IX. Reminds us of a long-forgotten and long-neglected aspect of history. 284.5'09.B16

Barker, Ernest. *The Crusades.* London: Oxford University Press, 1923.

Contains a short, provocative introduction to the Crusades. More detailed treatments may be found in Runciman's *History of the Crusades* (3 vols.; 1951-54), and Setton's *A History of the Crusades* (1955-). 274.2.B24

Bede's Ecclesiastical History of the English

People. Edited by Bertram Colgrave and R. A. B. Mynors. Oxford: At the Clarendon Press, 1969.

One of the only major accounts of the Anglo-Saxon invasion and the beginnings of Christianity in England. The present edition makes use for the first time of a mid-eighth-century manuscript from Leningrad, takes into consideration all the extant manuscripts, and updates the invaluable work of Plummer published over seventy years ago. First published in 731. 274.2.B39C 1969

Bryce, James. *The Holy Roman Empire.* New ed. London: Macmillan Co., 1919.

Remains a valuable treatment. Clear, concise, factual. 940.1.B84 1919

The Cambridge Medieval History. Edited by H. M. Gwatkin and J. B. Whitney. 9 vols. Cambridge: At the University Press, 1924-36.

A valuable companion volume to the *Cambridge Ancient History.* Covers the period from Constantine to the close of the Middle Ages. Each chapter has been written by an expert in the field, and each volume is complete with its own index and bibliography. Volume 9 contains maps pertaining to the Middle Ages. A condensed edition by C. W. Previte-Orton appeared in 1952 in two volumes and incorporates the results of recent scholarship. 940.1.C14

*Cannon, William Ragsdale. *History of Christianity in the Middle Ages.* Nashville: Abingdon Press, 1960.

Traces the events in the history of the Christian church from the fall of Rome in 476 to the fall of Constantinople in 1453, and surveys the men and movements, theology and philosophy that shaped the world of that time. Provides a complete picture of Eastern and Western medieval Christianity. 270.2.C16

Chesteron, Gilbert Keith. *Saint Thomas Aquinas.* Garden City: Doubleday and Co., 1957.

An introductory study to the work of the medieval philosopher-theologian. 282.44.AC8

Daniel-Rops, Henry [pseud]. *The Church in the Dark Ages.* Translated by Audrey Butler. New York: Dutton and Co., 1959.

This work by Jules Charles Henri Petiot ably treats the period of the ecumenical councils. Roman Catholic. 270.22.D22

Drummond, Robert Blackley. *Erasmus: His Life and Character as Shown by His Correspondence and Works.* 2 vols. London: Smith, Elder and Company, 1873.

A careful assessment of the life and career of one whose influence was clearly felt upon the church of the Reformation era, upon his friends, and upon biblical scholarship for the next one hundred years. 282.492.ER1.D84

Duffield, G. E., ed. *The Work of William Tyndale.* London: Falcon Books, 1965.

Appraises the genius of Tyndale and assesses his theological beliefs. Rightly places his life and labors in the context of Reformation history. Makes available primary source material found only in compendious tomes of the Parker Society. 274.2.T97D

Erasmus, Desiderius. *Eramus and His Age: Selected Letters.* Edited by Hans J. Hillerbrand. New York: Harper and Row Publishers, 1970.

Ideal for those who wish to obtain insights into the man, his philosophy, and his place in the Reformation movement. 274.2.ER1

Gardiner, James. *Lollardy and the Reformation in England.* 4 vols. London: Macmillan Co., 1908.

A well-written, interpretive treatise of the origin and influence of the Lollards, their persecution, and their place in Reformation history. 272.2.G16

Gaskoin, Charles Jacinth Bellairs. *Alcuin, His Life and Work.* New York: Russell and Russell, 1966.

Remains one of the most balanced

treatments of Alcuin's influence. First published in 1904. 274.3.AL1

Greenslade, Stanley Lawrence. *The Work of William Tindale*. London: Blaikie and Son, 1938.

Supplements Mozley's *William Tyndale*, and concentrates attention on the translation work of this great British reformer. 282.42.T97.G85

Hyma, Albert. *The Renaissance to the Reformation*. Rev. ed. Grand Rapids: Wm. B. Eerdmans Publishing Co., 1955.

An old, valuable survey. 270.5.H99 1955

John Hus at the Council of Constance. Translated by Matthew Spinka. New York: Columbia University Press, 1965.

A mature interpretation of the Reformer and the events leading up to his death. 284.37.H95

Lamb, Harold. *Charlemagne: The Legend and the Man*. Garden City: Doubleday and Co., 1954.

A vivid account of Charles the Great, his victories and defeats, the school he founded, the Renaissance that flourished under his patronage, and his influence upon the Christian church. 943.01.L16

————. *The Crusades*. Garden City: Doubleday and Co., 1931.

Originally published in two volumes. Contains the thrilling story of the Crusades from their beginning to the fall of Jerusalem, and from the struggle for supremacy in the Holy Land to the epic encounters of Richard the Lion-Hearted with Saladin the Wise. Lamb captures the impetus of these events and writes of them with fervor and insight. 940.18.L16

Lea, Henry Charles. *A History of the Inquisition in the Middle Ages*. 3 vols. New York: Russell and Russell, 1955.

This factual study exposes the horrors of the Inquisition. First published in 1888. An indispensable work. 272.2.L46 1955

Lechler, Gotthard Victor. *John Wiclif and His England Precursors*. Translated by Peter Lorimer. Edited by S. G. Green. London: The Religious Tract Society, 1904.

A popular, well-written study of Wycliffe and the Lollards. 282.42.W97

Lloyd, Roger Brodshaigh. *The Stricken Lute*. Port Washington, N.Y.: Kennikat Press, 1970.

This account of the life of Peter Abelard is interpretive as well as historical and serves the purpose of acquainting the reader with Abelard's thought. First published in 1932. 282.44.AB3 1970

Menzies, Lucy. *Saint Columba of Iona: A Study of His Life, His Times and His Influence*. London: J.M. Dent, 1920.

Canonization by the Church of Rome has detracted from Columba's place in history. What he accomplished on Iona may well serve as a model for modern theological education. 282.42.C72.M52

Milman, Henry Hart. *History of Latin Christianity; Including that of the Popes to the Pontificate of Nicolas V*. 9 vols. London: John Murray, 1883.

Continues the author's *History of Christianity*. Deals admirably with the main movements within the Church of Rome, including the various heretical movements that arose, the wars of the period, and the power struggles of popes and prelates, barons and dukes, kings and conquerors. 282'.09.M63

*****Parker, G. H. W.** *The Morning Star. The Advance of Christianity through the Centuries*. Grand Rapids: Wm. B. Eerdmans Publishing Co., 1965.

A careful, satisfying study of the influential people and events that contributed directly to the Reformation. Of particular value is the author's discussion of John Wycliffe. 270.B83 V. 3 (Alt. DDC 270.5)

Plaidy, Gene. *The Spanish Inquisition: Its Rise, Growth and End*. New York: Citadel Press, 1967.

A complete story of one of history's

worst epochs. 272.2'09.P69

Poole, Austin Lane. *From Domesday Book to Magna Carta, 1087-1216.* 2d ed. Oxford: At the Clarendon Press, 1955.

Covering the fortunes (or *mis*fortunes) of those in England following the death of William the Conqueror, this work records more than the struggle of two separate peoples—the Norman aristocracy and the English peasantry. It is also a record of the struggle for religious and political freedom, of great and good men and women, as well as of the selfish and powerful, indolent and corrupt. 942'.02.P78

Rice, Eugene F. *The Foundations of Early Modern Europe, 1460-1559.* New York: W. W. Norton, 1970.

A distinctive, well-documented presentation of the history of Europe during the period of the Renaissance and the Reformation. 940.2.R36

Rigg, James McMullen. *St. Anselm of Canterbury: A Chapter in the History of Religion.* London: Methuen and Company, 1896.

The author, a barrister, has provided a clear and in many respects authoritative biography of Anselm as churchman and political strategist. The theological insights into Anselm's thought are of the utmost merit. 283.42.AN7.R44

Runciman, Steven. *The Great Church in Captivity.* Cambridge: At the University Press, 1968.

A study of the Patriarchate of Constantinople from the eve of the Turkish conquest to the Greek War of Independence. 281.9.R87

————. *A History of the Crusades.* 3 vols. Cambridge: At the University Press, 1951.

Whether we regard the Crusades as the most romantic of Christian adventures or as the last of the barbarian invasions, they form a central fact in medieval history. Before their inception, the center of our civilization was placed in Byzantium and in the lands of the Arab caliphate. Before they faded out, the hegemony in civilization had passed to Western Europe. Out of this transformation modern history was born. In chronicling this transformation, Sir Steven Runciman has a written a book that, from beginning to end, enthrals the layman as completely as it satisfies the historian. The excitement of battle, the horror of senseless massacre, the interplay of personalities and ambitions, the effect on the whole development of European history—these are his themes. The whole tale is one of faith and folly, courage and greed, hope and disillusion. 270.4.R87

*****Schaff, David Schley.** *John Hus—His Life, Teachings and Death—After 500 Years.* New York: Charles Scribner's Sons, 1915.

While not as definitive as Spinka's works, this well-documented study surveys the life of the Czech reformer, pays tribute to his debt to Wycliffe, records his rise to national prominence as a leader of the people, and describes his open resistance to the pope and the fateful events leading up to the Council of Constance. 284.37.H95S

Smith, Herbert Maynard. *Pre-Reformation England.* New York: Russell and Russell, 1963.

A supplement to Bready's *England—Before and After Wesley.* Makes interesting reading, but now out-of-date. First published in 1938. 274.2.SM5 1963

Spinka, Matthew. *John Hus: A Biography.* Princeton: Princeton University Press, 1968.

After examining the life and writings of John Hus from every point of view, Spinka reveals the pitfalls and failures of Hus, and the religious and political narrow-mindedness that pervaded the era in which he lived. 274.37.SP4

————, **ed.** *Advocates of Reform: From*

Wyclif to Erasmus. Library of Christian Classics. Philadelphia: Westminster Press, 1953.

Of special value because it includes a selection of material not generally accessible to students of the period. 270.5.SP4

Stokes, George Thomas. *Ireland and the Celtic Church: A History of Ireland from St. Patrick to the English Conquest of 1172.* London: Hodder and Stoughton, 1886.

More and more attention is being focused on the Celtic church—its origin, missionary fervor, and message—and this account places within our hands a competent summary. 274.15.C33.ST6

Thompson, Alexander Hamilton, ed. *Bede: His Life, Times, and Writings.* New York: Russell and Russell, 1966.

Essays commemorating the twelfth centenary of Bede's death. 274.42.B39T

Turberville, Arthur Stanley. *Medieval Heresy and the Inquisition.* Hamden, Conn.: Archon Books, 1964.

An important introduction to the movements, intrigues, betrayals, and persecutions. 270.5.T79

Ullmann, Walter. *The Growth of Papal Government in the Middle Ages.* 2d ed. London: Methuen Co., 1962.

An informative treatise tracing the relationship between theory and institutions from the sixth century to the time of papal hegemony. For a further discus-

sion of this theme, see the writer's *Medieval Papalism: The Political Theories of the Medieval Canonists.* 270.4.UL4 1962

_____. *The Origins of the Great Schism.* Hamden, Conn.: Archon Books, 1967.

A scholarly assessment of fourteenth-century ecclesiastical church polity. 270.5.UL5 1967

*Walker, G. S. M. *The Growing Storm.* Advance of Christianity through the Centuries. Grand Rapids: Wm. B. Eerdmans Publishing Co., 1961.

Traces the rise and fall of the medieval papacy, and stresses the positive contribution of this period. The writer's treatment is judicious, his appraisal of events from A.D. 600 to 1350 is fair, and he combines exemplary scholarship with a fascinating presentation. 270.B83. v. 2 (Alt. DDC 270.4)

Warner, Henry James. *The Albigensian Heresy.* Rev. ed. 2 vols. New York: Russell and Russell, 1967.

An important historical study that focuses on the Manichaean dualism and allegorical interpretation of the sect, but it does not deal adequately with their persecution. 284.4.W24

Watkinson, William Lonsdale. *John Wicklif.* London: Epworth Press, n.d.

A thematic presentation of the life and labors of the reformer. 274.2.W97W

THE MODERN CHURCH (1517—PRESENT)

THE REFORMATION ERA (1517-1648)

*Anderson, James. *The Ladies of the Covenant.* London: Blackie and Son, 1850.

A companion volume to *Ladies of the Reformation.* Focuses on distinguished Scottish women during the period of the Covenanters. 270.8'092.AN2

*_____. *Ladies of the Reformation.* London: Blackie and Son, 1855.

The captivating story of distinguished women in England, Scotland, and the Netherlands who stood for their faith in spite of persecution and the threat of martyrdom. 270.6'092.AN2

Atkinson, James. *The Great Light: Luther and the Reformation.* The Advance of Christianity through the Centuries.

Grand Rapids: Wm. B. Eerdmans Publishing Co., 1968.

Covers almost the entire sixteenth century. Deals with Luther, Zwingli, Calvin, and the British Reformation. The treatment is uneven, but the material is well presented. Valuable. 270.B83 v. 4 (Alt. DDC 270.6).

―――. *The Trial of Luther.* London: B. T. Batsford, 1971.

A definitive study of Luther's defense at the Diet of Worms, 1521. 270.6.AT5

***Bainton, Roland Herbert.** *Here I Stand: A Life of Luther.* Nashville: Abingdon Press, 1951.

A brilliant treatment of the life of the great Reformer. Authoritative and well written. 284.143.L97B

―――. *The Reformation of the Sixteenth Century.* Boston: Beacon Press, 1952.

A clear, candid introduction. Of particular value is the correlation of the major events that took place in different parts of Europe during this period. 270.6.B16

―――. *Women of the Reformation in Germany and Italy.* Minneapolis: Augsburg Publishing House, 1971.

Frequently neglected, these women were faithful to their commitments and frequently displayed courage equal to that of the Reformers. 270.6'092.B16W

Bender, Harold Stauffer. *Conrad Grebel.* N.P.: By the author, 1936.

A definitive study. 284.3.G79

Bromiley, Geoffery William, ed. *Zwingli and Bullinger.* Library of Christian Classics. Philadelphia: Westminster Press, 1953.

Contains well-selected documents illustrative of the movement that grew up around these two men. Indispensable. 284.249.B78

***Cadier, Jean.** *The Man God Mastered.* Translated by O. R. Johnston. Grand Rapids: Wm. B. Eerdmans Publishing Co., 1960.

A brilliant translation of an important biography of John Calvin. 284.294.C13C

Calvin: Theological Treatises. Translated and edited by J. K. S. Reid Library of Christian Classics. Philadelphia: Westminster Press, 1954.

An able translation of such primary source material as "The Genevan Confession," "The Lausanne Articles," and documents on church organization, service, supervision, the Lord's Supper, and "The Necessity of Reforming the Church." 284.2.C13R

Carpenter, Spencer Cecil. *The Church in England,* 1597-1688. London: John Murray, 1954.

A thorough study of an important era in Anglican history. 283.09.C22

Chadwick, Owen. *The Reformation.* Grand Rapids: Wm. B. Eerdmans Publishing Co., 1965.

This general survey includes a thorough treatment of the Counter-Reformation, an account of how the Reformation affected the Eastern Orthodox church, and the influence of the Reformation on the ministry, worship, and the liturgy. 270.6.C34

Cowin, Henry. *John Knox: The Hero of the Scottish Reformation.* New York: AMS Press, 1970.

First appeared in 1905 as part of the *Heroes of the Reformation* series. The writer's treatment of the reformer's life is sympathetic and thorough, and his interpretation of events is more valuable than Percy's fine treatment. Well documented. 284.241.K77C 1970

Cranmer, Thomas. *The Works of Thomas Cranmer.* London: Falcon Books, 1965.

Cranmer left behind him a rich heritage. This account of his labors is testimony to his influence in ecclesiastical politics, as well as to his stature as a theologian. 283.42.C85 1965

***D'Aubigné, Jean Henri Merle.** *History of the Great Reformation of the Sixteenth*

Century in Germany, Switzerland, etc. 5 vols. London: D. Walther, 1837.

A masterly, well-documented treatment. Should be in the library of every evangelical pastor, and should be read at frequent intervals. 270.6.D26C

———. *The Life and Times of Martin Luther.* Translated by H. White. Chicago: Moody Press, n.d.

Contains selections from the author's famous *History of the Reformation in the Sixteenth Century.* Can be read with pleasure and enjoyment even by those who are not familiar with sixteenth-century Europe. 284.143.L97D

*———. *The Reformation in England.* Edited by S. M. Houghton. 2 vols. London: Banner of Truth Trust, 1962-63.

Selected writings published in 1853 and between 1866-78. Provides an indispensable guide to the place of the Bible in the Reformation of England. No one can read the writings of D'Aubigné and be the same afterward. 270.6.D26E

*Demaus, Robert L.** *Hugh Latimer: A Biography.* New ed. London: Religious Tract Society, 1903.

A pleasing, comprehensive study of the saintly Bishop of Worcester who was burned at the stake for refusing to accept the medieval doctrine of transubstantiation and the sacrifice of the Mass. 282.42.L34

Duffield, Gervase E., ed. *John Calvin: A Collection of Essays.* Courtenay Studies in Reformation Theology. Grand Rapids: Wm. B. Eerdmans Publishing Co., 1966.

A series of essays by an international team of Reformation scholars. Presents an accurate and less forbidding picture of Calvin. Particularly helpful for its assessment of his aims, achievements, and place in history. 284.294.C13.D87

———, **ed.** *Studies in John Calvin.* The Courtenay Studies in Reformation Theology. Grand Rapids: Wm. B. Eerdmans

Publishing Co., 1966.

Informative essays on different facets of Calvin's life and labors, theological system and teaching. 284.294.C13D

*Estep, William Roscoe.** *The Anabaptist Story.* Nashville: Broadman Press, 1963.

Desiring to vindicate the Anabaptists from the misrepresentation that has obscured and distorted their origin, teaching, and growth, the writer sets forth the growth of the free church movement in Europe and the development of their ideological beliefs. 284.3.ES8

*Grimm, Harold John.** *The Reformation Era.* Rev. ed. New York: Macmillan Co., 1965.

A clear presentation of the historical and cultural milieu of the Reformation period. 270.6.G88 1965

Harbison, Elmore Harris. *The Christian Scholar in the Age of the Reformation.* New York: Charles Scribner's Sons, 1956.

A study of the great personalities of the Reformation period. 270.6'092.H21

Hoogstra, Jacob Tunis, ed. *John Calvin, Contemporary Prophet.* Grand Rapids: Baker Book House, 1959.

Written to commemorate the 450th anniversary of Calvin's birth and the 400th anniversary of the final edition of the "Magna Charta" of the Reformation, *The Institutes of the Christian Religion,* this symposium focuses on the person of Calvin, his writings, and the relevancy of his theology to 1959. 284.294.C13H

*Knox, John.** *History of the Reformation in Scotland.* Edited by William Croft Dickinson. 2 vols. New York: Philosophical Library, 1950.

A readable edition of the reformer's famous works. 274.41.K77

Lindsay, Thomas Martin. *Luther and the German Reformation.* Freeport, N.Y.: Books for Libraries Press, 1970.

This work remains one of the best

treatments on the life and thought of Luther. Scholarly. First published in 1900. 270.643.L64 1970

Littell, Franklin Hamlin. *The Anabaptist View of the Church: A Study in the Origins of Sectarian Protestantism.* 2d ed. Beacon Hill, Boston: Starr King Press, 1958.

A thorough analysis of the Radical Reformation, with an evaluation of the Anabaptist doctrines and principles of church organization and administration. 284.3.L73 1958

*Loane, Marcus Lawrence. *Masters of the English Reformation.* London: Church Bookroom Press, 1956.

A delightful study of Thomas Bilney, William Tyndale, Hugh Latimer, Nicholas Ridley, and Thomas Cranmer. 274.2.L78M (Alt. DDC 283.42)

*_____. *Pioneers of the Reformation in England.* London: Church Book Room Press, 1964.

Covers four of the lesser-known personalities involved in the Reformation movement in England. They never rose to great eminence because their lives were cut short by those who opposed their evangelical teaching. 283.42.L78

Martin Luther. *The Career of the Reformer.* Philadelphia: Fortress Press, 1957-60.

Comprises volumes 31-34 of *Luther's Works.* Contains Luther's disputations and treatises, miscellaneous writings and historical incidents. Provides primary source material for all who would engage in a serious study of his life. 270.643.L97

_____. *Luther's Works.* Edited by Jaroslav Pelikan and Helmut T. Lehmann. 55 vols. Philadelphia: Fortress Press, 1955.

A project begun by Concordia Publishing House, St. Louis, and continued by the present publishers. The most extensive and definite translation of Luther's works available today. Includes his commentaries, sermons, and teach-

ings on theological themes, as well as an evaluation of his life, the liturgy, and his hymns. 284.143.L97P

*MacGregor, Geddes. *The Thundering Scott: A Portrait of John Knox.* Philadelphia: Westminster Press, 1957.

A brilliantly written treatment that ably blends the political forces and spiritual power that swept across Scotland and brought about the Reformation. 284.241.K77

Mackinnon, James. *Calvin and the Reformation.* 2 vols. New York: Russell and Russell, 1962.

An examination of Calvin's unique contribution to the Reformation. A valuable work. 270.6.M21C

_____. *Luther and the Reformation.* 4 vols. New York: Russell and Russell, 1962.

Contains an abundance of material based on an evaluation of original sources, and propounds in a judicious manner the writer's thoughts on Luther and the movements that brought about the Reformation. First published 1925-30. 270.G.M21L

*MacPherson, Hector. *Scotland's Battles for Spiritual Independence.* London: Hodder and Stoughton, 1905.

Ably delineates between the quest for power (ecclesiastical as well as political) and a true spirit of independence based upon biblical principles. Describes the struggle between church and state, and lays justifiable stress upon the far-ranging effects of the battles they fought and won. 284.241.M24

*McCrie, Thomas. *The Life of John Knox.* Inverness, Scotland: Free Presbyterian Church of Scotland, 1960.

A classic work. 284.241.K77M

*Manschreck, Clyde Leonard. *Melanchthon, The Quiet Reformer.* Nashville: Abingdon Press, 1958.

Defends Melanchthon's indiscretions, vindicates his actions, and shows him to be widely misunderstood by students of the period. 284.143.M48M

McNeill, John Thomas. *The History and Character of Calvinism.* New York: Oxford University Press, 1967.

A comprehensive account of Calvin's life, with information on the spread of Calvinism. Weak in its presentation of Calvin's theology, and makes tedious reading. 284.2.M23

Nixon, Leroy. *John Calvin, Expository Preacher.* Grand Rapids: Wm. B. Eerdmans Publishing Co., 1950.

Growing out of the author's thesis at Princeton Theological Seminary, this work explores Calvin's homiletic style, reveals the uniqueness of his approach when set against the spirit of his times, and provides readers with a clear revelation of Calvin's commitment to the Word of God. 284.294.C13.N65

*Parker Society, London. *The Parker Society . . . for the Publication of the Works of the Fathers and Early Writers of the Reformed English Church.* 55 vols. Cambridge: At the University Press, 1841-55.

An indispensable set containing the writings—sermons, tracts, treatises, prayers, and theological works—of the leading evangelical scholars in England during the Reformation and post-Reformation eras. 274.2.RE25.P22

Penning, Louwrens. *Genius of Geneva: A Popular Account of the Life and Times of John Calvin.* Translated by B. S. Berrington. Grand Rapids: Wm. B. Eerdmans Publishing Co., 1954.

In spite of the pedantic style, this is a stimulating account of Calvin and the movement that bears his name. Readily reveals the far-reaching influence of the reformer. 284.294.C13P

Percy, Eustace. *John Knox.* Richmond: John Knox Press, 1965.

Historically accurate, but less discerning than the works of MacGregor and Ridley. Deserves reading. 284.241.K77P

Pollard, Albert Frederick. *Thomas Cranmer and the English Reformation, 1489-1556.* Hamden, Conn.: Archon Books, 1965.

Seeks to clear up some of the mysteries surrounding Cranmer, his influence on church life, the convictions he chose to adhere to in the face of Tudor tyranny, and the events which brought about his martyrdom. Based on the 1905 edition. 283.42.C85P

*Renwick, A.M. *The Story of the Scottish Reformation.* Grand Rapids: Wm. B. Eerdmans Publishing Co., 1960.

A brilliantly written, captivating account of the spiritual, political and social forces that prevailed at the time of the Reformation in Scotland. 274.41.R29

*Ridley, Jasper Godwin. *John Knox.* Oxford: At the University Press, 1968.

A fresh account of Knox's activities in Scotland, England, Germany, and Switzerland. Focuses on Knox's political overtones and his theological presuppositions. 284.241.K77R

*_____. *Thomas Cranmer.* Oxford: At the Clarendon Press, 1962.

This work is objective, comprehensive, emphasizes the negative aspects more fully than is necessary, but provides a very informative, helpful study of the man who contributed to the English Reformation. 283.42.C85R

*Rilliet, Jean Horace. *Zwingli: Third Man of the Reformation.* Translated by Harold Knight. Philadelphia: Westminster Press, 1964.

Blends Zwingli's principle writings with a history of the times, deals at length with the Eucharistic controversy, and provides his readers with a most informative biography. 284.249.Z9R

Rupp, Ernest Gordon. *Luther's Progress to the Diet of Worms.* New York: Harper and Row, 1964.

An important, brief reconstruction of the reformer's early life and ministry.

Ably evaluates the technical aspects of salvation in the writings of the Schoolmen, and also contributes an informative study on Luther's nominalism. Should be read in the light of the writer's *Patterns of Reformation.* 270.6.R87

Schreiber, Clara Seuel. *Katherine, Wife of Luther.* Philadelphia: Muhlenberg Press, 1954.

An informative study of Katherine von Bora, Luther's "rib." Takes readers behind the scenes, and paints an intimate picture of the reformer's home life. 274.3.L97.SCH7

Singer, Charles Gregg. *John Calvin: His Roots and Fruits.* Philadelphia: Presbyterian and Reformed Publishing Co., 1967.

A brief evaluation of Calvin's view of the world, life, and history. 284.294.C13S

Smith, Herbert Maynard. *Henry VIII and the Reformation.* New York: Russell and Russell, 1962.

A critical evaluation of Henry's role in the separation of the English church from Roman rule, and of the kind of reformation he tried to bring about. 942.052.T815

Smith, Henry Preserved. *The Age of the Reformation.* New York: Henry Holt and Co., 1920.

†Contains important insights, but is marred by the writer's theological position. Bainton on *Luther,* Wendell on *Calvin,* and Rilliet on *Zwingli* are more reliable. 940.22.SM5

Smyth, Charles Hugh Egerton. *Cranmer and the Reformation under Edward VI.* Westport, Conn.: Greenwood Press, 1970.

Surveys the continuing results of the Reformation under the son of Henry VIII. Reprinted from the 1926 edition. 283.42.C85S 1970

*Stupperich, Robert. *Melanchthon.* Translated by Robert H. Fischer. Philadelphia: Westminster Press, 1965.

This record of one of the enigmatic figures of the sixteenth century describes the place of the reformer in the events that surrounded the followers and friends of Luther. 284.143.M48S

Taylor, F. J., ed. *Melanchthon and Bucer.* Library of Christian Classics. Philadelphia: Westminster Press.

An important contribution. Makes available primary source material that otherwise might be unobtainable. 270.6.T21

*Vedder, Henry C. *Balthasar Hübmaier.* New York: G. P. Putnam's Sons, 1905.

Builds on primary source material. Provides his readers with a well-written, readable study of the leader of the Anabaptists. 284.343.H86

Walker, Williston. *John Calvin.* New York: Schocken Books, 1906.

An old work that still retains its value. 284.294.C13W

Warburton, Ben A. *Calvinism.* Grand Rapids: Wm. B. Eerdmans Publishing Co., 1955.

An extensive investigation into the history and basic principles, benefits, and future prospects of Calvinism. 284.2.W19

Wenger, John Christian. *Even Unto Death.* Richmond: John Knox Press, 1961.

An account of the heroic witness of the sixteenth-century Anabaptists that corrects many of the distortions of the past. An important study. 284.3.W48

Whitehorn, R. D. and **Norman Sykes, eds.** *English Reformers.* Library of Christian Classics. Philadelphia: Westminster Press, 1966.

An important selection of documents illustrating the ecclesiastical conflicts of the period. 283.42.W58

*Williams, George Huntston. *The Radical Reformation.* Philadelphia: Westminster Press, 1962.

Deals with certain movements within the Reformation that have been largely ignored until the twentieth century. Includes the Anabaptists, the rationally inclined humanists, and the mystically inclined spiritualists. Worthy of detailed study in spite of the fact that the writer leans toward Unitarianism. 270.6.W67

_____ and **Angel M. Mergal, eds.** *Spiritual and Anabaptist Writers.* Library of Christian Classics. Philadelphia: Westminster Press, 1957.

A valuable collection of material pertaining to the radical movement of the Reformation. 284.3.W67

Wood, Arthur Skevington. *Captive to the Word: Martin Luther and the Bible.* Grand Rapids: Wm. B. Eerdmans Publishing Company, 1969.

A rewarding though not impartial study. 270.643.L97W

The Works of James Arminius. Translated by James Nichols. 3 vols. Grand Rapids: Baker Book House, 1956.

These lectures deal with the nature and scope of Arminius's theological system and show him to be much closer to Calvin's doctrine than many of his followers. First published in English in 1853. 284.9.AR5 1956

THE RISE OF
DENOMINATIONALISM
(1648—1789)

Baxter, Richard. *The Autobiography of Richard Baxter.* Abridged with an introduction and notes by J. M. Lloyd Thomas. London: J.M. Dent and Sons, 1925.

A clear, easy-to-read account of the life of one of the great nonconformists of the 17th century, replete with accounts of political and ecclesiastical intrigue and all that militates against the development of piety and the work of the Lord. 283.42.B33A

_____. *The Practical Works of the Rev. Richard Baxter.* 5 vols. London: Richard Edwards, 1825.

In a day when God's people are again perishing for lack of knowledge (cf. Hosea 6:4), it is refreshing to read how this great preacher of yesteryear made the profound truths of Holy Writ understandable. 283.42.B33

Bradford John. *Bradford's "History of Plymouth Plantation."* Boston: Wright and Potter, 1898.

A reproduction of the original manuscript, together with "a report of the proceedings incident to the return of the manuscript to Massachusetts." 277.1.B72

Bready, John Wesley. *England: Before and After Wesley.* London: Hodder and Stoughton, 1938.

Traces the evangelical revival and the social reform that saved England from revolution. 274.2.B74

***Brown, John.** *John Bunyan: His Life, Times and Work.* London: Hulbert Publishing Co., 1928.

The tercentenary edition of the Bedford tinker's life and ministry, preaching and dissent, and travail for religious liberty. 286.142.B88B

Brown, William James. *Jeremy Taylor.* London: SPCK, 1925.

Concentrates on Taylor's literary achievements, and refers only incidentally to the trials that plagued him throughout his life and brought about his early death. 283.15.T21

Buchan, John. *Oliver Cromwell.* London: Hodder and Stoughton, 1934.

More recognition is due the "Lord Protector" than is commonly conceded, for Cromwell, more than any other politician up to his time, laid a foundation for the establishment of democracy and the independence of church and state. 283.42.C88.B85

Channing, William Ellery. *The Works of William E. Channing, D. D.* 6 vols. Boston: James Munroe and Company, 1845.

†Those who wish to study Channing's brand of Unitarianism will find his views defended in these volumes. 288.73.C36

Clark, Henry William. *History of English Non-conformity.* 2 vols. London: Chapman and Hall, 1911.

Tackles successfully the period from Wycliffe to the close of the nineteenth century. Furnishes readers with an indispensable account of the struggle for religious freedom undertaken at such great cost by those who secured freedom of worship. An excellent treatment. Ought to be read repeatedly. 274.2.C54

The Complete Writings of Menno Simons. Translated by Leonard Verduin. Edited by John Christian Wenger. Scottsdale, Penn.: Herald Press, 1966.

This extensive study provides an indispensable reference book to early Anabaptist history. Includes a biographical sketch by Harold S. Bender. First published in 1956. 284.3.SI5

*Dallimore, Arnold A. *George Whitefield.* London: Banner of Truth Trust, 1970-.

Scheduled for two volumes. Volume 1 deals with the life and times of the great evangelist and the early revivals that attended his ministry in England and America. Gives promise of becoming the most definitive study of George Whitefield. 285.873.W58D

*Douglas, James Dixon. *Light in the North. The Advance of the Christianity through the Centuries.* Grand Rapids: Wm. B. Eerdmans Publishing Co., 1964.

A forthright presentation of the rise and influence of the Scottish Covenanters. 270.B83 V. 7 (Alt. DDC 285.241)

Dunn, Richard S. *The Age of Religious Wars, 1559-1689.* New York: W. W. Norton, 1970.

An indispensable assessment of the history of this period. 940.22.D92

Durnbaugh, Donald F. *The Believers' Church: The History and Character of Radical Protestantism.* New York: Macmillan Co., 1968.

A synopsis of independent movements within Christendom since the Reformation. Surveys the initial concept of the "Believers' Church," catalogs its history, and concludes with an assessment of their characteristics and theological beliefs. 280.4.D93

Easton, Emily. *Roger Williams: Prophet and Pioneer.* Freeport, N.Y.: Books for Libraries Press, 1969.

First published in 1930, this is perhaps one of the most sensitive biographies ever written of this great Christian statesman. 286.173.W67.EA7 1969

*Edwards, Jonathan. *The Diary of David Brainerd.* Chicago: Moody Press, 1955.

This autobiographical treatment recounts Brainerd's early life as a student and his missionary work among the Indians. In addition to being a record of his physical labors, it is the document of his inner struggle to know and do the will of God. An inspirational volume. First published in 1749. 285.173.B73E 1955

*Flavel, John. *The Works of John Flavel.* 6 vols. London: Banner of Truth Trust, 1968.

Prefaced with an account of Flavel's life, this work contains his theological and devotional studies, sermons and works of counsel, and studies on different portions of the Bible. First published in 1701. 284.242.F61 1968

Gaustad, Edwin Scott. *The Great Awakening in New England.* New York: Harper and Brothers, 1957.

A thorough, illuminating study. A welcome addition. 277.4.G23

*George Whitefield's Journals. London: Banner of Truth Trust, 1960.

Containing the *Seven Journals* first published between 1738 and 1741, together with other material by the evangelist and *An Unpublished Journal* first printed in 1938, this intimate account of Whitefield's ministry shows how he attracted the masses to hear the gospel and provides an informative study of his prayer life. 285.873.W58 1960

Gill, Frederick Cyril. *Charles Wesley: The First Methodist.* Nashville: Abingdon Press, 1964.

This biographical work draws on primary and secondary sources and provides a vivid account of the life and labors of the cofounder of Methodism. 287.142.W51G

Greaves, Richard L. *John Bunyan.* Courtenay Studies in Reformation Theology. Grand Rapids: Wm. B. Eerdmans Publishing Co., 1969.

An informative study of the theology of the tinker who became one of England's most popular preachers. 286.142.B88G

Grossart, Alexander B. *Representative Nonconformists: With the Message of their Life-work for Today.* London: Hodder and Stoughton, 1879.

The Spring Lectures of the Presbyterian Church of England, London, these studies provide important interpretative clues to the personalities of John Howe, Richard Baxter, Samuel Rutherford, and Matthew Henry. Makes inspirational reading. 284.G91

Harmon, Rebecca Lamar. *Susanna, Mother of the Wesleys.* Nashville: Abingdon Press, 1968.

A candid evaluation of the powerful influence Susanna Wesley exerted on her family. 287.142.W51H

Heimert, Alan E. and **Perry Miller.** *The Great Awakening: Documents Illustrating the Crisis and Its Consequences.* The American Heritage Series. Indianapolis: Bobbs-Merrill Co., 1967.

A valuable collection of sermons, letters, pamphlets, poems, and satires associated with the Great Awakening of the 1740s. 277.4.H36

Henry, Stuart Clark. *George Whitefield: Wayfaring Witness.* Nashville: Abingdon Press, 1957.

A modern evaluation of "The Man" and "His Message." Surveys his early life, and then concentrates on the type of messages he preached. 287.173.W58H

Hillerbrand, Hans Joachim. *A Fellowship of Discontent.* New York: Harper and Row, 1967.

A study of reformers, schismatics, heretics, apostates, sectarians, and radicals, from the time of the Reformation to the nineteenth century. 270.6'08.H55

Hooker, Richard. *The Works of the Learned and Judicious Divine, Mr. Richard Hooker.* 2 vols. Oxford: At the Clarendon Press, 1875.

Hooker was *par excellence* the apologist of the Elizabethan Settlement of 1559, and perhaps the most accomplished advocate Anglicanism has ever had. He developed his doctrines in his *Treatise on the Laws of Ecclesiastical Polity.* Of the five books that appeared in Hooker's lifetime, 1-4 were published in 1594, and 5 in 1597. Books 6 (certainly spurious in its present form) and 8 did not appear until 1648, and Book 7 until 1662. These volumes contain his complete writings. 283.42.H76 1875

Jackson, Robert Wise. *Jonathan Swift: Dean and Pastor.* London: Society for the Promotion of Christian Knowledge, 1939.

A short yet complete biography of Jonathan Swift—literary genius, discerning political critic, and insightful theologian. Also describes him as a family man who was a capable and dedicated pastor. 283.415.SW5.J13

The Journal of George Fox. Revised by J. L. Nickalls. Cambridge: At the University Press, 1952.

Records the events in the life of the founder of the Society of Friends. Contains extracts from William Penn's preface and Henry J. Cadbury's assessment of Fox's later years. 289.642.F83 1952

Kellogg, Samuel Henry. *The Genesis*

and Growth of Religion. New York: Macmillan Co., 1892.

Made up of the L. P. Stone Lectures, Princeton Theological Seminary, for 1892. Surveys the origin and growth of religion in the post-Reformation era, and deals particularly with the attacks of atheists and the approaches of the philosophers during the period of the Enlightenment. Particularly helpful in exposing the weaknesses of theologians and their systems of thought from Schleiermacher to the end of the nineteenth century. 270.7.K29

Law, William. *The Works of the Reverend William Law, M. A. . . .* 9 vols. London: J. Richardson, 1762.

Apart from Law's lengthy letters, readers will find here his fine treatise on "The Spirit of Prayer," "The Way of Divine Knowledge," work on Christian perfection, and so on. Many of these independent studies are worthy of reprinting as individual monographs. 283.42.L41

Lewis, Arthur James. *Zinzendorf, the Ecumenical Pioneer.* Philadelphia: Westminster Press, 1962.

A modern assessment of the Moravian contribution to Christian mission and unity. 284.643.Z6

The Letters of the Rev. John Wesley. Edited by John Telford. 8 vols. London: Epworth Press, 1931.

Builds on all earlier editions, and takes pains to insure completeness. Many of the letters contained in these volumes are controversial; some are intimate; some deal with doctrine and others with practical holiness; but all of them reveal much about the man and his times. 287.142.W51L

Mather, Cotton. *Magnalia Christi Americana.* Edited and abridged by Raymond J. Cunningham. New York: Frederick C. Ungar, 1970.

An ecclesiastical history of New England by one of the great theologians of

the period. 277.4.M42 1970

Miller, Perry. *Errand into the Wilderness.* Cambridge: Belknap Press of Harvard University Press, 1956.

A readable work on early American civilization, religion, and philosophical thought. 917.3.M61

————. *The New England Mind.* Boston: Beacon Press, 1954.

A fascinating study of early Americana. 917.4.M61

————. *Orthodoxy in Massachusetts.* New York: Harper and Row, 1970.

An important study, but one that misunderstands the nature of religious orthodoxy. 277.44.M61

———— and **T. H. Johnson, eds.** *The Puritans: A Sourcebook of Their Writings.* 2 vols. Rev. ed. New York: Harper and Row, 1963.

This thematic consideration of primary source material covers the major epochs of early American puritanism. It includes the Puritan's views on the state and society, this world and the next, poetry, education, and so on. First published in 1938. 810.822.M61

Moriarty, Gerald P. *Dean Swift and His Writings.* London: Seely and Company, 1893.

Apart from *Gulliver's Travels,* little is known of Jonathan Swift, dean of St. Patrick's Cathedral, Dublin, and one of the most influential theologians of his day. This study focuses on his political writings, novels, letters, and poetry, all of which provide us with a better understanding of his character. 283.415.SW5.M82

Murdock, Kenneth Ballard. *Increase Mather, The Foremost American Puritan.* New York: Russell and Russell, 1966.

Introduces readers to the life and thought of this renowned civic and ecclesiastical leader. First published in 1925. 285.873.M42

*Nichols, James Hastings. *History of*

Christianity, 1650-1950. Secularization of the West. New York: Ronald Press, 1956.

After carefully studying the history of the Christian church in the post-Reformation period, the writer comes to the conclusion that Western Christendom has become secularized. This scholarly work supports his thesis. 270.7.N51

Niebuhr, Reinhold. *Faith and History: A Comparison of Christian and Modern Views of History.* New York: Charles Scribner's Sons, 1949.

†Much of what the writer presents in this volume is helpful. Refutes the idea that historical development is of itself redemptive, and stresses that man's life can be made intelligible only with the larger role of meaning discerned by faith. 901.N55

Outler, Albert Cook, ed. *John Wesley.* Oxford: At the Clarendon Press, 1964.

By systematically arranging material under specific headings, the editor tries to bring into sharp focus the great revivalist's theological views. 287.142.W51

*Owen, John. *The Works of John Owen.* Edited by William H. Goold. 16 vols. London: Banner of Truth Trust, 1965.

A complete, unabridged edition of this famous Puritan's doctrinal, practical, and controversial writings. 285.842.OW2 1965

Rudolph, L. C. *Francis Asbury.* Nashville: Abingdon Press, 1966.

By deftly combining thorough research with a balanced interpretation of the data, the writer portrays the character and personality, sacrifice and service of America's first Methodist bishop. 287.173.AS1R

Rutherford, Samuel. *The Letters of Samuel Rutherford.* Chicago: Moody Press, 1951.

Imprisoned for his faith, Rutherford wrote letters of encouragement and consolation to others who were enduring trials and distress. These letters manifest a devout and reverent spirit and have become the valued heritage of the Christian church. 284.241.R93

Schmidt, Martin. *John Wesley: A Theological Biography.* Translated by Norman P. Goldhawk. London: Epworth Press, 1962-.

An excellent survey of the development of Wesley's doctrine. 287.442.W51S

*Smellie, Alexander. *Men of the Covenant.* London: Banner of Truth Trust, 1960.

Recounts the events in seventeenth-century Scotland in which men and women, bound by "covenant" to Christ, laid down their lives for His cause. Recaptures the intensity, zeal, heroism, and faith of these martyrs, as well as the craftiness and cruelty of their persecutors. First published in 1903. 284.241.SM3

*Strauss, Oscar S. *Roger Williams: The Pioneer of Religious Liberty.* Freeport, N.Y.: Books for Libraries Press, 1970.

First published in 1894, this graphic, well-written book deals honestly and impartially with the strengths and weaknesses of this great New Englander. 286.173.W67.ST8

Telford, John. *The Life of John Wesley.* London: Epworth Press, 1960.

Has long remained one of the most extensive treatments of Wesley's life and labors. Well written. First published in 1947. 287.142.W51T

*_____. *The Life of the Rev. Charles Wesley.* London: Wesleyan Methodist Book Room, 1900.

Begins with the ancestry and parentage of the Wesleys, moves quickly to missionary work in Georgia, describes in detail his conversion, and focuses on the different stages of the evangelical revival attending the ministry of John and Charles. 287.142.W51

Tracy, Joseph. *The Great Awakening.* New York: Arno Press, 1969.

Long out of print. Traces the history of revival in the time of Jonathan Edwards and George Whitefield. First published in 1845. 277.4.T67 1969

Turnbull, Ralph G. *Jonathan Edwards the Preacher.* Grand Rapids: Baker Book House, 1958.

A careful study of the character of Edwards as a preacher and the factors that contributed to his greatness. 285.873.ED9T

Tyerman, Luke. *The Life of the Rev. George Whitefield.* 2 vols. New York: Anson D.F. Randolph, 1877.

One of the truly great biographies of Whitefield. Traces his rise to prominence from his humble origins in Gloucester, through his studies at Oxford, to his ministry on both sides of the Atlantic. 285.873.W58.T96

Wardlaw, Ralph. *Discourses on the Principal Points of the Socinian Controversy.* 4th ed., enl. London: Longman, Rees, Orme, Brown and Green, 1828.

This vindication of Christ's deity also treats the doctrine of the atonement, the deity and personality of the Holy Spirit, and concludes with a discussion of the relation of doctrine to Christian character. Thorough. A most important treatise. 230.8.SO1.W21 1828

Weinlick, John Rudolf. *Count Zinzendorf.* Nashville: Abingdon Press, 1956.

Succeeds in providing an informative, well-written study of the founder of the Herrnhuter "Brüdergemeine." 284.643.Z6W

Wesley, John. *The Journal of the Rev. John Wesley.* Edited by Nehemiah Curmock. 8 vols. London: Epworth Press, 1938.

A special edition of Wesley's journal, letters, and other papers issued to commemorate the bicentary of John Wesley's conversion. Contains a complete reprint of the earlier material, together with some newly discovered writings and a supplementary volume. This informative work highlights the labors of the founder of Methodism, and also provides interesting data on the culture and customs of the times. In addition, there is an informative essay by Wesley himself on the rise and design of Oxford Methodism. 287.142.W51C

Williams, Roger. *Complete Writings of Roger Williams.* 7 vols. New York: Russell and Russell, 1963.

Shows how Williams's beliefs became the focal point of those who shared his values and goals. Lays a solid foundation both biblically and experientially for the separation of church and state. A valuable acquisition. 286.1.W67 1963

Winslow, Ola Elizabeth. *Jonathan Edwards.* New York: Collier Books, 1961.

This study is both factual and interpretive. First published in 1940. 285.873.ED9W

————. *John Eliot, Apostle to the Indians.* Boston: Houghton Mifflin Co., 1968.

Aptly describes and ably presents the ministry of Eliot to the Indians of Massachusetts. Blends a history of the times with the activity and ministry of the biographee. The author lacks sympathy with her subject. 285.873.EL4

***Wood, Arthur Skevington.** *The Inextinguishable Blaze.* The Advance of Christianity Through the Centuries. Grand Rapids: Wm. B. Eerdmans Publishing Co., 1960.

An in-depth study of the Wesleyan Revival of the eighteenth century. Traces its abiding results. 270.B83 V. 6 (Alt. DDC 270.7)

————. *John Wesley: The Burning Heart.* Grand Rapids: Wm. B. Eerdmans Publishing Co., 1969.

Records with candor and warmth the successes and failures of the rationalistic skeptic whose heart was "strangely warmed" by the gospel. 287.142.W51W

The Works of John Wesley. 3d ed. 14 vols.

Grand Rapids: Zondervan Publishing House, 1958-59.

This complete and unabridged edition is a reproduction of the authorized edition published by the Wesleyan Conference office in London, 1872. 287.142.W51

Wynbeek, David. *David Brainerd: Beloved Yankee.* Grand Rapids: Wm. B. Eerdmans Publishing Co., 1961.

An absorbing narrative based upon the diaries of this pioneer missionary. 285.173.B73W

THE ERA OF DIVERGENCE
(1789—   )

Abbott, Walter M., ed. *Documents of Vatican II.* New York: Association Press, 1966.

A compilation of the sixteen official documents produced by the council, together with speeches by Pope John and Pope Paul. 282.09.AB2

Alexander, William Lindsay. *Memoirs of the Life and Writings of Ralph Wardlaw.* 2d ed. Edinburgh: Adam and Charles Black, 1856.

"As the life of a great man is, in the general, composed of the history of his thoughts and actions . . ." so it is fitting that these memoirs should focus upon what Dr. Wardlaw accomplished during his lifetime: the church he pastored for fifty years, the books he wrote, the seminary he founded, and the impact of his life on the work of evangelism and importance of foreign missions. 285.841.W21.AL2 1856

Asbury, Francis. *Journal and Letters of Francis Asbury.* 3 vols. Edited by E. T. Clark. Nashville: Abingdon Press, 1958.

Asbury was one of the greatest explorers of the American frontier—a tower of strength in the early Methodist church and nation. He and his circuit riders went into every new community

and nearly every log cabin in the wilderness. In their saddlebags, they carried the fundamentals of civilization—the Bible, the hymnbook, and religious literature of a varied nature. They helped to make godly, law-abiding citizens out of people who might have become criminal. Asbury preached a gospel of personal salvation throughout his ministry, and he is deserving of a lasting and unique place in early American history. 287.173.AS1

The Autobiography of Peter Cartwright. Edited by W. P. Strickland. Nashville: Abingdon Press, 1956.

An intriguing account of the labors of one of the earliest and best-known circuit riders of early Methodism. First published in 1857. 287.173.C24

Bacon, Ernest Wallace. *Spurgeon: Heir of the Puritans.* Grand Rapids: William B. Eerdmans Publishing Co., 1968.

A biographical sketch that pays particular attention to the Puritan tradition out of which Spurgeon came. 286.142.SP9B

*Barbour, George Freeland. *The Life of Alexander Whyte.* 7th ed., rev. London: Hodder and Stoughton, 1925.

A fascinating study of the great Edinburgh preacher. 284.241.W62 1925

Bates, Miner Searle and **Wilhelm Pauck, eds.** *The Prospects of Christianity Throughout the World.* New York: Charles Scribner's Sons, 1964.

†Essays on the state of church and mission in various parts of the world. Ecumenical. 270.9.B31

*Boettner, Loraine. *Roman Catholicism.* London: Banner of Truth Trust, 1966.

A perceptive evaluation of Roman Catholic doctrine. 282.B63

Bonar, Andrew Alexander. *Robert Murray M'Cheyne: Memoir and Remains.* London: Banner of Truth Trust, 1966.

This work merited Spurgeon's approval as "one of the best and most profitable volumes ever published." Reprinted from the enlarged 1892 edition. 284.241.M13B 1966

*Bonar, Marjory, ed. *Andrew A. Bonar: Diary and Life.* London: Banner of Truth Trust, 1960.

A panoramic view of one of the most fascinating periods of Scottish church history. 284.241.B64 1960

Bonhoeffer, Dietrich. *Letters and Papers From Prison.* New York: Macmillan Co., 1962.

†Imprisoned by the Nazis during World War II, the writer continued to keep in touch with Christian leaders in Germany. This book contains his correspondence. Exposes his deep sensitivity to the needs of the hour, shows his faith in God, and reveals his theological presuppositions. 284.143.B64

Bramwell-Booth, Catherine. *Catherine Booth: The Story of Her Loves.* London: Hodder and Stoughton, 1970.

A pleasing story of the great wife of a great man; and one who, under God, labored as faithfully and as diligently as her husband—never for a moment as a shadowy figure behind the scenes, and never in any way as one inferior to the one to whom she was married. 267.15.B64.B73

*Brown, Harold O. J. *The Protest of a Troubled Protestant.* New Rochelle: Arlington House, 1969.

A vigorous apologetic for biblical Christianity, coupled with a defense of the historic beliefs against the inroads of materialism, secularism, and ecumenism. 280.4.B81

Breunig, Charles. *The Age of Revolution and Reaction, 1789-1850.* New York: W. W. Norton, 1970.

An original, well-balanced treatment of trends within Europe and their influence on the church. 940.27.B75

Cairns, Earle E. *Christianity in the United States.* Chicago: Moody Press, 1964.

Covers American religion in the colonial era to the middle of the twentieth century, coupled with a survey of present-day religious trends. 277.3.C12

The Cambridge Modern History. Edited by A. W. Ward, G. W. Prothero, and Stanley Lathes. 13 vols. Cambridge: At the University Press, 1934.

Covers the Renaissance, Reformation, the wars on religion, the Thirty Years War, the age of Louis XIV, the eighteenth century, the United States, the French Revolution, the Napoleonic wars, the Restoration, and the expansion that followed the turn of the century. Volume 13 contains tables and index. Has now been replaced by *The New Cambridge Modern History* (1957-65). 940.2.C14M

Campbell, Robert Edward, ed. *Spectrum of Protestant Beliefs.* New Rochelle: M. M. Bruce, 1968.

Compiled and edited by a Roman Catholic, this book surveys topics including the Trinity, the Bible, the virgin birth, the origin of sin, heaven and hell, premarital sex, racial integration, anti-Semitism, the ecumenical movement, and so on. The contributors are Carl Henry (neoevangelical), John Warwick Montgomery (confessional Lutheran), James Pike (liberal Episcopalian), William Hamilton (radical) and Bob Jones, Jr. The variety of opinion on these diverse subjects is sometimes humorous, and always provocative. A most unusual book. 280.4.C15

Carlile, John Charles. *Alexander Maclaren: The Man and His Message.* London: S. W. Partridge and Co., 1901.

A brief character sketch of the man who was widely regarded as the "prince of Bible expositors" of the last century. 286.142.M22

Carson, Herbert M. *The New Catholicism.* London: Banner of Truth Trust, 1965.

This brief booklet serves as a supplement to Carson's *Roman Catholicism Today.* Attempts to avoid the extremes of dismissing Catholicism altogether or accepting it without proper evaluation. 282.C23

Charles Grandison Finney: An Autobiography. Westwood, N.J.: Fleming H. Revell Co., reprint.

The remarkable story of a man completely mastered by the Spirit of God. First published in 1876. 285.873.F49

Curtis, Richard Kenneth. *They Called Him Mr. Moody.* Grand Rapids: Wm. B. Eerdmans Publishing Co., 1966.

A revealing biography of a colorful and unconventional man. Objective and sympathetic. 285.873.M77C

Dale, Alfred William Winterslow. *The Life of R. W. Dale of Birmingham.* London: Hodder and Stoughton, 1905.

In a day when most pastorates last three years or less, preachers have much to learn from a man of Dale's stature (though they should not err as he did in his understanding of the atonement). 285.842.D15.D15

***Davies, Alfred Mervyn.** Foundation of American Freedom.* Nashville: Abingdon Press, 1955.

Traces the history of democracy and the American constitution to the foundation for liberty and freedom that Calvin laid in his writings, and discourses on secular ideals and history. Forcibly reminds readers that America's concept of government rests ultimately on the authority of the Scriptures. 323.44.D28

Dillenberger, John and **Claude Welch.** *Protestant Christianity.* New York: Charles Scribner's Sons, 1954.

†Attempts to explain the nature of Protestant Christianity in the light of the development of its theology. 284.D58

Donaldson, August B. *Henry Parry Liddon.* London: Rivingtons, 1905.

While there is much to learn from Liddon's life, our interest in him focuses

more on him as a NT scholar and preacher. His *Analytical Exposition of Romans* and *I Timothy* still are eagerly sought after. 283.42.L61.D71

Douglas, W. M. *Andrew Murray and His Message.* Fort Washington, Penn.: Christian Literature Crusade, 1957.

The fascinating story of the Dutch Reformed minister, Keswick speaker, and author of numerous books on prayer and Christian living. 276.8.M96

***Edman, Victor Raymond.** Finney Lives On.* New York: Fleming H. Revell Co., 1951.

Narrates the life, work, and thought of the great revivalist by providing first of all a biographical sketch, then an exposition of Finney's evangelist methods, and lastly, a digest of his beliefs. 285.873.F49E

————. *Out of My Life.* Grand Rapids: Zondervan Publishing Co., 1961.

The author shares with his readers lessons he learned from the Scriptures and from the events in his life. Warmly devotional. 286.573.ED5

Ervine, St. John. *God's Soldier: General William Booth.* 2 vols. New York: Macmillan Co., 1935.

Building upon personal experience with the Salvation Army, Ervine supplies what may well be regarded as the definitive biography of the great founder of the movement. 267.15.B64.ER9

Fant, David Jones. *A. W. Tozer: A Twentieth Century Prophet.* Harrisburg: Christian Publications, 1964.

A sympathetic biography. Sorely needed. Reminds us of the simple faith of a great man of God. 286.573.T66

Farrar, Reginald. *The Life of Frederic William Farrar.* London: James Nisbet and Co., 1904.

While naturally sympathetic with his father's position on certain issues, Reginald Farrar succeeds in providing his readers with a vivid portrait of this great

Church of England preacher, administrator, teacher, historian, commentator, and family man. 283.42.F24.F24

Findlay, James F., Jr. *Dwight L. Moody: American Evangelist, 1837-1899.* Chicago: University of Chicago Press, 1969.

A modern assessment of one who has been called the "father of modern evangelism." 285.873.M77F

Fletcher, Joseph. *The History of the Revival and Progress of Independency in England.* 4 vols. London: John Snow, 1862.

A full and refreshing account of the need for independence, both personal and denominational, if individuals as well as the churches to which they belong are to be able to keep pace with the times and grow toward maturity in accordance with the teaching of the NT. 274.2.F63

Fullerton, William Young. *Charles Haddon Spurgeon: A Biography.* Chicago: Moody Press, 1966.

A thematic study of the "Prince of Preachers." Reprinted from the 1934 edition. 286.142.SP9F 1966

————. *F. B. Meyer: A Biography.* New York: Christian Alliance Publishing Co., 1930.

The life story of a man whose influence and ministry were felt on both sides of the Atlantic and who, for many years, gave the Bible readings at the Keswick Convention. 286.142.F95

Gaustad, Edwin Scott. *A Religious History of America.* New York: Harper and Row, 1966.

†A fascinating portrayal of the role of religion in the history of America. Well illustrated, and based on a careful study of the original documents. Deserves careful reading. 277.3.G23

Gilbert, Arthur. *The Vatican Council and the Jews.* Cleveland: World Publishing Co., 1968.

A Jewish rabbi reports on the events behind the Second Vatican Council's "statement on the Jews." 282.G37

Gilbert, Felix. *The End of the European Era, 1890 to the Present.* New York: W. W. Norton, 1970.

A definitive study of Europe at the turn of the century. Analyzes the pressures that gave rise to the clash of national interests and culminated in World War I, together with an evaluation of the efforts made to achieve political and economic stability, and of the rise of totalitarianism. Closes with the reconstruction of Europe and the dawning of the nuclear age. Of value for its synthesis of material and interpretation of events. 940.28.G37

Gill, Everett. *A. T. Robertson: A Biography.* New York: Macmillan Co., 1943.

An intimate portrait of the private and public life of the great Baptist NT scholar. 286.173.R54

Gordon, Ernest Barron. *Adoniram Judson Gordon: A Biography.* 2d ed. New York: Fleming H. Revell Co., 1896.

A brief, biographical sketch of the pastor of the Clarendon Street Baptist Church, Boston, and one of the founders of Gordon College and Divinity School. 286.173.G65 1896

————. *Ecclesiastical Octopus.* Boston: Fellowship Press, 1948.

A popular study of ecumenism in the U.S. 280.6273.G65

————. *The Leaven of the Sadducees.* Chicago: Bible Institute Colportage Association, 1926.

A vigorous expose of Unitarianism, tracing the history of the movement and its effect upon Christianity in the U.S.A. 288.G65

Handy, Robert T. *A Christian America: Protestant Hopes and Historical Realities.* New York: Oxford University Press, 1971.

The author deals effectively with the early optimism of the founding fathers, bases his conclusions largely on a fresh examination of primary source material, records the disillusionment of Christians during the colonial period, pursues with some skepticism the goals of the early revivalists. Concludes with an analysis of the faded Protestant dream of a Christian America, with its resultant disorientation of denominational life and the related cultural problems. 277.3.H19

Hanna, William. *Memoirs of the Life and Writings of Thomas Chalmers.* 3 vols. Edinburgh: Sutherland and Knox, 1849.

By using Chalmers's letters and diary, Hanna allows his father-in-law to become his own biographer. Of interest is the way in which Chalmers changed his religious opinions and eventually became one of Scotland's leading conservative theologians. Makes rewarding reading. 284.421.C35.H19

Harries, John. *G. Campbell Morgan: The Man and His Ministry.* New York: Fleming H. Revell Company, 1930.

Published before Morgan's death in 1945, this work does not deal with the influence of this great British preacher upon the people of England during World War II, nor does it treat Morgan's influence during the last years of his life. Instead, stress is placed upon his study habits and pulpit acumen. As such, it provides a revealing and stimulating analysis of the secret of Morgan's greatness, and those who aspire to excellence as expositors of God's Word would do well to dwell upon what Harries has written. 285.842.M82.H23

Hennell, Michael Murray. *John Venn and the Clapham Sect.* London: Lutterworth Press, 1958.

A captivating account of an evangelical Church of England clergyman who, while rector of Clapham, founded the Church Missionary Society and engaged in extensive philanthropic activity. 283.42.V55

Hiscox, Edward Thurston. *The New Directory for Baptist Churches.* Rev. ed.

Grand Rapids: Kregel Publications, 1970.

An old, standard work. 286.1.H62

*Hodge, Archibald Alexander. *The Life of Charles Hodge.* New York: Arno Press, 1969.

Traces the life and ministry of the renowned Princeton Seminary theologian. Reprinted from the 1881 edition. 285.173.H66 1969

Hudson, Winthrop Still. *American Protestantism.* Chicago History of American Civilization. Chicago: University of Chicago Press, 1961.

An interpretive assessment. 277.3.H86

Irwin, Grace Lillian. *Servant of Slaves.* Grand Rapids: Wm. B. Eerdmans Publishing Co., 1961.

A biographical novel of John Newton. Traces his life both as a profane and immoral slave trader, and later as a devoted servant of Jesus Christ. Excellent. 283.42.N48

James, Powhatan Wright. *George W. Truett, A Biography.* Nashville: Broadman Press, 1953.

A well-written, intimate study. 286.132.T76

Kilby, Clyde S. *Minority of One: The Biography of Jonathan Blanchard.* Grand Rapids: Wm. B. Eerdmans Publishing Co., 1959.

A full-scale portrait of the man who established two colleges and who exerted great influence in the shaping of events by his own rigorous and uncompromising life. 286.573.B59

Lang, George Henry. *An Ordered Life: An Autobiography.* London: Paternoster Press, 1959.

A painstaking assessment of the impact of the unchanging Word of God on the needs and circumstances of a changing, formative society, and of the influence of a man whose life was ordered by God. 286.542.L25

Latourette, Kenneth Scott. *Beyond the Ranges.* Grand Rapids: Wm. B. Eerdmans Publishing Co., 1967.

A brief autobiography. 286.173.L35

————. *Christianity in a Revolutionary Age: A History of Christianity in the Nineteenth and Twentieth Centuries.* 5 vols. New York: Harper and Brothers, 1958-62.

A comprehensive survey of the theological and ecclesiastical trends in the nineteenth and twentieth centuries, with an account of the influence of Christianity on the social, political, and educational situation. 270.8.L35

Leighton, Robert. *The Whole Works of . . . Robert Leighton, D.D. [with] a Life of the Author by J. N. Pearson.* 2 vols. London: James Duncan, 1835.

Leighton is known for his masterful commentary on 1 Peter. This set contains in addition his sermons on the Apostle's Creed, the Ten Commandments, Communion messages, ordination addresses, and so on. 283.41.L53

LeTourneau, Robert G. *Mover of Men and Mountains.* Englewood Cliffs, N.J.: Prentice-Hall, 1967.

The autobigraphy of an engineer and inventor who found God faithful even in times of depression. 287.973.L56

Macaulay, Joseph Cordner. *Truth vs. Dogma.* Chicago: Moody Press, 1946.

A pre-Vatican II study of Catholicism. 282.M11

MacFarlane, John. *The Life and Times of George Lawson, D.D., Selkirk.* Edinburgh: Oliphant, Anderson and Ferrier, 1861.

" . . . a faithful and sympathetic narrative of the career and works of one of the greatest Scottish divines of his day." —*The Scotsman.* 284.841.L44. M16

MacGregor, Geddes. *Coming Reformation.* Philadelphia: Westminster Press, 1960.

†Challenges Protestant leadership to recapture the high ideals and principles of the Reformers and to reinterpret them in twentieth-century settings. 284.M17

***MacKenzie, Robert.** *John Brown of Haddington.* London: Banner of Truth Trust, 1964.

The encouraging story of a peasant farmer who became a great preacher. 284.241.B81

McGurn, Barret. *A Reporter Looks at American Catholicism.* New York: Hawthorn Books, 1966.

An outline of the changes that have taken place in American Catholic life as they affect the man in the pew, bishops and priests, nuns and brothers, Catholic education and the Catholic press, the place of women in the church, and relations with the pope. 282.73.M17

Maier, Paul L. *A Man Spoke, A World Listened: The Story of Walter A. Maier.* New York: McGraw-Hill Book Co., 1963.

This biography of "The Man of the Lutheran Hour" covers his life as a seminary professor, radio preacher, husband, father, author, and theologian. 284.173.M28

Malcolm, Charles W. *Twelve Hours in the Day.* London: Marshall, Morgan and Scott, 1956.

A biography of Australian evangelist Lionel B. Fletcher. Traces his long and influential ministry, and shows how his service for the Lord was accompanied by unusual manifestations of the Spirit's presence and power. 285.894.F63

***Manhattan, Avro.** *Vatican Imperialism in the Twentieth Century.* Grand Rapids: Zondervan Publishing House, 1965.

Accompanied by very thorough documentation, this study exposes the ambitious, world-wide schemes of Romanism. A masterly critique that underscores apocalyptic study. 282.M31

***Marrat, Jabez.** *The Vicar of Madeley.* London: Charles H. Kelly, 1902.

A well-written biography of John Fletcher. 287.142.F63M

Marshall, Catherine (Wood). *A Man Called Peter: The Story of Peter Marshall.* New York: McGraw-Hill Book Co., 1951.

A true-to-life account of a young Scot who became the influential pastor and chaplain of the United States Senate. A moving account showing something of Marshall's commitment, inner struggles, and infectious sense of humor. 285.173.M35

***Meeter, John E., ed.** Selected Shorter Writings of Benjamin B. Warfield.* In process. Nutley, N.J.: Presbyterian and Reformed Publishing Co., 1970-.

Based upon articles that formerly appeared in a ten-volume set of Warfield's writings published by Oxford University Press 1887-1921. 285.173.W23.M47

Moulton, William Fiddian. *James Hope Moulton.* London: Epworth Press, 1919.

A sympathetic biographical sketch of the Methodist scholar who gave us such indispensable NT resources as the *Grammar of the New Testament Greek* (vol. 1) and, with G. Milligan, the *Vocabulary of the Greek Testament,* along with numerous other important works. 287.142.M86.M86

————. *William F. Moulton: A Memoir.* New York: E. P. Dutton and Co., 1899.

This biography of a leading Wesleyan NT scholar deals briefly with his earlier life and influences, and then focuses upon the high points of his career. A chapter of his biblical work and opinions has been added by J. H. Moulton. 287.142.M86

***Murch, James DeForest.** The Protestant Revolt.* Arlington, Va.: Crestwood Books, 1967.

Provides a clear critique of the NCC and its method of operation, and cites specifics. Shows how the NCC has infiltrated large churches and undermined the doctrinal distinctives of leading denominations, educational institutions, missionary societies, publishing houses,

and radio and television stations. 280.4.M93

***Murray, Iain Hamish.** The Forgotten Spurgeon.* London: Banner of Truth Trust, 1966.

The author believes that Spurgeon survives in evangelical circles only in anecdotes and encomiums, and that the real essence of Spurgeon's preaching has been forgotten. He writes to encourage his readers to acquaint themselves with Spurgeon's writings and theology. 286.142.SP9M

The New Cambridge Modern History. Edited by G. R. Potter, et al. 14 vols. Cambridge: At the University Press, 1957-65.

This new edition covers essentially the same material as the *Cambridge Modern History* (1934), but it incorporates all the advances of the last half century. Indispensable in tracing the trend of the times and the events that have led to the present situation. 940.2.C14N

Newman, John Henry. *Apologia Pro Vita Sua.* New York: Oxford University Press, 1964.

When Newman, an Anglican priest, became a Roman Catholic bishop, he wrote this autobiography to defend his actions. Graphically portrays the tumultuous years that led to his decision. Describes the turbulent religious life in England at that time. 282.42.N46

Newton, John. *The Voice of the Heart: Cardiphonia.* Chicago: Moody Press, 1950.

A Christian classic of rare excellence and great value. Exposes a pastor's heart, and reveals his concern for those who have been touched by the Holy Spirit. 283.42.N48V 1950

Nicoll, William Robertson. *Princes of the Church.* London: Hodder and Stoughton, 1921.

"Thumbnail sketches" of notable figures in the Christian world during the latter part of the nineteenth and the early

part of the twentieth centuries.
274.'092.N51

Niebuhr, Reinhold. *The Irony of American History.* New York: Charles Scribner's Sons, 1952.

†A provocative, original, and satirical work exploring the ironic element in America's history in terms of the contrast between the hopes of our forefathers and the reality of our present situation. Emphasizes the need for social action. 973.N55

*Olmstead, Clifton E. *History of Religion in the United States.* Englewood Cliffs, N.J.: Prentice-Hall, 1960.

†A detailed study of the history of Christianity in the U.S. 277.3.OL5

Overton, John Henry and **Elizabeth Wordsworth.** *Christopher Wordsworth: Bishop of Lincoln, 1807-1885.* London: Rivingtons, 1888.

Wordsworth lived at a time when literary greatness was frequently matched with theological acumen and an evangelical faith. As a conservative and erudite scholar, Wordsworth made a lasting contribution to biblical scholarship. 283.42.W89.OV2

Pelikan, Jaroslav. *The Riddle of Roman Catholicism.* Nashville: Abingdon Press, 1959.

A pre-Vatican II critique. 282. P36

Pierson, Arthur Tappan, *George Müller of Bristol.* Rev. ed. Westwood, N.J.: Fleming H. Revell Co., 1954.

The authorized account of Müller's life of faith and how, for sixty years, he trusted God to provide for his own needs and the needs of the two thousand orphaned children for whom he cared. First published in the U.S. in 1901. 286.542.M91

*Pollock, John Charles. *Moody: A Biographical Portrait of the Pacesetter in Modern Mass Evangelism.* Grand Rapids: Zondervan Publishing House, 1967.

A colorful account of a colorful life.

The writer captures some of Moody's enthusiasm as he recounts the events of Moody's life and ministry. 285.873.M77P

Pope, Richard Martin. *The Church and Its Culture.* St. Louis: Bethany Press, 1965.

A history of the church in the midst of changing cultures. First published in 1952. 270'.09.P81

Rich, Norman. *The Age of Nationalism and Reform, 1850-1890.* New York: W. W. Norton, 1970.

An analysis of the relationship between political events and intellectualism following the revolutions of 1848. Valuable for its historical summation of the period. 940.285.R37

Sangster, Paul. *Dr. Sangster.* London: Epworth Press, 1962.

An important study of one of Methodism's most distinguished twentieth-century preachers. 285.842.SA5

*Singer, Charles Gregg. *A Theological Interpretation of American History.* International Library of Philosophy and Theology. Philadelphia: Presbyterian and Reformed Publishing Co., 1964.

A devastating critique of theological liberalism, which the author claims has been the root cause for the decline of the constitution in the political life of the people and in the formation of a highly centralized government. 320.973.SI6

*Spurgeon, Charles Haddon. *C. H. Spurgeon: The Early Years, 1834-1859.* London: Banner of Truth Trust, 1962.

Intended to be the republication of Spurgeon's autobiography, this volume, in its revised edition, represents only one-half of the earlier work. It is regrettable that the publishers appear to have abandoned the idea of issuing the second part of this autobiography. 286.142.SP9 v. 1

*Stonehouse, Ned Bernard. *J. Gresham Machen.* Grand Rapids: Wm. B. Eerdmans Publishing Co., 1955.

A learned theologian and apologist, Machen taught at Princeton Seminary. Following the modernist-fundamentalist debates, he left Princeton and founded the Westminster Theological Seminary. This biography preserves for posterity a record of his greatness. 285.173.M18

Tarr, L. K. *Shields of Canada.* Grand Rapids: Baker Book House, 1967.

A sympathetic study of a highly controversial Canadian Baptist preacher. 286.092.T17

Thompson, Henry L. *Henry George Liddell, D.D., Dean of Christ Church, Oxford. A Memoir.* New York: Henry Holt and Company, 1899.

Liddell is best known for the Greek lexicon he edited with Robert Scott. In this volume we are introduced to him as a family man, scholar, and churchman. The author of these memoirs was vicar of St. Mary's, Oxford, and knew Liddell and his family well. 283.43.L61.T37

Townsend, Henry. *The Claims of the Free Churches.* London: Hodder and Stoughton, 1949.

Not designed as a history of the Free Church movement, but intended instead as an objective study of the emergence of principles of growth, personal and corporate, that have affected the life of English-speaking peoples throughout the world. 274.2.T66

Townsend, W. J., H. B. Workman and **G. Eayrs, eds.** *A New History of Methodism.* 2 vols. London: Hodder and Stoughton, 1909.

Quite apart from the fact that this is an able sketch of the history of Methodism, this work also treats an important facet of noncomformity and as such is of value even to those who are not Methodists. 287.T66

Tyerman, Luke. *Wesley's Designated Successor: The Life, Letters, and Literary Labors of John William Fletcher.* New York: Phillips and Hunt, 1883.

An authoritative volume on the "Vicar of Madeley." Provides numerous insights into his sanctity and devotion to his work among the Shropshire colliers. 287.142.F63T

Vidler, Alexander Roper. *The Church in an Age of Revolution.* Pelican History of the Church. Grand Rapids: Wm. B. Eerdmans Publishing Co., 1961.

Containing a history of Christianity from 1789 to 1961, these chapters provide a fresh approach to a familiar era of church history. 270.8.V66

Warfield, Benjamin Breckenridge. *Works of B. B. Warfield.* 10 vols. New York: Oxford University Press, 1927.

Makes available in a single series the major writings of this great American theologian. Highly recommended. 285.173.W23

Westcott, Arthur. *Life and Letters of Brooke Foss Westcott.* 2 vols. London: Macmillan and Co., 1903.

Among evangelicals, Westcott's stature continues to grow. These volumes permit us to see the heart of the man and glimpse the secret of his greatness. 283.42.W52.W52

The Works of the Rev. John Fletcher. 8 vols. London: John Mason, 1846.

This important set includes Fletcher's famous "Checks to Antinomianism," which was occasioned by the dispute between the Arminians and Calvinists. 287.142.F63

14

Comparative Religions

When God spoke to His ancient people, Israel, through Hosea, He lamented that His people were perishing for lack of knowledge. They had neglected the teaching of His Word. The same is true today. People are suffering mentally and emotionally, relationally and spiritually because they have been deprived of the counsel of Scripture (cf. Amos 8:11). They desperately feel the need for a sense of *belonging, worth,* and *competence.* And this is just what the cults and false religions attempt to provide.

Man's innate need may be traced back to the Garden of Eden. When God made Adam and Eve, He made them in His image (Gen. 1:26-27). They were His special creation. They drew their identity from their relationship with Him. In a very real sense they belonged to Him.

Adam and Eve were also made for each other (Gen. 2:18). This gave them a unique sense of oneness (Gen. 2:23). They belonged to each other. In addition, God prepared a beautiful garden for Adam and Eve to live in (Gen. 2:8,15). This completed their sense of *belonging*—vertically, relationally, environmentally.

Adam and Eve were the apex of God's creative handiwork (Gen. 2:7). He fellowshipped with them in the cool of the day (Gen. 3:8). In a very real sense, they knew they were unique. They enjoyed true *worth.*

God further gave Adam and Eve work to do. They were to "rule" or "have dominion over" the earth that He had created (Gen. 1:26,28; 2:15). All of creation was benign so that the work could be done easily and without strain (contrast Gen. 3:17-19). Adam and Eve enjoyed a sense of *competence.*

When sin entered the world, however, all of this was lost. Sin separated Adam and Eve from God, and they hid from Him. They were later expelled from the garden (Gen. 3:23-24). Gone now was their feeling of belonging.

As a result of sin, Adam and Eve had a new sensation of shame. Their thoughts turned inward upon themselves (Gen. 3:10). They became conscious of self, and with this came an awareness of their nakedness. They no longer possessed feelings of true worth.

Furthermore, the ground was cursed and would no longer be conducive to sustaining life. Hardship and toil were to be the legacy of disobedience (Gen. 3:17-19). Gone now was their feeling of competence.

Fortunately for Adam and Eve, God bridged the gap and in grace provided for their spiritual and physical needs (Gen. 3:15,21).

All of us, however, have continuing needs for feelings of belonging, worth, and competence. Each religion and cult tries to meet these needs in one way or another. Only in the beliefs and practices of the historic Judeo-Christian faith, can these be met as God intended. All others are counterfeit.

In the plan and purpose of God, provision has been made whereby all believers in Jesus Christ can have these basic needs met. *The solution lies in the development of a unique relationship with each member of the Godhead.*

As Christians, we have been brought into a new and vital relationship with God the Father. We have been made members of His family. We are accepted by Him and have access into His presence (Eph. 1:3-6; Heb. 4:16; 1 John 3:1-2; 4:16,18). We call Him "Father." In a very real sense, therefore, we *belong* to Him.

This relationship with God the Father serves as an antidote to feelings of anxiety (cf. 1 Pet. 5:7; Prov. 3:5-6).

A realization of our true worth is derived from our relationship with Christ the Son (1 John 4:9,17). As we meditate on the price He paid for our redemption (1 Pet. 1:18-19; cf. Ps. 49:7-9) and realize that we have been made heirs of all the glories of His kingdom (Rom. 8:17), we come to realize our true *worth*. This is quite apart from any work we may perform.

This relationship with the Lord Jesus Christ satisfactorily takes care of feelings of guilt (2 Cor. 7:9-11) through confession (1 John 1:9), which leads to restoration.

Finally, our ability to cope with the harsh realities of life is restored as we allow God the Holy Spirit to control our lives (Eph. 5:18). He indwells us and enables us to deal with each situation as it arises (John 14:16-17; 1 John 2:20). Through our relationship with Him, we again experience a feeling of *competence*.

This relationship with the Holy Spirit satisfactorily takes care of feelings of anger (arising out of our frustrations over things we cannot control or circumstances causing us to feel rejected or humiliated).

In a very real sense, therefore, God graciously meets our basic needs through a vital relationship with each Member of the Trinity. Feelings of security, significance, and satisfaction can be ours as we avail ourselves of the resources He has given us.

Pagan beliefs and practices *cannot* meet these needs in an entirely satisfactory manner or over an extended period of time. At best they provide an artificial environment where a devotee, for a time, feels accepted, affirmed, and adequate. This is a far cry, however, from what God in Christ planned for each one of His own.

SECTS AND CULTS

Baalen, Jan Karel van. *The Chaos of the Cults.* 4th ed. Grand Rapids: Wm. B. Eerdmans Publishing Co., 1962.

This well-known reference volume examines thirteen separate movements, including astrology, spiritism, Anglo-Israelism, and moral rearmament. Summarizes their historical development, evaluates their teachings, and provides questions for discussions. First published in 1938. 280.973.B11 1962

———. *The Gist of the Cults.* Grand Rapids: Wm. B. Eerdmans Publishing Co., 1944.

A brief summary of the teachings of some of the major cults. 289.B11

Davies, Horton. *Christian Deviations.* Rev. ed. Philadelphia: Westminster Press, 1965.

An assessment of the doctrines of eight church groups that have broken away from the Christian tradition. 290.D28 1965

*****Gerstner, John H.** *Theology of the Major Sects.* Grand Rapids: Baker Book House, 1960.

A handy reference volume designed to acquaint readers with the erroneous doctrines of various modern sects. Recommended. 289.G32

*****Hoekema, Anthony A.** *The Four Major Cults.* Grand Rapids: Wm. B. Eerdmans Publishing Co., 1963.

A thorough evaluation of the doctrinal teachings of Mormonism, Seventh-Day Adventism, Christian Science, and Jehovah's Witnesses. Particularly helpful to pastors. 289.H67

*****Martin, Walter Ralston.** *The Kingdom of the Cults.* Grand Rapids: Zondervan Publishing House, 1965.

An evaluation of the teachings of different sects, including Zen Buddhism, the Black Muslims, Unity, Bahai, Herbert Armstrong, and Rosicrucianism. Each chapter contains a short history,

brief quotations from the leading exponents, and a refutation of their teachings. Concludes with chapters on the psychology of cultism and the best methods of cult evangelism. 289.73.M36

Sanders, John Oswald. *Cults and Isms, Ancient and Modern.* 8th rev. ed. Grand Rapids: Zondervan Publishing House, 1963.

An old, standard work. 289.SA5 1963

SEVENTH-DAY ADVENTISM

Biederwolf, William Edward. *Seventh-Day Adventism.* Grand Rapids: Wm. B. Eerdmans Publishing Co., n.d.

A brief evaluation. Candid, insightful. 286.7.B47

Douty, Norman Franklin. *Another Look at Seventh-Day Adventism.* Grand Rapids: Baker Book House, 1962.

Working from original sources, Douty shows the areas in which Seventh-Day Adventism differs from the teaching of God's Word. Helpful. 286.7.D74

Martin, Walter Ralston. *The Truth About Seventh-Day Adventism.* Grand Rapids: Zondervan Publishing House, 1960.

A comprehensive and thorough study of their history and doctrinal beliefs. Advocates acceptance of them as Christians, not as a cult. 286.7.M36

MORMONISM

Biederwolf, William Edward. *Mormonism Under the Searchlight.* Grand Rapids: Wm. B. Eerdmans Publishing Co., n.d.

Provides a critique of the pagan origin and superstitious beliefs of Mormons. 289.3.B47

Brodie, Fawn (McKay). *No Man Knows My History.* 2d rev. ed. New York: Alfred P. Knopf, 1971.

†The life story of Joseph Smith, the self-styled Mormon "prophet."
289.3'09.B78 1971

Fraser, Gordon H. *What Does the Book of Mormon Teach?* Chicago: Moody Press, 1964.

An examination of the historical and supposedly scientific statements found in the Book of Mormon. 289.3.F86

Green, Nelson Winch. *Mormonism: Its Rise, Progress, and Present Condition.* New York: AMS Press, 1972.

Records the experiences of Mrs. Mary Ettie V. Smith during a fifteen-year residence with the Mormons. Provides a full and authentic sociological appraisal of their early religious beliefs and political practices. Originally published in 1870. 289.3'3.G82 1972

Martin, Walter Ralston. *Mormonism.* Grand Rapids: Zondervan Publishing House, 1963.

A brief handbook for lay people who are troubled by its doctrine. 289.3.M36

———. *The Maze of Mormonism.* Grand Rapids: Zondervan Publishing House, 1962.

An authoritative critique of America's fastest-growing cult. 289.3.M36M

Smith, John L. *Has Mormonism Changed . . . ?* Clearfield: Utah Evangelical Press, 1961.

A discussion of Mormonism both past and present, their modern practices of polygamy, proselytizing, strange doctrines, and rapid growth. Insightful. 289.3.SM6

———. *Hope or Despair?* Rev. ed. Clearfield: Utah Evangelical Press, 1959.

The writer examines the claims of Mormonism in the light of the Scriptures. 289.3.SM6 1959

CHRISTIAN SCIENCE

Biederwolf, William Edward. *The Unvarnished Facts About Christian Science.* Grand Rapids: Wm. B. Eerdmans Publishing Co., n.d.

An evaluation of Christian Science doctrine in the light of the Bible. 289.5.B47

Martin, Walter Ralston and **Norman H. Klann.** *The Christian Science Myth.* Grand Rapids: Zondervan Publishing House, 1955.

Exhibits a remarkable amount of research. Discusses and evaluates the claims of Mary Baker Eddy and, after sifting through her writings, compares the teachings of Christian Science with the Bible, exposing their fraudulent claims and antibiblical beliefs. 289.5.M36

PENTECOSTALISM

Burdick, Donald W. *Tongues: To Speak or Not to Speak.* Chicago: Moody Press, 1969.

Seeks to explain the present-day phenomenon of glossolalia. Burdick also gives his interpretation of the biblical teaching on tongues. 289.9.B89

Gelpi, Donald L. *Pentecostalism: A Theological Viewpoint.* Glen Rock, N.J.: Paulist Press, 1970.

The reflections of a Jesuit philosopher on the Catholic charismatic movement. Insightful, but not theologically reliable. 289.9.G28 (Alt. DDC 282)

***Gromacki, Robert Glenn.** *The Modern Tongues Movement.* Philadelphia: Presbyterian and Reformed Publishing Co., 1967.

An evaluation of the rise of Pentecostalism and the glossolalia phenomenon. A most welcome volume. 289.9.G89

Hoekema, Anthony A. *What About Tongue-Speaking?* Grand Rapids: Wm. B. Eerdmans Publishing Co., 1966.

Traces the tongues movement historically and biblically. A clear, forceful presentation. 289.9.H67

Koch, Kurt. *The Strife of Tongues.* Grand Rapids, Kregel Publications, 1969.

Provides the author's closely reasoned evaluation of the biblical teaching on tongues. Summarizes the teaching of leaders in the history of the Christian church, carefully sifts the evidence of "case histories," and provides the author's statement of the "biblical counterpart." 289.9.K81

Lightner, Robert Paul. *Speaking in Tongues and Divine Healing.* Des Plaines, Ill.: Regular Baptist Press, 1965.

A brief, clear exposition of the teachings of Scripture on these two subjects. 289.9.L62

Mills, Watson E. *Understanding Speaking in Tongues.* Grand Rapids: Wm. B. Eerdmans Publishing Co., 1970.

Insists that a distinction must be drawn between the form and the meaning of glossolalia. Claims that those who reject the form of glossolalia as no longer relevant should be prepared to concede that tongue-speaking may attest to genuine experience. 289.9.M62

Synan, Vinson. *The Holiness Pentecostal Movement in the United States.* Grand Rapids: Wm. B. Eerdmans Publishing Co., 1970.

A sympathetic study of the origin and growth of the Pentecostal and Holiness movements. Of particular interest is his recounting of recent developments and the growth of the charismatic movement in non-Pentecostal denominations. 289.9'09.SY7

*Stegall, Carroll. *The Modern Tongues and Healing Movement.* Shalimar, Fla.: The Author, n.d.

A penetrating analysis and critique. Hard to obtain, but worthy of careful reading. 289.9.ST3

FAITH HEALING

Bingham, Rowland Victor. *The Bible and the Body: Healing in the Scriptures.* Toronto: Evangelical Publishers, 1952.

Examines the biblical teaching on faith healing. First published in 1921. 289.9.B51 1952

Boggs, Wade H., Jr. *Faith Healing and the Christian Faith.* Richmond: John Knox Press, 1956.

A comprehensive assessment of the techniques used by faith healers like Oral Roberts, Agnes Sanford, Aimee Semple McPherson, "Little David," Christian Science, the Lourdes Shrine healings, the New Thought and Unity movements, Father Divine, and others. 289.9.B63

Edmunds, Vincent and **C. Gordon Scorer.** *Some Thoughts on Faith Healing.* London: Tyndale Press, 1966.

An evaluation of faith healing by two British M.D.'s. 289.9.ED5

JEHOVAH'S WITNESSES

Gruss, Edmond Charles. *Apostles of Denial.* Grand Rapids: Baker Book House, 1970.

A careful exposé of the history, doctrines, and aims of Jehovah's Witnesses. 289.9.G92

Martin, Walter Ralston. *Jehovah's Witnesses.* Grand Rapids: Zondervan Publishing House, 1963.

An abridgment of *Jehovah of the Watchtower.* 289.9.M36

*_____ and **Norman H. Klann.** *Jehovah of the Watchtower.* Grand Rapids: Zondervan Publishing House, 1953.

A most significant, pertinent evaluation of the antibiblical teachings of Jehovah's Witnesses. 289.9.M36J

*Schnell, William J. *Thirty Years a Watch Tower Slave.* Grand Rapids: Baker Book House, 1956.

The author recounts how he became enmeshed in the movement, his rise to positions of authority, the hopelessness of his situation, and his remarkable conversion. 289.9.SCH5

OTHER SECTS

Cassara, Ernest. *Universalism in America.* Boston: Beacon Press, 1971.

A documentary history of the rise of Universalism in the United States. 289.1'73.C26

Darms, Anton. *The Delusion of British-Israelism.* New York: Loizeaux Brothers, n.d.

A well-presented, documented exposé of the salient points in the British-Israelite creed. 289.9.D25

Martin, Walter Ralston. *Herbert W. Armstrong and the Radio Church of God in the Light of the Bible.* Minneapolis: Bethany Fellowship, 1968.

A serious investigation of Armstrongism. A sorely needed monograph. 289.9.M36H

WORLD RELIGIONS

Adams, Walter Marsham. *The Book of the Master of the Hidden Places.* London: John Murray, 1898.

A presentation of the Egyptian doctrine of the mother goddess. 299.31.AD1

*Anderson, James Norman Dairymple. *Christianity and Comparative Religions.* Downers Grove: Inter-Varsity Press, 1970.

Informative insights into the comparisons and contrasts between Christianity and Eastern religions. 291.AN2C

————, ed. *The World's Religions.* Grand Rapids: Wm. B. Eerdmans Publishing Co., 1950.

A factual and informative survey of Animism, Judaism, Islam, Hinduism, Buddhism, Shintoism, and Confucianism. 290.AN2W

Barthell, Edward E., Jr. *Gods and Goddesses of Ancient Egypt.* Coral Gables: University of Miami Press, 1970.

A modern treatment of the role of the gods in the worship of the ancient Egyptians. 292.211.B31

Bevan, Edwyn Robert, ed. *Hellenism and Christianity.* London: Allen and Unwin, 1921.

Insightful essays on the Greek background of the gospels. 291'.1'08.B46

Braden, Charles Samuel. *The Scriptures of Mankind: An Introduction.* New York: Macmillan Co., 1952.

A general introduction to the sacred literature of some of the world's major religions. 291.8.B73

Brandon, Samuel George Frederick. *Dictionary of Comparative Religion.* New York: Charles Scribner's Sons, 1970.

†Brings the most recent liberal scholarship to bear on the entire spectrum of world religions—Asian, Western, ancient, and primitive. 291'.03.B73

————. *The Judgment of the Dead.* New York: Charles Scribner's Sons, 1969.

A comparative survey of the ways in which the concept of the last judgment has found expression in the ancient cults of Egypt and Greece, as well as in the religions of Christianity and Islam. 291.2'3.B73

————. *Religion in Ancient History: Studies in Ideas, Men and Events.* New York: Charles Scribner's Sons, 1969.

†A collection of twenty-five essays dealing with the remarkable discoveries that have increased our knowledge of the history and religion of ancient civilizations. 291.B73

Branston, Brian. *Gods of the North.* London: Thames and Hudson, 1955.

By making use of original sources—*Verse Edda* and *Prose Edda* and other sagas—Branston unfolds the cosmological beliefs of the Norsemen and others

from the continent of Europe.
293.21.B73

Breasted, James Henry. *Development of Religion and Thought in Ancient Egypt.* Gloucester, Mass.: Peter Smith, 1970.

First published in 1912, this work by the "father of modern Egyptology" has now been superseded by the writings of Alan Gardiner, John Wilson, and others. 299.31.B74 1970

Bruce, Frederick Fyvie and **E. G. Rupp, eds.** *Holy Book and Holy Tradition.* Grand Rapids: Wm. B. Eerdmans Publishing Co., 1968.

Contains the lectures delivered at the International InterFaith colloquium held in the Faculty of Theology, University of Manchester, England. Surveys the relationship between Scripture and tradition, and includes papers on Judeo-Christian, Protestant, and modern Catholic theology. 291.8.B83

Butterworth, E. A. S. *The Tree at the Navel of the Earth.* Berlin: Walter De Gruyter and Co., 1970.

By studying certain of the symbols that are common in ancient art and appear in various forms in ancient literature, the writer seeks to elucidate the religious disciplines and attitudes represented by them. This study of the various forms of the fertility cult is helpful and provides interesting background material for the religions prevalent in both Old Testament and New Testament times. A valuable supplement to James's *The Tree of Life.* 291.B98

Campbell, Lewis. *Religion in Greek Literature.* Freeport, N.Y.: Books for Libraries Press, 1970.

Long recognized as a work of considerable merit. It sketches briefly and concisely the main tenets of Greek religion, traces their origin and development, and shows the incipient reasons for their decay. First published in 1898. 292'.08.C15

Carter, George William. *Zoroastrianism and Judaism.* New York: AMS Press, 1970.

Outlines the influence of Zoroastrianism upon Judaism in the postexilic period. First published in 1918. 295.1.C24

Cassuto, Umberto. *The Goddess 'Anat: Canaanite Epics of the Patriarchal Age.* Translated by Israel Abrahams, Jerusalem: Magnes Press, 1971.

Based upon the original texts, with Hebrew translation and commentary. A standard work on the Semitic goddess 'Anat and the Phoenician deity Baal. Illuminates the biblical record, and supplements the Old Testament narrative with material from the Ugaritic texts. 291.211.C27

Conrad, Jack Randolph. *The Horn and the Sword.* London: McGibon and Kee, 1959.

A definitive history of the bull as a symbol of power and fertility. Ably illustrates the pagan worship of the Old Testament and, by implication, explains God's jealousy over His wayward people when they became involved in the practices associated with the worship of Baal and the Ashtoreth. 291.212.C76

Driver, Godfrey Rolles. *Canaanite Myths and Legends.* Edinburgh: T. and T. Clark, 1956.

An important work by one of the great Semitic scholars of the present day. 299.24.D83

Ferguson, John. *The Religions of the Roman Empire.* Ithaca: Cornell University Press, 1970.

This modern treatment presents a comprehensive survey of the religions that flourished in Rome during the first few centuries of the Christian era. Describes the many new cults that sprang up during this period, and shows how they either fused with or reacted against the traditional religion of the times. 292.07.F38

*Finegan, Jack. *The Archaeology of World Religions.* Princeton: Princeton University Press, 1952.

A survey of the background of pagan religions like Primitivism, Zoroastrianism, Hinduism, Jainism, Buddhism, Confucianism, Taoism, Shintoism, Islam, and Sikhism, with an analysis of their beliefs based upon careful archaeological research. 290.9.F49

Frankfort, Henri. *The Problem of Similarity in Ancient Near Eastern Religions.* New York: Oxford University Press, 1951.

A brief but important study emphasizing that the parallels between Eastern religions should be considered when studying, for example, the religion of Israel. 299.32.F85

Frazer, James George. *The Fear of the Dead in Primitive Religion.* 3 vols. London: Macmillan and Co., 1933.

The William Wyse Foundation lectures, Trinity College, Cambridge, 1932-33. These far-ranging discussions of primitive superstition and mythology reveal unsophisticated man's awe of the unknown, as well as his deep-seated belief in a future life. Excellent. 291.23.F86

*_____. *The New Golden Bough.* Edited with notes and foreword by Theodore H. Gaster. New York: F. G. Phillips, 1968.

An abridgment of Frazer's classic work, with extensive critical notes on the customs, magical superstitions, taboos, sexual practices, and wizardry of ancient primitive civilizations. 291.F86

*Gaster, Theodor Harzl. *Thespis: Ritual, Myth and Drama in the Ancient Near East.* Rev. ed. Garden City: Doubleday and Co., 1961.

An extraordinary book uncovering the circumstances that inspired ancient literature and demonstrating the full meaning of ancient ritual and practices for students of drama today. 291.093.G21 1961

*Grant, Frederick Clifton. *Roman Hellenism and the New Testament.* Edinburgh: Oliver and Boyd, 1962.

†An examination of the Hellenistic background of the New Testament. 292.G76

Grand, Michael. *Roman Myths.* New York: Charles Scribner's Sons, 1971.

A survey of the myths that underlay Roman culture. Provides important sidelights of Paul's ministries in Ephesus and Corinth, and highlights the study of his epistles. 292'.07.G76

Habel, Norman C. *Yahweh versus Baal: A Conflict of Religious Cultures.* New York: Bookman Associates, 1964.

A study based on the relevent Ugaritic materials and their relationship to the faith of Israel. 291.2.H11

*Hamilton, Edith. *Mythology.* Boston: Little, Brown and Co., 1942.

A popular synthesis of Greek and Roman legends about their gods and heroes. Makes fascinating reading. 292.H18

*Hislop, Alexander. *The Two Babylons.* Neptune, N.J.: Loizeaux Brothers, 1953.

Traces the history of the worship established by Nimrod and his wife, Semiramis, and the growth of the mother-child cult. First published in 1916. Indispensable—a *must* for every pastor. 291.2.H62

Hooke, Samuel Henry, ed. *The Labyrinth: Further Studies in the Relation Between Myth and Ritual in the Ancient World.* London: Society for Promoting Christian Knowledge, 1935.

†This sequel to *Myth and Ritual* continues to stress the basic similarities in Near Eastern religious beliefs in which the central figure was the king, a god, who died and was resurrected. The contributors pave the way for the final two essays, in which these pagan beliefs are supposedly carried over into Christianity. 291.213.H76L

_____, **ed.** *Myth and Ritual: Essays on the Myth and Ritual of the Hebrews in Relation to the Culture Pattern of the Ancient East.* London: Oxford University Press, 1933.

†A disappointing series of essays that, for all their brilliance, fail to do away with special revelation and provide a cultic basis for the interpretation of the Old Testament. 291.213.H76

*****James, Edwin Oliver.** *The Ancient Gods: The History and Diffusion of Religion in the Ancient Near East and the Eastern Mediterranean.* New York: G.P. Putnam's Sons, 1960.

Not a "groundbreaker," but a synthesizer of a vast store of knowledge on ancient religious practices. The writer has mastered a complicated array of material and succinctly presents a synthesis that shows the higher aspects of Judaic and Christian theology as opposed to the pagan religions and practices of their contemporaries. Makes a real contribution to our knowledge of Egyptian, Assyrian, Babylonian, Hittite, and Ugaritic forms of worship; aptly describes the progress of the cult of the mother-goddess; and illumines the relationship between the gods and morality, life and culture, and the uniqueness of Israelite monotheism. 291.211.J23

_____. *Beginnings of Religion.* London: Hutchinson's University Library, n.d.

†An evaluation of the origins of religious belief based upon a judicious evaluation of archaeological evidence. Antisupernaturalistic. 291.J23

_____. *Christianity and Other Religions.* London: Hodder and Stoughton, 1968.

†Discusses the common aims Christianity shares with other religions. Evaluates the prehistoric background of religious monotheism and pantheism, and considers the varying views of salvation, sacrifices, immortality, and revelation. 291.J23C

_____. *Comparative Religion: An Intro-*

ductory and Historical Study. London: Methuen and Company, 1961.

†An important study and a worthy companion volume to the other writings by this author. Well documented. 290.J23

_____. *Concept of Deity: A Comparative and Historical Study.* London: Hutchinson Publishing Group, 1951.

Based on the Wilde Lectures in Natural and Comparative Religions, Oxford. Provides a valuable synthesis of the origin of ancient deities and modes of worship. Antisupernaturalistic. 291.211.J23C

*_____. *The Cult of the Mother-Goddess.* London: Thames and Hudson, 1959.

A fascinating account that makes clear the unique position occupied by the mother-goddess in the fertility myths and rituals of the ancient Near East, India, and the eastern Mediterranean. Clear and factual, yet cautious in interpretation. Has much to offer the student of comparative religions. 291.211.J23C

_____. *Myth and Ritual in the Ancient Near East: An Archaeological and Documentary Study.* London: Thames and Hudson, 1958.

Reexamines the role of myth and ritual in the ancient Near East and the eastern Mediterranean upon evidence obtained through excavation, decipherment, and translation of numerous texts discovered during the last quarter of a century. 290.J23

_____. *Nature and Function of Priesthood.* London: Thames and Hudson, 1961.

A historical study by a renowned comparative religionist who sees nothing unique in the worship ceremonies of the ancient Hebrews. 291.61.J23

_____. *Origins of Sacrifice: A Study in Comparative Religion.* Port Washington, N.Y.: Kennikat Press, 1970.

First published in 1933. Deals with the origin of blood sacrifices, fertility rights, human sacrifices, cannibalism, the mystery cults, and so on. 291.3.J23 1970

_____. *Prehistoric Religion: A Study in Prehistoric Archaeology.* London: Thames and Hudson, 1957.

A thorough, scholarly analysis of the earliest forms of burial, together with a definitive consideration of the beliefs and ritualistic practices associated with the mysteries of birth, fertility, and food supply. 290.J23P

_____. *The Tree of Life: An Archaeological Study.* Studies in the History of Religions. Leiden: E. J. Brill, 1966.

A scholarly evaluation of ancient forms of worship. 291.23.J23

_____. *The Worship of the Sky-God.* Oxford: Athlone Press, 1963.

Based on the Jordan Lectures on Comparative Religions for 1963. Ably highlights the pagan forms of worship associated with the sky-god. 291.212.J23W

Jastrow, Morris. *Aspects of Religious Belief and Practice in Babylonia and Assyria.* New York: B. Plom, 1971.

Part of the American lectures on the history of religions. First published in 1911. Contains a concise, scholarly analysis of Assyro-Babylonian religion. 299.21.J31 1971

Johnson, Aubrey Rodway. *The Cultic Prophet in Ancient Israel.* 2d ed. Cardiff: University of Wales Press, 1962.

A definitive study. Illumines much of the OT narrative. 291.63.J63 1962

Kapelrud, Arvid Schou. *Baal in the Ras Shamra Texts.* Copenhagen: G. E. C. Gad, 1952.

†A brief, well-documented assessment of Baal and his place in the Ugaritic pantheon. 299.26.K14

_____. *The Violent Goddess: Anat in the Ras Shamra Texts.* Oslo: Universitets Forlaget, 1969.

Provides a valuable historical link in the study of Near Eastern religions. 291.211.K14

*Kramer, Samuel Noah. *Mythologies of Ancient World.* Garden City: Doubleday and Co., 1961.

A valuable synthetic study by a recognized authority. 291.K85

_____. *The Sacred Marriage Rite: Aspects of Faith, Myth and Ritual in Ancient Sumer.* Bloomington: Indiana University Press, 1969.

A clear and authoritative account of the ancient Mesopotamian cult involving the shepherd-god Dumuzi and the goddess Inanna, with an analysis of the teaching of the sacred marriage rite. 299.2.K85

_____. *Sumerian Mythology.* Rev. ed. New York: Harper and Row, 1961.

A careful and, in many respects, definitive study of the spiritual and literary milieu of ancient Sumer. 299.2.K86 1961

Lang, Andrew. *Magic and Religion.* London: Longmans, Green and Co., 1901.

Contains an analysis of Sir George Frazer's book, *The Golden Bough.* Examines Frazer's hypotheses, refutes some of his theories, and corrects many of his conjectures. A valuable contribution to the study of the origin of different religious beliefs. 291.13.L25

The Laws of Manu. Translated by G. Buhler. New York: AMS Press, 1970.

A translation with extracts from seven commentaries. Helpful in understanding the rise of this form of religious belief. 294.5'92.M31 1970

Loverdo, Costa de. *Gods with Bronze Swords.* Translated by Nancy Amphoux. Garden City: Doubleday and Co., 1970.

A historical and archaeological assessment of Greek mythology and its influence upon the Graeco-Roman world. 292.13.L94

Neill, Stephen Charles. *Christian Faith and Other Faiths: The Christian Dialogue with Other Religions.* New York: Oxford University Press, 1961.

Based on the Moorhouse Lectures delivered in the Anglican Cathedral, Melbourne. Aims at achieving a basis for ecumenical understanding, and seeks to comprehend these faiths from "within and not merely to delineate them from without." 291.1.N31

Nida, Eugene A. and **W. A. Smalley.** *Introducing Animism.* New York: Friendship Press, 1959.

An evaluation of the mass of primitive religious beliefs and practices that frequently find expression in animistic worship. 291.211.N54

Noss, John Boyer. *Man's Religions.* 3d rev. ed. New York: Macmillan and Co., 1963.

†A definitive study of Hinduism, Jainism, Buddhism, Sikhism, Taoism, Confucianism, Shintoism, Zoroastrianism, Judaism, Christianity, and Islam. 291.N84 1963

Parrinder, Edward Geoffrey. *African Traditional Religion.* 3d rev. ed. London: SPCK, 1962.

A helpful monograph on the origin of primitive worship and the development of African religion. Written with verve and insight. 299.6.P24 1962

———. *Worship in the World's Religions.* New York: Association Press, 1961.

Synthesizes a vast amount of material in his presentation of the cults and practice of different world religions. 291.3.P24

Perry, W. J. *The Origin of Magic and Religion.* Port Washington, N.Y.: Kennikat Press, 1970.

First published in 1923. Recounts in a clear, unobtrusive way the story of the development of the magical in religious thought and practice. 291.3.P42 1970

Piggott, Stuart. *The Druids.* London: Thames and Hudson, 1968.

With Timothy Leary having proclaimed himself as the new "high priest" of the revived Druid religion in America, pastors may well find themselves confronted with these ancient customs in modern "dress." This work by Piggott is one of the best ever written on the religious practices of the Gauls and Britons who followed these early barbaric customs. 299.16.P62

Sayce, Archibald Henry. *Lectures on the Origin and Growth of Religion as Illustrated by the Ancient Babylonians.* 3d ed. London: Williams and Norgate, 1891.

The Hibbert Lectures for 1887, these studies by a renowned Assyriologist introduce the reader to such deities as Bel-Merodach, the supreme "Baal" of Babylon, other members of the pantheon, Tammuz and Istar, the sacred books of Chaldaea, and the cosmogonies and astrotheology of the Babylonians. 291.1.SA9 1891

Thompson, Henry O. *Mekal: The God of Beth-Shan.* Leiden: E. J. Brill, 1970.

This study of a leading Canaanite deity makes a valuable contribution to our knowledge of ancient antiquities in Israel. 299.26.T37

Toynbee, Arnold Joseph. *Christianity among the Religions of the World.* New York: Charles Scribner's Sons, 1956.

Surveys the position of Christianity and the other religions of the modern world in the face of the resurgence of the worship of ourselves in the shape of collective human power. 290.T66

Visser't Hooft, W. A. *No Other Name.* Philadelphia: Westminster Press, 1963.

†Speaks with enthusiasm about the validity of the historical Christian faith, and attacks religious syncretism, especially in Hinduism and Bahaism. Upholds the uniqueness of Christianity as

seen by the ecumenical movement. 290.V82

Vicedom, George Friedrick. *The Challenge of the World Religions.* Philadelphia: Fortress Press, 1963.

A modern presentation of the current pronouncements of the different religions of the world. 291.V66

*Vos, Howard Frederick, ed. *Religions in a Changing World.* Rev. ed. Chicago: Moody Press, 1959.

Most of the chapters comprised in this book have been written by missionaries who have had personal dealings with the religions about which they write. Includes a treatment of Communism, East-

ern Orthodoxy, Roman Catholicism, and Protestantism. A valuable work. 290.82.V92

Witt, R. E. *Isis in the Graeco-Roman World.* Ithaca: Cornell University Press, 1971.

A detailed study evaluating the place, worship, and doctrine of Isis in the Graeco-Roman world. Includes both a theological and an archaeological investigation. Aids in understanding the religious beliefs of the world into which Christ was born and in which the apostolic church was established. 291.211.W78

JUDAISM

*Abrahams, Israel. *Studies in Pharisaism and the Gospels.* 2 vols. Cambridge: At the University Press, 1924.

Provides a series of definitive discussions on aspects of Pharisaic Judaism, with insights upon the gospels. A work of genius. 296.812.AB85

Adler, Morris. *The World of the Talmud.* New York: Schocken Press, 1958.

A popular study stressing the ethical traditions of Reformed Judaism, 296.12.AD5

Albright, William Foxwell. *Yahweh and the Gods of Canaan: A Historical Analysis of Two Contrasting Faiths.* Garden City: Doubleday and Co., 1968.

Contains a historical analysis of Canaanite and Yahwistic worship. Illuminates much of the OT. 296.8.AL1

The Babylonian Talmud. Translated under the editorship of I. Epstein. 18 vols. London: Soncino Press, 1961.

Opens up for "English-speaking readers the most varied and indispensable index to the collective wisdom of the post-biblical Hebrew mind," and affords direct knowledge of the ordinances and teachings that have governed the reli-

gious life and social polity of the Jewish people through the ages. 296.125.EP8

*Bowker, John. *The Targums and Rabbinic Literature.* Cambridge: At the University Press, 1969.

An excellent, eminently readable account of the literature, with a clear definition of terms. Translation with comments on the material. 296.12.B67

Buckler, Adolf. *Studies in Sin and Atonement in the Rabbinic Literature of the First Century.* New York: Ktav Publishing House, 1967.

This great work penetrates the thinking of Jews in the postexilic period and shows what they actually believed with regard to sin and atonement. First published in 1928. Brought up to date with F. C. Grant's "Prolegomena." 296.3'85.B85

Daube, David. *Sin, Ignorance and Forgiveness in the Bible.* London: Liberal Jewish Synagogue, 1961.

A scholarly treatment. Deserves careful reading. 291.22.D26

*_____. *The New Testament and Rabbinic Judaism.* London: Athlone Press, 1956.

A work of great genius, but it suffers from the erratic form in which the material is presented. 296.3.D26

Davies, William David. *Torah in the Messianic Age and/or The Age to Come.* Philadelphia: Society of Biblical Literature, 1952.

Basing his analysis upon the Old Testament, Apocrypha, Pseudepigrapha, and Talmudic writings, the writer provides a study of what he believes the role of the law should be in the age of the Messiah. Lays the foundation for a summary of Jewish teaching and expectation during the intertestamental period. 296.D28

Davies, Thomas Witton. *Magic, Divination, and Demonology Among the Hebrews and Their Neighbors.* New York: Ktav Publishing House, 1970.

First published in 1898, this work on the lower forms of worship covers black magic, mysterious powers of the incantation, and the fetish. Provides an excellent backdrop for the study of demonism in biblical times, as well as a historical background for its present-day development. 291.32.D28 1970 (Alt. DDC 133.4)

*Dolman, D. H. *Simple Talks on the Tabernacle.* London: Marshall, Morgan and Scott, 1954.

A devout, reverent study of the typology of the Tabernacle. 296.4.D69 1954

Edersheim, Aldred. *History of the Jewish Nation After the Destruction of Jerusalem Under Titus.* Revised by Henry A. White. Grand Rapids: Baker Book House, 1954.

Based upon the 1856 edition, this work remains a standard work on the history of the Jewish nation from the first to nineteenth centuries. Of particular value for the light it throws on the gospels, the book of Acts, and subsequent church history. 933.09.ED2 1954

Epstein, Lewis M. *Sex Laws and Customs in Judaism.* New York: Ktav Publishing House, 1967.

A comprehensive study of the works of moralists and philosophers in Judaism in different places and at different times. 296.385.EP8

Farmer, William Reuben. *Maccabees, Zealots, and Josephus: An Inquiry into Jewish Nationalism in the Greco-Roman Period.* New York: Columbia University Press, 1956.

A defense of the writer's thesis that Josephus obscured the real connection between the Maccabees and the Jewish nationalists. Advances reasons for revising the history of Josephus in favor of his own theory. 296.8.F22

Finkel, Asher. *The Pharisees and the Teacher of Nazareth: A Study of Their Background, Their Halachic and Midrashic Teachings, Their Similarities and Differences.* Leiden: E. J. Brill, 1964.

A serious work dealing with Jewish oral tradition. Seeks to portray Jesus Christ against the background of His own times. 296.812.F49

Finkelstein, Louis. *The Pharisees: The Sociological Background of Their Faith.* 2 vols. New York: Jewish Publication Society of America, 1938.

A Jewish account of the origin and function of the Pharisees, with a vigorous defense of their attitudes and actions. 296.812.F49P

Fitzmyer, Joseph A. *Essays on the Semitic Background of the New Testament.* London: Jeffrey Chapman, 1971.

A collection of essays by a leading Aramaic scholar. 296.1.F57

Forster, W. *Palestinian Judaism in New Testament Times.* Edinburgh: Oliver and Boyd, 1964.

A valuable survey that includes the intertestamental period. 296.F77

Frazer, James George. *Folk-lore in the Old Testament.* London: Macmillan Co., 1923.

Deals with such matters as the mark of Cain, the great Flood and stories in pagan literature, the Tower of Babel, the covenant of Abraham, the heirship of Jacob. An intriguing work that enhances our understanding of the OT. 291.2.F86

Gaster, Theodor Herzl. *Festivals of the Jewish Year.* New York: Sloane Publishers, 1952.

A serious study of the origin of the customs and ceremonies associated with the feasts of Judaism. 296.4.G21

_____. *The Passover, Its History and Traditions.* Boston: Beacon Press, 1949.

Recounts the history of the festival, not only in terms of its accepted tradition, but also against the background of modern Judaism. 296.437.G21

Grant, Frederick Clifton. *Ancient Judaism and the New Testament.* Edinburgh: Oliver and Boyd, 1960.

A mediating work that attempts to minimize the conflicts between Judaism and early Christianity. 296.G76

Gray, George Buchanan. *Sacrifice in the Old Testament, Its Theory and Practice.* New York: Ktav Publishing House, 1970.

†Contains an abundance of material relating to the basic concepts and background involved in a proper understanding of OT sacrifice and the priesthood. 291.34.G79 1970

Herford, Robert Travers. *Christianity in Talmud and Midrash.* New York: Ktav Publishing House, 1965.

By emphasizing the historic roots of early Christianity, the writer shows rabbinical literature must be consulted if a thorough study of the rise and development of first-century Christianity is to be made. 296.12.H42

_____. *The Pharisees.* London: Allen and Unwin, 1924.

An old, standard work. Still worth reading. 296.81.H42

Higgens, Elford. *Hebrew Idolatry and Superstition.* Port Washington, N.Y.: Kennikat Press, 1970.

Reprinted from the 1893 edition. Surveys the critical works to that time, deals with the interchange of religious thought in the ancient Near East, and enlarges upon the pagan religious worship inherent in divination, witchcraft, and enchantment. 296.3.H53 1970

Jocz, Jakob. *The Jewish People and Jesus Christ.* London: SPCK, 1949.

A study centering in the difference between Judaism and the teaching of Jesus Christ. 296.81.J58

Kac, Arthur W. *The Rebirth of the State of Israel.* Chicago: Moody Press, 1958.

Contains an in-depth analysis of the biblical teaching concerning Israel and the prophetic truths behind Israel's restoration to the land of Palestine. 956.94.K11

_____. *The Spiritual Dilemma of the Jewish People.* Chicago: Moody Press, 1963.

An evaluation of present-day Judaism and the plight of the Jewish people. 296.K11

Klauser, Joseph. *From Jesus to Paul.* Translated by W. F. Stinespring. New York: Macmillan Co., 1943.

†A companion volume to this great Jewish scholar's earlier interpretation of Jesus. Together these volumes express the judgment of the synagogue on the church. 296.K66

Kraus, Hans-Joachim. *Worship in Israel: A Cultic History of the Old Testament.* Translated by G. Buswell. Richmond: John Knox Press, 1966.

†Based upon a historical survey of investigations from Wellhausen to de Vaux. Examines cultic calendars, regulations, and festivals, together with the role of the priests and Levites, cultic prophets, and the sacrificial system associated with Israel's worship. There are misprints throughout the book (e.g., *daleth* for *resh*), as well as some inaccurate bibli-

cal references. 296.4.K86

*McGee, John Vernon. *The Tabernacle: God's Portrait of Christ.* Los Angeles: Church of the Open Door, n.d.

A valuable, literal exposition of the passages in Exodus dealing with the Tabernacle, the altar and laver, table of shewbread, lampstand, and so on. 296.4.M17

*The Mishnah. Translated with brief explanatory notes by Herbert Danby. Oxford: Oxford University Press, 1933.

A valuable, informative study of Jewish oral law. Provides important information that highlights parts of the OT and the history of the intertestamental period. 296.123.M68

Montefiore, Claude Joseph Goldsmid. *Judaism and St. Paul.* London: Goschen, 1914.

Stresses the superiority of Reformed Judaism, and shows parallels between the teaching of Judaism and the theology of Paul. Of value to those who know how to cull information. 296.38.M76

———. *Lectures on the Origin and Growth of Religion as Illustrated by the Ancient Hebrews.* 3d ed. London: Williams and Norgate, 1897.

†A thoroughly critical, liberal work. Contains little of lasting value. 296.81.M76 1897

———. *Rabbinic Literature and Gospel Teachings.* London: Macmillan Co., 1930.

†A critical and provocative study supplementing the author's studies on the synoptic gospels with a treatment of the parallels between the religious and ethical teachings of the gospels and rabbinical literature. 296.81.M76

——— and **Herbert Martin James Loewe.** *A Rabbinic Anthology.* Cleveland: Meridian Books, 1960.

Explores with thoroughness, wisdom, sympathy, and tact the rabbinic tradition contained in the Talmud and Midrash as these have a bearing on the nature of

God, the law, virtue, prayer, faith, sin, charity, the Messiah, and the last judgment. First published in 1938. 296.1.M76 1960

Montefiore, Hugh. *Josephus and the New Testament.* London: A. R. Mowbray, 1960.

A scholarly study that, despite its erudition, is not as valuable as the treatment by Thackeray. 296.M76

Montgomery, James Alan. *The Samaritans: The Earliest Jewish Sect, Their History, Theology and Literature.* New York: Ktav Publishing House, 1968.

Focuses on the sect of the Samaritans in OT, intertestamental, and NT times. First published in 1907. 296.8.M76 1968

*Moore, George Foot. *Judaism in the First Centuries of the Christian Era.* 3 vols. Cambridge: Harvard University Press, 1927-30.

A monumental work on Jewish theology and ethics. Written from a rabbinic point of view. 296.M78

Moorehead, William Gallogly. *The Tabernacle.* Grand Rapids: Kregel Publications, 1957.

Includes a discussion of the Tabernacle, the priesthood, the sacrifices and feasts of ancient Israel. Easily understood. 296.4.M78 1957

*Mount, R. H., Jr. *The Law Prophesied.* 2d ed. Mansfield, Ohio: The author, 1963.

An engineer by profession, Mount has spent a lifetime studying the Tabernacle. His treatment and scale drawings, together with his comments on the text, are exceedingly helpful. 296.4.M86 1963

Odeberg, Hugo. *Pharisaism and Christianity.* Translated by J. M. Moe. St. Louis: Concordia Publishing House, 1964.

A graphic, understandable treatment highlighting the conflict between Christianity and Pharisaism. A valuable historical reference tool. 296.3.OD2

Oesterley, William Oscar Emil. *Judaism and Christianity.* New York: Ktav Publishing House, 1968.

†Contains a detailed investigation into the age of transition, the contact of Pharisaism with other cultures, and law and religion in ancient Israel. Unabridged. Originally published in three volumes in 1938. 296.8.OE8 1968

————. *Sacrifices in Ancient Israel: Their Origin, Purposes, and Development.* London: Hodder and Stoughton, 1937.

†Provocative lectures first delivered at King's College, London. Explores the purpose of sacrifices to the offerer—as gifts, to effect communion, and to liberate and give life. 291.34.OE8

———— and **G. H. Box.** *The Religion and Worship of the Synagogue: An Introduction to the Study of Judaism from the New Testament Period.* London: I. Pitman and Sons, 1911.

An able treatment of Jewish worship procedures that adopts a mediating position between historical criticism and form-criticism. 296.4.OE8

———— and **Theodore Henry Robinson.** *Hebrew Religion, Its Origin and Development.* London: SPCK, 1955.

†A standard work. Seeks to present the evolutionary development of Hebrew religion. Unreliable. 296.OE8

Olford, Stephen F. *The Tabernacle: Camping with God.* Neptune, N.J.: Loizeaux Brothers, 1971.

A stimulating and challenging devotional exposition of the typology of the Tabernacle. 296.4.OL2

Patai, Raphael. *The Hebrew Goddess.* New York: Ktav Publishing House, 1967.

Provides a vital link in the study of the Hebrew and Jewish religion that centered in the veneration of a goddess. Draws important parallels from ancient Near Eastern religions and early Catholicism to support the writer's views. 296.31.P27

Pfeiffer, Charles Franklin. *The Arab-Israeli Conflict.* Grand Rapids: Baker

Book House, 1972.

A modern appraisal of the events and circumstances that led up to this continuing conflict. 933.P47

Philo Judaeus. *The Works of Philo Judaeus.* Translated by C. D. Yonge. 3 vols. London: Henry G. Bohn, 1854.

A contemporary of Josephus, Philo has long been regarded as an important source to consult in the study of the Scriptures. He is well known for his allegorical interpretation, but, in spite of this, he provides numerous interesting sidelights on the biblical narrative. 932.0092.P54

Rabin, Chaim. *The Zadokite Documents.* Oxford: At the University Press, 1954.

An important study containing the text of these documents, an English translation, and a commentary. 296.817.R11

Rapaport, Samuel. *A Treasury of the Midrash.* New York: Ktav Publishing House, 1968.

An introductory approach to the Midrash, with chapters on demons, Ashmedai, and the Messiah. Valuable. 296.14.R18

Rappaport, Angelo Solomon. *Myth and Legend of Ancient Israel.* 3 vols. New York: Ktav Publishing House, 1965.

Based upon the 1928 edition, and updated with an introduction and notes by Raphael Patai. Surveys over one thousand years of ancient and medieval Jewish lore, and includes a study of folklore and anthropology pertaining to the biblical era. 296.31.R18 1965 (Alt. DDC 398.209174)

Ridout, Samuel. *Lectures on the Tabernacle.* New York: Loizeaux Brothers, 1952.

First published in 1914, these devotional messages have been held in high esteem by preachers for more than half a century. Plymouth Brethren. 296.4.R43 1952

Ringgren, Karl Wilhelm Helmer. *Sac-*

rifice in the Bible. London: Lutterworth Press, 1962.

A valuable supplement to de Vaux's treatment of the subject of OT sacrifices. 291.34.R47

Rowley, Harold Henry. *The Dead Sea Scrolls and Their Significance.* Oxford: Basil Blackwell, 1955.

An attempt to evaluate the importance and relevancy of the Qumran material. Dated. 296.817.R79

————. *Worship in Ancient Israel: Its Forms and Meaning.* Philadelphia: Fortress Press, 1967.

Based upon the Edward Cadbury Lectures delivered at the University of Birmingham, England, these studies survey worship practices from patriarchal times to the synagogue and include a definitive study of the period of the Exodus, the Temple, various forms of sacrifice, the use of psalmody and music, and so on. A scholarly volume. 296.4.R79

————. *The Zadokite Fragments and the Dead Sea Scrolls.* Oxford: Basil Blackwell, 1952.

A valuable work at the time it was published, but now superseded by Mansoor's *The Dead Sea Scrolls.* 296.817.R79

Samuel, Athanasius Yeshue. *Treasure of Qumran.* Philadelphia: Westminster Press, 1966.

The moving autobiography of the man who purchased the first of the Dead Sea Scrolls when they were found by the Ta'amireh Bedouins in the Judean desert. 296.817.SA4

Schurer, Emil. *A History of the Jewish People in the Time of Jesus Christ.* 5 vols. Translated by John MacPherson. Edinburgh: T. and T. Clark, 1890-91.

Still regarded as one of the most authoritative treatments of first-century Judaism. Covers the political history of Palestine from 175 B.C. to A.D. 135. 933.SCH8

Smith, William Robertson. *Lectures on the Religion of the Semites.* 3d ed. New York: Ktav Publishing House, 1969.

†The writer has been regarded as the founder of the modern comparative study of religion, and this seminal work provides an important introduction to his methodology. 299.2.SM6 1969

*Soltau, Henry W. *The Tabernacle, the Priesthood and the Offerings.* Harrisburg, Penn.: Christian Publications, n.d.

A classic study sufficiently detailed to be helpful. Avoids typology and fanciful spiritualization, and expounds the Scripture with reverence and clarity. 296.4.SO4

*————. *The Holy Vessels and Furniture of the Tabernacle.* Grand Rapids: Kregel Publications, 1970.

First published in 1851, this work by a lawyer is designed to give a correct exposition of the text relating to the Tabernacle and its furniture and to present the typical teaching with regard to Christ and His work. 296.4.SO4H 1970

Stewart, Roy A. *The Earlier Rabbinic Tradition.* London: Inter-Varsity Press, 1949.

A capable, thorough study. Ideal for those who desire a brief introduction. 296.J2.ST4

————. *Rabbinic Theology.* Edinburgh: Oliver and Boyd, 1961.

Without imposing any rigid framework on rabbinic thought, the author digresses to discuss the attitudes in his sources toward the Scriptures, women, Melchizedek, and so on. This treatment of rabbinism is fair, and the writings of the New Testament are used for comparison as well as illustration. 296.3.ST4

*Strack, Herman L. *Introduction to the Talmud and Midrash.* New York: Meridian Books, 1959.

The best, most concise introduction available. Replete with definitions, and provides an invaluable guide to the literature of the period. More complete than Bowker's *Targums and Rabbinic Literature.* 296.12.ST8

Thackeray, Henry St. John. *The Relation of St. Paul to Contemporary Jewish Thought.* London: Macmillan Co., 1900.

An extremely valuable study ably supported by recent evidence. 296.3.T32

Vaux, Roland de. *Studies in Old Testament Sacrifice.* Cardiff: University of Wales Press, 1964.

†In this work, de Vaux gathers together all the theories and archaeological data relating to the OT sacrificial system and interprets the information in the light of his presuppositions. His analysis of the opinions of others is valuable, but he stops short of the biblical teaching concerning the vicarious substitutionary atonement. 291.34.V46

Williams, Arthur Lukyn. *Talmudic Judaism and Christianity.* London: SPCK, 1933.

Makes the writer's vast scholarship available to students of the period. 296.12.W67

Wouk, Herman. *This Is My God.* Garden City: Doubleday and Co., 1959.

Deals with the Jewish people and their faith despite the culture of the West. 296.W91

Universal Jewish Encyclopedia. Edited by Isaac Landman, et al. 11 vols. New York: Universal Jewish Encyclopedia, 1939-44.

A multivolume work containing more than ten thousand articles on Jewish history, religion, culture, and customs, together with numerous biographical sketches. Covers every aspect of Judaism from the earliest times to the 1930s. Bible students will find its articles on the ark of Noah, the Atonement, Abraham's bosom and numerous other topics of great interest and importance. See also the *Jewish Encyclopedia* (1901-6) and the *Standard Jewish Encyclopedia*, 1959. 910.09.UN6

Yadin, Yigael. *The Message of the Scrolls.* London: Weidenfeld and Nicolson, 1957.

A valuable reconstruction of the history of the Scrolls, with an account of their purchase and translation. 296.817.Y1

BUDDHISM, CONFUCIANISM, ISLAM, AND HINDUISM

Anesaki, Masaharu. *History of Japanese Religion.* London: Kegan Paul, Trench, Trubaer and Company, 1930.

Originally made up of lectures delivered at Harvard University, 1913-15, these studies serve to introduce Westerners to Shintoism, Buddhism, and Confucianism. The work is characterized by an amazing thoroughness and lays a solid foundation for a consideration of contemporary developments within Japanese culture. 299.56.AN

Bhattacharji, Sukumari. *The Indian Theogony: A Comparative Study of Indian Mythology from the* Vedas *to the* Puranas. Cambridge: At the University Press, 1970.

A detailed, historical development of Indian mythology that ranks without peer in English literature. 291.13.B46

Cragg, Kenneth. *The Call of the Minaret.* New York: Oxford University Press, 1956.

A perceptive study of the teaching of Islam and its relation to Christianity. 297.C84

Eliot, Charles Norton Edgecumbe. *Hinduism and Buddhism; an Historical Sketch.* 3 vols. London: Routledge and Kegan Paul, 1968.

First published in 1921, this work has stood the test of time and ably introduces readers to the origin of, as well as the divisions within, each religious movement. Includes a discussion of their sacred writings, sacrifices, priesthoods, and so on. 294.EL4 1968

———. *Japanese Buddhism.* London: Routledge and Kegan Paul, 1969.

First published in 1935, this work retains its value. It remains one of the first historical sketches ever written. 294.32.EL4 1969

Gard, Richard Abbott, ed. *Buddhism.* New York: George Braziller, 1961.

Contains an overview of Buddha's life and thought, and shows how his religious ideals have accommodated themselves in over thirty Asian countries and in more than twenty different Asian languages. A seminal work. 294.3.G16

Gibb, Hamilton Alexander Rosskeen and **J. H. Kramers.** *Shorter Encyclopedia of Islam.* Ithaca: Cornell University Press, 1965.

An abridgment of the *Encyclopedia of Islam.* Retains the original articles in shortened or revised form, with a few new articles added. Arranged alphabetically by Arabic words, which have been transliterated into English. This makes the encyclopedia difficult to use unless one is particularly familiar with Arabic terminology. 297.03.G35

Hoffmann, Helmut. *The Religions of Tibet.* Translated by E. Fitzgerald. London: George Allen and Unwin, 1961.

By placing his emphasis upon the historic development of religious belief in Tibet, Hoffmann is able to show the penetration of Buddhism into Tibet and the eventual emergence of the Dalai Lamas. A fascinating chronicle. 294.329.H67

Hughes, Thomas Patrick. *A Dictionary of Islam.* Clifton, N.J.: Reference Book Publishers, 1965.

An encyclopedia of the doctrines, rites, ceremonies, customs, technical expressions, and theological terms of the Muslim religion. Arranged alphabetically using the English equivalent of Arabic terms. The article on Islam is

particularly well done. 297.03.H87

The I Ching, or Book of Changes. Translated into German by R. Wilhelm. Rendered into English by C. F. Baynes. 3d ed. Princeton: Princeton University Press, 1967.

Records the efforts of a Confucian scholar to find his place within the universe. As a manual on ethics, this work is permeated with practical wisdom. As a guide to the meaning of life, it falls short of divine revelation. 299.51'282.W64 1967

International Society for Krishna Consciousness. *Bhagavad-Gita.* Los Angeles: Bhaktivedanta Book Trust, 1968.

An abridged version of India's Vedic wisdom. Explains the religious significance behind yoga, karma, the quest for divine consciousness, and the perfection of renunciation. 294.5924.IN8

Johansson, Rune E. *The Psychology of Nirvana.* London: George Allen and Unwin, 1969.

Missionaries have often found the Pali writings conflicting and confusing. This work seeks to explore the heterogeneous morass of definitions surrounding the doctrine of Nirvana (or *nabbana*), with a view to explaining this aspect of Buddhist belief. 294.342.J59

Kitagawa, Joseph Mitsuo. *Religion in Japanese History.* New York: Columbia University Press, 1966.

Delineates the key elements of Japanese religion, describes the inner logic of each, and provides a historical and structural *Religionswissenschaft.* 299.56.K64

Maraini, Fosco. *Secret Tibet.* Translated by E. Mosbacher. London: Hutchinson and Company, 1952.

Perhaps Tibet will never again be known as Maraini and his illustrious forerunners—Bell, Tucci, Hedin, and Younghusband—knew it, for this demon-infested, saint-bearing mountain kingdom has fallen before Communism.

As a consequence, nearly a thousand years of monk-ruled feudalism have come to an end. 294.329.M32

Margoliouth, David Samuel. *The Early Development of Mohammedanism.* The Hibbert Lectures. London: Williams and Norgate, 1914.

These lectures, delivered in the University of London, 1913, draw from unpublished manuscripts as well as the writings of little-known Islamic authors. The result is a work of great interest as well as great merit. 297'.09.M33

Nikhilananda, Swami. *Hinduism: Its Meaning for the Liberation of the Spirit.* London: George Allen and Unwin, 1959.

Provides a brief account of the history and purposes of Hinduism, even to the point of advocating it as the highest form of Indian mystical achievement. 294.5.N58

———. *The Upanishads.* London: George Allen and Unwin, 1963.

An abridged edition of the author's four-volume work. Contains translations from the Sanskrit, with a brief outline of the metaphysics, psychology, and ethics of Vedic times. 294.5921.N58

Organ, Troy Wilson. *The Hindu Quest for the Perfection of Man.* Athens, Ohio: Ohio University Press, 1970.

Explores the quest for "liberation" in the various aspects of Hindu thought: *Artha, Kama, Dharma, Moksa, Bhakti,* and so on. Explains the various "ways" of perfectability (i.e., through thought, action, devotion, discipline). 294.5.OR3

Parrinder, Edward Geoffrey. *Jesus and the Qur'an.* New York: Barnes and Noble, 1965.

A study of the Islamic interpretations of Jesus Christ and the relationship of the Koran to the Bible. 297.122.P24

———. *Upanishads, Gita and Bible.* New York: Association Press, 1962.

A comparative study of the sacred writings of Hinduism and the Bible. 291.82.P24

***Pitt, Malcolm.** *Introducing Hinduism.* New York: Friendship Press, 1965.

A brief but informative study. 294.5.P68

Renou, Louis, ed. *Hinduism.* New York: George Braziller, 1961.

A brief overview of the principle groups within Hinduism, followed by excerpts from their Sanskrit writings. A work for the beginner. 294.5.R29

Saddhatissa, H. *Buddhist Ethics: Essence of Buddhism.* London: George Allen and Unwin, 1970.

When asked the secret of his success as secretary general of the United Nations—and how he managed to remain calm amid the stormy discussions of that diverse body—U Thant replied, "Because I am a Buddhist." This discussion of Buddhist ethics focuses on the volitional acts (or *karma*) that in turn determine one's future "fortune," and on the reflective wisdom that comes from a consideration of the teachings of the sages. The ultimate goal of such a life is "salvation"—or the ability to transcend the supramundane state of one's existence. 294.3SA1

Selections From the Sacred Writings of the Sikhs. Translated by T. Singh, et al. Revised by G. S. Fraser. London: George Allen and Unwin, 1965.

Described as the "authorized version" of certain of the sacred hymns of the Sikh scriptures, this material makes it possible for missiologists and students of comparative religions to trace the main tenets of Hindu religion, while also observing some of the similarities between Sikh and Islam. 294.6.SE4

Smith, D. Howard. *Chinese Religions.* London: Weidenfeld and Nicolson, 1968.

Assesses the place and importance of

religious beliefs in Chinese history while also describing the attention given to learning, piety, and devotion in the beliefs of the Confucian, Taoist, and Buddhist systems. 299.51.SM5

Thomas, Edward J. *The History of Buddhist Thought.* London: Routledge and Kegan Paul, 1951.

Begins with a brief biography of the founder, and then traces the rise of Buddhist dogma—often contradictory—to the various bodies who today claim to follow the teachings of Gotama. 294.3.T36

Watt, William Montgomery. *Companion to the Qur'an: Based on the Arberry Translation.* London: George Allen and Unwin, 1967.

Believing that the Koran is not easily understood, Montgomery provides an elucidation of its principal tenets. 297.1224.W34

Williams, John Alden, ed. *Islam.* New York: George Braziller, 1961.

A brief, popular overview of the history, rise, and influence of Islam. Not intended for the serious student. 297'.082.W67

Wilson, J. Christy. *Introducing Islam.* New York: Friendship Press, 1965.

An evaluation of the resurgence of Islamic belief in Asia, Africa, and the Far East. 297.W69

Wright, Arthur F., ed. *The Confucian Persuasion.* Stanford: Stanford University Press, 1960.

Sponsored by the Stanford Studies in the Civilizations of Eastern Asia, this work focuses attention on Confucian thought and the rich traditions of classical scholarship characterizing the practice of these beliefs in South China. 299.512.W93

Index of Authors

Index of Titles

Index of Subjects